GRUBER'S
COMPLETE
GRE*
2nd Edition
GUIDE 2013

GARY R. GRUBER, PhD

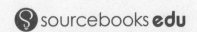

Published by Sourcebooks EDU, an imprint of Sourcebooks, Inc.
P.O. Box 4410, Naperville, Illinois 60567-4410
(630) 961-3900
Fax: (630) 961-2168
www.sourcebooks.com

Library of Congress Cataloging-in-Publication Data

Gruber, Gary R.
 Gruber's complete GRE guide 2013 / by Gary R. Gruber.—2nd ed.
   p. cm.
 1. Graduate Record Examination—Study guides. 2. Examinations—Scoring. I. Title. II. Title: Complete GRE guide 2013. III. Title: GRE guide 2013.
 LB2366.G78 2012
 378.1'662—dc23

2012016274

Printed and bound in the United States of America.
DR 10 9 8 7 6 5 4 3 2 1

Recent and Forthcoming Study Aids from Dr. Gary Gruber Include

Gruber's Complete SAT Guide 2013

Gruber's SAT 2400

Gruber's Complete SAT Math Workbook

Gruber's Complete SAT Critical Reading Workbook

Gruber's Complete SAT Writing Workbook

Gruber's SAT Word Master

Gruber's Complete PSAT/NMSQT Guide 2013

Gruber's Complete ACT Guide 2013

Gruber's Essential Guide to Test Taking: Grades 3–5

Gruber's Essential Guide to Test Taking: Grades 6–9

www.collegecountdown.com

www.sourcebooks.com

www.drgarygruber.com

www.mymaxscore.com

Important Note About This Book and Its Author

This book is the most up-to-date and complete book on the current GRE (Graduate Record Examinations). *Every exam* is patterned after the GRE, and *all* the strategies and techniques deal with the GRE. The GRE incorporates all the Gruber Critical Thinking Strategies.

This book was written by Dr. Gary Gruber, the leading authority on the GRE, who knows more than anyone else in the test-prep market exactly what is being tested in the GRE. In fact, the procedures to answer the GRE questions rely more heavily on the Gruber Critical Thinking Strategies than ever before, and this is the only book that has the exact thinking strategies you need to use to maximize your GRE score. Gruber's books are used by the nation's school districts more than any other books and are proven to get the highest documented school district standardized test scores.

Dr. Gruber has published more than 35 books with major publishers on test-taking and critical thinking methods, with more than 7 million copies sold. He has also authored more than 1,000 articles on his work in scholarly journals and nationally syndicated newspapers, has appeared on numerous television and radio shows, and has been interviewed in hundreds of magazines and newspapers. He has developed major programs for school districts and for city and state educational agencies for improving and restructuring curriculum, increasing learning ability and test scores, increasing motivation and developing a passion for learning and problem solving, and decreasing the student dropout rate. For example, PBS (Public Broadcasting System) chose Dr. Gruber to train the nation's teachers on how to prepare students for the SAT through a national satellite teleconference and videotape. His results have been lauded by people throughout the country from all walks of life.

Dr. Gruber is recognized nationally as the leading expert on standardized tests. It is said that no one in the nation is better at assessing the thinking patterns of how a person answers questions and providing the mechanism to improve faulty thinking approaches. GRE score improvements by students using Dr. Gruber's techniques have been the highest in the nation.

Gruber's unique methods have been and are being used by PBS, the nation's learning centers, international encyclopedias, school districts throughout the country, students in homes and workplaces across the nation, and a host of other entities.

His goal and mission is to get people's potential realized and the nation "impassioned" with learning and problem solving so that they don't merely try to get a fast, uncritical answer but actually enjoy and look forward to solving the problem and learning.

For more information on Gruber courses and additional Gruber products, visit www .drgarygruber.com.

Important: Many books do not reflect the current GRE questions. Don't practice with questions that misrepresent the actual questions on the GRE. For example, the math questions created by the test makers are oriented to allow someone to solve many problems without a calculator as fast as he or she could with one, and some can be solved faster without a calculator. This book reflects the GRE more accurately than any other commercial book, and the strategies contained in it are exactly those needed to be used on the GRE. It is said that only Dr. Gruber has the expertise and ability to reflect the exam far more closely than any competitor! Don't trust your future with less than the best material.

The Author Has Something Important to Tell You About How to Raise Your GRE Score

What Are Critical Thinking Skills?

First of all, I believe that intelligence can be taught. Intelligence, simply defined, is the aptitude or ability to reason things out. I am convinced that *you can learn* to *think logically* and figure things out better and faster, *particularly in regard to GRE Math and Verbal problems.* But someone must give you the tools. Let us call these tools *strategies.* And that's what Critical Thinking Skills are all about—*strategies.*

Learn the Strategies to Get More Points

The Critical Thinking Skills (beginning on page 65) will sharpen your reasoning ability so that you can increase your score on each part of the GRE.

These Critical Thinking Skills—5 General Strategies, 25 Math Strategies, and 17 Verbal Strategies—course right through this book. The Explanatory Answers for the 3 Practice Tests in the book direct you to those strategies that may be used to answer specific types of GRE questions. We can readily prove that the strategies in Part 4 of this book are usable for more than 90 percent of the questions that will appear on your GRE. It is obvious, then, that your *learning* and *using* the 46 easy-to-understand strategies in this book will very likely raise your GRE score substantially.

Are the Practice Tests in This Book Like an Actual GRE?

If you compare any one of the 3 Practice Tests in this book with an actual GRE, you will find the book test very much like the *actual* test in regard to *format, question types,* and *level of difficulty.* Compare our book tests with one of the official tests written by the GRE people.

Building Your Vocabulary Can Make a Difference on Your Test

Although antonyms no longer appear on the GRE, vocabulary will still be tested, especially on Sentence Completions and Reading Comprehension. This book includes four vital sections to build your vocabulary:

1. 3,400-Word List
2. 100 Vocabulary Tests
3. The Most Important/Frequently Used GRE Words
4. The Hot Prefixes and Roots

If you have time, it is important for you to study this word-building instructional material. You will find that *many, many words* in the 3,400-Word List will actually show up in the Sentence Completion and Reading Comprehension sections of the Verbal part of your GRE. We repeat that each additional correct answer adds approximately 10 points to your score (or adds approximately 1 point on the 130–170 point scale). Knowing the meanings of the words in the 3,400-Word List will, therefore, help you considerably to "rake in" those precious points.

Study the Latin and Greek Roots, Prefixes, and Suffixes

We have developed a list that contains roots, prefixes, and suffixes that give you the meaning of more than 150,000 words. Learning all of these will increase your vocabulary immensely. You may also wish to study the Hot Prefixes and Roots in Appendix A.

Study the Most Important/Frequently Used GRE Words

We have developed a list of the most frequently used words and their opposites related to specific categories for easy memorization. Study these words.

Study the Mini-Math Refresher

If you believe you are weak in basic math skills, study the Mini-Math Refresher. The material in the section is keyed to the Complete Math Refresher section for more thorough instruction.

Take the 101 Most Important Math Questions Test

To see what your weak basic math skills are, take the 101 Most Important Math Questions Test and look at the solutions to the questions. The questions are keyed to the Complete Math Refresher, so you can further brush up on your weak areas by referring to those pages in the Complete Math Refresher that are relevant for any questions you missed.

The Explanatory Answers to Questions Are Keyed to Specific Strategies and Basic Skills

The Explanatory Answers in this book are far from skimpy—unlike those of other GRE books. Our detailed answers will direct you to the strategy that will help you to arrive at a correct answer quickly. In addition, the math solutions in the book refer directly to the Math Refresher section, particularly useful in case your math skills are rusty.

Lift That GRE Score

By using the material in this book—that is, by taking the tests, learning the specific strategies, and refreshing your basic skills as described above—you should increase your GRE score substantially.

—**Gary Gruber**

Contents

PART 7

VOCABULARY BUILDING THAT IS GUARANTEED TO RAISE YOUR GRE SCORE 361

PART 8

ANALYTICAL WRITING SECTION 473

INTRODUCTION

I. Important Facts About the GRE

The Computer-Based GRE Test

When you take the computer-based test, you can edit or change your answers within a section.

You can skip and return later within a timed section.

You can use an on-screen calculator for the Quantitative Reasoning section.

You will have a question where you will have to highlight an answer within a reading passage.

My own personal feeling is that it is better to take the paper-based GRE test, since you do not have to rely on seeing the questions on a screen. You have them on paper and can mark on your paper and make use of strategies like drawing lines in a diagram or underlining statements in a paragraph right on the paper. Note that on the paper-based test, you will enter your answers in the test booklet rather than on a separate answer sheet.

Important Test Dates for the Paper-Based and Computer-Based GRE

For the latest test dates, go to http://www.ets.org/gre/revised_general/register/centers _dates/.

What Is on the GRE?

It will include two student-written essays. The essays will be the first part of the test. The Math section will include arithmetic, geometry, algebra I, and some advanced math covering topics in algebra II, statistics, probability, and data analysis. The test will measure reasoning ability and problem-solving skills. The other parts of the test will contain some long and shorter reading passages and sentence-completion questions.

How Will the Test Be Scored?

- The Verbal Reasoning and Quantitative Reasoning sections are reported on a 130−170 score scale, in 1-point increments.
- The Analytical Writing section is reported on a 0−6 score scale, in half-point increments.

How Long Will the Test Be?

The total time of the test will be 3 hours and 30 minutes for the paper-based test, and 3 hours and 45 minutes for the computer-based test.

What Verbal Background Must I Have?

The reading and vocabulary are at the 10th- to 12th-grade level, but strategies presented in this book will help you even if you are at a lower grade level.

- The Verbal Reasoning section features a deeper assessment of Reading Comprehension skills.
- The Quantitative Reasoning section emphasizes data interpretation and real-life scenarios.
- The Analytical Writing section includes tasks that require more focused responses.

What Math Background Must I Have?

The Math part will test arithmetic, first- and second-year algebra (Algebra I and II), geometry, and data analysis. However, if you use common sense, rely on just a handful of geometrical formulas, and learn the strategies and thinking skills presented in this book, you don't need to take a full course in geometry or memorize all the theorems. If you have not taken algebra, you should still be able to answer many of the Math questions using the strategies presented in this book.

Is Guessing Advisable?

Yes! There is no penalty for a wrong answer, so if you have to guess, do! However, in this book, I'll show you ways to make a very good guess if you can't answer the problem.

Can I Use a Calculator on the Math Portion of the Test?

Students will be provided a calculator on the paper-based test. While it is possible to solve every question without the use of a calculator, it is recommended that you use a calculator if you don't immediately see a faster way to solve the problem without one.

A Table of What's on the GRE (Paper-Based Test)

Measure	Number of Questions	Time
Analytical Writing	1 Analyze an Issue task and 1 Analyze an Argument task	30 minutes per task
Verbal Reasoning (2 sections)	25 questions per section	35 minutes per section
Quantitative Reasoning (2 sections)	25 questions per section (including Quantitative Comparison questions per section)	40 minutes per section

Question Types That Will Appear on the GRE

Verbal Reasoning

There will be two sections for the Verbal Reasoning part—25 questions in each section. For each section, there will be 12–13 Text Completion questions (Sentence Completions) where you will have to fill in blanks to make a meaningful sentence or passage. Four or 5 of these will contain single blanks where you will have to choose 2 correct choices from 6 answers.

Each section will contain a total of 12–13 Reading Comprehension questions. Some of these questions will be based on short passages, some on longer ones. There will be questions where you have to select more than one answer choice or passages where you will have to highlight a sentence within the reading passage to answer the question. Some questions will ask you to determine what will weaken or support material in the passage.

Quantitative Reasoning

There will be two sections for this part—25 questions in each section.

You will need to know basic math concepts of arithmetic, algebra, geometry, and data analysis.

Multiple-choice questions include some that have more than one correct answer so that you may have to select more than one answer.

In each section, there will be a total of 9 Quantitative Comparison questions which ask you to compare two quantities and see if one is greater, if they are equal, or if you cannot make a definite comparison. The remaining 16 questions in each section will consist of multiple-choice questions and about 2–3 numeric questions (without choices) where you'll have to "grid" in your answer numerically.

You will be given a calculator that you can use, if you wish, to answer the questions. Be aware that, as we describe in this book later on, you may find it faster sometimes not to use a calculator if you know some strategy.

Analytical Writing

There will be two sections for this part.

In each section, you will be given one topic and you will have to write about it. In the first section, you will be given a statement or passage and have to take a position of whether you agree or disagree with it and support your position.

In the second section, you will be given an argument in passage form and be asked how you would evaluate the argument and explain how additional evidence would weaken or strengthen the argument.

The tasks are specific and responses are measured to ensure that you can integrate your critical thinking and analytical writing by fully addressing the tasks with which you are presented.

Computer-Based Revised General Test

The Computer-Based GRE® Revised General Test contains six sections:
- an Analytical Writing section with two tasks, which always comes first in the test
- two Verbal Reasoning sections
- two Quantitative Reasoning sections
- one unscored section, typically a Verbal Reasoning or Quantitative Reasoning section, that may appear at any point in the test

Questions in the unscored section are being tried out either for possible use in future tests or to ensure that scores on new editions of the test are comparable to scores on earlier editions.

An identified research section may be included in place of the unscored section. The research section will always appear at the end of the test. Questions in this section are included for the purpose of Educational Testing Service (ETS) research and will not count toward your score.

The Verbal Reasoning, Quantitative Reasoning, and unidentified/unscored sections may appear in any order; therefore, you should treat each section as if it counts toward your score.

The Verbal Reasoning and Quantitative Reasoning measures are section-level adaptive. The computer selects the second section of a measure based on your performance on the first.

The Verbal Reasoning and Quantitative Reasoning measures allow you to preview other questions within the specific section on which you're working, review questions you've already answered, and change your answers.

Typical Computer-Based Revised General Test

Total testing time is 3 hours and 45 minutes, including the unscored section. The directions at the beginning of each Verbal Reasoning and Quantitative Reasoning section specify the total number of questions in the section and the time allowed for the section. For the Analytical Writing section, the timing for each task is shown when the task is presented.

Section	Number of Questions	Time
Analytical Writing (1 section)	2 separately timed writing tasks	30 min. per task
Verbal Reasoning (2 sections)	Approximately 20 questions per section	30 min. per section
Quantitative Reasoning (2 sections)	Approximately 20 questions per section	35 min. per section
Unscored*	Approximately 20 questions	30–35 min. per section
Research**	Varies	Varies

*An unidentified unscored section that does not count toward a score may be included and may appear in any order.
**An identified research section that is not scored may be included, and it will always be at the end of the test.

Should I Use My Test Booklet to Write on and to Do Calculations?

Always use your test booklet to draw on, or use scratch paper if you're taking the computer-based test. Many of my strategies expect you to label diagrams, draw and extend lines, circle important words and sentences, etc., so feel free to write anything in your booklet or on scratch paper. The booklets aren't graded—just the answers (see General Strategy 4, page 68).

Should I Be Familiar with the Directions to the Various Items on the GRE Before Taking the Test?

Make sure you are completely familiar with the directions to each of the item types on the GRE—the directions for answering the Sentence Completions, the Reading, the Essay, the Regular Math, and especially the Grid-Type and Quantitative Comparison questions (see General Strategy 2, page 66).

What Should a Student Bring to the Exam on the Test Date?

You should bring a few sharpened #2 pencils with erasers, your ID, and, of course, a watch.

A calculator will be provided at the test site. You may not use your own calculator. For the computer-based test, you can use an on-screen calculator. Be aware that every Math question on the GRE can be solved without a calculator; in many questions, it's actually easier not to use one.

How Should a Student Pace Himself/Herself on the Exam? How Much Time Should One Spend on Each Question?

Calculate the time allowed for the particular section. For example, 35 minutes. Divide by the number of questions. For example, 25. That gives you an average of spending $1\frac{2}{5}$ minutes per question in this example. However, the first set of questions within an item type in a section is easier, so spend less than a minute on the first set of questions and perhaps more than a minute on the last set. With the reading passages, you should give yourself only about 30 seconds a question and spend the extra time on the reading passages. Also, more difficult reading questions may take more time.

How Is the Exam Scored? Are Some Questions Worth More Points?

Each question is worth the same number of points. After getting a raw score—the number of questions right—this is equated to a "scaled" score from 130 to 170 in each of the Verbal Reasoning and Quantitative Reasoning sections. A scaled score of 150 in each part is considered average.

It's 3 Days Until the GRE; What Can I Do to Prepare?

Make sure you are completely familiar with the structure of the test (page xiv), the basic math skills needed (pages 175–184), and the basic verbal skills, such as prefixes and roots (pages 366–370). Take a few practice tests and refresh your understanding of the strategies used to answer the questions (see page xxvi for the 4-Hour Study Program).

What Percentage of GRE Study Time Should I Spend Learning Vocabulary Words?

A student should not spend too much time on this—perhaps 4 hours at most. To build your word recognition quickly, learn the Prefixes and Roots I have compiled, as well as the 3 Vocabulary Strategies. Students might also want to learn the Most Important/Frequently Used GRE Words and Their Opposites, a list that I have developed based on research of hundreds of actual GREs.

What Is the Most Challenging Type of Question on the Exam and How Does One Attack It?

Many questions on the test, especially at the end of a section, can be challenging. You should always attack challenging questions by using a specific strategy or strategies and common sense.

What Should a Student Do to Prepare the Night Before the Exam? Cram? Watch TV? Relax?

The night before the exam, I would just refresh my knowledge of the structure of the test, some strategies, and some basic skills (Verbal or Math). You want to do this to keep the thinking going so that it is continual right up to the exam. Don't overdo it, just do enough so that it's somewhat continuous—this will also relieve some anxiety so that you won't feel you are forgetting things before the exam.

The Paper Test Is Given in One Booklet. Can a Student Skip Between Sections?

No—you cannot skip between the sections. You have to work on the section until the time is called. If you get caught skipping sections or going back to earlier sections, then you risk being asked to leave the exam.

Should a Student Answer All Easy Questions First and Save Difficult Ones for Last?

The easy questions usually appear at the beginning of the section, the medium difficulty ones in the middle, and the hard ones toward the end. So, I would answer the questions as they are presented to you, and if you find you are spending more than 30 seconds on a question and not getting anywhere, go to the next question. You may, however, find that the more difficult questions toward the end are actually easy for you because you have learned the strategies in this book.

What Are the Most Crucial Strategies for Students?

All specific Verbal (Reading) and Math Strategies are crucial, including the general test-taking strategies (described starting on page 66): guessing, writing and drawing in your test booklet, and being familiar with question-type directions. The key Reading Strategy is to know the four general types of questions that are asked in reading—main idea, inference, specific details, and tone or mood. In Math, it's the translations strategy—words to numbers, drawing of lines, etc. Also make sure you know the basic math skills cold (see pages 175–184 for these rules—*make sure you know them*).

How Do Other Exams Compare with the GRE? Can I Use the Strategies and Examples in This Book for Them?

Most other exams are modeled after the GRE and SAT, and so the strategies used here are definitely useful when taking them. The GRE (Graduate Record Examinations, for entrance into graduate school) has questions that use the identical strategies used on the SAT. The questions are just sometimes worded at a slightly higher level. The ACT (American College Testing Program), another college entrance exam, reflects more than ever strategies that are used on the SAT and GRE.

How Does the Gruber Preparation Method Differ from Other Programs and GRE Books?

Many other GRE programs try to use "quick fix" methods or subscribe to memorization. So-called quick fix methods can be detrimental to effective preparation because the GRE people constantly change questions to prevent "gimmick" approaches. Rote memorization methods do not enable you to answer a variety of questions that appear in the GRE exam. In more than thirty years of experience writing preparation books for the GRE, Dr. Gruber has developed and honed the Critical Thinking Skills and Strategies that are based on all standardized tests' construction. So, while his method immediately improves your performance on the GRE, it also provides you with the confidence to tackle problems in all areas of study for the rest of your life. He remarkably enables you to be able to, without panic, look at a problem or question, extract something curious or useful from the problem, and lead you to the next step and finally to a solution, without rushing into a wrong answer or getting lured into a wrong choice. It has been said that test taking through his methodology becomes enjoyable rather than painful.

How Does Dr. Gruber Ensure That the Practice Questions in These Books Are Accurate Reflections of What Students Will See on the Actual Tests?

Dr. Gruber critically analyzes all the current questions and patterns on the actual tests to ensure that his questions review similar topics at a comparable level of difficulty. Additionally, Dr. Gruber is directly in touch with the research development teams that design the actual tests, getting first notice of any new items or methods used in the questions on any upcoming test.

II. The Inside Track on How GRE Questions Are Developed and How They Vary from Test to Test

When a GRE question is developed, it is based on a set of criteria and guidelines. Knowing how these guidelines work should demystify the test-making process and convince you why the strategies in this book are so critical to getting a high score.

Inherent in the GRE questions are Critical Thinking Skills, which present strategies that enable you to solve a question by the quickest method with the least amount of panic and brain-racking, and describe an elegance and excitement in problem solving. Adhering to and using the strategies (which the test makers use to develop the questions) will let you "sail" through the GRE.

Show me the solution to a problem, and I'll solve that problem. Show me a Gruber strategy for solving the problem, and I'll solve hundreds of problems.

Here's a sample of a set of guidelines presented for making up a GRE-type question in the math area:

The test maker is to make up a hard math problem in the regular math multiple-choice area, which involves

(A) algebra
(B) two or more equations
(C) two or more ways to solve: one way being standard substitution, the other, faster way using the *strategy* of merely *adding* or *subtracting* equations.*

Previous examples given to the test maker for reference:

1. If $x + y = 3$, $y + z = 4$, and $z + x = 5$, find the value of $x + y + z$.

   (A) 4
   (B) 5
   (C) 6
   (D) 7
   (E) 8

Solution: *Add* equations and get $2x + 2y + 2z = 12$; divide both sides of the equation by 2 and we get $x + y + z = 6$. (Answer C)

2. If $2x + y = 8$ and $x + 2y = 4$, find the value of $x - y$.

   (A) 3
   (B) 4
   (C) 5
   (D) 6
   (E) 7

Solution: *Subtract* equations and get $x - y = 4$. (Answer B)

3. If $y - x = 5$ and $2y + z = 11$, find the value of $x + y + z$.

   (A) 3
   (B) 6
   (C) 8
   (D) 16
   (E) 55

Solution: *Subtract* equation $y - x = 5$ from $2y + z = 11$. We get $2y - y + z - (-x) = 11 - 5$. So, $y + z + x = 6$. (Choice B)

Here's an example from a recent GRE.

$$7x + 3y = 12$$
$$3x + 7y = 6$$

If x and y satisfy the system of equations above, what is the value of $x - y$?

   (A) $\dfrac{2}{3}$
   (B) $\dfrac{3}{2}$
   (C) 1
   (D) 4
   (E) 6

Solution: Subtract equations. We get $4x - 4y = 6$

Factor now.
$$4(x - y) = 6$$
$$x - y = \frac{6}{4} = \frac{3}{2}$$

Note: See Math Strategy #13 on p. 103.

Quantitative Comparison:
Choose Choice A if Quantity A is greater than Quantity B.
Choose Choice B if Quantity A is less than Quantity B.
Choose Choice C if Quantity A is equal to Quantity B.
Choose D if a definite comparison cannot be made (that is, if neither Choice A, B, nor C is correct).

Given: $2x + y = 6$
$\qquad x + 2y = 9$

Quantity A	Quantity B
$x + y$	5

Solution: *Add* the given equations: We get $3x + 3y = 15$. Divide both sides of this equation by 3. We get $x + y = 5$. Since $x + y = 5$, the columns are equal, and so Choice C is correct.

Now let's look at the actual GRE examples that the test makers made up:

Choose Choice A if Quantity A is greater than Quantity B.
Choose Choice B if Quantity A is less than Quantity B.
Choose Choice C if Quantity A is equal to Quantity B.
Choose D if a definite comparison cannot be made (that is, if neither Choice A, B, nor C is correct).

Given:
$n + p + v = 50$
$n + p - v = 20$

Quantity A	Quantity B
v	15

Solution: Just *subtract* the equations above.

We get $n - n + p - p + v - (-v) = 30$.
$2v = 30$. $v = 15$. Quantities are equal, so Choice C is correct.

Choose Choice A if Quantity A is greater than Quantity B.
Choose Choice B if Quantity A is less than Quantity B.
Choose Choice C if Quantity A is equal to Quantity B.
Choose D if a definite comparison cannot be made (that is, if neither Choice A, B, nor C is correct).

Given:
$s = a - b$
$t = b - c$
$u = c - a$

Quantity A	Quantity B
$s + t + u$	0

Solution: Just *add* the equations:
$s + t + u = a - b + b - c + c - a = 0$.
So the quantities are equal and thus Choice C is correct.

III. What Are Critical Thinking Skills?

Critical Thinking Skills are generic skills for the creative and most effective way of solving a problem or evaluating a situation. The most effective way of solving a problem is to extract some piece of information or observe something curious from the problem and then use one or more of the specific strategies or Critical Thinking Skills (together with basic skills or information you already know) to get to the next step in the problem. This next step will catapult you toward a solution with further use of the specific strategies or thinking skills.

> 1. EXTRACT OR OBSERVE SOMETHING CURIOUS
> 2. USE SPECIFIC STRATEGIES TOGETHER WITH BASIC SKILLS

These specific strategies will enable you to focus on the process rather than just be concerned with the end result, which usually gets you into a fast, rushed, and wrong answer. The Gruber strategies have been shown to make test takers more comfortable with problem solving and to make the process enjoyable. The skills will last a lifetime, and you will develop a passion for problem solving. These Critical Thinking Skills show that conventional "drill and practice" is a waste of time unless the practice is based on these generic thinking skills.

Here's a simple example of how these Critical Thinking Skills can be used in a math problem:

> Which is greater, $7\frac{1}{7} \times 8\frac{1}{8} \times 6\frac{1}{6}$ or $8\frac{1}{8} \times 6\frac{1}{6} \times 7$?

Long and tedious way: Multiply $7\frac{1}{7} \times 8\frac{1}{8} \times 6\frac{1}{6}$ and compare it with $8\frac{1}{8} \times 6\frac{1}{6} \times 7$.

Error in doing the problem the "long way": You don't have to *calculate;* you just have to *compare,* so you need a *strategy* for *comparing* two quantities.

Critical Thinking Way: 1. *Observe:* There is a common $8\frac{1}{8}$ and $6\frac{1}{6}$.

2. *Use Strategy:* Since both $8\frac{1}{8}$ and $6\frac{1}{6}$ are just weighting factors, like the same quantities on both sides of a balance scale, just *cancel* them from both multiplied quantities above.

3. You are then left comparing $7\frac{1}{7}$ with 7, so the first quantity, $7\frac{1}{7}$, is greater. Thus $7\frac{1}{7} \times 8\frac{1}{8} \times 6\frac{1}{6}$ is greater than $8\frac{1}{8} \times 6\frac{1}{6} \times 7$.

Here's a simple example of how Critical Thinking Skills can be used for a Verbal problem:

If you see a word such as *delude* in a sentence or in a reading passage, you can assume that the word *delude* is negative and probably means "taking away from something" or "distracting," since the prefix *de-* means "away from" and thus has a negative connotation. Although you may not get the exact meaning of the word (in this case, the meaning is "deceive" or "mislead"), you can see how the word may be used in the context of the sentence it appears in, and thus get the flavor or feeling of the sentence, paragraph, or sentence completion. I have researched and developed more than 50 prefixes and roots (present in this book) that can let you make use of this context strategy.

Notice that the Critical Thinking approach gives you a fail-safe and exact way to the solution without superficially trying to solve the problem or merely guessing at it. This book contains all the Critical Thinking Strategies you need to know for the GRE test.

I have researched hundreds of GRE tests (thousands of GRE questions) and documented 42 Critical Thinking Strategies (all found in this book), powerful strategies that can be used to solve questions on every test. These strategies can be used for any Quantitative or Verbal Reasoning problem.

In short, you can learn how to solve a specific problem and thus find how to answer that specific problem, or you can learn a powerful strategy that will enable you to answer hundreds of problems.

IV. Multi-Level Approaches to the Solution of Problems

How a student answers a question is more important than the answer given by the student. For example, the student may have randomly guessed, the student may have used a rote and unimaginative method for solution, or the student may have used a very creative method. It seems that one should judge the student by the way he or she answers the question and not just by the answer to the question. Unfortunately, standardized tests such as the GRE do not work that way.

Example:

> **Question: Without using a calculator, which is greater:**
> **355×356 or 354×357?**

Case 1: **Rote Memory Approach** (a completely mechanical approach not realizing the fact that there may be a faster method that takes into account patterns or connections of the numbers in the question): The student multiplies 355×356, gets 126,380, and then multiplies 354×357 and gets 126,378.

Case 2: **Observer's Rote Approach** (an approach that makes use of a mathematical strategy that can be memorized and tried for various problems): The student does the following:

He or she divides both quantities by 354.

He or she then gets $\dfrac{355 \times 356}{354}$ compared with $\dfrac{354 \times 357}{354}$.

He or she then divides these quantities by 356 and then gets $\dfrac{355}{354}$ compared with $\dfrac{357}{356}$.

Now he or she realizes that $\dfrac{355}{354} = 1\dfrac{1}{354}$; $\dfrac{357}{356} = 1\dfrac{1}{356}$.

He or she then reasons that since the left side, $1\dfrac{1}{354}$, is greater than the right side, $1\dfrac{1}{356}$, the left side of the original quantities, 355×356, is greater than the right side of the original quantities, 354×357.

Case 3: **The Pattern Seeker's Method** (the most mathematically creative method—an approach in which the student looks for a pattern or sequence in the numbers and then is astute enough to represent the pattern or sequence in more general algebraic language to see the pattern or sequence more clearly):

Look for a pattern. Represent 355×356 and 354×357 by symbols.

Let $x = 354$.

Then $355 = x + 1$, $356 = x + 2$, $357 = x + 3$.

So $355 \times 356 = (x + 1)(x + 2)$ and $354 \times 357 = x(x + 3)$.

Multiplying the factors, we get

$355 \times 356 = x^2 + 3x + 2$ and $354 \times 357 = x^2 + 3x$.

The difference is $355 \times 356 - 354 \times 357 = x^2 + 3x + 2 - x^2 - 3x$,

which is just 2.

So 355×356 is greater than 354×357 by 2.

Note: You could have also represented 355 by x. Then $356 = x + 1$; $354 = x - 1$; $357 = x + 2$. We would then get $355 \times 356 = (x)(x + 1)$ and $354 \times 357 = (x - 1)(x + 2)$. Then we would use the method above to compare the quantities.

—OR—

You could have written 354 as a and 357 as b. Then $355 = a + 1$ and $356 = b - 1$. So $355 \times 356 = (a + 1)(b - 1)$ and $354 \times 357 = ab$. Let's see what $(355 \times 356) - (354 \times 357)$ is. This is the same as $(a + 1)(b - 1) - ab$, which is $(ab + b - a - 1) - ab$, which is in turn

$b - a - 1$. Since $b - a - 1 = 357 - 354 - 1 = 2$, the quantity $355 \times 356 - 354 \times 357 = 2$, so 355×356 is greater than 354×357 by 2.

Case 4: **The Astute Observer's Approach** (the simplest approach—an approach that attempts to figure out a connection between the numbers and uses that connection to figure out the solution):
$355 \times 356 = (354 + 1) \times 356 = (354 \times 356) + 356$ and
$354 \times 357 = 354 \times (356 + 1) = (354 \times 356) + 354$
One can see that the difference is just 2.

Case 5: **The Observer's Common Relation Approach** (the approach that people use when they want to connect two items to a third to see how the two items are related):
355×356 is greater than 354×356 by 356.
354×357 is greater than 354×356 by 354.
So this means that 355×356 is greater than 354×357.

Case 6: **Scientific, Creative, and Observational Generalization Method** (a highly creative method and the most scientific method, as it spots a critical and curious aspect of the sums being equal and provides for a generalization to other problems of that nature):
Represent $354 = a$, $357 = b$, $355 = c$, and $356 = d$
We have now that (1) $a + b = c + d$
$\qquad\qquad\qquad$ (2) $|b - a| > |d - c|$
We want to prove: $ab < dc$
Proof:
Square inequality (2): $(b - a)^2 > (d - c)^2$
Therefore: (3) $b^2 - 2ab + a^2 > d^2 - 2dc + c^2$
Multiply (3) by (-1) and this reverses the inequality sign:
$-(b^2 - 2ab + a^2) < -(d^2 - 2dc + c^2)$
or
(4) $-b^2 + 2ab - a^2 < -d^2 + 2dc - c^2$
Now square (1): $(a + b) = (c + d)$ and we get:
(5) $a^2 + 2ab + b^2 = c^2 + 2dc + d^2$
Add inequality (4) to equality (5) and we get:
$4ab < 4dc$
Divide by 4 and we get:
$ab < dc$
The generalization is that for any positive numbers a, b, c, d when $|b - a| > |d - c|$ and $a + b = c + d$, then $ab < dc$.
This also generalizes in a geometrical setting where for two rectangles whose perimeters are the same ($2a + 2b = 2c + 2d$), the rectangle whose absolute difference in sides $|d - c|$ is <u>least</u> has the <u>greatest</u> area.

Case 7: **Geometric and Visual Approach*** (the approach used by visual people or people that have a curious geometric bent and possess "out-of-the-box" insights):

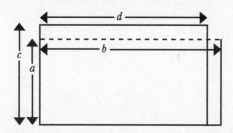

Where $a = 354$, $b = 357$, $c = 355$, and $d = 356$, we have two rectangles where the first one's length is d and width is c, and the second one's length is b (dotted line) and width is a.

*This method of solution was developed by and sent to the author from Dr. Eric Cornell, a Nobel laureate in physics.

Now the area of the first rectangle (dc) is equal to the area of the second (ab) minus the area of the rectangular slab, which is $(b - d)a$ plus the area of the rectangular slab $(c - a)d$. So we get: $cd = ab - (b - d)a + (c - a)d$. Since $b - d = c - a$, we get $cd = ab - (c - a)\,a + (c - a)d = ab + (d - a)(c - a)$.

Since $d > a$ and $c > a$, $cd > ab$. So $355 \times 356 > 354 \times 357$.

Note: Many people have thought that by multiplying units digits from one quantity and comparing that with the product of the units digits from the other quantity, they'd get the answer. For example, they would multiply $5 \times 6 = 30$ from 355×356, then multiply $4 \times 7 = 28$ from 354×357, and then say that 355×356 is greater than 354×357 because $5 \times 6 > 4 \times 7$. They would be lucky. That works if the sum of units digits of the first quantity is the same as or greater than the sum of units digits of the second quantity. However, if we want to compare something like $354 \times 356 = 126{,}024$ with $352 \times 359 = 126{,}368$, that method would not work.

V. A 4-Hour Study Program
for the GRE

For those who have only a few hours to spend in GRE preparation, I have worked out a *minimum* study program to get you by. It tells you what basic math skills you need to know, what vocabulary practice you need, and the most important strategies to focus on, from the 42 in this book.

General

Study General Strategies, pages 66–68.

Reading

Study the following Verbal Strategies beginning on page 136 (first 3 questions for each strategy):

Sentence Completion Strategies 1 and 2, pages 137–140
Vocabulary Strategies 1, 2, and 3, pages 168–173
Reading Comprehension Strategies 1, 2, and 10, pages 152–156 and 166–167

Study the Most Important/Frequently Used GRE Words and Their Opposites, page 373.

Math

Study the Mini-Math Refresher beginning on page 175.
Study the following Math Strategies beginning on page 72* (first 3 questions for each strategy):

Strategy 2, page 74   Strategy A, page 121
Strategy 4, page 83   Strategy B, page 123
Strategy 8, page 93   Strategy C, page 124
Strategy 12, page 101   Strategy D, page 127
Strategy 13, page 103
Strategy 14, page 105
Strategy 17, page 112
Strategy 18, page 115

If you have time, take Practice Test 1 starting on page 517. Do sections 1–4. Check your answers with the explanatory answers starting on page 565, and look again at the strategies and basic skills that apply to the questions you missed.

Writing

Look through the material in Part 8—Analytical Writing Section starting on page 473.

*Make sure you read pages 69–71 before you study Math Strategies.

VI. Longer-Range Study Program and Helpful Steps for Using This Book

1. Learn the 5 General Strategies for test taking on pages 66–68.
2. Take the Strategy Diagnostic GRE test on page 1 and follow the directions for diagnosis.
3. Take the GRE Practice Test 1 on page 517 and score yourself according to the instructions.
4. For those problems or questions that you answered incorrectly or were uncertain of, see the explanatory answers, beginning on page 565, and make sure that you learn the strategies keyed to the questions, beginning on page 65. For complete strategy development, it is a good idea to study *all* the strategies beginning on page 65, Part 4 of the Strategy Section, and learn how to do all the problems within each strategy.
5. If you are weak in basic math skills, take the 101 Most Important Math Questions Test beginning on page 37 and follow the directions for diagnosis.
6. To see if you are making use of the strategies you've learned, you should take the Shortest GRE Test on page 25 and follow the directions for diagnosis.

For Vocabulary Building

7. Learn the special Latin and Greek prefixes, roots, and suffixes beginning on page 366. This will significantly build your vocabulary. You may also want to study the Hot Prefixes and Roots in Appendix A beginning on page 717.
8. Study 100 words per day from the 3,400-Word List beginning on page 377.
9. Optional: Take the vocabulary tests beginning on page 426.
10. Study the Most Important/Frequently Used GRE Words and Their Opposites beginning on page 373.

For Math-Area Basic Skills Help

11. For the basic math skills keyed to the questions, study the Complete GRE Math Refresher beginning on page 185, or for a quicker review, look at the Mini-Math Refresher beginning on page 175.

For Writing Help

12. Look through Part 8—Analytical Writing Section beginning on page 473.

Now

13. Take the remaining two Practice GRE tests beginning on page 584, score yourself, and go over your answers with the explanatory answers. Always refer to the associated strategies and basic skills for questions you answered incorrectly or were not sure how to do.

PART 1

STRATEGY DIAGNOSTIC TEST FOR THE GRE

Take This Test to Find Out What Strategies You Don't Know

The purpose of this test is to find out *how* you approach GRE problems of different types and to reveal your understanding and command of the various strategies and Critical Thinking Skills. After checking your answers in the table at the end of the test, you will have a profile of your performance. You will know exactly what strategies you must master and where you may learn them.

Directions for Taking the
Diagnostic Test

For each odd-numbered question (1, 3, 5, 7, etc.), choose the best answer. In the even-numbered questions (2, 4, 6, 8, etc.), you will be asked how you solved the preceding odd-numbered question. Make sure that you answer the even-numbered questions carefully, as your answers will determine whether or not you used the right strategy. Be completely honest in your answers to the even-numbered questions, since you do want an accurate assessment in order to be helped. *Note*: Only the odd-numbered questions are SAT-type questions that would appear on the actual exam. The even-numbered questions are for self-diagnosis purposes only.

EXAMPLE:

1. The value of $17 \times 98 + 17 \times 2 =$

   (A) 1,550
   (B) 1,600
   (C) 1,700
   (D) 1,800
   (E) 1,850
   (The correct answer is Choice C.)

2. How did you get your answer?

   (A) I multiplied 17×98 and added that to 17×2.
   (B) I approximated and found the closest match in the choices.
   (C) I factored 17 to get $17(98 + 2)$.
   (D) I guessed.
   (E) By none of the above methods.

In question 2:

- If you chose A, you did the problem the long way unless you used a calculator.

- If you chose B, you probably approximated 98 by 100 and got 1,700.

- If you chose C, you factored out the 17 to get $17(98 + 2) = 17(100) = 1,700$. This was the best strategy to use.

- If you chose D, you probably didn't know how to solve the problem and just guessed.

- If you chose E, you did not use any of the methods above but used your own different method.

Note: In the even-numbered questions, you may have used a different approach from what will be described in the answer to that question. It is, however, a good idea to see if the alternate approach is described, as you may want to use that approach for solving other questions. Now turn to the next page to take the test.

Strategy Diagnostic Test
Answer Sheet

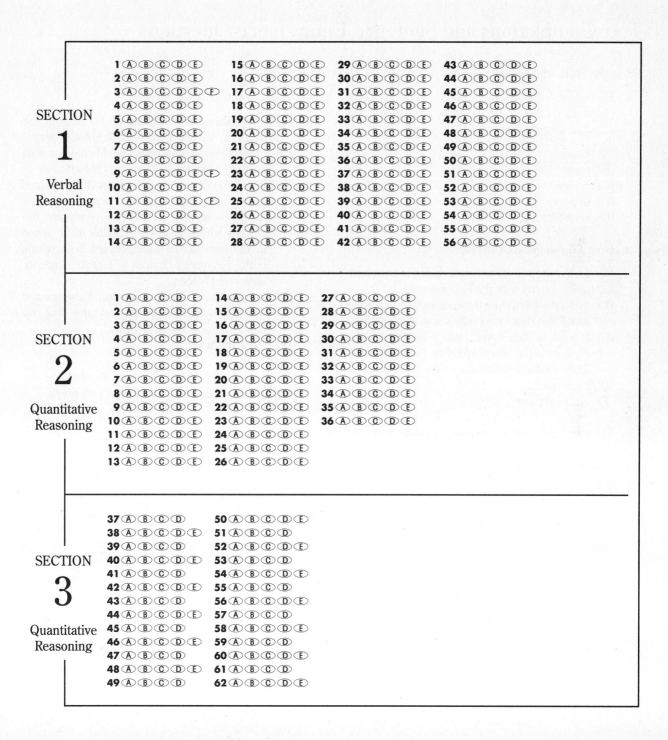

SECTION 1
Verbal Reasoning

1 Ⓐ Ⓑ Ⓒ Ⓓ Ⓔ   15 Ⓐ Ⓑ Ⓒ Ⓓ Ⓔ   29 Ⓐ Ⓑ Ⓒ Ⓓ Ⓔ   43 Ⓐ Ⓑ Ⓒ Ⓓ Ⓔ
2 Ⓐ Ⓑ Ⓒ Ⓓ Ⓔ   16 Ⓐ Ⓑ Ⓒ Ⓓ Ⓔ   30 Ⓐ Ⓑ Ⓒ Ⓓ Ⓔ   44 Ⓐ Ⓑ Ⓒ Ⓓ Ⓔ
3 Ⓐ Ⓑ Ⓒ Ⓓ Ⓔ Ⓕ   17 Ⓐ Ⓑ Ⓒ Ⓓ Ⓔ   31 Ⓐ Ⓑ Ⓒ Ⓓ Ⓔ   45 Ⓐ Ⓑ Ⓒ Ⓓ Ⓔ
4 Ⓐ Ⓑ Ⓒ Ⓓ Ⓔ   18 Ⓐ Ⓑ Ⓒ Ⓓ Ⓔ   32 Ⓐ Ⓑ Ⓒ Ⓓ Ⓔ   46 Ⓐ Ⓑ Ⓒ Ⓓ Ⓔ
5 Ⓐ Ⓑ Ⓒ Ⓓ Ⓔ   19 Ⓐ Ⓑ Ⓒ Ⓓ Ⓔ   33 Ⓐ Ⓑ Ⓒ Ⓓ Ⓔ   47 Ⓐ Ⓑ Ⓒ Ⓓ Ⓔ
6 Ⓐ Ⓑ Ⓒ Ⓓ Ⓔ   20 Ⓐ Ⓑ Ⓒ Ⓓ Ⓔ   34 Ⓐ Ⓑ Ⓒ Ⓓ Ⓔ   48 Ⓐ Ⓑ Ⓒ Ⓓ Ⓔ
7 Ⓐ Ⓑ Ⓒ Ⓓ Ⓔ   21 Ⓐ Ⓑ Ⓒ Ⓓ Ⓔ   35 Ⓐ Ⓑ Ⓒ Ⓓ Ⓔ   49 Ⓐ Ⓑ Ⓒ Ⓓ Ⓔ
8 Ⓐ Ⓑ Ⓒ Ⓓ Ⓔ   22 Ⓐ Ⓑ Ⓒ Ⓓ Ⓔ   36 Ⓐ Ⓑ Ⓒ Ⓓ Ⓔ   50 Ⓐ Ⓑ Ⓒ Ⓓ Ⓔ
9 Ⓐ Ⓑ Ⓒ Ⓓ Ⓔ Ⓕ   23 Ⓐ Ⓑ Ⓒ Ⓓ Ⓔ   37 Ⓐ Ⓑ Ⓒ Ⓓ Ⓔ   51 Ⓐ Ⓑ Ⓒ Ⓓ Ⓔ
10 Ⓐ Ⓑ Ⓒ Ⓓ Ⓔ   24 Ⓐ Ⓑ Ⓒ Ⓓ Ⓔ   38 Ⓐ Ⓑ Ⓒ Ⓓ Ⓔ   52 Ⓐ Ⓑ Ⓒ Ⓓ Ⓔ
11 Ⓐ Ⓑ Ⓒ Ⓓ Ⓔ Ⓕ   25 Ⓐ Ⓑ Ⓒ Ⓓ Ⓔ   39 Ⓐ Ⓑ Ⓒ Ⓓ Ⓔ   53 Ⓐ Ⓑ Ⓒ Ⓓ Ⓔ
12 Ⓐ Ⓑ Ⓒ Ⓓ Ⓔ   26 Ⓐ Ⓑ Ⓒ Ⓓ Ⓔ   40 Ⓐ Ⓑ Ⓒ Ⓓ Ⓔ   54 Ⓐ Ⓑ Ⓒ Ⓓ Ⓔ
13 Ⓐ Ⓑ Ⓒ Ⓓ Ⓔ   27 Ⓐ Ⓑ Ⓒ Ⓓ Ⓔ   41 Ⓐ Ⓑ Ⓒ Ⓓ Ⓔ   55 Ⓐ Ⓑ Ⓒ Ⓓ Ⓔ
14 Ⓐ Ⓑ Ⓒ Ⓓ Ⓔ   28 Ⓐ Ⓑ Ⓒ Ⓓ Ⓔ   42 Ⓐ Ⓑ Ⓒ Ⓓ Ⓔ   56 Ⓐ Ⓑ Ⓒ Ⓓ Ⓔ

SECTION 2
Quantitative Reasoning

1 Ⓐ Ⓑ Ⓒ Ⓓ Ⓔ   14 Ⓐ Ⓑ Ⓒ Ⓓ Ⓔ   27 Ⓐ Ⓑ Ⓒ Ⓓ Ⓔ
2 Ⓐ Ⓑ Ⓒ Ⓓ Ⓔ   15 Ⓐ Ⓑ Ⓒ Ⓓ Ⓔ   28 Ⓐ Ⓑ Ⓒ Ⓓ Ⓔ
3 Ⓐ Ⓑ Ⓒ Ⓓ Ⓔ   16 Ⓐ Ⓑ Ⓒ Ⓓ Ⓔ   29 Ⓐ Ⓑ Ⓒ Ⓓ Ⓔ
4 Ⓐ Ⓑ Ⓒ Ⓓ Ⓔ   17 Ⓐ Ⓑ Ⓒ Ⓓ Ⓔ   30 Ⓐ Ⓑ Ⓒ Ⓓ Ⓔ
5 Ⓐ Ⓑ Ⓒ Ⓓ Ⓔ   18 Ⓐ Ⓑ Ⓒ Ⓓ Ⓔ   31 Ⓐ Ⓑ Ⓒ Ⓓ Ⓔ
6 Ⓐ Ⓑ Ⓒ Ⓓ Ⓔ   19 Ⓐ Ⓑ Ⓒ Ⓓ Ⓔ   32 Ⓐ Ⓑ Ⓒ Ⓓ Ⓔ
7 Ⓐ Ⓑ Ⓒ Ⓓ Ⓔ   20 Ⓐ Ⓑ Ⓒ Ⓓ Ⓔ   33 Ⓐ Ⓑ Ⓒ Ⓓ Ⓔ
8 Ⓐ Ⓑ Ⓒ Ⓓ Ⓔ   21 Ⓐ Ⓑ Ⓒ Ⓓ Ⓔ   34 Ⓐ Ⓑ Ⓒ Ⓓ Ⓔ
9 Ⓐ Ⓑ Ⓒ Ⓓ Ⓔ   22 Ⓐ Ⓑ Ⓒ Ⓓ Ⓔ   35 Ⓐ Ⓑ Ⓒ Ⓓ Ⓔ
10 Ⓐ Ⓑ Ⓒ Ⓓ Ⓔ   23 Ⓐ Ⓑ Ⓒ Ⓓ Ⓔ   36 Ⓐ Ⓑ Ⓒ Ⓓ Ⓔ
11 Ⓐ Ⓑ Ⓒ Ⓓ Ⓔ   24 Ⓐ Ⓑ Ⓒ Ⓓ Ⓔ
12 Ⓐ Ⓑ Ⓒ Ⓓ Ⓔ   25 Ⓐ Ⓑ Ⓒ Ⓓ Ⓔ
13 Ⓐ Ⓑ Ⓒ Ⓓ Ⓔ   26 Ⓐ Ⓑ Ⓒ Ⓓ Ⓔ

SECTION 3
Quantitative Reasoning

37 Ⓐ Ⓑ Ⓒ Ⓓ   50 Ⓐ Ⓑ Ⓒ Ⓓ Ⓔ
38 Ⓐ Ⓑ Ⓒ Ⓓ Ⓔ   51 Ⓐ Ⓑ Ⓒ Ⓓ
39 Ⓐ Ⓑ Ⓒ Ⓓ   52 Ⓐ Ⓑ Ⓒ Ⓓ
40 Ⓐ Ⓑ Ⓒ Ⓓ Ⓔ   53 Ⓐ Ⓑ Ⓒ Ⓓ
41 Ⓐ Ⓑ Ⓒ Ⓓ   54 Ⓐ Ⓑ Ⓒ Ⓓ Ⓔ
42 Ⓐ Ⓑ Ⓒ Ⓓ Ⓔ   55 Ⓐ Ⓑ Ⓒ Ⓓ
43 Ⓐ Ⓑ Ⓒ Ⓓ   56 Ⓐ Ⓑ Ⓒ Ⓓ Ⓔ
44 Ⓐ Ⓑ Ⓒ Ⓓ Ⓔ   57 Ⓐ Ⓑ Ⓒ Ⓓ
45 Ⓐ Ⓑ Ⓒ Ⓓ   58 Ⓐ Ⓑ Ⓒ Ⓓ Ⓔ
46 Ⓐ Ⓑ Ⓒ Ⓓ Ⓔ   59 Ⓐ Ⓑ Ⓒ Ⓓ
47 Ⓐ Ⓑ Ⓒ Ⓓ   60 Ⓐ Ⓑ Ⓒ Ⓓ Ⓔ
48 Ⓐ Ⓑ Ⓒ Ⓓ Ⓔ   61 Ⓐ Ⓑ Ⓒ Ⓓ
49 Ⓐ Ⓑ Ⓒ Ⓓ   62 Ⓐ Ⓑ Ⓒ Ⓓ Ⓔ

Section 1: Verbal Reasoning

Text Completions and Sentence Equivalence Questions

Fill in the blank with the best choice.

1. He believed that because there is serious unemployment in our auto industry, we should not _____ foreign cars.

   (A) build
   (B) repair
   (C) review
   (D) import
   (E) consolidate

2. How did you get your answer?

   (A) I tried the word from each choice in the blank and came up with the best answer.
   (B) I chose a word from the choices that "sounded good" but that I am really not sure is correct.
   (C) I tried to figure out, *before* looking at the choices, what word would fit into the blank. Then I matched that word with the choices.
   (D) I guessed.
   (E) None of these.

3. Until we are able to improve substantially the _____ status of the underprivileged in our country, a substantial _____ in our crime rate is remote.

Blank 1	Blank 2
(A) financial	(D) ascension
(B) enormous	(E) development
(C) questionable	(F) attenuation

4. How did you get your answer?

   (A) I first tried combinations of words from the blanks to see which made for the best sentence.
   (B) I tried to see what words I could come up with for the blanks *before* looking at the choices.
   (C) I tried the first word from each of the choices in the first blank in the sentence to see which made the most sense. Then I eliminated the choices whose first words didn't make sense in the sentence. Finally, I tried both words in the remaining choices to further eliminate incorrect choices.
   (D) I noticed "until" indicated result. I also noticed that the word "improve" indicates that we could "reduce" the crime rate.
   (E) None of these.

5. Many buildings with historical significance are now being _____ instead of being torn down.
   (A) built
   (B) forgotten
   (C) destroyed
   (D) praised
   (E) repaired

6. How did you get your answer?

   (A) I tried each of the choices in the blank.
   (B) I tried to find my own word that would fit the blank *before* looking at the choices. Then I matched one of the choices with my word.
   (C) I looked for a word that meant the opposite of "being torn down."
   (D) I guessed.
   (E) None of these.

7. Being _____ person, he insisted at the conference that when he spoke he was not to be interrupted.

   (A) a successful
   (B) a delightful
   (C) a headstrong
   (D) an understanding
   (E) a solitary

8. How did you get your answer?

(A) I tried all the choices in the sentence and selected the best one.
(B) I realized, from the word *Being* and from the phrase after the comma, that there was a connection between the two parts of the sentence.
(C) I looked for the most difficult-sounding word.
(D) I guessed.
(E) None of these.

9. In spite of the ——— of her presentation, many people were ——— with the speaker's concepts and ideas.

Blank 1	Blank 2
(A) long-windedness	(D) enthralled
(B) formulation	(E) bored
(C) forcefulness	(F) gratified

10. How did you get your answer?

(A) I tried words from Blank 1 and words from Blank 2 to see which combination made sense in the sentence.
(B) I tried the first word from each choice in the first blank of the sentence to eliminate choices. Then I tried both words from the remaining choices to further eliminate choices.
(C) I realized that the words *in spite of* would create an opposition or contrast between the two parts of the sentence and therefore looked for words in the choices that were opposites.
(D) I guessed.
(E) None of these.

Select two answer choices that fit the sentence and give the sentence the same meaning.

11. Richard Wagner was frequently intolerant; moreover, his strange behavior caused most of his acquaintances to _____ the composer whenever possible. (Choose two answers)

(A) contradict
(B) interrogate
(C) shun
(D) revere
(E) tolerate
(F) reject

12. How did you get your answer?

(A) I tried all the choices in the blank and selected the best ones.
(B) I realized that the word *moreover* indicated support, so I looked for a choice that would represent a *support* of what was in the first part of the sentence.
(C) I tried to find my own words to fit the blank. Then I matched that word with a word in one of the choices.
(D) I guessed.
(E) None of these.

Each of the following questions consists of a word in capital letters, followed by five lettered words or phrases. Choose the word or phrase that is most nearly *opposite* in meaning to the word in capital letters. Since some of the questions require you to distinguish fine shades of meaning, consider all the choices before deciding which is best.

EXAMPLE:

GOOD: (A) sour (B) bad (C) red
(D) hot (E) ugly

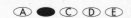

Note: Although antonyms are not a part of the GRE, we are still testing vocabulary through antonyms on this particular test, since it is important for you to develop vocabulary strategies for the Sentence Completions and Reading Comprehension parts of the GRE.

13. TENACIOUS:

(A) changing
(B) stupid
(C) unconscious
(D) poor
(E) antagonistic

14. How did you get your answer?

(A) I knew the meaning of the word *tenacious*.
(B) I knew what the root *ten* meant and looked for the opposite of that root.
(C) I did not know what *tenacious* meant but knew a word that sounded like *tenacious*.
(D) I guessed.
(E) None of these.

15. PROFICIENT:

(A) antiseptic
(B) unwilling
(C) inconsiderate
(D) retarded
(E) awkward

16. How did you get your answer?

(A) I knew what the prefix *pro-* meant and used it to figure out the capitalized word, but I didn't use any root of *proficient*.
(B) I used the meaning of the prefix *pro-* and the meaning of the root *fic* to figure out the meaning of the word *proficient*.
(C) I knew from memory what the word *proficient* meant.
(D) I guessed.
(E) None of these.

17. DELUDE:

(A) include
(B) guide
(C) reply
(D) upgrade
(E) welcome

18. How did you get your answer?

(A) I knew what the prefix *de-* meant and used it to figure out the meaning of the word *delude*, but I didn't use any root of *delude*.
(B) I used the meaning of the prefix *de-* and the meaning of the root *lud* to figure out the meaning of the word *delude*.
(C) I knew from memory what the word *delude* meant.
(D) I guessed.
(E) None of these.

19. POTENT:

(A) imposing
(B) pertinent
(C) feeble
(D) comparable
(E) frantic

20. How did you get your answer?

(A) I knew what the capitalized word meant.
(B) I knew a word or part of a word that sounded the same as *potent* or had a close association with the word *potent*.
(C) I knew a prefix or root of the capitalized word, which gave me a clue to the meaning of the word.
(D) I knew from a part of the capitalized word that the word had a negative or positive association. Thus, I selected a choice that was opposite in flavor (positive or negative).
(E) None of these.

21. RECEDE:

(A) accede
(B) settle
(C) surrender
(D) advance
(E) reform

22. How did you get your answer?

(A) I found a word opposite in meaning to the word *recede*, *without* looking at the choices. Then I matched my word with the choices.
(B) I used prefixes and/or roots to get the meaning of the word *recede*.
(C) I looked at the choices to see which word was opposite to *recede*. I *did not* try first to get my own word that was opposite to the meaning of *recede*, as in Choice A.
(D) I guessed.
(E) None of these.

23. THERMAL:

(A) improving
(B) possible
(C) beginning
(D) reduced
(E) frigid

24. How did you get your answer?

(A) I knew what the capitalized word meant.
(B) I knew a word or part of a word that sounded the same as *thermal* or had a close association with the word *thermal*.
(C) I knew a prefix or root of the capitalized word, which gave me a clue to the meaning of the word.
(D) I knew from a part of the capitalized word that the word had a negative or positive association. Thus, I selected a choice that was opposite in flavor (positive or negative).
(E) None of these.

25. SLOTHFUL:

(A) permanent
(B) ambitious
(C) average
(D) truthful
(E) plentiful

26. How did you get your answer?

(A) I knew what the capitalized word meant.
(B) I knew a word or part of a word that sounded the same as *sloth* or had a close association with the word *sloth*.
(C) I knew a prefix or root of the capitalized word, which gave me a clue to the meaning of the word.
(D) I knew from a part of the capitalized word that the word had a negative or positive association. Thus, I selected a choice that was opposite in flavor (positive or negative).
(E) None of these.

27. MUNIFICENCE:

(A) disloyalty
(B) stinginess
(C) dispersion
(D) simplicity
(E) vehemence

28. How did you get your answer?

(A) I knew what the capitalized word meant.
(B) I knew a word or part of a word that sounded the same as *munificence* or had a close association with the word *munificence*.
(C) I knew a prefix or root of the capitalized word, which gave me a clue to the meaning of the word.
(D) I knew from a part of the capitalized word that the word had a negative or positive association. Thus, I selected a choice that was opposite in flavor (positive or negative).
(E) None of these.

29. FORTITUDE:

(A) timidity
(B) conservatism
(C) placidity
(D) laxness
(E) ambition

30. How did you get your answer?

(A) I knew what the capitalized word meant.
(B) I knew a word or part of a word that sounded the same as *fortitude* or had a close association with the word *fortitude*.
(C) I knew a prefix or root of the capitalized word, which gave me a clue to the meaning of the word.
(D) I knew from a part of the capitalized word that the word had a negative or positive association. Thus, I selected a choice that was opposite in flavor (positive or negative).
(E) None of these.

31. DETRIMENT:

    (A) recurrence
    (B) disclosure
    (C) resemblance
    (D) enhancement
    (E) postponement

32. How did you get your answer?

    (A) I knew what the capitalized word meant.
    (B) I knew a word or part of a word that sounded the same as *detriment* or had a close association with the word *detriment*.
    (C) I knew a prefix or root of the capitalized word, which gave me a clue to the meaning of the word.
    (D) I knew from a part of the capitalized word that the word had a negative or positive association. Thus, I selected a choice that was opposite in flavor (positive or negative).
    (E) None of these.

33. CIRCUMSPECT:

    (A) suspicious
    (B) overbearing
    (C) listless
    (D) determined
    (E) careless

34. How did you get your answer?

    (A) I knew what the capitalized word meant.
    (B) I knew a word or part of a word that sounded the same as *circumspect* or had a close association with the word *circumspect*.
    (C) I knew a prefix or root of the capitalized word, which gave me a clue to the meaning of the word.
    (D) I knew from a part of the capitalized word that the word had a negative or positive association. Thus, I selected a choice that was opposite in flavor (positive or negative).
    (E) None of these.

35. LUCID:

    (A) underlying
    (B) complex
    (C) luxurious
    (D) tight
    (E) general

36. How did you get your answer?

    (A) I knew what the capitalized word meant.
    (B) I knew a word or part of a word that sounded the same as *lucid* or had a close association with the word *lucid*.
    (C) I knew a prefix or root of the capitalized word, which gave me a clue to the meaning of the word.
    (D) I knew from a part of the capitalized word that the word had a negative or positive association. Thus, I selected a choice that was opposite in flavor (positive or negative).
    (E) None of these.

Each of the following passages is followed by questions based on its content. Answer all questions following a passage on the basis of what is *stated* or *implied* in that passage.

She walked along the river until a policeman stopped her. It was one o'clock, he said. Not the best time to be walking alone by the side of a half-frozen river. He smiled at her, then offered to walk her home. It was the first day of the 5 new year, 1946, eight and a half months after the British tanks had rumbled into Bergen-Belsen.

That February, my mother turned twenty-six. It was difficult for strangers to believe that she had ever been a concentration camp inmate. Her face was smooth and 10 round. She wore lipstick and applied mascara to her large dark eyes. She dressed fashionably. But when she looked into the mirror in the mornings before leaving for work, my mother saw a shell, a mannequin who moved and spoke but who bore only a superficial resemblance to her real self. 15 The people closest to her had vanished. She had no proof that they were truly dead. No eyewitnesses had survived to vouch for her husband's death. There was no one living who had seen her parents die. The lack of confirmation haunted her. At night before she went to sleep and during the day as 20 she stood pinning dresses she wondered if, by some chance, her parents had gotten past the Germans or had crawled out of the mass grave into which they had been shot and were living, old and helpless, somewhere in Poland. What if only one of them had died? What if they had survived and had 25 died of cold or hunger after she had been liberated, while she was in Celle* dancing with British officers?

She did not talk to anyone about these things. No one, she thought, wanted to hear them. She woke up in the morning, went to work, bought groceries, went to the Jewish 30 Community Center and to the housing office like a robot.

*Celle is a small town in Germany.

37. The policeman stopped the author's mother from walking along the river because

(A) the river was dangerous
(B) it was the wrong time of day
(C) it was still wartime
(D) it was too cold
(E) she looked suspicious

38. Which part of the passage gives you the best clue for getting the right answer?

(A) Line 2: "It was one o'clock, he said."
(B) Lines 2–3: "It was one o'clock, he said. Not the best time to be walking alone."
(C) Lines 2–3: "It was one o'clock, he said. Not the best time to be walking alone by the side of a half-frozen river."
(D) None of these.
(E) I don't know.

39. The author states that his mother thought about her parents when she

(A) walked along the river
(B) thought about death
(C) danced with the officers
(D) arose in the morning
(E) was at work

40. Which part of the passage gives you the best clue for getting the right answer?

(A) Line 19: "At night before she went to sleep…"
(B) Lines 19–20: "…and during the day as she stood pinning dresses she wondered…"
(C) Lines 11–12: "But when she looked into the mirror in the mornings…"
(D) Lines 24–26: "What if they had survived and died of cold…while she was…dancing with British officers?"
(E) I don't know.

41. When the author mentions his mother's dancing with the British officers, he implies that his mother

(A) compared her dancing to the suffering of her parents
(B) had clearly put her troubles behind her
(C) felt it was her duty to dance with them
(D) felt guilty about dancing
(E) regained the self-confidence she once had

42. Which words expressed in the passage lead us to the right answer?

(A) Line 24: "had survived"
(B) Lines 24–25: "had died of cold or hunger"
(C) Line 21: "gotten past the Germans"
(D) Line 30: "like a robot"
(E) I don't know.

That one citizen is as good as another is a favorite American axiom, supposed to express the very essence of our Constitution and way of life. But just what do we mean when we utter that platitude? One surgeon is not as good 5 as another. One plumber is not as good as another. We soon become aware of this when we require the attention of either. Yet in political and economic matters we appear to have reached a point where knowledge and specialized training count for very little. A newspaper reporter is sent 10 out on the street to collect the views of various passersby on such a question as "Should the United States defend El Salvador?" The answer of the barfly who doesn't even

know where the country is located, or that it is a country, is quoted in the next edition just as solemnly as that of the
15 college teacher of history. With the basic tenets of democracy—that all men are born free and equal and are entitled to life, liberty, and the pursuit of happiness—no decent American can possibly take issue. But that the opinion of one citizen on a technical subject is just as authoritative
20 as that of another is manifestly absurd. And to accept the opinions of all comers as having the same value is surely to encourage a cult of mediocrity.

43. Which phrase best expresses the main idea of this passage?

(A) the myth of equality
(B) a distinction about equality
(C) the essence of the Constitution
(D) a technical subject
(E) knowledge and specialized training

44. Which is the best title for this passage?

(A) "Equality—for Everyone, for Every Situation?"
(B) "Dangers of Opinion and Knowledge"
(C) "The American Syndrome"
(D) "Freedom and Equality"
(E) I don't know.

45. The author most probably included the example of the question on El Salvador (lines 11−12) in order to

(A) move the reader to rage
(B) show that he is opposed to opinion sampling
(C) show that he has thoroughly researched his project
(D) explain the kind of opinion sampling he objects to
(E) provide a humorous but temporary diversion from his main point

46. The distinction between a "barfly" and a college teacher (lines 12−15) is that

(A) one is stupid, the other is not
(B) one is learned, the other is not
(C) one is anti-American, the other is not
(D) one is pro–El Salvadoran, the other is not
(E) I don't know.

47. The author would be most likely to agree that

(A) some men are born to be masters; others are born to be servants
(B) the Constitution has little relevance for today's world
(C) one should never express an opinion on a specialized subject unless he is an expert in that subject
(D) every opinion should be treated equally
(E) all opinions should not be given equal weight

48. Which lines give the best clue to the answer to this question?

(A) Lines 3−5
(B) Lines 4−6
(C) Lines 14−17
(D) Lines 18−22
(E) I don't know.

Mist continues to obscure the horizon, but above us the sky is suddenly awash with lavender light. At once the geese respond. Now, as well as their cries, a beating roar rolls across the water as if five thousand housewives have taken
5 it into their heads to shake out blankets all at one time. Ten thousand housewives. It keeps up—the invisible rhythmic beating of all those goose wings—for what seems a long time. Even Lonnie is held motionless with suspense.
Then the geese begin to rise. One, two, three hundred—
10 then a thousand at a time—in long horizontal lines that unfurl like pennants across the sky. The horizon actually darkens as they pass. It goes on and on like that, flock after flock, for three or four minutes, each new contingent announcing its ascent with an accelerating roar of cries and
15 wingbeats. Then gradually the intervals between flights become longer. I think the spectacle is over, until yet another flock lifts up, following the others in a gradual turn toward the northeastern quadrant of the refuge.
Finally the sun emerges from the mist; the mist itself
20 thins a little, uncovering the black line of willows on the other side of the wildlife preserve. I remember to close my mouth—which has been open for some time—and inadvertently shut two or three mosquitoes inside. Only a few straggling geese oar their way across the sun's red surface.
25 Lonnie wears an exasperated, proprietary expression, as if he had produced and directed the show himself and had just received a bad review. "It would have been better with more light," he says; "I can't always guarantee just when they'll start moving." I assure him I thought it was a fantastic sight.
30 "Well," he rumbles, "I guess it wasn't too bad."

49. In the descriptive phrase "shake out blankets all at one time" (line 5), the author is appealing chiefly to the reader's

    (A) background
    (B) sight
    (C) emotions
    (D) thoughts
    (E) hearing

50. Which words preceding the descriptive phrase "shake out blankets all at one time" (line 5) give us a clue to the correct answer to the previous question (question 49)?

    (A) "into their heads"
    (B) "lavender light"
    (C) "across the water"
    (D) "a beating roar"
    (E) I don't know.

51. The mood created by the author is one of

    (A) tranquility
    (B) excitement
    (C) sadness
    (D) bewilderment
    (E) unconcern

52. Which word in the passage is most closely associated with the correct answer?

    (A) mist
    (B) spectacle
    (C) geese
    (D) refuge
    (E) I don't know.

53. The main idea expressed by the author about the geese is that they

    (A) are spectacular to watch
    (B) are unpredictable
    (C) disturb the environment
    (D) produce a lot of noise
    (E) fly in large flocks

54. Which line(s) gives us a clue to the correct answer?

    (A) Line 1
    (B) Lines 16–17
    (C) Line 19
    (D) Line 30
    (E) I don't know.

55. Judging from the passage, the reader can conclude that

    (A) the speaker dislikes nature's inconveniences
    (B) the geese's timing is predictable
    (C) Lonnie has had the experience before
    (D) both observers are hunters
    (E) the author and Lonnie are the same person

56. Which gives us a clue to the right answer?

    (A) Lines 9–10
    (B) Line 19
    (C) Lines 21–22
    (D) Lines 28–29
    (E) I don't know.

Section 2: Quantitative Reasoning

Answer the following questions:

1. If $P \times \dfrac{11}{14} = \dfrac{11}{14} \times \dfrac{8}{9}$, then $P =$

   (A) $\dfrac{8}{9}$

   (B) $\dfrac{9}{8}$

   (C) 8

   (D) 11

   (E) 14

2. How did you get your answer?

   (A) I multiplied $\dfrac{11}{14}$ by $\dfrac{8}{9}$, *reducing first*.

   (B) I multiplied 11×8 and then divided the product by 14×9.

   (C) I canceled $\dfrac{11}{14}$ from both sides of the equals sign.

   (D) I guessed.

   (E) None of these.

3. Sarah is twice as old as John. Six years ago, Sarah was 4 times as old as John was then. How old is John now?

   (A) 3

   (B) 9

   (C) 18

   (D) 20

   (E) Cannot be determined.

4. How did you get your answer?

   (A) I substituted S for *Sarah*, $=$ for *is*, and J for *John* in the first sentence of the problem. Then I translated the second sentence into mathematical terms also.

   (B) I tried specific numbers for *Sarah* and/or *John*.

   (C) I racked my brain to figure out the ages but didn't write any equations down.

   (D) I guessed.

   (E) None of these.

5. 200 is what percent of 20?

   (A) $\dfrac{1}{10}$

   (B) 10

   (C) 100

   (D) 1,000

   (E) 10,000

6. How did you get your answer?

   (A) I translated *is* to $=$, *what* to a variable, *of* to $\times$, etc. Then I was able to set up an equation.

   (B) I just divided the two numbers and multiplied by 100 to get the percent.

   (C) I tried to remember how to work with *is-of* problems, putting the *of* over *is* or the *is* over *of*.

   (D) I guessed.

   (E) None of these.

7. In this diagram, $\triangle XYZ$ has been inscribed in a circle. If the circle encloses an area of 64, and the area of $\triangle XYZ$ is 15, then what is the area of the shaded region?

   (A) 25

   (B) 36

   (C) 49

   (D) 79

   (E) Cannot be determined.

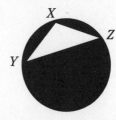

8. How did you get your answer?

   (A) I tried to calculate the area of the circle and the area of the triangle.

   (B) I used a special triangle or tried different triangles whose area was 15.

   (C) I subtracted 15 from 64.

   (D) I guessed.

   (E) None of these.

9. $66^2 + 2(34)(66) + 34^2 =$

   (A) 4,730
   (B) 5,000
   (C) 9,860
   (D) 9,950
   (E) 10,000

10. How did you get your answer?

    (A) I multiplied 66×66, $2 \times 34 \times 66$, and 34×34 and added the results.
    (B) I approximated a solution.
    (C) I noticed that $66^2 + 2(34)(66) + 34^2$ had the form of $a^2 + 2ab + b^2$ and set the form equal to $(a + b)^2$.
    (D) I guessed.
    (E) None of these.

11. The average height of three students is 68 inches. If two of the students have heights of 70 inches and 72 inches respectively, then what is the height (in inches) of the third student?

    (A) 60
    (B) 62
    (C) 64
    (D) 65
    (E) 66

12. How did you get your answer?

    (A) I used the following equation:

    $$(68 + 2) + (68 + 4) + x = 68 + 68 + 68$$

    Then I got:
    $68 + 68 + (x + 6) = 68 + 68 + 68$, and crossed off the two 68s on both sides of the equation to come up with $x + 6 = 68$.
    (B) I was able to eliminate the incorrect choices without figuring out a complete solution.

    (C) I got the equation $\dfrac{(70 + 72 + x)}{3} = 68$, then solved for x.
    (D) I guessed.
    (E) None of these.

13. If $0 < x < 1$, then which of the following must be true?

    I. $2x < 2$
    II. $x - 1 < 0$
    III. $x^2 < x$

    (A) I only
    (B) II only
    (C) I and II only
    (D) II and III only
    (E) I, II, and III

14. How did you get your answer?

    (A) I plugged in only one number for x in I, II, and III.
    (B) I plugged in more than one number for x and tried I, II, and III using each set of numbers.
    (C) I used the fact that $0 < x$ and $x < 1$ and manipulated those inequalities in I, II, and III.
    (D) I guessed.
    (E) None of these.

15. The sum of the cubes of any two consecutive positive integers is always

    (A) an odd integer
    (B) an even integer
    (C) the cube of an integer
    (D) the square of an integer
    (E) the product of an integer and 3

16. How did you get your answer?

    (A) I translated the statement into the form $x^3 + (x + 1)^3 =$ _____ and tried to see what I would get.
    (B) I tried numbers like 1 and 2 for the consecutive integers. Then I calculated the sum of the cubes of those numbers. I was able to eliminate some choices and then tried some other numbers for the consecutive integers to eliminate more choices.
    (C) I said, of two consecutive positive integers, one is even and therefore its cube is even. The other integer is odd; therefore its cube is odd. An odd + an even is an odd.
    (D) I guessed.
    (E) None of these.

17. If p is a positive integer, which *could* be an odd integer?

    (A) $2p + 2$
    (B) $p^3 - p$
    (C) $p^2 + p$
    (D) $p^2 - p$
    (E) $7p - 3$

18. How did you get your answer?

    (A) I plugged in a number or numbers for p and started testing all the choices, *starting with Choice A.*
    (B) I plugged in a number or numbers for p in each of the choices, *starting with Choice E.*
    (C) I looked at Choice E first to see if $7p - 3$ had the form of an even or an odd integer.
    (D) I guessed.
    (E) None of these.

19. In this figure, two points, B and C, are placed to the right of point A such that $4AB = 3AC$. The value of $\dfrac{BC}{AB}$

   (A) equals $\dfrac{1}{3}$

   (B) equals $\dfrac{2}{3}$

   (C) equals $\dfrac{3}{2}$

   (D) equals 3

   (E) cannot be determined.

$$A \bullet\!\!\rule[0.5ex]{3cm}{0.4pt}\!\! \ell$$

20. How did you get your answer?

   (A) I drew points B and C on the line and labeled AB as a and BC as b and then worked with a and b.
   (B) I substituted numbers for AB and AC.
   (C) I drew points B and C on the line and worked with equations involving BC and AB.
   (D) I guessed.
   (E) None of these.

21. A man rode a bicycle a straight distance at a speed of 10 miles per hour. He came back the same way, traveling the same distance at a speed of 20 miles per hour. What was the man's total number of miles for the trip back and forth if his total traveling time was one hour?

   (A) 15

   (B) $13\dfrac{1}{3}$

   (C) $7\dfrac{1}{2}$

   (D) $6\dfrac{2}{3}$

   (E) $6\dfrac{1}{3}$

22. How did you answer this question?

   (A) I used Rate × Time = Distance and plugged in my own numbers.
   (B) I averaged 10 and 20 and worked from there.
   (C) I called the times going back and forth by two different unknown variables but noted that the sum of these times was 1 hour.
   (D) I guessed.
   (E) None of these.

23. If the symbol ϕ is defined by the equation

$$a\phi b = a - b - ab$$

   for all a and b, then $\left(-\dfrac{1}{3}\right)\phi\,(-3) =$

   (A) $\dfrac{5}{3}$

   (B) $\dfrac{11}{3}$

   (C) $-\dfrac{13}{5}$

   (D) -4

   (E) -5

24. How did you get your answer?

   (A) I played around with the numbers $-\dfrac{1}{3}$ and -3 to get my answer. I didn't use any substitution method.
   (B) I substituted in $a\phi b = a - b - ab$, $\left(-\dfrac{1}{3}\right)$ for a and -3 for b.
   (C) I worked backward.
   (D) I guessed.
   (E) None of these.

25. If $y^8 = 4$ and $y^7 = \dfrac{3}{x}$, what is the value of y in terms of x?

   (A) $\dfrac{4x}{3}$

   (B) $\dfrac{3x}{4}$

   (C) $\dfrac{4}{x}$

   (D) $\dfrac{x}{4}$

   (E) $\dfrac{12}{x}$

26. How did you get your answer?

   (A) I solved for the value of y from $y^8 = 4$. Then I substituted that value of y in $y^7 = \dfrac{3}{x}$.
   (B) I took the seventh root of y in the second equation.
   (C) I divided the first equation by the second equation to get y alone in terms of x.
   (D) I guessed.
   (E) None of these.

27. If $4x + 5y = 10$ and $x + 3y = 8$, then $\dfrac{5x + 8y}{3} =$

   (A) 18
   (B) 15
   (C) 12
   (D) 9
   (E) 6

28. How did you get your answer?

   (A) I solved both simultaneous equations for x and for y, then substituted the values of x and y into

   $$\frac{(5x + 8y)}{3}.$$

   (B) I tried numbers for x and for y that would satisfy the first two equations.
   (C) I added both equations to get $5x + 8y$. Then I divided my result by 3.
   (D) I guessed.
   (E) None of these.

29. The circle with center A and radius AB is inscribed in the square here. AB is extended to C. What is the ratio of AB to AC?

   (A) $\sqrt{2}$

   (B) $\frac{\sqrt{2}}{4}$

   (C) $\frac{\sqrt{2} - 1}{2}$

   (D) $\frac{\sqrt{2}}{2}$

   (E) None of these.

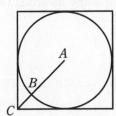

30. How did you get your answer?

   (A) I approximated the solution. I looked to see what the ratio of AB to AC might be from the diagram. Then I looked through the choices to see which choice was reasonable or to eliminate incorrect choices.
   (B) I saw a relationship between AB and AC but didn't draw any other lines.
   (C) I dropped a perpendicular from A to one of the sides of the square, then worked with the isosceles right triangle. I also labeled length AB by a single letter, and BC by another single letter.
   (D) I guessed.
   (E) None of these.

31. In the accompanying figure, side BC of triangle ABC is extended to D. What is the value of a?

   (A) 15
   (B) 17
   (C) 20
   (D) 24
   (E) 30

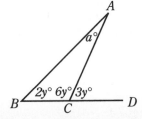

(Note: Figure is not drawn to scale.)

32. How did you get your answer?

   (A) I *first* said that $2y + 6y + a = 180$.
   (B) I *first* said that $6y + 3y = 180$, then solved for y.
   (C) I *first* said $3y = 2y + a$.
   (D) I guessed.
   (E) None of these.

33. What is the perimeter of the accompanying figure if B and C are right angles?

   (A) 14
   (B) 16
   (C) 18
   (D) 20
   (E) Cannot be determined.

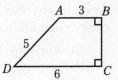

(Note: Figure is not drawn to scale.)

34. How did you get your answer?

   (A) I tried to first find angles A and D.
   (B) I drew a perpendicular from A to DC and labeled BC as an unknown (x or y, etc.).
   (C) I labeled BC as an unknown (x or y, etc.) but *did not* draw a perpendicular line from A to DC.
   (D) I guessed.
   (E) None of these.

35. Which of the angles below has a degree measure that can be determined?

   (A) $\angle WOS$
   (B) $\angle SOU$
   (C) $\angle WOT$
   (D) $\angle ROV$
   (E) $\angle WOV$

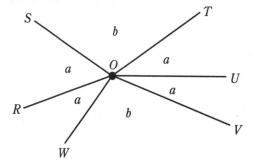

(Note: Figure is not drawn to scale.)

36. How did you get your answer?

   (A) I first said that $4a + 2b = 360$, got $2a + b = 180$, then looked through the choices.
   (B) I looked through the choices first.
   (C) I knew that the sum of the angles added up to 360 degrees but didn't know where to go from there.
   (D) I guessed.
   (E) None of these.

Section 3: Quantitative Reasoning (Quantitative Comparison)

For each of the odd questions from 37–61, compare Quantity A and Quantity B, using additional information centered above the two quantities if such information is given. Select one of the following four answer choices and fill in the corresponding circle to the right of the question.

   (A) Quantity A is greater.
   (B) Quantity B is greater.
   (C) The two quantities are equal.
   (D) The relationship cannot be determined from the information given.

A symbol that appears more than once in a question has the same meaning throughout the question.

	Quantity A	Quantity B	Correct Answer
Example 1:	$(2)(6)$	$2 + 6$	● Ⓑ Ⓒ Ⓓ

	Quantity A	Quantity B	Correct Answer
Example 2:	PS	SR	Ⓐ Ⓑ Ⓒ ●

(since equal lengths cannot be assumed, even though PS and SR appear equal)

SUMMARY DIRECTIONS FOR COMPARISON QUESTIONS

Choose A if the Quantity A is greater;
Choose B if the Quantity B is greater;
Choose C if the two quantities are equal;

Choose D if the relationship cannot be determined from the information given.

Quantity A	Quantity B
37. $\dfrac{1}{2} + \dfrac{1}{6} + \dfrac{1}{17}$	$\dfrac{1}{17} + \dfrac{1}{2} + \dfrac{1}{7}$

38. How did you get your answer?

   (A) I added the fractions in Column A and then added the fractions in Column B. Then I compared the results.

   (B) I canceled the $\dfrac{1}{2}$ and the $\dfrac{1}{17}$ from both columns.

   (C) I added the denominators.
   (D) I guessed.
   (E) None of these.

Quantity A	Quantity B
39. $24 \times 46 \times 35$	$46 \times 24 \times 36$

40. How did you get your answer?

   (A) I multiplied the numbers in Column A and multiplied the numbers in Column B. Then I compared results.

   (B) I approximated a solution for Column A and for Column B.

   (C) I canceled common quantities from both columns.

   (D) I guessed.
   (E) None of these.

	Quantity A	Quantity B

$$b > 1$$
$$a > 1$$
$$a \neq b$$

41. $\dfrac{a}{b}$ $\qquad\qquad\qquad\qquad$ $\dfrac{b}{a}$

42. How did you get your answer?

   (A) I tried different numbers for the variables to get different comparisons, making sure that $b > 1$, $a > 1$, and $a \neq b$.
   (B) I thought that because variables and not actual numbers were given that the answer was indeterminable.
   (C) I tried different numbers for the variables, not making sure that $b > 1$, $a > 1$, or $a \neq b$.
   (D) I guessed.
   (E) None of these.

	Quantity A	Quantity B

$$a > 0$$

43. $\dfrac{1}{a}$ $\qquad\qquad\qquad\qquad$ a

44. How did you get your answer?

   (A) I substituted different numbers for a, trying to get different comparisons.
   (B) I first found a number for a that would make the columns equal. Then I looked for a number for a that would make the columns unequal.
   (C) I thought because variables and not actual numbers were given in the columns that the answer was indeterminable.
   (D) I guessed.
   (E) None of these.

	Quantity A	Quantity B

45.   1 $\qquad\qquad\qquad\qquad$ $\dfrac{\frac{7}{9}}{\frac{9}{7}}$

46. How did you get your answer?

   (A) I first divided $\dfrac{7}{9}$ by $\dfrac{9}{7}$ in Column B.

   (B) I saw that in Column B, $\dfrac{7}{9}$ was less than $\dfrac{9}{7}$, so I realized that Column B must be less than 1.

   (C) I multiplied both columns by $\dfrac{9}{7}$ to get rid of the denominator in Column B.

   (D) I guessed.
   (E) None of these.

	Quantity A	Quantity B

$$ab \neq 0$$

47. $-a^2 b$ $\qquad\qquad\qquad\qquad$ ab

48. How did you get your answer?

   (A) I substituted numbers for a and b to get different comparisons.
   (B) I divided both columns by b, then divided both by a.
   (C) I divided both columns by ab since $ab \neq 0$.
   (D) I guessed.
   (E) None of these.

	Quantity A	Quantity B

$$30 > ab > 5$$
a and b are whole numbers

49. $a + b$ $\qquad\qquad\qquad\qquad$ ab

50. How did you answer this question?

   (A) I substituted whole numbers for a and b in the columns, making sure that $30 > ab > 5$. Then I substituted another set of whole numbers for a and for b in the columns, making sure again that $30 > ab > 5$.
   (B) I thought because only variables were given that the answer was obvious.
   (C) I tried different numbers for a and for b, not checking to see if $30 > ab > 5$.
   (D) I guessed.
   (E) None of these.

	Quantity A	Quantity B

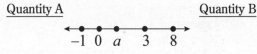

(Note: Figure is not drawn to scale.)

51. a $\qquad\qquad\qquad\qquad$ $8 - a$

52. How did you get your answer?

   (A) I added a to both columns and then divided by 2.
   (B) I let a be a number between 0 and 3, then substituted that number for the a in both columns.
   (C) I determined that $8 - a > 5$ since $a < 3$. Then I said $8 - a > 5 > 3 > a$.
   (D) I guessed.
   (E) None of these.

SUMMARY DIRECTIONS FOR COMPARISON QUESTIONS

Choose A if the Quantity A is greater;
Choose B if the Quantity B is greater;
Choose C if the two quantities are equal;

Choose D if the relationship cannot be determined from the information given.

Quantity A	Quantity B

$$m > n$$
$$n > p$$

53. m p

54. How did you get your answer?

(A) I substituted numbers for m and for n.
(B) I substituted n for p in Column B and n for m in Column A.
(C) I saw a relation between m and p from the given, $m > n$ and $n > p$.
(D) I guessed.
(E) None of these.

Quantity A	Quantity B

$$-5 < x < +5$$

55. -6 $-x$

56. How did you get your answer?

(A) I tried different values for x.
(B) I multiplied the number in each column by -1 to get 6 and x, respectively.
(C) I multiplied $-5 < x < +5$ by -1 to get $5 > -x > -5$ so that I could compare that with $-x$ and -6.
(D) I guessed.
(E) None of these.

Quantity A	Quantity B

57. $(a^3)^4$ a^7

58. How did you answer this question?

(A) I said $(a^3)^4 = a^{12}$ and then set $a^{12} > a^7$.
(B) I said $(a^3)^4 = a^7$ and then set $a^7 = a^7$.
(C) I said $(a^3)^4 = a^{12}$ and then tried $a = 1$ or $a = 0$ as one number for a in the columns.
(D) I said $(a^3)^4 = a^{12}$ and then tried numbers other than $a = 0$ or $a = 1$.
(E) None of these.

Quantity A	Quantity B

$$a > 0$$

59. $\sqrt{a} + \sqrt{3}$ $\sqrt{a + 3}$

60. How did you get your answer?

(A) I plugged in only one number for a.
(B) I plugged in two or more numbers for a.
(C) I squared both columns, then canceled the a and the 3 from both columns.
(D) I guessed.
(E) None of these.

Quantity A	Quantity B

61. $\sqrt{17} - \sqrt{3}$ $\sqrt{14}$

62. How did you get your answer?

(A) I first squared both columns.
(B) I approximated a solution by approximating $\sqrt{17}$, $\sqrt{3}$, and $\sqrt{14}$.
(C) I added $\sqrt{3}$ to both columns, first. Then I squared both columns.
(D) I guessed.
(E) None of these.

This is the end of the Strategy Diagnostic Test for the GRE. You've answered the questions in both the Verbal and Math sections, and you've recorded how you arrived at each answer.

Now you're ready to find out how you did. Go right to the table that follows for answer checking, diagnosis, and prescription.

Remember, the questions are in pairs: the odd-numbered ones are the questions themselves; the even-numbered ones, the approach you used to solve the questions. If either or both of your answers—solution and/or approach—fail to correspond to the answers given in the table, you should study the strategy for that pair.

The approximate time it should take to answer a particular question is also supplied. By using the best strategies throughout the actual GRE, you should increase accuracy, make the best use of your time, and thus improve your score dramatically.

Note: If the even-numbered answer (for questions 2, 4, 6, etc.) does not match your answer, you may want to look at the approach described in the answer, as you may be able to use that approach with other questions.

Strategy Diagnostic Test Answer and Diagnostic Table

Section 1: Verbal Reasoning			
Question number	Answer	*If either or both of your answers do not match the answers to the left, then refer to this strategy	Estimated time to solve each odd-numbered question (in seconds)
1	D	Sentence Completion 1,	
2	A	p. 137	20
3	A, F	Sentence Completion 3,	
4	D	p. 140	40
5	E	Sentence Completion 2,	
6	B	p. 138	30
7	C	Sentence Completion 3,	
8	B	p. 140	30
9	C, E	Sentence Completion 3,	
10	C	p. 140	40
11	C, F	Sentence Completion 3,	
12	B	p. 140	30
13	A	Vocabulary 1,	
14	B	p. 168	20
15	E	Vocabulary 1,	
16	B	p. 168	20
17	B	Vocabulary 1,	
18	B	p. 168	20
19	C	Vocabulary 3,	
20	B	p. 172	20
21	D	Vocabulary 1,	
22	B	p. 168	20
23	E	Vocabulary 3,	
24	B	p. 172	20
25	B	Vocabulary 2,	
26	B	p. 170	20
27	B	Vocabulary 2,	
28	B, C	p. 170	20

Strategy Diagnostic Test Answer and Diagnostic Table (Continued)

Section 1: Verbal Reasoning

Question number	Answer	*If either or both of your answers do not match the answers to the left, then refer to this strategy	Estimated time to solve each odd-numbered question (in seconds)
29	A	Vocabulary 3,	
30	B	p. 172	20
31	D	Vocabulary 2,	
32	B, C, D	p. 170	20
33	E	Vocabulary 1,	
34	B	p. 168	30
35	B	Vocabulary 3,	
36	B	p. 172	20
37	B	Reading Comprehension	
38	B	1, 2, pp. 152, 155	15
39	E	Reading Comprehension	
40	B	1, 2, pp. 152, 155	20
41	D	Reading Comprehension	
42	B	1, 2, pp. 152, 155	20
43	B	Reading Comprehension	
44	B	1, 2, pp. 152, 155	20
45	D	Reading Comprehension	
46	B	1, 2, pp. 152, 155	30
47	E	Reading Comprehension	
48	D	1, 2, pp. 152, 155	30
49	E	Reading Comprehension	
50	D	1, 2, pp. 152, 155	20
51	B	Reading Comprehension	
52	B	1, 2, pp. 152, 155	20
53	A	Reading Comprehension	
54	B	1, 2, pp. 152, 155	20
55	C	Reading Comprehension	
56	D	1, 2, pp. 152, 155	30

Strategy Diagnostic Test Answer and Diagnostic Table (Continued)

Section 2: Quantitative Reasoning

Question number	Answer	*If either or both of your answers do not match the answers to the left, then refer to this strategy	Estimated time to solve each odd-numbered question (in seconds)
1	A	Math 1, p. 72	10
2	C		
3	B	Math 2, p. 74	40
4	A		
5	D	Math 2, p. 74	30
6	A		
7	C	Math 3, p. 80	20
8	C		
9	E	Math 4, p. 83	40
10	C		
11	B	Math 5, p. 86	40
12	C		
13	E	Math 6, p. 88	50
14	C		
15	A	Math 7, p. 91	40
16	B, C		
17	E	Math 8, p. 93	30
18	B, C		
19	A	Math 14, p. 105	40
20	A		
21	B	Math 9, p. 95	60
22	C		
23	A	Math 11, p. 99	50
24	B		
25	A	Math 12 or 13, pp. 101, 103	30
26	C		
27	E	Math 13, p. 103	20
28	C		

Strategy Diagnostic Test Answer and Diagnostic Table (Continued)

Section 2: Quantitative Reasoning			
Question number	*Answer*	**If either or both of your answers do not match the answers to the left, then refer to this strategy*	*Estimated time to solve each odd-numbered question (in seconds)*
29 30	D C	Math 14, 18, pp. 105, 115	50
31 32	C B	Math 17, 18, pp. 112, 115	40
33 34	C B	Math 14, 18, pp. 105, 115	30
35 36	C A	Math 17, p. 112	40

Strategy Diagnostic Test Answer and Diagnostic Table (Continued)

Section 3: Quantitative Reasoning (Quantitative Comparison)			
Question number	Answer	*If either or both of your answers do not match the answers to the left, then refer to this strategy	Estimated time to solve each odd-numbered question (in seconds)
37†	A	Math A, p. 121	10
38†	B		
39†	B	Math B, p. 123	10
40†	C		
41†	D	Math C, p. 124	30
42†	A		
43†	D	Math C, p. 124	20
44†	B		
45†	A	Math D, p. 127	10
46†	B, C		
47†	D	Math C, p. 124	20
48†	A, C		
49†	D	Math C, p. 124	30
50†	A		
51†	B	Math D, p. 127	20
52†	A		
53†	A	Math E, p. 132	10
54†	C		
55†	B	Math E, p. 132	20
56†	C		
57†	D	Math C, p. 124	20
58†	C		
59†	A	Math D, p. 127	20
60†	C		
61†	B	Math D, p. 127	30
62†	C		

*Note: The solution to the odd-numbered question appears in the strategy section listed.

†Note: If more than 15 of your answers to questions with a dagger are incorrect, then review the introduction to the section of this book on quantitative comparison strategies (p. 120–121) before studying specific quantitative comparison strategies.

PART 2

THE SHORTEST GRE TEST— 20 QUESTIONS TO APPROXIMATE YOUR GRE SCORE

And the Exact Strategies You Need to Improve Your Score

Although it shouldn't take you more than 40 seconds to answer each Verbal (Reading) question and 1 minute to answer each Math question, you may take this test untimed and still get a fairly accurate prediction.

Verbal (Critical Reading)

Allow 7 minutes for this part.
Circle the correct answer(s).

Sentence Completions

Fill in the blank(s) with the appropriate choice:

Select one choice for each blank.

1. The instructor displayed extreme stubbornness; although he _____ the logic of the student's argument, he _____ to acknowledge her conclusion as correct.

Blank 1	Blank 2
(A) accepted	(D) refused
(B) denounced	(E) consented
(C) rejected	(F) decided

2. Select one choice for each blank.

In spite of the _____ of his presentation, many people were _____ with the speaker's concepts and ideas.

Blank 1	Blank 2
(A) long-windedness	(D) enthralled
(B) formulation	(E) bored
(C) forcefulness	(F) gratified

3. Select two answer choices that fit the sentence and give the sentence the same meaning.

Richard Wagner was frequently intolerant; moreover, his strange behavior caused most of his acquaintances to _____ the composer whenever possible.

(A) contradict
(B) interrogate
(C) shun
(D) revere
(E) tolerate
(F) reject

4. Select the correct answer choice for each blank.

Crusty and egotistical, Alfred A. Knopf, the publisher, wore _____ shirts from the most exclusive tailors; was a connoisseur of music, food, and wine; nurtured a garden of exotic plants; and enjoyed rare cigars. His self-assured, _____ manner, together with his insistence on the best of everything, shaped his ostentatious house's image as a _____ of work of enduring value.

Blank 1	Blank 2	Blank 3
(A) expensive	(D) decorous	(G) connoisseur
(B) immaculate	(E) irascible	(H) purveyor
(C) flamboyant	(F) congenial	(I) solicitor

Reading Comprehension

Read the following passage. Then answer the questions:

1 Sometimes the meaning of glowing water is ominous. Off the Pacific coast of North America, it may mean that the sea is filled with a minute plant that contains a poison of strange and terrible virulence. About four days after this
5 minute plant comes to alter the coastal plankton, some of the fishes and shellfish in the vicinity become toxic. This is because in their normal feeding, they have strained the poisonous plankton out of the water.

5. Fish and shellfish become toxic when they

(A) swim in poisonous water
(B) feed on poisonous plants or animals
(C) change their feeding habits
(D) give off a strange glow
(E) take strychnine into their systems

6. In the context of the passage, the word *virulence* in line 4 means

(A) strangeness
(B) color
(C) calamity
(D) potency
(E) powerful odor

7. The paragraph preceding the one in the passage most probably discussed the

(A) phenomena of the Pacific coastline
(B) poisons that affect man
(C) toxic plants in the sea
(D) characteristics of plankton
(E) phenomena of the sea

8. It can be assumed that "plankton" in line 5 are

(A) fish and shellfish
(B) small plants or animals
(C) sand deposits
(D) land parasites
(E) glacier or rock formations

Regular Math

Allow 7 minutes for this part.
Circle the correct answer.

Answer the following questions:

1. If $2x + 3y = 4$ and $y = 2$, find the value of x.

   (A) $+2$
   (B) $+1$
   (C) $\quad0$
   (D) -1
   (E) -2

2. Where $a \neq 1$, $\dfrac{a^7 - a^6}{a - 1} =$

   (A) $\dfrac{a}{a - 1}$

   (B) $\dfrac{1}{a - 1}$

   (C) $a^6 - a^5$
   (D) a^5
   (E) a^6

3. Sarah is twice as old as John. Six years ago Sarah was four times as old as John was then. In years, how old is John now?

   (A) 3
   (B) 9
   (C) 18
   (D) 20
   (E) Cannot be determined

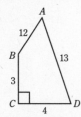

(Note: Figure is not drawn to scale.)

4. The area of the above figure $ABCD$

   (A) is 36
   (B) is 108
   (C) is 156
   (D) is 1872
   (E) cannot be determined

Directions for Questions 5–7:

In the following questions you must find an answer without referring to choices.

Examples of acceptable ways to use the grid:

Integer answer: 502 (either position is correct)

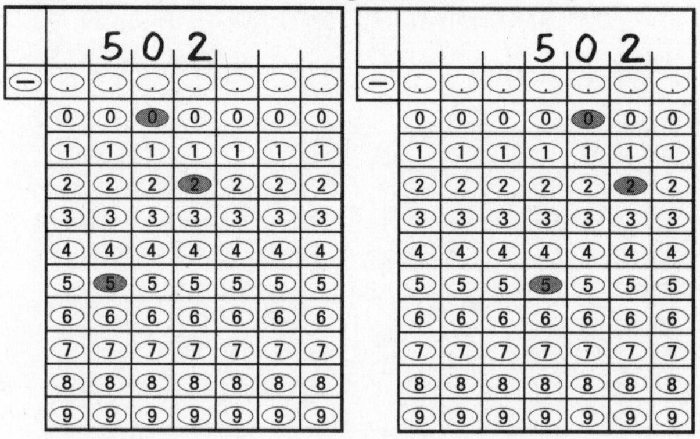

Decimal answer: -4.13 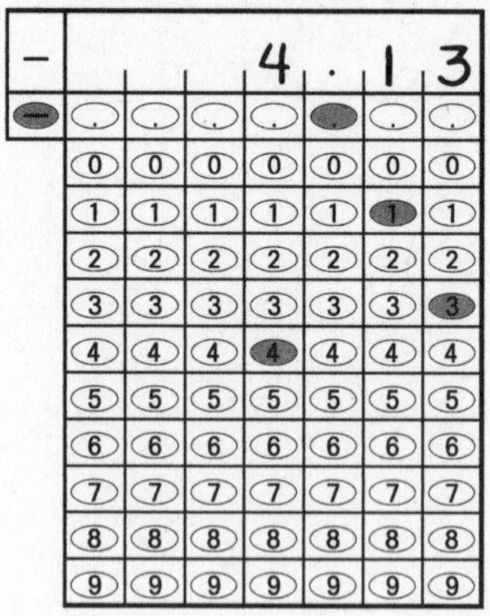   Fraction answer: $-\dfrac{2}{10}$

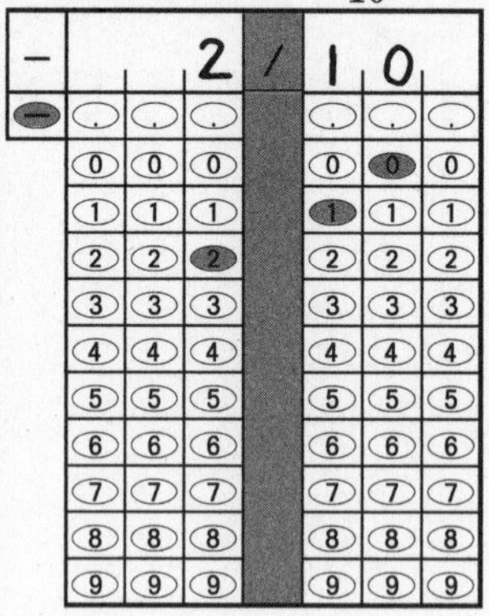

5. If $x + y = 7$ and $xy = 4$, then find the value of $x^2 + y^2$.

```
⊖ ○ ○ ○ ○ ○ ○ ○
  ⓪ ⓪ ⓪ ⓪ ⓪ ⓪ ⓪
  ① ① ① ① ① ① ①
  ② ② ② ② ② ② ②
  ③ ③ ③ ③ ③ ③ ③
  ④ ④ ④ ④ ④ ④ ④
  ⑤ ⑤ ⑤ ⑤ ⑤ ⑤ ⑤
  ⑥ ⑥ ⑥ ⑥ ⑥ ⑥ ⑥
  ⑦ ⑦ ⑦ ⑦ ⑦ ⑦ ⑦
  ⑧ ⑧ ⑧ ⑧ ⑧ ⑧ ⑧
  ⑨ ⑨ ⑨ ⑨ ⑨ ⑨ ⑨
```

6. If $y + 2q = 15$, $q + 2p = 5$ and $p + 2y = 7$, then find the value of $p + q + y$.

```
⊖ ○ ○ ○ ○ ○ ○ ○
  ⓪ ⓪ ⓪ ⓪ ⓪ ⓪ ⓪
  ① ① ① ① ① ① ①
  ② ② ② ② ② ② ②
  ③ ③ ③ ③ ③ ③ ③
  ④ ④ ④ ④ ④ ④ ④
  ⑤ ⑤ ⑤ ⑤ ⑤ ⑤ ⑤
  ⑥ ⑥ ⑥ ⑥ ⑥ ⑥ ⑥
  ⑦ ⑦ ⑦ ⑦ ⑦ ⑦ ⑦
  ⑧ ⑧ ⑧ ⑧ ⑧ ⑧ ⑧
  ⑨ ⑨ ⑨ ⑨ ⑨ ⑨ ⑨
```

7. On a street with 25 houses, 10 houses have *fewer than 6 rooms,* 10 houses have *more than 7 rooms,* and 4 houses have *more than 8 rooms.* What is the total number of houses on the street that are either 6-, 7-, or 8-room houses?

```
⊖ ○ ○ ○ ○ ○ ○ ○
  ⓪ ⓪ ⓪ ⓪ ⓪ ⓪ ⓪
  ① ① ① ① ① ① ①
  ② ② ② ② ② ② ②
  ③ ③ ③ ③ ③ ③ ③
  ④ ④ ④ ④ ④ ④ ④
  ⑤ ⑤ ⑤ ⑤ ⑤ ⑤ ⑤
  ⑥ ⑥ ⑥ ⑥ ⑥ ⑥ ⑥
  ⑦ ⑦ ⑦ ⑦ ⑦ ⑦ ⑦
  ⑧ ⑧ ⑧ ⑧ ⑧ ⑧ ⑧
  ⑨ ⑨ ⑨ ⑨ ⑨ ⑨ ⑨
```

Quantitative Comparison Math

Quantitative Comparison

The following questions each consist of two quantities, Quantity A and Quantity B. You are to compare the two quantities and on the answer sheet blacken space

A	if the Quantity A is greater;
B	if the Quantity B is greater;
C	if the two quantities are equal;
D	if the relationship cannot be determined from the information given.

Notes:
1. In certain questions, information concerning one or both of the quantities to be compared is centered above the two columns.
2. In a given question, a symbol that appears in both columns represents the same thing in Quantity A as it does in Quantity B.
3. Letters such as x, n, and k stand for real numbers.

SUMMARY DIRECTIONS FOR COMPARISON QUESTIONS

Choose A if the quantity A is greater;
Choose B if the quantity B is greater;
Choose C if the two quantities are equal;

Choose D if the relationship cannot be determined from the information given.

Write the correct answer A, B, C, D for each question.

Quantity A   Quantity B

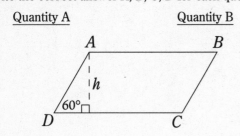

ABCD is a parallelogram.

8. $h \times AB$ $AD \times CD$

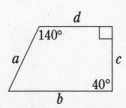

Note: Figure is not drawn to scale.

Quantity A	Quantity B
9. $a^2 - c^2$	$d^2 - b^2$

Quantity A	Quantity B

$$x > y > 0$$

Quantity A	Quantity B
10. $\sqrt{x + y} - \sqrt{x}$	$\sqrt{y}$

Quantity A	Quantity B

$$a \neq b \neq 0; \ a + b > 0$$

Quantity A	Quantity B
11. $\dfrac{2ab}{a+b}$	$\dfrac{a+b}{2}$

Quantity A	Quantity B

$$a > 1$$

Quantity A	Quantity B
12. $(a - 3)(2a + 1)$	$(a - 3)(a + 2)$

Answers

Verbal

1. A, D

2. C, E

3. C, F

4. C, E, H

5. B

6. D

7. E

8. B

Math

1. D

2. E

3. B

4. A

5. 41

6. 9

7. 11

8. B

9. C

10. B

11. B

12. D

Scoring

	Number Right		Approximate GRE Score	On 130–170 Point Scale
VERBAL				
	5	=	550–600	153–156
	6	=	650–700	160–163
	7	=	750	167
	8	=	800	170
	(*or* 6 or more = over 640)			over 159
MATH	8	=	600	157
	9	=	650	160
	10	=	700	163
	11	=	750	167
	12	=	800	170
	(*or* 8 or more = over 590)			over 156

Answers and Hints

VERBAL

1. A, D

Sentence Completion Strategy 3

Strategy: Watch for key words—*although* signals contrast—the blanks should be opposites. Notice that a key word is "stubbornness," which implies that the first blank is positive.

2. C, E

Sentence Completion Strategy 3

Strategy: Watch for key words. "In spite of" shows an opposite situation. Look for opposites in the choices.

3. C, F

Sentence Completion Strategy 3

Strategy: Watch for key words. "Moreover" is a key word adding to the already negative situation about the composer.

4. C, E, H

Sentence Completion Strategy 3, 4

Strategy: Watch for key words. Choices C, E, and H are correct. Look at the second blank first. Because of the key words *Crusty* and *egotistical*, it would appear that Choice E, the word *irascible*, meaning *hot-tempered*, would fit the second blank. And since there were so many things he had as described in the first sentence, Choice H, *purveyor* (one who spreads things throughout), would be a good fit. Because of the word *ostentatious* (showy), in the second sentence, you can see that Choice C, *flamboyant* (showy) would fit the first blank.

5. B

Reading Comprehension Strategy 2

Strategy: Underline important parts of passage, especially the last sentence.

6. D

Reading Comprehension Strategy 1, 5

Strategy: Look at grammar: adjectives modifying virulence.

7. E

Reading Comprehension Strategy 1

Strategy: Look at the phrase that introduces the passage.

8. B

Reading Comprehension Strategy 1, 5

Since the fish and shellfish become toxic (line 6), it can be inferred that they must eat the plankton, which could only be small animals or plants. Choice A is incorrect because "coastal plankton" is distinguished in the sentence from "fishes and shellfish." Choice D is incorrect because fish do not live on land, and it is assumed the situation takes place in water (see lines 1 and 3). Choices C and E are incorrect because it is unlikely that fish and shellfish would eat sand deposits or glacier or rock formations—they would eat plants or smaller animals.

MATH

1. (D)

Use **STRATEGY 7, Math Refresher 407**
Substitute numbers for variables.
Substitute $y = 2$ into the equation, $2x + 3y = 4$. You get $2x + 6 = 4$; $2x = -2$ so $x = -1$.

2. (E)

Use **STRATEGY 4, 12**
When dealing with complicated quantities or equations, it is sometimes simpler to <u>factor</u> to see the quantity take a different form. *Factor* out a^6 from the quantity $a^7 - a^6$. You get $a^6(a - 1)$. Thus

$$\frac{a^7 - a^6}{a - 1} = \frac{a^6(a - 1)}{a - 1} = a^6$$

3. (B)

Use **STRATEGY 2**
You won't rack your brains if you know how to translate from words to math. *Translate* Sarah to S, John to J, "is" to =, "Six years ago" to −6, "four times as old as John was then" to $4(J - 6)$. Then **Sarah is twice as old as John** translates to
(1) S = 2J.
And **Six years ago, Sarah was 4 times as old as John was then** translates to
(2) S − 6 = 4(J − 6), because John was **J − 6**, six years ago.
Substituting S = 2J in Equation 1, in Equation 2, we get:
$2J - 6 = 4(J - 6)$.
Then we get:
$2J - 6 = 4J - 24$. And then:
$-6 + 24 = 4J - 2J = 2J$. So
$2J = 18$ and $J = 9$.

4. (A)

Use **STRATEGY 14**
The best way to do the problem is to draw or extend lines to get more information. Draw *BD*, then find length *BD*. *BD* = 5 because triangle *BCD* is a 3–4–5 right triangle. Now triangle *BDA* is also a right triangle because a 5–12–13 triangle is a right triangle. We can then find the area of triangle *BCD* to be $3 \times \frac{4}{2} = 6$ and the area of triangle *BDA* to be $5 \times \frac{12}{12} = 30$. So the sum of these areas is the area of the figure *ABCD*. 36 is the answer.

5. 41

Don't try to solve for both *x* and *y*. You are not asked to do that—you are asked to find the value of $x^2 + y^2$, so try to manipulate the equations to get that quantity.
Use **STRATEGY 4**: Remember and Use Classic Forms, such as
$(x + y)^2 = x^2 + 2xy + y^2$.
We have
(1) $(x + y)^2 = x^2 + 2xy + y^2 = 7 \times 7 = 49$ and since $xy = 4$, we get
$2xy = 8$.
Substituting $2xy = 8$ in Equation 1 we get
$(x + y)^2 = x^2 + 2xy + y^2 = x^2 + 8 + y^2 = 49$.
Subtracting 8 from both sides of the last equation, we get
$x^2 + y^2 = 41$.

6. 9

I hope you didn't go through the tedium of substitution and solving for *q*, *p*, and *y*. You are *not* asked for the values of *each* of the variables. Use **STRATEGY 13**—when you have two or more equations, it is sometimes easier to just *add* or *subtract* them to get a result. *Add* equations, then *divide* by 3.

$$
\begin{array}{rcl}
y + 2q & = & 15 \\
q + 2p & = & 5 \\
+\ 2y + \quad p & = & 7 \\
\hline
3y + 3q + 3p & = & 27
\end{array}
$$

Factor 3: $3(q + p + y) = 27$; $q + p + y = 9$.

7. 11

Use **STRATEGY 17**

In many "logic" problems, it is sometimes easier to use an <u>indirect</u> approach or use the fact that *the whole equals the sum of its parts*. Use the *indirect* method: Don't try to get the number of 6-7-8 room houses directly. Instead, find houses that have fewer than 6 rooms (10) and more than 8 rooms (4), and what's left is the 6-7-8 room ones. Use the fact that *the whole equals the sum of its parts*. The total number of houses is 25 (given), and this must then equal the parts: 10 that have fewer than 6 rooms, plus 4 that have more than 8 rooms and whatever are remaining that have 6-7-8 rooms. Thus, 25 minus 10 minus 4 equals 11, which is the answer.

8. (B)

STRATEGY B, 14

Strategy: Label sides, then cancel quantities from Column A, B.

9. (C)

STRATEGY 17, 14, D

Strategy: Find remaining angle, draw diagonal, then add quantities to both columns to simplify.

10. (B)

STRATEGY D, A

Strategy: *Add or subtract* quantities to or from both columns to simplify. Add x to both columns, then *square* both columns. Then *cancel* common or like quantities from both columns.

11. (B)

STRATEGY D

Strategy: Cross-multiply, then subtract $4ab$ from both columns.

12. (D)

STRATEGY C

Strategy: Try to get a number for a that will *make the columns equal*. Then, just by looking at the columns, you can see that they are not always equal. Thus a definite relationship cannot be determined, and so Choice D is correct. Note that if you used Strategy B incorrectly and *canceled* the quantity $(a - 3)$ from both columns you would get the incorrect answer as A. The reason for this is that since $(a - 3)$ can be a negative, if for example $a = 2$, you could not cancel $(a - 3)$ from both quantities and preserve the same relationship in the columns.

PART 3

THE 101 MOST IMPORTANT MATH QUESTIONS YOU NEED TO KNOW HOW TO SOLVE

Take This Test to Determine Your Basic
(as Contrasted with Strategic) Math Weaknesses.
Diagnosis and Corrective Measures Follow Test.

101 Math Questions
Answer Sheet

A. Fractions
1.
2.
3.
4.
5.

B. Even–Odd Relationships
6.
7.
8.
9.
10.
11.
12.

C. Factors
13.
14.
15.
16.
17.
18.
19.
20.
21.

D. Exponents
22.
23.
24.
25.
26.
27.
28.
29.
30.
31.
32.

E. Percentages
33.
34.
35.

F. Equations
36.
37.
38.
39.
40.

G. Angles
41.
42.
43.
44.

H. Parallel Lines

45.
46.
47.
48.
49.
50.
51.

I. Triangles

52.
53.
54.
55.
56.
57.
58.
59.
60.
61.
62.
63.
64.
65.

J. Circles

66.
67.
68.
69.
70.

K. Other Figures

71.
72.
73.
74.
75.
76.
77.
78.
79.
80.

L. Number Lines

81.
82.

M. Coordinates

83.
84.
85.
86.

N. Inequalities

87.
88.
89.
90.
91.
92.

O. Averages

93.
94.

P. Shortcuts

95.
96.
97.
98.
99.
100.
101.

101 Math Questions
Test

Following are the 101 most important math questions you should know how to solve. After you take the test, check to see whether your answers are the same as those described, and whether or not you answered the question in the way described. After a solution, there is usually (where appropriate) a rule or generalization of the math concept just used in the solution. Make sure that you understand this generalization or rule, as it will apply to many other questions. Remember that these are the most important basic math questions you need to know how to solve. Make sure that you understand *all of them* before taking any standardized math test such as the GRE.

DO NOT GUESS AT ANY ANSWER! LEAVE THE ANSWER BLANK IF YOU DON'T KNOW HOW TO SOLVE THE PROBLEM.

A. Fractions

1. $\dfrac{\dfrac{a}{b}}{c} =$

   (A) $\dfrac{ab}{c}$

   (B) $\dfrac{ac}{b}$

   (C) $\dfrac{a}{bc}$

   (D) abc

   (E) None of these.

2. $\dfrac{1}{\dfrac{1}{y}} =$

   (A) y

   (B) y^2

   (C) $\dfrac{1}{y}$

   (D) infinity

   (E) None of these.

3. $\dfrac{\dfrac{a}{b}}{c} =$

   (A) $\dfrac{a}{bc}$

   (B) $\dfrac{ac}{b}$

   (C) $\dfrac{ab}{c}$

   (D) abc

   (E) None of these.

4. $\dfrac{1}{\dfrac{x}{y}} =$

   (A) xy

   (B) $\dfrac{x}{y}$

   (C) $\dfrac{y}{x}$

   (D) $\left(\dfrac{x}{y}\right)^2$

   (E) None of these.

5. $\dfrac{\dfrac{a}{b}}{\dfrac{b}{a}} =$

   (A) $\dfrac{b^2}{a^2}$

   (B) $\dfrac{a^2}{b^2}$

   (C) 1

   (D) $\dfrac{a}{b}$

   (E) None of these.

B. Even–Odd Relationships

6. ODD INTEGER × ODD INTEGER =

   (A) odd integer only
   (B) even integer only
   (C) even or odd integer

7. ODD INTEGER + or − ODD INTEGER =

(A) odd integer only
(B) even integer only
(C) even or odd integer

8. EVEN INTEGER × EVEN INTEGER =

(A) odd integer only
(B) even integer only
(C) even or odd integer

9. EVEN INTEGER + or − EVEN INTEGER =

(A) odd integer only
(B) even integer only
(C) even or odd integer

10. (ODD INTEGER)$^{\text{ODD POWER}}$ =

(A) odd integer only
(B) even integer only
(C) even or odd integer

11. (EVEN INTEGER)$^{\text{EVEN POWER}}$ =

(A) odd integer only
(B) even integer only
(C) even or odd integer

12. (EVEN INTEGER)$^{\text{ODD POWER}}$ =

(A) odd integer only
(B) even integer only
(C) even or odd integer

C. Factors

13. $(x + 3)(x + 2) =$

(A) $x^2 + 5x + 6$
(B) $x^2 + 6x + 5$
(C) $x^2 + x + 6$
(D) $2x + 5$
(E) None of these.

14. $(x + 3)(x - 2) =$

(A) $x^2 - x + 6$
(B) $x^2 + x + 5$
(C) $x^2 + x - 6$
(D) $2x + 1$
(E) None of these.

15. $(x - 3)(y - 2) =$

(A) $xy - 5y + 6$
(B) $xy - 2x - 3y + 6$
(C) $x + y + 6$
(D) $xy - 3y + 2x + 6$
(E) None of these.

16. $(a + b)(b + c) =$

(A) $ab + b^2 + bc$
(B) $a + b^2 + c$
(C) $a^2 + b^2 + ca$
(D) $ab + b^2 + ac + bc$
(E) None of these.

17. $(a + b)(a - b) =$

(A) $a^2 + 2ba - b^2$
(B) $a^2 - 2ba - b^2$
(C) $a^2 - b^2$
(D) 0
(E) None of these.

18. $(a + b)^2 =$

(A) $a^2 + 2ab + b^2$
(B) $a^2 + b^2$
(C) $a^2 + b^2 + ab$
(D) $2a + 2b$
(E) None of these.

19. $-(a - b) =$

(A) $a - b$
(B) $-a - b$
(C) $a + b$
(D) $b - a$
(E) None of these.

20. $a(b + c) =$

(A) $ab + ac$
(B) $ab + c$
(C) abc
(D) $ab + bc$
(E) None of these.

21. $-a(b - c) =$

(A) $ab - ac$
(B) $-ab - ac$
(C) $ac - ab$
(D) $ab + ac$
(E) None of these.

D. Exponents

22. $10^5 =$

(A) 1,000
(B) 10,000
(C) 100,000
(D) 1,000,000
(E) None of these.

23. $107076.5 = 1.070765 \times$

(A) 10^4
(B) 10^5
(C) 10^6
(D) 10^7
(E) None of these.

24. $a^2 \times a^5 =$

(A) a^{10}
(B) a^7
(C) a^3
(D) $(2a)^{10}$
(E) None of these.

25. $(ab)^7 =$

(A) ab^7
(B) a^7b
(C) a^7b^7
(D) $a^{14}b^{14}$
(E) None of these.

26. $\left(\dfrac{a}{c}\right)^8 =$

(A) $\dfrac{a^8}{c^8}$

(B) $\dfrac{a^8}{c}$

(C) $\dfrac{a}{c^8}$

(D) $\dfrac{a^7}{c}$

(E) None of these.

27. $a^4 \times b^4 =$

(A) $(ab)^4$
(B) $(ab)^8$
(C) $(ab)^{16}$
(D) $(ab)^{12}$
(E) None of these.

28. $a^{-3} \times b^5 =$

(A) $\dfrac{b^5}{a^3}$

(B) $(ab)^2$

(C) $(ab)^{-15}$

(D) $\dfrac{a^3}{b^5}$

(E) None of these.

29. $(a^3)^5 =$

(A) a^8
(B) a^2
(C) a^{15}
(D) a^{243}
(E) None of these.

30. $2a^{-3} =$

(A) $\dfrac{2}{a^3}$

(B) $2a^3$

(C) $2^3\sqrt{a}$

(D) a^{-6}

(E) None of these.

31. $2a^m \times \dfrac{1}{3}a^{-n} =$

(A) $\dfrac{2}{3}a^{m+n}$

(B) $\dfrac{2a^m}{3a^n}$

(C) $\dfrac{2}{3}a^{-mn}$

(D) $-\dfrac{2}{3}a^{-mn}$

(E) None of these.

32. $3^2 + 3^{-2} + 4^1 + 6^0 =$

(A) $8\dfrac{1}{9}$

(B) $12\dfrac{1}{9}$

(C) $13\dfrac{1}{9}$

(D) $14\dfrac{1}{9}$

(E) None of these.

E. Percentages

33. 15% of 200 =

(A) 3
(B) 30
(C) 300
(D) 3,000
(E) None of these.

34. What is 3% of 5?

    (A) $\frac{5}{3}\%$

    (B) 15

    (C) $\frac{3}{20}$

    (D) $\frac{3}{5}$

    (E) None of these.

35. What percent of 3 is 6?

    (A) 50
    (B) 20
    (C) 200

    (D) $\frac{1}{2}$

    (E) None of these.

F. Equations

36. If $y^2 = 16$, $y =$

    (A) +4 only
    (B) −4 only
    (C) ±4
    (D) ±8
    (E) None of these.

37. If $x - y = 10$, $y =$

    (A) $x - 10$
    (B) $10 + x$
    (C) $10 - x$
    (D) 10
    (E) None of these.

38. What is the value of x if $x + 4y = 7$ and $x - 4y = 8$?

    (A) 15

    (B) $\frac{15}{2}$

    (C) 7

    (D) $\frac{7}{2}$

    (E) None of these.

39. What is the value of x and y if $x - 2y = 2$ and $2x + y = 4$?

    (A) $x = 2, y = 0$
    (B) $x = 0, y = -2$
    (C) $x = -1, y = 2$
    (D) $x = 0, y = 2$
    (E) None of these.

40. If $\frac{x}{5} = \frac{7}{12}$, $x =$

    (A) $\frac{35}{12}$

    (B) $\frac{12}{35}$

    (C) $\frac{7}{60}$

    (D) $\frac{60}{7}$

    (E) None of these.

G. Angles

Questions 41–42 refer to the diagram below:

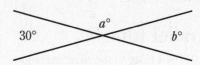

41. $a =$

    (A) 30
    (B) 150
    (C) 45
    (D) 90
    (E) None of these.

42. $b =$

    (A) 30
    (B) 150
    (C) 45
    (D) 90
    (E) None of these.

Question 43 refers to the diagram below:

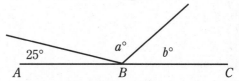

ABC is a straight line.

43. $a + b =$

    (A) 155
    (B) 165
    (C) 180
    (D) 145
    (E) None of these.

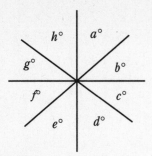

44. What is the value of $a + b + c + d + e + f + g + h$ in the diagram above?

(A) 180
(B) 240
(C) 360
(D) 540
(E) None of these.

H. Parallel Lines

Questions 45–51 refer to the diagram below:

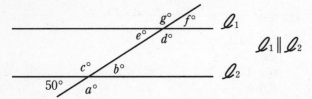

$\ell_1 \parallel \ell_2$

45. $a =$

(A) 50
(B) 130
(C) 100
(D) 40
(E) None of these.

46. $b =$

(A) 50
(B) 130
(C) 100
(D) 40
(E) None of these.

47. $c =$

(A) 50
(B) 130
(C) 100
(D) 40
(E) None of these.

48. $d =$

(A) 50
(B) 130
(C) 100
(D) 40
(E) None of these.

49. $e =$

(A) 50
(B) 130
(C) 100
(D) 40
(E) None of these.

50. $f =$

(A) 50
(B) 130
(C) 100
(D) 40
(E) None of these.

51. $g =$

(A) 50
(B) 130
(C) 100
(D) 40
(E) None of these.

I. Triangles

52.

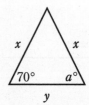

(Note: Figure is not drawn to scale.)

$a =$

(A) 70°
(B) 40°
(C) $\dfrac{xy}{70°}$
(D) Cannot be determined.
(E) None of these.

53.

(Note: Figure is not drawn to scale.)

$x =$

(A) 3
(B) $\dfrac{50}{3}$
(C) $3\sqrt{2}$
(D) Cannot be determined.
(E) None of these.

54.

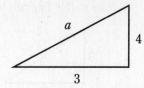

(Note: Figure is not drawn to scale.)

Which is a possible value for *a*?

(A) 1
(B) 6
(C) 10
(D) 7
(E) 8

55.

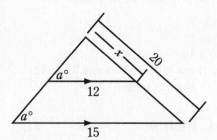

(Note: Figure is not drawn to scale.)

In the triangle above, *x* =

(A) 12
(B) 16
(C) 15
(D) 10
(E) None of these.

56.

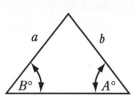

In the triangle above, if $B > A$, then

(A) $b = a$
(B) $b > a$
(C) $b < a$
(D) A relation between *b* and *a* cannot be determined.
(E) None of these.

57.

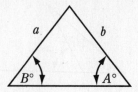

In the triangle above, if $b < a$, then

(A) $B > A$
(B) $B = A$
(C) $B < A$
(D) A relation between *B* and *A* cannot be determined.
(E) None of these.

58.

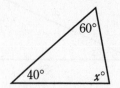

In the triangle above, *x* =

(A) 100
(B) 80
(C) 90
(D) 45
(E) None of these.

59.

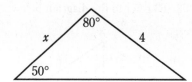

(Note: Figure is not drawn to scale.)

In the triangle above, *x* =

(A) $4\sqrt{2}$
(B) 8
(C) 4
(D) a number between 1 and 4
(E) None of these.

60.

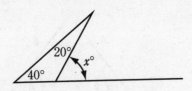

In the diagram above, $x =$

(A) 40
(B) 20
(C) 60
(D) 80
(E) None of these.

61.

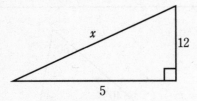

(Note: Figure is not drawn to scale.)

In the right triangle above, $x =$

(A) 17
(B) 13
(C) 15
(D) $12\sqrt{2}$
(E) None of these.

Questions 62−63 refer to the diagram below:

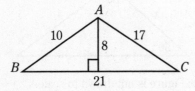

(Note: Figure is not drawn to scale.)

62. The perimeter of the triangle ABC is

(A) 16
(B) 48
(C) 168
(D) 84
(E) None of these.

63. The area of triangle ABC is

(A) 170
(B) 85
(C) 168
(D) 84
(E) None of these.

Questions 64−65 refer to the diagram below:

64. The area of the triangle is

(A) 6
(B) 7
(C) 12
(D) any number between 5 and 7
(E) None of these.

65. The perimeter of the triangle is

(A) 7
(B) 12
(C) 15
(D) any number between 7 and 12
(E) None of these.

J. Circles

Questions 66−67 refer to the diagram below:

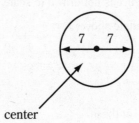

center

66. The area of the circle is

(A) 49
(B) 49π
(C) 14π
(D) 196π
(E) None of these.

67. The circumference of the circle is

(A) 14π
(B) 7π
(C) 49π
(D) 14
(E) None of these.

68.

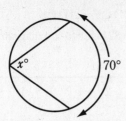

In the diagram above, $x =$

(A) 70°
(B) 35°
(C) 90°
(D) a number that cannot be determined
(E) None of these.

69.

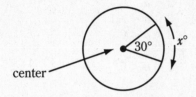

In the diagram above, $x =$

(A) 30°
(B) 60°
(C) 90°
(D) a number that cannot be determined
(E) None of these.

70.

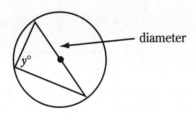

In the diagram above, $y =$

(A) 145°
(B) 60°
(C) 90°
(D) a number that cannot be determined
(E) None of these.

K. Other Figures

Questions 71–72 refer to the diagram below:

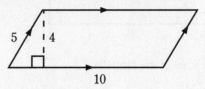

71. The area of the figure is

(A) 15
(B) 20
(C) 40
(D) 50
(E) None of these.

72. The perimeter of the figure is

(A) 15
(B) 30
(C) 40
(D) 50
(E) None of these.

Questions 73–75 refer to the figure below:

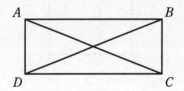

ABCD is a rectangle.

73. What is *BC* if *AD* = 6?

(A) 4
(B) 6
(C) 8
(D) 10
(E) 12

74. What is *DC* if *AB* = 8?

(A) 4
(B) 6
(C) 8
(D) 10
(E) 12

75. What is *DB* if *AC* = 10?

(A) 4
(B) 6
(C) 8
(D) 10
(E) 12

Questions 76–77 refer to the diagram below:

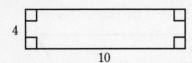

76. The area of the figure is

(A) 14
(B) 40
(C) 80
(D) 28
(E) None of these.

77. The perimeter of the figure is

(A) 14
(B) 28
(C) 36
(D) 40
(E) None of these.

Questions 78–79 refer to the figure below:

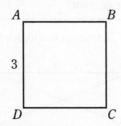

ABCD is a square; *AD* = 3.

78. What is the area of the square?

(A) 9
(B) 12
(C) 16
(D) 20
(E) None of these.

79. What is the perimeter of the square?

(A) 9
(B) 12
(C) 16
(D) 20
(E) None of these.

80. The volume of the rectangular solid below is

(A) 48
(B) 64
(C) 128
(D) 72
(E) None of these.

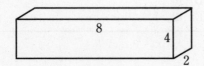

L. Number Lines

Questions 81–82 refer to the diagram below:

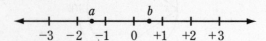

81. Which defines the range in values of *b* best?

(A) $-2 < b < 1$
(B) $0 < b < 2$
(C) $0 < b < 1$
(D) $-3 < b < 3$
(E) $0 < b$

82. Which defines the range in values of *a* best?

(A) $-2 < a$
(B) $-2 < a < -1$
(C) $-2 < a < 0$
(D) $a < -1$
(E) $-3 < a < 0$

M. Coordinates

Questions 83–85 refer to the diagram below:

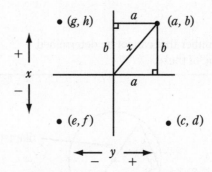

83. How many of the variables *a, b, c, d, e, f, g, h* are positive?

(A) 1
(B) 2
(C) 3
(D) 4
(E) 5

84. How many of the variables *a, b, c, d, e, f, g, h* are negative?

(A) 1
(B) 2
(C) 3
(D) 4
(E) 5

85. If $a = 3$, $b = 4$, what is x?

(A) 3
(B) 4
(C) 5
(D) 6
(E) None of these.

86.

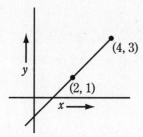

What is the slope of the line above?

(A) -1
(B) 0
(C) $+1$
(D) $+2$
(E) $+3$

N. Inequalities

Note: Any variable can be positive or negative or 0.

87. If $x > y$, then $4x > 4y$

(A) always
(B) sometimes
(C) never

88. If $x + y > z$, then $y > z - x$

(A) always
(B) sometimes
(C) never

89. If $-4 < -x$, then $+4 > +x$

(A) always
(B) sometimes
(C) never

90. If $m > n$, where q is any number, then $qm > qn$

(A) always
(B) sometimes
(C) never

91. If $x > y$ and $p > q$, then $x + p > y + q$

(A) always
(B) sometimes
(C) never

92. If $x > y$ and $p > q$, then $xp > qy$

(A) always
(B) sometimes
(C) never

O. Averages

93. What is the average of 30, 40, and 80?

(A) 150
(B) 75
(C) 50
(D) 45
(E) None of these.

94. What is the average speed in mph of a car traveling 40 miles in 4 hours?

(A) 160
(B) 10
(C) 120
(D) 30
(E) None of these.

P. Shortcuts

95. Which is greater? *Don't calculate a common denominator!*

$$\frac{7}{16} \text{ or } \frac{3}{7}$$

(A) $\dfrac{7}{16}$

(B) $\dfrac{3}{7}$

(C) They are equal.
(D) A relationship cannot be determined.

96. Add $\dfrac{7}{12} + \dfrac{3}{5} =$

(A) $1\dfrac{11}{60}$

(B) $1\dfrac{13}{60}$

(C) $1\dfrac{15}{60}$

(D) $\dfrac{10}{17}$

(E) None of these.

97. Subtract: $\dfrac{7}{12} - \dfrac{3}{5} =$

(A) $-\dfrac{1}{60}$

(B) $-\dfrac{3}{60}$

(C) $-1\dfrac{11}{60}$

(D) $\dfrac{4}{7}$

(E) None of these.

98. $\dfrac{4}{250} =$

(A) .016
(B) .04
(C) .004
(D) .025
(E) None of these.

Note: Do not divide 250 into 4 in the above question!

99. What is c if

$$200 = \frac{a + b + c}{2} \text{ and } 80 = \frac{a + b}{3}?$$

(A) 160
(B) 140
(C) 120
(D) 100
(E) None of these.

100. What is the value of $95 \times 75 - 95 \times 74$? (*Don't multiply* 95×75 *or* $95 \times 74!$)

(A) 65
(B) 75
(C) 85
(D) 95
(E) None of these.

101. Find the value of

$$\frac{140 \times 15}{5 \times 7} \quad (Don't\ multiply\ 140 \times 15!)$$

(A) 20
(B) 40
(C) 60
(D) 90
(E) None of these.

101 Math Questions:
Answers, Diagnoses, Solutions,
Generalizations, and Rules

101 Math Questions:
Answers

A. Fractions

1. B
2. A
3. A
4. C
5. B

B. Even–Odd Relationships

6. A
7. B
8. B
9. B
10. A
11. B
12. B

C. Factors

13. A
14. C
15. B
16. D
17. C
18. A
19. D
20. A
21. C

D. Exponents

22. C
23. B
24. B
25. C
26. A
27. A
28. A
29. C
30. A
31. B
32. D

E. Percentages

33. B
34. C
35. C

F. Equations

36. C
37. A
38. B
39. A
40. A

G. Angles

41. B
42. A
43. A
44. C

H. Parallel Lines

45. B
46. A
47. B
48. B
49. A
50. A
51. B

I. Triangles

52. A
53. A
54. B
55. B
56. B
57. C
58. B
59. C
60. C
61. B
62. B
63. D
64. A
65. B

J. Circles

66. B
67. A
68. B
69. A
70. C

K. Other Figures

71. C
72. B
73. B
74. C
75. D
76. B
77. B
78. A
79. B
80. B

L. Number Lines

81. C
82. B

M. Coordinates

83. D
84. D
85. C
86. C

N. Inequalities

87. A
88. A
89. A
90. B
91. A
92. B

O. Averages

93. C
94. B

P. Shortcuts

95. A
96. A
97. A
98. A
99. A
100. D
101. C

Basic Skills Math Diagnosis

Math area		Total questions	*If you got any of the answers to the following questions wrong, study answers to those questions.	Page in text for review	Complete Math Refresher: Refer to the numbered sections listed below of the Math Refresher (Part 6, starting on page 185) for a refresher on the applicable rules.
A.	Fractions	5	1–5	55	101–112, 123–128
B.	Even–Odd Relationships	7	6–12	55	603–611
C.	Factors	9	13–21	55–56	409
D.	Exponents	11	22–32	56	429–430
E.	Percentages	3	33–35	57	106, 107, 114
F.	Equations	5	36–40	57	406–409
G.	Angles	4	41–44	57–58	500–503
H.	Parallel Lines	7	45–51	58	504
I.	Triangles	14	52–65	58–60	306–308, 505–516
J.	Circles	5	66–70	61	310–311, 524–529
K.	Other Figures	10	71–80	61–62	303–305, 309, 312–316, 517–523
L.	Number Lines	2	81–82	62	410a
M.	Coordinates	4	83–86	62	410b–418
N.	Inequalities	6	87–92	63	419–428
O.	Averages	2	93–94	63	601
P.	Shortcuts	7	95–101	63–64	128, 609

Solutions, Generalizations, and Rules

A. Fractions

1. (B)

$$\frac{\dfrac{a}{b}}{c} = a \times \frac{c}{b} = \boxed{\dfrac{ac}{b}}$$

INVERT TO MULTIPLY

Alternate way:

$$\frac{\dfrac{a}{b}}{c} = \frac{\dfrac{a}{b}}{c} \times \frac{c}{c} = \frac{ac}{\dfrac{b}{c} \times c} = \boxed{\dfrac{ac}{b}}$$

2. (A)

$$\frac{\dfrac{1}{1}}{y} = 1 \times \frac{y}{1} = y$$

INVERT TO MULTIPLY

3. (A)

$$\frac{\dfrac{a}{b}}{c} = \frac{\dfrac{a}{b} \times b}{c \times b} = \frac{a}{cb} = \boxed{\dfrac{a}{bc}}$$

4. (C)

$$\frac{\dfrac{1}{x}}{y} = 1 \times \frac{y}{x} = \boxed{\dfrac{y}{x}}$$

INVERT TO MULTIPLY

5. (B)

$$\frac{\dfrac{a}{b}}{\dfrac{b}{a}} = \frac{a}{b} \times \frac{a}{b} = \boxed{\dfrac{a^2}{b^2}}$$

INVERT TO MULTIPLY

Alternate way:

$$\frac{\dfrac{a}{b}}{\dfrac{b}{a}} = \frac{\dfrac{a}{b} \times a}{\dfrac{b}{a} \times a} = \frac{\dfrac{a^2}{b}}{\dfrac{b}{a}a} = \frac{\dfrac{a^2}{b}}{b} = \frac{\dfrac{a^2}{b} \times b}{b \times b} = \boxed{\dfrac{a^2}{b^2}}$$

B. Even–Odd Relationships

6. (A) ODD × ODD = $\boxed{\text{ODD}}$

$3 \times 3 = 9; 5 \times 5 = 25$

7. (B) ODD + or − ODD = $\boxed{\text{EVEN}}$

$5 + 3 = 8$
$5 - 3 = 2$

8. (B) EVEN × EVEN = $\boxed{\text{EVEN}}$

$2 \times 2 = 4; 4 \times 2 = 8$

9. (B) EVEN + or − EVEN = $\boxed{\text{EVEN}}$

$6 + 2 = 8; 10 - 4 = 6$

10. (A) $(\text{ODD})^{\text{ODD}} = \boxed{\text{ODD}}$

$3^3 = 3 \times 3 \times 3 = 27$ (odd)

$1^{27} = 1$ (odd)

11. (B) $(\text{EVEN})^{\text{EVEN}} = \boxed{\text{EVEN}}$

$2^2 = 4$ (even); $4^2 = 16$ (even)

12. (B) $(\text{EVEN})^{\text{ODD}} = \boxed{\text{EVEN}}$

$2^3 = 2 \times 2 \times 2 = 8$ (even)
$4^1 = 4$ (even)

C. Factors

13. (A) $(x + 3)(x + 2) = x^2 \dots$

$(x + 3)(x + 2) = x^2 + 2x + 3x \dots$

$(x + 3)(x + 2) = x^2 + 2x + 3x + 6$

$(x + 3)(x + 2) = \boxed{x^2 + 5x + 6}$

14. (C) $(x + 3)(x - 2) = x^2 \dots$

$(x + 3)(x - 2) = x^2 - 2x + 3x \dots$

$(x + 3)(x - 2) = x^2 - 2x + 3x - 6$

$(x + 3)(x - 2) = \boxed{x^2 + x - 6}$

15. (B) $(x - 3)(y - 2) = xy \ldots$

$\overbrace{(x - 3)}(y - 2) = xy - 2x - 3y \ldots$

$(x - 3)(y - 2) = \boxed{xy - 2x - 3y + 6}$

16. (D) $(a + b)(b + c) = ab \ldots$

$\overbrace{(a + b)}(b + c) = ab + ac + b^2 \ldots$

$(a + b)(b + c) = \boxed{ab + ac + b^2 + bc}$

17. (C) $(a + b)(a - b) =$

$\underbrace{(a + b)}(a - b) = a^2$

$\overbrace{(a + b)(a - b)} = a^2 - ab + ba \ldots$

$(a + \underbrace{b)(a} - b) = a^2 - ab + ba - b^2$

$(a + b)(a - b) = a^2 - ab + ba - b^2$

$\boxed{(a + b)(a - b) = a^2 - b^2}$ MEMORIZE

18. (A) $(a + b)^2 = (a + b)(a + b)$

$\underbrace{(a + b)}(a + b) = a^2 \ldots$

$\overbrace{(a + b)(a + b)} = a^2 + ab + ba \ldots$

$(a + \underbrace{b)(a} + b) = a^2 + ab + ba + b^2$

$\boxed{(a + b)^2 = a^2 + 2ab + b^2}$ MEMORIZE

19. (D) $-(a - b) = -a - (-b)$

$-(a - b) = -a + b$

$\boxed{-(a - b) = b - a}$ MEMORIZE

20. (A) $a(b + c) =$

$\overbrace{a(b} + c) = \boxed{ab + ac}$

21. (C) $-a(b - c) =$

$-\overbrace{a(b} - c) = -ab - a(-c)$

$= -ab + ac = \boxed{ac - ab}$

D. Exponents

22. (C) $10^5 = 100,000$

$\qquad$ 5 zeroes

23. (B) $107076.5 = 1\,0\,7\,0\,7\,6.5$
$\qquad\qquad\qquad\quad {}_{5\ 4\ 3\ 2\ 1}$

$= 1.\overbrace{070765} \times \boxed{10^5}$

24. (B) Add exponents:

$a^2 \times a^5 = \boxed{a^7}\ a^m \times a^n = a^{m + n}$

25. (C) $(ab)^7 = \boxed{a^7 b^7}$

$(ab)^m = a^m b^m$

26. (A) $\left(\dfrac{a}{c}\right)^8 = \boxed{\dfrac{a^8}{c^8}}$

$\left(\dfrac{a}{c}\right)^m = \dfrac{a^m}{c^m}$

27. (A) $a^4 \times b^4 = \boxed{(ab)^4}$

$a^m \times b^m = (ab)^m$

28. (A) $a^{-3} \times b^5 = \boxed{\dfrac{b^5}{a^3}}$

$a^{-m} \times b^n = \dfrac{b^n}{a^m}$

29. (C) $(a^3)^5 = \boxed{a^{15}}$

MULTIPLY EXPONENTS

$(a^m)^n = a^{mn}$

30. (A) $2a^{-3} = \boxed{\dfrac{2}{a^3}}$

$ax^{-b} = \dfrac{a}{x^b}$ since $a^{-n} = \dfrac{1}{a^n}$

31. (B) $2a^m \times \dfrac{1}{3}a^{-n} = \dfrac{2}{3}a^m a^{-n}$

$= \dfrac{2}{3}a^{m-n}$ or $\boxed{\dfrac{2a^m}{3a^n}}$

32. (D) $3^2 + 3^{-2} + 4^1 + 6^0 =$

$3^2 = 3 \times 3 = 9$

$3^{-2} = \dfrac{1}{3^2} = \dfrac{1}{9}$

$4^1 = 4$

$6^0 = 1$ (any number to 0 power = 1)

$3^2 + 3^{-2} + 4^1 + 6^0 = 9 + \dfrac{1}{9} + 4 + 1 = \boxed{14\tfrac{1}{9}}$

E. Percentages

Translate: is → =

of → × (times)

percent (%) → $\dfrac{}{100}$

what → x (or y, etc.)

33. (B) 15%   of 200 =

↓↓   ↓ ↓ ↓

$15\dfrac{}{100} \times 200 =$

$\dfrac{15}{100} \times 200 =$

$\dfrac{15}{\cancel{100}} \times \cancel{200} = \boxed{30}$

34. (C) What is 3% of 5?

↓ ↓ ↓↓   ↓↓

$x = 3\dfrac{}{100} \times 5$

$x = \dfrac{3}{100} \times 5$

$x = \dfrac{15}{100} = \boxed{\dfrac{3}{20}}$

35. (C) What percent of   3   is   6?

↓   ↓   ↓   ↓   ↓ ↓

x $\dfrac{}{100}$ ×   3   =   6

$\dfrac{x}{100} \times 3 = 6$

$\dfrac{3x}{100} = 6$

$3x = 600$

$x = \boxed{200}$

F. Equations

36. (C) $y^2 = 16$

$\sqrt{y^2} = \pm\sqrt{16}$

$y = \boxed{\pm 4}$

37. (A) $x - y = 10$

Add y:

$x - y + y = 10 + y$

$x = 10 + y$

Subtract 10:

$x - 10 = 10 - 10 + y$

$\boxed{x - 10 = y}$

38. (B) Add equations:

$x + 4y = 7$

$x - 4y = 8$

$2x + \cancel{4y} - \cancel{4y} = 15$

$2x = 15$

$\boxed{x = \dfrac{15}{2}}$

39. (A) $x - 2y = 2$ $\boxed{1}$

$2x + y = 4$ $\boxed{2}$

Multiply $\boxed{1}$ by 2:

$2(x - 2y) = 2(2)$

We get:

$2x - 4y = 4$ $\boxed{3}$

Subtract $\boxed{2}$ from $\boxed{3}$:

$2x - 4y = 4$

$-\ (2x + y = 4)$

$0 - 5y = 0$

$\boxed{y = 0}$ $\boxed{4}$

Substitute $\boxed{4}$ into either $\boxed{1}$ or $\boxed{2}$:

In $\boxed{1}$:

$x - 2y = 2$

$x - 2(0) = 2$

$\boxed{x = 2}$

40. (A) $\dfrac{x}{5} = \dfrac{7}{12}$, $x =$

Cross-multiply x:

$$\left(\dfrac{x}{5} = \dfrac{7}{12}\right)$$

$12x = 35$

Divide by 12:

$\dfrac{12x}{12} = \dfrac{35}{12}$

$\boxed{x = \dfrac{35}{12} = 2\dfrac{11}{12}}$

G. Angles

This diagram refers to questions 41–42.

41. (B) $a°$ and 30° are supplementary angles (they add up to 180°).

So $a + 30 = 180$; $a = \boxed{150}$.

42. (A) $b°$ and 30° are *vertical* angles (vertical angles are equal).

So $b = \boxed{30}$.

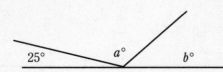

43. (A) $a°$, $b°$, and 25° make up a *straight* angle, which is 180°.

$a + b + 25 = 180$
$a + b = 180 - 25$
$a + b = \boxed{155}$

44. (C) The sum of the angles in the diagram is $\boxed{360°}$, the number of degrees around the circumference of a circle.

H. Parallel Lines

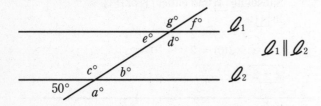

$\ell_1 \parallel \ell_2$

45. (B) $a + 50 = 180$

$a = \boxed{130}$

46. (A) $b = \boxed{50}$ (vertical angles)

47. (B) $c = a$ (vertical angles)

$= \boxed{130}$

48. (B) $d = c$ (alternate interior angles are equal)

$= \boxed{130}$

49. (A) $e = b$ (alternate interior angles)

$= \boxed{50}$

50. (A) $f = e$ (vertical angles)

$= \boxed{50}$

51. (B) $g = d$ (vertical angles)

$= \boxed{130}$

I. Triangles

52. (A)

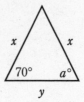

(Note: Figure is not drawn to scale.)

If two sides are equal, base angles are equal. Thus $a = \boxed{70°}$.

53. (A)

(Note: Figure is not drawn to scale.)

If base angles are equal, then sides are equal, so $\boxed{x = 3}$.

54. (B)

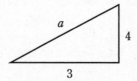

(Note: Figure is not drawn to scale.)

The sum of two sides must be *greater* than the third side. Try choices:

(A) $3 + 4 \not> 1$: (A) is not possible
(B) $3 + 4 > 6$; $6 + 3 > 4$; $4 + 6 > 3$...OK
(C) $3 + 4 \not> 10$: (C) is not possible
(D) $3 + 4 = 7$: (D) is not possible
(E) $3 + 4 \not> 8$: (E) is not possible

55. (B) Using similar triangles, write a *proportion* with x.

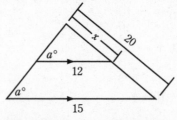

(Note: Figure is not drawn to scale.)

$$\frac{x}{20} = \frac{12}{15}$$
$$15x = 12 \times 20$$
$$x = \frac{12 \times 20}{15}$$
$$x = \frac{\overset{4}{\cancel{12}} \times \overset{4}{\cancel{20}}}{\underset{\cancel{5}}{\cancel{15}}} = \boxed{16}$$

In general:

$$\frac{m}{n} = \frac{q}{p} = \frac{r}{r+s}$$

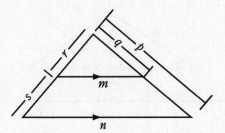

(Note: Figure is not drawn to scale.)

---

56. (B) The greater angle lies opposite the greater side and vice versa.

If $B > A$, $\boxed{b > a}$

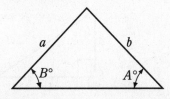

---

57. (C) The greater side lies opposite the greater angle and vice versa.

If $b < a$, then $\boxed{B < A}$

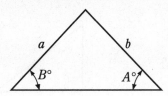

---

58. (B) Sum of angles of triangle = 180°.

So $40 + 60 + x = 180$
$100 + x = 180$
$\boxed{x = 80}$

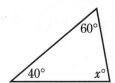

---

59. (C)

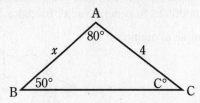

(Note: Figure is not drawn to scale.)

First calculate $\angle C$. Call it y.

$80 + 50 + y = 180$ (Sum of ∠s = 180°)

$y = 50$

Since $\angle C = y = 50$ and $\angle B = 50$, side AB = side AC.

$AB = \boxed{x = 4}$

---

60. (C) $x° = 20° + 40°$ (sum of *remote* interior angles = exterior angle)

$$\boxed{x = 60}$$

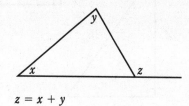

In general,

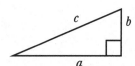

$z = x + y$

---

61. (B)

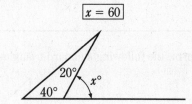

In right △, $a^2 + b^2 = c^2$
So for

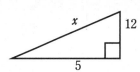

$$5^2 + 12^2 = x^2$$
$$25 + 144 = x^2$$
$$169 = x^2$$
$$\sqrt{169} = x$$
$$\boxed{13} = x$$

Note: Specific right triangles you should memorize; use multiples to generate other triangles.

Example of multiples:

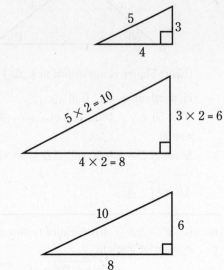

Memorize the following standard triangles:

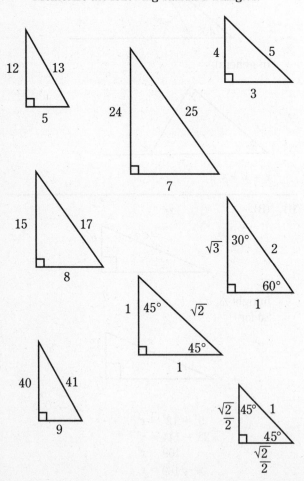

62. (B) Perimeter = sum of sides
10 + 17 + 21 = $\boxed{48}$

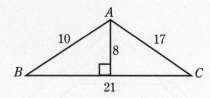

---

63. (D)

Area of $\triangle = \frac{1}{2}bh$

Area of $\triangle = \frac{1}{2}(21)(8) = \boxed{84}$

64. (A) Area of any triangle $= \frac{1}{2}$base × height

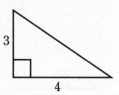

Here 4 is base and 3 is height. So area $= \frac{1}{2}(4 \times 3)$ $= \frac{1}{2}(12) = \boxed{6}$.

---

65. (B)

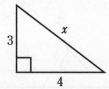

To find perimeter, we need to find the sum of the sides. The sum of the sides is $3 + 4 + x$.

We need to find x. From the solution in Question 61, we should realize that we have a 3–4–5 right triangle, so $x = 5$.

The perimeter is then $3 + 4 + 5 = \boxed{12}$.

Note that you could have found x by using the Pythagorean Theorem:

$3^2 + 4^2 = x^2$; $9 + 16 = x^2$; $25 = x^2$; $\sqrt{25} = x$; $5 = x$.

J. Circles

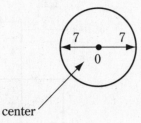

center

66. (B) Area $= \pi r^2 = \pi(7)^2$

$$= \boxed{49\pi}$$

---

67. (A) Circumference $= 2\pi r = 2\pi(7)$

$$= \boxed{14\pi}$$

---

68. (B) Inscribed angle $= \frac{1}{2}$ arc

$$x° = \frac{1}{2}(70°)$$

$$= \boxed{35°}$$

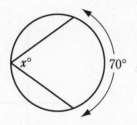

---

69. (A) Central angle = arc

$$\boxed{30°} = x°$$

Note: The *total* number of degrees around the circumference is 360°. So a central angle of 30°, like the one below, cuts $\frac{30}{360} = \frac{1}{12}$ the circumference.

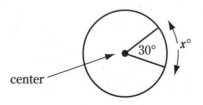

center

---

70. (C) The diameter cuts a 180° arc on the circle, so an inscribed angle $y = \frac{1}{2}$ arc $= \frac{1}{2}(180°) = \boxed{90°}$.
Here is a good thing to remember:

Any inscribed angle whose triangle base is a diameter is 90°.

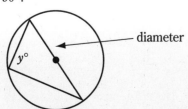

diameter

K. Other Figures

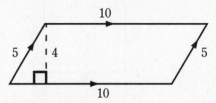

71. (C) Area of parallelogram = base × height = (10)(4) = $\boxed{40}$

72. (B) Perimeter = sum of sides = $5 + 5 + 10 + 10 = \boxed{30}$

ABCD is a rectangle.

73. (B) In a rectangle (as in a parallelogram), opposite sides are equal.

So $AD = BC = \boxed{6}$.

---

74. (C) In a rectangle (as in a parallelogram), opposite sides are equal.

So $DC = AB = \boxed{8}$.

---

75. (D) In a rectangle (but not in a parallelogram), the diagonals are equal.

So $DB = AC = \boxed{10}$.

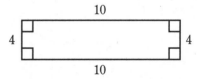

76. (B) Area of rectangle = length × width = 4 × 10 = $\boxed{40}$.

---

77. (B) Perimeter = sum of sides = $4 + 4 + 10 + 10 = \boxed{28}$.

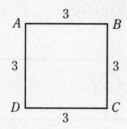

78. (A) Area of a square with side x is x^2. (All sides of a square are equal.) So length = width. Since $x = 3$, $x^2 = \boxed{9}$.

---

79. (B) Perimeter of a square is the sum of all sides of the square. Since all sides are equal, if one side is x, perimeter = $4x$.

$x = 3$, so $4x = \boxed{12}$.

---

80. (B) Volume of rectangular solid shown below = $a \times b \times c$

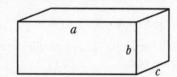

So for:

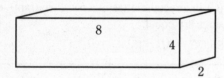

$a = 8, b = 4, c = 2$

and $a \times b \times c = 8 \times 4 \times 2 = \boxed{64}$.

Note: Volume of cube shown below = $a \times a \times a = a^3$

L. Number Lines

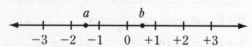

81. (C) b is between 0 and +1
so $\boxed{0 < b < 1}$.

82. (B) a is between -2 and -1
so $\boxed{-2 < a < -1}$.

M. Coordinates

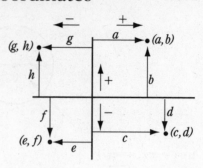

Horizontal right = +
Horizontal left = −
Vertical up = +
Vertical down = −

83. (D) a, b, c, h positive (4 letters)

84. (D) d, e, f, g negative (4 letters)

---

85. (C)

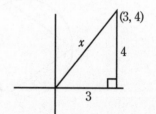

Remember the 3–4–5 right triangle. $\boxed{x = 5}$
You can also use the Pythagorean Theorem:
$3^2 + 4^2 = x^2$; $9 + 16 = x^2$; $x^2 = 25$; $\boxed{x = 5}$

86. (C)

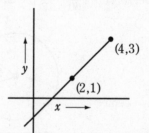

The slope of a line $y = mx + b$ is m. If two points (x_1, y_1) and (x_2, y_2) are on the line, then the slope is

$\dfrac{y_2 - y_1}{x_2 - x_1} = m$. Here $x_1 = 2$, $y_1 = 1$, $x_2 = 4$, $y_2 = 3$

So $\dfrac{y_2 - y_1}{x_2 - x_1} = \dfrac{3 - 1}{4 - 2} = \boxed{1}$.

N. Inequalities

87. (A) You can multiply an inequality by a positive number and retain the same inequality:

$x > y$

$\boxed{4x > 4y}$ $\boxed{\text{ALWAYS}}$

---

88. (A) You can subtract the same number from both sides of an inequality and retain the same inequality:

$$x + y > z$$
$$x + y - x > z - x$$

$\boxed{y > z - x}$ $\boxed{\text{ALWAYS}}$

---

89. (A) If you multiply an inequality by a minus sign, you *reverse* the original inequality sign:

$$-4 < -x$$
$$-(-4 < -x)$$

$\boxed{+4 > +x}$ $\boxed{\text{ALWAYS}}$

---

90. (B) If $m > n$,

$qm > qn$ if q is *positive*

$qm < qn$ if q is *negative*

$qm = qn$ if q is *zero*

So, $\boxed{qm > qn}$ $\boxed{\text{SOMETIMES}}$

---

91. (A) You can always add inequality relations to get the same inequality relation:

$$x > y$$
$$+\ p > q$$
$$\overline{x + p > y + q}$$ $\boxed{\text{ALWAYS}}$

---

92. (B) You can't always multiply inequality relations to get the same inequality relation. For example:

$3 > 2$	$3 > 2$
$\times -2 > -3$	$\times\ 2 > 1$
$-6 \not> -6$	$6 > 2$

However, if x, y, p, q are positive, then if $x > y$ and $p > q$, $xp > yq$. $\boxed{\text{SOMETIMES}}$

O. Averages

93. (C) Average of 30, 40, and 80 =

$\dfrac{30 + 40 + 80}{3} = \boxed{50}$

Average of $x + y + z + t + \ldots = \dfrac{x + y + z + t + \ldots}{\textit{number of terms}}$

---

94. (B) Average speed = $\dfrac{\text{TOTAL DISTANCE}}{\text{TOTAL TIME}}$

Distance = 40 miles, time = 4 hours

Average speed $= \dfrac{40 \text{ miles}}{4 \text{ hours}} = \boxed{10 \text{ miles per hour}}$

P. Shortcuts

95. (A) Don't get a common denominator if you can do something more easily:

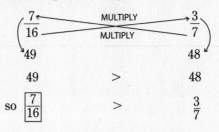

$49 \qquad > \qquad 48$

so $\boxed{\dfrac{7}{16}} \qquad > \qquad \dfrac{3}{7}$

---

96. (A)

$$\dfrac{7}{12} \overset{\text{MULTIPLY}}{\underset{\text{MULTIPLY}}{+}} \dfrac{3}{5} = \dfrac{7 \times 5 + 3 \times 12}{12 \times 5}$$

$$= \dfrac{35 + 36}{60}$$

$$= \dfrac{71}{60} = \boxed{1\ \dfrac{11}{60}}$$

---

97. (A)

$$\dfrac{7}{12} \overset{\text{MULTIPLY}}{\underset{\text{MULTIPLY}}{-}} \dfrac{3}{5} = \dfrac{7 \times 5 - 3 \times 12}{12 \times 5}$$

$$= \dfrac{35 - 36}{60}$$

$$= \boxed{-\dfrac{1}{60}}$$

---

98. (A) Don't divide by 250! Multiply both numerator and denominator by 4:

$\dfrac{4}{250} \times \dfrac{4}{4} = \dfrac{16}{1,000} = \boxed{0.016}$

---

99. (A) Get rid of denominators!

$200 = \dfrac{a + b + c}{2}$ $\boxed{1}$

Multiply $\boxed{1}$ by 2:

$200 \times 2 = a + b + c$ $\boxed{2}$

$80 = \dfrac{a + b}{3}$ $\boxed{3}$

Multiply $\boxed{3}$ by 3:

$80 \times 3 = a + b$ $\boxed{4}$

Now subtract $\boxed{4}$ from $\boxed{2}$:

$200 \times 2 - 80 \times 3 = a + b + c - (a + b)$

$= \cancel{a} + \cancel{b} + c - \cancel{a} - \cancel{b}$

$400 - 240 = c$

$\boxed{160} = c$

100. (D) Don't multiply 95×75 or 95×74!

Factor *common* 95:

$$95 \times 75 - 95 \times 74 = 95(75 - 74)$$
$$= 95(1)$$
$$= \boxed{95}$$

---

101. (C) $\dfrac{140 \times 15}{5 \times 7}$

Don't multiply 140×15 if you can first *reduce*.

$$\dfrac{\overset{20}{\cancel{140}} \times 15}{\underset{1}{5 \times \cancel{7}}} = \dfrac{20 \times 15}{5}$$

Further reduce:

$$\dfrac{20 \times \overset{3}{\cancel{15}}}{\underset{1}{\cancel{5}}} = \boxed{60}$$

PART 4

STRATEGY SECTION

Using Critical Thinking Skills to Score High on the GRE

5 General Strategies

General Strategies for Taking the GRE Examination

Before studying the 42 specific strategies for the Math and Critical Reading questions, you will find it useful to review the following 5 General Strategies for taking the GRE.

Strategy 1

DON'T RUSH INTO GETTING AN ANSWER WITHOUT THINKING. BE CAREFUL IF YOUR ANSWER COMES TOO EASILY, ESPECIALLY IF THE QUESTION IS TOWARD THE END OF THE SECTION.

Beware of Choice A If You Get the Answer Fast or Without Really Thinking

Everybody panics when they take an exam like the GRE. And what happens is that they rush into getting answers. That's OK, except that you have to think carefully. If a problem looks too easy, beware! And especially beware of the Choice A answer. It's usually a "lure" choice for those who rush into getting an answer without critically thinking about it. Here's an example:

Below is a picture of a digital clock. The clock shows that the time is 6:06. Consider all the times on the clock where the hour is the same as the minute like in the clock shown below. Another such "double" time would be 8:08 or 9:09. What is the smallest time period between any two such doubles?

(A) 61 minutes
(B) 60 minutes
(C) 58 minutes
(D) 50 minutes
(E) 49 minutes

$$6{:}06$$

Did you subtract 7:07 from 8:08 and get 1 hour and 1 minute (61 minutes)? If you did, you probably chose Choice A: the *lure choice*. Think—do you really believe that the test maker would give you such an easy question? The fact that you figured it out so easily and saw

that Choice A was your answer should make you think twice. The thing you have to realize is that there is another possibility: 12:12 to 1:01 gives 49 minutes, and so Choice E is correct.

So, in summary, if you get the answer fast and without doing much thinking, and it's a Choice A answer, think again. You may have fallen for the Choice A lure.

NOTE: Choice A is often a "lure choice" for those who quickly get an answer without doing any real thinking. However, you should certainly realize that Choice A answers can occur, especially if there is no "lure choice."

Strategy 2

KNOW AND LEARN THE DIRECTIONS TO THE QUESTION TYPES BEFORE YOU TAKE THE ACTUAL TEST.

Never Spend Time Reading Directions During the Test or Doing Sample Questions That Don't Count

All GREs are standardized. For example, all the Regular Math questions have the same directions from test to test, as do the Sentence Completions, etc. So, it's a good idea to learn these sets of directions and familiarize yourself with the types of questions early in the game, before you take your actual GRE.

Here's an example of a set of GRE directions, together with an accompanying example for the Quantitative Reasoning/Quantitative Comparison type of questions.

Section 3: Quantitative Reasoning

Time—40 minutes
25 Questions

For each question, indicate the best answer, using the directions given.

Notes: All numbers used are real numbers.

All figures are assumed to lie in a plane unless otherwise indicated.

Geometric figures, such as lines, circles, triangles, and quadrilaterals, **are not necessarily** drawn to scale. That is, you should **not** assume that quantities such as lengths and angle measures are as they appear in a figure. You should assume, however, that lines shown as straight are actually straight, points on a line are in the order shown, and, more generally, all geometric objects are in the relative positions shown. For questions with geometric figures, you should base your answers on geometric reasoning, not on estimating or comparing quantities by sight or by measurement.

Coordinate systems, such as *xy*-planes and number lines, **are** drawn to scale; therefore, you can read, estimate, or compare quantities in such figures by sight or by measurement.

Graphical data presentations, such as bar graphs, circle graphs, and line graphs, **are** drawn to scale; therefore, you can read, estimate, or compare data values by sight or by measurement.

For Questions 1–9, compare Quantity A and Quantity B, using additional information centered above the two quantities if such information is given. Select one of the following four answer choices and fill in the corresponding circle to the right of the question.

(A) **Quantity A is greater.**
(B) **Quantity B is greater.**
(C) **The two quantities are equal.**
(D) **The relationship cannot be determined from the information given.**

A symbol that appears more than once in a question has the same meaning throughout the question.

	Quantity A	Quantity B	Correct Answer
Example 1:	(2) (6)	2 + 6	Ⓐ ⓑ ⓒ ⓓ

Example 2:	*PS*	*SR*	Ⓐ ⓑ ⓒ ⓓ

(since equal lengths cannot be assumed, even though *PS* and *SR* appear equal)

If on your actual test you spend time reading these directions and/or answering the sample question, you will waste valuable time.

As you go through this book, you will become familiar with all the question types so that you won't have to read their directions on the actual test.

Strategy 3

DO NOT LEAVE ANY ANSWER BLANK.

You don't get a penalty for a wrong answer, so it is always important to put some answer on your answer sheet.

Strategy 4

WRITE AS MUCH AS YOU WANT IN YOUR TEST BOOKLET.

Test Booklets Aren't Graded—So Use Them as You Would Scrap Paper

On the paper-based test, many students are afraid to mark up their test booklets. But the booklets are not graded! Make any marks you want. In fact, some of the strategies demand that you extend or draw lines in geometry questions or label diagrams, circle incorrect answers, etc. That's why when I see computer programs that show only the questions on a screen and prevent the student from marking a diagram or circling an answer, I realize that such programs prevent the student from using many powerful strategies. *So, write all you want in your test booklet—use your test paper as you would scrap paper.*

Just make sure you don't make any marks near the answer circles on the paper-based GRE tests.

On the computer-based test, you will be provided with scrap paper. Make sure you redraw diagrams on the paper so you can mark them up by extending lines, drawing angles, etc.

Strategy 5

USE YOUR OWN CODING SYSTEM TO INDICATE WHICH QUESTIONS YOU NEED TO RETURN TO. (This applies to the paper-based GRE test.)

If You Have Extra Time after Completing a Test Section, You'll Know Exactly Which Questions Need More Attention

When you are sure that you have answered a question correctly, for the paper-based test, mark your question paper with ✓. For questions you are not sure of but for which you have eliminated some of the choices, use **?**. For questions that you're not sure of at all or for which you have not been able to eliminate any choices, use **??**. This will give you a bird's-eye view of what questions you should return to if you have time left after completing a particular test section.

Put these marks next to the question number, not near the answer circles.

For the computerized test, you may want to note on your scrap paper which questions you should return to if you weren't sure of the answer.

42 Easy-to-Learn Strategies

25 Math Strategies + 17 Verbal (Critical Reading) Strategies

Critical thinking is the ability to think clearly in order to solve problems and answer questions of all types—GRE questions, for example, both math and verbal!

Educators who are deeply involved in research on critical thinking skills tell us that such skills are straightforward, practical, teachable, and learnable.

The 25 Math Strategies and 17 Verbal Strategies in this section are critical thinking skills. These strategies have the potential to raise your GRE scores dramatically from approximately 50 points to 300 points (5 to 30 points on the new GRE scale) in verbal and quantitative reasoning. Since each correct GRE question gives you an additional 10 points or an additional 1 point on the new GRE scale, it is reasonable to assume that if you can learn and then use these valuable GRE strategies, you can boost your GRE scores phenomenally!

BE SURE TO LEARN AND USE THE STRATEGIES THAT FOLLOW!

How to Learn the Strategies

1. For each strategy, look at the heading describing the strategy.

2. Try to answer the first example without looking at the EXPLANATORY ANSWER.

3. Then look at the EXPLANATORY ANSWER, and if you got the right answer, see if the method described will enable you to solve the question in a better way with a faster approach.

4. Then try each of the next EXAMPLES without looking at the EXPLANATORY ANSWERS.

5. Use the same procedure as in (3) for each of the EXAMPLES.

The MATH STRATEGIES start on page 72, and the VERBAL STRATEGIES start on page 136. However, before you start the Math Strategies, it would be wise for you to look at the *Important Note on the Allowed Use of Calculators on the GRE*; the *Important Note on Math Questions on the GRE*, page 70; and *The Grid-Type Math Question*, page 70.

Important Note on the Allowed Use of Calculators on the GRE

Although the use of calculators on the GRE will be allowed, using a calculator may be sometimes more tedious, when in fact you can use another problem-solving method or shortcut. So you must be selective on when and when not to use a calculator on the test.

Here's an example of when a calculator should *not* be used:

$$\frac{2}{5} \times \frac{5}{6} \times \frac{6}{7} \times \frac{7}{8} \times \frac{8}{9} \times \frac{9}{10} \times \frac{10}{11} =$$

(A) $\frac{9}{11}$ (B) $\frac{2}{11}$ (C) $\frac{11}{36}$ (D) $\frac{10}{21}$ (E) $\frac{244}{360}$

Here the use of a calculator may take some time. However, if you use the strategy of canceling numerators and denominators (Math Strategy 1, Example 3 on page 73) as shown,

Cancel numerators/denominators:

$$\frac{2}{\cancel{5}} \times \frac{\cancel{5}}{\cancel{6}} \times \frac{\cancel{6}}{\cancel{7}} \times \frac{\cancel{7}}{\cancel{8}} \times \frac{\cancel{8}}{\cancel{9}} \times \frac{\cancel{9}}{\cancel{10}} \times \frac{\cancel{10}}{11} = \frac{2}{11}$$

you can see that the answer comes easily as $\frac{2}{11}$.

Here's an example where using a calculator may get you the solution *as fast as* using a strategy without the calculator:

25 percent of 16 is equivalent to $\frac{1}{2}$ of what number?

(A) 2   (B) 4   (C) 8   (D) 16   (E) 32

Using a calculator, you'd use Math Strategy 2 (page 74) (translating *of* to *times* and *is* to *equals*), first calculating 25 percent of 16 to get 4. Then you'd say 4 = half of what number and you'd find that number to be 8.

Without using a calculator, you'd still use Math Strategy 2 (the translation strategy), but you could write 25 percent as $\frac{1}{4}$, so you'd figure out that $\frac{1}{4} \times 16$ was 4. Then you'd call the number you want to find x, and say $4 = \frac{1}{2}(x)$. You'd find $x = 8$.

Note that both methods, with and without a calculator, are about equally efficient; however, the technique in the second method can be used for many more problems and hones more thinking skills.

Important Note on Math Questions on the GRE

There are three types of math questions on the GRE.

1. The Regular Math, which has choices. The strategies for these start on page 72.

2. The Grid-Type Math Question (numeric-entry question), which is described below.

   Note: The numeric-entry questions can be solved using the Regular Math Strategies.

3. The Quantitative Comparison Questions. To solve these questions, you have to compare the value of two quantities and decide whether one quantity is greater than the other, whether the quantities are equal, or whether you cannot make any of the above comparisons.

The Grid-Type Math Question

There will be some questions on the GRE where you will have to grid in your answer rather than choose from a set of choices. Here are the directions to the grid-type question. Make sure that you understand these directions completely before you answer any of the grid-type questions.

Here are the directions to the grid-type questions on the paper-based GRE test (on the computer GRE test, you simply type in your answer):

Questions 10–25 have several different formats. Unless otherwise directed, select a single answer choice. For Numeric-Entry questions, follow the instructions below.

Numeric-Entry Questions

To answer these questions, enter a number by filling in circles in a grid.

- Your answer may be an integer, a decimal, or a fraction, and it may be negative.

- Equivalent forms of the correct answer, such as 2.5 and 2.50, are all correct. Although fractions do not need to be reduced to lowest terms, they may need to be reduced to fit in the grid.

- Enter the exact answer unless the question asks you to round your answer.

- If a question asks for a fraction, the grid will have a built-in division slash (/). Otherwise, the grid will have a decimal point.

- Start your answer in any quantity, space permitting. Fill in no more than one circle in any quantity of the grid. Columns not needed should be left blank.

- Write your answer in the boxes at the top of the grid and fill in the corresponding circles. **You will receive credit only if the circles are filled in correctly, regardless of the number written in the boxes at the top.**

Examples of acceptable ways to use the grid:

Integer answer: 502 (either position is correct)   Decimal answer: −4.13   Fraction answer: $-\frac{2}{10}$

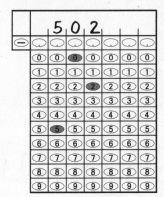

Examples of how to grid the answer to a problem:

Example 1:

Find a quantity that has a value between 1/4 and 1/3.

You can grid in any decimal quantity between 1/4 = 0.25 and 1/3 = .33333...

Here are some ways to grid the answer to the above question:

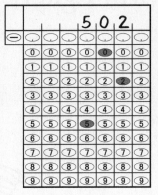

Example 2:

Find a fraction that has a value between 1/4 and 1/3.

This can be a hard problem if you don't use a strategy of somehow relating 1/4 to 1/3. For 1/4, multiply both numerator and denominator by 3. You get 3/12. Now for 1/3, similarly multiply both numerator and denominator by 4 to get 4/12. So 1/4 = 3/12 and 1/3 = 4/12.

But there is no obvious fraction between 3/12 and 4/12. So multiply both numerators and denominators of the fractions 3/12 and 4/12 by 2. We get:

1/4 = 3/12 = 6/24, and 1/3 = 4/12 = 8/24. You can see that **7/24** is in between the two fractions 1/4 and 1/3. You can also multiply both numerator and denominator of 1/4 by 12 to get 12/48 and multiply both numerator and denominator of 1/3 by 16 to get **16/48**. Thus, fractions in between 1/4 and 1/3 would be **13/48**, **14/48** = **7/24**, or **15/48**. Other fractions are **2/7**, **3/10**, and **3/11**.

Here are some ways to grid the answer to the above question:

25 Math Strategies

Using Critical Thinking Skills in Math Questions

MATH STRATEGY 1

Cancel Quantities to Make the Problem Simpler

Cancel numbers or expressions that appear on both sides of an equation; cancel same numerators and denominators. But make sure that you don't divide by 0 in what you're doing! You will save precious time by using this strategy. You won't have to make any long calculations.

EXAMPLE 1

If $P \times \dfrac{11}{14} = \dfrac{11}{14} \times \dfrac{8}{9}$, then $P =$

(A) $\dfrac{8}{9}$

(B) $\dfrac{9}{8}$

(C) 8

(D) 11

(E) 14

Choice A is correct. Do not multiply $\dfrac{11}{14} \times \dfrac{8}{9}$!

Cancel the common $\dfrac{11}{14}$:

$P \times \dfrac{\cancel{11}}{\cancel{14}} = \dfrac{\cancel{11}}{\cancel{14}} \times \dfrac{8}{9}$

$P = \dfrac{8}{9}$ *(Answer)*

Note: You can cancel the $\dfrac{11}{14}$ because you are *dividing* both sides by the same nonzero number. Suppose you had a problem like the following:

If $R \times a = a \times \dfrac{4}{5}$, then $R =$

(A) $\dfrac{2}{3}$

(B) $\dfrac{4}{5}$

(C) 1

(D) $\dfrac{5}{4}$

(E) Cannot be determined.

What do you think the answer is? It's not Choice B! It is Choice E, because you cannot cancel the *a*, because *a* may be 0 and you cannot divide by 0. So if $a = 0$, R can be *any* number.

EXAMPLE 2

If $y + \dfrac{7}{13} + \dfrac{6}{19} = \dfrac{3}{5} + \dfrac{7}{13} + \dfrac{6}{19}$, then $y =$

(A) $\dfrac{6}{19}$

(B) $\dfrac{13}{32}$

(C) $\dfrac{7}{13}$

(D) $\dfrac{3}{5}$

(E) $\dfrac{211}{247}$

Choice D is correct. *Do not add the fractions!*

Don't add: $\frac{3}{5} + \frac{7}{13} + \frac{6}{19}$! You waste a lot of time! There is a much shorter way to do the problem. Cancel $\frac{7}{13} + \frac{6}{19}$ from both sides of the equation. Thus,

$$y + \frac{\cancel{7}}{\cancel{13}} + \frac{\cancel{6}}{\cancel{19}} = \frac{3}{5} + \frac{\cancel{7}}{\cancel{13}} + \frac{\cancel{6}}{\cancel{19}}$$

$$y = \frac{3}{5} \ (Answer)$$

EXAMPLE 3

$$\frac{2}{5} \times \frac{5}{6} \times \frac{6}{7} \times \frac{7}{8} \times \frac{8}{9} \times \frac{9}{10} \times \frac{10}{11} =$$

(A) $\dfrac{9}{11}$

(B) $\dfrac{2}{11}$

(C) $\dfrac{11}{36}$

(D) $\dfrac{10}{21}$

(E) $\dfrac{244}{360}$

Choice B is correct.

Cancel numerators/denominators:

$$\frac{2}{\cancel{5}} \times \frac{\cancel{5}}{\cancel{6}} \times \frac{\cancel{6}}{7} \times \frac{7}{\cancel{8}} \times \frac{\cancel{8}}{\cancel{9}} \times \frac{\cancel{9}}{\cancel{10}} \times \frac{\cancel{10}}{11} = \frac{2}{11}$$

EXAMPLE 4

If $a + b > a - b$, which must follow?

(A) $a < 0$
(B) $b < 0$
(C) $a > b$
(D) $b > a$
(E) $b > 0$

Choice E is correct.

$$a + b > a - b$$

Cancel common as:

$$\cancel{a} + b > \cancel{a} - b$$
$$b > -b$$
$$\text{Add } b: \ b + b > b - b$$
$$2b > 0$$
$$b > 0$$

EXAMPLE 5

If $7\frac{2}{9} = 6 + \frac{y}{27}$, $y =$

(A) 8
(B) 30
(C) 35
(D) 37
(E) 33

Choice E is correct.

Subtract 6 from both sides:

$$7\frac{2}{9} - 6 = 6 + \frac{y}{27} - 6$$
$$1\frac{2}{9} = \frac{y}{27}$$
$$\frac{11}{9} = \frac{y}{27}$$
$$\frac{33}{27} = \frac{y}{27}$$
$$y = 33$$

MATH STRATEGY 2

Translate English Words into Mathematical Expressions

Many of the GRE problems are word problems. Being able to translate word problems from English into mathematical expressions or equations will help you to score high on the test. The following table translates some commonly used words into their mathematical equivalents:

TRANSLATION TABLE

Words	Math Way to Say It
is, as, was, has, cost	$=$ (equals)
of	$\times$ (times)
percent	$/100$ (the percent number over 100)
x percent	$x/100$
which, what	x (or any other variable)
x and y	$x + y$
the sum of x and y	$x + y$
the difference between x and y	$x - y$
x more than y	$x + y$
x less than y	$y - x$
the product of x and y	xy
the square of x	x^2
x is greater than y	$x > y$ (or $y < x$)
x is less than y	$x < y$ (or $y > x$)
y years ago	$- y$
y years from now	$+ y$
c times as old as John	$c \times$ (John's age)
x older than y	$x + y$
x younger than y	$y - x$
the increase from x to y	$y - x$
the decrease from x to y	$x - y$
the percent increase from x to y ($y > x$)	$\left(\dfrac{y - x}{x}\right)100$
the percent decrease from x to y ($y < x$)	$\left(\dfrac{x - y}{x}\right)100$
the percent of increase	$\left(\dfrac{\text{amount of increase}}{\text{original amount}}\right) \times 100$
the percent of decrease	$\left(\dfrac{\text{amount of decrease}}{\text{original amount}}\right) \times 100$
n percent greater than x	$x + \left(\dfrac{n}{100}\right)x$
n percent less than x	$x - \left(\dfrac{n}{100}\right)x$

By knowing this table, you will find word problems much easier to do.

OPTIONAL QUIZ ON TRANSLATION TABLE

Take this quiz to see if you understand the translation table before attempting the problems in Strategy #2 that follow.

1. **Mary is five years older than John** translates to:

   (A) $J = 5 + M$
   (B) $M + J = 5$
   (C) $M > 5 + J$
   (D) $M = 5 + J$
   (E) None of these.

   (D) Translate: **Mary** to M; **John** to J; **is** to =; **older than** to +
   So **Mary is five years older than John** becomes:

   $$\downarrow \quad \downarrow \quad \downarrow \qquad \qquad \downarrow \qquad \qquad \downarrow$$
   $$M \quad = \quad 5 \qquad \qquad + \qquad \qquad J$$

2. **3 percent of 5** translates to:

   (A) 3/5
   (B) 3/100 divided by 5
   (C) $(3/100) \times 5$
   (D) $3 \times 100 \times 5$
   (E) None of these.

   (C) percent or % = /100; of = ×; so

   3% of 5 translates to:
   $$\downarrow \quad \downarrow\downarrow$$
   $$\frac{3}{100} \times 5$$

3. **What percent of 3** translates to:

   (A) $x(100) \times 3$
   (B) $(x/100) \times 3$
   (C) $(x/100)$ divided by 3
   (D) $(3/100)x$
   (E) None of these.

   (B) Translate: what to x; percent to /100. Thus

   What percent of 3 becomes:
   $$\downarrow \qquad \downarrow \quad \downarrow\downarrow$$
   $$x \quad /100 \ \times 3$$

4. **Six years ago, Sarah was 4 times as old as John was then** translates to:

   (A) $S - 6 = 4J$
   (B) $6 - S = 4J$
   (C) $6 - S = 4(J - 6)$
   (D) $S - 6 = 4(J - 6)$
   (E) None of these.

   (D) **Six years ago, Sarah was** translates to $S - 6 =$. **4 times as old as John is** would be $4J$. However, **4 times as old as John *was then*** translates to $4(J - 6)$. Thus **Six years ago, Sarah was 4 times as old as John was then** translates to: $S - 6 = 4 \times (J - 6)$

5. **The percent increase from 5 to 10** is

   (A) $[(10 - 5)/5] \times 100$
   (B) $[(5 - 10)/5] \times 100$
   (C) $[(10 - 5)/10] \times 100$
   (D) $[(5 - 10)/10] \times 100$
   (E) None of these.

   (A) Percent increase from a to b is $[(b - a)/a] \times 100$. So **the percent increase from 5 to 10** would be $[(10 - 5)/5] \times 100$.

6. **Harry is older than John, and John is older than Mary** translates to:

   (A) $H > J > M$
   (B) $H > J < M$
   (C) $H > M > J$
   (D) $M > H > J$
   (E) None of these.

   (A) **Harry is older than John** translates to $H > J$. **John is older than Mary** translates to $J > M$. So we have $H > J$ and $J > M$, which, consolidated, becomes $H > J > M$.

7. **Even after Phil gives Sam 6 compact discs, he still has 16 more compact discs than Sam has** translates to:

   (A) $P - 6 = 16 + S$
   (B) $P - 6 = 16 + S + 6$
   (C) $P + 6 = 16 + S + 6$
   (D) $P + 6 + 16 + S$
   (E) None of these.

   (B) **Even after Phil gives Sam 6 compact discs** translates to:
   $P - 6$ $\boxed{1}$
   He still has 16 more compact discs than Sam has translates to:
   $= 16 + S + 6$ $\boxed{2}$
   since Sam has gotten 6 additional compact discs. Thus, combining $\boxed{1}$ and $\boxed{2}$, we get $P - 6 = 16 + S + 6$.

8. **q is 10% greater than p** translates to:

(A) $q = (10/100)q + p$
(B) $q > (10/100)p$
(C) $q = (10/100)p + p$
(D) $q = (10/100) + p$
(E) None of these.

(C) **q is** translates to $q =$
10% greater than p translates to
(10/100)p + p so

$$\begin{array}{c} \textbf{q is 10\% greater than p} \\ \text{translates to:} \quad \downarrow\downarrow \overbrace{\phantom{\text{xxxxxxxxxxxx}}} \\ q = (10/100)p + p \end{array}$$

9. **200 is what percent of 20** translates to:

(A) $200 = x \times 100 \times 20$
(B) $200 = (x/100)$ divided by 20
(C) $200 = (x/100) \times 20$
(D) $200 = x \times 20$
(E) None of these.

(C) Translate **is** to $=$; **what** to x; **percent** to /100; **of** to $\times$, so we get that:

$$\begin{array}{ccccc} & \textbf{200 is what percent of 20} & & & \\ \text{translates to:} & \downarrow \quad \downarrow \overbrace{\phantom{\text{xxxxxxx}}} & \downarrow \quad \downarrow & \\ & 200 \;=\; & x/100 & \times\; 20 \end{array}$$

10. **The product of the sums of x and y and y and z is 5** translates to:

(A) $xy + yz = 5$
(B) $x + y + y + z = 5$
(C) $(x + y)(yz) = 5$
(D) $(x + y)(y + z) = 5$
(E) None of these.

(D) **The sum of x and y is $x + y$. The sum of y and z is $y + z$. So the product of those sums is $(x + y)(y + z)$.**

Thus **The product of the sums of x and y and y and z is 5** translates to:
$(x + y)(y + z) = 5$

STRATEGY 2, EXAMPLE 1

Sarah is twice as old as John. Six years ago, Sarah was 4 times as old as John was then. How old is John now?

(A) 3
(B) 9
(C) 18
(D) 20
(E) impossible to determine

Choice B is correct. Translate:

Sarah is twice as old as John.
$$\downarrow \quad \downarrow \quad \downarrow \quad \downarrow \qquad \downarrow$$
$$S \;=\; 2 \;\times\; J$$
$$S = 2J \qquad \boxed{1}$$

Six years ago Sarah was 4 times as old as John was then
$$\downarrow \qquad\quad \downarrow \quad \downarrow\downarrow\;\downarrow \qquad\qquad \downarrow$$
$$-6 \qquad S \;=\; 4 \;\times\; (J-6)$$
This becomes $S - 6 = 4(J - 6)$ $\qquad \boxed{2}$

Substituting $\boxed{1}$ into $\boxed{2}$:

$$2J - 6 = 4(J - 6)$$
$$2J - 6 = 4J - 24$$
$$18 = 2J$$
$$9 = J \quad (Answer)$$

EXAMPLE 2

200 is what percent of 20?

(A) $\frac{1}{10}$
(B) 10
(C) 100
(D) 1,000
(E) 10,000

Choice D is correct. Translate:

200 is what percent of 20
$$\downarrow\;\downarrow\;\downarrow \qquad \downarrow \qquad \downarrow\;\downarrow$$
$$200 \;=\; x \quad \overline{100} \;\times\; 20$$

$200 = \frac{x}{100}(20)$

Divide by 20: $10 = \frac{x}{100}$

Multiply by 100: $1,000 = x$ (*Answer*)

EXAMPLE 3

If A is 250 percent of B, what percent of A is B?

(A) 125%
(B) $\frac{1}{250}$%
(C) 50%
(D) 40%
(E) 400%

Choice D is correct.

"If A is 250 percent of B" becomes
$$\downarrow\downarrow\;\downarrow \quad \downarrow \quad \downarrow\downarrow$$
$$A = 250\;/100 \;\times B$$

"What percent of A is B?" becomes
$$\downarrow \qquad \downarrow \quad \downarrow\downarrow\downarrow$$
$$x \quad /100 \;\times A = B$$

Set up the equations:

$$A = \frac{250}{100}B \qquad \boxed{1}$$

$$\frac{x}{100}A = B \qquad \boxed{2}$$

Divide equation $\boxed{1}$ by equation $\boxed{2}$:

$$\frac{A}{\frac{x}{100}A} = \frac{\frac{250}{100}B}{B}$$

We get:

$$\frac{1}{\frac{x}{100}} = \frac{250}{100}$$

Inverting, we get:

$$\frac{x}{100} = \frac{100}{250}$$
$$x = \frac{10,000}{250}$$

To simplify, multiply both numerator and denominator by 4:

$$x = \frac{10,000 \times 4}{250 \times 4}$$

$$x = \frac{40,000}{1,000} = 40$$

Alternate way:

Let $B = 100$ (choose any number for B).
We get (after translation)

$$A = \left(\frac{250}{100}\right)100 \qquad \boxed{1}$$

$$\left(\frac{x}{100}\right)A = 100 \qquad \boxed{2}$$

From $\boxed{1}$,

$$A = 250 \qquad \boxed{3}$$

Substituting $\boxed{3}$ into $\boxed{2}$, we get

$$\left(\frac{x}{100}\right)250 = 100 \qquad \boxed{4}$$

Multiplying both sides of $\boxed{4}$ by 100,

$$(x)(250) = (100)(100)$$

Dividing by 250:

$$x = \frac{100 \times 100}{250}$$

Simplify by multiplying numerator and denominator by 4:

$$x = \frac{100 \times 100 \times 4}{250 \times 4} = \frac{40,000}{1,000}$$
$$= 40$$

EXAMPLE 4

John is now m years old and Sally is 4 years older than John. Which represents Sally's age 6 years ago?

(A) $m + 10$
(B) $m - 10$
(C) $m - 2$
(D) $m - 4$
(E) $4m - 6$

Choice C is correct.

Translate:

John is now m years old
$\downarrow\ \downarrow\qquad\ \downarrow$
$J\ =\qquad m$

Sally is 4 years older than John
$\downarrow\ \downarrow\downarrow\qquad\ \downarrow\qquad\quad \downarrow$
$S\ = 4\qquad\ +\qquad J$

Sally's age 6 years ago
$\downarrow\qquad\quad \downarrow$
$S\ \ -\quad 6$

So we get: $\quad J = m$
$\qquad\qquad\quad S = 4 + J$

and find: $S - 6 = 4 + J - 6$
$\qquad\qquad S - 6 = J - 2$
$\qquad\qquad S - 6 = m - 2$ (substituting m for J)

See Math Strategy 7, Example 2 (page 91) for an alternate approach to solving this problem, using a

different strategy: **Use Specific Numerical Examples to Prove or Disprove Your Guess**.

EXAMPLE 5

Phil has three times as many DVDs as Sam has. Even after Phil gives Sam 6 DVDs, he still has 16 more DVDs than Sam has. What was the original number of DVDs that Phil had?

(A) 20
(B) 24
(C) 28
(D) 33
(E) 42

Choice E is correct.

Translate:

Phil has three times as many DVDs as Sam has
$\downarrow\ \downarrow\quad \downarrow\qquad \downarrow\qquad\qquad\qquad\qquad \downarrow$
$P\ =\quad 3\quad \times\qquad\qquad\qquad\qquad S$

Even after Phil gives Sam 6 DVDs, he still has 16
$\qquad\quad \downarrow\quad \downarrow\qquad \downarrow\qquad\qquad\qquad \downarrow\ \downarrow$
$\qquad\quad P\ \ -\qquad 6\qquad\qquad\qquad = 16$

more DVDs than Sam has
$\downarrow$
$+\qquad\qquad S+6$

Sam now has $(S + 6)$ DVDs because Phil gave Sam 6 DVDs. So we end up with the equations:

$P = 3S$

$P - 6 = 16 + S + 6$

Find P; get rid of S:

$$P = 3S; \qquad \frac{P}{3} = S$$

$$P - 6 = 16 + \frac{P}{3} + 6$$

$$P - 6 = \frac{48 + P + 18}{3}$$

$$3P - 18 = 48 + P + 18$$
$$2P = 84$$
$$P = 42$$

EXAMPLE 6

If q is 10% greater than p and r is 10% greater than y, qr is what percent greater than py?

(A) 1%
(B) 20%
(C) 21%
(D) 30%
(E) 100%

Choice C is correct.

Translate:

If q is <u>10% greater than p</u>

$$\downarrow \downarrow \qquad \qquad \downarrow$$
$$q = \qquad \frac{10}{100}\, p + p$$

and r is <u>10% greater than y</u>

$$\downarrow \downarrow \qquad \qquad \downarrow$$
$$r = \qquad \frac{10}{100}\, y + y$$

qr is <u>what percent greater than py</u>?

$$\downarrow \downarrow \qquad \qquad \downarrow$$
$$qr = \qquad \frac{x}{100}\, py + py$$

So we have three equations:

$$q = \frac{10}{100}\, p + p = \left(\frac{10}{100} + 1\right) p \qquad \boxed{1}$$

$$r = \frac{10}{100}\, y + y = \left(\frac{10}{100} + 1\right) y \qquad \boxed{2}$$

$$qr = \frac{x}{100}\, py + py = \left(\frac{x}{100} + 1\right) py \qquad \boxed{3}$$

Multiply $\boxed{1}$ and $\boxed{2}$:

$$qr = \left(\frac{10}{100} + 1\right)^2 py \qquad \boxed{4}$$

Now equate $\boxed{4}$ with $\boxed{3}$:

$$qr = \left(\frac{x}{100} + 1\right) py = \left(\frac{10}{100} + 1\right)^2 py \qquad \boxed{4}$$

You can see that $\left(\frac{10}{100} + 1\right)^2 = \frac{x}{100} + 1$, canceling py.

So, $\left(\frac{10}{100} + 1\right)^2 = \frac{100}{10,000} + 2\left(\frac{10}{100}\right) + 1 = \frac{x}{100} + 1$

$$\frac{100}{10,000} + \frac{20}{100} = \frac{21}{100} = \frac{x}{100}$$

$$21 = x$$

The answer is $x = 21$.

Alternate approach: Choose numbers for p and for y:

Let $p = 10$ and $y = 20$

Then, since q is 10% greater than p:

$$q = 10\% \text{ greater than } 10$$

$$q = \left(\frac{10}{100}\right)10 + 10 = 11$$

Next, r is 10% greater than y:

$$r = 10\% \text{ greater than } 20$$

$$\text{Or, } r = \left(\frac{10}{100}\right)20 + 20 = 22$$

Then:

$$qr = 11 \times 22$$

$$\text{and } py = 20 \times 10$$

So, to find what percent qr is greater than py, you would need to find:

$$\frac{qr - py}{py} \times 100 \text{ or}$$

$$\frac{11 \times 22 - 20 \times 10}{20 \times 10} \times 100$$

This is:

$$\frac{42}{200} \times 100 = 21$$

EXAMPLE 7

<u>Sales of Item X</u>
<u>Jan–June, 2004</u>

Month	Sales ($)
Jan	800
Feb	1,000
Mar	1,200
Apr	1,300
May	1,600
Jun	1,800

According to the above table, the percent increase in sales was greatest for which of the following periods?

(A) Jan–Feb
(B) Feb–Mar
(C) Mar–Apr
(D) Apr–May
(E) May–Jun

Choice A is correct.

The percent increase from Month A to Month B =

$$\frac{\text{Sales (Month B)} - \text{Sales (Month A)}}{\text{Sales (Month A)}} \times 100$$

Month	Sales ($)	Periods	% Increase in Sales
Jan	800	Jan–Feb	$\frac{1,000 - 800}{800} \times 100 = \frac{200}{800} \times 100$
Feb	1,000	Feb–Mar	$\frac{1,200 - 1,000}{1,000} \times 100 = \frac{200}{1,000} \times 100$
Mar	1,200	Mar–Apr	$\frac{1,300 - 1,200}{1,200} \times 100 = \frac{100}{1,200} \times 100$
Apr	1,300	Apr–May	$\frac{1,600 - 1,300}{1,300} \times 100 = \frac{300}{1,300} \times 100$
May	1,600	May–Jun	$\frac{1,800 - 1,600}{1,600} \times 100 = \frac{200}{1,600} \times 100$
Jun	1,800		

You can see that $\frac{200}{800} \times 100$ (Jan–Feb) is the greatest.

MATH STRATEGY **3**

> # Know How to Find Unknown Quantities (Areas, Lengths, Arc and Angle Measurements) from Known Quantities (the Whole Equals the Sum of Its Parts)

When asked to find a particular area or length, instead of trying to calculate it directly, find it by subtracting two other areas or lengths—a method based on the fact that the whole minus a part equals the remaining part.

This strategy is very helpful in many types of geometry problems. A very important equation to remember is

The whole = the sum of its parts $\boxed{1}$

Equation $\boxed{1}$ is often disguised in many forms, as seen in the following examples:

EXAMPLE 1

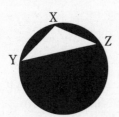

In the diagram above, $\triangle XYZ$ has been inscribed in a circle. If the circle encloses an area of 64, and the area of $\triangle XYZ$ is 15, then what is the area of the shaded region?

(A) 25
(B) 36
(C) 49
(D) 79
(E) It cannot be determined from the information given.

Choice C is correct. Use equation $\boxed{1}$. Here, the whole refers to the area within the circle, and the parts refer to the areas of the shaded region and the triangle. Thus,

> Area within circle =
> Area of shaded region +
> Area of $\triangle XYZ$

64 = Area of shaded region + 15

or Area of shaded region = 64 − 15 = 49
(*Answer*)

EXAMPLE 2

In the diagram below, $\overline{AE}$ is a straight line, and F is a point on $\overline{AE}$. Find an expression for $m\angle DFE$.

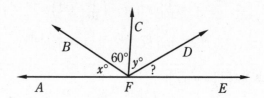

(A) $x + y - 60$
(B) $x + y + 60$
(C) $90 - x - y$
(D) $120 - x - y$
(E) $180 - x - y$

Choice D is correct. Use equation $\boxed{1}$. Here, the whole refers to the straight angle, $\angle AFE$, and its parts refer to $\angle AFB$, $\angle BFC$, $\angle CFD$, and $\angle DFE$. Thus,

$$m\angle AFE = m\angle AFB + m\angle BFC + \\ m\angle CFD + m\angle DFE$$
$$180 = x + 60 + y + m\angle DFE$$
or
$$m\angle DFE = 180 - x - 60 - y$$
$$m\angle DFE = 120 - x - y \ (Answer)$$

EXAMPLE 3

In the diagram below, $AB = m$, $BC = n$, and $AD = 10$. Find an expression for CD.

(Note: Diagram represents a straight line.)

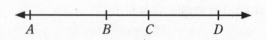

(A) $10 - mn$
(B) $10 - m - n$
(C) $m - n + 10$
(D) $m + n - 10$
(E) $m + n + 10$

Choice B is correct. Use equation $\boxed{1}$. Here, the whole refers to AD, and its parts refer to AB, BC, and CD. Thus,

$$AD = AB + BC + CD$$
$$10 = m + n + CD$$
or $$CD = 10 - m - n \ (Answer)$$

EXAMPLE 4

The area of triangle $ACE = 64$. The sum of the areas of the shaded triangles ABF and FDE is 39. What is the side of square $BFDC$?

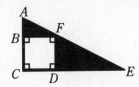

(A) 5
(B) 4
(C) $\sqrt{5}$
(D) $\sqrt{44}$
(E) Cannot be determined.

EXPLANATORY ANSWER

Choice A is correct.

Since we are dealing with areas, let's establish the area of the square $BFDC$, which will then enable us to get its side.

Now, the area of square $BFDC$ = area of triangle ACE − (area of triangles ABF + FDE)

Area of square $BFDC = 64 - 39$
$$= 25$$
Therefore, the side of square $BFDC = 5$.

EXAMPLE 5

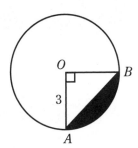

In the figure above, O is the center of the circle. Triangle AOB has side 3 and angle $AOB = 90°$. What is the area of the shaded region?

(A) $9\left(\dfrac{\pi}{4} - \dfrac{1}{2}\right)$

(B) $9\left(\dfrac{\pi}{2} - 1\right)$

(C) $9(\pi - 1)$

(D) $9\left(\dfrac{\pi}{4} - \dfrac{1}{4}\right)$

(E) Cannot be determined.

EXPLANATORY ANSWER

Choice A is correct.

<u>Subtract knowns from knowns:</u>

Area of shaded region = area of quarter circle AOB − area of triangle AOB

Area of quarter circle $AOB = \dfrac{\pi (3)^2}{4}$ (since $OA = 3$ and area of a quarter of a circle = $\dfrac{1}{4} \times \pi \times$ radius^2).

Area of triangle $AOB = \dfrac{3 \times 3}{2}$ (since $OB = 3$ and area of a triangle = $\dfrac{1}{2}$ base × height).

Thus, area of shaded region = $\dfrac{9\pi}{4} - \dfrac{9}{2} = 9\left(\dfrac{\pi}{4} - \dfrac{1}{2}\right)$.

EXAMPLE 6

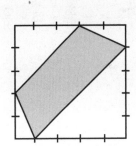

The sides in the square above are each divided into five equal segments. What is the value of

$$\frac{\text{Area of square}}{\text{Area of shaded region}}?$$

(A) $\dfrac{50}{29}$

(B) $\dfrac{50}{21}$

(C) $\dfrac{25}{4}$

(D) $\dfrac{29}{25}$

(E) None of these.

EXPLANATORY ANSWER

Choice B is correct.

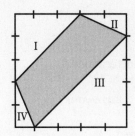

Subtract knowns from knowns:

Area of square = $5 \times 5 = 25$

Area of shaded region = area of square − area of I − area of II − area of III − area of IV

$$\text{Area of I} = \frac{3 \times 3}{2} = \frac{9}{2}$$

$$\text{Area of II} = \frac{2 \times 1}{2} = 1$$

$$\text{Area of III} = \frac{4 \times 4}{2} = 8$$

$$\text{Area of IV} = \frac{2 \times 1}{2} = 1$$

$$\text{Area of shaded region} = 25 - \frac{9}{2} - 1 - 8 - 1 = \frac{21}{2}$$

$$\frac{\text{Area of square}}{\text{Area of shaded region}} = \frac{25}{\frac{21}{2}} = 25 \times \frac{2}{21} = \frac{50}{21}$$

EXAMPLE 7

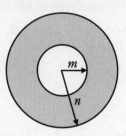

Two concentric circles are shown above with inner radius of m and outer radius of n. What is the area of the shaded region?

(A) $\pi(n - m)^2$

(B) $\pi(n^2 + m^2)$

(C) $\pi(n^2 - m^2)$

(D) $2\pi(n - m)$

(E) $2\pi(n + m)$

EXPLANATORY ANSWER

Choice C is correct.

Subtract knowns from knowns:

Area of shaded region = area of circle of radius n − area of circle of radius m

Area of circle of radius $n = \pi n^2$

Area of circle of radius $m = \pi m^2$

$$\text{Area of shaded region} = \pi n^2 - \pi m^2$$
$$= \pi(n^2 - m^2)$$

MATH STRATEGY 4

Remember Classic Expressions Such as

$$x^2 - y^2, x^2 + 2xy + y^2, x^2 - 2xy + y^2, \frac{x+y}{xy}$$

Memorize the following factorizations and expressions:

$$x^2 - y^2 = (x + y)(x - y) \qquad \boxed{\text{Equation 1}}$$

$$x^2 + 2xy + y^2 = (x + y)(x + y) = (x + y)^2 \quad \boxed{\text{Equation 2}}$$

$$x^2 - 2xy + y^2 = (x - y)(x - y) = (x - y)^2 \quad \boxed{\text{Equation 3}}$$

$$\frac{x + y}{xy} = \frac{1}{x} + \frac{1}{y} \quad x, y \neq 0 \qquad \boxed{\text{Equation 4}}$$

$$\frac{x - y}{xy} = \frac{1}{y} - \frac{1}{x} \quad x, y \neq 0 \qquad \boxed{\text{Equation 4A}}$$

$$xy + xz = x(y + z) \qquad \boxed{\text{Equation 5}}$$

$$xy - xz = x(y - z) \qquad \boxed{\text{Equation 5A}}$$

Examples 1, 3, 4, and 11 (as follows) can also be solved with the aid of a calculator and some with the aid of a calculator allowing for exponential calculations. However, to illustrate the effectiveness of Math Strategy 4, we did not use the calculator method of solution for these examples.

Use algebra to see patterns.

EXAMPLE 1

$$66^2 + 2(34)(66) + 34^2 =$$

(A) 4,730
(B) 5,000
(C) 9,860
(D) 9,950
(E) 10,000

Choice E is correct. Notice that there is a 34 and 66 running through the left side of the equality. To see a pattern, *use algebra*. Substitute *a* for 66 and *b* for 34. You get:

$$66^2 + 2(34)(66) + 34^2 =$$
$$a^2 + 2(b)(a) + b^2$$

But from Equation 2,

$$a^2 + 2ab + b^2 = \qquad \boxed{1}$$
$$(a + b)(a + b) =$$
$$(a + b)^2$$

Now substitute the numbers 34 and 66 *back into* $\boxed{1}$ to get:

$$66^2 + 2(34)(66) + 34^2 =$$
$$(66 + 34)(66 + 34) =$$
$$100 \times 100 =$$

10,000   (*Answer*)

EXAMPLE 2

If $(x + y) = 9$ and $xy = 14$, find $\frac{1}{x} + \frac{1}{y}$.

(Note: $x, y > 0$)

(A) $\frac{1}{9}$

(B) $\frac{2}{7}$

(C) $\frac{9}{14}$

(D) 5

(E) 9

Choice C is correct. We are given:

$$(x + y) = 9 \qquad \boxed{1}$$
$$xy = 14 \qquad \boxed{2}$$
$$x, y > 0 \qquad \boxed{3}$$

I hope that you did not solve $\boxed{2}$ for x (or y), and then substitute it into $\boxed{1}$. If you did, you obtained a quadratic equation.

Here is the FAST method. Use Equation 4:

$$\frac{1}{x} + \frac{1}{y} = \frac{x + y}{xy} \qquad \boxed{4}$$

From $\boxed{1}$ and $\boxed{2}$, we find that $\boxed{4}$ becomes

$$\frac{1}{x} + \frac{1}{y} = \frac{9}{14} \text{ (Answer)}$$

EXAMPLE 3

The value of $100 \times 100 - 99 \times 99 =$

(A) 1
(B) 2
(C) 99
(D) 199
(E) 299

Choice D is correct.

Write a for 100 and b for 99 to see a pattern:

$100 \times 100 - 99 \times 99$

$a \times a - b \times b = a^2 - b^2$. Use Equation 1:

Use the fact that $a^2 - b^2 = (a + b)(a - b)$ $\boxed{1}$

Put back 100 for a and 99 for b in $\boxed{1}$:

$a^2 - b^2 = 100^2 - 99^2 = (100 + 99)(100 - 99) = 199$

EXAMPLE 4

Use factoring to make problems simpler.

$$\frac{8^7 - 8^6}{7} =$$

(A) $\dfrac{8}{7}$

(B) 8^7

(C) 8^6

(D) 8^5

(E) 8^4

Choice C is correct.

Factor: $8^7 - 8^6 = 8^6(8^1 - 1)$ (Equation 5a)

$\qquad\qquad = 8^6(8 - 1)$

$\qquad\qquad = 8^6(7)$

So $\dfrac{8^7 - 8^6}{7} = \dfrac{8^6(7)}{7} = \dfrac{8^6\cancel{(7)}}{\cancel{7}} = 8^6$

EXAMPLE 5

Use factoring to make problems simpler.

$\sqrt{(88)^2 + (88)^2(3)} =$

(A) 88

(B) 176

(C) 348

(D) 35

(E) 352

Choice B is correct. Factor:

$(88)^2 + (88)^2(3) = 88^2(1 + 3) = 88^2(4)$ (Equation 5)

So:

$\sqrt{(88)^2 + (88)^2(3)} = \sqrt{88^2(4)}$

$\qquad\qquad\qquad\quad = \sqrt{88^2} \times \sqrt{4}$

$\qquad\qquad\qquad\quad = 88 \times 2$

$\qquad\qquad\qquad\quad = 176$

EXAMPLE 6

If $y + \dfrac{1}{y} = 9$, then $y^2 + \dfrac{1}{y^2} =$

(A) 76

(B) 77

(C) 78

(D) 79

(E) 81

Choice D is correct.

Square $\left(y + \dfrac{1}{y}\right) = 9$

Substituting y for x and $\dfrac{1}{y}$ for y in Equation 2, we get:

$\left(y + \dfrac{1}{y}\right)^2 = 81 = y^2 + 2(y)\left(\dfrac{1}{y}\right) + \left(\dfrac{1}{y}\right)^2$

$\qquad\qquad\qquad = y^2 + 2 + \left(\dfrac{1}{y}\right)^2$

$\qquad\qquad\qquad = y^2 + 2 + \dfrac{1}{y^2}$

$\qquad 79 = y^2 + \dfrac{1}{y^2}$

EXAMPLE 7

If $a - b = 4$ and $a + b = 7$, then $a^2 - b^2 =$

(A) $5\dfrac{1}{2}$

(B) 11

(C) 28

(D) 29

(E) 56

Choice C is correct.

Use $(a - b)(a + b) = a^2 - b^2$ (Equation 1)

$\qquad\qquad a - b = 4$

$\qquad\qquad a + b = 7$

$(a - b)(a + b) = 28 = a^2 - b^2$

EXAMPLE 8

If $x^2 - y^2 = 66$ and $x + y = 6$, what is the value of x?

(A) 11

(B) $\dfrac{21}{2}$

(C) $\dfrac{17}{2}$

(D) $\dfrac{13}{2}$

(E) $\dfrac{11}{2}$

Choice C is correct. Use

$$x^2 - y^2 = (x + y)(x - y) \qquad \text{(Equation 1)}$$
$$(x + y)(x - y) = 66$$

But we already know $x + y = 6$, so

$$6(x - y) = 66$$
$$x - y = 11$$

Now compare your two equations:
$$x + y = 6$$
$$x - y = 11$$

Adding these equations (see Strategy 13) gets you
$$2x = 17$$

$$x = \frac{17}{2}$$

EXAMPLE 9

What is the least possible value of $\dfrac{x + y}{xy}$ if $2 \le x < y \le 11$ and x and y are integers?

(A) $\dfrac{22}{121}$

(B) $\dfrac{5}{6}$

(C) $\dfrac{21}{110}$

(D) $\dfrac{13}{22}$

(E) 1

Choice C is correct.

Use $\dfrac{x + y}{xy} = \dfrac{1}{x} + \dfrac{1}{y}$ \qquad (Equation 4)

$\dfrac{1}{x} + \dfrac{1}{y}$ is *least* when x is *greatest* and y is *greatest*.

Since it was given that x and y are integers and that $2 \le x < y \le 11$, the greatest value of x is 10 and the greatest value of y is 11.

So the *least* value of $\dfrac{1}{x} + \dfrac{1}{y} = \dfrac{x + y}{xy} = \dfrac{10 + 11}{10 \times 11} = \dfrac{21}{110}$.

EXAMPLE 10

If $(a + b)^2 = 20$ and $ab = -3$, then $a^2 + b^2 =$

(A) 14
(B) 20
(C) 26
(D) 32
(E) 38

Choice C is correct.

Use $(a + b)^2 = a^2 + 2ab + b^2 = 20$ \qquad (Equation 2)

$$ab = -3$$

So, $2ab = -6$

Substitute $2ab = -6$ in:

$$a^2 + 2ab + b^2 = 20$$

We get:

$$a^2 - 6 + b^2 = 20$$
$$a^2 + b^2 = 26$$

EXAMPLE 11

If $998 \times 1{,}002 > 10^6 - x$, x could be

(A) 4 but not 3
(B) 4 but not 5
(C) 5 but not 4
(D) 3 but not 4
(E) 3, 4, or 5

Choice C is correct.

Use $(a + b)(a - b) = a^2 - b^2$ \qquad (Equation 1)

Write: $998 \times 1{,}002 = (1{,}000 - 2)(1{,}000 + 2) > 10^6 - x$
$$= 1{,}000^2 - 4 > 10^6 - x$$
$$= (10^3)^2 - 4 > 10^6 - x$$
$$= 10^6 - 4 > 10^6 - x$$

Multiply by -1; *reverse inequality sign*:

$$-1(-4 > -x)$$
$$+4 < +x$$

EXAMPLE 12

If $x^2 + y^2 = 2xy$ and $x > 0$ and $y > 0$, then

(A) $x = 0$ only
(B) $y = 0$ only
(C) $x = 1, y = 1$, only
(D) $x > y > 0$
(E) $x = y$

Choice E is correct. In the given equation $x^2 + y^2 = 2xy$, subtract $2xy$ from both sides to get it to look like what you have in Equation 3.

$$x^2 + y^2 - 2xy = 2xy - 2xy = 0$$
$$\text{So, } x^2 - 2xy + y^2 = 0.$$

We have:

$$x^2 - 2xy + y^2 = (x - y)^2 = 0 \quad \text{(Equation 3)}$$
$$x - y = 0, \text{ and thus } x = y.$$

MATH STRATEGY 5

Know How to Manipulate Averages

Almost all problems involving averages can be solved by remembering that

$$\text{Average} = \frac{\text{Sum of the individual quantities or measurements}}{\text{Number of quantities or measurements}}$$

(*Note:* Average is also called Arithmetic Mean.)

EXAMPLE 1

The average height of three students is 68 inches. If two of the students have heights of 70 inches and 72 inches respectively, then what is the height (in inches) of the third student?

(A) 60
(B) 62
(C) 64
(D) 65
(E) 66

Choice B is correct. Recall that

$$\text{Average} = \frac{\text{Sum of the individual measurements}}{\text{Number of measurements}}$$

Let x = height (in inches) of the third student. Thus,

$$68 = \frac{70 + 72 + x}{3}$$

Multiplying by 3,

$$204 = 70 + 72 + x$$
$$204 = 142 + x$$
$$x = 62 \text{ inches}$$

EXAMPLE 2

The average of 30 numbers is 65. If one of these numbers is 65, the sum of the remaining numbers is

(A) 65×64
(B) 30×64
(C) 29×30
(D) 29×64
(E) 29×65

Choice E is correct.

$$\text{Average} = \frac{\text{sum of numbers}}{30}$$

Call the numbers a, b, c, d, etc.

$$\text{So } 65 = \frac{a + b + c + d + \ldots}{30}$$

Now immediately get rid of the fractional part: Multiply by 30 to get: $65 \times 30 = a + b + c + d + \ldots$.

Since we were told *one of the numbers is 65,* let $a = 65$:

$65 \times 30 = 65 + b + c + d + \ldots$
So $65 \times 30 - 65 = b + c + d + \ldots$

$b + c + d + \ldots$ = <u>sum of remaining numbers</u>

Factor:

$65 \times 30 - 65 = 65(30 - 1) =$ sum of remaining numbers
$65 \times 29 =$ sum of remaining numbers

EXAMPLES 3–6

3. The average length of 6 objects is 25 cm. If 5 objects are each 20 cm in length, what is the length of the sixth object in cm?

   (A) 55
   (B) 50
   (C) 45
   (D) 40
   (E) 35

4. Scores on five tests range from 0 to 100 inclusive. If Don gets 70 on the first test, 76 on the second, and 75 on the third, what is the minimum score Don may get on the fourth test to average 80 on all five tests?

   (A) 76
   (B) 79
   (C) 82
   (D) 89
   (E) 99

5. Eighteen students attained an average score of 70 on a test, and 12 students on the same test scored an average of 90. What is the average score for all 30 students on the test?

   (A) 78
   (B) 80
   (C) 82
   (D) 85
   (E) Cannot be determined.

6. The average length of 10 objects is 25 inches. If the average length of 2 of these objects is 20 inches, what is the average length of the remaining 8 objects?

(A) $22\frac{1}{2}$ inches

(B) 24 inches

(C) $26\frac{1}{4}$ inches

(D) 28 inches

(E) Cannot be determined.

EXPLANATORY ANSWERS FOR EXAMPLES 3–6

3. (B) *Use the formula:*

$$\text{Average} = \frac{\text{Sum of individual items}}{\text{Number of items}}$$

Now call the length of the sixth item, x. Then:

$$25 = \frac{20 + 20 + 20 + 20 + 20 + x}{6}$$

or $25 = \frac{20 \times 5 + x}{6}$

Multiply by 6:

$$25 \times 6 = 20 \times 5 + x$$
$$150 = 100 + x$$
$$50 = x$$

4. (B) *Use the formula:*

$$\text{Average} = \frac{\text{Sum of scores on tests}}{\text{Number of tests}}$$

Let x be the score on the fourth test and y be the score on the fifth test.

Then:

$$80 = \text{Average} = \frac{70 + 76 + 75 + x + y}{5}$$

The minimum score x Don can get is the *lowest* score he can get. The higher the score y is, the lower the score x can be. The greatest value y can be is 100. So:

$$80 = \frac{70 + 76 + 75 + x + 100}{5}$$
$$80 = \frac{321 + x}{5}$$

Multiply by 5:

$$400 = 321 + x$$
$$79 = x$$

5. (A) *Use the formula:*

$$\text{Average} = \frac{\text{Sum of scores}}{\text{Number of students}}$$

"Eighteen students attained an average of 70 on a test" translates mathematically to:

$$70 = \frac{\text{Sum of scores of 18 students}}{18} \quad \boxed{1}$$

"Twelve students on the same test scored an average of 90" translates to:

$$90 = \frac{\text{Sum of scores of other 12 students}}{12} \quad \boxed{2}$$

Now what you are looking for is the *average score of all 30 students*. That is, you are looking for:

$$\text{Average of 30 students} = \frac{\text{Sum of scores of all 30 students}}{30} \quad \boxed{3}$$

So, if you can find the *sum of scores of all 30 students*, you can find the required average.

Now, the sum of all 30 students = sum of scores of 18 students + sum of scores of other 12 students.

And this can be gotten from $\boxed{1}$ and $\boxed{2}$:

From $\boxed{1}$: 70×18 = sum of scores of 18 students

From $\boxed{2}$: 90×12 = sum of scores of other 12 students

So adding:

$70 \times 18 + 90 \times 12$ = sum of scores of 18 students + sum of scores of other 12 students = sum of scores of 30 students

Put all this in $\boxed{3}$:

$$\text{Average of 30 students} = \frac{70 \times 18 + 90 \times 12}{30}$$
$$= \frac{7\!\!\!\diagup 0 \times 18 + 9\!\!\!\diagup 0 \times 12}{3\!\!\!\diagup 0}$$
$$= \frac{7 \times 18 + 9 \times 12}{3}$$
$$= \frac{7 \times \overset{6}{\cancel{18}} + \overset{3}{\cancel{9}} \times 12}{\cancel{3}}$$
$$= 42 + 36 = 78$$

6. **(C)** Denote the lengths of the objects by a, b, c, d, etc. Since the average length of 10 objects is given to be 25 inches, establish an equation for the average length:

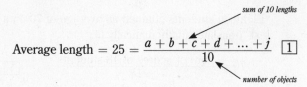

$$\text{Average length} = 25 = \frac{a + b + c + d + \dots + j}{10} \quad \boxed{1}$$

The question also says that the average length of 2 of these objects is 20. Let the lengths of two we choose be a and b. So,

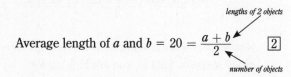

$$\text{Average length of } a \text{ and } b = 20 = \frac{a + b}{2} \quad \boxed{2}$$

Now we want to find the average length of the *remaining* objects. There are 8 remaining objects of lengths $c, d, e, \dots j$. Call the average of these lengths x, which is what we want to find.

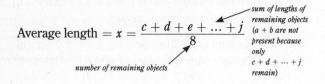

$$\text{Average length} = x = \frac{c + d + e + \dots + j}{8}$$

sum of lengths of remaining objects ($a + b$ are not present because only $c + d + \dots + j$ remain)

number of remaining objects

Use equations $\boxed{1}$ and $\boxed{2}$:

$$25 = \frac{a + b + c + \dots + j}{10} \quad \boxed{1}$$

$$20 = \frac{a + b}{2} \quad \boxed{2}$$

Now, remember, we want to find the value of x:

$$x = \frac{c + d + e + \dots + j}{8}$$

Multiply Equation $\boxed{1}$ by 10 to get rid of the denominator. We get:

$$25 \times 10 = 250 = a + b + c + \dots + j$$

Now multiply Equation $\boxed{2}$ by 2 to get rid of the denominator:

$$20 \times 2 = 40 = a + b$$

Subtract these two new equations:

$$250 = a + b + c + \dots + j$$
$$- [40 = a + b]$$

You get: $210 = c + d + \dots + j$

Now you just have to divide by 8 to get:

$$\frac{210}{8} = \frac{c + d + \dots + j}{8} = x$$

$$= 26\frac{1}{4}$$

MATH STRATEGY 6

Know How to Manipulate Inequalities

Most problems involving inequalities can be solved by remembering one of the following statements.

If $x > y$, then $x + z > y + z$ $\boxed{\text{Statement 1}}$

If $x > y$ and $w > z$, then $x + w > y + z$ $\boxed{\text{Statement 2}}$

(Note that $\boxed{\text{Statement 1}}$ and $\boxed{\text{Statement 2}}$ are also true if all the ">" signs are changed to "<" signs.)

If $w > 0$ and $x > y$, then $wx > wy$ $\boxed{\text{Statement 3}}$

If $w < 0$ and $x > y$, then $wx < wy$ $\boxed{\text{Statement 4}}$

If $x > y$ and $y > z$, then $x > z$ $\boxed{\text{Statement 5}}$

$x > y$ is the same as $y < x$ $\boxed{\text{Statement 6}}$

$a < x < b$ is the same as both $a < x$ and $x < b$ $\boxed{\text{Statement 7}}$

If $x > y > 0$ and $w > z > 0$, then $xw > yz$ $\boxed{\text{Statement 8}}$

If $x < 0$ and $z = x + y$, then $z > y$ $\boxed{\text{Statement 9}}$

If $x < 0$, then $\begin{cases} x^n < 0 \text{ if } n \text{ is odd} \\ x^n > 0 \text{ if } n \text{ is even} \end{cases}$ $\boxed{\text{Statement 10}}$ $\boxed{\text{Statement 11}}$

If $xy > 0$, then $x > 0$ and $y > 0$ or $x < 0$ and $y < 0$ $\boxed{\text{Statement 12}}$

If $xy < 0$, then $x > 0$ and $y < 0$ or $x < 0$ and $y > 0$ $\boxed{\text{Statement 13}}$

EXAMPLE 1

If $0 < x < 1$, then which of the following must be true?

  I. $2x < 2$
 II. $x - 1 < 0$
III. $x^2 < x$

(A) I only
(B) II only
(C) I and II only
(D) II and III only
(E) I, II, and III

Choice E is correct. We are told that $0 < x < 1$. Using

    $\boxed{\text{Statement 7}}$, we have

$$0 < x \qquad \boxed{1}$$
$$x < 1 \qquad \boxed{2}$$

For Item I, we multiply $\boxed{2}$ by 2.

See $\boxed{\text{Statement 3}}$

$$2x < 2$$

Thus, Item I is true.
For Item II, we add -1 to both sides of $\boxed{2}$.

See $\boxed{\text{Statement 1}}$ to get
$$x - 1 < 0$$

Thus Item II is true.
For Item III, we multiply $\boxed{2}$ by x.

See $\boxed{\text{Statement 3}}$ to get
$$x^2 < x$$

Thus, Item III is true.

All items are true, so Choice E is correct.

EXAMPLE 2

Given that $\dfrac{a}{b}$ is less than 1, $a > 0$, $b > 0$. Which of the following must be greater than 1?

(A) $\dfrac{a}{2b}$

(B) $\dfrac{b}{2a}$

(C) $\dfrac{\sqrt{b}}{a}$

(D) $\dfrac{b}{a}$

(E) $\left(\dfrac{a}{b}\right)^2$

Choice D is correct.

$$\textit{Given:} \quad \frac{a}{b} < 1 \qquad \boxed{1}$$
$$a > 0 \qquad \boxed{2}$$
$$b > 0 \qquad \boxed{3}$$

See $\boxed{\text{Statement 3}}$: Multiply $\boxed{1}$ by b. We get

$$b\left(\frac{a}{b}\right) < b\,(1)$$
$$a < b \qquad \boxed{4}$$

Use $\boxed{\text{Statement 3}}$ where $w = \dfrac{1}{a}$. Divide $\boxed{4}$ by a. We get

$$\frac{a}{a} < \frac{b}{a}$$
$$1 < \frac{b}{a}$$

or

$$\frac{b}{a} > 1$$

EXAMPLE 3

Which combination of the following statements can be used to demonstrate that x is positive?

  I. $x > y$
 II. $1 < y$

(A) I alone but not II
(B) II alone but not I
(C) I and II taken together but neither taken alone
(D) Both I alone and II alone
(E) Neither I nor II nor both

Choice C is correct. We want to know which of the following

$$x > y \qquad \boxed{1}$$
$$1 < y \qquad \boxed{2}$$

is enough information to conclude that

$$x > 0 \qquad \boxed{3}$$

$\boxed{1}$ alone is not enough to determine $\boxed{3}$ because $0 > x > y$ could be true. (Note: x is greater than y, but they both could be negative.)

$\boxed{2}$ alone is not enough to determine $\boxed{3}$ because we don't know whether x is greater than, less than, or equal to y.

However, if we use $\boxed{1}$ and $\boxed{2}$ together, we can compare the two:

$$1 < y \text{ is the same as } y > 1$$

Therefore, $x > y$ with $y > 1$ yields: $\boxed{\text{Statement 5}}$

$$x > 1 \qquad \boxed{4}$$

Since $1 > 0$ is always true, then from $\boxed{4}$

$$x > 0 \text{ is always true}$$

EXAMPLE 4

What are all values of x such that $(x - 7)(x + 3)$ is positive?

(A) $x > 7$
(B) $-7 < x < 3$
(C) $-3 < x < 7$
(D) $x > 7$ or $x < -3$
(E) $x > 3$ or $x < -7$

Choice D is correct.

$$(x - 7)(x + 3) > 0 \text{ when}$$
$$x - 7 > 0 \text{ and } x + 3 > 0 \qquad \boxed{1}$$
$$\text{or} \quad x - 7 < 0 \text{ and } x + 3 < 0 \qquad \boxed{2}$$

| Statement 12 |

From $\boxed{1}$ we have $x > 7$ and $x > -3$ $\qquad \boxed{3}$
Thus $x > 7$; $\qquad \boxed{4}$
From $\boxed{2}$, we have $x < 7$ and $x < -3$ $\qquad \boxed{5}$
Thus $x < -3$; $\qquad \boxed{6}$

EXAMPLE 5

If p and q are nonzero real numbers and if $p^2 + q^3 < 0$ and if $p^3 + q^5 > 0$, which of the following number lines shows the relative positions of p, q, and 0?

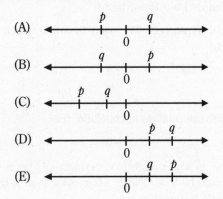

Choice B is correct.

Method 1: Given: $p^2 + q^3 < 0$ $\qquad \boxed{1}$
$p^3 + q^5 > 0$ $\qquad \boxed{2}$

Subtracting p^2 from $\boxed{1}$ and q^5 from $\boxed{2}$, we have

$$q^3 < -p^2 \qquad \boxed{3}$$
$$p^3 > -q^5 \qquad \boxed{4}$$

and

since the square of any real number is greater than 0, $p^2 > 0$ and so $-p^2 < 0$. $\qquad \boxed{5}$

Using | Statement 5 |, combining $\boxed{3}$ and $\boxed{5}$ we get

$q^3 < -p^2 < 0$ $\qquad \boxed{6}$
and get $q^3 < 0$. $\qquad \boxed{7}$

Thus, $q < 0$. $\qquad \boxed{8}$
From $\boxed{8}$, we can say $q^5 < 0$ or $-q^5 > 0$. $\qquad \boxed{9}$

Using | Statement 5 |, combining $\boxed{4}$ and $\boxed{9}$,
$p^3 > -q^5 > 0$ and $p^3 > 0$. Thus $p > 0$. $\qquad \boxed{10}$

Using $\boxed{8}$ and $\boxed{10}$, it is easily seen that Choice B is correct.

Method 2: **(Use Strategy 6: Know how to manipulate inequalities.)**

$$\text{Given: } p^2 + q^3 < 0 \qquad \boxed{1}$$
$$p^3 + q^5 > 0 \qquad \boxed{2}$$

Since p^2 is always > 0, using this with $\boxed{1}$, we know that $q^3 < 0$ and, therefore, $q < 0$. $\qquad \boxed{3}$

If $q^3 < 0$, then $q^5 < 0$. $\qquad \boxed{4}$

Using $\boxed{4}$ and $\boxed{2}$, we know that
$$p^3 > 0, \text{ and therefore } p > 0 \qquad \boxed{5}$$

Using $\boxed{3}$ and $\boxed{5}$, only Choice B is correct.

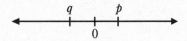

EXAMPLE 6

Janie is older than Tammy, but she is younger than Lori. Let j, t, and l be the ages in years of Janie, Tammy, and Lori, respectively. Which of the following is true?

(A) $j < t < l$
(B) $t < j < l$
(C) $t < l < j$
(D) $l < j < t$
(E) $l < t < j$

Choice B is correct. **(First, use Strategy 2: Translate English words into mathematical expressions.)** "Janie is older than Tammy but she is younger than Lori," translates to:

$$\text{Janie's age} > \text{Tammy's age} \qquad \boxed{1}$$
$$\text{Janie's age} < \text{Lori's age} \qquad \boxed{2}$$
$$\text{Given:} \quad \text{Janie's age} = j \qquad \boxed{3}$$
$$\text{Tammy's age} = t \qquad \boxed{4}$$
$$\text{Lori's age} = l \qquad \boxed{5}$$

Substituting $\boxed{3}$, $\boxed{4}$, and $\boxed{5}$ into $\boxed{1}$ and $\boxed{2}$, we get

$$j > t \qquad \boxed{6}$$
$$j < l \qquad \boxed{7}$$

Use | Statement 5 |. Reversing $\boxed{6}$, we get

$$t < j \qquad \boxed{8}$$

Combining $\boxed{8}$ and $\boxed{7}$, we get

$$t < j < l$$

STRATEGY SECTION • 91

MATH
STRATEGY 7

Use Specific Numerical Examples to Prove or Disprove Your Guess

When you do not want to do a lot of algebra, or when you are unable to prove what you think is the answer, you may want to substitute numbers.

EXAMPLE 1

The sum of the cubes of any two consecutive positive integers is always

(A) an odd integer
(B) an even integer
(C) the cube of an integer
(D) the square of an integer
(E) the product of an integer and 3

Choice A is correct. Try specific numbers. Call consecutive positive integers 1 and 2.
Sum of cubes:

$$1^3 + 2^3 = 1 + 8 = 9$$

You have now eliminated choices B and C. You are left with choices A, D, and E.

Now try two other consecutive integers: 2 and 3.

$$2^3 + 3^3 = 8 + 27 = 35$$

Choice A is acceptable. Choice D is false. Choice E is false.

Thus, Choice A is the only choice remaining.

EXAMPLE 2

John is now m years old, and Sally is 4 years older than John. Which represents Sally's age 6 years ago?

(A) $m + 10$
(B) $m - 10$
(C) $m - 2$
(D) $m - 4$
(E) $4m - 6$

Choice C is correct.

<u>Try a specific number.</u>

Let $m = 10$

John is 10 years old.
Sally is 4 years older than John, so Sally is 14 years old.
Sally's age 6 years ago was 8 years.

Now look for the choice that gives you 8 with $m = 10$.

(A) $m + 10 = 10 + 10 = 20$
(B) $m - 10 = 10 - 10 = 0$
(C) $m - 2 = 10 - 2 = 8$—that's the one

See Math Strategy 2, Example 4 (page 78) for an alternate approach to solving this problem, using a different strategy: **Translate English Words into Mathematical Expressions**.

EXAMPLE 3

If $x \neq 0$, then $\dfrac{(-3x)^3}{-3x^3} =$

(A) -9
(B) -1
(C) 1
(D) 3
(E) 9

Choice E is correct.

<u>Try a specific number.</u>
Let $x = 1$. Then:

$$\frac{(-3x)^3}{-3x^3} = \frac{(-3x(1))^3}{-3(1^3)} = \frac{(-3)^3}{-3} = 9$$

EXAMPLE 4

If $a = 4b$, then the average of a and b is

(A) $\dfrac{1}{2}b$

(B) $\dfrac{3}{2}b$

(C) $\dfrac{5}{2}b$

(D) $\dfrac{7}{2}b$

(E) $\dfrac{9}{2}b$

Choice C is correct.

Try a specific number.

Let $b = 1$. Then $a = 4b = 4$. So the average =

$$\frac{1+4}{2} = \frac{5}{2}.$$

Look at choices where $b = 1$. The only choice that gives $\frac{5}{2}$ is Choice C.

EXAMPLE 5

The sum of three consecutive even integers is P. Find the sum of the next three consecutive *odd* integers that follow the greatest of the three even integers.

(A) $P + 9$
(B) $P + 15$
(C) $P + 12$
(D) $P + 20$
(E) None of these.

Choice B is correct.

Try specific numbers.

Let the three consecutive even integers be 2, 4, 6.

So, $2 + 4 + 6 = P = 12$.

The next three consecutive odd integers that follow 6 are:

$$7, 9, 11$$

So the sum of

$$7 + 9 + 11 = 27$$

Now, where $P = 12$, look for a choice that gives you 27:

(A) $P + 9 = 12 + 9 = 21$—NO
(B) $P + 15 = 12 + 15 = 27$—YES

EXAMPLE 6

If $3 > a$, which of the following is *not* true?

(A) $3 - 3 > a - 3$
(B) $3 + 3 > a + 3$
(C) $3(3) > a(3)$
(D) $3 - 3 > 3 - a$
(E) $\frac{3}{3} > \frac{a}{3}$

Choice D is correct.

Try specific numbers.
Work backward from Choice E if you wish.
Let $a = 1$.
Choice E:

$$\frac{3}{3} > \frac{a}{3} = \frac{1}{3} \qquad\qquad \text{TRUE STATEMENT}$$

Choice D:

$$3 - 3 > 3 - a = 3 - 1, \text{ or } 0 > 2 \quad \text{FALSE STATEMENT}$$

EXAMPLE 7

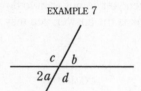

In the figure of intersecting lines above, which of the following is equal to $180 - a$?

(A) $a + d$
(B) $a + 2d$
(C) $c + b$
(D) $b + 2a$
(E) $c + d$

Choice A is correct.

Try a specific number.
Let $\boxed{a = 20°}$

Then $2a = 40°$.
Be careful now—all of the other angles are now determined, so don't choose any more.
Because vertical angles are equal, $2a = b$, so

$$\boxed{b = 40°}$$

Now $c + b = 180°$, so $c + 40 = 180$ and

$$\boxed{c = 140°}$$

Thus, $\boxed{d = 140°}$ (vertical angles are equal).
Now look at the question:

$$180 - a = 180 - 20 = 160$$

Which is the correct choice?

(A) $a + d = 20 + 140 = 160$—that's the one!

See Math Strategy 17, Example 2 (page 113) for an alternate approach to solving this problem, using a different strategy: **Use the Given Information Effectively (and Ignore Irrelevant Information).**

MATH STRATEGY 8

When Each Choice Must Be Tested, Start with Choice E and Work Backward

If you must check each choice for the correct answer, start with Choice E and work backward. The reason for this is that the test maker of a question *in which each choice must be tested* often puts the correct answer as Choice D or E in order to trick the careless student who starts testing with choice A. So if you're trying all the choices, start with the last choice, then the next to last choice, etc. See example 8 for an instance of when this strategy should not be used.

EXAMPLE 1

If p is a positive integer, which *could* be an odd integer?

(A) $2p + 2$
(B) $p^3 - p$
(C) $p^2 + p$
(D) $p^2 - p$
(E) $7p - 3$

Choice E is correct. Start with Choice E first, since you have to *test* out the choices.

Method 1: Try a number for p. Let $p = 1$. Then (starting with Choice E):

$7p - 3 = 7(1) - 3 = 4$. 4 is even, so try another number for p to see whether $7p - 3$ is odd. Let $p = 2$.

$7p - 3 = 7(2) - 3 = 11$. 11 is odd. Therefore, Choice E is correct.

Method 2: Look at Choice E. $7p$ could be even or odd, depending on what p is. If p is even, $7p$ is even. If p is odd, $7p$ is odd. Accordingly, $7p - 3$ is either even or odd. Therefore, Choice E is correct.

Note: By using either Method 1 or Method 2, it is not necessary to test the other choices.

EXAMPLE 2

If $y = x^2 + 3$, then for which value of x is y divisible by 7?

(A) 10
(B) 8
(C) 7
(D) 6
(E) 5

Choice E is correct. Since you must check all of the choices, start with Choice E:

$$y = 5^2 + 3 = 25 + 3 = 28$$
$$28 \text{ is divisible by 7}$$

If you had started with Choice A, you would have had to test four choices instead of one choice before finding the correct answer.

EXAMPLE 3

Which fraction is greater than $\frac{1}{2}$?

(A) $\frac{4}{9}$

(B) $\frac{17}{35}$

(C) $\frac{6}{13}$

(D) $\frac{12}{25}$

(E) $\frac{8}{15}$

Choice E is correct.

<u>Look at Choice E first.</u>

$$\text{Is } \frac{8}{15} > \frac{1}{2}?$$

Use the cross-multiplication method.

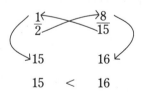

$$15 \quad < \quad 16$$

So, $\frac{1}{2} < \frac{8}{15}$.

You also could have looked at Choice E, said $\frac{8}{16} = \frac{1}{2}$, and realized that $\frac{8}{15} > \frac{1}{2}$ because $\frac{8}{15}$ has a smaller denominator than $\frac{8}{16}$.

EXAMPLE 4

If n is an even integer, which of the following is an odd integer?

(A) $n^2 - 2$
(B) $n - 4$
(C) $(n - 4)^2$
(D) n^3
(E) $n^2 - n - 1$

Choice E is correct.

Look at Choice E first.

$$n^2 - n - 1$$
If n is even,
n^2 is even
n is even
1 is odd

So, $n^2 - n - 1 =$ even − even − odd = odd.

EXAMPLE 5

Which of the following is an odd number?

(A) 7×22
(B) $59 - 15$
(C) $55 + 35$
(D) $75 \div 15$
(E) 4^7

Choice D is correct.

Look at Choice E first.

4^7 is even, since $4 \times 4 \times 4 \ldots$ is even.
So now look at Choice D: $\frac{75}{15} = 5$, which is odd.

EXAMPLE 6

$$\begin{array}{r} 3\,\#\,2 \\ \times \quad 8 \\ \hline 28 \star 6 \end{array}$$

If # and ⋆ are different digits in the correctly calculated multiplication problem above, then # could be

(A) 1
(B) 2
(C) 3
(D) 4
(E) 6

Choice E is correct.

Try Choice E first.

$$\begin{array}{r} 3\,\#\,2 \\ \times \quad 8 \\ \hline 28 \star 6 \end{array} \qquad \begin{array}{r} 3\,⑥\,2 \\ \times \quad 8 \\ \hline 28\,⑨\,6 \end{array}$$

9 and 6 are different numbers, so Choice E is correct.

EXAMPLE 7

Which choice describes a pair of numbers that are *unequal*?

(A) $\frac{1}{6}, \frac{11}{66}$

(B) $3.4, \frac{34}{10}$

(C) $\frac{15}{75}, \frac{1}{5}$

(D) $\frac{3}{8}, 0.375$

(E) $\frac{86}{24}, \frac{42}{10}$

Choice E is correct.

Look at Choice E first.

$$\frac{86}{24} \qquad ? \qquad \frac{42}{10}$$

Cross-multiply:

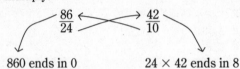

860 ends in 0 24×42 ends in 8

Thus, the numbers must be *different* and *unequal*.

When *Not* to Use This Strategy:

If you can spot something in the question that shows you how to solve the problem readily without having to test each choice, there's no need to go through every answer by working backwards.

EXAMPLE 8

If $|6 - 5y| > 20$, which of the following is a possible value of y?

(A) -3
(B) -1
(C) 1
(D) 3
(E) 5

Choice A is correct.

Instead of plugging in values for y, starting with Choice E, you should realize there will only be one answer listed for which $6 - 5y > 20$. So which choice gives you the largest product for $-5y$? Start by checking the *most negative* choice, or $y = -3$.

This gives you $|6 - 5(-3)| = |6 + 15| = |21|$, which is greater than 20.

Know How to Solve Problems Using the Formula R × T = D

Almost every problem involving motion can be solved using the formula

$$R \times T = D$$
or
rate × elapsed time = distance

EXAMPLE 1

The diagram below shows two paths: Path 1 is 10 miles long, and Path 2 is 12 miles long. If Person X runs along Path 1 at 5 miles per hour and Person Y runs along Path 2 at y miles per hour, and if it takes exactly the same amount of time for both runners to run their whole path, then what is the value of y?

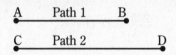

(A) 2

(B) $4\frac{1}{6}$

(C) 6

(D) 20

(E) 24

Choice C is correct. Let T = Time (in hours) for either runner to run the whole path.

Using $R \times T = D$, for Person X, we have
(5 mi/hr)(T hours) = 10 miles
or $5T = 10$, or   ☐1
         $T = 2$

For Person Y, we have
(y mi/hr)(T hours) = 12 miles
or $yT = 12$
Using ☐1, $y(2) = 12$, or $y = 6$

EXAMPLE 2

A car traveling at 50 miles per hour for two hours travels the same distance as a car traveling at 20 miles per hour for x hours. What is x?

(A) $\frac{4}{5}$

(B) $\frac{5}{4}$

(C) 5

(D) 2

(E) $\frac{1}{2}$

Choice C is correct.

Use $R \times T = D$. Call the distance both cars travel D (since the distance is the same for both cars).

So we get:

$$50 \times 2 = D = 100 \qquad \boxed{1}$$
$$20 \times x = D = 100 \qquad \boxed{2}$$

Solving $\boxed{2}$, you can see that $x = 5$.

EXAMPLE 3

John walks at a rate of 4 miles per hour. Sally walks at a rate of 5 miles per hour. If John and Sally both start at the same point, how many miles is one person from the other after t hours of walking? (*Note:* Both are walking on the same road in the same direction.)

(A) $\frac{t}{2}$

(B) t

(C) $2t$

(D) $\frac{4}{5}t$

(E) $\frac{5}{4}t$

Choice B is correct.

Draw a diagram:

John (4 mph)

(*t hours*)

$\vdash\!\!-\!\!D_J\!\!-\!\!\rightarrow$

Sally (5 mph)

(*t hours*)

$\vdash\!\!-\!\!-\!\!D_S\!\!-\!\!-\!\!\rightarrow$

Let D_J be distance that John walks in t hours.
Let D_S be distance that Sally walks in t hours.
Then, using $R \times t = D$,

for John: $4 \times t = D_J$
for Sally: $5 \times t = D_S$

The distance between Sally and John after t hours of walking is:

$$D_S - D_J = 5t - 4t = t$$

EXAMPLE 4

A man rode a bicycle a straight distance at a speed of 10 miles per hour and came back the same distance at a speed of 20 miles per hour. What was the man's total number of miles for the trip back and forth, if his total traveling time was 1 hour?

(A) 15

(B) $7\frac{1}{2}$

(C) $6\frac{1}{3}$

(D) $6\frac{2}{3}$

(E) $13\frac{1}{3}$

Choice E is correct.

Always use $R \times T = D$ (Rate $\times$ Time = Distance) in problems like this. Call the first distance D and the time for the first part T_1. Since he rode at 10 mph:

$$10 \times T_1 = D \qquad \boxed{1}$$

Now for the trip back. He rode at 20 mph. Call the time it took to go back T_2. Since he came back the *same* distance, we can call that distance D also. So for the trip back using $R \times T = D$, we get:

$$20 \times T_2 = D \qquad \boxed{2}$$

Since it was given that the total traveling time was 1 hour, the total traveling time is:

$$T_1 + T_2 = 1$$

Now here's the trick: Let's make use of the fact that $T_1 + T_2 = 1$. Dividing Equation $\boxed{1}$ by 10, we get:

$$T_1 = \frac{D}{10}$$

Dividing Equation $\boxed{2}$ by 20, we get:

$$T_2 = \frac{D}{20}$$

Now add $T_1 + T_2$ and we get:

$$T_1 + T_2 = 1 = \frac{D}{10} + \frac{D}{20}$$

Factor D:

$$1 = D\left(\frac{1}{10} + \frac{1}{20}\right)$$

Add $\frac{1}{10} + \frac{1}{20}$. Remember the fast way of adding fractions?

$$\frac{1}{10} \quad\overset{\times}{+}\quad \frac{1}{20} = \frac{20 + 10}{20 \times 10} = \frac{30}{200}$$

So:

$$1 = (D)\frac{30}{200}$$

Multiply by 200 and divide by 30 and we get:

$$\frac{200}{30} = D; D = 6\frac{2}{3}$$

Don't forget, we're looking for $2D$: $2D = 13\frac{1}{3}$

EXAMPLE 5

What is the average rate of a bicycle traveling at 10 mph a distance of 5 miles and at 20 mph the same distance?

(A) 15 mph
(B) 20 mph

(C) $12\frac{1}{2}$ mph

(D) $13\frac{1}{3}$ mph

(E) 16 mph

Choice D is correct.

Ask yourself, what does *average rate* mean? It *does not* mean the average of the rates! If you thought it did, you would have selected Choice A as the answer (averaging 10 and 20 to get 15)—the "lure" choice.

Average is a word that *modifies* the word *rate* in this case. So you must define the word *rate* first, before you do anything with averaging. Since Rate $\times$ Time = Distance,

$$\text{Rate} = \frac{\text{Distance}}{\text{Time}}$$

Then *average* rate must be:

$$\text{Average rate} = \frac{\text{TOTAL distance}}{\text{TOTAL time}}$$

The *total distance* is the distance covered on the whole trip, which is $5 + 5 = 10$ miles.
The *total time* is the time traveled the first 5 miles at 10 mph added to the time the bicycle traveled the next 5 miles at 20 mph.
Let t_1 be the time the bicycle traveled the first 5 miles.
Let t_2 be the time the bicycle traveled the next 5 miles.
Then the *total time* $= t_1 + t_2$.
Since $R \times T = D$,

for the first 5 miles: $10 \times t_1 = 5$
for the next 5 miles: $20 \times t_2 = 5$

Finding t_1: $t_1 = \dfrac{5}{10}$

Finding t_2: $t_2 = \dfrac{5}{20}$

So, $t_1 + t_2 = \dfrac{5}{10} + \dfrac{5}{20}$

$= \dfrac{1}{2} + \dfrac{1}{4}$ (remembering how to quickly add
$= \dfrac{4+2}{8}$ fractions)

$= \dfrac{6}{8} = \dfrac{3}{4}$

$$\text{Average rate} = \frac{\text{TOTAL distance}}{\text{TOTAL time}}$$

$$= \frac{5+5}{\dfrac{3}{4}}$$

$$= (5+5) \times \frac{4}{3}$$

$$= 10 \times \frac{4}{3} = \frac{40}{3} = 13\frac{1}{3} \; (Answer)$$

Here's a formula you can memorize:
If a vehicle travels a certain distance at a mph and travels the same distance at b mph, the *average rate* is

$$\frac{2ab}{a+b}$$

Try doing the problem using this formula:

$$\frac{2ab}{a+b} = \frac{2 \times 10 \times 20}{10 + 20} = \frac{400}{30} = 13\frac{1}{3}$$

Caution: Use this formula only when you are looking for *average rate and when the distance is the same for both speeds.*

MATH STRATEGY 10

Know How to Use Units of Time, Distance, Area, or Volume to Find or Check Your Answer

By knowing what the units in your answer must be, you will often have an easier time finding or checking your answer. A very helpful thing to do is to treat the units of time or space as variables (like *x* or *y*). Thus, you should substitute, multiply, or divide these units as if they were ordinary variables. The following examples illustrate this idea.

EXAMPLE 1

What is the distance in miles covered by a car that traveled at 50 miles per hour for 5 hours?

(A) 10
(B) 45
(C) 55
(D) 200
(E) 250

Choice E is correct. Although this is an easy $R \times T = D$ problem, it illustrates this strategy very well.

Recall that

rate × time $= $ distance
$(50 \text{ mi/hr})(5 \text{ hours}) = $ distance

Notice that when I substituted into $R \times T = D$, *I kept the units of rate and time* (miles/hour and hours). Now I will *treat these units as if they were ordinary variables.* Thus,

distance $= (50 \text{ mi/hr})(5 \text{ hours})$

I have canceled the variable "hour(s)" from the numerator and denominator of the right side of the equation. Hence,

$$\text{distance} = 250 \text{ miles}$$

The distance has units of "miles," as I would expect. In fact, if the units in my answer had been "miles/hour" or "hours," then I would have been in error.

Thus, *the general procedure* for problems using this strategy is:

Step 1. <u>Keep the units given in the question.</u>

Step 2. <u>Treat the units as ordinary variables.</u>

Step 3. <u>Make sure the answer has units that you would expect.</u>

EXAMPLE 2

How many inches is equivalent to 2 yards, 2 feet, and 7 inches?

(A) 11
(B) 37
(C) 55
(D) 81
(E) 103

Choice E is correct.
Remember that

$$1 \text{ yard } = 3 \text{ feet} \qquad \boxed{1}$$
$$1 \text{ foot } = 12 \text{ inches} \qquad \boxed{2}$$

Treat the units of length as variables! Divide $\boxed{1}$ by 1 yard, and $\boxed{2}$ by 1 foot, to get

$$1 = \frac{3 \text{ feet}}{1 \text{ yard}} \qquad \boxed{3}$$

$$1 = \frac{12 \text{ inches}}{1 \text{ foot}} \qquad \boxed{4}$$

We can multiply any expression by 1 and get the same value. Thus, 2 yards + 2 feet + 7 inches =

$$(2 \text{ yards})(1)(1) + (2 \text{ feet})(1) + 7 \text{ inches} \qquad \boxed{5}$$

Substituting $\boxed{3}$ and $\boxed{4}$ into $\boxed{5}$, 2 yards + 2 feet + 7 inches

$$= 2 \text{ yards}\left(\frac{3 \text{ feet}}{\text{yard}}\right)\left(\frac{12 \text{ inches}}{\text{foot}}\right) + 2 \text{ feet}\left(\frac{12 \text{ inches}}{\text{foot}}\right) + 7 \text{ inches}$$

$$= 72 \text{ inches} + 24 \text{ inches} + 7 \text{ inches}$$

$$= 103 \text{ inches}$$

Notice that the answer is in "inches," as I expected. If the answer had come out in "yards" or "feet," then I would have been in error.

EXAMPLE 3

A car wash cleans x cars per hour, for y hours, at z dollars per car. How much money in *cents* does the car wash receive?

(A) $\dfrac{xy}{100z}$

(B) $\dfrac{xyz}{100}$

(C) $100xyz$

(D) $\dfrac{100x}{yz}$

(E) $\dfrac{yz}{100x}$

Choice C is correct.

Use units:

$$\left(\frac{x \text{ cars}}{\text{hour}}\right)(y \text{ hours})\left(\frac{z \text{ dollars}}{\text{car}}\right) = xyz \text{ dollars} \qquad \boxed{1}$$

Since there are 100 cents to a dollar, we multiply $\boxed{1}$ by 100. We get $100xyz$ cents.

EXAMPLE 4

There are 3 feet in a yard and 12 inches in a foot. How many yards are there altogether in 1 yard, 1 foot, and 1 inch?

(A) $1\dfrac{1}{3}$

(B) $1\dfrac{13}{36}$

(C) $1\dfrac{11}{18}$

(D) $2\dfrac{5}{12}$

(E) $4\dfrac{1}{12}$

Choice B is correct. **Know how to work with units.**

> *Given:* 3 feet = 1 yard
> 12 inches = 1 foot

Thus,

$$1 \text{ yard} + 1 \text{ foot} + 1 \text{ inch} \qquad =$$

$$1 \text{ yard} + 1 \text{ foot}\left(\frac{1 \text{ yard}}{3 \text{ feet}}\right) \qquad +$$

$$1 \text{ inch}\left(\frac{1 \text{ foot}}{12 \text{ inches}}\right)\left(\frac{1 \text{ yard}}{3 \text{ feet}}\right) \qquad =$$

$$1 + \frac{1}{3} + \frac{1}{36} \text{ yards} \qquad =$$

$$1 + \frac{12}{36} + \frac{1}{36} \text{ yards} \qquad =$$

$$1\frac{13}{36} \text{ yards}$$

Use New Definitions and Functions Carefully

Some GRE questions may use new symbols, functions, or definitions that were created in the question. At first glance, these questions may seem difficult because you are not familiar with the new symbol, function, or definition. *However, most of these questions can be solved through simple substitution or application of a simple definition.*

EXAMPLE 1

If the symbol ϕ is defined by the equation

$$a \phi b = a - b - ab$$

for all a and b, then $\left(-\frac{1}{3}\right) \phi (-3) =$

(A) $\dfrac{5}{3}$

(B) $\dfrac{11}{3}$

(C) $-\dfrac{13}{3}$

(D) -4

(E) -5

Choice A is correct. All that is required is substitution:

$$a \phi b = a - b - ab$$

$$\left(-\tfrac{1}{3}\right)\phi(-3)$$

Substitute $-\frac{1}{3}$ for a and -3 for b in $a - b - ab$:

$$\left(-\frac{1}{3}\right)\phi(-3) = -\frac{1}{3} - (-3) - \left(-\frac{1}{3}\right)(-3)$$

$$= -\frac{1}{3} + 3 - 1$$

$$= 2 - \frac{1}{3}$$

$$= \frac{5}{3} \ (Answer)$$

EXAMPLE 2

Let $\boxed{x} = \begin{cases} \dfrac{5}{2}(x+1) & \text{if } x \text{ is an odd integer} \\ \dfrac{5}{2}x & \text{if } x \text{ is an even integer} \end{cases}$

Find $\boxed{2y}$, where y is an integer.

(A) $\dfrac{5}{2}y$

(B) $5y$

(C) $\dfrac{5}{2}y + 1$

(D) $5y + \dfrac{5}{2}$

(E) $5y + 5$

Choice B is correct. All we have to do is substitute $2y$ into the definition of $\boxed{x}$. In order to know which definition of $\boxed{x}$ to use, we want to know if $2y$ is even. Since y is an integer, then $2y$ is an even integer. Thus,

$$\boxed{2y} = \frac{5}{2}(2y)$$

$$\text{or } \boxed{2y} = 5y \ (Answer)$$

EXAMPLE 3

As in Example 1, ø is defined as
$$a \text{ ø } b = a - b - ab.$$

If $a \text{ ø } 3 = 6$, $a =$

(A) $\dfrac{9}{2}$

(B) $\dfrac{9}{4}$

(C) $-\dfrac{9}{4}$

(D) $-\dfrac{4}{9}$

(E) $-\dfrac{9}{2}$

Choice E is correct.
$$a \text{ ø } b = a - b - ab$$
$$a \text{ ø } 3 = 6$$

Substitute a for a, 3 for b:
$$a \text{ ø } 3 = a - 3 - a(3) = 6$$
$$= a - 3 - 3a = 6$$
$$= -2a - 3 = 6$$
$$2a = -9$$
$$a = -\dfrac{9}{2}$$

EXAMPLE 4

The symbol $\left(\ x\ \right)$ is defined as the greatest integer less than or equal to x.

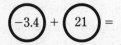 =

(A) 16
(B) 16.6
(C) 17
(D) 17.6
(E) 18

Choice C is correct.

$\left(-3.4\right)$ is defined as the *greatest integer less than or equal to* -3.4. This is -4, since $-4 < -3.4$.

$\left(21\right)$ is defined as the *greatest integer less than or equal to* 21. That is just 21, since $21 = 21$.

Thus, $-4 + 21 = 17$.

EXAMPLE 5

 is defined as $xz - yt$.

$\begin{pmatrix} 2 & 1 \\ 1 & 1 \end{pmatrix} =$

(A) $\begin{pmatrix} 1 & 1 \\ 1 & 1 \end{pmatrix}$

(B) $\begin{pmatrix} 3 & 2 \\ 2 & 1 \end{pmatrix}$

(C) $\begin{pmatrix} 4 & 3 \\ 2 & 1 \end{pmatrix}$

(D) $\begin{pmatrix} 5 & 4 \\ 4 & 2 \end{pmatrix}$

(E) $\begin{pmatrix} 3 & 1 \\ 1 & 2 \end{pmatrix}$

Choice E is correct.

$$\begin{pmatrix} x & y \\ z & t \end{pmatrix} = xz - yt; \quad \begin{pmatrix} 2 & 1 \\ 1 & 1 \end{pmatrix} = ?$$

Substituting 2 for x, 1 for z, 1 for y, and 1 for t,

$$\begin{pmatrix} 2 & 1 \\ 1 & 1 \end{pmatrix} = (2)(1) - (1)(1)$$
$$= 1$$

Now work from Choice E:

(E) $\begin{pmatrix} 3 & 1 \\ 1 & 2 \end{pmatrix} = xz - yt = (3)(1) - (1)(2)$
$$= 3 - 2 = 1$$

EXAMPLE 6

If for all numbers a, b, c the operation ● is defined as
$$a ● b = ab - a$$
then
$$a ● (b ● c) =$$

(A) $a(bc - b - 1)$

(B) $a(bc + b + 1)$

(C) $a(bc - c - b - 1)$

(D) $a(bc - b + 1)$

(E) $a(b - a + c)$

Choice A is correct.

$$a \bullet b = ab - a$$

$$a \bullet (b \bullet c) = ?$$

Find $(b \bullet c)$ first. <u>Use substitution:</u>

$$\begin{array}{c} a \bullet b = ab - a \\ \uparrow \quad \uparrow \\ b \quad c \end{array}$$

Substitute b for a and c for b:

$$b \bullet c = b(c) - b$$

Now, $a \bullet (b \bullet c) = a \bullet (bc - b)$
Use definition $a \bullet b = ab - a$
Substitute a for a and $bc - b$ for b:

$$a \bullet b = ab - a$$

$$\begin{aligned} a \bullet (bc - b) &= a(bc - b) - a \\ &= abc - ab - a \\ &= a(bc - b - 1) \end{aligned}$$

MATH STRATEGY 12

Try Not to Make Tedious Calculations, Since There Is Usually an Easier Way

In many of the examples given in these strategies, it has been explicitly stated that one should not calculate complicated quantities. In some of the examples, we have demonstrated a fast and a slow way of solving the same problem. On the actual exam, if you find that your solution to a problem involves a tedious and complicated method, then you are probably doing the problem in a long, hard way.* Almost always, there will be an easier way.

Examples 5 and 6 can also be solved with the aid of a calculator and some with the aid of a calculator allowing for exponential calculations. However, to illustrate the effectiveness of Math Strategy 12, we did not use the calculator method of solving these examples.

EXAMPLE 1

If $x = 1 + 2 + 2^2 + 2^3 + 2^4 + 2^5 + 2^6 + 2^7 + 2^8 + 2^9$ and $y = 1 + 2x$, then $y - x =$

(A) 2^7
(B) 2^8
(C) 2^9
(D) 2^{10}
(E) 2^{11}

Choice D is correct. I hope you did not calculate $1 + 2 + \ldots 2^9$. If you did, then you found that $x = 1,023$ and $y = 2,047$ and $y - x = 1,024$.

Here is the FAST method. Instead of making these tedious calculations, observe that since

$$\begin{aligned} x = 1 + 2 + 2^2 + 2^3 + 2^4 + 2^5 + 2^6 \\ + 2^7 + 2^8 + 2^9 \end{aligned} \qquad \boxed{1}$$

then $2x = 2 + 2^2 + 2^3 + 2^4 + 2^5 + 2^6 + 2^7$
$\qquad\qquad + 2^8 + 2^9 + 2^{10}$ $\qquad \boxed{2}$

and $y = 1 + 2x = 1 + 2 + 2^2 + 2^3 + 2^4$
$\qquad\qquad + 2^5 + 2^6 + 2^7 + 2^8 + 2^9 + 2^{10}$ $\qquad \boxed{3}$

Thus, calculating $\boxed{3} - \boxed{1}$, we get

$$\begin{aligned} y - x = 1 + 2 + 2^2 + 2^3 + 2^4 + 2^5 + 2^6 + 2^7 \\ + 2^8 + 2^9 + 2^{10} \\ - (1 + 2 + 2^2 + 2^3 + 2^4 + 2^5 + 2^6 + 2^7 \\ + 2^8 + 2^9) \\ = 2^{10} \; (Answer) \end{aligned}$$

EXAMPLE 2

If $16r - 24q = 2$, then $2r - 3q =$

(A) $\dfrac{1}{8}$

(B) $\dfrac{1}{4}$

(C) $\dfrac{1}{2}$

(D) 2

(E) 4

Choice B is correct.

---

* Many times, you can DIVIDE, MULTIPLY, ADD, SUBTRACT, or FACTOR to simplify.

Divide by 8:

$$\frac{16r - 24q}{8} = \frac{2}{8}$$

$$2r - 3q = \frac{1}{4}$$

EXAMPLE 3

If $(a^2 + a)^3 = x(a + 1)^3$, where $a + 1 \neq 0$, then $x =$

(A) a

(B) a^2

(C) a^3

(D) $\dfrac{a + 1}{a}$

(E) $\dfrac{a}{a + 1}$

Choice C is correct.

Isolate x first:

$$x = \frac{(a^2 + a)^3}{(a + 1)^3}$$

Now use the fact that $\left(\dfrac{x^3}{y^3}\right) = \left(\dfrac{x}{y}\right)^3$:

$$\frac{(a^2 + a)^3}{(a + 1)^3} = \left(\frac{a^2 + a}{a + 1}\right)^3$$

Now factor $a^2 + a = a(a + 1)$

So:

$$\left(\frac{a^2 + a}{a + 1}\right)^3 = \left[\frac{a(a + 1)}{a + 1}\right]^3$$

$$= \left[\frac{a\,(a\!\!\!\not{+}\!\!\!1)}{a\!\!\!\not{+}\!\!\!1}\right]^3$$

$$= a^3$$

EXAMPLE 4

If $\dfrac{p + 1}{r + 1} = 1$ and $p,\ r$ are nonzero, and p is not equal to -1, and r is not equal to -1, then

(A) $2 > p/r > 1$ always

(B) $p/r < 1$ always

(C) $p/r = 1$ always

(D) p/r can be greater than 2

(E) $p/r = 2$ always

Choice C is correct.

Get rid of the fraction. Multiply both sides of the equation

$$\frac{p + 1}{r + 1} = 1 \text{ by } (r + 1)$$

$$\left(\frac{p + 1}{r + 1}\right)\!\!\not{r + 1} = r + 1$$

$$p + 1 = r + 1$$

Cancel the 1s:

$$p = r$$

So:

$$\frac{p}{r} = 1$$

EXAMPLE 5

$$\frac{4}{250} =$$

(A) 0.16

(B) 0.016

(C) 0.0016

(D) 0.00125

(E) 0.000125

Choice B is correct.

Don't divide 4 into 250! Multiply:

$$\frac{4}{250} \times \frac{4}{4} = \frac{16}{1,000}$$

Now $\dfrac{16}{100} = .16$, so $\dfrac{16}{1,000} = .016$.

EXAMPLE 6

$$(3 \times 4^{14}) - 4^{13} =$$

(A) 4

(B) 12

(C) 2×4^{13}

(D) 3×4^{13}

(E) 11×4^{13}

Choice E is correct.

Factor 4^{13} from
$(3 \times 4^{14}) - 4^{13}$
We get $4^{13}[(3 \times 4^1) - 1]$
or $4^{13}(12 - 1) = 4^{13}(11)$

You will see more of the technique of dividing, multiplying, adding, and subtracting in the next strategy, Math Strategy 13.

MATH STRATEGY 13

Know How to Find Unknown Expressions by Adding, Subtracting, Multiplying, or Dividing Equations or Expressions

When you want to calculate composite quantities like $x + 3y$ or $m - n$, often you can do it by adding, subtracting, multiplying, or dividing the right equations or expressions.

EXAMPLE 1

If $4x + 5y = 10$ and $x + 3y = 8$, then $\dfrac{5x + 8y}{3} =$

(A) 18
(B) 15
(C) 12
(D) 9
(E) 6

Choice E is correct. Don't solve for x, then for y.

Try to get the quantity $\dfrac{5x + 8y}{3}$ by adding or subtracting the equations. In this case, add equations.

$$\begin{aligned} 4x + 5y &= 10 \\ + \quad x + 3y &= 8 \\ \hline 5x + 8y &= 18 \end{aligned}$$

Now divide by 3:

$$\frac{5x + 8y}{3} = \frac{18}{3} = 6 \; (Answer)$$

EXAMPLE 2

If $25x + 8y = 149$ and $16x + 3y = 89$, then

$$\frac{9x + 5y}{5} =$$

(A) 12
(B) 15
(C) 30
(D) 45
(E) 60

Choice A is correct. We are told

$$25x + 8y = 149 \qquad \boxed{1}$$
$$16x + 3y = 89 \qquad \boxed{2}$$

The long way to do this problem is to solve $\boxed{1}$ and $\boxed{2}$ for x and y, and then substitute these values into $\dfrac{9x + 5y}{5}$.

The fast way to do this problem is to subtract $\boxed{2}$ from $\boxed{1}$ and get

$$9x + 5y = 60 \qquad \boxed{3}$$

Now all we have to do is to divide $\boxed{3}$ by 5:

$$\frac{9x + 5y}{5} = 12 \quad (Answer)$$

EXAMPLE 3

If $21x + 39y = 18$, then $7x + 13y =$

(A) 3
(B) 6
(C) 7
(D) 9
(E) It cannot be determined from the information given.

Choice B is correct. We are given

$$21x + 39y = 18 \qquad \boxed{1}$$

Divide $\boxed{1}$ by 3:

$$7x + 13y = 6 \; (Answer)$$

EXAMPLE 4

If $x + 2y = 4$, then $5x + 10y - 8 =$

(A) 10
(B) 12
(C) −10
(D) −12
(E) 0

Choice B is correct.

Multiply $x + 2y = 4$ by 5 to get:
$$5x + 10y = 20$$

Now subtract 8:
$$\begin{aligned} 5x + 10y - 8 &= 20 - 8 \\ &= 12 \end{aligned}$$

EXAMPLE 5

If $6x^5 = y^2$ and $x = \dfrac{1}{y}$, then $y =$

(A) x^6

(B) $\dfrac{x^5}{6}$

(C) $6x^6$

(D) $\dfrac{6x^5}{5}$

(E) $\dfrac{x^5}{5}$

Choice C is correct.

Multiply $6x^5 = y^2$ by $x = \dfrac{1}{y}$ to get:

$$6x^6 = y^2 \times \dfrac{1}{y} = y$$

EXAMPLE 6

If $y^8 = 4$ and $y^7 = \dfrac{3}{x}$,

what is the value of y in terms of x?

(A) $\dfrac{4x}{3}$

(B) $\dfrac{3x}{4}$

(C) $\dfrac{4}{x}$

(D) $\dfrac{x}{4}$

(E) $\dfrac{12}{x}$

Choice A is correct.

Don't solve for the *value* of y first, by finding $y = 4^{\frac{1}{8}}$.

Just divide the two equations:

(Step 1) $y^8 = 4$

(Step 2) $y^7 = \dfrac{3}{x}$

(Step 3) $\dfrac{y^8}{y^7} = \dfrac{4}{\dfrac{3}{x}}$

(Step 4) $y = 4 \times \dfrac{x}{3}$

(Step 5) $y = \dfrac{4x}{3}$ *(Answer)*

EXAMPLE 7

If $x > 0$, $y > 0$, and $x^2 = 27$ and $y^2 = 3$, then $\dfrac{x^3}{y^3} =$

(A) 9
(B) 27
(C) 36
(D) 48
(E) 54

Choice B is correct.

Divide: $\dfrac{x^2}{y^2} = \dfrac{27}{3} = 9$

Take square root: $\dfrac{x}{y} = 3$

So $\left(\dfrac{x}{y}\right)^3 = \dfrac{x^3}{y^3} = 3^3 = 27$

EXAMPLE 8

If $\dfrac{m}{n} = \dfrac{3}{8}$ and $\dfrac{m}{q} = \dfrac{4}{7}$, then $\dfrac{n}{q} =$

(A) $\dfrac{12}{15}$

(B) $\dfrac{12}{56}$

(C) $\dfrac{56}{12}$

(D) $\dfrac{32}{21}$

(E) $\dfrac{21}{32}$

Choice D is correct.

First get rid of fractions!

Cross-multiply $\dfrac{m}{n} = \dfrac{3}{8}$ to get $8m = 3n$. $\boxed{1}$

Now cross-multiply $\dfrac{m}{q} = \dfrac{4}{7}$ to get $7m = 4q$. $\boxed{2}$

Now divide equations $\boxed{1}$ and $\boxed{2}$:

$$\dfrac{8m}{7m} = \dfrac{3n}{4q} \qquad \boxed{3}$$

The ms cancel and we get:

$$\dfrac{8}{7} = \dfrac{3n}{4q} \qquad \boxed{4}$$

Multiply Equation $\boxed{4}$ by 4 and divide by 3 to get

$$\dfrac{8 \times 4}{7 \times 3} = \dfrac{n}{q}$$

Thus $\dfrac{n}{q} = \dfrac{32}{21}$.

EXAMPLE 9

If $\dfrac{a + b + c + d}{4} = 20$

And $\dfrac{b + c + d}{3} = 10$

Then $a =$

(A) 50
(B) 60
(C) 70
(D) 80
(E) 90

Choice A is correct.

We have

$$\dfrac{a + b + c + d}{4} = 20 \qquad \boxed{1}$$

$$\dfrac{b + c + d}{3} = 10 \qquad \boxed{2}$$

Multiply Equation $\boxed{1}$ by 4:

We get: $a + b + c + d = 80$ $\qquad \boxed{3}$

Now multiply Equation $\boxed{2}$ by 3:

We get: $b + c + d = 30$ $\qquad \boxed{4}$

Now subtract Equation $\boxed{4}$ from Equation $\boxed{3}$:

$$a + b + c + d = 80 \qquad \boxed{3}$$
$$- \; (b + c + d = 30) \qquad \boxed{4}$$

We get $a = 50$.

Draw or Extend Lines in a Diagram to Make a Problem Easier; Label Unknown Quantities

EXAMPLE 1

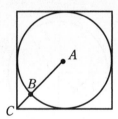

The circle with center A and radius AB is inscribed in the square above. AB is extended to C. What is the ratio of AB to AC?

(A) $\sqrt{2}$

(B) $\dfrac{\sqrt{2}}{4}$

(C) $\dfrac{\sqrt{2} - 1}{2}$

(D) $\dfrac{\sqrt{2}}{2}$

(E) None of these.

Choice D is correct. Always draw or extend lines to get more information. Also label unknown lengths, angles, or arcs with letters.

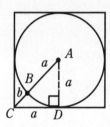

Label $AB = a$ and $BC = b$.
Draw perpendicular AD. Note it is just the radius, a. CD also $= a$, because each side of the square is length $2a$ (the diameter) and CD is $\frac{1}{2}$ the side of the square.

We want to find $\dfrac{AB}{AC} = \dfrac{a}{a + b}$

Now $\triangle ADC$ is an isosceles right triangle, so $AD = CD = a$.

By the Pythagorean Theorem, $a^2 + a^2 = (a + b)^2$ where $a + b$ is the hypotenuse of a right triangle.

We get: $2a^2 = (a + b)^2$
Divide by $(a + b)^2$:

$$\dfrac{2a^2}{(a + b)^2} = 1$$

Divide by 2:

$$\frac{a^2}{(a+b)^2} = \frac{1}{2}$$

Take square roots of both sides:

$$\frac{a}{(a+b)} = \frac{1}{\sqrt{2}} =$$

$$= \frac{1}{\sqrt{2}}\left(\frac{\sqrt{2}}{\sqrt{2}}\right)$$

$$= \frac{\sqrt{2}}{2} \quad (Answer)$$

EXAMPLE 2

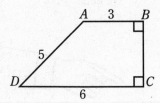

What is the perimeter of the above figure if B and C are right angles?

(A) 14
(B) 16
(C) 18
(D) 20
(E) Cannot be determined.

Choice C is correct.

Draw perpendicular AE. Label side $BC = h$. You can see that $AE = h$.

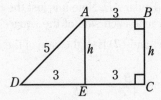

$ABCE$ is a rectangle, so $CE = 3$. This makes $ED = 3$ since the whole $DC = 6$.

Now use the Pythagorean Theorem for triangle AED:

$$h^2 + 3^2 = 5^2$$
$$h^2 = 5^2 - 3^2$$
$$h^2 = 25 - 9$$
$$h^2 = 16$$
$$h = 4$$

So the perimeter is $3 + h + 6 + 5 = 3 + 4 + 6 + 5 = 18$. (*Answer*)

EXAMPLE 3

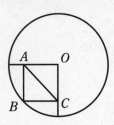

In the figure above, O is the center of a circle with a radius of 6, and $AOCB$ is a square. If point B is on the circumference of the circle, the length of $AC =$

(A) $6\sqrt{2}$
(B) $3\sqrt{2}$
(C) 3
(D) 6
(E) $6\sqrt{3}$

Choice D is correct.

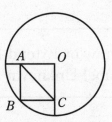

This is tricky if not impossible if you don't draw OB. So draw OB:

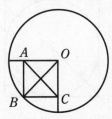

Since $AOCB$ is a square, $OB = AC$; and since $OB =$ radius $= 6$, $AC = 6$.

EXAMPLE 4

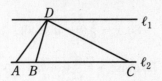

Lines ℓ_1 and ℓ_2 are parallel. $AB = \frac{1}{3} AC$.

$$\frac{\text{The area of triangle } ABD}{\text{The area of triangle } DBC} =$$

(A) $\frac{1}{4}$

(B) $\frac{1}{3}$

(C) $\frac{3}{8}$

(D) $\frac{1}{2}$

(E) Cannot be determined.

Choice D is correct.

$AB = \frac{1}{3} AC$

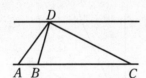

Ask yourself, what is the area of a triangle? It is $\frac{1}{2}$ (height × base). So let's get the heights and the bases of the triangles ABD and DBC. First <u>draw the altitude</u> (call it h).

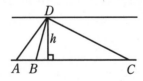

Now label $AB = \frac{1}{3}AC$ (given).

This makes $BC = \frac{2}{3}AC$, since $AB + BC = AC$.

Thus the area of $\triangle ABD = \frac{1}{2}h(AB) = \frac{1}{2}h\left(\frac{1}{3}AC\right)$

Area of $\triangle DBC = \frac{1}{2}h(BC) = \frac{1}{2}h\left(\frac{2}{3}AC\right)$

$$\frac{\text{Area of } ABD}{\text{Area of } DBC} = \frac{\frac{1}{2}h\left(\frac{1}{3}AC\right)}{\frac{1}{2}h\left(\frac{2}{3}AC\right)}$$

$$= \frac{\frac{1}{3}}{\frac{2}{3}} = \frac{1}{3} \times \frac{3}{2} = \frac{1}{2}$$

EXAMPLE 5

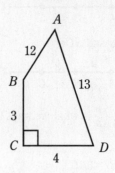

(Note: Figure is not drawn to scale.)

The area of the above figure $ABCD$

(A) is 36
(B) is 108
(C) is 156
(D) is 1,872
(E) Cannot be determined.

Choice A is correct.

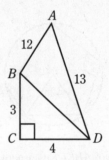

Draw BD. BCD is a 3–4–5 right triangle, so $BD = 5$. Now remember that a 5–12–13 triangle is also a right triangle, so angle ABD is a right angle. The area of triangle BCD is $(3 \times 4)/2 = 6$ and the area of triangle BAD is $(5 \times 12)/2 = 30$, so the total area is 36.

EXAMPLE 6

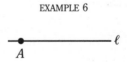

In the above figure, two points, B and C, are placed to the right of point A such that $4AB = 3AC$. The value of $\frac{BC}{AB}$

(A) equals $\frac{1}{3}$

(B) equals $\frac{2}{3}$

(C) equals $\frac{3}{2}$

(D) equals 3

(E) Cannot be determined.

Choice A is correct.

Place B and C to the right of A:

$$\bullet_{A} \quad \bullet_{B} \quad \bullet_{C} \quad\ell$$

Now label $AB = a$ and $BC = b$:

$$\bullet_{A} \overset{a}{\quad} \bullet_{B} \overset{b}{\quad} \bullet_{C} \quad\ell$$

$$\frac{BC}{AB} = \frac{b}{a} \left(\frac{b}{a} \text{ is what we want to find}\right)$$

We are given $4AB = 3AC$.

So, $4a = 3(a + b)$

Expand: $4a = 3a + 3b$

Subtract $3a$: $a = 3b$

Divide by 3 and a: $\frac{1}{3} = \frac{b}{a}$

But remember $\frac{BC}{AB} = \frac{b}{a}$, so $\frac{BC}{AB} = \frac{1}{3}$

EXAMPLE 7

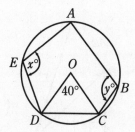

In the figure above, $ABCDE$ is a pentagon inscribed in the circle with center at O. $\angle DOC = 40°$. What is the value of $x + y$?

(A) 80
(B) 100
(C) 180
(D) 200
(E) Cannot be determined.

Choice D is correct.

Label degrees in each arc.

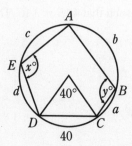

$\angle x$ is measured by $\frac{1}{2}$ the arc it cuts.

So, $x = \frac{1}{2}(b + a + 40)$

Likewise, $y = \frac{1}{2}(c + d + 40)$

You want to find $x + y$, so add:

$$x = \frac{1}{2}(b + a + 40)$$
$$y = \frac{1}{2}(c + d + 40)$$
$$\overline{}$$
$$x + y = \frac{1}{2}(b + a + 40 + c + d + 40)$$

But what is $a + b + c + d + 40$? It is the total number of degrees around the circumference, which is 360.

So, $x + y = \frac{1}{2}(\underbrace{b + a + c + d + 40} + 40)$

$$= \frac{1}{2}(360 + 40)$$

$$= \frac{1}{2}(400) = 200$$

EXAMPLE 8

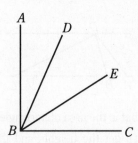

In the above figure, if $\angle ABE = 40°$, $\angle DBC = 60°$, and $\angle ABC = 90°$, what is the measure of $\angle DBE$?

(A) 10°
(B) 20°
(C) 40°
(D) 100°
(E) Cannot be determined.

Choice A is correct.

Label angles first.

Now $\angle ABE = 40$, so $a + b = 40$
$\angle DBC = 60$, so $b + c = 60$
$\angle ABC = 90$, so $a + b + c = 90$

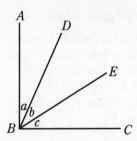

You want to find $\angle DBE$. $\angle DBE = b$, and you want to get the value of b from:

$$a + b = 40 \qquad \boxed{1}$$
$$b + c = 60 \qquad \boxed{2}$$
$$a + b + c = 90 \qquad \boxed{3}$$

Add $\boxed{1}$ and $\boxed{2}$:

$$\begin{aligned} a + b &= 40 \\ + b + c &= 60 \\ \hline a + 2b + c &= 100 \end{aligned}$$

Subtract $\boxed{3}$:

$$\begin{aligned} -(a + b + c &= 90) \\ \hline b &= 10 \end{aligned}$$

EXAMPLE 9

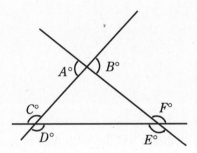

In the figure above, three lines intersect at the points shown. What is the value of $A + B + C + D + E + F$?

(A) 1,080
(B) 720
(C) 540
(D) 360
(E) Cannot be determined.

Choice B is correct.

Relabel, using the fact that *vertical angles are equal*.

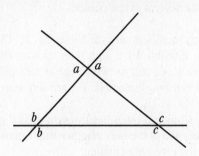

Now use the fact that a straight angle has 180° in it:

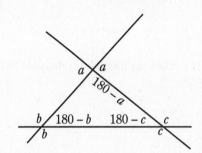

Now use the fact that the sum of the angles of a triangle = 180°:

$$180 - a + 180 - b + 180 - c = 180$$
$$540 - a - b - c = 180$$
$$540 - 180 = a + b + c$$
$$360 = a + b + c$$

Now remember what we are looking to find (the sum):

$$a + a + b + b + c + c = 2a + 2b + 2c$$

But this is just $2(a + b + c) = 2(360) = 720$.

MATH STRATEGY 15

Know How to Eliminate Certain Choices

Instead of working out a lot of algebra, you may be able to eliminate several of the choices at first glance. In this way you can save yourself a lot of work. The key is to remember to use pieces of the given information to eliminate several of the choices at once.

EXAMPLE 1

The sum of the digits of a three-digit number is 15. If this number is not divisible by 2 but is divisible by 5, which of the following is the number?

(A) 384
(B) 465
(C) 635
(D) 681
(E) 780

Choice B is correct. Use pieces of the given information to eliminate several of the choices.

Which numbers are divisible by 2? Choices A and E are divisible by 2 and, thus, can be eliminated. Of Choices B, C, and D, which are *not* divisible by 5? Choice D can be eliminated. We are left with Choices B and C.

Only Choice B (465) has the sum of its digits equal to 15. Thus, 465 is the only number that satisfies all the pieces of the given information.

If you learn to use this method well, you can save loads of time.

EXAMPLE 2

Which of the following numbers is divisible by 5 and 9, but not by 2?

(A) 625
(B) 639
(C) 650
(D) 655
(E) 675

Choice E is correct. Clearly, a number is divisible by 5 if, and only if, its last digit is either 0 or 5. A number is also divisible by 2 if, and only if, its last digit is divisible by 2. *Certain choices are easily eliminated.* Thus we can *eliminate* Choices B and C.

Method 1: To eliminate some more choices, remember that a number is divisible by 9 if, and only if, the sum of its digits is divisible by 9. Thus, Choice E is the only correct answer.

Method 2: If you did not know the test for divisibility by 9, divide the numbers in Choices A, D, and E by 9 to find the answer.

EXAMPLE 3

If the last digit and the first digit are interchanged in each of the numbers below, which will result in the number with the *largest* value?

(A) 5,243
(B) 4,352
(C) 4,235
(D) 2,534
(E) 2,345

Choice E is correct.
The number with the largest last digit will become the largest number after interchanging.　　　　　　　1

Certain choices are easily eliminated.

Using 1, we see that Choices C and E each end in 5. All others end in digits less than 5 and may be eliminated. Start with Choice E (see Strategy 8),
Choice E, 2,345, becomes 5,342.　　　　　2
Choice C, 4,235, becomes 5,234.　　　　　3
2 is larger than 3.

EXAMPLE 4

Which of the following could be the value of 3^x where x is an integer?

(A) 339,066
(B) 376,853
(C) 411,282
(D) 422,928
(E) 531,441

Choice E is correct. Let's look at what 3^x looks like for integral values of x:

$3^1 = 3$
$3^2 = 9$
$3^3 = 27$
$3^4 = 81$
$3^5 = 243$
$3^6 = \ldots 9$
$3^7 = \ldots 7$
$3^8 = \ldots 1$

Note that 3^x always has the *units* digit of 3, 9, 7, or 1. So we can eliminate choices A, C, and D since those choices end in other numbers than 3, 9, 7, or 1. We are left with Choices B and E. The number in the correct choice must be exactly divisible by 3, since it is of the form 3^x ($= 3 \times 3 \times 3 \ldots$) where x is an integer. This is a good time to use your calculator. Divide the number in choice B by 3: You get 125,617.66. That's *not* an integer. So the only remaining choice is Choice E.

MATH STRATEGY 16

> Watch Out for Questions That Seem Very Easy but That Can Be Tricky—Beware of Choice A as a "Lure Choice"

When questions appear to be solved very easily, think again! Watch out especially for the "lure," Choice A.

EXAMPLE 1*

$$6{:}06$$

The diagram above shows a 12-hour digital clock whose hours value is the same as the minutes value. Consider each time when the same number appears for both the hour and the minutes as a "double time" situation. What is the shortest elapsed time period between the appearance of one double time and an immediately succeeding double time?

(A) 61 minutes
(B) 60 minutes
(C) 58 minutes
(D) 50 minutes
(E) 49 minutes

Choice E is correct. Did you think that just by subtracting something like 8:08 from 9:09 you would get the answer (1 hour and 1 minute = 61 minutes)? That's Choice A, which is wrong. So beware, because your answer came too easily for a test like the GRE. You must realize that there is another possibility of "double time" occurrence—12:12 and 1:01, whose difference is 49 minutes. This is Choice E, the correct answer.

EXAMPLE 2

The letters d and m are integral digits in a certain number system. If $0 \leq d \leq m,$ how many different possible values are there for d?

(A) m
(B) $m - 1$
(C) $m - 2$
(D) $m + 1$
(E) $m + 2$

Choice D is correct. Did you think that the answer was m? Do not be careless! The list 1, 2, 3, …, m contains m elements. If 0 is included in the list, then there are $m + 1$ elements. Hence, if $0 \leq d \leq m$ where d is integral, then d can have $m + 1$ different values.

EXAMPLE 3

There are some flags hanging in a horizontal row. Starting at one end of the row, the U.S. flag is 25th. Starting at the other end of the row, the U.S. flag is 13th. How many flags are in the row?

(A) 36
(B) 37
(C) 38
(D) 39
(E) 40

Choice B is correct. **The obvious may be tricky!**

Method 1: Given:

The U.S. flag is 25th from one end. [1]
The U.S. flag is 13th from the other end. [2]

At first glance it may appear that adding [1] and [2], 25 + 13 = 38, will be the correct answer. This is WRONG!

The U.S. flag is being counted twice: Once as the 25th and again as the 13th from the other end. The correct answer is

$$25 + 13 - 1 = 37.$$

Method 2:

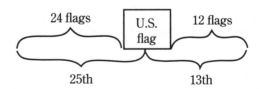

24 flags | U.S. flag | 12 flags

25th 13th

24 + 12 + U.S. flag = 36 + U.S. flag = 37

Note: This problem also appears in Strategy 1 of the 5 General Strategies on page 66.

EXAMPLE 4

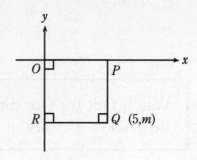

$OR = RQ$ in the figure above. If the coordinates of Q are $(5,m)$, find the value of m.

(A) -5
(B) $-\sqrt{5}$
(C) 0
(D) $\sqrt{5}$
(E) 5

Choice A is correct.

Given: $OR = RQ$ $\boxed{1}$
Coordinates of $Q = (5,m)$ $\boxed{2}$
From $\boxed{2}$, we get $RQ = 5$ $\boxed{3}$
Substitute $\boxed{3}$ into $\boxed{1}$. We get
$$OR = 5$$

The obvious may be tricky! Since Q is below the x-axis, its y-coordinate is negative. Thus $m = -5$.

Use the Given Information Effectively (and Ignore Irrelevant Information)

You should always use first the piece of information that tells you the most, gives you a useful idea, or brings you closest to the answer.

EXAMPLE 1

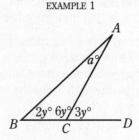

(Note: Figure is not drawn to scale.)

In the figure above, side BC of triangle ABC is extended to D. What is the value of a?

(A) 15
(B) 17
(C) 20
(D) 24
(E) 30

Choice C is correct.

Use the piece of information that will give you something definite. You might have first thought of using the fact that the sum of the angles of a triangle $= 180°$. However, that will give you

$$a + 2y + 6y = 180$$

That's not very useful. However, if you use the fact that the sum of the angles in a straight angle is 180, we get:

$$6y + 3y = 180$$
$$\text{and we get } 9y = 180$$
$$y = 20$$

Now we have gotten something useful. At this point, we can use the fact that the sum of the angles in a triangle is 180.

$$a + 2y + 6y = 180$$

Substituting 20 for y, we get

$$a + 2(20) + 6(20) = 180$$
$$a = 20 \quad \textit{(Answer)}$$

EXAMPLE 2

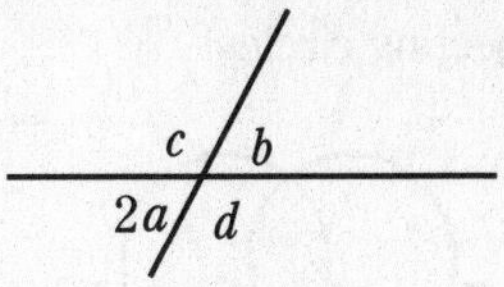

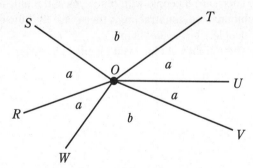

In the figure of intersecting lines above, which of the following is equal to $180 - a$?

(A) $a + d$
(B) $a + 2d$
(C) $c + b$
(D) $b + 2a$
(E) $c + d$

Choice A is correct. Try to get something you can work with. From the diagram,

$$2a + d = 180.$$

So, to find $180 - a$, just subtract a from both sides of the above equation.

$$2a + d - a = 180 - a.$$

You get:

$$a + d = 180 - a.$$

See Math Strategy 7, Example 7 (page 92) for an alternate approach to solving this problem, using a different strategy: **Use Specific Numerical Examples to Prove or Disprove Your Guess**.

EXAMPLE 3

S T
b
a O a
U
a
R a
b V
W

(Note: Figure is not drawn to scale.)

Which of the above angles has a degree measure that can be determined?

(A) $\angle WOS$
(B) $\angle SOU$
(C) $\angle WOT$
(D) $\angle ROV$
(E) $\angle WOV$

Choice C is correct.

Use information that will get you something useful.

$4a + 2b = 360$ (sum of all angles $= 360°$)

Divide by 2 to simplify:

$$2a + b = 180$$

Now try all the choices. You could work backward from Choice E, but we'll start with Choice A:

(A) $\angle WOS = 2a$—You know that $2a + b = 180$ but don't know the value of $2a$.
(B) $\angle SOU = b + a$—You know $2a + b = 180$ but don't know the value of $b + a$.
(C) $\angle WOT = b + 2a$—You know that $2a + b = 180$, so you know the value of $b + 2a$.

EXAMPLE 4

If a ranges in value from 0.003 to 0.3 and b ranges in value from 3.0 to 300.0, then the minimum value of $\frac{a}{b}$ is

(A) 0.1
(B) 0.01
(C) 0.001
(D) 0.0001
(E) 0.00001

Choice E is correct.

Start by using the definitions of *minimum* and *maximum*.

The minimum value of $\frac{a}{b}$ is when a is *minimum* and b is *maximum*.

The minimum value of $a = .003$
The maximum value of $b = 300$

So the minimum value of $\frac{a}{b} = \frac{.003}{300} = \frac{.001}{100} = .00001$.

EXAMPLE 5

If $xry = 0$, $yst = 0$, and $rxt = 1$, then which must be 0?

(A) r
(B) s
(C) t
(D) x
(E) y

Choice E is correct.

Use information that will give you something to work with.

$rxt = 1$ tells you that $r \neq 0$, $x \neq 0$, and $t \neq 0$.
So if $xry = 0$, then y must be 0.

EXAMPLE 6*

On a street with 25 houses, 10 houses have *fewer than 6 rooms,* 10 houses have *more than 7 rooms,* and 4 houses have *more than 8 rooms.* What is the total number of houses on the street that are either 6-, 7-, or 8-room houses?

(A) 5
(B) 9
(C) 11
(D) 14
(E) 15

Choice C is correct.

There are three possible situations:

(a) Houses that have *fewer than 6 rooms* (call the number *a*)
(b) Houses that have *6, 7, or 8 rooms* (call the number *b*)
(c) Houses that have *more than 8 rooms* (call the number *c*)

$a + b + c$ must total 25 (given).   ☐1

a is 10 (given).   ☐2

c is 4 (given).   ☐3

Substituting ☐2 and ☐3 in ☐1 we get $10 + b + 4 = 25$. *b* must therefore be 11.

EXAMPLE 7

In a room, there are 5 *blue-eyed blonds.* If altogether there are 14 *blonds* and 8 people with *blue eyes* in the room, how many people are there in the room? (Assume that everyone in the room is blond, has blue eyes, or is a blue-eyed blond.)

(A) 11
(B) 17
(C) 22
(D) 25
(E) 27

Choice B is correct.

Method 1:

Draw two intersecting circles.

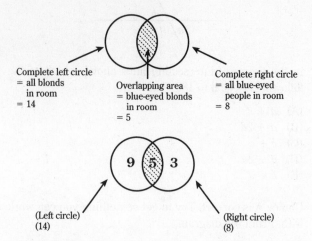

Complete left circle = all blonds in room = 14
Overlapping area = blue-eyed blonds in room = 5
Complete right circle = all blue-eyed people in room = 8

(Left circle) (14)
(Right circle) (8)

Above, subtracting: all blonds (14) − blue-eyed blonds (5), we get 9.
Above, subtracting: all blue-eyed people (8) − blue-eyed blonds (5), we get 3.
So the number of people in the room is $9 + 5 + 3 = 17$.

Method 2:

Total number of people are:

(a) blonds *without* blue eyes
(b) blue-eyed people *who are not* blond
(c) blue-eyed blonds

(a) There are 14 blonds and 5 blue-eyed blonds, so, subtracting, there are 9 blonds *without* blue eyes.
(b) There are 8 people with blue eyes and 5 blue-eyed blonds, so, subtracting, there are 3 blue-eyed people who are *not* blond.
(c) The number of blue-eyed blonds is 5 (given).

Adding the number of people in (a), (b), and (c), we get $9 + 3 + 5 = 17$.

*Note: This problem also appears in the 20 Shortest GRE Questions, Part 2.

Know and Use Facts about Triangles

By remembering these facts about triangles, you can often save yourself a lot of time and trouble.

I.

    If $a = b$, then $x = y$

The base angles of an isosceles triangle are equal.

    If $x = y$, then $a = b$

If the base angles of a triangle are equal, the triangle is isosceles.

II.

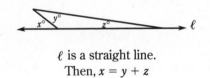

ℓ is a straight line.
Then, $x = y + z$

The measure of an exterior angle is equal to the sum of the measures of the remote interior angles.

III.

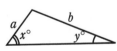   If $a < b$, then $y < x$

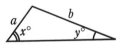   If $y < x$, then $a < b$

In a triangle, the greatest angle lies opposite the greatest side.

IV.

Similar Triangles

 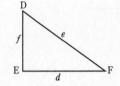

If $\triangle ABC \sim \triangle DEF$, then
$$m\angle A = m\angle D$$
$$m\angle B = m\angle E$$
$$m\angle C = m\angle F$$

and $\dfrac{a}{d} = \dfrac{b}{e} = \dfrac{c}{f}$

V.

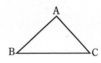 $m\angle A + m\angle B + m\angle C = 180°$

The sum of the interior angles of a triangle is 180 degrees.

VI.

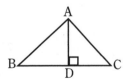   Area of $\triangle ABC = \dfrac{AD \times BC}{2}$

The area of a triangle is one-half the product of the altitude to a side and the side.

Note: If $m\angle A = 90°$,

Area also $= \dfrac{AB \times AC}{2}$

VII.

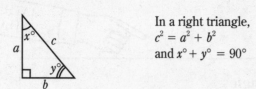

In a right triangle,
$c^2 = a^2 + b^2$
and $x° + y° = 90°$

(A) 20
(B) 25
(C) 26
(D) 45
(E) 48

Choice C is correct.

Method 1: Use VII above. Then,

$$x^2 = 24^2 + 10^2$$
$$= 576 + 100$$
$$= 676$$

Thus, $x = 26$ (*Answer*)

Method 2: Look at VIII. Notice that $\triangle MNP$ is similar to one of the standard triangles:

VIII. Memorize the following standard triangles:

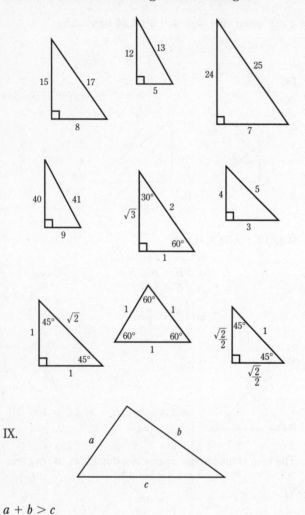

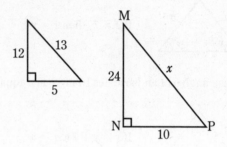

This is true because

$$\frac{12}{24} = \frac{5}{10} \text{ (Look at IV).}$$

Hence, $\frac{12}{24} = \frac{13}{x}$ or $x = 26$ (*Answer*)

EXAMPLE 2

If Masonville is 50 kilometers due north of Adamston and Elvira is 120 kilometers due east of Adamston, then the minimum distance between Masonville and Elvira is

(A) 125 kilometers
(B) 130 kilometers
(C) 145 kilometers
(D) 160 kilometers
(E) 170 kilometers

Choice B is correct. *Draw a diagram first.*

IX.

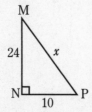

$a + b > c$
$a + c > b$
$b + c > a$

The sum of the lengths of two sides of a triangle is greater than the length of the third side. (This is like saying that the shortest distance between two points is a straight line.)

EXAMPLE 1

In the diagram below, what is the value of x?

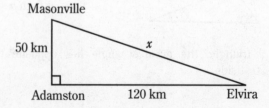

The given information translates into the diagram above. Note Statement VIII. The triangle above is a multiple of the special 5–12–13 right triangle.

$$50 = 10(5)$$
$$120 = 10(12)$$
$$\text{Thus, } x = 10(13) = 130 \text{ kilometers}$$

(*Note:* The Pythagorean Theorem could also have been used: $50^2 + 120^2 = x^2$.)

EXAMPLE 3

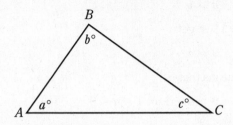

(Note: Figure is not drawn to scale.)

In triangle *ABC*, if $a > c$, which of the following is true?

(A) $BC = AC$
(B) $AB > BC$
(C) $AC > AB$
(D) $BC > AB$
(E) $BC > AC$

Choice D is correct. (Remember triangle inequality facts.) From basic geometry, Statement III, we know that, since $m\angle BAC > m\angle BCA$, then leg opposite $\angle BAC >$ leg opposite $\angle BCA$, or

$$BC > AB$$

EXAMPLE 4

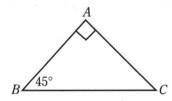

(Note: Figure is not drawn to scale.)

The triangle above has side $BC = 10$, angle $B = 45°$, and angle $A = 90°$. The area of the triangle

(A) is 15
(B) is 20
(C) is 25
(D) is 30
(E) Cannot be determined.

Choice C is correct.

First find angle C using Statement V.

$$90° + 45° + m\angle C = 180°$$

So $m\angle C = 45°$.
Using Statement I, we find $AB = AC$,
since $m\angle B = m\angle C = 45°$.

Since our right triangle *ABC* has $BC = 10$, using Statement VIII (the right triangle $\frac{\sqrt{2}}{2}, \frac{\sqrt{2}}{2}, 1$), multiply by 10 to get a right triangle:

$$\frac{10\sqrt{2}}{2}, \frac{10\sqrt{2}}{2}, 10$$

Thus side $AB = \frac{10\sqrt{2}}{2} = 5\sqrt{2}$

side $AC = \frac{10\sqrt{2}}{2} = 5\sqrt{2}$

Now the area of triangle *ABC*, according to Statement VI, is

$$\frac{5\sqrt{2} \times 5\sqrt{2}}{2} = \frac{25 \times 2}{2} = 25$$

EXAMPLE 5

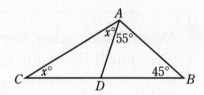

In the figure above, what is the value of x?

(A) 30
(B) 40
(C) 50
(D) 80
(E) 100

Choice B is correct.

Remember triangle facts. Use Statement II.

$\angle ADB$ is an exterior angle of $\triangle ACD$, so

$$m\angle ADB = x + x = 2x \qquad \boxed{1}$$

In $\triangle ADB$, the sum of its angles $= 180$ (Statement V), so

$$m\angle ADB + 55 + 45 = 180$$
or $\qquad m\angle ADB + 100 = 180$
or $\qquad\qquad m\angle ADB = 80 \qquad \boxed{2}$

Equating $\boxed{1}$ and $\boxed{2}$, we have

$$2x = 80$$
$$x = 40 \text{ (} \textit{Answer} \text{)}$$

EXAMPLE 6

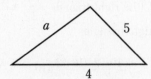

(Note: Figure is not drawn to scale.)

Which of the following represent all of the possibilities for the value of a in the figure above?

(A) $1 < a < 9$
(B) $4 < a < 5$
(C) $0 < a < 9$
(D) $4 < a < 9$
(E) $5 < a < 9$

Choice A is correct. From Statement IX, since the sum of the lengths of two sides of a triangle is greater than the length of the third side, we have:

$$a + 5 > 4 \qquad \boxed{1}$$
$$a + 4 > 5 \qquad \boxed{2}$$
$$5 + 4 > a \qquad \boxed{3}$$

From $\boxed{2}$ we get:

$$a > 1.$$

From $\boxed{3}$ we get:

$$9 > a.$$

This means that

$$9 > a > 1, \text{ or } 1 < a < 9.$$

When Calculating Answers, Never Multiply and/or Do Long Division If Reducing Can Be Done First

Note: On the GRE exam, because calculators are permitted, you may do the following problems with a calculator also. But it would be wise for you to see the other approach too—how the problem can be solved *without* the use of a calculator.

EXAMPLE 1

If $w = \dfrac{81 \times 150}{45 \times 40}$, then $w =$

(A) 3
(B) $6\frac{3}{4}$
(C) $7\frac{1}{4}$
(D) 9
(E) $20\frac{1}{4}$

Do not multiply in this case. 81×150 and 45×40 to get
$$\dfrac{12,150}{1,800}$$

Factor first: $\dfrac{\overbrace{9 \times 9}^{81} \times \overbrace{15 \times 10}^{150}}{\underbrace{9 \times 5}_{45} \times \underbrace{4 \times 10}_{40}}$

Then cancel like factors in numerator and denominator:

$$\dfrac{\cancel{9} \times 9 \times 15 \times \cancel{10}}{\cancel{9} \times 5 \times 4 \times \cancel{10}}$$

Reduce further: $\dfrac{9 \times \cancel{5} \times 3}{\cancel{5} \times 4}$

Then simplify: $\dfrac{27}{4} = 6\frac{3}{4}$ *(Answer)*

Thus, Choice B is correct.

EXAMPLE 2

$$\dfrac{4^2 + 4^2 + 4^2}{3^3 + 3^3 + 3^3} =$$

(A) $\dfrac{16}{27}$

(B) $\dfrac{8}{9}$

(C) $\dfrac{4}{3}$

(D) $\dfrac{64}{27}$

(E) $\dfrac{512}{81}$

Choice A is correct.

$$\frac{4^2 + 4^2 + 4^2}{3^3 + 3^3 + 3^3} =$$

Factor and reduce: $\quad \dfrac{\cancel{3}\,(4^2)}{\cancel{3}\,(3^3)} =$

$$\frac{16}{27}$$

EXAMPLE 3

If $6 \times 7 \times 8 \times 9 = \dfrac{12 \times 14 \times 18}{x}$, then $x =$

(A) $\dfrac{1}{2}$

(B) 1

(C) 4

(D) 8

(E) 12

Choice B is correct.

Given: $6 \times 7 \times 8 \times 9 = \dfrac{12 \times 14 \times 18}{x}$ $\qquad$ $\boxed{1}$

so that $\quad x = \dfrac{12 \times 14 \times 18}{6 \times 7 \times 8 \times 9}$ $\qquad$ $\boxed{2}$

Do *not* multiply the numbers out in the numerator and denominator of $\boxed{2}$! It is too much work! Rewrite $\boxed{2}$.

Factor and reduce:

$$x = \frac{12 \times 14 \times 18}{6 \times 7 \times 8 \times 9} = \frac{2 \times \cancel{6} \times 2 \times \cancel{7} \times 2 \times \cancel{9}}{\cancel{6} \times \cancel{7} \times 8 \times \cancel{9}}$$

$$= \frac{2 \times 2 \times 2}{8} = \frac{\cancel{8}}{\cancel{8}} = 1 \qquad (Answer)$$

EXAMPLE 4

If $\dfrac{81 \times y}{27} = 21$, then $y =$

(A) $\dfrac{1}{21}$

(B) $\dfrac{1}{7}$

(C) 3

(D) 7

(E) 21

Choice D is correct.

Given: $\dfrac{81 \times y}{27} = 21$

Multiply both sides by 27 to get $81 \times y = 21 \times 27$.

$$y = \frac{21 \times 27}{81}$$

Factor and reduce:

$$y = \frac{3 \cdot 7 \times 3 \cdot \cancel{9}}{9 \cdot \cancel{9}}$$

$$= \frac{\cancel{3} \cdot 7 \times \cancel{3}}{\cancel{3} \cdot \cancel{3}}$$

$$y = 7 \qquad\qquad (Answer)$$

EXAMPLE 5

Find the value of $\dfrac{y^2 - 7y + 10}{y - 2}$ rounded to the nearest whole number if $y = 8.000001$.

(A) 2

(B) 3

(C) 5

(D) 6

(E) 16

Choice B is correct.

Given: $\dfrac{y^2 - 7y + 10}{y - 2}$ $\qquad$ $\boxed{1}$

Factor and reduce:

Factor the numerator of $\boxed{1}$. We get

$$\frac{(y - 5)\,\cancel{(y - 2)}}{\cancel{y - 2}} = y - 5 \qquad \boxed{2}$$

Substitute 8.000001 in $\boxed{2}$. We have

$$8.000001 - 5 =$$
$$3.000001 \approx 3 \qquad (Answer)$$

Quantitative Comparison Strategies

Introduction

In the quantitative comparison question, you are presented with quantities under two columns. You have to determine whether the Quantity A is less than, greater than, or equal to the Quantity B. There is also a possibility that a definite comparison cannot be made. In very, very few cases will you ever have to calculate quantities. Since you just have to compare the relative values, you can usually manipulate the columns to get a simple comparison, as you will see.

Things You Must Know First

1. Memorize directions for quantitative comparison questions. The following rewording of the standard directions given on the GRE tells you *precisely* how to choose an answer:

- If Quantity A is *always greater* than Quantity B (or if Quantity B is always less than Quantity A), select Choice A.

- If Quantity A is *always less* than Quantity B (or if Quantity B is always greater than Quantity A), select Choice B.

- If Quantity A is *always equal* to Quantity B, select Choice C.

- If there is no way to make any of the above definite comparisons, select Choice D. (In other words, if a definite comparison or relationship cannot be made, select Choice D.)

Note: If there is a quantity centered between the columns, you may use that information in the columns. A symbol such as x, a, etc., means the same thing in both columns. All variables like x, n, a, represent real numbers. Make sure that you memorize these directions.

EXAMPLE

Quantity A	Quantity B
1	$\frac{1}{2}$

In this example you would select Choice A, since Quantity A > Quantity B.

2. When there's a quantity between the columns, use the *middle quantity* in both columns.

EXAMPLE

$$x = 2$$

Quantity A	Quantity B
x	$x + 1$

In this example, substitute 2 for x:

2	$(2 + 1)$

Quantity A < Quantity B, so Choice B is correct.

3. You can add or subtract the same quantity to (or from) both columns and still get the same comparison.

EXAMPLE

Quantity A	Quantity B	
$8 - 3$	7	(Quantity A < Quantity B)

Add 3 to both columns:

Quantity A	Quantity B	
8	$7 + 3$	(Quantity A < Quantity B)

SUMMARY DIRECTIONS FOR COMPARISON QUESTIONS

Choose A if Quantity A is greater;
Choose B if Quantity B is greater;
Choose C if the two quantities are equal;

Choose D if the relationship cannot be determined from the information given.

4. You can multiply or divide both columns by the *same positive* number and still get the same comparison.

EXAMPLE

Quantity A	Quantity B	
$\frac{7}{4}$	$\frac{9}{4}$	(Quantity A < Quantity B)

Multiply by 4:

7	9	(Quantity A < Quantity B)

5. REMEMBER THE FOLLOWING:

- Any variable like x, a, etc., can be *negative, positive, 0,* or a fraction unless otherwise specified.

- If you get different comparisons when you try different numbers (for example, if you were to find that in one case Quantity A > Quantity B and in another Quantity A < Quantity B), then Choice D is correct.

- Never divide or multiply columns by a negative number or by 0.

MATH STRATEGY A

Cancel Numbers or Expressions Common to Both Columns by Addition or Subtraction

If the same expression or number appears in both columns, we can then subtract it from both columns.

Examples 1, 4, and 5 can also be solved with the aid of a calculator. However, to illustrate the effectiveness of Math Strategy A, we did not use the calculator method of solution in these examples.

EXAMPLE 1

Quantity A	Quantity B
$\frac{1}{2} + \frac{1}{6} + \frac{1}{17}$	$\frac{1}{17} + \frac{1}{2} + \frac{1}{7}$

Choice A is correct.
Don't add fractions in columns! Cancel common quantities:

Quantity A	Quantity B
$\cancel{\frac{1}{2}} + \frac{1}{6} + \cancel{\frac{1}{17}}$	$\cancel{\frac{1}{17}} + \cancel{\frac{1}{2}} + \frac{1}{7}$
$\frac{1}{6}$	$\frac{1}{7}$

Quantity A > Quantity B.

EXAMPLE 2

Quantity A	Quantity B
	$y > 0$
$w + x$	$w + x + y$

Choice B is correct. Since $w + x$ appears in both columns, we can subtract $w + x$ from both columns to get

Quantity A	Quantity B
0	y

and from the given information we know that $y > 0$.

EXAMPLE 3

Quantity A	Quantity B
y is an integer	
$y < 0$	
-1	$\frac{1}{y} - 1$

Choice A is correct.

SUMMARY DIRECTIONS FOR COMPARISON QUESTIONS

Choose A if Quantity A is greater;
Choose B if Quantity B is greater;
Choose C if the two quantities are equal;

Choose D if the relationship cannot be determined from the information given.

Quantity A	Quantity B
-1	$\dfrac{1}{y} - 1$

Cancel -1: $-\cancel{1}$ $\qquad$ $\dfrac{1}{y} - \cancel{1}$

$\downarrow$ $\qquad\qquad$ $\downarrow$

0 $\qquad\qquad$ $\dfrac{1}{y}$

Since $y < 0$, $\dfrac{1}{y} < 0$, and Quantity A > Quantity B.

EXAMPLE 4

Quantity A	Quantity B
$5 - 0.005$	$5 - 0.0055$

Choice A is correct.

Quantity A	Quantity B
$5 - 0.005$	$5 - 0.0055$

Cancel 5:

$\cancel{5} - 0.005$	$\cancel{5} - 0.0055$
-0.0050	-0.0055
-0.0050 $\quad > \quad$	-0.0055

EXAMPLE 5

Quantity A	Quantity B
	$a \le 15$	
$7 + 3 + 15$	$7 + 3 + a$

Choice D is correct.

Quantity A	Quantity B
	$a \le 15$	
$7 + 3 + 15$	$7 + 3 + a$

Cancel $7 + 3$:

$\cancel{7} + \cancel{3} + 15$	$\cancel{7} + \cancel{3} + a$
15	a

Since $15 \ge a$ (given), you can't make a definite comparison.

EXAMPLE 6

Quantity A	Quantity B

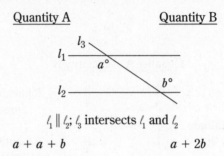

$l_1 \parallel l_2$; l_3 intersects l_1 and l_2

$a + a + b$	$a + 2b$

Choice C is correct.

Quantity A	Quantity B
$a + a + b$	$a + 2b$

Subtract a, b from both columns:

$\cancel{a} + a + \cancel{b}$	$\cancel{a} + 2b$
$-\cancel{a} - \cancel{b}$	$-\cancel{a} - b$
$\downarrow$	$\downarrow$
a	b

Now $a = b$ because if $l_1 \parallel l_2$, alternate interior angles a and b are equal.

Cancel Numbers or Expressions (Positive Quantities Only!!) Common to Both Columns by Multiplication or Division

If the same expression or number (positive quantities only which may be multiplied by other expressions) appears in both columns, we can then divide it from both columns. NEVER divide both columns by zero or a negative number.

Examples 1 and 3 can also be solved with the aid of a calculator. However, to illustrate the effectiveness of Math Strategy B, we did not use the calculator method of solution in these examples.

EXAMPLE 1

Quantity A	Quantity B
$24 \times 46 \times 35$	$46 \times 24 \times 36$

Choice B is correct.

Don't multiply out! Cancel 24×46 from both columns (by dividing both columns by 24×46).

Quantity A	Quantity B
$\cancel{24} \times \cancel{46} \times 35$	$\cancel{46} \times \cancel{24} \times 36$

Quantity A < Quantity B.

EXAMPLE 2

Quantity A	Quantity B

$$m > 1$$
$$n > 0$$

Quantity A	Quantity B
mn	n

Choice A is correct.

Since $n > 0$ and n appears in both columns, we can divide it from both columns to get

Quantity A	Quantity B
m	1

and we are given that $m > 1$.

EXAMPLE 3

Quantity A	Quantity B
$\dfrac{3}{14} \times \dfrac{5}{7} \times \dfrac{2}{3}$	$\dfrac{5}{7} \times \dfrac{3}{14} \times \dfrac{3}{4}$

Choice B is correct.

Quantity A	Quantity B
$\dfrac{3}{14} \times \dfrac{5}{7} \times \dfrac{2}{3}$	$\dfrac{5}{7} \times \dfrac{3}{14} \times \dfrac{3}{4}$

Cancel common fractions:

Quantity A	Quantity B
$\cancel{\dfrac{3}{14}} \times \cancel{\dfrac{5}{7}} \times \dfrac{2}{3}$	$\cancel{\dfrac{5}{7}} \times \cancel{\dfrac{3}{14}} \times \dfrac{3}{4}$
$\dfrac{2}{3}$	$\dfrac{3}{4}$
$\dfrac{2}{3}$ <	$\dfrac{3}{4}$

EXAMPLE 4

Quantity A	Quantity B

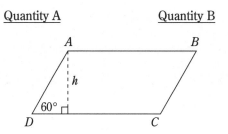

$ABCD$ is a parallelogram

$h \times AB$	$AD \times CD$

Choice B is correct.

SUMMARY DIRECTIONS FOR COMPARISON QUESTIONS

Choose A if Quantity A is greater; Choose B if Quantity B is greater; Choose C if the two quantities are equal;	Choose D if the relationship cannot be determined from the information given.

Label $AB = a$ and $AD = b$

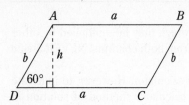

$AB = a$ $AD = b$ $CD = a$

	Quantity A	Quantity B
	$h \times AB$	$AD \times CD$
So	$h \times a$	$b \times a$

Cancel a:

$$h \qquad\qquad b$$

Since b is the hypotenuse of the right triangle, it must be greater than h. So $h < b$.

MATH STRATEGY C

When a Comparison of the Two Columns Is Difficult, Use Numbers in Place of Variables

Sometimes by using numbers in place of variables, you can show that different comparisons exist, making choice D correct.

EXAMPLE 1

Quantity A	Quantity B
	$b > 1$
	$a > 1$
	$a \neq b$
$\dfrac{a}{b}$	$\dfrac{b}{a}$

Choice D is correct. Let us take numerical examples that satisfy $a, b > 1$.

CASE 1

$a = 6, b = 3$ Then the columns become

Quantity A	Quantity B
$\dfrac{6}{3} = 3$	$\dfrac{3}{6} = \dfrac{1}{2}$

and the quantity in Quantity A is greater.

CASE 2

$$a = 4, b = 12$$

Then the columns become

Quantity A	Quantity B
$\dfrac{4}{12} = \dfrac{1}{3}$	$\dfrac{12}{4} = 3$

and the quantity in *Quantity B is greater.*

In one case, Quantity A > Quantity B. In the second case, Quantity B > Quantity A. Thus, a definite comparison *cannot* be made.

EXAMPLE 2

Quantity A	Quantity B
	$a > 0$
$\dfrac{1}{a}$	a

Choice D is correct.

Often you can find a number for the variable that makes the columns equal. Then all you have to find is another number that will make them unequal. In the above example, choose $a = 1$. This makes the columns equal. You can see that any other value of a, like $a = 100$, will make the columns unequal. Thus, a definite relation *cannot* be obtained.

EXAMPLE 3

Quantity A	Quantity B
$30 > ab > 5$	
a and b are whole numbers	
$a + b$	ab

Choice D is correct.

Try $a = 6$, $b = 4$. We get:

Quantity A		Quantity B
$6 + 4$		6×4
10		24
10	$<$	24

Try $a = 1$, $b = 6$. We get:

Quantity A		Quantity B
$1 + 6$		1×6
7		6
7	$>$	6

A definite comparison cannot be made.

EXAMPLES 4–6

	Quantity A	Quantity B
4.	$a > b > 1$	
	a and b are whole numbers	
	a^b	b^a

	Quantity A	Quantity B
5.	x is an integer	
	x^{x+1}	$(x+1)^x$

	Quantity A	Quantity B
6.	$ab \neq 0$	
	$-a^2b$	ab^2

EXPLANATORY ANSWERS FOR EXAMPLES 4–6

	Quantity A		Quantity B
4. (D)	$a > b > 1$		
	a^b		b^a
	Let $a = 3$, $b = 2$:		
	3^2		2^3
	9	$>$	8
	Let $a = 4$, $b = 2$:		
	4^2		2^4
	16	$=$	16

A definite comparison cannot be made.

	Quantity A		Quantity B
5. (D)	x is an integer		
	x^{x+1}		$(x+1)^x$
	Try $x = 1$:		
	1^{1+1}		$(1+1)^1$
	1	$<$	2
	Try $x = 2$:		
	2^{2+1}		$(2+1)^2$
	8	$<$	9
	Make sure. Try $x = 3$:		
	3^{3+1}		$(3+1)^3$
	81	$>$	64

In one case Quantity A $<$ Quantity B; in another case Quantity A $>$ Quantity B. Thus, a definite comparison cannot be made.

	Quantity A		Quantity B
6. (D)	$ab \neq 0$		
	$-a^2b$		ab^2

You can't cancel or divide by a or b because a or b *may be negative*. Try $a = 1$, $b = 1$. We get:

-1	$<$	1

Try $a = -1$, $b = 1$. We get:

-1	$=$	-1

A definite comparison cannot be made.

For examples 7–10, use the Gruber equal/not equal method to prove that Choice D is correct

If Possible, Find a Number (or Numbers) That Makes the Columns Equal and Another Number (or Numbers) That Makes Them Unequal to Ensure That Choice D Is the Right Answer.

If you feel that a definite comparison cannot be made, try to find one particular number that when substituted for the variable in the columns will make the columns *equal*. All you then have to do to prove that Choice D is correct is find another number that will make the columns *unequal*.

EXAMPLE 7

Quantity A	Quantity B
$x^2 = y^2$	
x^2	xy

Choice D is correct.

SUMMARY DIRECTIONS FOR COMPARISON QUESTIONS

Choose A if Quantity A is greater;
Choose B if Quantity B is greater;
Choose C if the two quantities are equal;

Choose D if the relationship cannot be determined from the information given.

Quantity A	Quantity B

$$x^2 = y^2$$

| x^2 | xy |

You can't divide by x since x may be negative.
Try $x = 1, y = 1$.

| 1^2 | $(1)(1)$ |
| 1   = | 1 |

Now try $x = -1$, and $y = +1$.

$(-1)^2$	$(-1)(+1)$
↓	↓
+1 >	−1

Thus a definite comparison cannot be made.

EXAMPLE 8

Quantity A	Quantity B

$$0 > a$$

| $(a + 4)(a + 5)$ | $(a + 4)^2$ |

Choice D is correct.

You may be tempted to cancel $(a + 4)$ from both columns. Because $(a + 4)$ *may be zero* or negative, you are not allowed to do this. If you did, you'd get

Quantity A	Quantity B
$a + 5$	$a + 4$
5 >	4

and you would think Choice A correct, which is *wrong*! Here's the best way:

Let $a = -4$. That way the columns become equal (both equal to 0).
Now let $a = -1$:

$$(-1 + 4)(-1 + 5) \quad \neq \quad (-1 + 4)^2$$

Don't bother to calculate out, because you can see that the columns aren't equal. Thus a definite comparison cannot be made.

EXAMPLE 9

Quantity A	Quantity B

$$x > 0, y > 0, z > 0$$

| $\dfrac{1}{x+y+z}$ | $x + y + z$ |

Choice D is correct.

Let $x = y = z = \frac{1}{3}$ to get the columns *equal*.

Thus:

$$\dfrac{1}{\frac{1}{3}+\frac{1}{3}+\frac{1}{3}} = 1 \qquad\qquad 1$$

Any other numbers, such as $x = 2, y = 2, z = 2$, will make the columns *unequal*:

$$\dfrac{1}{2+2+2} \qquad \neq \qquad 2 + 2 + 2$$

Therefore, Choice D is correct.

EXAMPLE 10

Quantity A	Quantity B
$(a^3)^4$	a^7

Choice D is correct.

Quantity A	Quantity B
$(a^3)^4$	a^7

First calculate $(a^3)^4 = a^{12}$ (remember your basic math skills?). The columns become:

| a^{12} | a^7 |

Now try $a = 1$ to get the columns equal. If we then try $a = 2$, we can see that the columns are unequal. Thus a definite comparison cannot be made.

MATH STRATEGY **D**

> ## To Make a Comparison Simpler—Especially of Fractions—Multiply, Divide, Add to, or Subtract from Both Columns by a Quantity (Never Multiply or Divide by Zero or by a Negative Number)

Examples 1, 3, 4, 12, 13, 16, and 18 can also be solved with the aid of a calculator and some with the aid of a calculator allowing for exponential calculations. However, to illustrate the effectiveness of Math Strategy D, we did not use the calculator method of solution in these examples.

EXAMPLE 1

Quantity A	Quantity B
1	$\dfrac{\frac{7}{9}}{\frac{9}{7}}$

Choice A is correct.

Don't divide 7/9 by 9/7. <u>Multiply</u> both columns by 9/7 to get rid of the complicated fraction in Quantity B:

Quantity A	Quantity B
$1 \times 9/7$	$\dfrac{7/9}{\cancel{9/7}} \times \cancel{9/7}$
9/7	7/9

Quantity A > Quantity B.

EXAMPLE 2

Quantity A	Quantity B

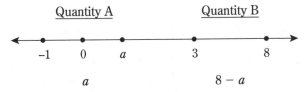

a	$8 - a$

Choice B is correct.

Get rid of the minus sign by <u>adding</u> a to both columns:

Quantity A	Quantity B
$a + a$	$8 - a + a$
$2a$	8

Divide by 2: a 4

Now look at the diagram: $a < 3$, so $a < 4$.
Quantity A < Quantity B.

EXAMPLE 3

Quantity A	Quantity B
$\sqrt{19} - \sqrt{3}$	$\sqrt{16}$

Choice B is correct. First, get rid of the minus sign by adding $\sqrt{3}$ to both columns.

Quantity A	Quantity B
$\sqrt{19}$	$\sqrt{16} + \sqrt{3}$

Now *square* both columns.

Quantity A	Quantity B
$(\sqrt{19})^2$	$(\sqrt{16} + \sqrt{3})^2$
19	$16 + 3 + 2\sqrt{16}\sqrt{3}$
19	$19 + 2\sqrt{16}\sqrt{3}$

Cancel the 19s:

Quantity A	Quantity B
Quantity B > Quantity A.	
0	$2\sqrt{16}\sqrt{3}$

For Examples 4–7, try to get rid of minus signs by adding.

To Simplify a Problem, You Can Often Get Rid of Minus Signs Just by Adding the Same Quantity to Both Columns.

You learned addition before you learned subtraction, and addition *is* more fundamental and basic than subtraction. Thus it would seem that it is easier and more natural to add whenever you can rather than to subtract. So try not to deal with minus signs or subtraction if the problem looks tedious—try to use addition.

SUMMARY DIRECTIONS FOR COMPARISON QUESTIONS

Choose A if Quantity A is greater;
Choose B if Quantity B is greater;
Choose C if the two quantities are equal;

Choose D if the relationship cannot be determined from the information given.

EXAMPLES 4–7

Quantity A	Quantity B
4. $\dfrac{7}{12} - \dfrac{1}{14}$	$\dfrac{6}{14}$

5. $0 > a > b$

| $-3b$ | a |

6.

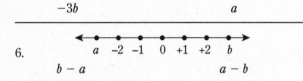

| $b - a$ | $a - b$ |

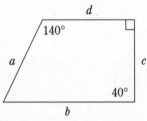

Note: Figure is not drawn to scale.

7. $a^2 - c^2$ \qquad\qquad $d^2 - b^2$

EXPLANATORY ANSWERS FOR EXAMPLES 4–7

Quantity A	Quantity B
4. (A) $\dfrac{7}{12} - \dfrac{1}{14}$	$\dfrac{6}{14}$

Add $\dfrac{1}{14}$ to both columns to get rid of the minus sign:

$$\dfrac{7}{12} - \dfrac{1}{14} + \dfrac{1}{14} \qquad\qquad \dfrac{6}{14} + \dfrac{1}{14}$$

$$\dfrac{7}{12} - \dfrac{\not1}{\not14} + \dfrac{\not1}{\not14} \qquad\qquad \dfrac{7}{14}$$

$$\dfrac{7}{12} \quad > \quad \dfrac{7}{14}$$

Quantity A	Quantity B
5. (A)	$0 > a > b$
$-3b$	a

Add $3b$ to both columns:

$-3b + 3b$	$a + 3b$
$\downarrow$	$\downarrow$
0	$a + 3b$

Since $0 > a$ and $0 > b$, $a + 3b$ is *negative*. So Quantity A > Quantity B.

Quantity A	Quantity B

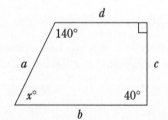

| $b - a$ | $a - b$ |

6. (A)

Add a to both columns; then add b to both columns to get rid of minus signs:

	$b - a$	$a - b$
Add a:	$b - \not a + \not a$	$a - b + a$
	b	$2a - b$
Add b:	$b + b$	$2a - \not b + \not b$
	$2b$	$2a$
Divide by 2:	b	a
From diagram:	b	$>$	a

7. (C)

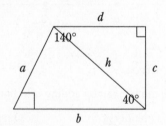

Note: Figure is not drawn to scale.

The sum of the internal angles of a quadrilateral is 360 degrees. Find remaining angle:

$$140 + 40 + 90 + x = 360$$
$$x = 90$$

Now <u>draw</u> line and <u>label</u> it h.

Note: Figure is not drawn to scale.

By the Pythagorean Theorem,

$$a^2 + b^2 = h^2$$
$$d^2 + c^2 = h^2$$
$$\text{so } a^2 + b^2 = d^2 + c^2$$

Add c^2 and b^2 to both columns:

$\boxed{1}$

Quantity A	Quantity B
$a^2 - c^2$	$d^2 - b^2$
Add c^2: a^2	$d^2 - b^2 + c^2$
Add b^2: $a^2 + b^2$	$d^2 + c^2$

The columns are therefore equal because of $\boxed{1}$.

For Examples 8–14, multiply or divide to simplify the problem, but never multiply by 0 or by a negative number.

Often You Can Multiply or Divide Each Quantity by the Same Number to Simplify the Problem and Avoid Tedious Calculations.

EXAMPLES 8–14

	Quantity A		Quantity B
8.		$a \neq 0$	
	0		$\dfrac{5}{a^2}$
9.		$a > 0$	
	$2a$		$\dfrac{a}{0.4}$
10.		$a > 0$	
	$\dfrac{1}{a}$		a
11.		$a > b > 0$	
	$\dfrac{a^2 + b^2}{a - b}$		$a - b$
12.	7×8^{12}		8×7^{12}
13.	35×65		34×66
14.		$a > b > 0$	
	$\dfrac{2ab}{a + b}$		$\dfrac{a+b}{2}$

EXPLANATORY ANSWERS FOR EXAMPLES 8–14

8. (B)

Quantity A		Quantity B
	$a \neq 0$	
0		$\dfrac{5}{a^2}$

Since $a^2 > 0$ (even if a is negative, $a^2 > 0$) <u>you can multiply by a^2:</u>

0		$\dfrac{5}{a^2}$
$0 \times a^2$		$\dfrac{5}{\not{a^2}} \times \not{a^2}$
0		5
0	$<$	5

9. (B)

Quantity A		Quantity B
	$a > 0$	
$2a$		$\dfrac{a}{0.4}$

<u>Multiply by 0.4 to get rid of the denominator:</u>

$(2a)(0.4)$		$\dfrac{a}{\not{0.4}} \not{0.4}$
$\downarrow$		$\downarrow$
$0.8a$		a

Since $a > 0$, <u>divide by a:</u>

$\dfrac{0.8\not{a}}{\not{a}}$		$\dfrac{\not{a}}{\not{a}}$
$\downarrow$		$\downarrow$
0.8		1
0.8	$<$	1

10. (D)

Quantity A		Quantity B
	$a > 0$	
$\dfrac{1}{a}$		a

Since $a > 0$, <u>multiply both columns by a:</u>

$$a > 0$$

$\dfrac{1}{\not{a}} \times \not{a}$		$a \times a$
1		a^2

Now you have to be careful: If $a > 1$, certainly $a^2 > 1$. But if a is a fraction such as $\dfrac{1}{4}$, then $a^2 = \dfrac{1}{16} < 1$, so a definite comparison cannot be made. This is because in one case, $a^2 > 1$, and in another case, $a^2 < 1$.

SUMMARY DIRECTIONS FOR COMPARISON QUESTIONS

Choose A if Quantity A is greater;
Choose B if Quantity B is greater;
Choose C if the two quantities are equal;

Choose D if the relationship cannot be determined from the information given.

Quantity A	Quantity B

11. (A) $a > b > 0$

$$\frac{a^2 + b^2}{a - b} \qquad a - b$$

Since $a > b$, $a - b > 0$,
So we can <u>multiply both columns by $a - b$</u>:

$$\frac{a^2 + b^2}{a-b} \times \cancel{a-b} \qquad (a - b)(a - b)$$

$$a^2 + b^2 \qquad a^2 - 2ab + b^2$$

Cancel $a^2 + b^2$ from both columns:

$$0 \qquad -2ab$$

Since $a > b > 0$, $2ab > 0$ and $-2ab < 0$. Thus Quantity A > Quantity B.

Quantity A	Quantity B

12. (A) 7×8^{12} $\qquad$ 8×7^{12}

Use logic. It's obviously too hard to calculate 7×8^{12} and 8×7^{12}. So let's try to take advantage of the curious form of the numbers. <u>Divide</u> both columns by 7 and then divide by 8:

$$\frac{7 \times 8^{12}}{7} \qquad \frac{8 \times 7^{12}}{7}$$

$$8^{12} \qquad 8 \times 7^{11}$$

Now divide by 8:

$$\frac{8^{12}}{8} \qquad \frac{8 \times 7^{11}}{8}$$

$$8^{11} \qquad 7^{11}$$

Quantity A > Quantity B.

Quantity A	Quantity B
35×65	34×66

13. (A) You *do not* have to multiply 35×65 and 34×66! *Note the relationship of the numbers in the columns:* That is, between 35 and 34 and 65 and 66. Divide 34 into the quantities in both columns and divide 65 into the quantities in both columns. We get

Quantity A	Quantity B
$\dfrac{35 \times 65}{34 \times 65}$	$\dfrac{34 \times 66}{34 \times 65}$

Simplified, this becomes

Quantity A	Quantity B
$\dfrac{35}{34}$	$\dfrac{66}{65}$

Now $\dfrac{35}{34}$ is $1\dfrac{1}{34}$ and $\dfrac{66}{65}$ is $1\dfrac{1}{65}$. Since $\dfrac{1}{34} > \dfrac{1}{65}$, the quantity in Quantity A is greater than the quantity in Quantity B, and Choice A is correct.

14. (A)

Quantity A	Quantity B

$$a > b > 0$$

$$\frac{2ab}{a + b} \qquad \frac{a + b}{2}$$

<u>Multiply</u> both columns by $a + b$ and by 2 to get rid of fractions:

Quantity A	Quantity B
$2(a+b) \times \dfrac{2ab}{a+b}$	$2(a+b)\dfrac{a+b}{2}$
↓	↓
$2(\cancel{a+b}) \times \dfrac{2ab}{\cancel{a+b}}$	$\dfrac{\cancel{2}(a+b)(a+b)}{\cancel{2}}$
↓	↓
$4ab$	$(a+b)(a+b)$
↓	↓
$4ab$	$a^2 + 2ab + b^2$
↓	↓

Subtract $4ab$:

$4ab - 4ab$	$a^2 + 2ab + b^2 - 4ab$
↓	↓
0	$a^2 - 2ab + b^2$
↓	↓
0	$(a - b)(a - b)$

Since $a > b > 0$, $(a - b)(a - b) > 0$
So Quantity B > Quantity A.

For Examples 15–18, square both columns to get rid of square roots.

In Comparing Square Roots, Instead of Calculating or Substituting Numbers, You Can Usually Just Square the Square Roots to Get Rid of Square Root Signs.

EXAMPLE 15

Quantity A	Quantity B
$a > 0$	
$\sqrt{a} + \sqrt{3}$	$\sqrt{a+3}$

Choice A is correct.
Square both columns:

Quantity A	Quantity B
$(\sqrt{a} + \sqrt{3})^2$	$(\sqrt{a+3})^2$
$\downarrow$	$\downarrow$
$a + 3 + 2\sqrt{a}\sqrt{3}$	$a + 3$

Cancel $a + 3$:

$a + 3 + 2\sqrt{a}\sqrt{3}$	$a + 3$
$\downarrow$	$\downarrow$
$2\sqrt{a}\sqrt{3}$	0
$2\sqrt{a}\sqrt{3}$ $\quad>\quad$	0

EXAMPLES 16–18

	Quantity A	Quantity B
16.	$\sqrt{19}$	$\sqrt{6} + \sqrt{13}$
17.	$x > y > 0$	
	$\sqrt{x+y}$	$\sqrt{x} + \sqrt{y}$
18.	$\sqrt{17} - \sqrt{3}$	$\sqrt{14}$

EXPLANATORY ANSWERS FOR EXAMPLES 16–18

16. (B)

Quantity A	Quantity B
$\sqrt{19}$	$\sqrt{6} + \sqrt{13}$

Square both columns:

$\sqrt{19} \times \sqrt{19}$	$(\sqrt{6} + \sqrt{13})(\sqrt{6} + \sqrt{13})$
19	$6 + 13 + 2\sqrt{13}\sqrt{6}$

Cancel 19:

0 $\quad<\quad$	$2\sqrt{13}\sqrt{6}$

Quantity A	Quantity B
$x > y > 0$	

17. (B) $\sqrt{x+y}$ $\qquad$ $\sqrt{x} + \sqrt{y}$

Square both columns:

$(\sqrt{x+y})(\sqrt{x+y})$	$(\sqrt{x} + \sqrt{y})(\sqrt{x} + \sqrt{y})$
$x + y$	$x + y + 2\sqrt{x}\sqrt{y}$

Cancel *common* $x + y$ from both columns:

0	$2\sqrt{x}\sqrt{y}$

Quantity A < Quantity B.

Quantity A	Quantity B
18. (B) $\sqrt{17} - \sqrt{3}$	$\sqrt{14}$

First, *add* $\sqrt{3}$ to both columns to get rid of $(-\sqrt{3})$ from Quantity A. (It is usually easier to work with + than with −.)

$\sqrt{17} - \sqrt{3} + \sqrt{3}$	$\sqrt{14} + \sqrt{3}$

Now square both columns:

17	$(\sqrt{14} + \sqrt{3})^2$
17	$14 + 3 + 2\sqrt{14}\sqrt{3}$
17 $\quad<\quad$	$17 + 2\sqrt{14}\sqrt{3}$

For Examples 19–22, make sure you don't divide by 0 or by a negative number.

When Canceling a Quantity from Both Columns, Make Sure You Are Not Actually Dividing by 0 or by a Negative Number.

EXAMPLE 19

Quantity A	Quantity B
$0 > a$	
$b > 2$	
$\dfrac{a}{b}$	ab

Choice A is correct.
Don't divide by a, because $a < 0$. But you can multiply by b:

Quantity A	Quantity B
$\dfrac{a}{b} \times b$	$ab \times b$

Now since a is negative and $b > 2$, you can see that $a > ab^2$, and so Quantity A is greater than Quantity B.

EXAMPLES 20–22

	Quantity A	Quantity B
20.	bc	ab
		$c > b > a$
21.	ab	b
		$0 > a > b$
22.	a^2	a
		$a < 1$

SUMMARY DIRECTIONS FOR COMPARISON QUESTIONS

Choose A if Quantity A is greater;
Choose B if Quantity B is greater;
Choose C if the two quantities are equal;

Choose D if the relationship cannot be determined from the information given.

EXPLANATORY ANSWERS FOR EXAMPLES 20–22

20. (D)

Quantity A	Quantity B
$c > b > a$	
bc	ab

Don't cancel b since b may be negative.
Suppose $b = 0$. Then the columns are =
Suppose $b = 1$. Then Quantity A > Quantity B since $c > a$. Therefore, you cannot make a definite comparison.

21. (A)

Quantity A	Quantity B
$0 > a > b$	
ab	b

Since $b < 0$, don't cancel b.
But think—if $0 > a$ and $0 > b$, then ab is *positive*.
So:

Quantity A		Quantity B
positive number		negative number
positive number	>	negative number

22. (D)

Quantity A	Quantity B
$a < 1$	
a^2	a

We don't know if $a = 0$, so we can't divide by a to get a comparison. However, we know that a^2 (Quantity A) is always positive or zero. If a is negative, Quantity A > Quantity B. If $a = 0$, Quantity A = Quantity B. In one case, Quantity A > Quantity B, in another Quantity A = Quantity B. So a definite comparison cannot be made.

MATH STRATEGY E

Try to Get the Columns and the Given to Look Similar

The quantities to be compared in the columns and the information given may look different. Whenever it is possible, you should try to get the columns to look like what is given, or try to get the given to look like what is in the columns.

EXAMPLE 1

Quantity A	Quantity B
$m > n$	
$n > p$	
m	p

Choice A is correct. We want to compare m and p. However, the given information,

$$m > n \quad \boxed{1}$$
$$n > p \quad \boxed{2}$$

does not directly relate to m and p. So we should try to get the given information to look similar to what we want to compare. By comparing $\boxed{1}$ and $\boxed{2}$ we have

$$m > p$$

This is the piece of information we need in order to compare the two columns. Clearly, Choice A is correct.

EXAMPLE 2

Quantity A	Quantity B
$-5 < x < +5$	
-6	$-x$

Choice B is correct.
Try to get the given to look like what's in the columns. Multiply the given by -1. You get

$$-1(-5 < x < +5) \to +5 > -x > -5$$

remembering to reverse the inequality signs when multiplying by a negative number.

Now we found $-x > -5$. Now look at the columns:

If $-x > -5$, surely

$$-x > -6 \text{ and Quantity A} < \text{Quantity B.}$$

EXAMPLES 3–8

Quantity A	Quantity B
3.	$-y = x$	
0	$x + y$

Quantity A	Quantity B
4.	$66 < 6a < 140$	
23.4	a

Quantity A	Quantity B
5.	18% of $4x = 86$	
43	18% of $42x$

Quantity A	Quantity B
6.	$5x < 30 < 6x$	
6	x

Quantity A	Quantity B
7.	$a + b + c = 8$	
	$a - b + c = 4$	
$2a + 2c$	13

Quantity A	Quantity B
8.	$3 > 12a + 12$	
0	a

EXPLANATORY ANSWERS FOR EXAMPLES 3–8

Quantity A	Quantity B
3. (C)	$-y = x$	
0	$x + y$

Get the given to look like what's in the columns.
$$-y = x, \text{ so } x + y = 0$$
Now you can see that Quantity A = Quantity B.

Quantity A	Quantity B
4. (A)	$66 < 6a < 140$	
23.4	a

Get the given to look like what's in the columns.
Divide the given by 6:
$$\frac{66}{6} < \frac{6a}{6} < \frac{140}{6}$$
$$11 < a < 23\frac{1}{3}$$
Now $23\frac{1}{3} > a$ and 23.4 (Quantity A) $> 23\frac{1}{3}$
So, $23.4 > 23\frac{1}{3} > a$ and $23.4 > a$.

Quantity A	Quantity B
5. (C)	18% of $4x = 86$	
43	18% of $2x$

Get the given to look like what's in the columns.
Divide the given by 2:
$$\frac{18\% \text{ of } 4x}{2} = \frac{86}{2}$$
$$18\% \text{ of } 2x = 43$$
Quantity A = Quantity B.

Quantity A	Quantity B
6. (A)	$5x < 30 < 6x$	
6	x

Get the given to look like what's in the columns.
You want to get something like $x > 6$ or $6 > x$
from the given $5x < 30 < 6x$.
So divide by 5:
$$\frac{5x}{5} < \frac{30}{5} < \frac{6x}{5}$$
$$x < 6 < \frac{6x}{5}$$
NOTE: If you had divided $5x < 30 < 6x$ by 6, you
would have gotten:
$$\frac{5x}{6} < 5 < x$$
but that wouldn't have given you $x > 6$ or $6 > x$.

Quantity A	Quantity B
7. (B)	$a + b + c = 8$	
	$a - b + c = 4$	
$2a + 2c$	13

Relate the given to the columns:
Add:
$$\begin{array}{r} a + b + c = 8 \\ a - b + c = 4 \\ \hline 2a + 2c = 12 \end{array}$$
Substitute $2a + 2c = 12$ in Quantity A to get:

12	13
$12 < 13$	

Quantity A	Quantity B
8. (A)	$3 > 12a + 12$	
0	a

Relate the given to the columns:
Divide the given by 12:
$$\frac{3}{12} > \frac{12a + 12}{12}$$
$$\frac{1}{4} > \frac{12a}{12} + \frac{12}{12}$$
$$\frac{1}{4} > a + 1$$
Subtract 1 to get a alone.
$$\frac{1}{4} - 1 > a$$
$$-\frac{3}{4} > a$$
Since $0 > -\frac{3}{4}$ and $-\frac{3}{4} > a$, then $0 > -\frac{3}{4} > a$
and $0 > a$.

SUMMARY DIRECTIONS FOR COMPARISON QUESTIONS

Choose A if Quantity A is greater,
Choose B if Quantity B is greater,
Choose C if the two quantities are equal;

Choose D if the relationship cannot be determined from the information given.

MATH STRATEGY F

Use the Choice C Method When Straightforward Computations Must Be Made

---

This strategy should be used only if you must guess the answer or if you do not have the time to work out tedious arithmetic. When the answer to a problem requires only a straightforward computation and if there are very specific numbers (such as 17 or 23) involved in the problem, Choice C is almost always correct. The reason is that the test maker has a logical reason to make Choice C the answer. We see this in the following problem.

EXAMPLE 1

Quantity A	Quantity B
$5x + 12 = 27$	
x	3

Choice C is correct. Look at all the specific numbers that are involved in this question: 5, 12, 27, and 3. These numbers were not accidentally chosen! The solution to this problem involves a straightforward calculation!

$$5x + 12 = 27 \qquad \boxed{1}$$
$$5x = 15$$
$$x = 3$$

Why did the test maker want Choice C as the answer? The reason is that if you could not solve $\boxed{1}$, then you guessed what x should be. You probably guessed that x is some number greater than 3 or less than 3. In addition, if you made a mistake solving $\boxed{1}$, then you obtained a value for x that was greater than 3 or less than 3. Either way, you wrote Choice A or B as your answer. You may even have written Choice D if you could not do the problem correctly. Thus, the test maker felt that only someone who really knew how to solve the problem would write Choice C. Let us look at another problem.

EXAMPLE 2

Last year, Jack had 60 CDs. This year Jack has 75 CDs.

Quantity A	Quantity B
The percent increase in the number of CDs Jack has this year from the number of CDs Jack had last year.	25%

Choice C is correct. Look at all the specific numbers in this problem: 60, 75, and 25.

The percent increase in the number of CDs Jack had since last year =

$$\frac{\text{Number of CDs Jack has now} - \text{Number of CDs Jack had last year}}{\text{Number of CDs Jack had last year}} \times 100$$

$$= \frac{75 - 60}{60} \times 100$$

$$= \frac{15}{60} \times 100$$

$$= 25\% \ (\textit{Answer})$$

Anyone who guessed the answer or who made a mistake in the above calculation probably wrote A, B, or D as the answer. Only someone who really solved the problem correctly was able to get the right answer, Choice C.

EXAMPLE 3

Quantity A	Quantity B
The length of the hypotenuse of a right triangle whose legs are 7 inches and 24 inches long.	The length of the hypotenuse of a right triangle whose legs are 15 inches and 20 inches long.

Choice C is correct. Look at all the specific numbers in this question: 7, 24, 15, and 20. These numbers were not accidentally chosen! The solution to this problem involves straightforward calculation!

$$(\text{hypotenuse})^2 = (\text{first leg})^2 + (\text{second leg})^2$$

Thus, for Quantity A,

$$(\text{hypotenuse})^2 = 7^2 + 24^2$$
$$= 49 + 576$$
$$= 625$$

Hypotenuse in Quantity A = 25 $\boxed{1}$

For Quantity B

$$(\text{hypotenuse})^2 = 15^2 + 20^2$$
$$= 225 + 400$$
$$= 625$$

Hypotenuse in Quantity B = 25 $\boxed{2}$

From $\boxed{1}$ and $\boxed{2}$ the answer is clear. Anyone who guessed the answer or who made a mistake in the above calculation probably wrote A, B, or D as the answer. Only someone who really solved the problem correctly was able to get the right answer.

17 Verbal (Reading) Strategies

Using Critical Thinking Skills in
Verbal Questions (Reading Sections) and
Sentence Completions (Text Completions
and Sentence Equivalence Questions)

4 Sentence Completion (Text Completion and Sentence Equivalence) Strategies

Note: For these questions it is important that you learn the meaning of vocabulary words in part 7 and then the vocabulary strategies on page 168.

One-Blank Sentences

SENT. COMPL. STRATEGY 1

> For a Sentence with Only One Blank, Fill in the Blank with Each Choice to See the Best Fit.* In the Six-Choice Questions, You Will Have to Choose Two Answers That Both Work.

Before you decide which is the best choice, fill in the blank with each of the five or six answer choices to see which word will fit best into the sentence as a whole.

FIVE-CHOICE QUESTIONS

EXAMPLE 1

He believed that because there is serious unemployment in our auto industry, we should not _____ foreign cars.

(A) discuss
(B) regulate
(C) research
(D) import
(E) disallow

EXPLANATORY ANSWER

Choice D is correct. The word "import" means to bring in from another country or place. The sentence now makes good sense. The competition resulting from importation of foreign cars reduces the demand for American-made cars. This throws many American auto workers out of jobs.

EXAMPLE 2

His attempt to _____ his guilt was betrayed by the tremor of his hand as he picked up the paper.

(A) extenuate
(B) determine
(C) conceal
(D) intensify
(E) display

EXPLANATORY ANSWER

Choice C is correct. The word "conceal" means to keep secret or to hide. The sentence now makes good sense. The nervousness caused by his guilty conscience is shown by the shaking of his hand. He is thus prevented in his attempt to hide his guilt.

EXAMPLE 3

In large cities, the number of family-owned grocery stores has fallen so sharply that the opportunity to shop in such a place is _____ occasion.

(A) a celebrated
(B) an old
(C) a fanciful
(D) a rare
(E) an avid

EXPLANATORY ANSWER

Choice D is correct. A rare occasion is one that you seldom have the opportunity to participate in. Shopping in a family-owned grocery store in a large city today is, indeed, a rare occasion.

*Strategy 1 is considered the Master Strategy for *one-blank* Sentence Completion questions because it can be used effectively to answer every *one-blank* Sentence Completion question. However, it is important that you learn all of the other Sentence Completion strategies, because they can be used to double-check your answers.

SIX-CHOICE QUESTIONS
Choose two answer choices that fit the sentence
and give the sentence the same meaning.

EXAMPLE 4

It is unthinkable for a prestigious conductor to agree to include _____ musicians in his orchestra.

(A) capable
(B) seasoned
(C) mediocre
(D) recommended
(E) professional
(F) amateur

EXPLANATORY ANSWER

Choices C and F are correct. The word "mediocre" (meaning average, ordinary) completes the sentence so that it makes good sense. Also, "amateur" would work. The other choices do *not* work.

EXAMPLE 5

A desire to be applauded by those in attendance, not his sensitivity to the plight of the underprivileged, was the reason for his _____ at the charity affair.

(A) shyness
(B) discomfort
(C) speaking
(D) arrogance
(E) generosity
(F) magnanimity

EXPLANATORY ANSWER

Choices E and F are correct. No other choice makes sense in the sentence. It is clear that the person was primarily interested in being appreciated for his donation. Note that although Choice C, speaking, fits the sentence, it does not impart the same meaning as the words in Choices E and F.

You can sometimes use this strategy in a two-blank question. Here's an example.

EXAMPLE 6

Legal _____ initiated by the government necessitate that manufacturers use _____ in choosing food additives.

Blank 1	Blank 2
(A) entanglements	(D) knowledge
(B) restraints	(E) moderation
(C) proclivities	(F) caution

EXPLANATORY ANSWER

Choices B and F are correct. Although this is a two-blank question, we should use Sentence Completion Strategy 1. Try the words in each of the choices in the blanks in the sentence.

Choices A and D are two more possibilities. But the point of the sentence evidently is that government prohibitions of certain food additives necessitate care by manufacturers in choosing food additives that are permitted. Thus Choices A and D are not as good as Choices B and F.

SENT. COMPL. STRATEGY 2

Try to Complete the Sentence in Your Own Words Before Looking at the Choices

This strategy often works well, especially with one-blank sentences. You may be able to fill in the blank with a word of your own that makes good sense. Then look at the answer choices to see whether any of the choices has the same meaning as your own word.

EXAMPLE 1

Many buildings with historical significance are now being _____ instead of being torn down.

(A) built
(B) forgotten
(C) destroyed
(D) praised
(E) repaired

EXPLANATORY ANSWER

Choice E is correct. The key words "instead of" constitute an *opposition indicator*. The words give us a good clue— we should fill in the blank with an antonym (opposite) for "torn down." If you used the strategy of trying to complete the sentence *before* looking at the five choices, you might have come up with any of the following appropriate words:

remodeled
reconstructed
remade
renovated

These words all mean the same as the correct Choice E word, "repaired."

EXAMPLE 2

Wishing to _____ the upset passenger who found a nail in his steak, the flight attendant offered him a complimentary bottle of champagne.

(A) appease
(B) berate
(C) disregard
(D) reinstate
(E) acknowledge

EXPLANATORY ANSWER

Choice A is correct. Since the passenger was upset, the flight attendant wished to do something to make him feel better. If you used the strategy of trying to complete the sentence *before* looking at the five choices, you might have come up with the following words that would have the meaning "to make someone feel better":

pacify
soothe
satisfy
conciliate
relieve

These words all mean the same as the Choice A word, "appease."

EXAMPLE 3

Just as the person who is kind brings happiness to others, so does he bring _____ to himself.

(A) wisdom
(B) guidance
(C) satisfaction
(D) stinginess
(E) insecurity

EXPLANATORY ANSWER

Choice C is correct. You must look for a word that balances with "happiness." Here are some of the words:

joy
goodness
satisfaction
enjoyment

All these words can be linked to Choice C.

SIX-CHOICE QUESTIONS
Select the two answer choices that fit the sentence and give the sentence the same meaning.

EXAMPLE 4

Actors are sometimes very _____ since they must believe strongly in their own worth and talents.

(A) taciturn
(B) unequivocal
(C) tedious
(D) egotistic
(E) reticent
(F) arrogant

EXPLANATORY ANSWER

Choices D and F are correct. "Since" signifies *result*. So the second clause of the sentence, starting with "since," really tells us that the missing word or words must be one of the following:

boastful
very much interested in one's own self
egotistic
self-centered
headstrong
arrogant

Thus, Choices D and F are correct.

EXAMPLE 5

Hunger has reached epidemic proportions nationwide, leaving up to 20 million people _____ to illness and fear.

(A) agreeable
(B) vulnerable
(C) obvious
(D) acclimated
(E) sensitive
(F) susceptible

EXPLANATORY ANSWER

Choices B and F are correct. You might have come up with any of the following words:

open (to)
unprotected (from)

These words all mean about the same as the correct one, Choice B: "vulnerable," or Choice F: "susceptible."

Note: In many of the six-choice questions the correct answers are synonyms.

One- or Two-Blank Sentences

SENT. COMPL. STRATEGY 3

Pay Close Attention to the Key Words in the Sentence

A key word may indicate what is happening in the sentence. Here are some examples of key words and what these words may indicate.

Key Word	Indicating
although however in spite of rather than nevertheless on the other hand but	OPPOSITION
Key Word	Indicating
moreover besides additionally furthermore in fact	SUPPORT
Key Word	Indicating
therefore consequently accordingly because when so	RESULT

There are many other words—in addition to these—that can act as key words to help you considerably in getting the right answer. A key word *frequently* appears in the sentence. Watch for it!

SINGLE-BLANK QUESTIONS

EXAMPLE 1

Richard Wagner was frequently intolerant; moreover, his strange behavior caused most of his acquaintances to _____ the composer whenever possible.

(A) contradict
(B) interrogate
(C) shun
(D) revere
(E) tolerate

EXPLANATORY ANSWER

Choice C is correct. The word "moreover" is a *support indicator* in this sentence. As we try each choice word in the blank, we find that "shun" (avoid) is the only logical word that fits. You might have selected Choice A ("con-tradict"), but very few would seek to contradict an intolerant man with strange behavior.

SINGLE-BLANK, SIX-CHOICE QUESTIONS

Select the two answer choices that fit the sentence and give the sentence the same meaning.

EXAMPLE 2

Being _____ person, he insisted at the conference that when he spoke he was not to be interrupted.

(A) a flamboyant
(B) a rejoiceful
(C) a headstrong
(D) a contemplative
(E) a solitary
(F) a dictatorial

EXPLANATORY ANSWER

Choices C and F are correct. The main clause of the sentence—"he insisted...not be interrupted"—*supports* the idea expressed in the first three words of the sentence. Accordingly, Choice C, "headstrong" (meaning stubborn), and Choice F, "dictatorial" (meaning "ruling"), are the only correct choices.

EXAMPLE 3

Although Grete Waitz is a celebrated female marathon runner, she is noted for her _____ .

(A) vigor
(B) indecision
(C) modesty
(D) deference
(E) endurance
(F) perspicacity

EXPLANATORY ANSWER

Choices C and D are correct. The beginning word "Although" constitutes an *opposition indicator.* We can then expect the second part of the sentence to indicate an idea that is opposite to what is said in the first part of the sentence. Choice C "modesty" (courteous respect) and Choice D "deference" (yielding in opinion) provide the words that give us the closest to an opposite idea. Since Waitz is celebrated, we expect her to be immodest and have little deference. The words in the other choices do *not* give us that opposite idea. (*Perspicacity* means keen judgment.)

For two-blank sentences, look for contrasts or opposition in the two parts of the sentence—then look for opposite relationships in the choices.

DOUBLE-BLANK QUESTIONS

EXAMPLE 4

Until we are able to improve substantially the _____ status of the underprivileged in our country, a substantial _____ in our crime rate is remote.

Blank 1	Blank 2
(A) financial	(D) ascension
(B) enormous	(E) development
(C) questionable	(F) attenuation

EXPLANATORY ANSWER

Choices A and F are correct. Watch for key words like "Until," which is a *result indicator.* You can see that we can either increase or reduce the crime rate. The word "improve" indicates that we would "reduce" the crime rate, thus leading to Choice F (attenuate) as a correct choice. And what we would want to improve is the "financial" status.

EXAMPLE 5

All of the efforts of the teachers will bring about no _____ changes in the scores of the students because books and other _____ educational materials are not available.

Blank 1	Blank 2
(A) impartial	(D) reflected
(B) spiritual	(E) necessary
(C) marked	(F) inspiring

EXPLANATORY ANSWER

Choices C and E are correct. The word "because" is a *result indicator*. You can see that if educational materials are not available, the students will not do well on the tests. So "marked" and "necessary" would fit well in the sentence.

Sometimes you can look for contrasts or opposition in the two parts of the sentence—then look for opposite relationships in the choices.

EXAMPLE 6

In spite of the _____ of his presentation, many people were _____ with the speaker's concepts and ideas.

Blank 1	Blank 2
(A) long-windedness	(D) enthralled
(B) formulation	(E) bored
(C) forcefulness	(F) gratified

EXPLANATORY ANSWER

Choices C and E are correct. "In spite of" signals an *opposite* or contrast in the sentence. The contrasting words that have opposite connotation are *forcefulness* and *bored*. Note that the word *formulation* (Choice B) is really the same as the speaker's concepts and ideas, so it wouldn't make sense to describe what the people felt about the speaker's concepts and ideas.

Three-Blank Sentence Completions

SENT. COMPL. STRATEGY 4

Look for the Overall Flavor of the Passage and Use Sentence Completion Strategy 3 of Noting *Key Words*

Know which blank to fill in first. Try to get an overall sense of the passage.

Many times you will be able to fill in the correct choice in the second column or third column of the choices. Then you will be able to see what the correct choice in the first column is. So it is not always good to first deal with the first column of choices.

EXAMPLE 1

The novel *Uncle Tom's Cabin*, which effectively _____ the unfairness toward black people, was a major influence in _____ the antislavery movement and set the stage that _____ the true flavor of the United States' Constitutional premise.

Blank 1	Blank 2	Blank 3
(A) predicted	(D) pacifying	(G) triggered
(B) portrayed	(E) appraising	(H) echoed
(C) complied with	(F) strengthening	(I) counteracted

EXPLANATORY ANSWER

Choices B, F, and H are correct. Look at the second blank first. Because of the flavor of the first part of the sentence, *The novel* Uncle Tom's Cabin, *which effectively _____ the unfairness toward black people*, the word in the second blank should be *strengthening*, Choice F. Now you can see that the first blank should be Choice B, *portrayed*. Consequently, the third blank word would represent the true flavor of the Constitution. That word would be *echoed*, Choice H.

Here's a three-blank question with more difficult words in the choices.

EXAMPLE 2

Crusty and egotistical, Alfred A. Knopf, the publisher, wore _____ shirts from the most exclusive tailors; was a connoisseur of music, food, and wine; nurtured a garden of exotic plants; and enjoyed rare cigars. His self-assured, _____ manner, together with his insistence on the best of everything, shaped his ostentatious publishing house's image as a _____ of works of enduring value.

Blank 1	Blank 2	Blank 3
(A) expensive	(D) decorous	(G) connoisseur
(B) immaculate	(E) irascible	(H) purveyor
(C) flamboyant	(F) congenial	(I) solicitor

EXPLANATORY ANSWER

Choices C, E, and H are correct. Look at the second blank first. Because of the key words *Crusty* and *egotistical*, it would appear that Choice E, the word *irascible*, meaning "hot-tempered," would fit the second blank. And since there were so many things he had as described in the first sentence, Choice H, *purveyor* (one who spreads things throughout) would be a good fit. Because of the word *ostentatious* (showy) in the second sentence, you can see that Choice C, *flamboyant* (showy), would fit the first blank.

Reading Strategies

Introduction

Before getting into the detailed strategies, I want to say that the most important way to really understand what you're reading is to **get involved** with the passage—as if a friend of yours was reading the passage to you and you had to be interested so you wouldn't slight your friend. When you see the passage on paper it is also a good idea to **underline** important parts of the passage, which we'll also go over later in one of the strategies. For the computer-based GRE, please see the footnote on the following page.

So many students ask, How do I answer reading comprehension questions? How do I read the passage effectively? Do I look at the questions before reading the passage? Do I underline things in the passage? Do I have to memorize details and dates? How do I get interested and involved in the passage?

All of these are good questions. They will be answered carefully and in the right sequence.

What Reading Comprehension Questions Ask

First of all, it is important to know that most reading comprehension questions ask about one of four things:

---

1. The MAIN IDEA of the passage
2. INFORMATION SPECIFICALLY MENTIONED in the passage
3. INFORMATION IMPLIED (not directly stated) in the passage
4. The TONE or MOOD of the passage

For example, following are some typical question stems. Each lets you immediately know which of the above is being asked about.

1. It can be inferred from the passage that... (IMPLIED INFORMATION)

2. According to the author... (MAIN IDEA)

3. The passage is primarily concerned with... (MAIN IDEA)

4. The author's statement that... (SPECIFIC INFORMATION)

5. Which of the following describes the mood of the passage? (TONE or MOOD)

6. The author implies that... (IMPLIED INFORMATION)

7. The use of paper is described in lines 14–16... (SPECIFIC INFORMATION)

8. The main purpose of the passage... (MAIN IDEA)

9. The author's tone is best described as... (TONE or MOOD)

10. One could easily see the author as... (IMPLIED INFORMATION)

Getting Involved with the Passage

Now, let's first put aside the burning question: Should I read the questions first before reading the passage? The answer is NO! If you have in mind the four main question types given previously, you will not likely be in for any big surprises. Many questions, when you get to them, will be reassuringly familiar in the way they're framed and in their intent. You can best answer them by reading the passage first, allowing yourself to become involved with it.

To give you an idea of what I mean, look over the following passage. When you have finished, I'll show you how you might read it so as to get involved with it and with the author's intent.

Introductory Passage 1

We should also know that "greed" has little to do with the environmental crisis. The two main causes are population pressures, especially the pressures of large metropolitan populations, and the desire—a highly commendable one—to bring a decent living at the lowest possible cost to the largest possible number of people.

The environmental crisis is the result of success—success in cutting down the mortality of infants (which has given us the population explosion), success in raising farm output sufficiently to prevent mass famine (which has given us contamination by pesticides and chemical fertilizers), and success in getting the people out of the tenements of the 19th-century cities and into the greenery and privacy of the single-family home in the suburbs (which has given us urban sprawl and traffic jams). The environmental crisis, in other words, is largely the result of doing too much of the right sort of thing.

To overcome the problems that success always creates, one must build on it. But where to start? Cleaning up the environment requires determined, sustained effort with clear targets and deadlines. It requires, above all, concentration of effort. Up to now we have tried to do a little bit of everything—and tried to do it in the headlines—when what we ought to do first is draw up a list of priorities.

Breakdown and Underlining of the Passage*

Before going over the passage with you, I want to suggest some underlining you might want to make and show what different parts of the passage refer to.

We should also know that "greed" has little to do with the environmental crisis. The two main causes are <u>population pressures,</u> especially the pressures of large metropolitan populations, and the <u>desire</u>—a highly commendable one—<u>to bring a decent living at the lowest possible cost</u> to the largest possible number of people.

Sets stage.

<u>The environmental crisis is the result of success</u>—success in cutting down the mortality of infants (which has given us the population explosion), success in raising farm output sufficiently to prevent mass famine (which has given us contamination by pesticides and chemical fertilizers), and success in getting the people out of the tenements of the 19th-century cities and into the greenery and privacy of the single-family home in the suburbs (which has given us urban sprawl and traffic jams). The environmental crisis, in other words, is largely the result of doing <u>too much of the right sort of thing.</u>

This should interest and surprise you.

Examples of success.

Summary of the success examples.

To overcome the problems that success always creates, <u>one must build on it</u>. But where to start? Cleaning up the environment requires determined, <u>sustained effort with clear targets and deadlines</u>. It requires, above all, <u>concentration of effort.</u> Up to now we have tried to do a little bit of everything—and tried to do it in the headlines—when what we ought to do first is <u>draw up a list of priorities.</u>

Solutions.

Now I'll go over the passage with you, showing you what might go through your mind as you read. This will let you see how to get involved with the passage, and how this involvement facilitates answering the questions that follow the passage. In many cases, you'll actually be able to anticipate the questions. Of course, when you are preparing for the GRE, you'll have to develop this skill so that you do it rapidly and almost automatically.

Let's look at the first sentence:

We should also know that "greed" has little to do with the environmental crisis.

Immediately you should say to yourself, "So something else must be involved with the environmental crisis." Read on:

The two main causes are population pressures, especially the pressures of large metropolitan populations, and the desire—a highly commendable one—to bring a decent living at the lowest possible cost to the largest possible number of people.

Now you can say to yourself, "Oh, so population pressures and the desire to help the people in the community caused the environmental crisis." You should

*On the computer-based GRE, you might want to make some notes on your scrap paper since you will not be able to underline on the computer screen.

also get a feeling that the author is not really against these causes of the environmental crisis and that he or she believes that the crisis is in part a side effect of worthwhile efforts and enterprises. Read on:

The environmental crisis is the result of success—success in cutting down the mortality of infants (which has given us the population explosion), success in raising farm output sufficiently to prevent mass famine (which has given us contamination by pesticides and chemical fertilizers), and success in getting the people out of the tenements of the 19th-century city and into the greenery and privacy of the single-family home in the suburbs (which has given us urban sprawl and traffic jams).

Now you should say to yourself, "It seems that for every positive thing that the author mentions, there is a negative occurrence that leads to the environmental crisis."

Now read the last sentence of this paragraph:

The environmental crisis, in other words, is largely the result of doing too much of the right sort of thing.

Now you can say to yourself, "Gee, we wanted to do the right thing, but we created something bad. It looks like you can't have your cake and eat it, too!"

Now you should anticipate that in the next and final paragraph, the author will discuss what may be done to reduce the bad effects that come from the good. Look at the first sentence of the third paragraph:

To overcome the problem that success always creates, one must build on it.

Now you can say to yourself, "Well, how?" In fact, in the next sentence the author asks the very question you just asked: *But where to start?* Read on to find out the author's answer.

Cleaning up the environment requires determined, sustained effort with clear targets and deadlines. It requires, above all, concentration and effort.

So now you can say to yourself, "Oh, so that's what we need—definite goals, deadlines for reaching those goals, and genuine effort to achieve the goals."

The author then discusses what you may have already thought about:

Up to now we have tried to do a little bit of everything...

What the author is saying (and you should realize this) is that up to now, we haven't concentrated on one particular problem at a time. We used "buckshot instead of bullets." Read on:

—and tried to do it in the headlines—when what we ought to do first is draw up a list of priorities.

So you can now see that, in the author's opinion, making a list of priorities and working on them one at a time, with a target in mind, may get us out of the environmental crisis and still preserve our quality of life.

How to Answer Reading Comprehension Questions Most Effectively

Before we start to answer the questions, let me tell you the best and most effective way of answering passage questions. You should read the question and proceed to look at the choices in the order of Choice A, Choice B, etc. If a choice (such as Choice A) doesn't give you the definite feeling that it is correct, don't try to analyze it further. Go on to Choice B. Again, if that choice (Choice B) doesn't make you feel that it's the right one, and you really have to think carefully about the choice, go on to Choice C and the rest of the choices and choose the best one.

Suppose you have gone through all five choices, and you don't know which one is correct, or you don't see any one that stands out as obviously being correct. Then quickly guess or leave the question blank if you wish and go on to the next question. You can go back after you have answered the other questions relating to the passage. But remember, when you return to the questions you weren't sure of, don't spend too much time on them. Try to forge ahead on the test.

Let's proceed to answer the questions now. Look at the first question:

1. This passage assumes the desirability of
   (A) using atomic energy to conserve fuel
   (B) living in comfortable family lifestyles
   (C) settling disputes peacefully
   (D) combating cancer and heart disease with energetic research
   (E) having greater government involvement in people's daily lives

Look at Choice A. That doesn't seem correct. Now look at Choice B. Do you remember that the author claimed that the environmental crisis is the result of the successful attempt to get people out of their tenements and into a better environment? We can only feel that the author *assumes* this desirability of *living in comfortable family lifestyles* (Choice B) since the author uses the word *success* in describing the transition from living in tenements to living in single-family homes. Therefore, Choice B is correct. You don't need to analyze or even consider the other choices, since we have zeroed in on Choice B.

Let's look at Question 2:

2. According to this passage, one early step in any effort to improve the environment would be to

(A) return to the exclusive use of natural fertilizers
(B) put a high tax on profiteering industries
(C) ban the use of automobiles in the cities
(D) study successful efforts in other countries
(E) set up a timetable for corrective actions

Again, let's go through the choices in the order Choice A, Choice B, etc., until we come up with the right choice. Choices A, B, C, and D seem unlikely to be correct. So look at Choice E. We remember that the author said that we should establish clear targets and deadlines to improve the environment. That makes Choice E look like the correct answer.

Let's look at Question 3:

3. The passage indicates that the conditions that led to overcrowded roads also brought about

(A) more attractive living conditions for many people
(B) a healthier younger generation
(C) greater occupational opportunities
(D) the population explosion
(E) greater concentration of population pressures

Here we would go back to the part of the passage that discussed overcrowded roads. This is where (second paragraph) the author says that urban sprawl and traffic jams are one result of success in getting people out of tenements and into single-family homes. So you can see that Choice A is correct. Again, there is no need to consider other choices, since you should be fairly comfortable with Choice A.

Let's look at Question 4:

4. It could logically be assumed that the author of this passage would support legislation to

(A) ban the use of all pesticides
(B) prevent the use of automobiles in the cities
(C) build additional conventional power plants immediately
(D) organize an agency to coordinate efforts to cope with environmental problems
(E) restrict the press coverage of protests led by environmental groups

This is the type of question that asks you to determine how the author might feel about something else, when you already know something about the author's sentiments on one particular subject.

Choices A, B, and C do not seem correct. But look at Choice D. The author said that the way to get out of the energy crisis is to set targets and deadlines in order to cope with specific problems. The author would therefore probably want to organize an agency to do this. Choice D is correct.

Let's look at another passage, and what I'm going to tell you is what would be going through my mind as I read it. The more you can get involved with the passage in an active and not a passive way, the faster you'll read it, and the more you'll get out of it.

Introductory Passage 2

Some scraps of evidence bear out those who hold a very high opinion of the average level of culture among the Athenians of the great age. The funeral speech of Pericles is the most famous indication from Athenian literature that its level was indeed high. Pericles was, however, a politician, and he may have been flattering his audience. We know that thousands of Athenians sat hour after hour in the theater listening to the plays of the great Greek dramatists. These plays, especially the tragedies, are at a very high intellectual level throughout. There are no letdowns, no concessions to the lowbrows or to the demands of "realism," such as the scene of the grave-diggers in *Hamlet*. The music and dancing woven into these plays were almost certainly at an equally high level. Our opera—not Italian opera, not even Wagner, but the restrained, difficult opera of the 18th century—is probably the best modern parallel. The comparison is no doubt dangerous, but can you imagine almost the entire population of an American city (in suitable installments, of course) sitting through performances of Mozart's *Don Giovanni* or Gluck's *Orpheus*? Perhaps the Athenian masses went to these plays because of a lack of other amusements. They could at least understand something of what went on, since the subjects were part of their folklore. For the American people, the subjects of grand opera are not part of their folklore.

Let's start reading the passage:

Some scraps of evidence bear out those who hold a very high opinion of the average level of culture among the Athenians of the great age.

Now this tells you that the author is going to talk about the culture of the Athenians. Thus the stage is set. Go on reading now:

The funeral speech of Pericles is the most famous indication from Athenian literature that its level was indeed high.

At this point you should say to yourself, "That's interesting, and there was an example of the high level of culture."

Read on:

Pericles was, however, a politician, and he may have been flattering his audience.

Now you can say, "So that's why those people were so attentive in listening—they were being flattered."

Read on:

We know that thousands of Athenians sat hour after hour in the theater listening to the plays of the great Greek dramatists. These plays, especially the tragedies, are at a very high intellectual level throughout. There are no letdowns, no concessions to the lowbrows or to the demands of "realism"…

At this point you should say to yourself, "That's strange—it could not have been just flattery that kept them listening hour after hour. How did they do it?" You can almost anticipate that the author will now give examples and contrast what he is saying to our plays and our audiences.

Read on:

The music and dancing woven into these plays were almost certainly at an equally high level. Our opera—not Italian opera… is probably the best modern parallel. The comparison is no doubt dangerous, but can you imagine almost the entire population of an American city…sitting through performances of…

Your feeling at this point should be, "No, I cannot imagine that. Why is that so?" So you should certainly be interested to find out.

Read on:

Perhaps the Athenian masses went to these plays because of a lack of other amusements. They could at least understand something of what went on, since the subjects were part of their folklore.

Now you can say, "So that's why those people were able to listen hour after hour—the material was all part of their folklore!"

Read on:

For the American people, the subjects…are not part of their folklore.

Now you can conclude, "So that's why the Americans cannot sit through these plays and perhaps cannot understand them—they were not part of their folklore!"

Here are the questions that follow the passage:

1. The author seems to question the sincerity of

   (A) politicians
   (B) playwrights
   (C) operagoers
   (D) lowbrows
   (E) gravediggers

2. The author implies that the average American

   (A) enjoys *Hamlet*
   (B) loves folklore
   (C) does not understand grand opera
   (D) seeks a high cultural level
   (E) lacks entertainment

3. The author's attitude toward Greek plays is one of

   (A) qualified approval
   (B) grudging admiration
   (C) studied indifference
   (D) partial hostility
   (E) great respect

4. The author suggests that Greek plays

   (A) made great demands upon their actors
   (B) flattered their audiences
   (C) were written for a limited audience
   (D) were dominated by music and dancing
   (E) stimulated their audiences

Let's try to answer them.

Question 1: Remember the statement about Pericles? This statement was almost unrelated to the passage since it was not discussed or referred to again. And here we have a question about it. Usually, if you see something that you think is irrelevant in a passage, you may be pretty sure that a question will be based on that irrelevancy. It is apparent that the author seems to question the sincerity of politicians (*not* playwrights), since Pericles was a politician. Therefore Choice A is correct.

Question 2: We know that it was implied that the average American does not understand grand opera. Therefore Choice C is correct.

Question 3: From the passage, we see that the author is very positive about the Greek plays. Thus the author must have great respect for the plays. Note that the author may not have respect for Pericles, but Pericles was not a playwright; he was a politician. Therefore Choice E (not Choice A) is correct.

Question 4: It is certainly true that the author suggests that the Greek plays stimulated their audiences. They didn't necessarily flatter their audiences—there was only one indication of flattery, and that was by Pericles, who was not a playwright, but a politician. Therefore Choice E (not Choice B) is correct.

Example of Underlinings*

Some scraps of evidence bear out those who hold a <u>very high</u>   ← *sets stage*
<u>opinion of the average level of culture among the Athenians</u> of
the great age. The funeral speech of Pericles is the most famous
indication from Athenian literature that its level was indeed
high. Pericles was, however, <u>a politician</u>, and he may have <u>been</u>   } ← *example*
<u>flattering his audience.</u> We know that thousands of Athenians
sat hour after hour in the theater listening to the plays of the
great Greek dramatists. These plays, especially the tragedies,
are <u>at a very high intellectual</u> level throughout. There are no   ← *qualification*
letdowns, no concessions to the lowbrows or to the demands
of "realism," such as the scene of the gravediggers in *Hamlet*.   ← *further*
The music and dancing woven into these plays were almost   *examples*
certainly at an equally high level. <u>Our opera</u>—not Italian opera,   ✓
not even Wagner, but the restrained, difficult opera of the 18th
century—<u>is probably the best modern parallel.</u> The comparison   ← *comparison*
is no doubt dangerous, but can you imagine almost the entire
population of an American city (in suitable installments, of
course) sitting through performances of Mozart's *Don Giovanni*
or Gluck's *Orpheus*? <u>Perhaps the Athenian masses went to these</u>   }
<u>plays because of a lack of other amusements.</u> They could at least
understand something of what went on, since <u>the subjects were</u>   } ← *explanation*
<u>part of their folklore.</u> For the American people, the subjects of   *of previous*
grand opera are not part of their folklore.   *statements*

Now the whole purpose of analyzing this passage
the way I did was to show you that if you get involved
and interested in the passage, you will not only anticipate many of the questions, but when you answer them
you will be able to zero in on the right question choice
without having to necessarily analyze or eliminate the
wrong choices first. That's a great time-saver on a
standardized test such as the GRE.

Now here's a short passage from which four questions were derived. Let's see if you can answer them
after you've read the passage.

Introductory Passage 3

Sometimes the meaning of glowing water is ominous. Off
the Pacific Coast of North America, it may mean that the
sea is filled with a minute plant that contains a poison of
strange and terrible virulence. About four days after this
5 minute plant comes to alter the coastal plankton, some of
the fishes and shellfish in the vicinity become toxic. This
is because in their normal feeding, they have strained the
poisonous plankton out of the water.

1. Fish and shellfish become toxic when they

   (A) swim in poisonous water
   (B) feed on poisonous plants
   (C) change their feeding habits
   (D) give off a strange glow
   (E) take strychnine into their systems

2. One can most reasonably conclude that plankton
   are

   (A) minute organisms
   (B) mussels
   (C) poisonous fish
   (D) shellfish
   (E) fluids

3. In the context of the passage, the word "virulence"
   in line 4 means

   (A) strangeness
   (B) color
   (C) calamity
   (D) potency
   (E) powerful odor

4. The paragraph preceding this one most probably
   discussed

   (A) phenomena of the Pacific coastline
   (B) poisons that affect man
   (C) the culture of the early Indians
   (D) characteristics of plankton
   (E) phenomena of the sea

EXPLANATORY ANSWERS

1. Choice B is correct. Look at the last three
   sentences. Fish become toxic when they feed on
   poisonous plants. Don't be fooled by using the first
   sentence, which seemingly leads to Choice A.

*On the computer-based GRE, you might want to make some notes on your scrap paper since you will not be able to underline on the
computer screen.

2. Choice A is correct. Since we are talking about *minute* plants (second sentence), it is reasonable to assume that plankton are *minute* organisms.

3. Choice D is correct. We understand that the poison is very strong and toxic. Thus it is "potent," virulent.

4. Choice E is correct. Since the second and not the first sentence was about the Pacific Coast, the paragraph preceding this one probably didn't discuss the phenomena of the Pacific coastline. It might have, if the first sentence—the sentence that links the ideas in the preceding paragraph—were about the Pacific coastline. Now, since we are talking about glowing water being ominous (first sentence), the paragraph preceding the passage is probably about the sea or the phenomena of the sea.

Summary

So in summary:

1. Make sure that you get involved with the passage. You may even want to select first the passage that interests you most. For example, if you're interested in science, you may want to choose the science passage first. Just make sure that you make some notation so that you don't mismark your answer sheet by putting the answers in the wrong answer boxes.

2. Pay attention to material that seems unrelated in the passage—there will probably be a question or two based on that material.

3. Pay attention to the mood created in the passage or the tone of the passage. Here again, especially if the mood is striking, there will probably be a question relating to mood.

4. Don't waste valuable time looking at the questions before reading the passage.

5. When attempting to answer the questions (after reading the passage), it is sometimes wise to try to figure out the answer before going through the choices. This will enable you to zero in on the correct answer without wasting time with all of the choices.

6. You may want to underline any information in the passages involving dates, specific names, etc., on your test to have as a ready reference when you come to the questions. Note: on the computer-based GRE, you might want to make some notes on your scrap paper since you will not be able to underline on the computer screen.

7. Always try to see the overall attempt of the author of the passage or try to get the main gist of why the passage was being written. Try to get involved by asking yourself if you agree or disagree with the author, etc.

The 10 Reading Comprehension Strategies begin on page 152.

10 Reading Comprehension Strategies

This section of Reading Comprehension Strategies includes several passages. These passages, though somewhat shorter than the passages that appear on the actual GRE and in the 3 GRE Practice Tests in this book, illustrate the general nature of the real GRE reading passages.

Each of the 10 Reading Comprehension Strategies that follow is accompanied by at least two different passages followed by questions and explanatory answers in order to explain how the strategy is used.

READ. COMP. STRATEGY 1

> ## As You Read Each Question, Determine the Type: Main Idea, Detecting Details, Inference, or Tone/Mood

Here are the four major abilities tested in Reading Comprehension questions:

1. **Main Idea.** Selection of the main thought of a passage; ability to judge the general significance of a passage; ability to select the best title of a passage.

2. **Detecting Details.** Ability to understand the writer's explicit statements; to get the literal meaning of what is written; to identify details.

3. **Inferential Reasoning.** Ability to weave together the ideas of a passage and to see their relationships; to draw correct inferences; to go beyond literal interpretation to the implications of the statements.

4. **Tone/Mood.** Ability to determine from the passage the tone or mood that is dominant in the passage—humorous, serious, sad, mysterious, etc.

EXAMPLE 1

The fight crowd is a beast that lurks in the darkness behind the fringe of white light shed over the first six rows by the incandescents atop the ring, and is not to be trusted with pop bottles or other hardware.

5 People who go to prize fights are sadistic.

When two prominent pugilists are scheduled to pummel one another in public on a summer's evening, men and women file into the stadium in the guise of human beings, and thereafter become a part of a gray thing that
10 squats in the dark until, at the conclusion of the blood-letting, they may be seen leaving the arena in the same guise they wore when they entered.

As a rule, the mob that gathers to see men fight is unjust, vindictive, swept by intense, unreasoning hatreds,
15 and proud of its swift recognition of what it believes to be sportsmanship. It is quick to greet the purely phony move of the boxer who extends his gloves to his rival who has slipped or been pushed to the floor, and to reward this stimulating but still baloney gesture with a pattering of
20 hands that indicates the following: "You are a good sport. We recognize that you are a good sport, and we know a sporting gesture when we see one. Therefore we are all good sports, too. Hurrah for us!"

The same crowd doesn't see the same boxer stick his
25 thumb in his opponent's eye or try to cut him with the laces of his glove, butt him or dig him a low one when the referee

isn't in a position to see. It roots consistently for the smaller man, and never for a moment considers the desperate psychological dilemma of the larger of the two. It howls
30 with glee at a good finisher making his kill. The Roman hordes were more civilized. Their gladiators asked them whether the final blow should be administered or not. The main attraction at the modern prize fight is the spectacle of a man clubbing a helpless and vanquished opponent into
35 complete insensibility. The referee who stops a bout to save a slugged and punch-drunken man from the final ignominy is hissed by the assembled sportsmen.

QUESTIONS

1. The tone of the passage is chiefly

   (A) disgusted
   (B) jovial
   (C) matter-of-fact
   (D) satiric
   (E) devil-may-care

2. Which group of words from the passage best indicates the author's opinion?

   (A) "referee," "opponent," "finisher"
   (B) "gladiators," "slugged," "sporting gesture"
   (C) "stimulating," "hissing," "pattering"
   (D) "beast," "lurks," "gray thing"
   (E) "dilemma," "hordes," "spectacle"

3. Apparently, the author believes that boxing crowds find the referee both

   (A) gentlemanly and boring
   (B) entertaining and essential
   (C) blind and careless
   (D) humorous and threatening
   (E) necessary and bothersome

EXPLANATORY ANSWERS

1. Choice A is correct. The author is obviously much offended (disgusted) by the inhuman attitude of the crowd watching the boxing match. For example, see these lines:

   Line 1: "The fight crowd is a beast."
   Line 5: "People who go to prize fights are sadistic."
   Lines 13–14: "…the mob that gathers to see men fight is unjust, vindictive, swept by intense…hatreds."
   Lines 30–31: "The Roman hordes were more civilized."

   To answer this question, you must be able to determine the tone that is dominant in the passage. Accordingly, this is a TONE/MOOD type of question.

2. Choice D is correct. The author's opinion is clearly one of disgust and discouragement because of the behavior of the fight crowd. Accordingly, you would expect the author to use words that were condemnatory, like "beast," and gloom-filled words like "lurks" and "gray thing." To answer this question, you must see relationships between words and feelings. So we have here an INFERENTIAL REASONING question type.

3. Choice E is correct. Lines 24–27 show that the referee is *necessary:* "The same crowd doesn't see the same boxer stick his thumb into his opponent's eye…when the referee isn't in a position to see." Lines 35–37 show that the referee is *bothersome:* "The referee who stops a bout…is hissed by the assembled sportsmen." To answer this question, you must have the ability to understand the writer's specific statements. Accordingly, this is a DETECTING DETAILS type of question.

EXAMPLE 2*

Mist continues to obscure the horizon, but above us the sky is suddenly awash with lavender light. At once the geese respond. Now, as well as their cries, a beating roar rolls across the water as if five thousand housewives have taken
5 it into their heads to shake out blankets all at one time. Ten thousand housewives. It keeps up—the invisible rhythmic beating of all those goose wings—for what seems a long time. Even Lonnie is held motionless with suspense.

Then the geese begin to rise. One, two, three
10 hundred—then a thousand at a time—in long horizontal lines that unfurl like pennants across the sky. The horizon actually darkens as they pass. It goes on and on like that, flock after flock, for three or four minutes, each new contingent announcing its ascent with an accelerating roar of
15 cries and wingbeats. Then gradually the intervals between flights become longer. I think the spectacle is over, until yet another flock lifts up, following the others in a gradual turn toward the northeastern quadrant of the refuge.

Finally the sun emerges from the mist; the mist itself
20 thins a little, uncovering the black line of willows on the other side of the wildlife preserve. I remember to close my mouth—which has been open for some time—and inadvertently shut two or three mosquitoes inside. Only a few straggling geese oar their way across the sun's red
25 surface. Lonnie wears an exasperated, proprietary expression, as if he had produced and directed the show himself and had just received a bad review. "It would have been better with more light," he says; "I can't always guarantee just when they'll start moving." I assure him I thought it
30 was a fantastic sight. "Well," he rumbles, "I guess it wasn't too bad."

*Note this example also appears in Part 1, Strategy Diagnostic Test for the GRE.

QUESTIONS

1. In the descriptive phrase "shake out blankets all at one time" (line 5), the author is appealing chiefly to the reader's

   (A) background
   (B) sight
   (C) emotions
   (D) thoughts
   (E) hearing

2. The mood created by the author is one of

   (A) tranquility
   (B) excitement
   (C) sadness
   (D) bewilderment
   (E) unconcern

3. The main idea expressed by the author about the geese is that they

   (A) are spectacular to watch
   (B) are unpredictable
   (C) disturb the environment
   (D) produce a lot of noise
   (E) fly in large flocks

4. Judging from the passage, the reader can conclude that

   (A) the speaker dislikes nature's inconveniences
   (B) the geese's timing is predictable
   (C) Lonnie has had the experience before
   (D) both observers are hunters
   (E) the author and Lonnie are the same person

EXPLANATORY ANSWERS

1. Choice E is correct. See lines 3–5: "…a beating roar rolls across the water…shake out blankets all at one time." The author, with these words, is no doubt appealing to the reader's hearing. To answer this question, the reader has to identify those words dealing with sound and noise. Therefore, we have here a DETECTING DETAILS type of question. It is also an INFERENTIAL REASONING question, in that the "sound" words such as "beating" and "roar" lead the reader to infer that the author is appealing to the auditory (hearing) sense.

2. Choice B is correct. Excitement courses right through this passage. Here are examples:
   Lines 6–7: "…the invisible rhythmic beating of all those goose wings…"
   Line 8: "Even Lonnie is held motionless with suspense."
   Lines 9–10: "Then the geese begin to rise…a thousand at a time…"
   Lines 13–15: "…flock after flock…roar of cries and wingbeats."

   To answer this question, you must determine the dominant tone in this passage. Therefore, we have here a TONE/MOOD question.

3. Choice A is correct. The word "spectacular" means *dramatic, thrilling, impressive*. There is considerable action expressed throughout the passage. Sometimes there is a lull—then the action begins again. See lines 16–17: "I think the spectacle is over, until yet another flock lifts up, following the others…" To answer this question, you must have the ability to judge the general significance of the passage. Accordingly, we have here a MAIN IDEA question.

4. Choice C is correct. See lines 25–29: "Lonnie wears an exasperated, proprietary expression… when they'll start moving.'" To answer this question, you must be able to draw a correct inference. Therefore, we have here an INFERENTIAL REASONING question.

READ. COMP. STRATEGY 2

Underline the Key Parts of the Reading Passage*†

The underlinings will help you to answer questions. Practically every question will ask you to detect the following:

a)   the main idea

or

b)   information that is specifically mentioned in the passage

or

c)   information that is implied (not directly stated) in the passage

or

d)   the tone or mood of the passage.

If you find out quickly what the question is aiming for, you will more easily arrive at the correct answer by referring to your underlinings in the passage.

EXAMPLE 1

That one citizen is as good as another is a favorite American axiom, supposed to express the very essence of our Constitution and way of life. But just what do we mean when we utter that platitude? One surgeon is not as good
5 as another. One plumber is not as good as another. We soon become aware of this when we require the attention of either. Yet in political and economic matters we appear to have reached a point where knowledge and specialized training count for very little. A newspaper reporter is sent
10 out on the street to collect the views of various passersby on such a question as "Should the United States defend El Salvador?" The answer of the barfly who doesn't even know where the country is located, or that it is a country, is quoted in the next edition just as solemnly as that of the
15 college teacher of history. With the basic tenets of democracy—that all men are born free and equal and are entitled to life, liberty, and the pursuit of happiness—no decent American can possibly take issue. But that the opinion of one citizen on a technical subject is just as authoritative
20 as that of another is manifestly absurd. And to accept the opinions of all comers as having the same value is surely to encourage a cult of mediocrity.

QUESTIONS

1. Which phrase best expresses the main idea of this passage?

    (A) the myth of equality
    (B) a distinction about equality
    (C) the essence of the Constitution
    (D) a technical subject
    (E) knowledge and specialized training

2. The author most probably included the example of the question on El Salvador (lines 11–12) in order to

    (A) move the reader to rage
    (B) show that he is opposed to opinion sampling
    (C) show that he has thoroughly researched his project
    (D) explain the kind of opinion sampling he objects to
    (E) provide a humorous but temporary diversion from his main point

3. The author would be most likely to agree that

    (A) some men are born to be masters; others are born to be servants
    (B) the Constitution has little relevance for today's world
    (C) one should never express an opinion on a specialized subject unless he is an expert in that subject
    (D) every opinion should be treated equally
    (E) all opinions should not be given equal weight

EXPLANATORY ANSWERS

1. Choice B is correct. See lines 1–7: "That one citizen...attention of either." These lines indicate that there is quite a distinction about equality when we are dealing with all the American people.

2. Choice D is correct. See lines 9–15: "A newspaper reporter...college teacher of history." These lines show that the author probably included the example of the question of El Salvador in order to explain the kind of opinion sampling he objects to.

* Strategy 2 is considered the Master Reading Comprehension Strategy because it can be used effectively in every Reading Comprehension question. However, it is important that you learn the other Reading Comprehension Strategies because they can often be used to double-check your answers.
†Unfortunately, on the computer-based GRE you cannot underline on the computer screen. However, you can make notes on your scrap paper.

3. Choice E is correct. See lines 18–22: "But that the opinion…to encourage a cult of mediocrity." Accordingly, the author would be most likely to agree that all opinions should *not* be given equal weight.

EXAMPLE 2

She walked along the river until a policeman stopped her. It was one o'clock, he said. Not the best time to be walking alone by the side of a half-frozen river. He smiled at her, then offered to walk her home. It was the first day of the
5 new year, 1946, eight and a half months after the British tanks had rumbled into Bergen-Belsen.

That February, my mother turned twenty-six. It was difficult for strangers to believe that she had ever been a concentration-camp inmate. Her face was smooth and
10 round. She wore lipstick and applied mascara to her large, dark eyes. She dressed fashionably. But when she looked into the mirror in the mornings before leaving for work, my mother saw a shell, a mannequin who moved and spoke but who bore only a superficial resemblance to her real self.
15 The people closest to her had vanished. She had no proof that they were truly dead. No eyewitnesses had survived to vouch for her husband's death. There was no one living who had seen her parents die. The lack of confirmation haunted her. At night before she went to sleep and during the day as
20 she stood pinning dresses she wondered if, by some chance, her parents had gotten past the Germans or had crawled out of the mass grave into which they had been shot and were living, old and helpless, somewhere in Poland. What if only one of them had died? What if they had survived and had
25 died of cold or hunger after she had been liberated, while she was in Celle* dancing with British officers?

She did not talk to anyone about these things. No one, she thought, wanted to hear them. She woke up in the mornings, went to work, bought groceries, went to the Jewish
30 Community Center and to the housing office like a robot.

*Celle is a small town in Germany.

QUESTIONS

1. The policeman stopped the author's mother from walking along the river because

   (A) the river was dangerous
   (B) it was the wrong time of day
   (C) it was still wartime
   (D) it was so cold
   (E) she looked suspicious

2. The author states that his mother thought about her parents when she

   (A) walked along the river
   (B) thought about death
   (C) danced with officers
   (D) arose in the morning
   (E) was at work

3. When the author mentions his mother's dancing with the British officers, he implies that his mother

   (A) compared her dancing to the suffering of her parents
   (B) had clearly put her troubles behind her
   (C) felt it was her duty to dance with them
   (D) felt guilty about dancing
   (E) regained the self-confidence she once had

EXPLANATORY ANSWERS

1. Choice B is correct. See lines 1–4: "She walked along…offered to walk her home." The policeman's telling her that it was not the best time to be walking alone indicates clearly that "it was the wrong time of day."

2. Choice E is correct. Refer to lines 19–20: "…and during the day as she stood pinning dresses she wondered…"

3. Choice D is correct. See lines 24–26: "What if they had survived…dancing with British officers?"

Look Back at the Passage When in Doubt

Sometimes while you are answering a question, you are not quite sure whether you have chosen the correct answer. Often, the underlinings that you have made in the reading passage will help you to determine whether a certain choice is the only correct choice.

EXAMPLE 1

All museum adepts are familiar with examples of *ostrakoi*, the oystershells used in balloting. As a matter of fact, these "oystershells" are usually shards of pottery, conveniently glazed to enable the voter to express his wishes in writing.
5 In the Agora, a great number of these have come to light, bearing the thrilling name Themistocles. Into rival jars were dropped the ballots for or against his banishment. On account of the huge vote taken on that memorable date, it was to be expected that many ostrakoi would be found,
10 but the interest of this collection is that a number of these ballots are inscribed in an *identical* handwriting. There is nothing mysterious about it! The Boss was on the job, then as now. He prepared these ballots and voters cast them—no doubt for the consideration of an obol or two. The *ballot box*
15 *was stuffed*.

How is the glory of the American boss diminished! A vile imitation, he. His methods as old as Time!

QUESTION

The title that best expresses the ideas of this passage is

(A) An Odd Method of Voting
(B) Themistocles, an Early Dictator
(C) Democracy in the Past
(D) Political Trickery—Past and Present
(E) The Diminishing American Politician

EXPLANATORY ANSWER

Choice D is correct. An important idea that you might have underlined is expressed in lines 12–13: "The Boss was on the job, then as now."

EXAMPLE 2

But the weather predictions that an almanac always contains are, we believe, mostly wasted on the farmer. He can take a squint at the moon before turning in. He can "smell" snow or tell if the wind is shifting dangerously east.
5 He can register forebodingly an extra twinge in a rheumatic shoulder. With any of these to go by, he can be reasonably sure of tomorrow's weather. He can return the almanac to the nail behind the door and put a last stick of wood in the stove. For an almanac, a zero night or a morning's drifted
10 road—none of these has changed much since Poor Richard wrote his stuff and barns were built along the Delaware.

QUESTION

The author implies that, in predicting weather, there is considerable value in

(A) reading the almanac
(B) placing the last stick of wood in the stove
(C) sleeping with one eye on the moon
(D) keeping an almanac behind the door
(E) noting rheumatic pains

EXPLANATORY ANSWER

Choice E is correct. Important ideas that you might have underlined are the following:
Lines 2–3: "He can take a squint at the moon."
Lines 3–4: "He can 'smell' snow…"
Lines 5–6: "He can register forebodingly an extra twinge in a rheumatic shoulder."

These underlinings will reveal that, in predicting weather, the quote in lines 5–6 gives you the correct answer.

Before You Start Answering the Questions, Read the Passage *Carefully*

A great advantage of careful reading of the passage is that you will, thereby, get a very good idea of what the passage is about. If a particular sentence is not clear to you as you read, then reread that sentence to get a better idea of what the author is trying to say.

EXAMPLE 1

The American Revolution is the only one in modern history which, rather than devouring the intellectuals who prepared it, carried them to power. Most of the signatories of the Declaration of Independence were intellectuals.
5 This tradition is ingrained in America, whose greatest statesmen have been intellectuals—Jefferson and Lincoln, for example. These statesmen performed their political function, but at the same time they felt a more universal responsibility, and they actively defined this responsibility.
10 Thanks to them there is in America a living school of political science. In fact, it is at the moment the only one perfectly adapted to the emergencies of the contemporary world, and one that can be victoriously opposed to communism. A European who follows American politics
15 will be struck by the constant reference in the press and from the platform to this political philosophy, to the historical events through which it was best expressed, to the great statesmen who were its best representatives.

[Underlining important ideas as you are reading this passage is strongly urged.]

QUESTIONS

1. The title that best expresses the ideas of this passage is

   (A) Fathers of the American Revolution
   (B) Jefferson and Lincoln—Ideal Statesmen
   (C) The Basis of American Political Philosophy
   (D) Democracy vs. Communism
   (E) The Responsibilities of Statesmen

2. According to the passage, intellectuals who pave the way for revolutions are usually

   (A) honored
   (B) misunderstood
   (C) destroyed
   (D) forgotten
   (E) elected to office

3. Which statement is true according to the passage?

   (A) America is a land of intellectuals.
   (B) The signers of the Declaration of Independence were well educated.
   (C) Jefferson and Lincoln were revolutionaries.
   (D) Adaptability is a characteristic of American political science.
   (E) Europeans are confused by American politics.

EXPLANATORY ANSWERS

1. Choice C is correct. Throughout this passage, the author speaks about the basis of American political philosophy. For example, see lines 5–11: "This tradition is ingrained in America,…a living school of political science."

2. Choice C is correct. See lines 1–3: "The American Revolution is the only one…carried them to power." These lines may be interpreted to mean that intellectuals who pave the way for revolutions—other than the American Revolution—are usually destroyed.

3. Choice D is correct. The word "adaptability" means the ability to adapt—to adjust to a specified use or situation. Now see lines 10–14: "…there is in America…opposed to communism."

EXAMPLE 2

The microscopic vegetables of the sea, of which the diatoms
are most important, make the mineral wealth of the water
available to the animals. Feeding directly on the diatoms
and other groups of minute unicellular algae are the marine
5 protozoa, many crustaceans, the young of crabs, barnacles,
sea worms, and fishes. Hordes of small carnivores, the first
link in the chain of flesh eaters, move among these peaceful
grazers. There are fierce little dragons half an inch long,
the sharp-jawed arrowworms. There are gooseberrylike
10 comb jellies, armed with grasping tentacles, and there are
the shrimplike euphausiids that strain food from the water
with their bristly appendages. Since they drift where the
currents carry them, with no power or will to oppose that
of the sea, this strange community of creatures and the
15 marine plants that sustain them are called plankton, a word
derived from the Greek, meaning wandering.

[Underlining important ideas as you are reading this
passage is strongly urged.]

QUESTIONS

1. According to the passage, diatoms are a kind of

(A) mineral
(B) alga
(C) crustacean
(D) protozoan
(E) fish

2. Which characteristic of diatoms does the passage
emphasize?

(A) size
(B) feeding habits
(C) activeness
(D) numerousness
(E) cellular structure

EXPLANATORY ANSWERS

1. Choice B is correct. See lines 3–5: "Feeding
directly on the diatoms…minute unicellular algae
are the marine protozoa…" These lines indicate
that diatoms are a kind of alga.

2. Choice A is correct. See lines 1–4: "The microscopic vegetables of the sea…minute unicellular
algae…." In these lines, the words "microscopic"
and "minute" emphasize the small size of the
diatoms.

READ. COMP. STRATEGY **5**

Get the Meanings of Tough Words by Using the Context Method

Suppose you don't know the meaning of a certain word in a passage. Then try to determine
the meaning of that word from the context—that is, from the words that are close in position
to that word whose meaning you don't know. Knowing the meanings of difficult words in the
passage will help you to better understand the passage as a whole.

EXAMPLE 1

Like all insects, it wears its skeleton on the outside—a
marvelous chemical compound called chitin which sheathes
the whole of its body. This flexible armor is tremendously tough, light, shatterproof, and resistant to alkali
5 and acid compounds that would eat the clothing, flesh, and
bones of man. To it are attached muscles so arranged
around catapult-like hind legs as to enable the hopper to
hop, if so diminutive a term can describe so prodigious a
leap as ten or twelve feet—about 150 times the length of
10 the one-or-so-inch-long insect. The equivalent feat for a man

would be a casual jump, from a standing position, over the
Washington Monument.

QUESTIONS

1. The word "sheathes" (line 2) means

(A) strips
(B) provides
(C) exposes
(D) encases
(E) excites

2. The word "prodigious" (line 8) means

(A) productive
(B) frightening
(C) criminal
(D) enjoyable
(E) enormous

EXPLANATORY ANSWERS

1. Choice D is correct. The words in line 1, "it wears its skeleton on the outside," give us the idea that "sheathes" probably means "covers" or "encases."

2. Choice E is correct. See the surrounding words in lines 7–10, "enable the hopper to hop…so prodigious a leap as ten or twelve feet—about 150 times the length of the one-or-so-inch–long insect." We may easily infer that the word "prodigious" means "great in size," "enormous."

EXAMPLE 2

Since the days when the thirteen colonies, each so jealous of its sovereignty, got together to fight the British soldiers, the American people have exhibited a tendency—a genius—to maintain widely divergent viewpoints in normal
5 times, but to unite and agree in times of stress. One reason the federal system has survived is that it has demonstrated this same tendency. Most of the time the three coequal divisions of the general government tend to compete. In crises they tend to cooperate, and not only during war. A
10 singular instance of cooperation took place in the opening days of the first administration of Franklin D. Roosevelt, when the harmonious efforts of the executive and the legislature to arrest the havoc of depression brought the term *rubber-stamp Congress* into the headlines. On the
15 other hand, when in 1937 Roosevelt attempted to bend the judiciary to the will of the executive by "packing" the Supreme Court, Congress rebelled. This frequently proved flexibility—this capacity of both people and government to shift from competition to cooperation and back again as
20 circumstances warrant—suggests that the federal system will be found equal to the very real dangers of the present world situation.

QUESTIONS

1. The word "havoc" (line 13) means

(A) possession
(B) benefit
(C) destruction
(D) symptom
(E) enjoyment

2. The word "divergent" (line 4) means

(A) interesting
(B) discussed
(C) flexible
(D) differing
(E) appreciated

EXPLANATORY ANSWERS

1. Choice C is correct. The prepositional phrase "of depression," which modifies "havoc," should indicate that this word has an unfavorable meaning. The only choice that has an unfavorable meaning is Choice C—"destruction."

2. Choice D is correct. See lines 3–5: "…the American people…widely divergent viewpoints…but to unite and agree in times of stress." The word "but" in this sentence is an *opposition indicator*. We may, therefore, assume that a "divergent viewpoint" is a "differing" one from the idea expressed in the words "to unite and agree in times of stress."

READ. COMP.
STRATEGY 6

Circle Transitional Words in the Passage*

There are certain transitional words—also called "bridge" or "key" words—that will help you to discover logical connections in a reading passage. *Circling* these transitional words will help you to get a better understanding of the passage.

Here are examples of commonly used transitional words and what these words may indicate.

Transitional Word	Indicating
although however in spite of rather than nevertheless on the other hand but	OPPOSITION

Transitional Word	Indicating
moreover besides additionally furthermore in fact	SUPPORT

Transitional Word	Indicating
therefore consequently accordingly because when so	RESULT

EXAMPLE 1

Somewhere between 1860 and 1890, the dominant emphasis in American literature was radically changed. But it is obvious that this change was not necessarily a matter of conscious concern to all writers. In fact, many writers
5 may seem to have been actually unaware of the shifting emphasis. Moreover, it is not possible to trace the steady march of the realistic emphasis from its first feeble notes to its dominant trumpet-note of unquestioned leadership. The progress of realism is to change the figure to that of a small
10 stream, receiving accessions from its tributaries at unequal points along its course, its progress now and then balked by the sandbars of opposition or the diffusing marshes of error and compromise. Again, it is apparent that any attempt to classify rigidly, as romanticists or realists, the writers of this
15 period is doomed to failure, since it is not by virtue of the writer's conscious espousal of the romantic or realistic creed that he does much of his best work, but by virtue of that writer's sincere surrender to the atmosphere of the subject.

QUESTIONS

1. The title that best expresses the ideas of this passage is

(A) Classifying American Writers
(B) Leaders in American Fiction
(C) The Sincerity of Writers
(D) The Values of Realism
(E) The Rise of Realism

2. Which characteristic of writers does the author praise?

(A) their ability to compromise
(B) their allegiance to a "school"
(C) their opposition to change
(D) their awareness of literary trends
(E) their intellectual honesty

EXPLANATORY ANSWERS

1. Choice E is correct. Note some of the transitional words that help you to interpret the passage and see why a title of "The Rise of Realism" would be warranted. In line 6, "Moreover" is a key word that is connected to "realistic emphasis" in line 7. This idea is also connected to the sentence involving the "progress of realism" in line 9. The word "again" in line 13 is also connected with this rise in realism.

2. Choice E is correct. See lines 15–18: "...since it is not by virtue of...but by virtue of that writer's sincere...of the subject." The transitional word "but" helps us to arrive at the correct answer, which is "their intellectual honesty."

*Unfortunately, on the computer-based GRE, you cannot circle on the computer screen. However, you can make notes on your scrap paper.

EXAMPLE 2

A humorous remark or situation is, furthermore, always a pleasure. We can go back to it and laugh at it again and again. One does not tire of the *Pickwick Papers,* or of the humor of Mark Twain, any more than the child tires of a
5 nursery tale that he knows by heart. Humor is a feeling, and feelings can be revived. But wit, being an intellectual and not an emotional impression, suffers by repetition. A witticism is really an item of knowledge. Wit, again, is distinctly a gregarious quality, whereas humor may abide
10 in the breast of a hermit. Those who live by themselves almost always have a dry humor. Wit is a city, humor a country, product. Wit is the accomplishment of persons who are busy with ideas; it is the fruit of intellectual cultivation and abounds in coffeehouses, in salons, and in literary
15 clubs. But humor is the gift of those who are concerned with persons rather than ideas, and it flourishes chiefly in the middle and lower classes.

QUESTION

1. It is probable that the paragraph preceding this one discussed the

(A) *Pickwick Papers*
(B) characteristics of literature
(C) characteristics of human nature
(D) characteristics of humor
(E) nature of human feelings

EXPLANATORY ANSWER

1. Choice D is correct. See lines 1–2: "A humorous remark or situation is, furthermore, always a pleasure." The transitional word "furthermore" means "in addition." We may, therefore, assume that something dealing with humor has been discussed in the previous paragraph.

READ. COMP. STRATEGY 7

Don't Answer a Question on the Basis of Your Own Opinion

Answer each question on the basis of the information given or suggested in the passage itself. Your own views or judgments may sometimes conflict with what the author of the passage is expressing. Answer the question according to what the author believes.

EXAMPLE 1

The drama critic, on the other hand, has no such advantages. He cannot be selective; he must cover everything that is offered for public scrutiny in the principal playhouses of the city where he works. The column space that
5 seemed, yesterday, so pitifully inadequate to contain his comments on *Long Day's Journey into Night* is roughly the same as that which yawns today for his verdict on some inane comedy that has chanced to find for itself a numskull backer with five hundred thousand dollars to lose. This
10 state of affairs may help to explain why the New York theater reviewers are so often, and so unjustly, stigmatized as baleful and destructive fiends. They spend most of their professional lives attempting to pronounce intelligent judgments on plays that have no aspiration to intelligence. It is
15 hardly surprising that they lash out occasionally; in fact, what amazes me about them is that they do not lash out more violently and more frequently. As Shaw said of his fellow-critics in the 1890s, they are "a culpably indulgent body of men." Imagine the verbal excoriations that would
20 be inflicted if Lionel Trilling, or someone of comparable eminence, were called on to review five books a month of which three were novelettes composed of criminal confessions. The butchers of Broadway would seem lambs by comparison.

QUESTIONS

1. In writing this passage, the author's purpose seems to have been to

(A) comment on the poor quality of our plays
(B) show why book reviewing is easier than play reviewing
(C) point out the opinions of Shaw
(D) show new trends in literary criticism
(E) defend the work of the play critic

2. The passage suggests that, as a play, *Long Day's Journey into Night* was

(A) inconsequential
(B) worthwhile
(C) poorly written
(D) much too long
(E) pleasant to view

EXPLANATORY ANSWERS

1. Choice E is correct. Throughout the passage, the author is defending the work of the play critic. See, for example, lines 9–14: "This state of affairs... plays that have no aspiration to intelligence." Be sure that you do not answer a question on the basis of your own views. You yourself may believe that the plays presented on the stage today are of poor quality (Choice A) generally. The question, however, asks about the *author's opinion*— not yours.

2. Choice B is correct. See lines 4–9: "The column space...dollars to lose." You yourself may believe that *Long Day's Journey into Night* is a bad play (Choice A or C or D). But remember—the author's opinion, not yours, is asked for.

EXAMPLE 2

History has long made a point of the fact that the magnificent flowering of ancient civilization rested upon the institution of slavery, which released opportunity at the top of the art and literature that became the glory of antiq-
5 uity. In a way, the mechanization of the present-day world produces the condition of the ancient in that the enormous development of labor-saving devices and of contrivances that amplify the capacities of mankind affords the base for the leisure necessary to widespread cultural pursuits.
10 Mechanization is the present-day slave power, with the difference that in the mechanized society there is no group of the community that does not share in the benefits of its inventions.

QUESTION

1. The author's attitude toward mechanization is one of

   (A) awe
   (B) acceptance
   (C) distrust
   (D) fear
   (E) devotion

EXPLANATORY ANSWER

1. Choice B is correct. Throughout the passage, the author's attitude toward mechanization is one of acceptance. Such acceptance on the part of the author is indicated particularly in lines 10–13: "Mechanization is...the benefits of its inventions." You yourself may have a feeling of distrust (Choice C) or fear (Choice D) toward mechanization. But the author does not have such feelings.

READ. COMP. STRATEGY 8

After Reading the Passage, Read Each Question *Carefully*

Be sure that you read *with care* not only the stem (beginning) of a question, but also *each* of the five choices. Some students select a choice just because it is a true statement—or because it answers part of a question. This can get you into trouble.

EXAMPLE 1

The modern biographer's task becomes one of discovering the "dynamics" of the personality he is studying rather than allowing the reader to deduce that personality from documents. If he achieves a reasonable likeness, he need
5 not fear too much that the unearthing of still more material will alter the picture he has drawn; it should add dimension to it, but not change its lineaments appreciably. After all, he has had more than enough material to permit him to reach conclusions and to paint his portrait. With this abundance
10 of material he can select moments of high drama and find episodes to illustrate character and make for vividness. In any event, biographers, I think, must recognize that the writing of a life may not be as "scientific" or as "definitive" as we have pretended. Biography partakes of a large part
15 of the subjective side of man; and we must remember that those who walked abroad in our time may have one appearance for us—but will seem quite different to posterity.

QUESTION

1. According to the author, which is the real task of the modern biographer?

   (A) interpreting the character revealed to him by study of the presently available data
   (B) viewing the life of the subject in the biographer's own image
   (C) leaving to the reader the task of interpreting the character from contradictory evidence
   (D) collecting facts and setting them down in chronological order
   (E) being willing to wait until all the facts on his subject have been uncovered

EXPLANATORY ANSWER

1. Choice A is correct. See lines 1–7: "The modern biographer's task…but not change its lineaments appreciably." The word "dynamics" is used here to refer to the physical and moral forces that exerted influence on the main character of the biography. The lines quoted indicate that the author believes that the real task of the biographer is to study the *presently available data*. Choice D may also appear to be a correct choice since a biographer is likely to consider his job to be collecting facts and setting them down in chronological order. But the passage does not directly state that a biographer has such a procedure.

EXAMPLE 2

Although patience is the most important quality a treasure hunter can have, the trade demands a certain amount of courage too. I have my share of guts, but make no boast about ignoring the hazards of diving. As all good divers
5 know, the business of plunging into an alien world with an artificial air supply as your only link to the world above can be as dangerous as stepping into a den of lions. Most of the danger rests within the diver himself.

The devil-may-care diver who shows great bravado
10 underwater is the worst risk of all. He may lose his bearings in the glimmering dim light that penetrates the sea and become separated from his diving companions. He may dive too deep, too long and suffer painful, sometimes fatal, bends.

QUESTION

1. According to the author, an underwater treasure hunter needs above all to be

   (A) self-reliant
   (B) adventuresome
   (C) mentally alert
   (D) patient
   (E) physically fit

EXPLANATORY ANSWER

1. Choice D is correct. See lines 1–3: "Although patience is the most important…courage too." Choice E ("physically fit") may also appear to be a correct choice, since an underwater diver certainly has to be physically fit. Nevertheless, the passage nowhere states this directly.

READ. COMP. STRATEGY 9

Increase Your Vocabulary to Boost Your Reading Comprehension Score

1. You can increase your vocabulary tremendously by learning Latin and Greek roots, prefixes, and suffixes. Knowing the meanings of difficult words will thereby help you to understand a passage better.

   Sixty percent of all the words in our English language are derived from Latin and Greek. By learning certain Latin and Greek roots, prefixes, and suffixes, you will be able to understand the meanings of more than 150,000 additional English words. See "The Gruber Prefix-Root-Suffix List" beginning on page 366.

2. This book also includes a "GRE 3,400-Word List" beginning on page 377. This Word List will prove to be a powerful vocabulary builder for you.

   There are other steps—in addition to the two steps explained above—to increase your vocabulary. Here they are:

3. Take vocabulary tests like the 100 Tests to Strengthen Your Vocabulary beginning on page 426.
4. Read as widely as possible—novels, nonfiction, newspapers, magazines.
5. Listen to people who speak well. Many TV programs have very fine speakers. You can pick up many new words listening to such programs.
6. Get into the habit of using a dictionary often. You can get a dictionary app for your phone or look up words online.
7. Play word games—crossword puzzles will really build up your vocabulary.

EXAMPLE 1

Acting, like much writing, is probably a compensation for and release from the strain of some profound maladjustment of the psyche. The actor lives most intensely by proxy. He has to be somebody else to be himself. But it is
5 all done openly and for our delight. The dangerous man, the enemy of nonattachment or any other wise way of life, is the born actor who has never found his way into the Theater, who never uses a stage door, who does not take a call and then wipe the paint off his face. It is the intrusion
10 of this temperament into political life, in which at this day it most emphatically does not belong, that works half the mischief in the world. In every country you may see them rise, the actors who will not use the Theater, and always they bring down disaster from the angry gods who like to
15 see mountebanks in their proper place.

QUESTIONS

1. The meaning of "maladjustment" (lines 2–3) is a

    (A) replacement of one thing for another
    (B) profitable experience in business
    (C) consideration for the feelings of others
    (D) disregard of advice offered by others
    (E) poor relationship with one's environment

2. The meaning of "psyche" (line 3) is

    (A) person
    (B) mind
    (C) personality
    (D) psychology
    (E) physique

3. The meaning of "intrusion" (line 9) is

    (A) entering without being welcome
    (B) acceptance after considering the facts
    (C) interest that has developed after a period of time
    (D) fear as the result of imagination
    (E) refusing to obey a command

4. The meaning of "mountebanks" (line 15) is

    (A) mountain climbers
    (B) cashiers
    (C) high peaks
    (D) fakers
    (E) mortals

EXPLANATORY ANSWERS

1. Choice E is correct. The prefix *mal-* means "bad." Obviously a maladjustment is a bad adjustment— that is, a poor relationship with one's environment.

2. Choice B is correct. The root *psyche* means the mind functioning as the center of thought, feeling, and behavior.

3. Choice A is correct. The prefix *in-* means "into" in this case. The root *trud, trus* means "pushing into"—or entering without being welcome.

4. Choice D is correct. The root *mont* means "to climb." The root *banc* means a "bench." A mountebank is literally "one who climbs on a bench." The actual meaning of *mountebank* is a quack (faker) who sells useless medicines from a platform in a public place.

EXAMPLE 2

The American Museum of Natural History has long portrayed various aspects of man. Primitive cultures have been shown through habitat groups and displays of man's tools, utensils, and art. In more recent years, there has been a
5 tendency to delineate man's place in nature, displaying his destructive and constructive activities on the earth he inhabits. Now, for the first time, the Museum has taken man apart, enlarged the delicate mechanisms that make him run, and examined him as a biological phenomenon.
10 In the new Hall of the Biology of Man, Museum technicians have created a series of displays that are instructive to a degree never before achieved in an exhibit hall. Using new techniques and new materials, they have been able to produce movement as well as form and color. It is a human
15 belief that beauty is only skin deep. But nature has proved to be a master designer, not only in the matter of man's bilateral symmetry but also in the marvelous packaging job that has arranged all man's organs and systems within his skin-covered case. When these are taken out of the
20 case, greatly enlarged, and given color, they reveal form and design that give the lie to that old saw. Visitors will be surprised to discover that man's insides, too, are beautiful.

QUESTIONS

1. The meaning of "bilateral" (line 17) is

    (A) biological
    (B) two-sided
    (C) natural
    (D) harmonious
    (E) technical

2. The meaning of "symmetry" (line 17) is

    (A) simplicity
    (B) obstinacy
    (C) sincerity
    (D) appearance
    (E) proportion

EXPLANATORY ANSWERS

1. Choice B is correct. The prefix *bi-* means "two." The root *latus* means "side." Therefore, *bilateral* means "two-sided."

2. Choice E is correct. The prefix *sym-* means "together." The root *metr* means "measure." The word *symmetry*, therefore, means "proportion," "harmonious relation of parts," "balance."

READ. COMP. STRATEGY 10

> # Know How to Deal with Questions That Ask You to Find Statements That *Support* or *Weaken* the Arguments in a Passage or Statements That the Passage Does Not Provide Any Information About

Children should be required to play a musical instrument at an early age so that they will develop an appreciation for music. Furthermore, they should be exposed to classical music and be made knowledgeable of the history in the
5 composer's time so that they can associate the composer's music with the particular period in time. By incorporating these aspects in the children's educational program, the children will develop an appreciation and understanding of classical music.

SUPPORTING AN ARGUMENT

Which of the following statements, if true, is supported by the passage?

(A) Great musicians have developed their talents at an early age.

(B) Adults who love classical music are aware of the historical period of the compositions they listen to.

(C) Children who play an instrument show greater affinity for appreciation of classical music later in life.

(D) Children who are exposed to and listen to classical music develop an appreciation for music in their teenage and adult years.

(E) Classical music develops the intellect of the mind and provides carryover for creativity in other disciplines.

EXPLANATORY ANSWER

Choice C is correct: See lines 1–2. Choice A is incorrect: The passage doesn't describe how great musicians developed their talent. Choice B is incorrect: The passage does not say that a "love" or even "appreciation"

for classical music is associated specifically with the knowledge of the period in history of the compositions. Choice D is incorrect: The passage only says that appreciation for music is based on the playing of a musical instrument. Choice E is incorrect: This is not mentioned in the passage.

WEAKENING AN ARGUMENT

Which of the following, if true, seriously weakens the arguments in the passage? Choose two choices.

(A) Children who have difficulty in playing an instrument diminish their interest in music.

(B) Playing an instrument and learning historical musical facts are only a part of why someone will enjoy music later in life.

(C) Students who are talented in another area such as mathematics will primarily develop an interest in that area.

EXPLANATORY ANSWER

Choice A is correct: See lines 1–2. It says that children playing an instrument develop appreciation in music. If the children who have difficulty in playing an instrument diminish their interest in music, this would weaken the argument. Choice B is correct: If playing an instrument and learning historical facts are only a part of why someone will enjoy music later in life, this would undermine the contention in the passage. Choice C is incorrect: This would not weaken the arguments in the passage. Students who are talented in other areas would not affect what is described in the passage.

PROVIDING INFORMATION

The passage provides information on each of the following EXCEPT

(A) The role of active participation in music.
(B) The importance of learning about the historical events in the composer's time.
(C) The importance of the exposure to classical music at a young age.
(D) The reason for the requirement to play an instrument.
(E) The emotional effect that music has on a child.

EXPLANATORY ANSWER

Choice E is correct. Nowhere in the passage is described the "emotional" effect music has on a child. The statements in all of the other choices can be found in the passage. Choice A: See lines 1–2. Choice B: See lines 3–6. Choice C: See lines 2–6. Choice D: See lines 1–2.

3 Vocabulary Strategies

Introduction

Although **antonyms** (opposites of words) are not on the GRE, it is still important for you to know vocabulary and the strategies to figure out the meanings of words, since there are many questions involving difficult words in all the sections on the Verbal Reasoning part of the GRE, that is, the **Sentence Completions** and **Reading Comprehension.**

VOCABULARY STRATEGY 1

Use Roots, Prefixes, and Suffixes to Get the Meanings of Words

You can increase your vocabulary tremendously by learning Latin and Greek roots, prefixes, and suffixes. Sixty percent of all the words in our English language are derived from Latin and Greek. By learning certain Latin and Greek roots, prefixes, and suffixes, you will be able to understand the meanings of more than 150,000 additional English words. See "The Gruber Prefix-Root-Suffix List" beginning on page 366 and "Hot Prefixes and Roots" in Appendix A beginning on page 717.

EXAMPLE 1

Opposite of PROFICIENT:

(A) antiseptic
(B) unwilling
(C) inconsiderate
(D) neglectful
(E) awkward

EXPLANATORY ANSWER

Choice E is correct. The prefix *pro-* means "forward, for the purpose of." The root *fic* means "to make" or "to do." Therefore, *proficient* literally means "doing something in a forward way." The definition of proficient is "skillful, adept, capable." The antonym of *proficient* is, accordingly, *awkward, incapable.*

EXAMPLE 2

Opposite of DELUDE:

(A) include
(B) guide
(C) reply
(D) upgrade
(E) welcome

EXPLANATORY ANSWER

Choice B is correct. The prefix *de-* means "downward, against." The root *lud* means "to play (a game)." Therefore, *delude* literally means "to play a game against." The definition of delude is "to deceive, to mislead." The antonym of *delude* is, accordingly, *to guide.*

EXAMPLE 3

Opposite of LAUDATORY:

(A) vacating
(B) satisfactory
(C) revoking
(D) faultfinding
(E) silent

Choice D is correct. The root *laud* means "praise." The suffix *-ory* means "a tendency toward." Therefore, *laudatory* means "having a tendency toward praising someone." The definition of *laudatory* is praising. The antonym of *laudatory* is, accordingly, *faultfinding*.

EXAMPLE 4

Opposite of SUBSTANTIATE:

(A) reveal
(B) intimidate
(C) disprove
(D) integrate
(E) assist

Choice C is correct. The prefix *sub-* means "under." The root *sta* means "to stand." The suffix *-ate* is a verb form indicating "the act of." Therefore, *substantiate* literally means "to perform the act of standing under." The definition of *substantiate* is "to support with proof or evidence." The antonym is, accordingly, *disprove*.

EXAMPLE 5

Opposite of TENACIOUS:

(A) changing
(B) stupid
(C) unconscious
(D) poor
(E) antagonistic

Choice A is correct. *Ten* = to hold; *tenacious* = constant, holding. OPPOSITE = *changing*.

EXAMPLE 6

Opposite of RECEDE:

(A) accede
(B) settle
(C) surrender
(D) advance
(E) reform

Choice D is correct. *Re-* = back; *ced* = to go; *recede* = to go back. OPPOSITE = *advance*.

EXAMPLE 7

Opposite of CIRCUMSPECT:

(A) suspicious
(B) overbearing
(C) listless
(D) determined
(E) careless

Choice E is correct. *Circum-* = around; *spect* = to look or see; *circumspect* = looking all around or making sure that you see everything, careful. OPPOSITE = *careless*.

EXAMPLE 8

Opposite of MALEDICTION:

(A) sloppiness
(B) praise
(C) health
(D) religiousness
(E) proof

Choice B is correct. *Mal* = bad; *dict* = to speak; *malediction* = to speak badly about. OPPOSITE = *praise*.

EXAMPLE 9

Opposite of PRECURSORY:

(A) succeeding
(B) flamboyant
(C) cautious
(D) simple
(E) cheap

Choice A is correct. *Pre-* = before; *curs* = to run; *precursory* = coming before. OPPOSITE = *succeeding.*

EXAMPLE 10

Opposite of CIRCUMVENT:

(A) to go the straight route
(B) alleviate
(C) to prey on one's emotions
(D) scintillate
(E) perceive correctly

Choice A is correct. *Circum-* = around (like a circle); *vent* = to come; *circumvent* = to come around. OPPOSITE = *to go the straight route.*

VOCABULARY STRATEGY 2

Pay Attention to the Sound or Feeling of the Word—Whether Positive or Negative, Harsh or Mild, Big or Little, Etc.

If the word sounds harsh or terrible, such as "obstreperous," the meaning probably is something harsh or terrible. If you're looking for a word opposite in meaning to "obstreperous," look for a word or words that have a softer sound, such as "pleasantly quiet or docile." The sense of "obstreperous" can also seem to be negative—so if you're looking for a synonym, look for a negative word. If you're looking for an opposite (antonym), look for a positive word.

EXAMPLE 1

Opposite of BELLIGERENCY:

(A) pain
(B) silence
(C) homeliness
(D) elegance
(E) peace

Choice E is correct. The word *belligerency* imparts a tone of forcefulness or confusion and means "warlike." The opposite would be calmness or peacefulness. The closest choices are B or E, with E a little closer to the opposite in tone for the capitalized word. Of course, if you knew the root *belli* means "war," you could see the opposite as (E) peace.

EXAMPLE 2

Opposite of DEGRADE:

(A) startle
(B) elevate
(C) encircle
(D) replace
(E) assemble

Choice B is correct. Here you can think of the *de-* in *degrade* as a prefix that is negative (bad) and means *down,* and in fact *degrade* does mean "to debase or lower." So you should look for an opposite that would be a word with a *positive* (good) meaning. The best word from the choices is (B) elevate.

EXAMPLE 3

Opposite of OBFUSCATION:

(A) illumination
(B) irritation
(C) conviction
(D) minor offense
(E) stable environment

Choice A is correct. The prefix *ob-* is usually negative, as in *obstacle* or *obliterate*, and in fact *obfuscate* means "darken, bewilder, obscure, or confuse." So since we are looking for an opposite, you would look for a *positive* word. Choices A and E are positive, and you should go for the more positive of the two, which is Choice A.

EXAMPLE 4

Opposite of MUNIFICENCE:

(A) disloyalty
(B) stinginess
(C) dispersion
(D) simplicity
(E) vehemence

EXPLANATORY ANSWER

Choice B is correct because *munificence* means "generosity." Many of the words ending in *-ence*, like *opulence*, *effervescence*, *luminescence*, *quintessence*, etc., represent or describe something big or bright. So the opposite of one of these words would denote something small or dark.

You can associate the prefix *muni-* with money, as in "municipal bonds," so the word *munificence* must deal with money and in a big way. The opposite deals with money in a small way. Choice B fits the bill.

EXAMPLE 5

Opposite of DETRIMENT:

(A) recurrence
(B) disclosure
(C) resemblance
(D) enhancement
(E) postponement

EXPLANATORY ANSWER

Choice D is correct. The prefix *de-* can also mean "against" and is negative, and *detriment* means something that causes damage or loss. So you should look for a positive word. The only one is D, enhancement.

EXAMPLE 6

Opposite of UNDERSTATE:

(A) embroider
(B) initiate
(C) distort
(D) pacify
(E) violate

EXPLANATORY ANSWER

Choice A is correct. *Understate* means something said in a restrained or downplayed manner. You see "under" in *understate*, so look for a choice that gives you the impression of something that is "over," as in "overstated." The only choice is A, embroider, which means to embellish.

EXAMPLE 7

Opposite of DISHEARTEN:

(A) engage
(B) encourage
(C) predict
(D) dismember
(E) misinform

EXPLANATORY ANSWER

Choice B is correct. You see *heart* in *dishearten*. The *dis-* is negative and means "not to," or "not to have heart," and *dishearten* does mean to discourage. So you want to look for a *positive* word. Choice B, encourage, fits the bill.

EXAMPLE 8

Opposite of FIREBRAND:

(A) an intellect
(B) one who is charitable
(C) one who makes peace
(D) a philanthropist
(E) one who is dishonest

EXPLANATORY ANSWER

Choice C is correct. You see *fire* in *firebrand*. So think of something fiery or dangerous. The opposite of *firebrand* must be something that's calm or safe. The best choice is Choice C, whereas a *firebrand* is someone who causes trouble.

Use Word Associations to Determine Word Meanings and Their Opposites

Looking at the root or part of any capitalized word may suggest an association with another word that looks similar and whose meaning you know. This new word's meaning may give you a clue as to the meaning of the original word or the opposite in meaning to the original word if you need an opposite. For example, *extricate* reminds us of the word "extract," the opposite of which is "to put together."

EXAMPLE 1

Opposite of STASIS:

(A) stoppage
(B) reduction
(C) depletion
(D) fluctuation
(E) completion

EXPLANATORY ANSWER

Choice D is correct. Think of *static* or *stationary*. The opposite would be motion or fluctuation, since *stasis* means "a stopping or retarding of movement."

EXAMPLE 2

Opposite of APPEASE:

(A) criticize
(B) analyze
(C) correct
(D) incense
(E) develop

EXPLANATORY ANSWER

Choice D is correct. *Appease* means "to placate." Think of *peace* in *appease*. The opposite would be something violent or *incense*.

EXAMPLE 3

Opposite of COMMISERATION:

(A) undeserved reward
(B) lack of sympathy
(C) unexpected success
(D) absence of talent
(E) inexplicable danger

EXPLANATORY ANSWER

Choice B is correct. Think of *misery* in the word *commiseration*. *Commiseration* means the sharing of misery. Choice B is the only appropriate choice.

EXAMPLE 4

Opposite of JOCULAR:

(A) unintentional
(B) exotic
(C) muscular
(D) exaggerated
(E) serious

EXPLANATORY ANSWER

Choice E is correct. Think of *joke* in the word *jocular*, which means "given to joking." The opposite would be *serious*.

EXAMPLE 5

Opposite of ELONGATE:

(A) melt
(B) wind
(C) confuse
(D) smooth
(E) shorten

EXPLANATORY ANSWER

Choice E is correct. Think of the word *long* in *elongate*, which means "to lengthen." The opposite would be short or *shorten*.

EXAMPLE 6

Opposite of SLOTHFUL:

(A) permanent
(B) ambitious
(C) average
(D) truthful
(E) plentiful

EXPLANATORY ANSWER

Choice B is correct. Think of *sloth*, a very, very slow animal. So *slothful*, which means "lazy or sluggish," must be slow and unambitious. The opposite would be *ambitious*.

EXAMPLE 7

Opposite of FORTITUDE:

(A) timidity
(B) conservatism
(C) placidity
(D) laxness
(E) ambition

EXPLANATORY ANSWER

Choice A is correct. *Fortitude* means "strength in the face of adversity"; you should think of *fort* or *fortify* as something strong. The opposite would be weakness, or *timidity.*

EXAMPLE 8

Opposite of LUCID:

(A) underlying
(B) abstruse
(C) luxurious
(D) tight
(E) general

EXPLANATORY ANSWER

Choice B is correct. *Lucid* means "easily understood or clear"; you should think of *lucite*, a clear plastic. The opposite of clear is "hard to see through," or abstruse. *Note:* The *ab-* in *abstruse* makes Choice B the only *negative* choice, which is the opposite of the positive word *lucid.*

EXAMPLE 9

Opposite of POTENT:

(A) imposing
(B) pertinent
(C) feeble
(D) comparable
(E) frantic

EXPLANATORY ANSWER

Choice C is correct. Think of the word *potential* or *powerful.* To have potential is to have the ability or power to be able to do something. So the opposite would be feeble. You could also have thought of *potent* as a positive word. The opposite would be a negative word. The only two choices that are negative are choices C and E.

PART 5

MINI-MATH REFRESHER

The Most Important Basic Math Rules and Concepts You Need to Know

Make sure that you understand each of the following math rules and concepts. It is a good idea to memorize them all. Refer to the section of the Complete Math Refresher (Part 6 starting on page 185) shown in parentheses, e.g., (409), for a complete explanation of each.

Algebra and Arithmetic

(409)
$$a(b + c) = ab + ac$$
Example:
$$5(4 + 5) = 5(4) + 5(5)$$
$$= 20 + 25$$
$$= 45$$

(409)
$$(a + b)(c + d) = ac + ad + bc + bd$$
Example:
$$(2 + 3)(4 - 6) = (2)(4) + (2)(-6)$$
$$+ (3)(4) + (3)(-6)$$
$$= 8 - 12 + 12 - 18$$
$$= -10$$

(409)
$$(a + b)^2 = a^2 + 2ab + b^2$$

(409)
$$(a - b)^2 = a^2 - 2ab + b^2$$

(429)
$$a^2 = (a)(a)$$
Example:
$$2^2 = (2)(2) = 4$$
$$a^3 = (a)(a)(a)$$

(429)
$$\frac{a^x}{a^y} = a^{x-y}$$
Examples:
$$\frac{a^3}{a^2} = a^{3-2} = a$$
$$\frac{2^3}{2^2} = 2^{3-2} = 2$$

(409)
$$(a + b)(a - b) = a^2 - b^2$$

(429)
$$a^x a^y = a^{x+y}$$
Examples:
$$a^2 \times a^3 = a^5$$
$$2^2 \times 2^3 = 2^5 = 32$$

(409)
$$-(a - b) = b - a$$

(429)
$$a^0 = 1$$
$$10^0 = 1$$
$$10^1 = 10$$
$$10^2 = 100$$
$$10^3 = 1,000, \text{ etc.}$$
Example:
$$8.6 \times 10^4 = 8.6\underset{1}{0}\underset{2}{0}\underset{3}{0}\underset{4}{0}.0$$

(429)
$$(a^x)^y = a^{xy}$$
Examples:
$$(a^3)^5 = a^{15}; (2^3)^5 = 2^{15}$$

(429)
$$(ab)^x = a^x b^x$$
Examples:
$$(2 \times 3)^3 = 2^3 \times 3^3; (ab)^2 = a^2 b^2$$

(430)

If $y^2 = x$, then $y = \pm\sqrt{x}$

Example:

If $y^2 = 4$,

then $y = \pm\sqrt{4} = \pm 2$

(429)

$a^{-y} = \dfrac{1}{a^y}$

Example: $2^{-3} = \dfrac{1}{2^3} = \dfrac{1}{8}$

Percentage Problems

(107)

Percentage

$x\% = \dfrac{x}{100}$

Example:

$5\% = \dfrac{5}{100}$

RULE: "What" becomes x

"percent" becomes $\dfrac{1}{100}$

"of" becomes $\times$ (times)

"is" becomes $=$ (equals)

(107)

Examples:

(1) What percent of 5 is 2?

$$\dfrac{x}{100} \qquad \times\ 5\ =\ 2$$

or

$$\left(\dfrac{x}{100}\right)(5) = 2$$

$$\dfrac{5x}{100} = 2$$

$$5x = 200$$

$$x = 40$$

Answer $= 40\%$

(107)

(2) 6 is what percent of 24?

$$6\ =\ \dfrac{x}{100} \qquad \times\ 24$$

$$6 = \dfrac{24x}{100}$$

$$600 = 24x$$

$$100 = 4x \text{ (dividing both sides by 6)}$$

$$25 = x$$

Answer $= 25\%$

Equations

(409)

Example: $x^2 - 2x + 1 = 0$. Solve for x.
  Procedure:
  Factor: $(x-1)(x-1) = 0$
$$x - 1 = 0$$
$$x = 1$$
In the example $x^2 - 2x + 1 = 0$, where $m = 1$, $n = 1$, $b = -1$, $c = -1$,
$(x - 1)(x - 1) = (1)(1)x^2 + (-1)(1)x + (1)x(-1) + (-1)(-1)$
$$= x^2 + -x + -x + 1$$
$$= x^2 + -2x + 1$$

Note that in general:

$(mx + b)(nx + c) = mnx^2 + bnx + mxc + bc$

---

(407)

Example: $x + y = 1$; $x - y = 2$. Solve for x and y.
  Procedure:
  Add equations:
$$x + y = 1$$
$$\underline{x - y = 2}$$
$$2x + 0 = 3$$
Therefore $2x = 3$ and $x = \dfrac{3}{2}$

Substitute $x = \dfrac{3}{2}$ back into one of the equations:
$$x + y = 1$$
$$\frac{3}{2} + y = 1$$
$$y = -\frac{1}{2}$$

Equalities

(402)

$$a + b = c$$
$$\underline{+ \quad\quad d = d}$$
$$a + b + d = c + d$$

$$3 + 4 = 7$$
$$\underline{+ \quad\quad 2 = 2}$$
$$3 + 4 + 2 = 7 + 2$$

Inequalities

(419–425)

$>$ means greater than, $<$ means less than, $\geq$ means greater than or equal to, etc.

$$b > c$$
$$\underline{+ \quad d > e}$$
$$b + d > c + e$$

$$4 > 3$$
$$\underline{+ \quad 7 > 6}$$
$$11 > 9$$

$$4 > 3$$
$$\underline{-6 > -7}$$
$$-2 > -4$$

$$5 > 4$$
$$(6)\, 5 > 4\, (6)$$
Thus
$$30 > 24$$

$$-5 < -4$$
$$-(-5) > -(-4) \quad \text{(reversing inequality)}$$
$$5 > 4$$

If $\;-2 < x < +2$
then $+2 > -x > -2$

$a > b > 0$
Thus $a^2 > b^2$

Geometry

(504)

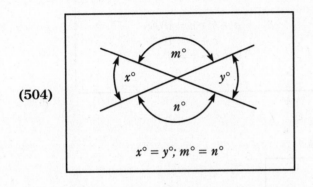

$x° = y°; m° = n°$

(501)

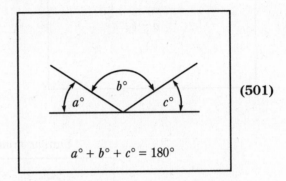

$a° + b° + c° = 180°$

(504)

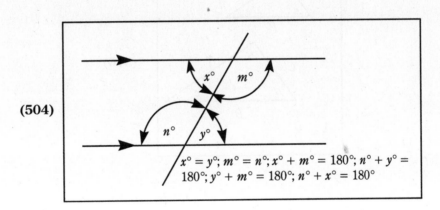

$x° = y°; m° = n°; x° + m° = 180°; n° + y° = 180°; y° + m° = 180°; n° + x° = 180°$

(506)

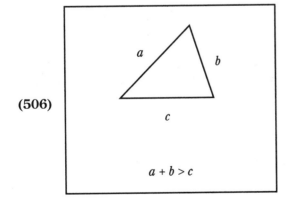

$a + b > c$

(506)

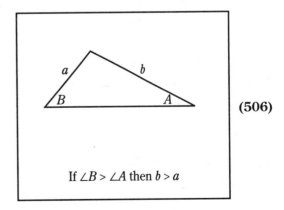

If $\angle B > \angle A$ then $b > a$

(507)

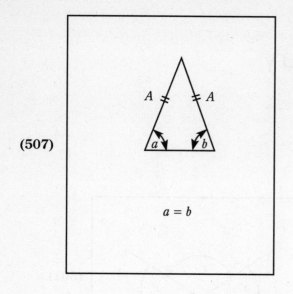

$a = b$

(501)

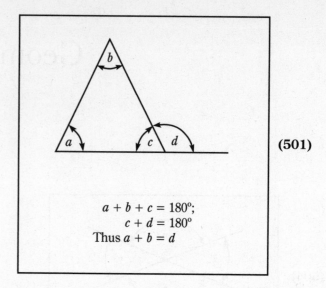

$a + b + c = 180°;$
$c + d = 180°$
Thus $a + b = d$

Similar Triangles

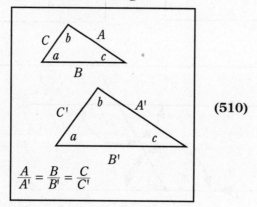

(510)

$$\frac{A}{A'} = \frac{B}{B'} = \frac{C}{C'}$$

Areas & Perimeters

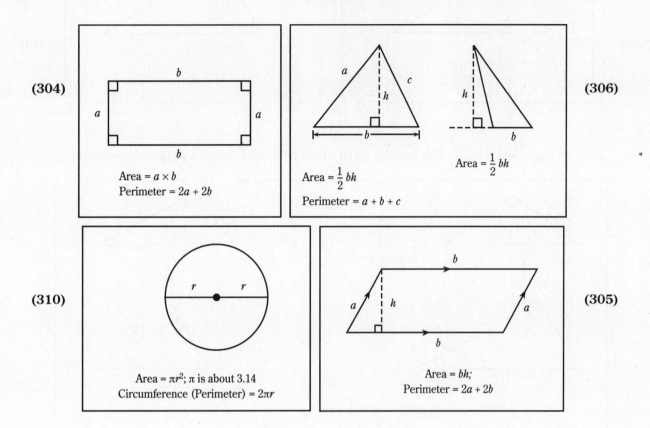

(304)

Area = $a \times b$
Perimeter = $2a + 2b$

(306)

Area = $\frac{1}{2} bh$
Perimeter = $a + b + c$

Area = $\frac{1}{2} bh$

(310)

Area = πr^2; π is about 3.14
Circumference (Perimeter) = $2\pi r$

(305)

Area = bh;
Perimeter = $2a + 2b$

More on Circles

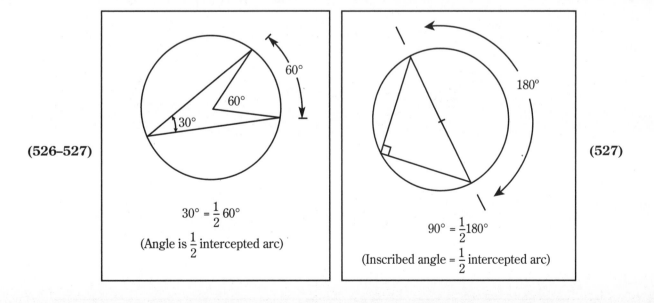

(526–527)

$30° = \frac{1}{2} 60°$

(Angle is $\frac{1}{2}$ intercepted arc)

(527)

$90° = \frac{1}{2} 180°$

(Inscribed angle = $\frac{1}{2}$ intercepted arc)

(509)

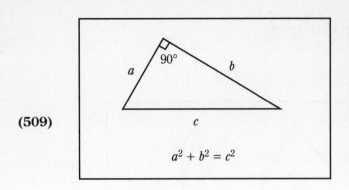

$$a^2 + b^2 = c^2$$

(509)

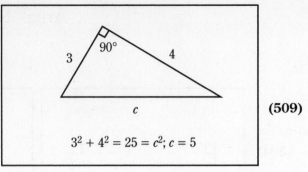

$$3^2 + 4^2 = 25 = c^2; c = 5$$

Here are some right triangles (not drawn to scale) whose relationship of sides you should memorize:

(509)

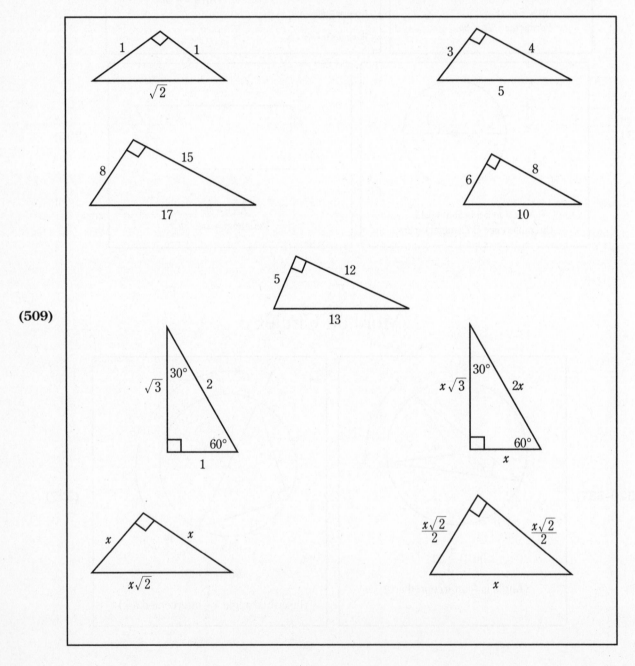

Coordinate Geometry

(410)

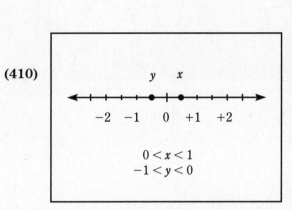

$$0 < x < 1$$
$$-1 < y < 0$$

(410–411)

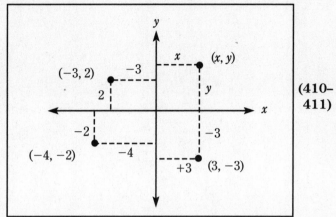

(411)

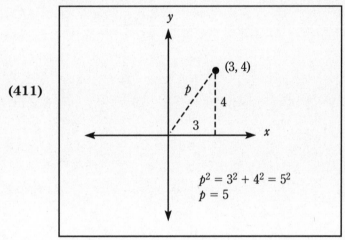

$$p^2 = 3^2 + 4^2 = 5^2$$
$$p = 5$$

(416)

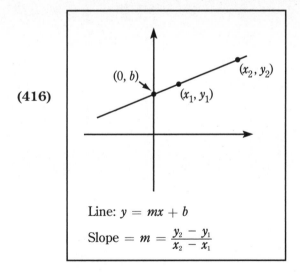

Line: $y = mx + b$

Slope $= m = \dfrac{y_2 - y_1}{x_2 - x_1}$

PART 6

COMPLETE GRE MATH REFRESHER

There are many GRE exam takers whose math background is not quite up to par—probably because their basic math skills are "rusty" or because they never did do well in their math classes. For these math-troubled students, this Math Refresher section will be "manna from heaven." The pages that follow constitute a complete basic math course that will help students greatly in preparing for the math part of the GRE.

This Math Refresher offers the following:

1. a systematic review of every math area covered by the questions in the math part of the GRE

and

2. short review tests throughout the Refresher to check whether the student has grasped the math principles that he or she has just studied.

The review tests will also provide students with valuable reinforcement so that they will remember how to go about solving math problems they would otherwise have difficulty with on the actual GRE.

Each of the 8 "Sessions" in this Math Refresher has a review test ("Practice Test"). Almost every review test has 50 questions followed by 50 detailed solutions. All of the solutions for the 8 review tests include a number (or numbers) in parentheses *after each solution*. The number refers to a specific instructional section where the rules and principles involved in the question are explained simply and clearly.

There is another very important purpose that this Math Refresher serves. You will find, after every solution in the Math sections of the 3 GRE Practice Tests in this book, a key to the mathematical principles of this Math Refresher. For example, a solution may direct you to Math Refresher 202, which deals with Distance and Time problems. If you happen to be weak in this mathematical operation, the 202 Math Refresher explanation will immediately clarify for you how to do Distance and Time problems. In other words, for those who are weak in any phase of basic math, this invaluable keying system will help you get the right answer to your GRE Math question—and thereby add approximately 10 points to your GRE score or 1 point on the new GRE scale.

MATH REFRESHER*
SESSION 1

Fractions, Decimals, Percentages, Deviations, Ratios and Proportions, Variations, and Comparison of Fractions

Fractions, Decimals, Percentages

These problems involve the ability to perform numerical operations quickly and correctly. It is essential that you learn the arithmetical procedures outlined in this section.

101.　Four different ways to write "a divided by b" are $a \div b$, $\frac{a}{b}$, $a : b$, $b \overline{)a}$.

　　Example: 7 divided by 15 is $7 \div 15 = \frac{7}{15} = 7 : 15 = 15\overline{)7}$.

102.　The numerator of a fraction is the upper number, and the denominator is the lower number.

　　Example: In the fraction $\frac{8}{13}$, the numerator is 8 and the denominator is 13.

103.　Moving a decimal point one place to the right multiplies the value of a number by 10, whereas moving the decimal point one place to the left divides a number by 10. Likewise, moving a decimal point two places to the right multiplies the value of a number by 100, whereas moving the decimal point two places to the left divides a number by 100.

　　Example:　$24.35 \times 10 = 243.5$ (decimal point moved to *right*)
　　　　　　　$24.35 \div 10 = 2.435$ (decimal point moved to *left*)

104.　To change a fraction to a decimal, divide the numerator of the fraction by its denominator.

　　Example: Express $\frac{5}{6}$ as a decimal. We divide 5 by 6, obtaining 0.83.

$$\frac{5}{6} = 5 \div 6 = 0.833\ldots$$

105.　To convert a decimal to a fraction, delete the decimal point and divide by whatever unit of 10 the number of decimal places represents.

　　Example: Convert 0.83 to a fraction. First, delete the decimal point. Second, two decimal places represent hundredths, so divide 83 by 100: $\frac{83}{100}$.

$$0.83 = \frac{83}{100}$$

106. To change a fraction to a percent, find its decimal form, multiply by 100, and add a percent sign.

> **Example:** Express $\frac{3}{8}$ as a percent. To convert $\frac{3}{8}$ to a decimal, divide 3 by 8, which gives us 0.375. Multiplying 0.375 by 100 gives us 37.5%.

107. To change a percent to a fraction, drop the percent sign and divide the number by 100.

> **Example:** Express 17% as a fraction. Dropping the % sign gives us 17, and dividing by 100 gives us $\frac{17}{100}$.

108. To *reduce* a fraction, divide the numerator and denominator by the largest number that divides them both evenly.

> **Example:** Reduce $\frac{10}{15}$. Dividing both the numerator and denominator by 5 gives us $\frac{2}{3}$.

> **Example:** Reduce $\frac{12}{36}$. The largest number that divides into both 12 and 36 is 12.
> Reducing the fraction, we have $\dfrac{\overset{1}{\cancel{12}}}{\underset{3}{\cancel{36}}} = \dfrac{1}{3}$.

> *Note:* In both examples, the reduced fraction is exactly equal to the original fraction:
> $$\frac{2}{3} = \frac{10}{15} \text{ and } \frac{12}{36} = \frac{1}{3}.$$

109. To add fractions with like denominators, add the numerators of the fractions, keeping the same denominator.

> **Example:** $\frac{1}{7} + \frac{2}{7} + \frac{3}{7} = \frac{6}{7}$.

110. To add fractions with different denominators, you must first change all of the fractions to *equivalent fractions* with the same denominators.

STEP 1. Find the *lowest (or least) common denominator,* the smallest number divisible by all of the denominators.

> **Example:** If the fractions to be added are $\frac{1}{3}$, $\frac{1}{4}$, and $\frac{5}{6}$, then the lowest common denominator is 12, because 12 is the smallest number that is divisible by 3, 4, and 6.

STEP 2. Convert all of the fractions to *equivalent fractions,* each having the lowest common denominator as its denominator. To do this, multiply the numerator of each fraction by the number of times that its denominator goes into the lowest common denominator. The product of this multiplication will be the *new numerator.* The denominator of the equivalent fractions will be the lowest common denominator. (See Step 1 above.)

> **Example:** The lowest common denominator of $\frac{1}{3}$, $\frac{1}{4}$, and $\frac{5}{6}$ is 12. Thus, $\frac{1}{3} = \frac{4}{12}$, because 12 divided by 3 is 4, and 4 times 1 = 4. $\frac{1}{4} = \frac{3}{12}$, because 12 divided by 4 is 3, and 3 times 1 = 3. $\frac{5}{6} = \frac{10}{12}$, because 12 divided by 6 is 2, and 2 times 5 = 10.

STEP 3. Now add all of the equivalent fractions by adding the numerators.

> **Example:** $\frac{4}{12} + \frac{3}{12} + \frac{10}{12} = \frac{17}{12}$

STEP 4. Reduce the fraction if possible, as shown in Section 108.

Example: Add $\frac{4}{5}$, $\frac{2}{3}$ and $\frac{8}{15}$. The lowest common denominator is 15, because 15 is the smallest number that is divisible by 5, 3, and 15. Then, $\frac{4}{5}$ is equivalent to $\frac{12}{15}$; $\frac{2}{3}$ is equivalent to $\frac{10}{15}$; and $\frac{8}{15}$ remains as $\frac{8}{15}$. Adding these numbers gives us $\frac{12}{15} + \frac{10}{15} + \frac{8}{15} = \frac{30}{15}$. Both 30 and 15 are divisible by 15, giving us $\frac{2}{1}$, or 2.

111. To *multiply fractions,* follow this procedure:

STEP 1. To find the numerator of the product, multiply all the numerators of the fractions being multiplied.

STEP 2. To find the denominator of the product, multiply all of the denominators of the fractions being multiplied.

STEP 3. Reduce the product.

Example: $\frac{5}{7} \times \frac{2}{15} = \frac{5 \times 2}{7 \times 15} = \frac{10}{105}$. Reduce by dividing both the numerator and denominator by 5, the common factor. $\frac{10}{105} = \frac{2}{21}$.

112. To *divide fractions,* follow this procedure:

STEP 1. Invert the divisor. That is, switch the positions of the numerator and denominator in the fraction you are dividing *by.*

STEP 2. Replace the division sign with a multiplication sign.

STEP 3. Carry out the multiplication indicated.

STEP 4. Reduce the product.

Example: Find $\frac{3}{4} \div \frac{7}{8}$. Inverting $\frac{7}{8}$, the divisor, gives us $\frac{8}{7}$. Replacing the division sign with a multiplication sign gives us $\frac{3}{4} \times \frac{8}{7}$. Carrying out the multiplication gives us $\frac{3}{4} \times \frac{8}{7} = \frac{24}{28}$. The fraction $\frac{24}{28}$ may then be reduced to $\frac{6}{7}$ by dividing both the numerator and the denominator by 4.

113. To *multiply decimals*, follow this procedure:

STEP 1. Disregard the decimal point. Multiply the factors (the numbers being multiplied) as if they were whole numbers.

STEP 2. In each factor, count the number of digits to the *right* of the decimal point. Find the total number of these digits in all the factors. In the product, start at the right and count to the left this (total) number of places. Put the decimal point there.

Example: Multiply 3.8×4.01. First, multiply 38 and 401, getting 15,238. There is a total of 3 digits to the right of the decimal points in the factors. Therefore, the decimal point in the product is placed 3 units to the left of the digit farthest to the right (8).

$$3.8 \times 4.01 = 15.238$$

Example: 0.025×3.6. First, multiply 25×36, getting 900. In the factors, there is a total of 4 digits to the right of the decimal points; therefore, in the product, we place the decimal point 4 units to the left of the digit farthest to the right in 900. However, there are only 3 digits in the product, so we add a 0 to the left of the 9, getting 0900. This makes it possible to place the decimal point correctly, thus: .0900, or .09. From this example, we can derive the rule that in the product we add as many zeros as are needed to provide the proper number of digits to the left of the digit farthest to the right.

114. To find a percent of a given quantity:

STEP 1. Replace the word "of" with a multiplication sign.

STEP 2. Convert the percent to a decimal: drop the percent sign and divide the number by 100. This is done by moving the decimal point two places to the left, adding zeros where necessary.

> **Examples:** 30% = 0.30   2.1% = 0.021   78% = 0.78

STEP 3. Multiply the given quantity by the decimal.

> **Example:** Find 30% of 200.

> 30% of 200 = 30% × 200 = 0.30 × 200 = 60.00

Deviations

Estimation problems arise when dealing with *approximations,* that is, numbers that are not mathematically precise. The error, or *deviation,* in an approximation is a measure of the closeness of that approximation.

115. *Absolute error,* or *absolute deviation,* is the difference between the estimated value and the real value (or between the approximate value and the exact value).

> **Example:** If the actual value of a measurement is 60.2 and we estimate it as 60, then the absolute deviation (absolute error) is 60.2 − 60 = 0.2.

116. *Fractional error,* or *fractional deviation,* is the ratio of the absolute error to the exact value of the quantity being measured.

> **Example:** If the exact value is 60.2 and the estimated value is 60, then the fractional error is

$$\frac{60.2 - 60}{60.2} = \frac{0.2}{60.2} = \frac{0.2 \times 5}{60.2 \times 5} = \frac{1}{301}$$

117. *Percent error,* or *percent deviation,* is the fractional error expressed as a percent. (See Section 106 for the method of converting fractions to percents.)

118. Many business problems, including the calculation of loss, profit, interest, and so forth, are treated as deviation problems. Generally, these problems concern the difference between the original value of a quantity and some new value after taxes, after interest, etc. The following chart shows the relationship between business and estimation problems.

Business Problems	*Estimation Problems*
original value	= exact value
new value	= approximate value
net profit net loss net interest	= absolute error
fractional profit fractional loss fractional interest	= fractional error
percent profit percent loss percent interest	= percent error

Example: An item that originally cost \$50 is resold for \$56. Thus the *net profit* is \$56 − \$50 = \$6. The *fractional profit* is $\dfrac{\$56 - \$50}{\$50} = \dfrac{\$6}{\$50} = \dfrac{3}{25}$. The *percent profit* is equal to the percent equivalent of $\dfrac{3}{25}$, which is 12%. (See Section 106 for converting fractions to percents.)

119. When there are two or more *consecutive changes in value,* remember that the new value of the first change becomes the original value of the second; consequently, successive fractional or percent changes may not be added directly.

Example: Suppose that a \$100 item is reduced by 10% and then by 20%. The first reduction puts the price at \$90 (10% of \$100 = \$10; \$100 − \$10 = \$90). Then, reducing the \$90 (the new original value) by 20% gives us \$72 (20% of \$90 = \$18; \$90 − \$18 = \$72). Therefore, it is *not* correct to simply add 10% and 20% and then take 30% of \$100.

Ratios and Proportions

120. A proportion is an equation stating that two ratios are equal. For example, $3 : 2 = 9 : x$ and $7 : 4 = a : 15$ are proportions. To solve a proportion:

STEP 1. First change the ratios to fractions. To do this, remember that $a : b$ is the same as $\dfrac{a}{b}$, or $1 : 2$ is equivalent to $\dfrac{1}{2}$, or $7 : 4 = a : 15$ is the same as $\dfrac{7}{4} = \dfrac{a}{15}$.

STEP 2. Now cross-multiply. That is, multiply the numerator of the first fraction by the denominator of the second fraction. Also multiply the denominator of the first fraction by the numerator of the second fraction. Set the first product equal to the second. This rule is sometimes stated as "The product of the means equals the product of the extremes."

Example: When cross-multiplying in the equation $\dfrac{3}{2} = \dfrac{9}{y}$, we get $3 \times y = 2 \times 9$, or $3y = 18$.

When we cross-multiply in the equation $\dfrac{a}{2} = \dfrac{4}{8}$, we get $8a = 8$, and by dividing each side of the equation by 8 to reduce, $a = 1$.

STEP 3. Solve the resulting equation. This is done algebraically.

Example: Solve for a in the proportion $7 : a = 6 : 18$.

Change the ratios to the fractional relation $\dfrac{7}{a} = \dfrac{6}{18}$. Cross-multiply: $7 \times 18 = 6 \times a$, or $126 = 6a$.

Solving for a gives us $a = 21$.

121. In solving proportions that have units of measurement (feet, seconds, miles, etc.), each ratio must have the same units. For example, if we have the ratio 5 inches : 3 feet, we must convert the 3 feet to 36 inches and then set up the ratio 5 inches : 36 inches, or 5 : 36. We might wish to convert inches to feet. Noting that 1 inch = $\dfrac{1}{12}$ foot, we get 5 inches : 3 feet = $5\left(\dfrac{1}{12}\right)$ feet : 3 feet = $\dfrac{5}{12}$ feet : 3 feet.

Example: On a blueprint, a rectangle measures 6 inches in width and 9 inches in length. If the actual width of the rectangle is 16 inches, how many feet are there in the length?

Solution: We set up the proportions, 6 inches : 9 inches = 16 inches : x feet. Since x feet is equal to $12x$ inches, we substitute this value in the proportion. Thus, 6 inches : 9 inches = 16 inches : $12x$ inches. Since all of the units are now the same, we may work with the numbers alone. In fractional terms we have $\dfrac{6}{9} = \dfrac{16}{12x}$. Cross-multiplication gives us $72x = 144$, and solving for x gives us $x = 2$. The rectangle is 2 feet long.

Variations

122. In a variation problem, you are given a relationship between certain variables. The problem is to determine the change in one variable when one or more of the other variables changes.

Direct Variation (Direct Proportion)

If x varies directly with y, this means that $x/y = k$ (or $x = ky$) where k is a constant.

> **Example:** If the cost of a piece of glass varies directly with the area of the glass, and a piece of glass of 5 square feet costs $20, then how much does a piece of glass of 15 square feet cost?

Represent the cost of the glass as c and the area of the piece of glass as A. Then we have $c/A = k$.

Now since we are given that a piece of glass of 5 square feet costs $20, we can write $20/5 = k$, and we find $k = 4$.

Let's say a piece of glass of 15 square feet costs x. Then we can write $x/15 = k$. But we found $k = 4$, so $x/15 = 4$ and $x = 60$. $60 is then the answer.

Inverse Variation (Inverse Proportion)

If x varies inversely with y, this means that $xy = k$ where k is a constant.

> **Example:** If a varies inversely with b and when $a = 5$, $b = 6$, then what is b when $a = 10$?

We have $ab = k$. Since $a = 5$ and $b = 6$, $5 \times 6 = k = 30$. So if $a = 10$, $10 \times b = k = 30$ and $b = 3$.

Other Variations

> **Example:** In the formula $A = bh$, if b doubles and h triples, what happens to the value of A?

STEP 1. Express the new values of the variables in terms of their original values, i.e., $b' = 2b$ and $h' = 3h$.

STEP 2. Substitute these values in the formula and solve for the desired variable: $A' = b'h' = (2b)(3h) = 6bh$.

STEP 3. Express this answer in terms of the original value of the variable, i.e., since the new value of A is $6bh$, and the old value of A was bh, we can express this as $A_{new} = 6A_{old}$. The new value of the variable is expressed with a prime mark and the old value of the variable is left as it was. In this problem, the new value of A would be expressed as A' and the old value as A. $A' = 6A$.

> **Example:** If $V = e^3$ and e is doubled, what happens to the value of V?
>
> *Solution:* Replace e with $2e$. The new value of V is $(2e)^3$. Since this is a new value, V becomes V'. Thus $V' = (2e)^3$, or $8e^3$. Remember, from the original statement of the problem, that $V = e^3$. Using this, we may substitute V for e^3 found in the equation $V' = 8e^3$. The new equation is $V' = 8V$. Therefore, the new value of V is 8 times the old value.

Comparison of Fractions

In fraction comparison problems, you are given two or more fractions and are asked to arrange them in increasing or decreasing order, or to select the larger or the smaller. The following rules and suggestions will be very helpful in determining which of two fractions is greater.

123. If fractions A and B have the same denominators, and A has a larger numerator, then fraction A is larger. (We are assuming here, and for the rest of this Refresher Session, that numerators and denominators are positive.)

Example: $\frac{56}{271}$ is greater than $\frac{53}{271}$ because the numerator of the first fraction is greater than the numerator of the second.

124. If fractions A and B have the same numerator, and A has a larger denominator, then fraction A is smaller.

Example: $\frac{37}{256}$ is smaller than $\frac{37}{254}$.

125. If fraction A has a larger numerator and a smaller denominator than fraction B, then fraction A is larger than B.

Example: $\frac{6}{11}$ is larger than $\frac{4}{13}$. (If this does not seem obvious, compare both fractions with $\frac{6}{13}$.)

126. Another method is to convert all of the fractions to equivalent fractions. To do this follow these steps:

STEP 1. First find the *lowest common denominator* of the fractions. This is the smallest number that is divisible by all of the denominators of the original fractions. See Section 110 for the method of finding lowest common denominators.

STEP 2. The fraction with the greatest numerator is the largest fraction.

127. Still another method is the *conversion to approximating decimals*.

Example: To compare $\frac{5}{9}$ and $\frac{7}{11}$, we might express both as decimals to a few places of accuracy: $\frac{5}{9}$ is approximately equal to 0.555, while $\frac{7}{11}$ is approximately equal to 0.636, so $\frac{7}{11}$ is obviously greater. To express a fraction as a decimal, divide the numerator by the denominator.

128. If all of the fractions being compared are very close in value to some easy-to-work-with number, such as $\frac{1}{2}$ or 5, you may subtract this number from each of the fractions without changing this order.

Example: To compare $\frac{151}{75}$ with $\frac{328}{163}$ we notice that both of these fractions are approximately equal to 2. If we subtract 2 (that is, $\frac{150}{75}$ and $\frac{326}{163}$, respectively) from each, we get $\frac{1}{75}$ and $\frac{2}{163}$, respectively. Since $\frac{1}{75}$ $\left(\text{or } \frac{2}{150}\right)$ exceeds $\frac{2}{163}$, we see that $\frac{151}{75}$ must also exceed $\frac{328}{163}$.

An alternative method of comparing fractions is to change the fractions to their decimal equivalents and then compare the decimals. (See Sections 104 and 127.) You should weigh the relative amount of work and difficulty involved in each method when you face each problem.

129.   The following is a quick way of comparing fractions.

Example: Which is greater, $\frac{3}{8}$ or $\frac{7}{18}$?

Procedure:

$$\frac{3}{8} \xleftarrow{\text{MULTIPLY}} \quad \xrightarrow{\text{MULTIPLY}} \frac{7}{18}$$

Multiply the 18 by the 3. We get 54. Put the 54 on the *left* side.

$$54$$

Now *multiply* the 8 by the 7. We get 56. Put the 56 on the *right* side.

$$54 \qquad\qquad\qquad 56$$

Since $56 > 54$ and 56 is on the *right* side, the fraction $\frac{7}{18}$ (which was also originally on the *right* side) is *greater* than the fraction $\frac{3}{8}$ (which was originally on the *left* side).

Example: If $y > x$, which is greater, $\frac{1}{x}$ or $\frac{1}{y}$? (x and y are positive numbers.)

Procedure:

$$\frac{1}{x} \xleftarrow{\text{MULTIPLY}} \quad \xrightarrow{\text{MULTIPLY}} \frac{1}{y}$$

Multiply y by 1. We get y. Put y on the left side:

$$y$$

Multiply x by 1. We get x. Put x on the right side:

$$y \qquad\qquad\qquad x$$

Since $y > x$ (given), $\frac{1}{x}$ (which was originally on the left) is greater than $\frac{1}{y}$ (which was originally on the right).

Example: Which is greater?

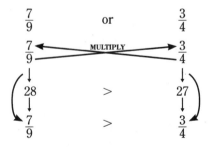

Practice Test 1

Fractions, Decimals, Percentages, Deviations, Ratios and Proportions, Variations, and Comparison of Fractions

Correct answers and solutions follow each test.

1. A B C D E

1. Which of the following answers is the sum of the following numbers:

$2\frac{1}{2}, \frac{21}{4}, 3.350, \frac{1}{8}$?

(A) 8.225
(B) 9.825
(C) 10.825
(D) 11.225
(E) 12.350

2. A B C D E

2. A chemist was preparing a solution that should have included 35 milligrams of a chemical. If she actually used 36.4 milligrams, what was her percentage error (to the nearest 0.01%)?

(A) 0.04%
(B) 0.05%
(C) 1.40%
(D) 3.85%
(E) 4.00%

3. A B C D E

3. A retailer buys a radio from the wholesaler for $75.00. He then marks up the price by $\frac{1}{3}$ and sells it at a discount of 20%. What was his profit on the radio (to the nearest cent)?

(A) $5.00
(B) $6.67
(C) $7.50
(D) $10.00
(E) $13.33

4. A B C D E

4. On a blueprint, $\frac{1}{4}$ inch represents 1 foot. If a window is supposed to be 56 inches wide, how wide would its representation be on the blueprint?

(A) $1\frac{1}{6}$ inches

(B) $4\frac{2}{3}$ inches

(C) $9\frac{1}{3}$ inches

(D) 14 inches

(E) $18\frac{2}{3}$ inches

5. A B C D E

5. If the radius of a circle is increased by 50%, what will be the percent increase in the circumference of the circle? (Circumference $= 2\pi r$)

(A) 25%
(B) 50%
(C) 100%
(D) 150%
(E) 225%

6. A B C D E

6. Which of the following fractions is the greatest?

(A) $\dfrac{403}{134}$

(B) $\dfrac{79}{26}$

(C) $\dfrac{527}{176}$

(D) $\dfrac{221}{73}$

(E) $\dfrac{99}{34}$

7. A B C D E

7. A store usually sells a certain item at a 40% profit. One week the store has a sale, during which the item is sold for 10% less than the usual price. During the sale, what is the percent profit the store makes on each of these items?

(A) 4%
(B) 14%
(C) 26%
(D) 30%
(E) 36%

8. A B C D E

8. What is 0.05 percent of 6.5?

(A) 0.00325
(B) 0.013
(C) 0.325
(D) 1.30
(E) 130.0

9. A B C D E

9. What is the value of $\dfrac{3\frac{1}{2} + 3\frac{1}{4} + 3\frac{1}{4} + 3\frac{1}{2}}{4\frac{1}{2}}$?

(A) $1\frac{1}{2}$

(B) $2\frac{1}{4}$

(C) 3

(D) $3\frac{1}{4}$

(E) $3\frac{3}{8}$

10. A B C D E

10. If 8 men can chop down 28 trees in one day, how many trees can 20 men chop down in one day?

(A) 28 trees
(B) 160 trees
(C) 70 trees
(D) 100 trees
(E) 80 trees

11. A B C D E

11. What is the product of the following fractions: $\frac{3}{100}, \frac{15}{49}, \frac{7}{9}$?

(A) $\frac{215}{44,100}$

(B) $\frac{1}{140}$

(C) $\frac{1}{196}$

(D) $\frac{25}{158}$

(E) $\frac{3}{427}$

12. A B C D E

12. In calculating the height of an object, Mrs. Downs mistakenly observed the height to be 72 cm instead of 77 cm. What was her percentage error (to the nearest hundredth of a percent)?

(A) 6.49%
(B) 6.69%
(C) 6.89%
(D) 7.09%
(E) 7.19%

13. A B C D E

13. A businessman buys 1,440 dozen pens at $2.50 a dozen and then sells them at a price of 25¢ apiece. What is his total profit on the lot of pens?

(A) $60.00
(B) $72.00
(C) $720.00
(D) $874.00
(E) $8,740.00

14. A B C D E

14. On a map, 1 inch represents 1,000 miles. If the area of a country is actually 16 million square miles, what is the area of the country's representation on the map?

(A) 4 square inches
(B) 16 square inches
(C) 4,000 square inches
(D) 16,000 square inches
(E) 4,000,000 square inches

15. A B C D E

15. The formula for the volume of a cone is $V = \frac{1}{3}\pi r^2 h$. If the radius (r) is doubled and the height (h) is divided by 3, what will be the ratio of the new volume to the original volume?

(A) 2 : 3
(B) 3 : 2
(C) 4 : 3
(D) 3 : 4
(E) None of these.

16. A B C D E

16. Which of the following fractions has the smallest value?

(A) $\frac{34.7}{163}$

(B) $\frac{125}{501}$

(C) $\frac{173}{700}$

(D) $\frac{10.9}{42.7}$

(E) $\frac{907}{3,715}$

17. A B C D E

17. Mr. Cutler usually makes a 45% profit on every radio he sells. During a sale, he reduces his margin of profit to 40%, while his sales increase by 10%. What is the ratio of his new total profit to the original profit?

(A) 1 : 1
(B) 9 : 8
(C) 9 : 10
(D) 11 : 10
(E) 44 : 45

18. A B C D E

18. What is 1.3 percent of 0.26?

(A) 0.00338
(B) 0.00500
(C) 0.200
(D) 0.338
(E) 0.500

19. A B C D E

19. What is the average of the following numbers: $3.2, \frac{47}{12}, \frac{10}{3}$?

(A) 3.55

(B) $\frac{10}{3}$

(C) $\frac{103}{30}$

(D) $\frac{209}{60}$

(E) $\frac{1,254}{120}$

20. A B C D E

20. If it takes 16 faucets 10 hours to fill 8 tubs, how long will it take 12 faucets to fill 9 tubs?

(A) 10 hours
(B) 12 hours
(C) 13 hours
(D) 14 hours
(E) 15 hours

21. A B C D E

21. If the 8% tax on a sale amounts to 96¢, what is the final price (tax included) of the item?

(A) $1.20
(B) $2.16
(C) $6.36
(D) $12.00
(E) $12.96

22. A B C D E

22. In a certain class, 40% of the students are girls, and 20% of the girls wear glasses. What percent of the children in the class are girls who wear glasses?

(A) 6%
(B) 8%
(C) 20%
(D) 60%
(E) 80%

23. A B C D E

23. What is 1.2% of 0.5?

(A) 0.0006
(B) 0.006
(C) 0.06
(D) 0.6
(E) 6.0

24. A B C D E

24. Which of the following quantities is the largest?

(A) $\dfrac{275}{369}$

(B) $\dfrac{134}{179}$

(C) $\dfrac{107}{144}$

(D) $\dfrac{355}{476}$

(E) $\dfrac{265}{352}$

25. A B C D E

25. If the length of a rectangle is increased by 120%, and its width is decreased by 20%, what happens to the area of the rectangle?

(A) It decreases by 4%.
(B) It remains the same.
(C) It increases by 24%.
(D) It increases by 76%.
(E) It increases by 100%.

26. A B C D E

26. A merchant buys an old rug for $25.00. He spends $15.00 to have it restored to good condition and then sells the rug for $50.00. What is the percent profit on his total investment?

(A) 20%
(B) 25%
(C) 40%
(D) $66\dfrac{2}{3}\%$
(E) 100%

27. A B C D E

27. Of the following sets of fractions, which one is arranged in *decreasing* order?

(A) $\dfrac{5}{9}, \dfrac{7}{11}, \dfrac{3}{5}, \dfrac{2}{3}, \dfrac{10}{13}$

(B) $\dfrac{2}{3}, \dfrac{3}{5}, \dfrac{7}{11}, \dfrac{5}{9}, \dfrac{10}{13}$

(C) $\dfrac{3}{5}, \dfrac{5}{9}, \dfrac{7}{11}, \dfrac{10}{13}, \dfrac{2}{3}$

(D) $\dfrac{10}{13}, \dfrac{2}{3}, \dfrac{7}{11}, \dfrac{3}{5}, \dfrac{5}{9}$

(E) None of these.

28. A B C D E

28. If the diameter of a circle doubles, the circumference of the larger circle is how many times the circumference of the original circle? (Circumference $= \pi d$)

(A) π
(B) 2π
(C) 1
(D) 2
(E) 4

29. A B C D E

29. The scale on a set of plans is 1 : 8. If a man reads a certain measurement on the plans as 5.6″, instead of 6.0″, what will be the resulting approximate percent error on the full-size model?

(A) 6.7%
(B) 7.1%
(C) 12.5%
(D) 53.6%
(E) 56.8%

30. A B C D E   **30.** A salesman bought 2 dozen television sets at $300 each. He sold two-thirds of them at a 25% profit but was forced to take a 30% loss on the rest. What was his total profit (or loss) on the television sets?

      (A) a loss of $200
      (B) a loss of $15
      (C) no profit or loss
      (D) a gain of $20
      (E) a gain of $480

31. A B C D E   **31.** The sum of $\frac{1}{2}$, $\frac{1}{3}$, $\frac{1}{8}$, and $\frac{1}{15}$ is:

      (A) $\frac{9}{8}$

      (B) $\frac{16}{15}$

      (C) $\frac{41}{40}$

      (D) $\frac{65}{64}$

      (E) $\frac{121}{120}$

32. A B C D E   **32.** What is $\frac{2}{3}$% of 90?

      (A) 0.006
      (B) 0.06
      (C) 0.6
      (D) 6.0
      (E) 60

33. A B C D E   **33.** A man borrows $360. If he pays it back in 12 monthly installments of $31.50, what is his interest rate?

      (A) 1.5%
      (B) 4.5%
      (C) 10%
      (D) 5%
      (E) 7.5%

34. A B C D E   **34.** A merchant marks a certain lamp up 30% above original cost. Then he gives a customer a 15% discount. If the final selling price of the lamp was $86.19, what was the original cost?

      (A) $66.30
      (B) $73.26
      (C) $78.00
      (D) $99.12
      (E) $101.40

35. A B C D E   **35.** In a certain recipe, $2\frac{1}{4}$ cups of flour are called for to make a cake that serves 6. If Mrs. Jenkins wants to use the same recipe to make a cake for 8, how many cups of flour must she use?

      (A) $2\frac{1}{3}$ cups

      (B) $2\frac{3}{4}$ cups

      (C) 3 cups

      (D) $3\frac{3}{8}$ cups

      (E) 4 cups

36. A B C D E

36. If 10 men can survive for 24 days on 15 cans of rations, how many cans will be needed for 8 men to survive for 36 days?

(A) 15 cans
(B) 16 cans
(C) 17 cans
(D) 18 cans
(E) 19 cans

37. A B C D E

37. If, on a map, $\frac{1}{2}$ inch represents 1 mile, how long is a border whose representation is $1\frac{1}{15}$ feet long?

(A) $2\frac{1}{30}$ miles

(B) $5\frac{1}{15}$ miles

(C) $12\frac{4}{5}$ miles

(D) $25\frac{3}{5}$ miles

(E) $51\frac{1}{5}$ miles

38. A B C D E

38. In the formula $e = hf$, if e is doubled and f is halved, what happens to the value of h?

(A) h remains the same.
(B) h is doubled.
(C) h is divided by 4.
(D) h is multiplied by 4.
(E) h is halved.

39. A B C D E

39. Which of the following expresses the ratio of 3 inches to 2 yards?

(A) $3 : 2$
(B) $3 : 9$
(C) $3 : 12$
(D) $3 : 24$
(E) $3 : 72$

40. A B C D E

40. If it takes Mark twice as long to earn $6.00 as it takes Carl to earn $4.00, what is the ratio of Mark's pay per hour to Carl's pay per hour?

(A) $2 : 1$
(B) $3 : 1$
(C) $3 : 2$
(D) $3 : 4$
(E) $4 : 3$

41. A B C D E

41. What is the lowest common denominator of the following set of fractions:

$$\frac{1}{6}, \frac{13}{27}, \frac{4}{5}, \frac{3}{10}, \frac{2}{15}?$$

(A) 27
(B) 54
(C) 135
(D) 270
(E) None of these.

A B C D E
42. 42. The average grade on a certain examination was 85. Ralph, on the same examination, scored 90. What was Ralph's *percent* deviation from the average score (to the nearest tenth of a percent)?

(A) 5.0%
(B) 5.4%
(C) 5.5%
(D) 5.8%
(E) 5.9%

A B C D E
43. 43. Successive discounts of 20% and 12% are equivalent to a single discount of:

(A) 16.0%
(B) 29.6%
(C) 31.4%
(D) 32.0%
(E) 33.7%

A B C D E
44. 44. On a blueprint of a park, 1 foot represents $\frac{1}{2}$ mile. If an error of $\frac{1}{2}$ inch is made in reading the blueprint, what will be the corresponding error on the actual park?

(A) 110 feet
(B) 220 feet
(C) 330 feet
(D) 440 feet
(E) None of these.

A B C D E
45. 45. If the two sides of a rectangle change in such a manner that the rectangle's area remains constant, and one side increases by 25%, what must happen to the other side?

(A) It decreases by 20%
(B) It decreases by 25%
(C) It decreases by $33\frac{1}{3}$%
(D) It decreases by 50%
(E) None of these.

A B C D E
46. 46. Which of the following fractions has the smallest value?

(A) $\dfrac{6,043}{2,071}$

(B) $\dfrac{4,290}{1,463}$

(C) $\dfrac{5,107}{1,772}$

(D) $\dfrac{8,935}{2,963}$

(E) $\dfrac{8,016}{2,631}$

A B C D E
47. 47. A certain company increased its prices by 30% during 2003. Then, in 2004, it was forced to cut back its prices by 20%. What was the net change in price?

(A) −4%
(B) −2%
(C) +2%
(D) +4%
(E) 0%

48. A B C D E

48. What is 0.04%, expressed as a fraction?

(A) $\frac{2}{5}$

(B) $\frac{1}{25}$

(C) $\frac{4}{25}$

(D) $\frac{1}{250}$

(E) $\frac{1}{2,500}$

49. A B C D E

49. What is the value of the fraction

$$\frac{16 + 12 + 88 + 34 + 66 + 21 + 79 + 11 + 89}{25}?$$

(A) 15.04
(B) 15.44
(C) 16.24
(D) 16.64
(E) None of these.

50. A B C D E

50. If coconuts are twice as expensive as bananas, and bananas are one-third as expensive as grapefruits, what is the ratio of the price of one coconut to one grapefruit?

(A) 2 : 3
(B) 3 : 2
(C) 6 : 1
(D) 1 : 6
(E) None of these.

Answer Key for Practice Test 1

1. D	14. B	27. D	39. E
2. E	15. C	28. D	40. D
3. A	16. A	29. A	41. D
4. A	17. E	30. E	42. E
5. B	18. A	31. C	43. B
6. B	19. D	32. C	44. A
7. C	20. E	33. D	45. A
8. A	21. E	34. C	46. C
9. C	22. B	35. C	47. D
10. C	23. B	36. D	48. E
11. B	24. E	37. D	49. D
12. A	25. D	38. D	50. A
13. C	26. B		

Answers and Solutions for Practice Test 1

1. Choice D is correct. First, convert the fractions to decimals, as the final answer must be expressed in decimals: $2.500 + 5.250 + 3.350 + 0.125 = 11.225$. (104, 127, 128)

2. Choice E is correct. This is an estimation problem. Note that the correct value was 35, not 36.4. Thus the *real* value is 35 mg and the *estimated* value is 36.4 mg. Thus, percent error is equal to $(36.4 - 35) \div 35$, or 0.04, expressed as a percent, which is 4%. (117)

3. Choice A is correct. This is a business problem. First, the retailer marks up the wholesale price by $\frac{1}{3}$, so the marked-up price equals $\$75\left(1 + \frac{1}{3}\right)$, or $100; then it is reduced 20% from the $100 price, leaving a final price of $80. Thus, the net profit on the radio is $5.00. (118)

4. Choice A is correct. Here we have a proportion problem: length on blueprint : actual length $= \frac{1}{4}$ inch : 1 foot. The second ratio is the same as 1 : 48 because 1 foot = 12 inches. In the problem the actual length is 56 inches, so that if the length on the blueprint equals x, we have the proportion $x : 56 = 1 : 48$; $\frac{x}{56} = \frac{1}{48}$. $48x = 56$; so $x = \frac{56}{48}$, or $1\frac{1}{6}$ inches. (120)

5. Choice B is correct. Since $C = 2\pi r$ (where r is the radius of the circle, and C is its circumference), the new value of r, r', is $(1.5)r$ (since r is increased by 50%). Using this value of r', we get the new C, $C' = 2\pi r' = 2\pi(1.5)r = (1.5)2\pi r$. Remembering that $C = 2\pi r$, we get that $C' = (1.5)C$. Since the new circumference is 1.5 times the original, there is an increase of 50%. (122)

6. Choice B is correct. In this numerical comparison problem, it is helpful to realize that all of these fractions are approximately equal to 3. If we subtract 3 from each of the fractions, we get $\frac{1}{134}$, $\frac{1}{26}$, $-\frac{1}{176}$, $\frac{2}{73}$, and $-\frac{3}{34}$, respectively. Clearly, the greatest of these is $\frac{1}{26}$, which therefore shows the greatest of the five given fractions. Another method of solving this type of numerical comparison problem is to convert the fractions to decimals by dividing the numerator by the denominator. (127, 128)

7. Choice C is correct. This is another business problem, this time asking for percentage profit. Let the original price be P. A 40% profit means that the store will sell the item for $100\%P + 40\%P$, which is equal to $140\%P$, which in turn is equal to $\left(\frac{140}{100}\right)P = 1.4P$. Then the marked-up price will be $1.4(P)$. Ten percent is taken off this price, to yield a final price of $(0.90)(1.40)(P)$, or $(1.26)(P)$. Thus, the fractional increase is 0.26, so the percent increase is 26%. (118)

8. Choice A is correct. Remember that in the phrase "percent of," the word "of" may be replaced by a multiplication sign. Thus, $0.05\% \times 6.5 = 0.0005 \times 6.5$, so the answer is 0.00325. (114)

9. Choice C is correct. First, add the fractions in the numerator to obtain $13\frac{1}{2}$. Then divide $13\frac{1}{2}$ by $4\frac{1}{2}$. If you cannot see immediately that the answer is 3, you can convert the halves to decimals and divide, or you can express the fractions in terms of their common denominator, thus: $13\frac{1}{2} = \frac{27}{2}$; $4\frac{1}{2} = \frac{9}{2}$; $\frac{27}{2} \div \frac{9}{2} = \frac{27}{2} \times \frac{2}{9} = \frac{54}{18} = 3$. (110, 112)

10. Choice C is correct. This is a proportion problem. If x is the number of men needed to chop down 20 trees, then we form the proportion 8 men : 28 trees = 20 men : x trees, or $\frac{8}{28} = \frac{20}{x}$. Solving for x, we get $x = \frac{(28)(20)}{8}$, or $x = 70$. (120)

11. Choice B is correct. $\frac{3}{100} \times \frac{15}{49} \times \frac{7}{9} = \frac{3 \times 15 \times 7}{100 \times 49 \times 9}$. Canceling 7 out of the numerator and denominator gives us $\frac{3 \times 15}{100 \times 7 \times 9}$. Canceling 5 out of the numerator and denominator gives us $\frac{3 \times 3}{20 \times 7 \times 9}$. Finally, canceling 9 out of both numerator and denominator gives us $\frac{1}{20 \times 7}$, or $\frac{1}{140}$. (111)

12. Choice A is correct. Percent error = (absolute error) ÷ (correct measurement) = 5 ÷ 77 = 0.0649 (approximately) × 100 = 6.49%. (117)

13. Choice C is correct. Profit on each dozen pens = selling price − cost = 12(25¢) − $2.50 = $3.00 − $2.50 = 50¢ profit per dozen. Total profit = profit per dozen × number of dozens = 50¢ × 1440 = $720.00. (118)

14. Choice B is correct. If 1 inch represents 1,000 miles, then 1 square inch represents 1,000 miles squared, or 1,000,000 square miles. Thus, the area would be represented by 16 squares of this size, or 16 square inches. (120)

15. Choice C is correct. Let V' equal the new volume. Then if $r' = 2r$ is the new radius, and $h' = \frac{h}{3}$ is the new height, $V' = \frac{1}{3}\pi(r')^2(h') = \frac{1}{3}\pi(2r)^2\left(\frac{h}{3}\right) = \frac{4}{9}\pi r^2 h = \frac{4}{3}V$, so the ratio $V' : V$ is equal to $4 : 3$. (122)

16. Choice A is correct. Using a calculator, we get: $\frac{34.7}{163} = 0.2128$ for Choice A; $\frac{125}{501} = 0.2495$ for Choice B; $\frac{173}{700} = 0.2471$ for Choice C; $\frac{10.9}{42.7} = 0.2552$ for Choice D; and $\frac{907}{3,715} = 0.2441$ for Choice E. Choice A is the smallest value. (104, 127)

17. Choice E is correct. Let N = the original cost of a radio. Then, original profit = 45% × N. New profit = 40% × 110%N = 44% × N. Thus, the ratio of new profit to original profit is 44 : 45. (118)

18. Choice A is correct.
1.3% × 0.26 = 0.013 × 0.26 = 0.00338. (114)

19. Choice D is correct. Average = $\frac{1}{3}\left(3.2 + \frac{47}{12} + \frac{10}{3}\right)$. The decimal $3.2 = \frac{320}{100} = \frac{16}{5}$, and the lowest common denominator of the three fractions is 60; then $\frac{16}{5} = \frac{192}{60}, \frac{47}{12} = \frac{235}{60}$ and $\frac{10}{3} = \frac{200}{60}$. Then, $\frac{1}{3}\left(\frac{192}{60} + \frac{235}{60} + \frac{200}{60}\right) = \frac{1}{3}\left(\frac{627}{60}\right) = \frac{209}{60}$.
(101, 105, 109)

20. Choice E is correct. This is an inverse proportion. If it takes 16 faucets 10 hours to fill 8 tubs, then it takes 1 faucet 160 hours to fill 8 tubs (16 faucets : 1 faucet = x hours : 10 hours; $\frac{16}{1} = \frac{x}{10}$; $x = 160$). If it takes 1 faucet 160 hours to fill 8 tubs, then (dividing by 8) it takes 1 faucet 20 hours to fill 1 tub. If it takes 1 faucet 20 hours to fill 1 tub, then it takes 1 faucet 180 hours (9 × 20 hours) to fill 9 tubs. If it takes 1 faucet 180 hours to fill 9 tubs, then it takes 12 faucets $\frac{180}{12}$, or 15 hours, to fill 9 tubs. (120)

21. Choice E is correct. Let P be the original price. Then $0.08P = 96¢$, so that $8P = \$96$, or $P = \$12$. Adding the tax, which equals 96¢, we obtain our final price of $12.96. (118)

22. Choice B is correct. The number of girls who wear glasses is 20% of 40% of the children in the class. Thus, the indicated operation is multiplication; 20% × 40% = 0.20 × 0.40 = 0.08 = 8%. (114)

23. Choice B is correct. 1.2% × 0.5 = 0.012 × 0.5 = 0.006. (114)

24. Choice E is correct. Using a calculator to find the answer to three decimal places, we get: $\frac{275}{369} = 0.745$ for Choice A; $\frac{134}{179} = 0.749$ for Choice B; $\frac{107}{144} = 0.743$ for Choice C; $\frac{355}{476} = 0.746$ for Choice D; $\frac{265}{352} = 0.753$ for Choice E. Choice E is the largest value. (104, 127)

25. Choice D is correct. Area = length × width. The new area will be equal to the new length × the new width. The new length = (100% + 120%) × old length = 220% × old length = $\frac{220}{100}$ × old length = 2.2 × old length. The new width = (100% − 20%) × old width = 80% × old width = $\frac{80}{100}$ × old width = .8 × old width. The new area = new width × new length = 2.2 × .8 × old length × old width. So the new area = 1.76 × old area, which is 176% of the old area. This is an increase of 76% from the original area. (122)

26. Choice B is correct. Total cost to merchant = $25.00 + $15.00 = $40.00.

Profit = selling price − cost = $50 − $40 = $10. Percent profit = profit ÷ cost = $10 ÷ $40 = 25%. (118)

27. Choice D is correct. We can convert the fractions to decimals or to fractions with a lowest common denominator. Inspection will show that all sets of fractions contain the same members; therefore, if we convert one set to decimals or find the lowest common denominator for one set, we can use our results for all sets. Converting a fraction to a decimal involves only one operation, a single division, whereas converting to the lowest common denominator involves a multiplication, which must be followed by a division and a multiplication to change each fraction to one with the lowest common denominator. Thus, conversion to decimals is often the simpler method: $\frac{10}{13} = 0.769$; $\frac{2}{3} = 0.666$; $\frac{7}{11} = 0.636$; $\frac{3}{5} = 0.600$; $\frac{5}{9} = 0.555$.

However, in this case there is an even simpler method. Convert two of the fractions to equivalent fractions: $\frac{3}{5} = \frac{6}{10}$ and $\frac{2}{3} = \frac{8}{12}$. We now have $\frac{5}{9}$, $\frac{6}{10}, \frac{7}{11}, \frac{8}{12}$, and $\frac{10}{13}$. Remember this rule: When the numerator and denominator of a fraction are both positive, adding 1 to both will bring the value of the fraction closer to 1. (For example, $\frac{3}{4} = \frac{2+1}{3+1}$, so $\frac{3}{4}$ is closer to 1 than $\frac{2}{3}$ and is therefore the greater fraction.) Thus we see that $\frac{5}{9}$ is less than $\frac{6}{10}$, which is less than $\frac{7}{11}$, which is less than $\frac{8}{12}$, which is less than $\frac{9}{13}$. $\frac{9}{13}$ is obviously less than $\frac{10}{13}$, so $\frac{10}{13}$ must be the greatest fraction. Thus, in decreasing order the fractions are $\frac{10}{13}, \frac{2}{3}, \frac{7}{11}, \frac{3}{5}$, and $\frac{5}{9}$. This method is a great time-saver once you become accustomed to it. (104)

28. Choice D is correct. The formula governing this situation is $C = \pi d$, where C = circumference and d = diameter. Thus, if the new diameter is $d' = 2d$, then the new circumference is $C' = \pi d' = 2\pi d = 2C$. Thus, the new, larger circle has a circumference twice that of the original circle. (122)

29. Choice A is correct. The most important feature of this problem is recognizing that the scale does not affect percent (or fractional) error, since it simply results in multiplying the numerator and denominator of a fraction by the same factor. Thus, we need only calculate the original percent error. Although it would not be incorrect to calculate the full-scale percent error, it would be time-consuming and might result in unnecessary errors. Absolute error = 0.4″. Actual measurement = 6.0″. Therefore, percent error = (absolute error ÷ actual measurement) × 100% = $\frac{0.4}{6.0}$ × 100%, which equals 6.7% (approximately). (117)

30. Choice E is correct. Total cost = number of sets × cost of each = 24 × $300 = $7,200.

Revenue = (number sold at 25% profit × price at 25% profit) + (number sold at 30% loss × price at 30% loss)
= (16 × $375) + (8 × $210) = $6,000 + $1,680 = $7,680.

Profit = revenue − cost = $7,680 − $7,200 = $480. (118)

31. Choice C is correct. $\frac{1}{2} + \frac{1}{3} + \frac{1}{8} + \frac{1}{15} = \frac{60}{120} + \frac{40}{120} + \frac{15}{120} + \frac{8}{120} = \frac{123}{120} = \frac{41}{40}$. (110)

32. Choice C is correct. $\frac{2}{3}\% \times 90 = \frac{2}{300} \times 90 = \frac{180}{300} = \frac{6}{10} = 0.6$. (114)

33. Choice D is correct. If the man makes 12 payments of $31.50, he pays back a total of $378.00. Since the loan is for $360.00, his net interest is $18.00. Therefore, his rate of interest is $\frac{\$18.00}{\$360.00}$, which can be reduced to 0.05, or 5%. (118)

34. Choice C is correct. Final selling price = 85% × 130% × cost = 1.105 × cost. Thus, $86.19 = 1.105C, where C = cost. C = $86.19 ÷ 1.105 = $78.00 (exactly). (118)

35. Choice C is correct. If x is the amount of flour needed for 8 people, then we can set up the proportion $2\frac{1}{4}$ cups : 6 people = x : 8 people. Solving for x gives us $x = \frac{8}{6} \times 2\frac{1}{4}$ or $\frac{8}{6} \times \frac{9}{4} = 3$. (120)

36. Choice D is correct. If 10 men can survive for 24 days on 15 cans, then 1 man can survive for 240 days on 15 cans. If 1 man can survive for 240 days on 15 cans, then 1 man can survive for $\frac{240}{15}$, or 16 days, on 1 can. If 1 man can survive for 16 days on 1 can, then 8 men can survive for $\frac{16}{8}$, or 2 days, on 1 can. If 8 men can survive for 2 days on 1 can, then for 36 days 8 men need $\frac{36}{2}$, or 18 cans, to survive. (120)

37. Choice D is correct. $1\frac{1}{15}$ feet = $1\frac{1}{15} \times 12$ inches = $\frac{16}{15} \times 12$ inches = 12.8 inches. So we have a proportion, $\frac{\frac{1}{2}\text{ inch}}{1\text{ mile}} = \frac{12.8\text{ inches}}{x\text{ miles}}$. Cross-multiplying, we get $\frac{1}{2}x = 12.8$, so $x = 25.6 = 25\frac{3}{5}$. (120)

38. Choice D is correct. If $e = hf$, then $h = \frac{e}{f}$. If e is doubled and f is halved, then the new value of h, $h' = \left(\frac{2e}{\frac{1}{2}f}\right)$. Multiplying the numerator and denominator by 2 gives us $h' = \frac{4e}{f}$. Since $h = \frac{e}{f}$ and $h' = \frac{4e}{f}$, we see that $h' = 4h$. This is the same as saying that h is multiplied by 4. (122)

39. Choice E is correct. 3 inches : 2 yards = 3 inches : 72 inches = 3 : 72. (121)

40. Choice D is correct. If Carl and Mark work for the same length of time, then Carl will earn $8.00 for

every \$6.00 Mark earns (since in the time Mark can earn one \$6.00 wage, Carl can earn *two* \$4.00 wages). Thus, their hourly wage rates are in the ratio \$6.00 (Mark) : \$8.00 (Carl) = 3 : 4.　(120)

41. Choice D is correct. The lowest common denominator is the smallest number that is divisible by all of the denominators. Thus we are looking for the smallest number that is divisible by 6, 27, 5, 10, and 15. The smallest number that is divisible by 6 and 27 is 54. The smallest number that is divisible by 54 and 5 is 270. Since 270 is divisible by 10 and 15 also, it is the lowest common denominator.　(110, 126)

42. Choice E is correct.

Percent deviation = $\dfrac{\text{absolute deviation}}{\text{average score}} \times 100\%$.

Absolute deviation = Ralph's score − average score = 90 − 85 = 5.

Percent deviation = $\dfrac{5}{85} \times 100\%$ = 500% ÷ 85 = 5.88% (approximately).

5.88% is closer to 5.9% than to 5.8%, so 5.9% is correct.　(117)

43. Choice B is correct. If we discount 20% and then 12%, we are, in effect, taking 88% of 80% of the original price. Since "of" represents multiplication, when we deal with percent we can multiply 88% × 80% = 70.4%. This is a deduction of 29.6% from the original price.　(119, 114)

44. Choice A is correct. This is a simple proportion: $\dfrac{1 \text{ foot}}{\frac{1}{2} \text{ mile}} = \dfrac{\frac{1}{2} \text{ inch}}{x}$. Our first step must be to convert all these measurements to one unit. The most logical unit is the one our answer will take—feet.

Thus, $\dfrac{1 \text{ ft}}{2{,}640 \text{ ft}} = \dfrac{\frac{1}{24} \text{ ft}}{x}$. (1 mile equals 5,280 feet.) Solving for x, we find $x = \dfrac{2{,}640}{24}$ feet = 110 feet.

(120, 121)

45. Choice A is correct. Let side a increase by 25%. Then $a' = (100 + 25)\%a = 125\%a = \dfrac{125}{100}a = 1.25a = \dfrac{5a}{4}$. We also have that $ab = a'b'$. Substituting $a' = \dfrac{5a}{4}$, we get $ab = \dfrac{5a}{4}b'$. The a's cancel and we get $b = \dfrac{5}{4}b'$. So $b' = \dfrac{4}{5}b$, a decrease of $\dfrac{1}{5}$, or 20%.

(122)

46. Choice C is correct. Using a calculator, we get: $\dfrac{6{,}043}{2{,}071}$ = 2.9179 for Choice A; $\dfrac{4{,}290}{1{,}463}$ = 2.9323 for Choice B; $\dfrac{5{,}107}{1{,}772}$ = 2.8820 for Choice C; $\dfrac{8{,}935}{2{,}963}$ = 3.0155 for Choice D; and $\dfrac{8{,}016}{2{,}631}$ = 3.0467 for Choice E. Choice C has the smallest value.　(104, 127).

47. Choice D is correct. Let's say that the price was \$100 during 2003. 30% of \$100 = \$30, so the new price in 2003 was \$130. In 2004, the company cut back its prices 20%, so the new price in 2004 = $\$130 - \left(\dfrac{20}{100}\right)\$130 = \$130 - \left(\dfrac{1}{5}\right)\$130 = \$130 - \$26 = \$104$.

The net change is \$104 − \$100 = \$4. \$4/\$100 = 4% increase.　(118)

48. Choice E is correct. $0.04\% = \dfrac{0.04}{100} = \dfrac{4}{10{,}000} = \dfrac{1}{2{,}500}$.　(107)

49. Choice D is correct. Before adding, you should examine the numbers to be added. They form pairs, like this: 16 + (12 + 88) + (34 + 66) + (21 + 79) + (11 + 89), which equals 16 + 100 + 100 + 100 + 100 = 416. Dividing 416 by 25, we obtain $16\dfrac{16}{25}$, which equals 16.64.　(112)

50. Choice A is correct. We can set up a proportion as follows:

$\dfrac{1 \text{ coconut}}{1 \text{ banana}} = \dfrac{2}{1}, \dfrac{1 \text{ banana}}{1 \text{ grapefruit}} = \dfrac{1}{3}$, so by multiplying the two equations together $\left(\dfrac{1 \text{ coconut}}{1 \text{ banana}} \times \dfrac{1 \text{ banana}}{1 \text{ grapefruit}} = \dfrac{2}{1} \times \dfrac{1}{3}\right)$ and canceling the bananas and the 1s in the numerators and denominators, we get: $\dfrac{1 \text{ coconut}}{1 \text{ grapefruit}} = \dfrac{2}{3}$, which can be written as 2 : 3.　(120)

MATH REFRESHER
SESSION 2

Rate Problems: Distance and Time, Work, Mixture, and Cost

Word Problem Setup

200. Some problems require translation of words into algebraic expressions or equations. For example: 8 more than 7 times a number is 22. Find the number. Let n = the number. We have

$$7n + 8 = 22 \qquad\qquad 7n = 14 \qquad\qquad n = 2$$

Another example: There are 3 times as many boys as girls in a class. What is the ratio of boys to the total number of students? Let n = number of girls. Then

$$3n = \text{number of boys}$$
$$4n = \text{total number of students}$$

$$\frac{\text{number of boys}}{\text{total students}} = \frac{3n}{4n} = \frac{3}{4}$$

201. Rate problems concern a special type of relationship that is very common: rate × input = output. This results from the definition of rate as *the ratio between output and input*. In these problems, input may represent any type of "investment," but the most frequent quantities used as inputs are time, work, and money. Output is usually distance traveled, work done, or money spent.

Note that the word *per*, as used in rates, signifies a ratio. Thus a rate of 25 miles per hour signifies the ratio between an output of 25 miles and an input of 1 hour.

Frequently, the word *per* will be represented by the fraction sign, thus $\dfrac{25 \text{ miles}}{1 \text{ hour}}$.

> **Example:** Peter can walk a mile in 10 minutes. He can travel a mile on his bicycle in 2 minutes. How far away is his uncle's house if Peter can walk there and bicycle back in 1 hour exactly?

To solve a rate problem such as the one above, follow these steps:

STEP 1. Determine the names of the quantities that represent input, output, and rate in the problem you are doing. In the example, Peter's input is *time*, and his output is *distance*. His rate will be *distance per unit of time*, which is commonly called *speed*.

STEP 2. Write down the fundamental relationship in terms of the quantities mentioned, making each the heading of a column. In the example, set up the table like this:

$$\text{speed} \times \text{time} = \text{distance}$$

STEP 3. Directly below the name of each quantity, write the unit of measurement in terms of the answer you want. Your choice of unit should be the most convenient one, but remember, once you have chosen a unit, you must convert all quantities to that unit.

We must select a unit of time. Since a *minute* was the unit used in the problem, it is the most logical choice. Similarly, we will choose a *mile* for our unit of distance. *Speed* (which is the ratio of distance to time) will therefore be expressed in *miles per minute*, usually abbreviated as mi/min. Thus, our chart now looks like this:

speed × time = distance

mi/min	minutes	miles

STEP 4. The problem will mention various situations in which some quantity of input is used to get a certain quantity of output. Represent each of these situations on a different line of the table, leaving blanks for unknown quantities.

In the sample problem, four situations are mentioned: Peter can walk a mile in 10 minutes; he can bicycle a mile in 2 minutes; he walks to his uncle's house; and he bicycles home. On the diagram, with the appropriate boxes filled, the problem will look like this:

speed × time = distance

	mi/min	minutes	miles
1. walking		10	1
2. bicycling		2	1
3. walking			
4. bicycling			

STEP 5. From the chart and from the relationship at the top of the chart, quantities for filling some of the empty spaces may become obvious. Fill in these values directly.

In the example, on the first line of the chart, we see that the walking speed × 10 equals 1.

Thus, the walking *speed* is 0.1 mi/min (mi/min × 10 = 1 mi; mi/min = $\frac{1\,\text{mi}}{10\,\text{min}}$ = 0.1).

Similarly, on the second line we see that the bicycle speed equals 0.5 mi/min. Furthermore, his walking speed shown on line 3 will be 0.1, the same speed as on line 1; and his bicycling speed shown on line 4 will equal the speed (0.5) shown on line 2. Adding this information to our table, we get:

speed × time = distance

	mi/min	minutes	miles
1. walking	0.1	10	1
2. bicycling	0.5	2	1
3. walking	0.1		
4. bicycling	0.5		

STEP 6. Next, fill in the blanks with algebraic expressions to represent the quantities indicated, being careful to take advantage of simple relationships stated in the problem or appearing in the chart.

Continuing the example, we represent the time spent traveling shown on line 3 by x. According to the fundamental relationship, the distance traveled on this trip must be $(0.1)x$. Similarly, if y represents the time shown on line 4, the distance traveled is $(0.5)y$. Thus our chart now looks like this:

speed × time = distance

	mi/min	minutes	miles
1. walking	0.1	10	1
2. bicycling	0.5	2	1
3. walking	0.1	x	$(0.1)x$
4. bicycling	0.5	y	$(0.5)y$

STEP 7. Now, from the statement of the problem, you should be able to set up enough equations to solve for all the unknowns. In the example, there are two facts that we have not used yet. First, since Peter is going to his uncle's house and back, it is assumed that the distances covered on the two trips are equal. Thus we get the equation $(0.1)x = (0.5)y$. We are told that the total time to and from his uncle's house is one hour. Since we are using minutes as our unit of time, we convert the one hour to 60 minutes. Thus we get the equation: $x + y = 60$. Solving these two equations ($0.1x = 0.5y$ and $x + y = 60$) algebraically, we find that $x = 50$ and $y = 10$. (See Section 407 for the solution of simultaneous equations.)

STEP 8. Now that you have all the information necessary, you can calculate the answer required. In the sample problem, we are required to determine the distance to the uncle's house, which is $(0.1)x$ or $(0.5)y$. Using $x = 50$ or $y = 10$ gives us the distance as 5 miles.

Now that we have shown the fundamental steps in solving a rate problem, we shall discuss various types of rate problems.

Distance and Time

202. In *distance and time problems*, the fundamental relationship that we use is *speed × time = distance*. Speed is the rate, time is the input, and distance is the output. The example in Section 201 was this type of problem.

> **Example:** In a sports car race, David gives Kenny a head start of 10 miles. David's car goes 80 miles per hour and Kenny's car goes 60 miles per hour. How long should it take David to catch up to Kenny if they both leave their starting marks at the same time?

STEP 1. Here the fundamental quantities are *speed*, *time*, and *distance*.

STEP 2. The fundamental relationship is speed × time = distance. Write this at the top of the chart.

STEP 3. The unit for *distance* in this problem will be a *mile*. The unit for *speed* will be *miles per hour*. Since the speed is in miles per hour, our *time* will be in *hours*. Now our chart looks like this:

speed × time = distance

mi/hr	hours	miles

STEP 4. The problem offers us certain information that we can add to the chart. First we must make two horizontal rows, one for Kenny and one for David. We know that Kenny's speed is 60 miles per hour and that David's speed is 80 miles per hour.

STEP 5. In this case, none of the information in the chart can be used to calculate other information in the chart.

STEP 6. Now we must use algebraic expressions to represent the unknowns. We know that both Kenny and David travel for the same amount of time, but we do not know for how much time, so we will place an x in the space for each boy's time. Now from the relationship of speed $\times$ time = distance, we can calculate Kenny's distance as $60x$ and David's distance as $80x$. Now the chart looks like this:

	speed $\times$	time =	distance
	mi/hr	hours	miles
Kenny	60	x	$60x$
David	80	x	$80x$

STEP 7. From the statement of the problem we know that David gave Kenny a 10-mile head start. In other words, David's distance is 10 more miles than Kenny's distance. This can be stated algebraically as $60x + 10 = 80x$. That is, Kenny's distance + 10 miles = David's distance.

Solving for x gives us $x = \frac{1}{2}$.

STEP 8. The question asks how much time is required for David to catch up to Kenny. If we look at the chart, we see that this time is x, and x has already been calculated as $\frac{1}{2}$, so the answer is $\frac{1}{2}$ hour.

Work

203. In *work problems* the input is time and the output is the amount of work done. The rate is the work per unit of time.

> **Example:** Jack can chop down 20 trees in 1 hour, whereas it takes Ted $1\frac{1}{2}$ hours to chop down 18 trees. If the two of them work together, how long will it take them to chop down 48 trees?

> *Solution:* By the end of Step 5 your chart should look like this:

	rate $\times$	time =	work
	trees/hr.	hours	trees
1. Jack	20	1	20
2. Ted	12	$1\frac{1}{2}$	18
3. Jack	20		
4. Ted	12		

In Step 6, we represent the time that it takes Jack by x in line 3. Since we have the relationship that rate $\times$ time = work, we see that in line 3 the work is $20x$. Since the two boys work together (therefore, for the same amount of time), the time in line 4 must be x, and the work must be $12x$. Now, in Step 7, we see that the total work is 48 trees. From lines 3 and 4, then, $20x + 12x = 48$. Solving for x gives us $x = 1\frac{1}{2}$. We are asked to find the number of hours needed by the boys to chop down the 48 trees together, and we see that this time is x, or $1\frac{1}{2}$ hours.

Mixture

204. In *mixture problems* you are given a percent or a fractional composition of a substance, and you are asked questions about the weights and compositions of the substance. The basic relationship here is that the percentage of a certain substance in a mixture × the amount of the mixture = the amount of substance.

Note that it is often better to change percents to decimals because it makes it easier to avoid errors.

Example: A chemist has two quarts of 25% acid solution and one quart of 40% acid solution. If he mixes these, what will be the concentration of the mixture?

Solution: Let x = concentration of the mixture. At the end of Step 6, our table will look like this:

concentration × amount of sol = amount of acid

	$\dfrac{\text{qt (acid)}}{\text{qt (sol)}}$	qts (sol)	qts (acid)
25% solution	0.25	2	0.50
40% solution	0.40	1	0.40
mixture	x	3	$3x$

We now have one additional bit of information: The amount of acid in the mixture must be equal to the total amount of acid in each of the two parts, so $3x = 0.50 + 0.40$. Therefore x is equal to 0.30, which is the same as a 30% concentration of the acid in the mixture.

Cost

205. In *cost problems* the rate is the *price per item*, the input is the *number of items*, and the output is the *value* of the items considered. When you are dealing with dollars and cents, you must be very careful to use the decimal point correctly.

Example: Jim has $3.00 in nickels and dimes in his pocket. If he has twice as many nickels as he has dimes, how many coins does he have altogether?

Solution: After Step 6, our chart should look like this (where c is the number of dimes Jim has):

rate × number = value

	cents/coin	coins	cents
nickels	5	$2c$	$10c$
dimes	10	c	$10c$

Now we recall the additional bit of information that the total value of the nickels and dimes is $3.00, or 300 cents. Thus, $5(2c) + 10c = 300$; $20c = 300$; so $c = 15$, the number of dimes. Jim has twice as many nickels, so $2c = 30$.

The total number of coins is $c + 2c = 3c = 45$.

The following table will serve as review for this Refresher Section.

TYPE OF PROBLEM	FUNDAMENTAL RELATIONSHIP
distance	speed × time = distance
work	rate × time = work done
mixture	concentration × amount of solution = amount of ingredient
cost	rate × number of items = value

Practice Test 2

Rate Problems: Distance and Time, Work, Mixture, and Cost

Correct answers and solutions follow each test.

1. A B C D E

1. A man rowed 3 miles upstream (against the current) in 90 minutes. If the river flowed with a current of 2 miles per hour, how long did the man's return trip (downstream) take?

   (A) 20 minutes
   (B) 30 minutes
   (C) 45 minutes
   (D) 60 minutes
   (E) 80 minutes

2. A B C D E

2. Charles can do a job in 1 hour, Bill can do the same job in 2 hours, and Bob can do the job in 3 hours. How long does it take them to do the job working together?

   (A) $\frac{6}{11}$ hour

   (B) $\frac{1}{2}$ hour

   (C) 6 hours

   (D) $\frac{1}{3}$ hour

   (E) $\frac{1}{6}$ hour

3. A B C D E

3. Mr. Smith had $2,000 to invest. He invested part of it at 5% per year and the remainder at 4% per year. After one year, his investment grew to $2,095. How much of the original investment was at the 5% rate?

   (A) $500
   (B) $750
   (C) $1,000
   (D) $1,250
   (E) $1,500

4. A B C D E

4. A man walks down the road for half an hour at an average speed of 3 miles per hour. He waits 10 minutes for a bus, which brings him back to his starting point at 3:15. If the man began his walk at 2:25 the same afternoon, what was the average speed of the bus?

   (A) 1.5 miles per hour
   (B) 3 miles per hour
   (C) 4.5 miles per hour
   (D) 6 miles per hour
   (E) 9 miles per hour

5. A B C D E

5. Faucet A lets water flow into a 5-gallon tub at a rate of 1.5 gallons per minute. Faucet B lets water flow into the same tub at a rate of 1.0 gallons per minute. Faucet A runs alone for 100 seconds; then the two of them together finish filling up the tub. How long does the whole operation take?

   (A) 120 seconds
   (B) 150 seconds
   (C) 160 seconds
   (D) 180 seconds
   (E) 190 seconds

6. A B C D E

6. Coffee A normally costs 75¢ per pound. It is mixed with Coffee B, which normally costs 80¢ per pound, to form a mixture that costs 78¢ per pound. If there are 10 pounds of the mix, how many pounds of Coffee A were used in the mix?

(A) 3
(B) 4
(C) 4.5
(D) 5
(E) 6

7. A B C D E

7. If a man can run p miles in x minutes, how long will it take him to run q miles at the same rate?

(A) $\dfrac{pq}{x}$ minutes

(B) $\dfrac{px}{q}$ minutes

(C) $\dfrac{q}{px}$ minutes

(D) $\dfrac{qx}{p}$ minutes

(E) $\dfrac{x}{pq}$ minutes

8. A B C D E

8. A train went 300 miles from City X to City Y at an average rate of 80 mph. At what speed did it travel on the way back if its average speed for the whole trip was 100 mph?

(A) 120 mph

(B) 125 mph

(C) $133\frac{1}{3}$ mph

(D) $137\frac{1}{2}$ mph

(E) 150 mph

9. A B C D E

9. A man spent exactly $2.50 on 3¢, 6¢, and 10¢ stamps. If he bought ten 3¢ stamps and twice as many 6¢ stamps as 10¢ stamps, how many 10¢ stamps did he buy?

(A) 5
(B) 10
(C) 12
(D) 15
(E) 20

10. A B C D E

10. If 6 workers can complete 9 identical jobs in 3 days, how long will it take 4 workers to complete 10 such jobs?

(A) 3 days
(B) 4 days
(C) 5 days
(D) 6 days
(E) more than 6 days

11. A B C D E

11. A barge travels twice as fast when it is empty as when it is full. If it travels 20 miles north with a cargo, spends 20 minutes unloading, and returns to its original port empty, taking 8 hours to complete the entire trip, what is the speed of the barge when it is empty?

(A) less than 3 mph
(B) less than 4 mph but not less than 3 mph
(C) less than 6 mph but not less than 4 mph
(D) less than 8 mph but not less than 6 mph
(E) 8 mph or more

A B C D E
12.

12. Bill can hammer 20 nails in 6 minutes. Jeff can do the same job in only 5 minutes. How long will it take them to finish if Bill hammers the first 5 nails, then Jeff hammers for 3 minutes, then Bill finishes the job?

(A) 4.6 minutes
(B) 5.0 minutes
(C) 5.4 minutes
(D) 5.8 minutes
(E) 6.0 minutes

A B C D E
13.

13. Jack has two quarts of a 30% acid solution and three pints of a 20% solution. If he mixes them, what will be the concentration (to the nearest percent) of the resulting solution? (1 quart = 2 pints.)

(A) 22%
(B) 23%
(C) 24%
(D) 25%
(E) 26%

A B C D E
14.

14. Robert has 12 coins totaling $1.45. None of his coins is larger than a quarter. Which of the following *cannot* be the number of quarters he has?

(A) 1
(B) 2
(C) 3
(D) 4
(E) 5

A B C D E
15.

15. Jim's allowance is $1.20 per week. Stan's is 25¢ per day. How long will they have to save, if they save both their allowances together, before they can get a model car set that costs $23.60?

(A) 6 weeks
(B) 8 weeks
(C) 10 weeks
(D) 13 weeks
(E) 16 weeks

A B C D E
16.

16. Chuck can earn money at the following schedule: $2.00 for the first hour, $2.50 an hour for the next two hours, and $3.00 an hour after that. He also has the opportunity of taking a different job that pays $2.75 an hour. He wants to work until he has earned $15.00. Which of the following is true?

(A) The first job will take him longer by 15 minutes or more.
(B) The first job will take him longer by less than 15 minutes.
(C) The two jobs will take the same length of time.
(D) The second job will take him longer by 30 minutes or more.
(E) The second job will take him longer by less than 10 minutes.

A B C D E
17.

17. If Robert can seal 40 envelopes in one minute, and Paul can do the same job in 80 seconds, how many minutes (to the nearest minute) will it take the two of them, working together, to seal 350 envelopes?

(A) 4 minutes
(B) 5 minutes
(C) 6 minutes
(D) 7 minutes
(E) 8 minutes

18. ABCDE

18. Towns A and B are 400 miles apart. If a train leaves A in the direction of B at 50 miles per hour, how long will it take before that train meets another train, going from B to A, at a speed of 30 miles per hour? (Note: The train that leaves B departs at the same time as the train that leaves A.)

(A) 4 hours

(B) $4\frac{1}{3}$ hours

(C) 5 hours

(D) $5\frac{2}{3}$ hours

(E) $6\frac{2}{3}$ hours

19. ABCDE

19. A tub is shaped like a rectangular solid, with internal measurements of 2 feet × 2 feet × 5 feet. If two faucets, each with an output of 2 cubic feet of water per minute, pour water into the tub simultaneously, how many minutes does it take to fill the tub completely?

(A) less than 3 minutes
(B) less than 4 minutes, but not less than 3
(C) less than 5 minutes, but not less than 4
(D) less than 6 minutes, but not less than 5
(E) 6 minutes or more

20. ABCDE

20. A 30% solution of barium chloride is mixed with 10 grams of water to form a 20% solution. How many grams were in the original solution?

(A) 10
(B) 15
(C) 20
(D) 25
(E) 30

21. ABCDE

21. Mr. Adams had a coin collection including only nickels, dimes, and quarters. He had twice as many dimes as he had nickels, and half as many quarters as he had nickels. If the total face value of his collection was $300.00, how many quarters did the collection contain?

(A) 75
(B) 100
(C) 250
(D) 400
(E) 800

22. ABCDE

22. A storekeeper stocks a high-priced pen and a lower-priced model. If he sells the high-priced pens, which yield a profit of $1.20 per pen sold, he can sell 30 in a month. If he sells the lower-priced pens, making a profit of 15¢ per pen sold, he can sell 250 pens in a month. Which type of pen will yield more profit per month, and by how much?

(A) The cheaper pen will yield a greater profit, by $1.50.
(B) The more expensive pen will yield a greater profit, by $1.50.
(C) The cheaper pen will yield a greater profit, by 15¢.
(D) The more expensive pen will yield a greater profit, by 15¢.
(E) Both pens will yield exactly the same profit.

23. ABCDE

23. At a cost of $2.50 per square yard, what would be the price of carpeting a rectangular floor, 18 feet × 24 feet?

(A) $120
(B) $360
(C) $750
(D) $1,000
(E) $1,080

24. A B C D E

24. Tom and Bill agreed to race across a 50-foot pool and back again. They started together, but Tom finished 10 feet ahead of Bill. If their rates were constant, and Tom finished the race in 27 seconds, how long did Bill take to finish it?

(A) 28 seconds
(B) 30 seconds
(C) $33\frac{1}{3}$ seconds
(D) 35 seconds
(E) 37 seconds

25. A B C D E

25. If four men need $24.00 worth of food for a three-day camping trip, how much will two men need for a two-week trip?

(A) $12.00
(B) $24.00
(C) $28.00
(D) $42.00
(E) $56.00

26. A B C D E

26. A man walks 15 blocks to work every morning at a rate of 2 miles per hour. If there are 20 blocks in a mile, how long does it take him to walk to work?

(A) $12\frac{1}{2}$ minutes

(B) 15 minutes

(C) $22\frac{1}{2}$ minutes

(D) $37\frac{1}{2}$ minutes

(E) 45 minutes

27. A B C D E

27. A certain river has a current of 3 miles per hour. A boat takes twice as long to travel upstream between two points as it does to travel downstream between the same two points. What is the speed of the boat in still water?

(A) 3 miles per hour
(B) 6 miles per hour
(C) 9 miles per hour
(D) 12 miles per hour
(E) The speed cannot be determined from the given information.

28. A B C D E

28. Stan can run 10 miles per hour, whereas Jack can run only 8 miles per hour. If they start at the same time from the same point and run in opposite directions, how far apart (to the nearest mile) will they be after 10 minutes?

(A) 1 mile
(B) 2 miles
(C) 3 miles
(D) 4 miles
(E) 5 miles

29. ABCDE

29. Machine A can produce 40 bolts per minute, whereas Machine B can produce only 30 per minute. Machine A begins alone to make bolts, but it breaks down after $1\frac{1}{2}$ minutes, and Machine B must complete the job. If the job requires 300 bolts, how long does the whole operation take?

(A) $7\frac{1}{2}$ minutes

(B) 8 minutes

(C) $8\frac{1}{2}$ minutes

(D) 9 minutes

(E) $9\frac{1}{2}$ minutes

30. ABCDE

30. Ten pints of 15% salt solution are mixed with 15 pints of 10% salt solution. What is the concentration of the resulting solution?

(A) 10%
(B) 12%
(C) 12.5%
(D) 13%
(E) 15%

31. ABCDE

31. Jeff makes $5.00 every day, from which he must spend $3.00 for various expenses. Pete makes $10.00 a day but has to spend $7.00 each day for expenses. If the two of them save together, how long will it take before they can buy a $150 car?

(A) 10 days
(B) 15 days
(C) 30 days
(D) 50 days
(E) 75 days

32. ABCDE

32. Two cities are 800 miles apart. At 3:00 P.M., Plane A leaves one city, traveling toward the other city at a speed of 600 miles per hour. At 4:00 the same afternoon, Plane B leaves the first city, traveling in the same direction at a rate of 800 miles per hour. Which of the following answers represents the actual result?

(A) Plane A arrives first, by an hour or more.
(B) Plane A arrives first, by less than an hour.
(C) The two planes arrive at exactly the same time.
(D) Plane A arrives after Plane B, by less than an hour.
(E) Plane A arrives after Plane B, by an hour or more.

33. ABCDE

33. Peter has as many nickels as Charlie has dimes; Charlie has twice as many nickels as Peter has dimes. If together they have $2.50 in nickels and dimes, how many nickels does Peter have?

(A) 1 nickel
(B) 4 nickels
(C) 7 nickels
(D) 10 nickels
(E) The answer cannot be determined from the given information.

34. ABCDE

34. A man can travel 120 miles in either of two ways. He can travel at a constant rate of 40 miles per hour, or he can travel halfway at 50 miles per hour, then slow down to 30 miles per hour for the second 60 miles. Which way is faster, and by how much?

(A) The constant rate is faster by 10 minutes or more.
(B) The constant rate is faster by less than 10 minutes.
(C) The two ways take exactly the same time.
(D) The constant rate is slower by less than 10 minutes.
(E) The constant rate is slower by 10 minutes or more.

35. A B C D E

35. John walks 10 miles at an average rate of 2 miles per hour and returns on a bicycle at an average rate of 10 miles per hour. How long (to the nearest hour) does the entire trip take him?

(A) 3 hours
(B) 4 hours
(C) 5 hours
(D) 6 hours
(E) 7 hours

36. A B C D E

36. If a plane can travel P miles in Q hours, how long will it take to travel R miles?

(A) $\dfrac{PQ}{R}$ hours

(B) $\dfrac{P}{QR}$ hours

(C) $\dfrac{QR}{P}$ hours

(D) $\dfrac{Q}{PR}$ hours

(E) $\dfrac{PR}{Q}$ hours

37. A B C D E

37. A boy can swim 75 feet in 12 seconds. What is his rate to the nearest mile per hour?

(A) 1 mph
(B) 2 mph
(C) 3 mph
(D) 4 mph
(E) 5 mph

38. A B C D E

38. How many pounds of a $1.20-per-pound nut mixture must be mixed with two pounds of a 90¢-per-pound mixture to produce a mixture that sells for $1.00 per pound?

(A) 0.5
(B) 1.0
(C) 1.5
(D) 2.0
(E) 2.5

39. A B C D E

39. A broken clock is set correctly at 12:00 noon. However, it registers only 20 minutes for each hour. In how many hours will it again register the correct time?

(A) 12
(B) 18
(C) 24
(D) 30
(E) 36

40. A B C D E

40. If a man travels p hours at an average rate of q miles per hour, and then r hours at an average rate of s miles per hour, what is his overall average rate of speed?

(A) $\dfrac{pq + rs}{p + r}$

(B) $\dfrac{q + s}{2}$

(C) $\dfrac{q + s}{p + r}$

(D) $\dfrac{p}{q} + \dfrac{r}{s}$

(E) $\dfrac{p}{s} + \dfrac{r}{q}$

41. A B C D E

41. If Walt can paint 25 feet of fence in an hour, and Joe can paint 35 feet in an hour, how many minutes will it take them to paint a 150-foot fence, if they work together?

(A) 150
(B) 200
(C) 240
(D) 480
(E) 500

42. A B C D E

42. If a man travels for a half hour at a rate of 20 miles per hour, and for another half hour at a rate of 30 miles per hour, what is his average speed?

(A) 24 miles per hour
(B) 25 miles per hour
(C) 26 miles per hour
(D) 26.5 miles per hour
(E) The answer cannot be determined from the given information.

43. A B C D E

43. New York is 3,000 miles from Los Angeles. Sol leaves New York aboard a plane heading toward Los Angeles at the same time that Robert leaves Los Angeles aboard a plane heading toward New York. If Sol is moving at 200 miles per hour and Robert is moving at 400 miles per hour, how soon will one plane pass the other?

(A) 2 hours
(B) $22\frac{1}{2}$ hours
(C) 5 hours
(D) 4 hours
(E) 12 hours

44. A B C D E

44. A man exchanged a dollar bill for change and received 7 coins, none of which were half dollars. How many of these coins were dimes?

(A) 0
(B) 1
(C) 4
(D) 5
(E) The answer cannot be determined from the information given.

45. A B C D E

45. A man adds two quarts of pure alcohol to a 30% solution of alcohol in water. If the new concentration is 40%, how many quarts of the original solution were there?

(A) 12
(B) 15
(C) 18
(D) 20
(E) 24

46. A B C D E

46. A certain power company charges 8¢ per kilowatt-hour for the first 1,000 kilowatt-hours, and 6¢ per kilowatt-hour after that. If a man uses a 900-watt toaster for 5 hours, a 100-watt lamp for 25 hours, and a 5-watt clock for 400 hours, how much is he charged for the power he uses? (1 kilowatt = 1,000 watts)

(A) 56¢
(B) 64¢
(C) 72¢
(D) $560.00
(E) $720.00

47.
47. At 30¢ per yard, what is the price of 96 inches of ribbon?

(A) 72¢
(B) 75¢
(C) 80¢
(D) 84¢
(E) 90¢

48.
48. A man travels for 6 hours at a rate of 50 miles per hour. His return trip takes him $7\frac{1}{2}$ hours. What is his average speed for the whole trip?

(A) 44.4 miles per hour
(B) 45.0 miles per hour
(C) 46.8 miles per hour
(D) 48.2 miles per hour
(E) 50.0 miles per hour

49.
49. Rachel puts $100 in the bank for two years at 5% interest compounded annually. At the end of the two years, what is her balance?

(A) $100.00
(B) $105.00
(C) $105.25
(D) $110.00
(E) $110.25

50.
50. A 12-gallon tub has a faucet that lets water in at a rate of 3 gallons per minute, and a drain that lets water out at a rate of 1.5 gallons per minute. If you start with 3 gallons of water in the tub, how long will it take to fill the tub completely? (Note that the faucet is on and the drain is open.)

(A) 3 minutes
(B) 4 minutes
(C) 6 minutes
(D) 7.5 minutes
(E) 8 minutes

Answer Key for Practice Test 2

1. B	14. A	27. C	39. B
2. A	15. B	28. C	40. A
3. E	16. B	29. E	41. A
4. E	17. B	30. B	42. B
5. C	18. C	31. C	43. C
6. B	19. D	32. B	44. E
7. D	20. C	33. E	45. A
8. C	21. D	34. A	46. C
9. B	22. A	35. D	47. C
10. C	23. A	36. C	48. A
11. D	24. B	37. D	49. E
12. C	25. E	38. B	50. C
13. E	26. C		

Answers and Solutions for Practice Test 2

1. **Choice B is correct.** The fundamental relationship here is: rate × time = distance. The easiest units to work with are miles per hour for the rate, hours for time, and miles for distance. Note that the word *per* indicates division, because when calculating a rate, we *divide* the number of miles (distance units) by the number of hours (time units).

We can set up our chart with the information given. We know that the upstream trip took $1\frac{1}{2}$ hours (90 minutes) and that the distance was 3 miles. Thus the upstream rate was 2 miles per hour. The downstream distance was also 3 miles, but we use t for the time, which is unknown. Thus the downstream rate was $\frac{3}{t}$. Our chart looks like this:

rate   ×   time   =   distance

	mi/hr	hours	miles
upstream	2	$1\frac{1}{2}$	3
downstream	$\frac{3}{t}$	t	3

We use the rest of the information to solve for t. We know that the speed of the current is 2 miles per hour. We assume the boat to be in still water and assign it a speed, s; then the upstream (against the current) speed of the boat is $s - 2$ miles per hour. Since $s - 2 = 2$, $s = 4$.

Now, the speed of the boat downstream (with the current) is $s + 2$, or 6 miles per hour. This is equal to $\frac{3}{t}$, and we get the equation $\frac{3}{t} = 6$, so $t = \frac{1}{2}$ hour.

We must be careful with our units because the answer must be in minutes. We can convert $\frac{1}{2}$ hour to 30 minutes to get the final answer. (201, 202)

2. **Choice A is correct.**

rate   ×   time   =   work

	job/hr	hours	jobs
Charles	1	1	1
Bill	$\frac{1}{2}$	2	1
Bob	$\frac{1}{3}$	3	1
together	r	t	1

Let r = rate together and t = time together.

Now, $r = 1 + \frac{1}{2} + \frac{1}{3} = \frac{11}{6}$ because *whenever two or more people are working together, their joint rate is the sum of their individual rates.* This is not necessarily true of the time or the work done. In this case, we know that $r \times t = 1$ and $r = \frac{11}{6}$, so $t = \frac{6}{11}$. (201, 203)

3. **Choice E is correct.**

rate   ×   principal = interest

	$/$	$	$
5%	0.05	x	0.05x
4%	0.04	y	0.04y

Let x = the part of the $2,000 invested at 5%. Let y = the part of $2,000 invested at 4%. We know that since the whole $2,000 was invested, $x + y$ must equal $2,000. Furthermore, we know that the sum of the interests on both investments equaled $95, so $0.05x + 0.04y = 95$. Since we have to solve only for x, we can express this as $0.01x + 0.04x + 0.04y = 95$. Then we factor out 0.04. Thus $0.01x + 0.04(x + y) = 95$. Since we know that $x + y = 2,000$, we have $0.01x + 0.04(2,000) = 95$; $0.01x + 80 = 95$, and $x = 1,500$. Thus, $1,500 was invested at 5%. (201, 205)

4. Choice E is correct.

rate $\times$ time = distance

	mi/min	min	miles
walk	$\frac{1}{20}$	30	a
wait	0	10	0
bus	r	t	a

Let a = distance the man walks. Since the man walks at 3 miles per hour, he walks at $\frac{3\,mi}{60\,min}$, or $\frac{1\,mi}{20\,min}$. From this we can find $a = \frac{1\,mi}{20\,min} \times 30\,min = 1\frac{1}{2}$ miles. The total time he spent was 50 minutes (the difference between 3:15 and 2:25), and 30 + 10 + t = 50, so t must be equal to 10 minutes. This reduces our problem to the simple equation $10r = 1\frac{1}{2}$ (where r = rate of the bus), and, on solving, r = 0.15 miles per minute. But the required answer is in miles per hour. In one hour, or 60 minutes, the bus can travel 60 times as far as the 0.15 miles it travels in one minute, so that the bus travels $60 \times 0.15 = 9$ miles per hour. (201, 202)

5. Choice C is correct.

rate $\times$ time = water

	gal/min	min	gal
A only	1.5	$\frac{5}{3}$*	2.5
B only	1.0	0	0
A and B	2.5	t	x

* $\frac{5}{3}$ min = 100 sec.

Let t = time faucets A and B run together.

Let x = amount of water delivered when A and B run together.

We know that the total number of gallons is 5, and A alone delivers 2.5 gallons (1.5 gal/min $\times \frac{5}{3}$ min = 2.5 gal), so x equals 2.5. This leads us to the simple equation $2.5t = 2.5$, so $t = 1$ minute, or 60 seconds.

Thus, the whole operation takes $\frac{5}{3}$ + t minutes, or 100 + 60 seconds, totaling 160 seconds. (201, 203)

6. Choice B is correct.

rate $\times$ amount = cost

	¢/lb	lb	¢
Coffee A	75	x	$75x$
Coffee B	80	y	$80y$
mix	78	10	780

Let x = weight of Coffee A in the mix.

Let y = weight of Coffee B in the mix.

We know that the weight of the mix is equal to the sum of the weights of its components. Thus, $x + y = 10$. Similarly, the cost of the mix is equal to the sum of the costs of the components. Thus, $75x + 80y = 780$. So we have $x + y = 10$ and $75x + 80y = 780$. Now $y = 10 - x$, so substituting $y = 10 - x$ in the second equation, we get,

$$75x + 80(10 - x) = 780$$
$$75x + 800 - 80x = 780$$
$$800 - 5x = 780$$
$$20 = 5x$$
$$4 = x$$

Thus 4 pounds of Coffee A were used.

(201, 204, 407)

7. Choice D is correct.

rate $\times$ time = distance

	mi/min	min	miles
first run	r	x	p
second run	r	t	q

Let r = rate of the man.

Let t = time it takes him to run q miles.

From the first line, we know that $rx = p$, then $r = \frac{p}{x}$. Substituting this in the second line, we get $\left(\frac{p}{x}\right)t = q$, so $t = q\left(\frac{x}{p}\right)$, or $\frac{qx}{p}$ minutes. (201, 202)

8. Choice C is correct.

rate × time = distance

	mi/hr	hrs	miles
X to Y	80	t	300
Y to X	r	s	300
whole trip	100	$s + t$	600

Let t = time from city X to city Y.

Let s = time from city Y to city X.

Let r = rate of the train from Y to X.

We know that $80t = 300$, so $t = \frac{300}{80}$, or $\frac{15}{4}$. Also, $100(s + t) = 600$, so $s + t = 6$. This and the last equation lead us to the conclusion that $s = 6 - \frac{15}{4}$, or $\frac{9}{4}$. Now, from the middle line of the table, we have $r\left(\frac{9}{4}\right) = 300$, so $r = \frac{400}{3}$, or $133\frac{1}{3}$ miles per hour.

(Note that the reason why we chose the equations in this particular order was that it is easiest to concentrate first on those with the most data already given.) (201, 202)

9. Choice B is correct.

rate × number = cost

	¢/stamp	stamps	¢
3¢ stamps	3	10	30
10¢ stamps	10	x	$10x$
6¢ stamps	6	$2x$	$12x$

Let x = the number of 10¢ stamps bought.

We know that the total cost is 250¢, so $30 + 10x + 12x = 250$. This is the same as $22x = 220$, so $x = 10$. Therefore, he bought ten 10¢ stamps. (201, 205)

10. Choice C is correct.

rate × time = work

	job/day	days	jobs
6 workers	$6r$	3	9
4 workers	$4r$	t	10

Let r = rate of one worker.

Let t = time for 4 workers to do 10 jobs.

From the first line, we have $18r = 9$, so $r = \frac{1}{2}$.

Substituting this in the second line, $4r = 2$, so $2t = 10$. Therefore $t = 5$. The workers will take 5 days. (201, 203)

11. Choice D is correct.

rate × time = distance

	mi/hr	hrs	miles
north	r	$\frac{20}{r}$	20
unload	0	$\frac{1}{3}$	0
return	$2r$	$\frac{10}{r}$	20

Let r = loaded rate; then $2r$ = empty rate.

Total time = $\frac{20}{r} + \frac{1}{3} + \frac{10}{r} = 8$ hours.

Multiplying by $3r$ on both sides, we get $90 = 23r$, so $r = 90 \div 23$, or about 3.9 miles per hour. However, the problem asks for the speed *when empty*, which is $2r$, or 7.8. This is less than 8 mph, but not less than 6 mph. (201, 202)

12. Choice C is correct.

rate × time = work

	nail/min	min	nails
Bill	r	6	20
Jeff	s	5	20
Bill	r	$\frac{5}{r}$	5
Jeff	s	3	$3s$
Bill	r	$\frac{x}{r}$	x

Let r = Bill's rate.

Let s = Jeff's rate.

x = number of nails left after Jeff takes his turn.

$6r = 20$, so $r = 3\frac{1}{3}$.

$5s = 20$, so $s = 4$.

Total work = $5 + 3s + x = 20 = 5 + 12 + x = 20$, so $x = 3$. Thus $\frac{x}{r} = 0.9$.

Total time = $\frac{5}{r} + 3 + \frac{x}{r} = 1.5 + 3 + 0.9 = 5.4$. (201, 203)

13. Choice E is correct.

concentration × volume = amount of acid

	% acid	pts	pts
old sol	30%	4	1.2
	20%	3	0.6
new sol	$x\%$	7	1.8

(2 qts = 4 pts)

Let $x\%$ = concentration of new solution.

4 pts of 30% + 3 pts of 20% = 7 pts of $x\%$

1.2 pts + 0.6 pt = 1.8 pts

$(x\%)(7) = 1.8$, so $x = 180 \div 7 = 25.7$ (approximately), which is closest to 26%.   (201, 204)

14. Choice A is correct.

coin × number = total value

	¢/coin	coins	cents
pennies	1	p	p
nickels	5	n	$5n$
dimes	10	d	$10d$
quarters	25	q	$25q$

Let p = number of pennies

$\quad n$ = number of nickels

$\quad d$ = number of dimes

$\quad q$ = number of quarters

Total number of coins = $p + n + d + q = 12$.

Total value = $p + 5n + 10d + 25q = 145$.

Now, if $q = 1$, then $p + n + d = 11$, $p + 5n + 10d = 120$. But in this case, the greatest possible value of the other eleven coins would be the value of eleven dimes, or 110 cents, which falls short of the amount necessary to give a total of 145 cents for the twelve coins put together. Therefore, Robert cannot have only one quarter.   (201, 205)

15. Choice B is correct.

rate × time = money

	¢/wk	weeks	cents
Jim	120	w	$120w$
Stan	175	w	$175w$
together	295	w	$295w$

(25¢/day = $1.75/week)

Let w = the number of weeks they save.

Total money = $295w = 2,360$.

Therefore, $w = 2,360 \div 295 = 8$.

So, they must save for 8 weeks.   (201, 205)

16. Choice B is correct.

rate × time = pay

	¢/hr	hours	¢
first job	200	1	200
	250	2	500
	300	x	$300x$
second job	275	y	$275y$

Let x = hours at $3.00.

Let y = hours at $2.75.

Total pay, first job = $200 + 500 + 300x = 1,500$, so $x = 2\frac{2}{3}$.

Total time, first job = $1 + 2 + 2\frac{2}{3} = 5\frac{2}{3}$.

Total pay, second job = $275y = 1,500$, so $y = 5\frac{5}{11}$.

Total time, second job = $5\frac{5}{11}$.

$\frac{2}{3}$ hour = 40 minutes

$\frac{5}{11}$ hour = 27.2727... minutes (less than $\frac{2}{3}$ hour).

Thus, the first job will take him longer by less than 15 minutes.   (201, 205)

17. Choice B is correct.

rate × time = work

	envelopes/min	min	envelopes
Robert	40	t	$40t$
Paul	30	t	$30t$
both	70	t	$70t$

Let t = time to seal 350 envelopes.

Paul's rate is 30 envelopes/minute, as shown by the proportion:

$$\text{rate} = \frac{40 \text{ envelopes}}{80 \text{ seconds}} = \frac{30 \text{ envelopes}}{60 \text{ seconds}}$$

Total work = $70t = 350$, so $t = 5$ minutes.

(201, 203)

18. Choice C is correct.

rate × time = distance

	mi/hr	hr	miles
A to B	50	t	$50t$
B to A	30	t	$30t$

Let t = time to meet.

Total distance traveled by two trains together equals $50t + 30t = 80t = 400$ miles, so $t = 5$ hrs.
(201, 202)

19. Choice D is correct.

rate × time = amount of water

	cu. ft./m	min	cu. ft.
2 faucets	4	t	20

Let t = time to fill the tub.

Volume of tub = 2 ft. × 2 ft. × 5 ft. = 20 cu. ft.

Rate = 2 × rate of each faucet = 2 × 2 cu. ft./min = 4 cu. ft./min.

$4t = 20$ cu. ft.

Therefore, $t = 5$ minutes. (201, 203)

20. Choice C is correct.

concentration × weight = amount of barium chloride

	%	grams	grams
original	30%	x	$0.30x$
water	0%	10	0
new	20%	$10 + x$	$0.30x$

Let x = number of grams of original solution.

Total weight and amounts of barium chloride may be added by column.

$(20\%) \times (10 + x) = 0.30x$, so $10 + x = 1.50x$, $x = 20$. (201, 204)

21. Choice D is correct.

coin × number = value

	¢/coin	coins	cents
nickels	5	n	$5n$
dimes	10	$2n$	$20n$
quarters	25	$\frac{n}{2}$	$\frac{25n}{2}$

Let n = number of nickels.

Total value = $5n + 20n + \frac{25n}{2} = \left(37\frac{1}{2}\right)n$
$= 30{,}000$.

Thus, $n = 30{,}000 \div 37\frac{1}{2} = 800$.

The number of quarters is then $\frac{n}{2} = \frac{800}{2} = 400$.
(201, 205)

22. Choice A is correct.

rate × number = profit

	¢/pen	pens	cents
high-price	120	30	3,600
low-price	15	250	3,750

Subtracting 3,600¢ from 3,750¢, we get 150¢.

Thus, the cheaper pen yields a profit of 150¢, or $1.50, more per month than the more expensive one. (201, 205)

23. Choice A is correct.

price × area = cost

$/sq. yd.	sq. yd.	dollars
2.50	48	120

Area must be expressed in square yards; 18 ft. = 6 yds., and 24 ft. = 8 yds., so 18 ft. × 24 ft. = 6 yds. × 8 yds. = 48 sq. yds. The cost would then be $2.50 × 48 = $120.00. (201, 205)

24. Choice B is correct.

rate × time = distance

	ft/sec	sec	feet
Tom	r	27	100
Bill	s	27	90
Bill	s	t	100

Let r = Tom's rate.
Let s = Bill's rate.

Let t = Bill's time to finish the race.

$27s = 90$, so $s = \dfrac{90}{27} = \dfrac{10}{3}$;

$st = 100$, and $s = \dfrac{10}{3}$, so $\dfrac{10t}{3} = 100$; thus $t = 30$.

(201, 202)

25. Choice E is correct. This is a rate problem in which the fundamental relationship is rate × time × number of men = cost. The rate is in dollars/man-days. Thus, our chart looks like this:

rate × time × number = cost

	\$/man-days	days	men	\$
1st trip	r	3	4	$12r$
2nd trip	r	14	2	$28r$

The cost of the first trip is \$24, so $12r = 24$ and $r = 2$.

The cost of the second trip is $28r$, or \$56. (201, 205)

26. Choice C is correct.

rate × time = distance

blocks/min.	min	blocks
$\dfrac{2}{3}$	t	15

Let t = time to walk to work.

2 miles/hr = 2(20 blocks)/(60 min) = $\dfrac{2}{3}$ blocks/minute.

$t = 15 \div \dfrac{2}{3} = 22\dfrac{1}{2}$ minutes. (201, 202)

27. Choice C is correct.

rate × time = distance

	mi/hr	hrs	miles
down	$r + 3$	h	$h(r + 3)$
up	$r - 3$	$2h$	$2h(r - 3)$

Let h = time to travel downstream.

Let r = speed of the boat in still water.

Since the two trips cover the same distance, we can write the equation: $h(r + 3) = 2h(r - 3)$. Dividing by h, $r + 3 = 2r - 6$, so $r = 9$. (201, 202)

28. Choice C is correct. We could treat this as a regular distance problem and make up a table that would solve it, but there is an easier way here, if we consider the quantity representing the distance

between the boys. This distance starts at zero and increases at the rate of 18 miles per hour. Thus, in 10 minutes, or $\dfrac{1}{6}$ hour, they will be 3 miles apart

($\dfrac{1}{6}$ hr × 18 $\dfrac{\text{mi}}{\text{hr}}$ = 3 mi). (201, 202)

29. Choice E is correct.

rate × time = work

	bolts/min	min	bolts
A	40	$1\dfrac{1}{2}$	60
B	30	t	240

Let t = time B works.

Since A produces only 60 out of 300 that must be produced, B must produce 240; then, $30t = 240$, so $t = 8$.

Total time = $t + 1\dfrac{1}{2} = 8 + 1\dfrac{1}{2} = 9\dfrac{1}{2}$. (201, 203)

30. Choice B is correct.

concentration × volume = amount of salt

	%	pints	"pints" of salt
15%	15	10	1.5
10%	10	15	1.5
Total	x	25	3.0

Let x = concentration of resulting solution.

$(x\%)(25) = 3.0$, so $x = 300 \div 25 = 12$. (201, 204)

31. Choice C is correct.

rate × time = pay (net)

	\$/day	days	\$
Jeff	2	d	$2d$
Pete	3	d	$3d$
total	5	d	$5d$

(Net pay = pay − expenses.)

Let d = the number of days it takes to save.

Total net pay = \$150.00, so $150 = 5d$; thus $d = 30$.

Do not make the mistake of using 5 and 10 as the rates! (201, 205)

32. Choice B is correct.

rate	×	time	=	distance
	mi/hr	hours	miles
plane A	600	h	800
plane B	0	1	0
plane B	800	t	800

Let h = time for trip at 600 mph.

Let t = time for trip at 800 mph.

Plane A: $600h = 800$, so $h = \frac{800}{600} = 1\frac{1}{3}$ hours = 1 hour, 20 minutes.

Plane B: $800t = 800$, so $t = 1$.

Total time for plane A = 1 hour, 20 minutes.

Total time for plane B = 1 hour + 1 hour = 2 hours.

Thus, plane A arrives before plane B by 40 minutes (less than an hour). (201, 202)

33. Choice E is correct.

coin	×	number	=	value
	¢/coin	coins	cents
Peter	5	n	$5n$
Peter	10	d	$10d$
Charlie	5	$2d$	$10d$
Charlie	10	n	$10n$

Let n = number of Peter's nickels.

Let d = number of Peter's dimes.

Total value of coins = $5n + 10d + 10d + 10n = 15n + 20d$.

Thus, $15n + 20d = 250$. This has many different solutions, each of which is possible (e.g., $n = 2$, $d = 11$, or $n = 6$, $d = 8$, etc.). (201, 205)

34. Choice A is correct.

rate	×	time	=	distance
	mi/hr	hours	miles
constant rate	40	h	120
two rates	50	m	60
	30	n	60

Let h = time to travel 120 miles at the constant rate.

Let m = time to travel 60 miles at 50 mi/hr.

Let n = time to travel 60 miles at 30 mi/hr.

Forming the equations for h, m, and n, and solving, we get:

$$40h = 120; \; h = \frac{120}{40}; \; h = 3$$

$$50m = 60; \; m = \frac{60}{50}; \; m = 1.2$$

$$30n = 60; \; n = \frac{60}{30}; \; n = 2$$

Total time with constant rate = h = 3 hours.

Total time with changing rate = $m + n$ = 3.2 hours.

Thus, the constant rate is faster by 0.2 hours, or 12 minutes. (201, 202)

35. Choice D is correct.

rate	×	time	=	distance
	mi/hr	hours	miles
walking	2	h	10
bicycling	10	t	10

Let h = time to walk.

Let t = time to bicycle.

Forming equations: $2h = 10$, so $h = 5$; and $10t = 10$, so $t = 1$.

Total time = $h + t = 5 + 1 = 6$. (201, 202)

36. Choice C is correct.

rate	×	time	=	distance
mi/hr	hours	miles
x	Q	P
x	y	R

Let x = rate at which the airplane travels.

Let y = time to travel R miles.

$Qx = P$, so $x = \frac{P}{Q}$.

$xy = \left(\frac{P}{Q}\right)y = R$, so $y = \frac{QR}{P}$ hours = time to travel R miles. (201, 202)

37. Choice D is correct.

rate × time = distance

mi/hr	hours	miles
r	$\frac{1}{300}$	$\frac{75}{5280}$

Let r = rate of swimming.

75 feet = $75\left(\frac{1}{5,280}\text{ mile}\right) = \frac{75}{5,280}$ mile

12 seconds = $12\left(\frac{1}{3,600}\text{ hour}\right) = \frac{1}{300}$ hour

$r = \frac{75}{5,280} \div \frac{1}{300} = \frac{22,500}{5,280} = 4.3$ (approximately)

= 4 mi/hr (approximately). (201, 202)

38. Choice B is correct.

price × amount = value

	¢/lb	lbs	cents
$1.20 nuts	120	x	$120x$
$0.90	90	2	180
mixture	100	$x + 2$	$180 + 120x$

Let x = pounds of $1.20 mixture.

Total value of mixture = $100(x + 2) = 180 + 120x$.
$100x + 200 = 180 + 120x$, so $x = 1$ pound.

(201, 204)

39. Choice B is correct.

rate × time = loss

hr/hr	hrs	hrs
$\frac{2}{3}$	t	12

(Loss is the amount by which the clock time differs from real time.)

Let t = hours to register the correct time.

If the clock registers only 20 minutes each hour, it loses 40 minutes, or $\frac{2}{3}$ hour each hour. The clock will register the correct time only if it has lost some multiple of 12 hours. The first time this can occur is after it has lost 12 hours. $\left(\frac{2}{3}\right)t = 12$, so $t = 18$ hours. (201)

40. Choice A is correct.

rate × time = distance

	mi/hr	hrs	miles
	q	p	pq
	s	r	rs
total	x	$p + r$	$pq + rs$

Let x = average speed.

We may add times of travel at the two rates, and also add the distances. Then, $x(p + r) = pq + rs$; thus, $x = \frac{pq + rs}{p + r}$. (201, 202)

41. Choice A is correct.

rate × time = work

	ft/hr	hrs	feet
Joe	35	x	$35x$
Walt	25	x	$25x$
Both	60	x	$60x$

Let x = the time the job takes.

Since they are working together, we add their rates and the amount of work they do. Thus, $60x = 150$, so $x = 2.5$ (hours) = 150 minutes. (201, 203)

42. Choice B is correct.

rate × time = distance

	mi/hr	hrs	miles
first $\frac{1}{2}$ hour	20	$\frac{1}{2}$	10
second $\frac{1}{2}$ hour	30	$\frac{1}{2}$	15
total	x	1	25

Let x = average speed.

We add the times and distances; then, using the rate formula, $(x)(1) = 25$, so $x = 25$ mi/hr. (201, 202)

43. Choice C is correct.

rate × time = distance

	mi/hr	hours	miles
Sol	200	t	200t
Robert	400	t	400t

Let t = time from simultaneous departure to meeting.

Sol's time is equal to Robert's time because they leave at the same time and then they meet. Their combined distance is 3,000 miles, so $200t + 400t = 3,000$, or $t = 5$ hours.   (201, 202)

44. Choice E is correct.

coin × number = value

	¢/coin	coins	¢
pennies	1	p	p
nickels	5	n	5n
dimes	10	d	10d
quarters	25	q	25q

Let p = number of pennies.
Let n = number of nickels.
Let d = number of dimes.
Let q = number of quarters.

Adding the numbers of coins and their values, we get $p + n + d + q = 7$, and $p + 5n + 10d + 25q = 100$. These equations are satisfied by several values of p, n, d, and q. For example, $p = 0$, $n = 0$, $d = 5$, $q = 2$ satisfies the equation, as does $p = 0$, $n = 3$, $d = 1$, $q = 3$, and other combinations. Thus, the number of dimes cannot be determined.   (201, 205)

45. Choice A is correct.

	%	**amt of solution**	**amount of alcohol**
concentration ×		qts	qts
pure alcohol	100%	2	2
solution	30%	x	0.30x
mixture	40%	2 + x	2 + 0.30x

Let x = quarts of original solution.

Amounts of solution and of alcohol may be added.

$(40\%)(2 + x) = 2 + 0.30x$; so $0.8 + 0.4x = 2.0 + 0.30x$; thus, $x = 12$.   (201, 204)

46. Choice C is correct.

rate × time = cost

	¢/kWh	kWh	¢
first 1,000 kWh	8	t	8t

(time expressed in kilowatt-hours, or kWh)

Let t = number of kWh.

This problem must be broken up into two different parts: (1) finding the total power or the total number of kilowatt-hours (kWh) used, and (2) calculating the charge for that amount.

(1) Total power used, $t = (900w)(5 \text{ hr}) + (100w)(25 \text{ hr}) + (5w)(400 \text{ hr}) = (4,500 + 2,500 + 2,000)$ watt-hours = 9,000 watt-hours.

(2) One thousand watt-hours equals one kilowatt-hour. Thus, $t = 9$ kilowatt-hours, so that the charge is $(8¢)(9) = 72¢$.   (201, 205)

47. Choice C is correct.

rate × amount = cost

	¢/in	in	¢
1 yard	r	36	30
96 inches	r	96	96r

Let r = cost per inch of ribbon.

From the table, $r \times 36 \text{ in} = 30¢$; $r = \dfrac{30¢}{36 \text{ in}} = \dfrac{5¢}{6 \text{ in}}$. Thus, $96r = 96\left(\dfrac{5}{6}\right) = 80¢$.   (201, 205)

48. Choice A is correct.

rate × time = distance

	mi/hr	hrs	miles
trip	50	6	300
return	r	$7\frac{1}{2}$	300
total	s	$13\frac{1}{2}$	600

Let r = rate for return.

Let s = average overall rate.

$\left(13\frac{1}{2}\right)(s) = 600$; thus, $s = 600 \div 13\frac{1}{2} = 44.4$ (approximately).   (201, 202)

49. Choice E is correct.

rate × principal = interest

	%/year	$	$/year
first year	5	100	5
second year	5	105	5.25

Interest first year equals rate × principal = 5% × $100 = $5.

New principal = $105.00.

Interest second year = rate × new principal = 5% × $105 = $5.25.

Final principal = $105.00 + $5.25 = $110.25.

(201, 205)

50. Choice C is correct.

rate × time = amount

	gal/min	min	gallons
in	3	x	$3x$
out	$1\frac{1}{2}$	x	$1\frac{1}{2}x$
net	$1\frac{1}{2}$	x	$1\frac{1}{2}x$

(Net = in − out.)

Let x = time to fill the tub completely.

Since only 9 gallons are needed (there are already 3 in the tub), we have $1\frac{1}{2}x = 9$, so $x = 6$.   (201)

MATH REFRESHER
SESSION 3

Area, Perimeter, and Volume Problems

Area, Perimeter, and Volume

301. *Formula Problems.* Here, you are given certain data about one or more geometric figures, and you are asked to supply some missing information. To solve this type of problem, follow this procedure:

STEP 1. If you are not given a diagram, draw your own; this may make the answer readily apparent or may suggest the best way to solve the problem. You should try to make your diagram as accurate as possible, but *do not waste time perfecting your diagram.*

STEP 2. Determine the formula that relates to the quantities involved in your problem. In many cases it will be helpful to set up tables containing the various data. (See Sections 303–317.)

STEP 3. Substitute the given information for the unknown quantities in your formulas to get the desired answer.

When doing volume, area, and perimeter problems, keep this hint in mind: Often the solutions to such problems can be expressed as the sum of the areas *or* volumes *or* perimeters of simpler figures. In such cases do not hesitate to break down your original figure into simpler parts.

In doing problems involving the following figures, these approximations and facts will be useful:

$\sqrt{2}$ is approximately 1.4. $\qquad$ $\sin 45° = \dfrac{\sqrt{2}}{2}$, which is approximately 0.71.

$\sqrt{3}$ is approximately 1.7.

$\sqrt{10}$ is approximately 3.16. $\qquad$ $\sin 60° = \dfrac{\sqrt{3}}{2}$, which is approximately 0.87.

π is approximately $\dfrac{22}{7}$ or 3.14.

$\sin 30° = \dfrac{1}{2}$

Example: The following figure contains a square, a right triangle, and a semicircle. If $ED = CD$ and the length of CD is 1 unit, find the area of the entire figure.

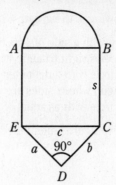

Solution: To calculate the area of the entire figure, we calculate the areas of the triangle, square, and semicircle and then add these together. In a right triangle, the area is $\frac{1}{2}ab$ where a and b are the sides of the triangle. In this case we will call side ED, a, and side CD, b. $ED = CD = 1$, so the area of the triangle is $\frac{1}{2}(1)(1)$, or $\frac{1}{2}$.

The area of a square is s^2, where s is a side. We see that the side EC of the square is the hypotenuse of the right triangle. We can calculate this length by using the formula $c^2 = a^2 + b^2$ where $a = b = 1$; then we can see that $c = \sqrt{2}$. Thus, in this case, $s = \sqrt{2}$, so the area of the square is $(\sqrt{2})^2 = 2$.

AB is the diameter of the semicircle, so $\frac{1}{2}AB$ is the radius. Since all sides of a square are equal, $AB = \sqrt{2}$, and the radius is $\frac{1}{2}\sqrt{2}$. Further, the area of a semicircle is $\frac{1}{2}\pi r^2$, where r is the radius, so the area of this semicircle is $\frac{1}{2}\pi\left(\frac{1}{2}\sqrt{2}\right)^2 = \frac{1}{4}\pi$.

The total area of the whole figure is equal to the area of the triangle plus the area of the square plus the area of the semicircle $= \frac{1}{2} + 2 + \frac{1}{4}\pi = 2\frac{1}{2} + \frac{1}{4}\pi$.

Example: If water flows into a rectangular tank with dimensions of 12 inches, 18 inches, and 30 inches at the rate of 0.25 cubic feet per minute, how long will it take to fill the tank?

Solution: This problem is really a combination of a rate problem and a volume problem. First we must calculate the volume, and then we must substitute in a rate equation to get our final answer. The formula for the volume of a rectangular solid is $V = lwh$, where l, w, and h are the length, width, and height, respectively. We must multiply the three dimensions of the tank to get the volume. However, if we look ahead to the second part of the problem, we see that we want the volume in cubic *feet;* therefore we convert 12 inches, 18 inches, and 30 inches to 1 foot, 1.5 feet, and 2.5 feet, respectively. Multiplying gives us a volume of 3.75 cubic feet. Now substituting in the equation *rate* × *time* = *volume*, we get 0.25 × time = 3.75; time $= \frac{3.75}{0.25}$; thus, the time is 15 minutes.

302. *Comparison problems.* Here you are asked to identify the largest, or smallest, of a group of figures, or to place them in ascending or descending order of size. The following procedure is the most efficient one:

STEP 1. Always diagram each figure before you come to any conclusions. Whenever possible, try to include two or more of the figures in the same diagram, so that their relative sizes are most readily apparent.

STEP 2. If you have not already determined the correct answer, then (and only then) determine the size of the figures (as you would have done in Section 301) and compare the results.

(Note that even if Step 2 is necessary, Step 1 should eliminate most of the possible choices, leaving only a few formula calculations to be done.)

Example: Which of the following is the greatest in length?

(A) The perimeter of a square with a side of 4 inches.
(B) The perimeter of an isosceles right triangle whose equal sides are 8 inches each.
(C) The circumference of a circle with a diameter of $4\sqrt{2}$ inches.
(D) The perimeter of a pentagon whose sides are all equal to 3 inches.
(E) The perimeter of a semicircle with a radius of 5 inches.

Solution: Diagramming the five figures mentioned, we obtain the following illustration:

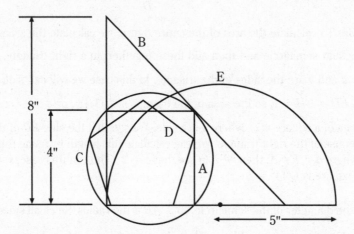

From the diagram, it is apparent that the square and the pentagon are both smaller than the circle. Further observation should show that the circle is smaller than the triangle. Thus we need only to see which is larger—the semicircle or the triangle. The perimeter of the semicircle is found by the formula: $P = 2r + \pi r$ (the sum of the diameter and the semicircular arc, where r is the radius). Since r in this case is 5 inches, the perimeter is approximately $10 + (3.14)5$, or 25.7 inches. The formula for the perimeter of a triangle is the sum of the sides. In this case, two of the sides are 8 inches and the third side can be found by using the relationship $c^2 = a^2 + b^2$, where a and b are the sides of a right triangle, and c is the hypotenuse. Since in our problem $a = b = 8$ inches, $c = \sqrt{8^2 + 8^2} = \sqrt{128} = \sqrt{2(64)} = 8\sqrt{2}$, which is the third side of the triangle. The perimeter is $8 + 8 + 8\sqrt{2}$, which is $16 + 8\sqrt{2}$. This is approximately equal to $16 + 8(1.4)$, or 27.2, so the triangle is the largest of the figures.

FORMULAS USED IN AREA, PERIMETER, AND VOLUME PROBLEMS

It is important that you know as many of these formulas as possible. Problems using these formulas appear frequently on tests of all kinds. You should not need to refer to the following tables when you do problems. Learn these formulas before you go any further.

---

303. *Square.* The area of a square is the square of one of its sides. Thus, if A represents the area, and s represents the length of a side, $A = s^2$. The area of a square is also one-half of the square of its diagonal and may be written as $A = \frac{1}{2}d^2$, where d represents the length of a diagonal. The perimeter of a square is 4 times the length of one of its sides, or $4s$.

Square

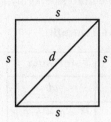

quantity	formula
area	$A = s^2$ $A = \frac{1}{2}d^2$
perimeter	$P = 4s$

304. *Rectangle.* Let a and b represent the length of two adjacent sides of a rectangle, and let A represent the area. Then the area of a rectangle is the product of the two adjacent sides: $A = ab$. The perimeter, P, is the sum of twice one side and twice the adjacent side: $P = 2a + 2b$.

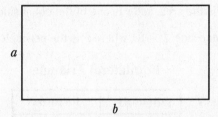

Rectangle

quantity	formula
area	$A = ab$
perimeter	$P = 2a + 2b$

305. *Parallelogram.* The area of a parallelogram is the product of a side and the altitude, h, to that side: $A = bh$ (in this case the altitude to side b). Let a and b represent the length of 2 adjacent sides of a parallelogram. Then, c is the included angle. The area can also be expressed as the product of two adjacent sides and the sine of the included angle: $A = ab \sin c$, where c is the angle included between side a and side b. The perimeter is the sum of twice one side and twice the adjacent side: $P = 2a + 2b$. A represents its area, P its perimeter, and h the altitude to one of its sides.

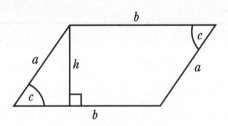

Parallelogram

quantity	formula
area	$A = bh$ $A = ab \sin c$
perimeter	$P = 2a + 2b$

306. *Triangle.* The area of any triangle is one-half of the product of any side and the altitude to that side: $A = \frac{1}{2} bh$, where b is a side, and h the altitude to that side. The area may be written also as one-half of the product of any two adjacent sides and the sine of the included angle: $A = \frac{1}{2}ab \sin c$, where A is the area, a and b are two adjacent sides, and c is the included angle. The perimeter of a triangle is the sum of the sides of the triangle: $P = a + b + c$, where P is the perimeter, and c is the third side.

Triangle

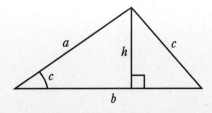

quantity	formula
area	$A = \frac{1}{2}bh$ $A = \frac{1}{2}ab \sin C$
perimeter	$P = a + b + c$

307. *Right triangle.* The area of a right triangle is one-half of the product of the two sides adjacent to the right angle: $A = \frac{1}{2}ab$, where A is the area, and a and b are the adjacent sides. The perimeter is the sum of the sides: $P = a + b + c$, where c is the third side, or hypotenuse.

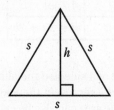

Right Triangle

quantity	formula
area	$A = \frac{1}{2}ab$
perimeter	$P = a + b + c$
hypotenuse	$c^2 = a^2 + b^2$

308. *Equilateral triangle.* The area of an equilateral triangle is one-fourth the product of a side squared and $\sqrt{3}$: $A = \frac{1}{4} s^2 \sqrt{3}$, where A is the area, and s is one of the equal sides. The perimeter of an equilateral triangle is 3 times one side: $P = 3s$, where P is the perimeter.

Equilateral Triangle

quantity	formula
area	$A = \frac{1}{4}s^2 \sqrt{3}$
perimeter	$P = 3s$
altitude	$h = \frac{1}{2}s \sqrt{3}$

> **NOTE: The equilateral triangle and the right triangle are special cases of the triangle, and any law that applies to the triangle applies to both the right triangle and the equilateral triangle.**

309. *Trapezoid.* The area of a trapezoid is one-half of the product of the altitude and the sum of the bases: $A = \frac{1}{2}h(B + b)$, where A is the area, B and b are the bases, and h is the altitude. The perimeter is the sum of the 4 sides: $P = B + b + c + d$, where P is the perimeter, and c and d are the other 2 sides.

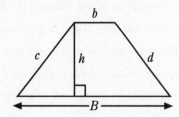

Trapezoid

quantity	formula
area	$A = \frac{1}{2}h(B + b)$
perimeter	$P = B + b + c + d$

310. *Circle*. The area of a circle is π (pi) times the square of the radius: $A = \pi r^2$, where A is the area, and r is the radius. The circumference is pi times the diameter, or pi times twice the radius: $C = \pi d = 2\pi r$, where C is the circumference, d the diameter, and r the radius.

Circle

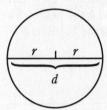

quantity	formula
area	$A = \pi r^2$
circumference	$C = \pi d = 2\pi r$

311. *Semicircle*. The area of a semicircle is one-half pi times the square of the radius: $A = \frac{1}{2}\pi r^2$, where A is the area, and r is the radius. The length of the curved portion of the semicircle is one-half pi times the diameter or pi times the radius: $C = \frac{1}{2}\pi d = \pi r$, where C is the circumference, d is the diameter, and r is the radius. The perimeter of a semicircle is equal to the circumference plus the length of the diameter: $P = C + d = \frac{1}{2}\pi d + d$, where P is the perimeter.

Semicircle

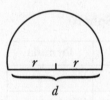

quantity	formula
area	$A = \frac{1}{2}\pi r^2$
circumference	$C = \frac{1}{2}\pi d = \pi r$
perimeter	$P = d\left(\frac{1}{2}\pi + 1\right)$

312. *Rectangular solid*. The volume of a rectangular solid is the product of the length, width, and height: $V = lwh$, where V is the volume, l is the length, w is the width, and h is the height. The volume is also the product of the area of one side and the altitude to that side: $V = Bh$, where B is the area of its base and h the altitude to that side. The surface area is the sum of the area of the six faces. $S = 2wh + 2hl + 2wl$, where S is the surface area.

Rectangular Solid

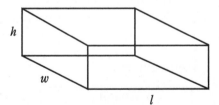

quantity	formula
volume	$V = lwh$ $V = Bh$
surface area	$S = 2wh + 2hl + 2wl$

313. *Cube*. The volume of a cube is its edge cubed: $V = e^3$, where V is the volume and e is an edge. The surface area is the sum of the areas of the six faces: $S = 6e^2$, where S is the surface area.

Cube

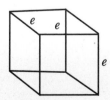

quantity	formula
volume	$V = e^3$
surface area	$S = 6e^2$

314. *Cylinder.* The volume of a cylinder is the area of the base times the height: $V = Bh$, where V is the volume, B is the area of the base, and h is the height. Note that the area of the base is the area of the circle, πr^2, where r is the radius of a base. The surface area not including the bases is the circumference of the base times the height: $S_1 = Ch = 2\pi rh$, where S_1 is the surface area without the bases, C the circumference, and h the height. The area of the bases $= 2\pi r^2$. Thus, the surface area of the cylinder, including the bases, is $S_2 = 2\pi rh + 2\pi r^2 = 2\pi r(h + r)$.

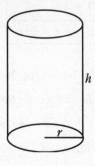

Cylinder

quantity	formula
volume	$V = Bh$ $V = \pi r^2 h$
surface area	$S_1 = 2\pi rh$ (without bases) $S_2 = 2\pi r(h + r)$ (with bases)

315. *Sphere.* The volume of a sphere is four-thirds π times the cube of the radius: $V = \frac{4}{3}\pi r^3$, where V is the volume and r is the radius. The surface area is 4π times the square of the radius: $S = 4\pi r^2$, where S is the surface area.

Sphere

quantity	formula
volume	$V = \frac{4}{3}\pi r^3$
surface area	$S = 4\pi r^2$

316. *Hemisphere.* The volume of a hemisphere is two-thirds π times the cube of the radius: $V = \frac{2}{3}\pi r^3$, where V is the volume and r is the radius. The surface area not including the area of the base is 2π times the square of the radius: $S_1 = 2\pi r^2$, where S_1 is the surface area without the base. The total surface area, including the base, is equal to the surface area without the base plus the area of the base: $S_2 = 2\pi r^2 + \pi r^2 = 3\pi r^2$, where S_2 is the surface area including the base.

Hemisphere

quantity	formula
volume	$V = \frac{2}{3}\pi r^3$
surface area	$S_1 = 2\pi r^2$ (without bases) $S_2 = 3\pi r^2$ (with bases)

317. *Pythagorean Theorem.* The Pythagorean Theorem states a very important geometrical relationship. It states that in a right triangle, if c is the hypotenuse (the side opposite the right angle), and a and b are the sides adjacent to the right angle, then $c^2 = a^2 + b^2$.

Pythagorean Theorem

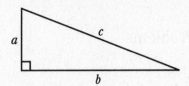

quantity	formula
square of hypotenuse	$c^2 = a^2 + b^2$
length of hypotenuse	$c = \sqrt{a^2 + b^2}$

Examples of right triangles are triangles with sides of 3, 4, and 5, or 5, 12, and 13. Any multiples of these numbers also form right triangles—for example, 6, 8, and 10, or 30, 40, and 50.

Using the Pythagorean Theorem to find the diagonal of a square, we get $d^2 = s^2 + s^2$ or $d^2 = 2s^2$, where d is the diagonal and s is a side. Therefore, $d = s\sqrt{2}$, or the diagonal of a square is $\sqrt{2}$ times the side.

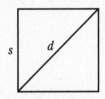

Square

quantity	formula
diagonal	$d = s\sqrt{2}$

318.   Another important fact to remember in doing area problems is that areas of two similar (having the same shape) figures are in the same ratio as the squares of corresponding parts of the figures.

Example: Triangles P and Q are similar. Side p of triangle P is 2 inches, the area of triangle P is 3 square inches, and corresponding side q of triangle Q is 4 inches. What is the area of triangle Q?

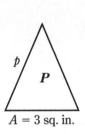

$A = 3$ sq. in.

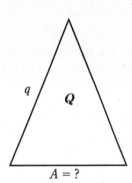

$A = ?$

Solution: The square of side p is to the square of side q as the area of P is to the area of Q. If we call x the area of triangle Q, then we get the following relationship: The square of side p is to the square of side q as the area of P is to the area of Q, or

$$\frac{2^2}{4^2} = \frac{3}{x} \text{ or } \frac{4}{16} = \frac{3}{x}$$

Therefore, $x = 12$ square inches.

Practice Test 3

Area, Perimeter, and Volume Problems

Correct answers and solutions follow each test.

1. A B C D E

1. Which of the following figures has the largest area?

    (A) a square with a perimeter of 12 inches
    (B) a circle with a radius of 3 inches
    (C) a right triangle with sides of 3, 4, and 5 inches
    (D) a rectangle with a diagonal of 5 inches and sides of 3 and 4 inches
    (E) a regular hexagon with a perimeter of 18 inches

2. A B C D E

2. If the area of the base of a rectangular solid is tripled, what is the percent increase in its volume?

    (A) 200%
    (B) 300%
    (C) 600%
    (D) 800%
    (E) 900%

3. A B C D E

3. How many yards of a carpeting that is 26 inches wide will be needed to cover a floor that is 12 ft. by 13 ft.?

    (A) 22 yards
    (B) 24 yards
    (C) 27 yards
    (D) 36 yards
    (E) 46 yards

4. A B C D E

4. If water flows into a rectangular tank at the rate of 6 cubic feet per minute, how long will it take to fill the tank, which measures $18'' \times 32'' \times 27''$?

    (A) less than one minute
    (B) less than two minutes, but not less than one minute
    (C) less than three minutes, but not less than two minutes
    (D) less than four minutes, but not less than three minutes
    (E) four minutes or more

5. A B C D E

5. The ratio of the area of a circle to the radius of the circle is

    (A) π
    (B) 2π
    (C) π^2
    (D) $4\pi^2$
    (E) not determinable

6. A B C D E

6. Which of the following figures has the smallest perimeter or circumference?

    (A) a circle with a diameter of 2 feet
    (B) a square with a diagonal of 2 feet
    (C) a rectangle with sides of 6 inches and 4 feet
    (D) a pentagon with each side equal to 16 inches
    (E) a hexagon with each side equal to 14 inches

7. In the figure shown, *DE* is parallel to *BC*. If the area of triangle *ADE* is half that of trapezoid *DECB*, what is the ratio of *AE* to *AC*?

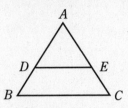

(A) 1 : 2
(B) 1 : $\sqrt{2}$
(C) 1 : 3
(D) 1 : $\sqrt{3}$
(E) 1 : $\sqrt{3} - 1$

8. At a speed of 22 revolutions per minute, how long will it take a wheel of radius 10 inches, rolling on its edge, to travel 10 feet? (Assume π equals $\frac{22}{7}$, and express answer to nearest 0.1 second.)

(A) 0.2 seconds
(B) 0.4 seconds
(C) 5.2 seconds
(D) 6.3 seconds
(E) 7.4 seconds

9. If the diagonal of a square is 16 inches long, what is the area of the square?

(A) 64 square inches
(B) $64\sqrt{2}$ square inches
(C) 128 square inches
(D) $128\sqrt{2}$ square inches
(E) 256 square inches

10. In the diagram shown, *ACDF* is a rectangle, and *GBHE* is a circle. If *CD* = 4 inches, and *AC* = 6 inches, what is the number of square inches in the darker shaded area?

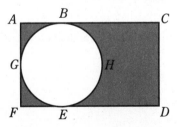

(A) $16 - 4\pi$ square inches
(B) $24 - 4\pi$ square inches
(C) $24 - 16\pi$ square inches
(D) $16 - 2\pi$ square inches
(E) $24 - 2\pi$ square inches

11. A B C D E

11. What is the area of an equilateral triangle with a side of 1 inch?

(A) 1 square inch

(B) $\frac{\sqrt{3}}{2}$ square inch

(C) $\frac{1}{2}$ square inch

(D) $\frac{\sqrt{3}}{4}$ square inch

(E) $\frac{1}{3}$ square inch

12. A B C D E

12. The measurements of a rectangle are 12 feet by 16 feet. What is the area of the smallest *circle* that can cover this rectangle entirely (so that no part of the rectangle is outside the circle)?

(A) 192 square feet
(B) 384 square feet
(C) 100π square feet
(D) 128π square feet
(E) 400π square feet

13. A B C D E

13. A man wishes to cover his floor with tiles, each one measuring $\frac{3}{4}$ inch by 2 inches. If his room is a rectangle, measuring 12 feet by 18 feet, how many such tiles will he need?

(A) 144
(B) 1,152
(C) 1,728
(D) 9,216
(E) 20,736

14. A B C D E

14. The volume of a sphere is equal to the volume of a cylinder. If the radius of the sphere is 4 meters and the radius of the cylinder is 8 meters, what is the height of the cylinder?

(A) 8 meters

(B) $\frac{4}{3}$ meters

(C) 4 meters

(D) $\frac{16}{3}$ meters

(E) 1 meter

15. A B C D E

15. A wheel travels 33 yards in 15 revolutions. What is its diameter? (Assume $\pi = \frac{22}{7}$.)

(A) 0.35 feet
(B) 0.70 feet
(C) 1.05 feet
(D) 1.40 feet
(E) 2.10 feet

16. A B C D E

16. If a rectangle with a perimeter of 48 inches is equal in area to a right triangle with legs of 12 inches and 24 inches, what is the rectangle's diagonal?

(A) 12 inches
(B) $12\sqrt{2}$ inches
(C) $12\sqrt{3}$ inches
(D) 24 inches
(E) The answer cannot be determined from the given information.

17. A B C D E

17. What is the approximate area that remains after a circle $3\frac{1}{2}''$ in diameter is cut from a square piece of cloth with a side of 8"? (Use $\pi = \frac{22}{7}$.)

(A) 25.5 square inches
(B) 54.4 square inches
(C) 56.8 square inches
(D) 142.1 square inches
(E) 284.2 square inches

18. A B C D E

18. A container is shaped like a rectangular solid with sides of 3 inches, 3 inches, and 11 inches. What is its approximate capacity, if 1 gallon equals 231 cubic inches? (1 gallon = 128 fluid ounces.)

(A) 14 ounces
(B) 27 ounces
(C) 55 ounces
(D) 110 ounces
(E) 219 ounces

19. A B C D E

19. The 20-inch-diameter wheels of one car travel at a rate of 24 revolutions per minute, while the 30-inch-diameter wheels of a second car travel at a rate of 18 revolutions per minute. What is the ratio of the speed of the second car to that of the first?

(A) 1 : 1
(B) 3 : 2
(C) 4 : 3
(D) 6 : 5
(E) 9 : 8

20. A B C D E

20. A circular garden twenty feet in diameter is surrounded by a path three feet wide. What is the area of the path?

(A) 9π square feet
(B) 51π square feet
(C) 60π square feet
(D) 69π square feet
(E) 90π square feet

21. A B C D E

21. What is the area of a semicircle with a diameter of 16 inches?

(A) 32π square inches
(B) 64π square inches
(C) 128π square inches
(D) 256π square inches
(E) 512π square inches

22. A B C D E

22. If the edges of a cube add up to 4 feet in length, what is the volume of the cube?

(A) 64 cubic inches
(B) 125 cubic inches
(C) 216 cubic inches
(D) 512 cubic inches
(E) None of these.

23. A B C D E

23. The inside of a trough is shaped like a rectangular solid, 25 feet long, 6 inches wide, and filled with water to a depth of 35 inches. If we wish to raise the depth of the water to 38 inches, how much water must be let into the tank?

(A) $\frac{25}{96}$ cubic feet

(B) $\frac{25}{8}$ cubic feet

(C) $\frac{75}{2}$ cubic feet

(D) 225 cubic feet
(E) 450 cubic feet

24. |A B C D E|

24. If 1 gallon of water equals 231 cubic inches, approximately how much water will fill a cylindrical vase 7 inches in diameter and 10 inches high? (Assume $\pi = \frac{22}{7}$.)

(A) 1.7 gallons
(B) 2.1 gallons
(C) 3.3 gallons
(D) 5.3 gallons
(E) 6.7 gallons

25. |A B C D E|

25. Tiles of linoleum, measuring 8 inches × 8 inches, cost 9¢ apiece. At this rate, what will it cost a man to cover a floor with these tiles, if his floor measures 10 feet by 16 feet?

(A) $22.50
(B) $25.00
(C) $28.00
(D) $32.40
(E) $36.00

26. |A B C D E|

26. Which of the following figures has the largest area?

(A) a 3–4–5 triangle with a hypotenuse of 25 inches
(B) a circle with a diameter of 20 inches
(C) a square with a 20-inch diagonal
(D) a regular hexagon with a side equal to 10 inches
(E) a rectangle with sides of 10 inches and 30 inches

27. |A B C D E|

27. If the radius of the base of a cylinder is tripled, and its height is divided by three, what is the ratio of the volume of the new cylinder to the volume of the original cylinder?

(A) 1 : 9
(B) 1 : 3
(C) 1 : 1
(D) 3 : 1
(E) 9 : 1

28. |A B C D E|

28. If 1 cubic foot of water equals 7.5 gallons, how long will it take for a faucet that flows at a rate of 10 gal/min to fill a cube 2 feet on each side (to the nearest minute)?

(A) 4 minutes
(B) 5 minutes
(C) 6 minutes
(D) 7 minutes
(E) 8 minutes

29. |A B C D E|

29. The ratio of the area of a square to the *square of its diagonal* is which of the following?

(A) 2 : 1
(B) $\sqrt{2}$: 1
(C) 1 : 1
(D) 1 : $\sqrt{2}$
(E) 1 : 2

A B C D E

30. If *ABCD* is a square, with side *AB* = 4 inches, and *AEB* and *CED* are semicircles, what is the area of the shaded portion of the diagram below?

(A) $8 - \pi$ square inches
(B) $8 - 2\pi$ square inches
(C) $16 - 2\pi$ square inches
(D) $16 - 4\pi$ square inches
(E) $16 - 8\pi$ square inches

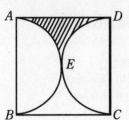

A B C D E

31. If the area of a circle is equal to the area of a rectangle, one of whose sides is equal to π, express the other side of the rectangle, *x*, in terms of the radius of the circle, *r*.

(A) $x = r$

(B) $x = \pi r$

(C) $x = r^2$

(D) $x = \sqrt{r}$

(E) $x = \dfrac{1}{r}$

A B C D E

32. If the volume of a cube is 27 cubic meters, find the surface area of the cube.

(A) 9 square meters
(B) 18 square meters
(C) 54 square meters
(D) 3 square meters
(E) 1 square meter

A B C D E

33. What is the area of a regular hexagon one of whose sides is 1 inch?

(A) $\dfrac{3\sqrt{3}}{4}$

(B) $\sqrt{3}$

(C) $\dfrac{3\sqrt{3}}{2}$

(D) 3

(E) 6

A B C D E

34. What is the area of the triangle pictured below?

(A) 18 square units
(B) 32 square units
(C) 24 square units
(D) 12 square units
(E) 124 square units

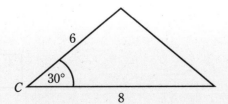

A B C D E

35. **35.** If a wheel travels 1 mile in 1 minute, at a rate of 600 revolutions per minute, what is the diameter of the wheel, in feet? (Use $\pi = \frac{22}{7}$.)

(A) 2.2 feet
(B) 2.4 feet
(C) 2.6 feet
(D) 2.8 feet
(E) 3.0 feet

A B C D E

36. **36.** Which of the following figures has the largest perimeter?

(A) a square with a diagonal of 5 feet
(B) a rectangle with sides of 3 feet and 4 feet
(C) an equilateral triangle with a side equal to 48 inches
(D) a regular hexagon whose longest diagonal is 6 feet
(E) a parallelogram with sides of 6 inches and 7 feet

A B C D E

37. **37.** A man has two containers: The first is a rectangular solid, measuring 3 inches × 4 inches × 10 inches; the second is a cylinder having a base with a radius of 2 inches and a height of 10 inches. If the first container is filled with water, and then this water is poured into the second container, which of the following occurs?

(A) There is room for more water in the second container.
(B) The second container is completely filled, without overflowing.
(C) The second container overflows by less than 1 cubic inch.
(D) The second container overflows by less than 2 (but not less than 1) cubic inches.
(E) The second container overflows by 2 or more cubic inches.

A B C D E

38. **38.** If, in this diagram, A represents a square with a side of 4″, and B, C, D, and E are semicircles, what is the area of the entire figure?

(A) $16 + 4\pi$ square inches
(B) $16 + 8\pi$ square inches
(C) $16 + 16\pi$ square inches
(D) $16 + 32\pi$ square inches
(E) $16 + 64\pi$ square inches

A B C D E

39. **39.** The area of a square is $81p^2$. What is the length of the square's diagonal?

(A) $9p$
(B) $9p\sqrt{2}$
(C) $18p$
(D) $9p^2$
(E) $18p^2$

A B C D E

40. **40.** The following diagram represents the floor of a room that is to be covered with carpeting at a price of $2.50 per square yard. What will be the cost of the carpeting?

(A) $70
(B) $125
(C) $480
(D) $630
(E) None of these.

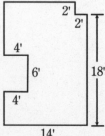

A B C D E
41.

41. Which of the following has the largest perimeter?

(A) a square with a diagonal of 10 inches
(B) a 3–4–5 right triangle with a hypotenuse of 15 inches
(C) a pentagon, each of whose sides is 5 inches
(D) a right isosceles triangle with an area of 72 square inches
(E) a regular hexagon with a radius of 5 inches

A B C D E
42.

42. If you double the area of the base of a rectangular solid, and also triple the solid's height, what is the ratio of the new volume to the old volume?

(A) $2:3$
(B) $3:2$
(C) $1:6$
(D) $6:1$
(E) None of these.

A B C D E
43.

43. A certain type of linoleum costs \$1.50 per square yard. If a room measures 27 feet by 14 feet, what will be the cost of covering it with linoleum?

(A) \$44.10
(B) \$51.60
(C) \$63.00
(D) \$132.30
(E) \$189.00

A B C D E
44.

44. How many circles, each with a 4-inch radius, can be cut from a rectangular sheet of paper, measuring 16 inches $\times$ 24 inches?

(A) 6
(B) 7
(C) 8
(D) 12
(E) 24

A B C D E
45.

45. The ratio of the area of an equilateral triangle, in square inches, to its perimeter, in inches, is

(A) $3:4$
(B) $4:3$
(C) $\sqrt{3}:4$
(D) $4:\sqrt{3}$
(E) The answer cannot be determined from the given information.

A B C D E
46.

46. What is the volume of a cylinder whose radius is 4 inches, and whose height is 10 inches? (Assume that $\pi = 3.14$.)

(A) 125.6 cubic inches
(B) 134.4 cubic inches
(C) 144.0 cubic inches
(D) 201.2 cubic inches
(E) 502.4 cubic inches

A B C D E
47.

47. The area of a square is $144s^2$. What is the square's diagonal?

(A) $12s$
(B) $12s\sqrt{2}$
(C) $24s$
(D) $144s$
(E) $144s^2$

48.   A B C D E

48. A circular pool is ten feet in diameter and five feet deep. What is its volume, in cubic feet?

(A) 50 cubic feet
(B) 50π cubic feet
(C) 125π cubic feet
(D) 250π cubic feet
(E) 500π cubic feet

49.   A B C D E

49. A certain type of carpeting is 30 inches wide. How many yards of this carpet will be needed to cover a floor that measures 20 feet by 24 feet?

(A) 48
(B) 64
(C) 144
(D) 192
(E) None of these.

50.   A B C D E

50. Two wheels have diameters of 12 inches and 18 inches, respectively. Both wheels roll along parallel straight lines at the same linear speed until the large wheel has revolved 72 times. At this point, how many times has the small wheel revolved?

(A) 32
(B) 48
(C) 72
(D) 108
(E) 162

Answer Key for Practice Test 3

1. B	**14.** B	**27.** D	**39.** B
2. A	**15.** E	**28.** C	**40.** A
3. B	**16.** B	**29.** E	**41.** D
4. B	**17.** B	**30.** B	**42.** D
5. E	**18.** C	**31.** C	**43.** C
6. B	**19.** E	**32.** C	**44.** A
7. D	**20.** D	**33.** C	**45.** E
8. C	**21.** A	**34.** D	**46.** E
9. C	**22.** A	**35.** D	**47.** B
10. B	**23.** B	**36.** D	**48.** C
11. D	**24.** A	**37.** A	**49.** B
12. C	**25.** D	**38.** B	**50.** D
13. E	**26.** B		

Answers and Solutions for Practice Test 3

1. Choice B is correct. This is a fairly difficult comparison problem, but the use of diagrams simplifies it considerably.

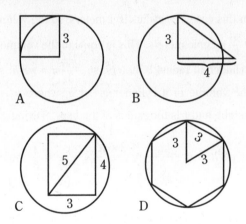

From diagram A it is apparent that the circle is larger than the square. Diagram B shows that the circle is larger than the right triangle. And, since a rectangle with a diagonal of 5 inches is made up of two right triangles, as shown in diagram C, the circle is larger than the rectangle. Finally, as shown in diagram D, the circle is larger than the hexagon. Thus, the circle is the largest of the five figures described. (302)

2. Choice A is correct. This is a formula problem: letting V_o represent the original volume, B_o represent the original area of the base, and h_o represent the original height of the figure, we have the formula $V_o = h_o B_o$. The new volume, V, is equal to $3h_o B_o$. Thus, the new volume is three times the original volume—an *increase* of 200%. (301)

3. Choice B is correct. Here, we must find the length of carpeting needed to cover an area of 12′ × 13′, or 156 square feet. The formula needed is: $A = lw$, where l = length and w = width, both expressed in *feet*. Now, since we know that $A = 156$ square feet, and $w = 26$ inches, or $\frac{26}{12}$ feet, we can calculate l as $156 \div \left(\frac{26}{12}\right)$, or 72 feet. But since the answer must be expressed in yards, we express 72 feet as 24 yards. (304)

4. Choice B is correct. First we must calculate the volume of the tank in cubic feet. Converting the dimensions of the box to feet, we get $1\frac{1}{2}$ feet × $2\frac{2}{3}$ feet × $2\frac{1}{4}$ feet, so the total volume is $\frac{3}{2} \times \frac{8}{3} \times \frac{9}{4}$, or 9, cubic feet. Thus, at a rate of 6 cubic feet per minute, it would take $\frac{9}{6}$, or $1\frac{1}{2}$, minutes to fill the tank. (312, 201)

5. Choice E is correct. Here, we use the formula $A = \pi r^2$, where A = area, and r = radius. Thus, the ratio of A to r is just $\frac{A}{r} = \pi r$. Since r is not a constant, the ratio cannot be determined. (310)

6. Choice B is correct. First, we diagram the circle and the square and see that the square has a smaller perimeter. Next, we notice that the circle, which has a larger circumference than the square, has circumference 2π, or about 6.3 feet. But the perimeters of the rectangle (9 feet), of the pentagon (5 × 16 inches = 80 inches = 6 feet, 8 inches), and of the hexagon (6 × 14 inches = 84 inches = 7 feet) are all greater than the circumference of the circle, and therefore also greater than the perimeter of the square. Thus, the square has the smallest perimeter. (302)

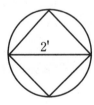

7. Choice D is correct. The formula involved here is $A_1 : A_2 = s_1^2 : s_2^2$, where A_1 represents the area of the triangle with one side of length s_1, and A_2 represents the area of the triangle corresponding to s_2. If we let s_1 represent AE, and s_2 represent AC, so that A_1 is the area of ADE and A_2 is the area of ABC, then we have the resulting formula $\frac{AE}{AC} = \frac{s_1}{s_2} = \sqrt{\frac{A_1}{A_2}}$. The area of the trapezoid $DECB$ is twice the area of ADE, or $2A_1$, so the area of ABC is equal to the sum of the area of ADE and $DECB$, which equal A_1 and

$2A_1$, respectively; thus, the area of ABC is $3A_1$. So, $A_1 : A_2 = 1 : 3$. Thus, $s_1 : s_2 = \sqrt{\dfrac{1}{3}} = 1 : \sqrt{3}$.　(318)

8. Choice C is correct. Since the radius of the circle is 10 inches, its circumference is $2\pi(10 \text{ inches})$, or $2\left(\dfrac{22}{7}\right)(10 \text{ inches})$, which equals $\dfrac{440}{7}$ inches. This is the distance the wheel will travel in one revolution. To travel 10 feet, or 120 inches, it must travel $120 \div \dfrac{440}{7}$, or $\dfrac{21}{11}$ revolutions. At a speed of 22 revolutions per minute, or $\dfrac{11}{30}$ revolutions per second, it will take $\dfrac{21}{11} \div \dfrac{11}{30}$, or $\dfrac{630}{121}$ seconds. Carrying the division to the nearest tenth of a second, we get 5.2 seconds.　(310)

9. Choice C is correct. If we let d represent the diagonal of a square, s represent the length of one side, and A represent the area, then we have two formulas: $d = s\sqrt{2}$, and $A = s^2$, relating the three quantities. However, from the first equation, we can see that $s^2 = \dfrac{d^2}{2}$, so we can derive a third formula, $A = \dfrac{d^2}{2}$, relating A and d. We are given that d equals 16″, so we can calculate the value of A as $\dfrac{(16 \text{ inches})^2}{2}$, or 128 square inches.　(303)

10. Choice B is correct. The area of the shaded figure is equal to the difference between the areas of the rectangle and the circle. The area of the rectangle is defined by the formula $A = bh$, where b and h are the two adjacent sides of the rectangle. In this case, A is equal to 4 inches × 6 inches, or 24 square inches. The area of the circle is defined by the formula $A = \pi r^2$, where r is the radius. Since BE equals the diameter of the circle and is equal to 4 inches, then the radius must be 2 inches. Thus, the area of the circle is $\pi(2 \text{ inches})^2$, or 4π square inches. Subtracting, we obtain the area of the shaded portion: $24 - 4\pi$ square inches. (304, 310)

11. Choice D is correct. We use the formula for the area of an equilateral triangle, $\dfrac{\sqrt{3}s^2}{4}$, where s is a side. If $s = 1$, then the area of the triangle is $\dfrac{\sqrt{3}}{4}$.　(308)

12. Choice C is correct. An angle, which is inscribed in a circle, whose sides cut off an arc of 180° (that is, it intersects the ends of a diameter) is a right angle. According to the Pythagorean Theorem, the diameter AC, being the hypotenuse of a triangle with sides of 12 feet and 16 feet, has a length of $\sqrt{12^2 + 16^2} = \sqrt{400} = 20$ feet. Therefore, if we call d the diameter, the area of the circle is $A = \pi\left(\dfrac{d}{2}\right)^2 = \pi\left(\dfrac{20}{2}\right)^2 = 100\pi$ square feet.

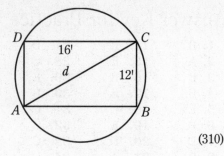

　(310)

13. Choice E is correct. The area of the room = 12 feet × 18 feet = 216 square feet. The area of one tile $= \dfrac{3}{4}$ inches × 2 inches $= \dfrac{3}{2}$ square inches. The number of tiles = area of the room ÷ area of one tile

$$= \dfrac{216 \text{ square feet}}{\dfrac{3}{2} \text{ square inches}} = \dfrac{216 \times 144 \text{ square inches}}{\dfrac{3}{2} \text{ square inches}}$$

$$= 216 \times \overset{48}{\cancel{144}} \times \dfrac{2}{3} = 20{,}736 \text{ tiles}.$$　(304)

14. Choice B is correct. The volume of a sphere is found by using the formula $\dfrac{4}{3}\pi r^3$, where r is the radius. In this case, the radius is 4 meters, so the volume is $\dfrac{256}{3}\pi$ cubic meters. This is equal to the volume of a cylinder of radius 8 meters, so $\dfrac{256}{3}\pi = \pi 8^2 h$, since the volume of a cylinder is $\pi r^2 h$, where h is the height, and r is the radius of the base. Solving $\dfrac{256\pi}{3} = \pi 8^2 h$: $h = \dfrac{\dfrac{256\pi}{3}}{\pi 64} = \dfrac{256\overset{4}{\cancel{\pi}}}{3} \times \dfrac{1}{\cancel{\pi}64} = \dfrac{4}{3}$ meters.　(314, 315)

15. Choice E is correct. 33 yards = 99 feet = 15 revolutions. Thus, 1 revolution $= \dfrac{99}{15}$ feet $= \dfrac{33}{5}$ feet = 6.6 feet. Since 1 revolution = the circumference of the wheel, the wheel's diameter = circumference ÷ π. 6.6 feet ÷ $\dfrac{22}{7}$ = 2.10 feet.　(310)

16. Choice B is correct. The area of the right triangle is equal to $\dfrac{1}{2}ab$, where a and b are the legs of the triangle. In this case, the area is $\dfrac{1}{2} \times 12 \times 24$, or 144 square inches. If we call the sides of the rectangle x and y we get $2x + 2y = 48$, or $y = 24 - x$. The area of the rectangle is xy, or $x(24 - x)$. This must be equal to 144, so we get the equation $24x - x^2 = 144$. Adding $x^2 - 24x$ to both sides of this last equation gives us $x^2 - 24x + 144 = 0$, or $(x - 12)^2 = 0$. Thus, $x = 12$. By the Pythagorean Theorem, the diagonal of the rectangle $= \sqrt{12^2 + 12^2} = \sqrt{144 + 144} = \sqrt{2(144)} = (\sqrt{2})(\sqrt{144}) = 12\sqrt{2}$.

　(304, 306, 317)

17. Choice B is correct. The area of the square is 64 square inches, since $A = s^2$ where s is the length of a side, and A is the area. The area of the circle is $\pi\left(\frac{7}{4}\right)^2 = \frac{22}{7} \times \frac{49}{16} = \frac{77}{8} = 9.625$. Subtracting, $64 - 9.625 = 54.375 = 54.4$ (approximately).

(304, 310)

18. Choice C is correct. The capacity of the volume ($V = lwh$, where l, w, h are the adjacent sides of the solid) of the container = (3 inches)(3 inches)(11 inches) = 99 cubic inches. Since 1 gallon equals 231 cubic inches, 99 cubic inches equal $\frac{99}{231}$ gallons (the fraction reduces to $\frac{3}{7}$). One gallon equals 128 ounces (1 gallon = 4 quarts; 1 quart = 2 pints; 1 pint = 16 ounces), so the container holds $\frac{384}{7}$ ounces = 55 ounces (approximately).

(312)

19. Choice E is correct. The speed of the first wheel is equal to its rate of revolution multiplied by its circumference, which equals 24×20 inches $\times \pi = 480\pi$ inches per minute. The speed of the second is 18×30 inches $\times \pi = 540\pi$ inches per minute. Thus, their ratio is $540\pi : 480\pi = 9 : 8$.

(310)

20. Choice D is correct. The area of the path is equal to the area of the ring between two concentric circles of radii 10 feet and 13 feet. This area is obtained by subtracting the area of the smaller circle from the area of the larger circle. The area of the larger circle is equal to $\pi \times$ its radius squared = $\pi(13)^2$ square feet = 169π square feet. By the same process, the area of the smaller circle = 100π square feet. The area of the shaded part = $169\pi - 100\pi = 69\pi$ square feet.

(310)

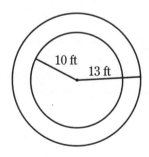

21. Choice A is correct. The diameter = 16 inches, so the radius = 8 inches. Thus, the area of the whole circle = $\pi(8 \text{ inches})^2 = 64\pi$ square inches. The area of the semicircle is one-half of the area of the whole circle, or 32π square inches.

(311)

22. Choice A is correct. A cube has 12 equal edges, so the length of one side of the cube is $\frac{1}{12}$ of 4 feet, or 4 inches. Thus, its volume is 4 inches $\times$ 4 inches $\times$ 4 inches = 64 cubic inches.

(313)

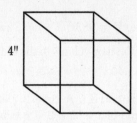

23. Choice B is correct. The additional water will take the shape of a rectangular solid measuring 25 feet $\times$ 6 inches $\times$ 3 inches (3" = the added depth) $= 25 \times \frac{1}{2} \times \frac{1}{4}$ cubic feet $= \frac{25}{8}$ cubic feet.

(312)

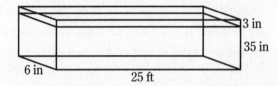

24. Choice A is correct. The volume of the cylinder $= \pi r^2 h = \left(\frac{22}{7}\right)\left(\frac{7}{2}\right)^2 (10)$ cubic inches = 385 cubic inches. 231 cubic inches = 1 gallon, so 385 cubic inches = $\frac{385}{231}$ gallons = $\frac{5}{3}$ gallons = 1.7 gallons (approximately).

(314)

25. Choice D is correct. The area of floor = 10 feet $\times$ 16 feet = 160 square feet. Area of one tile = 8 inches $\times$ 8 inches = 64 square inches = $\frac{64}{144}$ square feet = $\frac{4}{9}$ square feet. Thus, the number of tiles = area of floor $\div$ area of tile = $160 \div \frac{4}{9} = 360$. At 9¢ apiece, the tiles will cost $32.40.

(304)

26. Choice B is correct. Looking at the following three diagrams, we can observe that the triangle, square, and hexagon are all smaller than the circle.

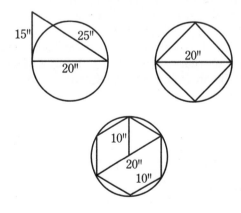

Comparing the areas of the circle and the rectangle, we notice that the area of the circle is $\pi(10 \text{ inches})^2 = 100\pi$ square inches, which is greater than (10 inches)(30 inches) = 300 square inches, the area of the rectangle. (π is approximately 3.14.)

(302)

27. Choice D is correct. In a cylinder, $V = \pi r^2 h$, where r is the radius of the base, and h is the height. The

new volume, $V' = \pi(3r)^2 \left(\dfrac{h}{3}\right) = 3\pi r^2 h = 3V$. Thus, the ratio of the new volume to the old volume is $3 : 1$.

(314)

28. Choice C is correct. A cube 2 feet on each side has a volume of $2 \times 2 \times 2 = 8$ cubic feet. Since 1 cubic foot equals 7.5 gallons, 8 cubic feet equals 60 gallons. If the faucet flows at the rate of 10 gallons/minute, it will take 6 minutes to fill the cube. (313)

29. Choice E is correct. Let s = the side of the square. Then, the area of the square is equal to s^2. The diagonal of the square is $s\sqrt{2}$, so the square of the diagonal is $2s^2$. Thus, the ratio of the area of the square to the square of the diagonal is $s^2 : 2s^2$, or $1 : 2$.

(303)

30. Choice B is correct. The area of the square $ABCD$ is equal to 4 inches $\times$ 4 inches = 16 square inches. The two semicircles can be placed together diameter-to-diameter to form a circle with a radius of 2 inches, and thus, an area of 4π. Subtracting the area of the circle from the area of the square, we obtain the combined areas of AED and BEC. But, since the figure is symmetrical, AED and BEC must be equal. The area of the remainder is $16 - 4\pi$; AED is one-half of this remainder, or $8 - 2\pi$ square inches.

(303, 310)

31. Choice C is correct. The area of the circle is equal to πr^2, and the area of the rectangle is equal to πx. Since these areas are equal, $\pi r^2 = \pi x$, and $x = r^2$.

(304, 310)

32. Choice C is correct. The volume of a cube is e^3 where e is the length of an edge. If the volume is 27 cubic meters, then $e^3 = 27$ and $e = 3$ meters. The surface area of a cube is $6e^2$, and if $e = 3$ meters, then the surface area is 54 square meters.

(313)

33. Choice C is correct. The area of a regular hexagon, one of whose sides is 1 inch, is equal to the sum of the areas of 6 equilateral triangles, each with a side of 1 inch. The area of an equilateral triangle with a side of 1 inch is equal to $\dfrac{\sqrt{3}}{4}$ square inches. (The formula for the area of an equilateral triangle with a side of s is $A = \dfrac{1}{4}s^2\sqrt{3}$.) The sum of 6 such triangles is $\dfrac{6\sqrt{3}}{4}$, or $\dfrac{3\sqrt{3}}{2}$.

(308)

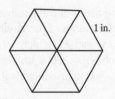

34. Choice D is correct. Draw a perpendicular line from the top of the triangle to the side, which is 8. You have created a 30–60–90 right triangle. The line drawn is $\dfrac{1}{2}$ of 6 = 3. The area of the whole triangle is the altitude multiplied by the base divided by 2. The altitude is 3 and the base is 8, so the area is $3 \times \dfrac{8}{2} = 12$.

(307)

35. Choice D is correct. Since the wheel takes 1 minute to make 600 revolutions and travels 1 mile in that time, we have the relation 1 mile = 5,280 feet = 600 revolutions. Thus, 1 revolution = $\dfrac{5,280}{600}$ feet = 8.8 feet = circumference = π(diameter) = $\left(\dfrac{22}{7}\right)$(diameter). Therefore, the diameter = 8.8 feet $\div \left(\dfrac{22}{7}\right)$ = 2.8 feet.

(310)

36. Choice D is correct. In this case, it is easiest to calculate the perimeters of the five figures. According to the Pythagorean Theorem, a square with a diagonal of 5 feet has a side of $\dfrac{5}{\sqrt{2}}$, which is equal to $\dfrac{5\sqrt{2}}{2}$. (This is found by multiplying the numerator and denominator of $\dfrac{5}{\sqrt{2}}$ by $\sqrt{2}$.) If each side of the square is $\dfrac{5\sqrt{2}}{2}$, then the perimeter is $\overset{2}{\cancel{4}} \times \dfrac{5\sqrt{2}}{\cancel{2}} = 10\sqrt{2}$ feet. A rectangle with sides of 3 feet and 4 feet has a perimeter of $2(3) + 2(4)$, or 14 feet. An equilateral triangle with a side of 48 inches, or 4 feet, has a perimeter of 12 feet. A regular hexagon whose longest diagonal is 6 feet has a side of 3 feet and, therefore, a perimeter of 18 feet. (See the diagram for Solution 33.) Finally, a parallelogram with sides of 6 inches, or $\dfrac{1}{2}$ foot, and 7 feet has a perimeter of 15 feet. Therefore, the hexagon has the largest perimeter.

(302, 317)

37. Choice A is correct. The volume of the first container is equal to 3 inches $\times$ 4 inches $\times$ 10 inches, or 120 cubic inches. The volume of the second container, the cylinder, is equal to $\pi r^2 h = \pi(2 \text{ inches})^2(10 \text{ inches})$, or 40π cubic inches, which is greater than 120 cubic inches (π is greater than 3). So the second container can hold more than the first. If the first container is filled and the contents poured into the second, there will be room for more water in the second.

(312, 314)

38. Choice B is correct. The area of the square is 16 square inches. The four semicircles can be added to form two circles, each of radius 2 inches, so the area of each circle is 4π square inches, and the two circles add up to 8π square inches. Thus, the total area is $16 + 8\pi$ square inches.

(303, 311)

39. Choice B is correct. Since the area of the square is $81p^2$, one side of the square will equal $9p$. According to the Pythagorean Theorem, the diagonal will equal $\sqrt{81p^2 + 81p^2} = 9p\sqrt{2}$. (303, 317)

40. Choice A is correct. We can regard the area as a rectangle, 20 ft × 14 ft, with two rectangles, measuring 4 ft × 6 ft and 2 ft × 2 ft, cut out. Thus, the area is equal to 280 square feet − 24 sq ft − 4 sq ft = 252 sq ft = $\frac{252}{9}$ square yards = 28 sq yds. (Remember, 1 square yard equals 9 square feet.) At $2.50 per square yard, 28 square yards will cost $70. (304)

41. Choice D is correct. The perimeter of the square is equal to four times its side; since a side is $\frac{1}{\sqrt{2}}$, or $\frac{\sqrt{2}}{2}$ times the diagonal, the perimeter of the square in question is $4 \times 5\sqrt{2} = 20\sqrt{2}$, which is approximately equal to 28.28 inches. The perimeter of a right triangle with sides that are in a 3–4–5 ratio, i.e., 9 inches, 12 inches, and 15 inches, is 9 + 12 + 15 = 36 inches. The perimeter of the pentagon is 5 × 5 inches, or 25 inches. The perimeter of the right isosceles triangle (with sides of 12 inches, 12 inches, and $12\sqrt{2}$ inches) is 24 + $12\sqrt{2}$ inches, which is approximately equal to 40.968 inches. The perimeter of the hexagon is 6 × 5 inches, or 30 inches. Thus, the isosceles right triangle has the largest perimeter of those figures mentioned. You should become familiar with the approximate value of $\sqrt{2}$, which is 1.414. (302)

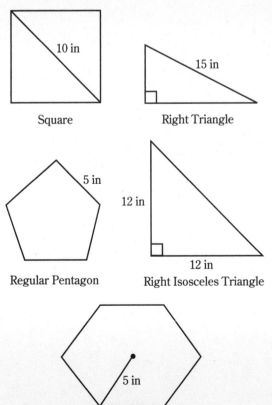

Square

Right Triangle

Regular Pentagon

Right Isosceles Triangle

Regular Hexagon

42. Choice D is correct. For rectangular solids, the following formula holds:

$V = Ah$, where A is the area of the base, and h is the height.

If we replace A with $2A$, and h with $3h$, we get $V' = (2A)(3h) = 6V$. Thus, $V' : V = 6 : 1$. (312)

43. Choice C is correct. The area of the room is 27 feet × 14 feet = 378 square feet. 9 square feet = 1 square yard, so the area of the room is 42 square yards. At $1.50 per square yard, the linoleum to cover the floor will cost $63.00. (304)

44. Choice A is correct. A circle with a 4-inch radius has an 8-inch diameter, so there can be only 2 rows of 3 circles each, or 6 circles. (310)

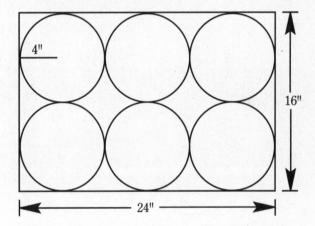

45. Choice E is correct. Let one side of the triangle be s. Then the area of the triangle is $\frac{s^2\sqrt{3}}{4}$. (Either memorize this formula or remember that it is derived by drawing an altitude to divide the triangle into two congruent 30–60–90 right triangles.) The perimeter of the equilateral triangle is $3s$, so the ratio of the area to the perimeter is $\frac{s^2\sqrt{3}}{4} : 3s$, or $s : 4\sqrt{3}$, which cannot be determined unless we know the value of s. (308)

46. Choice E is correct. The formula for volume of a cylinder is $V = \pi r^2 h$, where r is the radius of the base, and h is the height. Here, $r = 4$ inches, and $h = 10$ inches, while $\pi \approx 3.14$. (The symbol $\approx$ means "approximately equal to.") Thus $V \approx (4)^2(10)(3.14) = 160(3.14) = 502.4$ cubic inches. (314)

47. Choice B is correct. If the area of a square is $144s^2$, then one side will equal $12s$, so the diagonal will equal $12s\sqrt{2}$. (The Pythagorean Theorem may be used here to get $d = \sqrt{144s^2 + 144s^2}$, where d is the diagonal.) (303, 317)

48. Choice C is correct. The inside of the pool forms a cylinder of radius 5 feet, and height 5 feet. The volume is $\pi r^2 h$, or $\pi \times 5 \times 5 \times 5 = 125\pi$ cubic feet. (314)

49. Choice B is correct. The area of the floor is 20 feet $\times$ 24 feet = 480 square feet. 30 inches is equal to $2\frac{1}{2}$ feet, and we must find the length that, when multiplied by $2\frac{1}{2}$ feet, will yield 480 square feet. This length is 192 feet, which equals 64 yards (3 feet = 1 yard). (304)

50. Choice D is correct. The circumference of the larger wheel is 18π inches ($C = \pi d$). After 72 revolutions, the larger wheel will have gone a distance of $72(18\pi)$ inches. Since the smaller wheel moves at the same linear speed, it will also have gone $72(18\pi)$ inches. The circumference of the smaller wheel is 12π inches, and if we call the number of revolutions that the smaller wheel makes r, then we know that $12\pi r = 72(18\pi)$. Dividing both sides by 12π gives us $r = 6(18)$ or 108 revolutions. Note that in this problem we have used the relation *distance = rate × time*, where the time for both wheels is a fixed quantity. (310)

MATH REFRESHER
SESSION 4

Algebra Problems

Algebraic Properties

Algebra is the branch of mathematics that applies the laws of arithmetic to symbols that represent unknown quantities. The most commonly used symbols are the letters of the alphabet such as A, B, C, x, y, z, etc. These symbols can be added, subtracted, multiplied, and divided like numbers. For example, $3a + 2a = 5a$, $2x - x = x$, $3(5b) = 15b$, $\frac{6x}{3x} = 2$. These symbols can be raised to powers like a^3 or y^2. Remember that raising a number to a power means multiplying the number by itself a number of times. For example, $a^3 = a \cdot a \cdot a$. The power is 3, and a is multiplied by itself 3 times.

Generally, in algebra, a variable (an unknown represented by a symbol) appears in an *equation* (a statement that defines the relationship between certain quantities), and values of the variable that *satisfy* the equation must be found. For example, the equation $6a = 12$ is satisfied when the variable, a, is equal to 2. This section is a discussion on how to solve complicated algebraic equations and other related topics.

Fundamental Laws of Our Number System

The following list of laws applies to all numbers, and these laws are necessary to work with when doing arithmetic and algebra problems. Remember these laws and use them in doing problems.

401. If $x = y$ and $y = z$, then $x = z$. This property is called *transitivity*. For example, if $a = 3$ and $b = 3$, then $a = b$.

402. If $x = y$, then $x + z = y + z$, and $x - z = y - z$. This means that the same quantity can be added to or subtracted from both sides of an equation. For example, if $a = b$, then add any number to both sides, say 3, and $a + 3 = b + 3$. Or if $a = b$, then $a - 3 = b - 3$.

403. If $x = y$, then $x \cdot z = y \cdot z$ and $x \div z = y \div z$, unless $z = 0$ (see Section 404). This means that both sides of an equation can be multiplied by the same number. For example, if $a = n$, then $5a = 5n$. It also means that both sides of an equation can be divided by the same nonzero number. If $a = b$, then $\frac{a}{3} = \frac{b}{3}$.

404. *Never divide by zero.* This is a very important fact that must be remembered. The quotient of *any* quantity (except zero) divided by zero is infinity.

405. $x + y = y + x$, and $x \cdot y = y \cdot x$. Therefore, $2 + 3 = 3 + 2$, and $2 \cdot 3 = 3 \cdot 2$. Remember that this does not work for division and subtraction. $3 \div 2$ does not equal $2 \div 3$, and $3 - 2$ does not equal $2 - 3$. The property described here is called *commutativity*.

Algebraic Expressions

405a. Since the letters in an algebraic expression stand for numbers, and since we add, subtract, multiply, or divide them to get the algebraic expression, the algebraic expression itself stands for a number. When we are told what value each of the letters in the expression has, we can evaluate the expression. Note that $(+a) \times (+b) = +ab$; $(+a) \times (-b) = -ab$; $(-a) \times (+b) = -ab$; and $-a \times -b = +ab$.

In evaluating algebraic expressions, place the value you are substituting for a letter in parentheses. (This is important when a letter has a negative value.)

Example: What is the value of the expression $a^2 - b^3$ when $a = -2$, and $b = -1$? $a^2 - b^3 = (-2)^2 - (-1)^3 = 4 - (-1) = 5$.

If you can, simplify the algebraic expression before you evaluate it.

Example: Evaluate $\frac{32a^6b^2}{8a^4b^3}$ if $a = 4$, and $b = -2$.

First we divide:

$$\frac{32a^6b^2}{8a^4b^3} = \frac{4a^2}{b}. \text{ Then } \frac{4a^2}{b} = \frac{4(+4)^2}{-2} = -32.$$

Equations

406. *Linear equations in one unknown.* An equation of this type has only one variable, and that variable is always in the first power, e.g., x or y or a, but never a higher or fractional power, e.g., x^2, y^3, or $a^{1/2}$. Examples of linear equations in one unknown are $x + 5 = 7$, $3a - 2 = 7a + 1$, $2x - 7x = 8 + x$, $8 = -4y$, etc. To solve these equations, follow these steps:

STEP 1. Combine the terms on the left and right sides of the equality. That is, (1) add all of the numerical terms on each side, and (2) add all of the terms with variables on each side. For example, if you have $7 + 2x + 9 = 4x - 3 - 2x + 7 + 6x$, combining terms on the left gives you $16 + 2x$, because $7 + 9 = 16$, and $2x$ is the only variable term on that side. On the right we get $8x + 4$, since $4x - 2x + 6x = 8x$ and $-3 + 7 = 4$. Therefore the new equation is $16 + 2x = 8x + 4$.

STEP 2. Put all of the numerical terms on the right side of the equation and all of the variable terms on the left side. This is done by subtracting the numerical term on the left from both sides of the equation and by subtracting the variable term on the right side from both sides of the equation. In the example $16 + 2x = 8x + 4$, subtract 16 from both sides and obtain $2x = 8x - 12$; then subtracting $8x$ from both sides gives $-6x = -12$.

STEP 3. Divide both sides by the coefficient of the variable. In this case, where $-6x = -12$, dividing by -6 gives $x = 2$. This is the final solution to the problem.

Example: Solve for a in the equation $7a + 4 - 2a = 18 + 17a + 10$.

Solution: From Step 1, we combine terms on both sides to get $5a + 4 = 28 + 17a$. As in Step 2, we then subtract 4 and $17a$ from both sides to give $-12a = 24$. By Step 3, we then divide both sides of the equation by the coefficient of a, which is -12, to get $a = -2$.

Example: Solve for x in $2x + 6 = 0$.

Solution: Here Step 1 is eliminated because there are no terms to combine on either side. Step 2 requires that 6 be subtracted from both sides to get $2x = -6$. Then dividing by 2 gives $x = -3$.

407. *Simultaneous equations in two unknowns.* These are problems in which two equations, each with two unknowns, are given. These equations must be solved together (simultaneously) in order to arrive at the solution.

STEP 1. Rearrange each equation so that both are in the form that has the x term on the left side and the y term and the constant on the right side. In other words, put the equations in the form $Ax = By + C$, where A, B, and C are numerical constants. For example, if one of the equations is $9x - 10y + 30 = 11y + 3x - 6$, then subtract $-10y$ and 30 from both sides to get $9x = 21y + 3x - 36$. Subtracting $3x$ from both sides gives $6x = 21y - 36$, which is in the form of $Ax = By + C$.

The first equation should be in the form $Ax = By + C$, and the second equation should be in the form $Dx = Ey + F$, where $A, B, C, D, E,$ and F are numerical constants.

STEP 2. Multiply the first equation by the coefficient of x in the second equation (D). Multiply the second equation by the coefficient of x in the first equation (A). Now the equations are in the form $ADx = BDy + CD$ and $ADx = AEy + AF$. For example, in the two equations $2x = 7y - 12$ and $3x = y + 1$, multiply the first by 3 and the second by 2 to get $6x = 21y - 36$ and $6x = 2y + 2$.

STEP 3. Equate the right sides of both equations. This can be done because both sides are equal to ADx. (See Section 401 on transitivity.) Thus, $BDy + CD = AEy + AF$. So $21y - 36$ and $2y + 2$ are both equal to $6x$ and are equal to each other: $21y - 36 = 2y + 2$.

STEP 4. Solve for y. This is done in the manner outlined in Section 406. In the equation $21y - 36 = 2y + 2$, $y = 2$. By this method $y = \dfrac{AF-CD}{BD-AE}$.

STEP 5. Substitute the value of y into either of the original equations and solve for x. In the general equations we would then have either $x = \dfrac{B}{A}\left[\dfrac{AF-CD}{BD-AE}\right] + \dfrac{C}{A}$, or $x = \dfrac{E}{D}\left[\dfrac{AF-CD}{BD-AE}\right] + \dfrac{F}{D}$. In the example, if $y = 2$ is substituted into either $2x = 7y - 12$ or $3x = y + 1$, then $2x = 14 - 12$ or $3x = 3$ can be solved to get $x = 1$.

Example: Solve for a and b in the equations $3a + 4b = 24$ and $2a + b = 11$.

Solution: First note that it makes no difference in these two equations whether the variables are a and b instead of x and y. Subtract $4b$ from the first equation and b from the second equation to get the equations $3a = 24 - 4b$ and $2a = 11 - b$. Multiply the first by 2 and the second by 3. Thus, $6a = 48 - 8b$ and $6a = 33 - 3b$. Equate $48 - 8b$ and $33 - 3b$ to get $48 - 8b = 33 - 3b$. Solving for b in the usual manner gives us $b = 3$. Substituting the value of $b = 3$ into the equation $3a + 4b = 24$ obtains $3a + 12 = 24$. Solving for a gives $a = 4$. Thus the complete solution is $a = 4$ and $b = 3$.

408. *Quadratic equations.* Quadratic equations are expressed in the form $ax^2 + bx + c = 0$, where $a, b,$ and c are constant numbers (for example, $\frac{1}{2}, 4, -2$, etc.) and x is a variable. An equation of this form may be satisfied by two values of x, one value of x, or no values of x. Actually, when there are no values of x that satisfy the equation, there are only *imaginary* solutions. On the GRE, you will not have questions where you will have to use these formulas. To determine the number of solutions, find the value of the expression $b^2 - 4ac$ where $a, b,$ and c are the constant coefficients of the equation $ax^2 + bx + c = 0$.

> If $b^2 - 4ac$ is *greater* than 0, there are two solutions.
>
> If $b^2 - 4ac$ is *less* than 0, there are no solutions.
>
> If $b^2 - 4ac$ is *equal* to 0, there is one solution.

If solutions exist, they can be found by using the formulas:

$$x = \frac{-b + \sqrt{b^2-4ac}}{2a} \text{ and } x = \frac{-b - \sqrt{b^2-4ac}}{2a}$$

Note that if $b^2 - 4ac = 0$, the two above solutions will be the same and there will be one solution.

Example: Determine the solutions, if they exist, to the equation $x^2 + 6x + 5 = 0$.

Solution: First, noting $a = 1$, $b = 6$, and $c = 5$, calculate $b^2 - 4ac$, or $6^2 - 4(1)(5)$. Thus, $b^2 - 4ac = 16$. Since this is greater than 0, there are two solutions. They are, from the formulas:

$$x = \frac{-6 + \sqrt{6^2 - 4 \cdot 1 \cdot 5}}{2 \cdot 1} \text{ and } x = \frac{-6 - \sqrt{6^2 - 4 \cdot 1 \cdot 5}}{2 \cdot 1}$$

Simplify these to:

$$x = \frac{-6 + \sqrt{16}}{2} \text{ and } x = \frac{-6 - \sqrt{16}}{2}$$

As $\sqrt{16} = 4$, $x = \frac{-6 + 4}{2} = \frac{-2}{2}$ and $x = \frac{-6 - 4}{2} = \frac{-10}{2}$. Thus, the two solutions are $x = -1$ and $x = -5$.

Another method of solving quadratic equations is to *factor* the $ax^2 + bx + c$ into two expressions. This will be explained in the next section.

409. *Factoring.* Factoring is breaking down an expression into two or more expressions, the product of which is the original expression. For example, 6 can be factored into 2 and 3 because $2 \cdot 3 = 6$. $x^2 - x$ can be factored into x and $(x - 1)$ because $x^2 - x = x(x - 1)$. Then, if $x^2 + bx + c$ is factorable, it will be factored into two expressions in the form $(x + d)$ and $(x + e)$. If the expression $(x + d)$ is multiplied by the expression $(x + e)$, their product is $x^2 + (d + e)x + de$. For example, $(x + 3) \cdot (x + 2)$ equals $x^2 + 5x + 6$. To factor an expression such as $x^2 + 6x + 8$, find d and e such that $d + e = 6$ and $de = 8$. Of the various factors of 8, we find that $d = 4$ and $e = 2$. Thus $x^2 + 6x + 8$ can be factored into the expressions $(x + 4)$ and $(x + 2)$. Below are factored expressions.

$$x^2 + 2x + 1 = (x + 1)(x + 1) \qquad x^2 + 3x + 2 = (x + 2)(x + 1)$$
$$x^2 + 4x + 4 = (x + 2)(x + 2) \qquad x^2 + 5x + 6 = (x + 3)(x + 2)$$
$$x^2 - 4x + 3 = (x - 3)(x - 1) \qquad x^2 - 4x - 5 = (x - 5)(x + 1)$$
$$x^2 + 10x + 16 = (x + 8)(x + 2) \qquad x^2 + 4x - 5 = (x + 5)(x - 1)$$
$$x^2 - 5x + 6 = (x - 2)(x - 3) \qquad x^2 - x - 6 = (x - 3)(x + 2)$$

Notice if the expression is of the form $ax^2 + bx + c$. For example, we would factor $2x^2 + x + 1$ as $(2x + 1)(x - 1)$.

An important rule to remember in factoring is that $a^2 - b^2 = (a + b)(a - b)$. For example, $x^2 - 9 = (x + 3)(x - 3)$. You don't get a middle term in x because the $3x$ cancels with the $-3x$ in the product $(x + 3)(x - 3)$. To apply factoring in solving quadratic equations, factor the quadratic expression into two terms and set each term equal to zero. Then, solve the two resulting equations.

Example: Solve $x^2 - x - 6 = 0$.

Solution: First factor the expression $x^2 - x - 6$ into $x - 3$ and $x + 2$. Setting each of these equal to 0 gives $x - 3 = 0$ and $x + 2 = 0$. Solving these equations gives us $x = 3$ and $x = -2$.

Algebra of Graphs

410a. *Number Lines.* Numbers, positive and negative, can be represented as points on a straight line. Conversely, points on a line can also be represented by numbers. This is done by use of the number line.

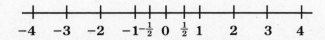

The diagram above is an example of a number line. On a number line, a point is chosen to represent the number zero. Then a point that is 1 unit to the right of 0 represents +1; a point that is $\frac{1}{2}$ unit to the right of 0 is $+\frac{1}{2}$; a point that is 2 units to the right of 0 is +2; and so on. A point that is 1 unit to the left of 0 is −1; a point that is $\frac{1}{2}$ unit to the left of 0 is $-\frac{1}{2}$; a point that is 2 units to the left of 0 is −2; and so on. As you can see, all points to the right of the 0 point represent positive numbers, and all those to the left of the 0 point represent negative numbers.

<u>To find the distance between two points on the line:</u>

1. Find the numbers that represent the points.
2. The distance is the smaller number subtracted from the larger.

For example: Find the distance between point *A* and point *B* on the number line.

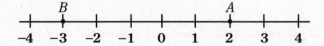

Point *A* is +2 on the number line and point *B* is −3. +2 is larger than −3, so the distance is +2 −(−3), or +2 + 3 = 5. By counting the number of units between *A* and *B*, the distance is also found to be 5.

410b. *Coordinate geometry.* These problems deal with the algebra of graphs. A graph consists of a set of points whose position is determined with respect to a set of axes usually labeled the *x*-axis and the *y*-axis and divided into appropriate units. Locate a point on the graph with an "*x*-coordinate" of *a* units and a "*y*-coordinate" of *b* units. First move *a* units along the *x*-axis (either to the right or the left depending on whether *a* is positive or negative). Then move *b* units along the *y*-axis (either up or down depending on the sign of *b*). A point with an *x*-coordinate of *a*, and a *y*-coordinate of *b*, is represented by (*a*,*b*). The points (2,3), (−1,4), (−2,−3), and (4,−2) are shown on the following graph.

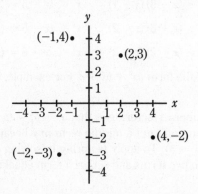

411. *Distance between two points.* If the coordinates of point *A* are (x_1, y_1) and the coordinates of point *B* are (x_2, y_2), then the distance on the graph between the two points is $d = \sqrt{(x_2 - x_1)^2 + (y_2 - y_1)^2}$.

Example: Find the distance between the point (2,−3) and the point (5,1).

Solution: In this case $x_1 = 2$, $x_2 = 5$, $y_1 = -3$, and $y_2 = 1$. Substituting into the above formula gives us

$$d = \sqrt{(5-2)^2 + [1-(-3)]^2} = \sqrt{3^2 + 4^2} = \sqrt{25} = 5$$

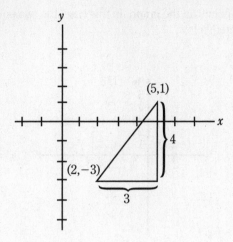

Note: This formula is a consequence of the Pythagorean Theorem. Pythagoras, an ancient Greek mathematician, discovered that the square of the length of the hypotenuse (longest side) of a right triangle is equal to the sum of the square of the lengths of the other two sides. See Sections 317 and 509.

412. *Midpoint of the line segment joining two points.* If the coordinates of the first point are (x_1, y_1) and the coordinates of the second point are (x_2, y_2), then the coordinates of the midpoint will be $\left(\dfrac{x_1 + x_2}{2}, \dfrac{y_1 + y_2}{2}\right)$. In other words, each coordinate of the midpoint is equal to the *average* of the corresponding coordinates of the endpoints.

Example: Find the midpoint of the segment connecting the points (2,4) and (6,2).

Solution: The average of 2 and 6 is 4, so the first coordinate is 4. The average of 4 and 2 is 3; thus the second coordinate is 3. The midpoint is (4,3). $\left[\dfrac{2+6}{2} = 4, \ \dfrac{4+2}{2} = 3\right]$

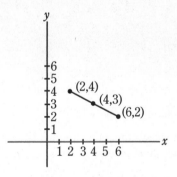

413. *Plotting the graph of a line.* An equation that can be put in the form of $y = mx + b$, where m and b are numerical constants, can be represented as a line on a graph. This means that all of the points on the graph that the line passes through will satisfy the equation. Remember that each point has an x and a y value that can be substituted into the equation. To plot a line, follow the steps below:

STEP 1. Select two values of x and two values of y that will satisfy the equation. For example, in the equation $y = 2x + 4$, the point $(x = 1, y = 6)$, will satisfy the equation, as will the point $(x = -2, y = 0)$. There is an infinite number of such points on a line.

STEP 2. Plot these two points on the graph. In this case, the two points are (1,6) and (−2,0). These points are represented below.

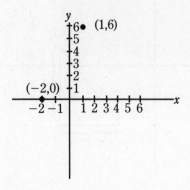

STEP 3. Draw a line connecting the two points. This is the line representing the equation.

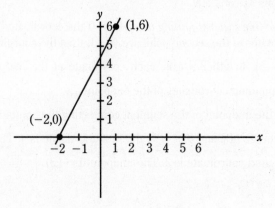

(Note: A straight line is completely specified by two points.)

Example: Graph the equation $2y + 3x = 12$.

Solution: Two points that satisfy this equation are (2,3) and (0,6). Plotting these points and drawing a line between them gives:

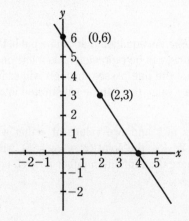

414. *Y-intercept.* The y-intercept of a line is the point where the line crosses the y-axis. At any point where a line crosses the y-axis, $x = 0$. To find the y-intercept of a line, simply substitute $x = 0$ into the equation of the line, and solve for y.

Example: Find the *y*-intercept of the equation $2x + 3y = 6$.

Solution: If $x = 0$ is substituted into the equation, it simplifies to $3y = 6$. Solving for *y* gives $y = 2$. Thus, 2 is the *y*-intercept.

If an equation can be put into the form of $y = mx + b$, then b is the *y*-intercept.

---

415. *X-intercept.* The point where a line intersects the *x*-axis is called the *x*-intercept. At this point $y = 0$. To find the *x*-intercept of a line, substitute $y = 0$ into the equation and solve for *x*.

Example: Given the equation $2x + 3y = 6$, find the *x*-intercept.

Solution: Substitute $y = 0$ into the equation, getting $2x = 6$. Solving for *x*, find $x = 3$. Thus the *x*-intercept is 3.

In the diagram below, the *y*- and *x*-intercepts of the equation $2x + 3y = 6$ are illustrated.

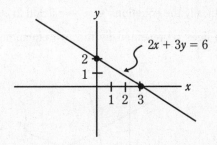

416. *Slope.* The slope of a line is the change in *y* caused by a 1-unit increase in *x*. If an equation is in the form of $y = mx + b$, then as *x* increases 1 unit, *y* will increase *m* units. Therefore the slope is *m*.

Example: Find the slope of the line $2x + 3y = 6$.

Solution: First put the equation into the form of $y = mx + b$. Subtract $2x$ from both sides and divide by 3. The equation becomes $y = -\frac{2}{3}x + 2$. Therefore the slope is $-\frac{2}{3}$.

The slope of the line joining two points, (x_1, y_1) and (x_2, y_2), is given by the expression $m = \frac{y_2 - y_1}{x_2 - x_1}$.

Example: Find the slope of the line joining the points $(3,2)$ and $(4,-1)$.

Solution: Substituting into the above formula gives us $m = \frac{-3}{1} = -3$, where $x_1 = 3$, $x_2 = 4$, $y_1 = 2$, $y_2 = -1$.

If two lines are perpendicular, the slope of one is the negative reciprocal of the other.

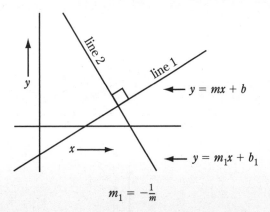

Example: What is the slope of a line perpendicular to the line $y = -3x + 4$?

Solution: Since the slope of the line $y = -3x + 4$ is -3, the slope of the line perpendicular to that line is the negative reciprocal, or $\frac{-1}{-3} = \frac{+1}{3}$

417. *Graphing simultaneous linear equations.* Recall that simultaneous equations are a pair of equations in two unknowns. Each of these equations is graphed separately, and each is represented by a straight line. The solution of the simultaneous equations (i.e., the pair of values that satisfies *both* equations at the same time) is represented by the intersection of two lines. Now, for any pair of lines, there are three possible relationships:

1. The lines intersect at one and only one point; in this case, this point represents the unique solution to the pair of equations. This is most often the case. Such lines are called *consistent*.

2. The lines coincide exactly; this represents the case where the two equations are equivalent (just different forms of the same mathematical relation). Any point that satisfies *either* of the two equations automatically satisfies *both*.

3. The lines are parallel and never intersect. In this case the equations are called *inconsistent*, and they have *no* solution at all. Two lines that are parallel will have the same slope.

Example: Solve graphically the equations $4x - y = 5$ and $2x + 4y = 16$.

Solution: Plot the two lines represented by the two equations. (See Section 413.) The graph is shown below.

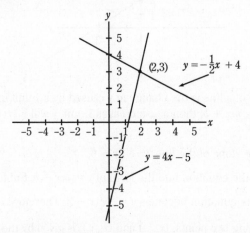

The two lines intersect in the point (2,3), which represents the solution $x = 2$ and $y = 3$. This can be checked by solving the equations as is done in Section 407.

Example: Solve $x + 2y = 6$ and $2x + 4y = 8$.

Solution: Find a point that satisfies each equation. The graph will look like this:

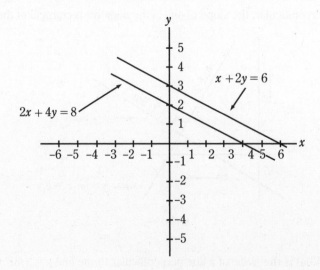

These lines will never intersect, and these equations are termed inconsistent. There is no solution.

Remember that two parallel lines have the same slope. This is an easy way to see whether two lines are consistent or inconsistent.

Example: Find the solution to $2x - 3y = 8$ and $4x = 6y + 16$.

Solution: On the graph these two lines are identical. This means that there is an infinite set of points that satisfy both equations.

Equations of identical lines are multiples of each other and can be reduced to a single equation.

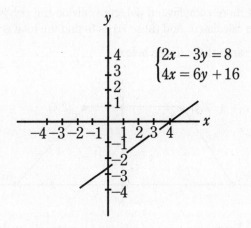

418. *Areas of polygons.* Often, an elementary geometric figure is placed on a graph to calculate its area. This is usually simple for figures such as triangles, rectangles, squares, parallelograms, etc.

Example: Calculate the area of the triangle in the figure below.

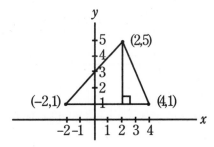

Solution: The area of a triangle is $\frac{1}{2}$ (base) (height). On the graph the length of the line joining $(-2,1)$ and $(4,1)$ is 6 units. The height, which goes from point $(2,5)$ to the base, has a length of 4 units. Therefore the area is $\frac{1}{2}(6)(4) = 12$.

Example: Calculate the area of the square pictured below.

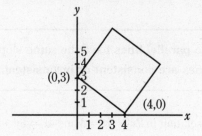

Solution: The area of a square is given by the square of the side. To find this area, first find the length of one side. The length of a segment whose endpoints are (x_1, y_1) and (x_2, y_2) is given by the formula $\sqrt{(x_2 - x_1)^2 + (y_2 - y_1)^2}$. Substituting in $(0,3)$ and $(4,0)$ gives a length of 5 units. Thus the length of one side of the square is 5. Using the formula area $=$ (side)^2 gives an area of 5^2, or 25 square units.

To find the area of more complicated polygons, divide the polygon into simple figures whose areas can be calculated. Add these areas to find the total area.

Example: Find the area of the figure below:

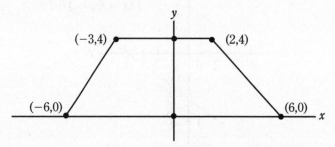

Solution: Divide the figure into two triangles and a rectangle by drawing vertical lines at $(-3,4)$ and $(2,4)$. Thus the polygon is now two triangles and a rectangle.

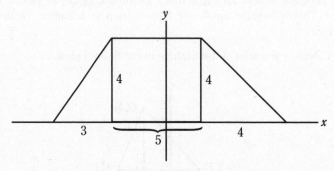

The height of the left triangle is 4 units, and the base is 3. Using $A = \frac{1}{2}bh$ gives the area as 6.

The height of the right triangle is 4, and the base is 4. The area is 8. The length of one side of the rectangle is 4, and the other side is 5. Using the formula area $=$ base $\cdot$ height gives the area as 20. Thus the total area is $6 + 8 + 20 = 34$.

Inequalities

419. *Inequalities.* These problems deal with numbers that are less than, greater than, or equal to other numbers. The following laws apply to all inequalities:

$<$ means "less than," thus $3 < 4$
$>$ means "greater than," thus $5 > 2$
$\leq$ means "less than or equal to," thus $x \leq y$ means $x < y$ or $x = y$
$\geq$ means "greater than or equal to," thus $x \geq y$ means $x > y$ or $x = y$

420. If equal quantities are added to or subtracted from both sides of an inequality, the direction of the inequality does *not* change.

$$\text{If } x < y, \text{ then } x + z < y + z \text{ and } x - z < y - z.$$

$$\text{If } x > y, \text{ then } x + z > y + z \text{ and } x - z > y - z.$$

For example, given the inequality $4 > 2$, with 1 added to or subtracted from both sides, the results, $5 > 3$ and $3 > 1$, have the same inequality sign as the original. If the problem is algebraic, e.g., $x + 3 < 6$, it is possible to subtract 3 from both sides to get the simple inequality $x < 3$.

421. Subtracting parts of an inequality from an equation *reverses* the order of the inequality.

$$\text{Given } z = z \text{ and } x < y, \text{ then } z - x > z - y.$$

$$\text{Given } z = z \text{ and } x > y, \text{ then } z - x < z - y.$$

For example, given that $3 < 5$, subtracting 3 from the left-hand and 5 from the right-hand sides of the equation $10 = 10$ results in $7 > 5$. Thus the direction of the inequality is reversed.

Note: Subtracting parts of an equation from an inequality does not reverse the inequality. For example, if $3 < 5$, then $3 - 10 < 5 - 10$.

422. Multiplying or dividing an inequality by a number greater than zero does not change the order of the inequality.

$$\text{If } x > y, \text{ and } a > 0, \text{ then } xa > ya \text{ and } \frac{x}{a} > \frac{y}{a}.$$

$$\text{If } x < y, \text{ and } a > 0, \text{ then } xa < ya \text{ and } \frac{x}{a} < \frac{y}{a}.$$

For example, if $4 > 2$, multiplying both sides by any arbitrary number (for instance, 5) gives $20 > 10$, which is still true. Or, if algebraically $6h < 3$, dividing both sides by 6 gives $h < \frac{1}{2}$, which is true.

423. Multiplying or dividing an inequality by a number less than 0 reverses the order of the inequality.

$$\text{If } x > y, \text{ and } a < 0, \text{ then } xa < ya \text{ and } \frac{x}{a} < \frac{y}{a}.$$

$$\text{If } x < y, \text{ and } a < 0, \text{ then } xa > ya \text{ and } \frac{x}{a} > \frac{y}{a}.$$

If $-3 < 2$ is multiplied through by -2 it becomes $6 > -4$, and the order of the inequality is reversed.

> **Note that negative numbers are always less than positive numbers. Note also that the greater the absolute value of a negative number, the smaller the number actually is. Thus, $-10 < -9$, $-8 < -7$, etc.**

---

424. The product of two numbers with like signs is positive.

$$\text{If } x > 0 \text{ and } y > 0, \text{ then } xy > 0.$$

$$\text{If } x < 0 \text{ and } y < 0, \text{ then } xy > 0.$$

For example, -3 times -2 is 6.

425. The product of two numbers with unlike signs is negative.

$$\text{If } x < 0 \text{ and } y > 0, \text{ then } xy < 0.$$

$$\text{If } x > 0 \text{ and } y < 0, \text{ then } xy < 0.$$

For example, -2 times 3 is -6. 8 times -1 is -8, etc.

426. *Linear inequalities in one unknown.* In these problems a first-power variable is given in an inequality, and this variable must be solved for in terms of the inequality. Examples of linear inequalities in one unknown are: $2x + 7 > 4 + x$, $8y - 3 \le 2y$, etc.

STEP 1. By ordinary algebraic addition and subtraction (as if it were an equality) get all of the constant terms on one side of the inequality and all of the variable terms on the other side. In the inequality $2x + 4 < 8x + 16$ subtract 4 and $8x$ from both sides and get $-6x < 12$.

STEP 2. Divide both sides by the coefficient of the variable. Important: If the coefficient of the variable is negative, you must reverse the inequality sign. For example, in $-6x < 12$, dividing by -6 gives $x > -2$. (The inequality is reversed.) In $3x < 12$, dividing by 3 gives $x < 4$.

Example: Solve for y in the inequality $4y + 7 \ge 9 - 2y$.

Solution: Subtracting $-2y$ and 7 from both sides gives $6y \ge 2$. Dividing both sides by 6 gives $y \ge \frac{1}{3}$.

Example: Solve for a in the inequality $10 - 2a < 0$.

Solution: Subtracting 10 from both sides gives $-2a < -10$. Dividing both sides by -2 gives $a > \frac{-10}{-2}$ or $a > 5$. Note that the inequality sign has been reversed because of the division by a negative number.

427. *Simultaneous linear inequalities in two unknowns.* These are two inequalities, each one in two unknowns. The same two unknowns are to be solved for in each equation. This means the equations must be solved simultaneously.

STEP 1. Plot both inequalities on the same graph. Replace the inequality sign with an equals sign and plot the resulting line. The side of the line that makes the inequality true is then shaded in. For example, graph the inequality $(2x - y > 4)$. First replace the inequality sign, getting $2x - y = 4$; then, plot the line. The x-intercept is 2. The y-intercept is -4. (See Sections 414 and 415 for determining x- and y-intercepts.)

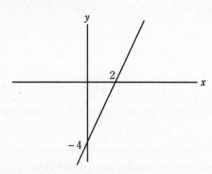

To decide which side of the line satisfies the inequality, choose a convenient point on each side and determine which point satisfies the inequality. Shade in that side of the line. In this case, choose the point (0,0). With this point the equation becomes $2(0) - 0 > 4$, or $0 > 4$. This is not true. Therefore, shade in the other side of the line.

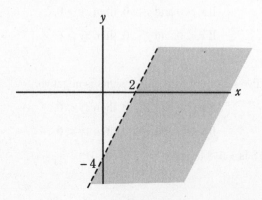

STEP 2. After both inequalities have been solved, the area that is common to both shaded portions is the solution to the problem.

Example: Solve $x + y > 2$ and $3x < 6$.

Solution: First graph $x + y > 2$ by plotting $x + y = 2$ and using the point $(4,0)$ to determine the region where the inequality is satisfied:

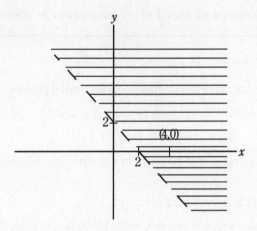

Graph the inequality $3x < 6$ on the same axes and get:

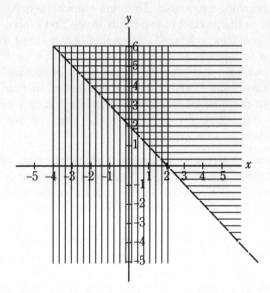

The solution is the double-shaded area.

428. *Higher-order inequalities in one unknown.* These are inequalities that deal with variables multiplied by themselves. For example, $x^2 + 3 \geq 0$, $(x - 1)(x + 2) < 4$ and $x^3 - 7x > 0$ are such inequalities. The basic rules to remember in doing such problems are:

---

1. The product of any number of positive numbers is positive.

For example, $2 \times 3 \times 4 \times 5 = 120$, which is positive, or $\frac{1}{2} \times \frac{1}{2} = \frac{1}{4}$, which is positive.

---

2. The product of an even number of negative numbers is positive.

For example, $(-3)(-2) = 6$ or $(-3)(-1)(-9)(-2) = 54$, which is positive.

> **3. The product of an odd number of negative numbers is negative.**

For example, $(-1)(-2)(-3) = -6$ or $\left(-\dfrac{1}{2}\right)(-2)(-3)(-6)(-1) = -18$.

> **4. Any number squared or raised to an even power is always positive or zero.**

For example, $x^2 \geq 0$ or $a^4 \geq 0$ for all x and for all a.

Often these basic rules will make the solution to an inequality problem obvious.

Example: Which of the following values can x^2 not have?

(A) 5   (B) -2 (C) 0   (D) 144   (E) 9

Solution: We know that $x^2 \geq 0$ for all x, so x^2 cannot be negative. -2 is negative, so x^2 cannot equal -2.

The steps in solving a higher-order inequality are:

STEP 1.   Bring all of the terms to one side of the inequality, making the other side zero. For example, in the inequality $x^2 > 3x - 2$, subtract $3x - 2$ from both sides to get $x^2 - 3x + 2 > 0$.

STEP 2.   Factor the resulting expression. To factor a quadratic expression means to write the original expression as the product of two terms in the first power, i.e., $x^2 = x \cdot x$. x is a factor of x^2. (See Section 409 for a detailed explanation of factoring.) The quadratic expression $x^2 - 3x + 2$ when factored is $(x - 2)(x - 1)$. Note that $x \cdot x = x^2$, $-2x - x = -3x$ and $(-1)(-2) = 2$. Most quadratic expressions can easily be factored by taking factors of the last term (in this case 2 and 1) and adding or subtracting them to or from x. Through trial and error, the right combination is found. Remember that $(a + b)(c + d) = ac + ad + bc + bd$. Example: $(x + 4)(x + 2) = x^2 + 4x + 2x + 8 = x^2 + 6x + 8$. Another is that $a^2 - b^2 = (a + b)(a - b)$. Example: $x^2 - 16 = (x + 4)(x - 4)$.

STEP 3.   Investigate which terms are positive and which terms are negative. For example, in $(x - 3)(x + 2) > 0$, either $(x - 3)$ and $(x + 2)$ are both positive, or $(x - 3)$ and $(x + 2)$ are both negative. If one were positive and the other were negative, the product would be negative and would not satisfy the inequality. If the factors are positive, then $x - 3 > 0$ and $x + 2 > 0$, which yields $x > 3$ and $x > -2$. For x to be greater than 3 and to be greater than -2, it must be greater than 3. If it is greater than 3, it is automatically greater than -2. Thus, with positive factors, $x > 3$ is the answer. If the factors are negative, $x - 3 < 0$ and $x + 2 < 0$, or $x < -2$. For x to be less than 3 and less than -2 it must be less than -2. Thus, with negative factors, $x < -2$ is the answer. As both answers are possible from the original equation, the solution to the original problem is $x > 3$ or $x < -2$.

Example: For which values of x is $x^2 + 5 < 6x$?

Solution: First subtract $6x$ from both sides to get $x^2 - 6x + 5 < 0$. The left side factors into $(x - 5)(x - 1) < 0$. Now for this to be true, one factor must be positive and one must be negative, i.e., their product is less than zero. Thus, $x - 5 > 0$ and $x - 1 < 0$, or $x - 5 < 0$ and $x - 1 > 0$. If $x - 5 < 0$ and $x - 1 > 0$, then $x < 5$ and $x > 1$, or $1 < x < 5$. If $x - 5 > 0$ and $x - 1 < 0$ then $x > 5$ and $x < 1$, which is impossible because x cannot be less than 1 *and* greater than 5. Therefore, the solution is $1 < x < 5$.

Example: For what values of x is $x^2 < 4$?

Solution: Subtract 4 from both sides to get $x^2 - 4 < 0$. Remember that $a^2 - b^2 = (a + b)(a - b)$; thus $x^2 - 4 = (x + 2)(x - 2)$. Hence, $(x + 2)(x - 2) < 0$. For this to be true $x + 2 > 0$ and $x - 2 < 0$, or $x + 2 < 0$ and $x - 2 > 0$. In the first case $x > -2$ and $x < 2$, or $-2 < x < 2$. The second case is $x < -2$ and $x > +2$, which is impossible because x cannot be less than -2 *and* greater than 2. Thus, the solution is $-2 < x < 2$.

Example: When is $(x^2 + 1)(x - 2)^2(x - 3)$ greater than or equal to zero?

Solution: This can be written as $(x^2 + 1)(x - 2)^2(x - 3) \geq 0$. This is already in factors. The individual terms must be investigated. $x^2 + 1$ is always positive because $x^2 \geq 0$, so $x^2 + 1$ must be greater than 0. $(x - 2)^2$ is a number squared, so this is always greater than or equal to zero. Therefore, the product of the first two terms is positive or equal to zero for all values of x. The third term $x - 3$ is positive when $x > 3$, and negative when $x < 3$. For the entire expression to be positive, $x - 3$ must be positive, i.e., $x > 3$. For the expression to be equal to zero, $x - 3 = 0$, i.e., $x = 3$, or $(x - 2)^2 = 0$, i.e., $x = 2$. Thus, the entire expression is positive when $x > 3$ and zero when $x = 2$ or $x = 3$.

Exponents and Roots

429. *Exponents.* An exponent is an easy way to express repeated multiplication. For example, $5 \times 5 \times 5 \times 5 = 5^4$. The 4 is the exponent. In the expression $7^3 = 7 \times 7 \times 7$, 3 is the exponent. 7^3 means 7 is multiplied by itself three times. If the exponent is 0, the expression always has a value of 1. Thus, $6^0 = 15^0 = 1$, etc. If the exponent is 1, the value of the expression is the number base. Thus, $4^1 = 4$ and $9^1 = 9$.

In the problem $5^3 \times 5^4$, we can simplify by counting the factors of 5. Thus $5^3 \times 5^4 = 5^{3+4} = 5^7$. When we multiply and the base number is the same, we keep the base number and add the exponents. For example, $7^4 \times 7^8 = 7^{12}$.

For division, we keep the same base number and subtract exponents. Thus, $8^8 \div 8^2 = 8^{8-2} = 8^6$.

A negative exponent indicates the reciprocal of the expression with a positive exponent, thus $3^{-2} = \dfrac{1}{3^2}$.

430. *Roots.* The square root of a number is a number whose square is the original number. For example, $\sqrt{16} = 4$, since $4 \times 4 = 16$. (The $\sqrt{}$ symbol always means a positive number.)

To simplify a square root, we factor the number.

$$\sqrt{32} = \sqrt{16 \cdot 2} = \sqrt{16} \cdot \sqrt{2} = 4\sqrt{2}$$
$$\sqrt{72} = \sqrt{36 \cdot 2} = \sqrt{36} \cdot \sqrt{2} = 6\sqrt{2}$$
$$\sqrt{300} = \sqrt{25 \cdot 12} = \sqrt{25} \cdot \sqrt{12}$$
$$= 5 \cdot \sqrt{12}$$
$$= 5 \cdot \sqrt{4 \cdot 3}$$
$$= 5 \cdot \sqrt{4} \cdot \sqrt{3}$$
$$= 5 \cdot 2\sqrt{3}$$
$$= 10\sqrt{3}$$

We can add expressions with the square roots only if the numbers inside the square root sign are the same. For example,

$$3\sqrt{7} + 2\sqrt{7} = 5\sqrt{7}$$
$$\sqrt{18} + \sqrt{2} = \sqrt{9 \cdot 2} + \sqrt{2} = \sqrt{9} \cdot \sqrt{2} + \sqrt{2} = 3\sqrt{2} + \sqrt{2} = 4\sqrt{2}.$$

431. *Evaluation of expressions.* To evaluate an expression means to substitute a value in place of a letter. For example: Evaluate $3a^2 - c^3$; if $a = -2, c = -3$.

$$3a^2 - c^3 = 3(-2)^2 - (-3)^3 = 3(4) - (-27) = 12 + 27 = 39$$

Given: $a \triangledown b = ab + b^2$. Find: $-2 \triangledown 3$.

Using the definition, we get

$$-2 \triangledown 3 = (-2)(3) + (3)^2$$
$$= -6 + 9$$
$$-2 \triangledown 3 = 3$$

Practice Test 4

Algebra Problems

Correct answers and solutions follow each test.

1.
A B C D E

1. For what values of x is the following equation satisfied: $3x + 9 = 21 + 7x$?

(A) -3 only
(B) 3 only
(C) 3 or -3 only
(D) no values
(E) an infinite number of values

2.
A B C D E

2. What values may z have if $2z + 4$ is greater than $z - 6$?

(A) any values greater than -10
(B) any values greater than -2
(C) any values less than 2
(D) any values less than 10
(E) None of these.

3.
A B C D E

3. If $ax^2 + 2x - 3 = 0$ when $x = -3$, what value(s) can a have?

(A) -3 only
(B) -1 only
(C) 1 only
(D) -1 and 1 only
(E) -3, -1, and 1 only

4.
A B C D E

4. If the coordinates of point P are $(0,8)$, and the coordinates of point Q are $(4,2)$, which of the following points represent the midpoint of PQ?

(A) $(0,2)$
(B) $(2,4)$
(C) $(2,5)$
(D) $(4,8)$
(E) $(4,10)$

5.
A B C D E

5. In the formula $V = \pi r^2 h$, what is the value of r, in terms of V and h?

(A) $\dfrac{\sqrt{V}}{\pi h}$

(B) $\pi\sqrt{\dfrac{V}{h}}$

(C) $\sqrt{\pi V h}$

(D) $\dfrac{\pi h}{\sqrt{V}}$

(E) $\sqrt{\dfrac{V}{\pi h}}$

6.
A B C D E

6. Solve the inequality $x^2 - 3x < 0$.

(A) $x < -3$
(B) $-3 < x < 0$
(C) $x < 3$
(D) $0 < x < 3$
(E) $3 < x$

7. A B C D E

7. Which of the following lines is parallel to the line represented by $2y = 8x + 32$?

    (A) $y = 8x + 32$
    (B) $y = 8x + 16$
    (C) $y = 16x + 32$
    (D) $y = 4x + 32$
    (E) $y = 2x + 16$

8. A B C D E

8. In the equation $4.04x + 1.01 = 9.09$, what value of x is necessary to make the equation true?

    (A) -1.5
    (B) 0
    (C) 1
    (D) 2
    (E) 2.5

9. A B C D E

9. What values of x satisfies the equation $(x + 1)(x - 2) = 0$?

    (A) 1 only
    (B) -2 only
    (C) 1 and -2 only
    (D) -1 and 2 only
    (E) any values between -1 and 2

10. A B C D E

10. What is the largest possible value of the following expression:
    $(x + 2)(3 - x)(2 + x)^2(2x - 6)(2x + 4)$?

    (A) -576
    (B) -24
    (C) 0
    (D) 12
    (E) Cannot be determined.

11. A B C D E

11. For what value(s) of k is the following equation satisfied:
    $2k - 9 - k = 4k + 6 - 3k$?

    (A) -5 only
    (B) 0
    (C) $\dfrac{5}{2}$ only
    (D) no values
    (E) more than one value

12. A B C D E

12. In the equation $p = aq^2 + bq + c$, if $a = 1$, $b = -2$, and $c = 1$, which of the following expresses p in terms of q?

    (A) $p = (q - 2)^2$
    (B) $p = (q - 1)^2$
    (C) $p = q^2$
    (D) $p = (q + 1)^2$
    (E) $p = (q + 2)^2$

13. A B C D E

13. If $A + B + C = 10$, $A + B = 7$, and $A - B = 5$, what is the value of C?

    (A) 1
    (B) 3
    (C) 6
    (D) 7
    (E) The answer cannot be determined from the given information.

14. A B C D E

14. If $5x + 15$ is greater than 20, which of the following best describes the possible values of x?

(A) x must be greater than 5
(B) x must be greater than 3
(C) x must be greater than 1
(D) x must be less than 5
(E) x must be less than 1

15. A B C D E

15. If $\frac{t^2-1}{t-1} = 2$, then what value(s) may t have?

(A) 1 only
(B) -1 only
(C) 1 or -1
(D) no values
(E) an infinite number of values

16. A B C D E

16. If $4m = 9n$, what is the value of $7m$, in terms of n?

(A) $\frac{63n}{4}$

(B) $\frac{9n}{28}$

(C) $\frac{7n}{9}$

(D) $\frac{28n}{9}$

(E) $\frac{7n}{4}$

17. A B C D E

17. The coordinates of a triangle are (0,2), (2,4), and (1,6). What is the area of the triangle in square units (to the nearest unit)?

(A) 2 square units
(B) 3 square units
(C) 4 square units
(D) 5 square units
(E) 6 square units

18. A B C D E

18. In the formula $s = \frac{1}{2}gt^2$, what is the value of t, in terms of s and g?

(A) $\frac{2s}{g}$

(B) $2\sqrt{\frac{s}{g}}$

(C) $\frac{s}{2g}$

(D) $\sqrt{\frac{s}{2g}}$

(E) $\sqrt{\frac{2s}{g}}$

19. A B C D E

19. In the triangle ABC, angle A is a 30° angle, and angle B is obtuse. If x represents the number of degrees in angle C, which of the following best represents the possible values of x?

(A) $0 < x < 60$
(B) $0 < x < 150$
(C) $60 < x < 180$
(D) $120 < x < 180$
(E) $120 < x < 150$

20. A B C D E

20. Which of the following sets of coordinates does *not* represent the vertices of an isosceles triangle?

(A) (0,2), (0,−2), (2,0)
(B) (1,3), (1,5), (3,4)
(C) (1,3), (1,7), (4,5)
(D) (2,2), (2,0), (1,1)
(E) (2,3), (2,5), (3,3)

21. A B C D E

21. If $2 < a < 5$, and $6 > b > 3$, what are the possible values of $a + b$?

(A) $a + b$ must equal 8.
(B) $a + b$ must be between 2 and 6.
(C) $a + b$ must be between 3 and 5.
(D) $a + b$ must be between 5 and 8.
(E) $a + b$ must be between 5 and 11.

22. A B C D E

22. The area of a square will be doubled if:

(A) the length of the diagonal is divided by 2.
(B) the length of the diagonal is divided by $\sqrt{2}$.
(C) the length of the diagonal is multiplied by 2.
(D) the length of the diagonal is multiplied by $\sqrt{2}$.
(E) None of the above.

23. A B C D E

23. Find the value of y that satisfies the equation $8.8y − 4 = 7.7y + 7$.

(A) 1.1
(B) 7.7
(C) 8.0
(D) 10.0
(E) 11.0

24. A B C D E

24. Which of the following is a factor of the expression $2x^2 + 1$?

(A) $x + 2$
(B) $x − 2$
(C) $x + \sqrt{2}$
(D) $x − \sqrt{2}$
(E) None of these.

25. A B C D E

25. A businessman has ten employees; his salary is equal to six times the *average* of the employees' salaries. If the eleven of them received a total of $640,000 in one year, what was the businessman's salary that year?

(A) $40,000
(B) $60,000
(C) $240,000
(D) $400,000
(E) $440,000

26. A B C D E

26. If $6x + 3 = 15$, what is the value of $12x − 3$?

(A) 21
(B) 24
(C) 28
(D) 33
(E) 36

27. If $2p + 7$ is greater than $3p - 5$, which of the following best describes the possible values of p?

(A) p must be greater than 2.
(B) p must be greater than 12.
(C) p must be less than 2.
(D) p must be less than 12.
(E) p must be greater than 2, but less than 12.

28. What is the value of q if $x^2 + qx + 1 = 0$, if $x = 1$?

(A) -2
(B) -1
(C) 0
(D) 1
(E) 2

29. What is the area (to the nearest unit) of the shaded figure in the diagram below, assuming that each of the squares has an area of 1?

(A) 12
(B) 13
(C) 14
(D) 15
(E) 16

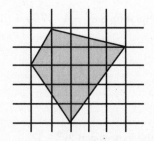

30. Which of the following statements is *false*?

(A) Any two numbers, a and b, have a sum equal to $a + b$.
(B) Any two numbers, a and b, have a product equal to $a \cdot b$.
(C) Any two numbers, a and b, have a difference equal to $a - b$.
(D) Any two numbers, a and b, have a quotient equal to $\dfrac{a}{b}$.
(E) Any two numbers, a and b, have an average equal to $\dfrac{(a + b)}{2}$.

31. If $(x - 1)(x - 2)(x^2 - 4) = 0$, what are the possible values of x?

(A) -2 only
(B) $+2$ only
(C) $-1, -2,$ or -4 only
(D) $+1, +2,$ or $+4$ only
(E) $+1, -2,$ or $+2$ only

32. If $P + Q = R$, and $P + R = 2Q$, what is the ratio of P to R?

(A) $1:1$
(B) $1:2$
(C) $2:1$
(D) $1:3$
(E) $3:1$

33. A B C D E

33. For what value(s) of r is $\dfrac{r^2 + 5r + 6}{r + 2}$ equal to 0?

    (A) −2 only
    (B) −3 only
    (C) +3 only
    (D) −2 or −3
    (E) +2 or +3

34. A B C D E

34. What is the value of $a^2b + 4ab^2 + 4b^3$, if $a = 15$ and $b = 5$?

    (A) 1,625
    (B) 2,125
    (C) 2,425
    (D) 2,725
    (E) 3,125

35. A B C D E

35. If $m + 4n = 2n + 8m$, what is the ratio of n to m?

    (A) 1 : 4
    (B) 1 : −4
    (C) −4 : 1
    (D) 2 : 7
    (E) 7 : 2

36. A B C D E

36. If the value of a lies between −5 and +2, and the value of b lies between −7 and +1, what are the possible values for the product, $a \cdot b$?

    (A) between −14 and +2
    (B) between −35 and +2
    (C) between +2 and +35
    (D) between −12 and +3
    (E) between −14 and +35

37. A B C D E

37. What is the area, in square units, of a triangle whose vertices lie on points (−5,1), (−5,4), and (2,4)?

    (A) 10.5 square units
    (B) 12.5 square units
    (C) 15.0 square units
    (D) 20.0 square units
    (E) 21.0 square units

38. A B C D E

38. If $A + B = 12$, and $B + C = 16$, what is the value of $A + C$?

    (A) −4
    (B) −28
    (C) +4
    (D) +28
    (E) The answer cannot be determined from the given information.

39. A B C D E

39. What is the solution to the equation $x^2 + 2x + 1 = 0$?

    (A) $x = 1$
    (B) $x = 0$
    (C) $x = 1$ and $x = -1$
    (D) $x = -1$
    (E) no real solutions

A B C D E
40.

40. Which of the following equations will have a vertical line as its graph?

(A) $x + y = 1$
(B) $x - y = 1$
(C) $x = 1$
(D) $y = 1$
(E) $xy = 1$

A B C D E
41.

41. For what values of x does $x^2 + 3x + 2$ equal zero?

(A) -1 only
(B) $+2$ only
(C) -1 or -2 only
(D) 1 or 2 only
(E) None of these.

A B C D E
42.

42. If $a + b$ equals 12, and $a - b$ equals 6, what is the value of b?

(A) 0
(B) 3
(C) 6
(D) 9
(E) The answer cannot be determined from the given information.

A B C D E
43.

43. For what values of m is $m^2 + 4$ equal to $4m$?

(A) -2 only
(B) 0 only
(C) $+2$ only
(D) $+4$ only
(E) more than one value

A B C D E
44.

44. If $x = 0$, $y = 2$, and $x^2yz + 3xz^2 + y^2z + 3y + 4x = 0$, what is the value of z?

(A) $-\dfrac{4}{3}$

(B) $-\dfrac{3}{2}$

(C) $+\dfrac{3}{4}$

(D) $+\dfrac{4}{3}$

(E) The answer cannot be determined from the given information.

A B C D E
45.

45. If $c + 4d = 3c - 2d$, what is the ratio of c to d?

(A) $1:3$
(B) $1:-3$
(C) $3:1$
(D) $2:3$
(E) $2:-3$

A B C D E
46.

46. If $3 < x < 7$, and $6 > x > 2$, which of the following best describes x?

(A) $2 < x < 6$
(B) $2 < x < 7$
(C) $3 < x < 6$
(D) $3 < x < 7$
(E) No value of x can satisfy both of these conditions.

47.

47. What are the coordinates of the midpoint of the line segment whose endpoints are (4,9) and (5,15)?

(A) (4,5)
(B) (5,9)
(C) (4,15)
(D) (4.5,12)
(E) (9,24)

48.

48. If $\dfrac{t^2 + 2t}{2t + 4} = \dfrac{t}{2}$, what does t equal?

(A) -2 only
(B) $+2$ only
(C) any value except $+2$
(D) any value except -2
(E) any value

49. A B C D E

49. If $x + y = 4$, and $x + z = 9$, what is the value of $(y - z)$?

(A) -5
(B) $+5$
(C) -13
(D) $+13$
(E) The answer cannot be determined from the given information.

50. A B C D E

50. Of the following statements, which are equivalent?

   I. $-3 < x < 3$

  II. $x^2 < 9$

  III. $\dfrac{1}{x} < \dfrac{1}{3}$

(A) I and II only
(B) I and III only
(C) II and III only
(D) I, II, and III
(E) None of the above.

Answer Key for Practice Test 4

1. A	**14.** C	**27.** D	**39.** D
2. A	**15.** D	**28.** A	**40.** C
3. C	**16.** A	**29.** B	**41.** C
4. C	**17.** B	**30.** D	**42.** B
5. E	**18.** E	**31.** E	**43.** C
6. D	**19.** A	**32.** D	**44.** B
7. D	**20.** E	**33.** B	**45.** C
8. D	**21.** E	**34.** E	**46.** C
9. D	**22.** D	**35.** E	**47.** D
10. C	**23.** D	**36.** E	**48.** D
11. D	**24.** E	**37.** A	**49.** A
12. B	**25.** C	**38.** E	**50.** A
13. B	**26.** A		

Answers and Solutions for Practice Test 4

1. Choice A is correct. The original equation is $3x + 9 = 21 + 7x$. First subtract 9 and $7x$ from both sides to get $-4x = 12$. Now divide both sides by the coefficient of x, -4, obtaining the solution, $x = -3$. (406)

2. Choice A is correct. Given $2z + 4 > z - 6$. Subtracting equal quantities from both sides of an inequality does not change the order of the inequality. Therefore, subtracting z and 4 from both sides gives a solution of $z > -10$. (419, 420)

3. Choice C is correct. Substitute -3 for x in the original equation to get the following:

$$a(-3)^2 + 2(-3) - 3 = 0$$
$$9a - 6 - 3 = 0$$
$$9a - 9 = 0$$
$$a = 1 \quad (406)$$

4. Choice C is correct. To find the midpoint of the line segment connecting two points, find the point whose x-coordinate is the average of the two given x-coordinates, and whose y-coordinate is the average of the two given y-coordinates. The midpoint here will be $\left(\dfrac{0+4}{2}, \dfrac{8+2}{2}\right)$, or (2,5). (412)

5. Choice E is correct. Divide both sides of the equation by πh:

$$\frac{V}{\pi h} = r^2$$

Take the square root of both sides:

$$r = \sqrt{\frac{V}{\pi h}}. \quad (408)$$

6. Choice D is correct. Factor the original expression into $x(x - 3) < 0$. In order for the product of two expressions to be less than 0 (negative), one must be positive and the other must be negative. Thus, $x < 0$ and $x - 3 > 0$; or $x > 0$ and $x - 3 < 0$. In the first case, $x < 0$ and $x > 3$. This is impossible because x cannot be less than 0 *and* greater than 3 at the same time. In the second case $x > 0$ and $x < 3$, which can be rewritten as $0 < x < 3$. (428)

7. Choice D is correct. Divide both sides of the equation $2y = 8x + 32$ by 2 to get $y = 4x + 16$. Now it is in the form of $y = mx + b$, where m is the slope of the line and b is the y-intercept. Thus the slope of the line is 4. Any line parallel to this line must have the same slope. The answer must have a slope of 4. This is the line $y = 4x + 32$. Note that all of the choices are already in the form of $y = mx + b$. (416)

8. Choice D is correct. Subtract 1.01 from both sides to give: $4.04x = 8.08$. Dividing both sides by 4.04 gives a solution of $x = 2$. (406)

9. Choice D is correct. If a product is equal to zero, then one of the factors must equal zero. If $(x + 1)(x - 2) = 0$, either $x + 1 = 0$, or $x - 2 = 0$. Solving these two equations, we see that either $x = -1$ or $x = 2$. (408, 409)

10. Choice C is correct. It is possible, but time-consuming, to examine the various ranges of x, but it will be quicker if you realize that the same factors appear, with numerical multiples, more than once in the expression. Properly factored, the expression becomes:

$$(x + 2)(2 + x)^2(2)(x + 2)(3 - x)(-2)(3 - x) =$$
$$-4(x + 2)^4(3 - x)^2$$

Since squares of real numbers can never be negative, the whole product has only one negative term and is therefore negative, except when one of the terms is zero, in which case the product is also zero. Thus, the product cannot be larger than zero for any x. (428)

11. Choice D is correct. Combine like terms on both sides of the given equations and obtain the equivalent form: $k - 9 = k + 6$. This is true for no values of k. If k is subtracted from both sides, -9 will equal 6, which is impossible. (406)

12. Choice B is correct. Substitute for the given values of a, b, and c, and obtain $p = q^2 - 2q + 1$; or, rearranging terms, $p = (q - 1)^2$. (409)

13. Choice B is correct. $A + B + C = 10$. Also, $A + B = 7$. Substitute the value 7 for the quantity $(A + B)$ in the first equation and obtain the new equation: $7 + C = 10$ or $C = 3$. $A - B = 5$ could be used with the other two equations to find the values of A and B. (406)

14. Choice C is correct. If $5x + 15 > 20$, then subtract 15 from both sides to get $5x > 5$. Now divide both sides by 5. This does not change the order of the inequality because 5 is a positive number. The solution is $x > 1$. (419, 426)

15. Choice D is correct. Factor $(t^2 - 1)$ to obtain the product $(t + 1)(t - 1)$. For any value of t, except 1, the equation is equivalent to $(t + 1) = 2$, or $t = 1$. One is the only possible value of t. However this value is not possible as $t - 1$ would equal 0, and the quotient $\dfrac{t^2 - 1}{t - 1}$ would not be defined. (404, 409)

16. Choice A is correct. If $4m = 9n$, then $m = \dfrac{9n}{4}$. Multiplying both sides of the equation by 7, we obtain: $7m = \dfrac{63n}{4}$. (403)

17. Choice B is correct. As the diagram shows, the easiest way to calculate the area of this triangle is to start with the area of the enclosing rectangle and subtract the three shaded triangles.

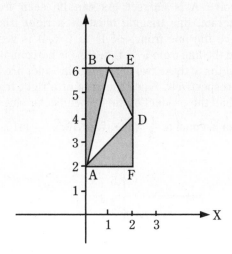

The area of the rectangle $ABEF = (2)(4) = 8$ square units.

The area of the triangle $ABC = \dfrac{1}{2}(1)(4) = 2$ square units.

The area of the triangle $CDE = \dfrac{1}{2}(1)(2) = 1$ square unit.

The area of the triangle $ADF = \dfrac{1}{2}(2)(2) = 2$ square units.

Thus the area of the triangle $ACD = 8 - 5 = 3$ square units. (418)

18. Choice E is correct. Since $s = \dfrac{1}{2}gt^2$, divide both sides of the equation by $\dfrac{1}{2}g$ to obtain the form, $\dfrac{2s}{g} = t^2$. Then, after taking the square roots, $t = \sqrt{\dfrac{2s}{g}}$. (403)

19. Choice A is correct. The sum of the three angles of a triangle must be 180°. Since angle A is 30°, and angle B is between 90° and 180° (it is obtuse), their sum is greater than 120° and less than 180° (the sum of all three angles is 180°). Their sum subtracted from the total of 180° gives a third angle greater than zero, but less than 60°. (419)

20. Choice E is correct. An isosceles triangle has two equal sides. To find the length of the sides, we use the distance formula, $\sqrt{(x_2 - x_1)^2 + (y_2 - y_1)^2}$. In the first case the lengths of the sides are 4, $2\sqrt{2}$ and $2\sqrt{2}$. Thus two sides have the same length, and it is an isosceles triangle. The only set of points that is not an isosceles triangle is the last one. (411)

21. Choice E is correct. The smallest possible value of a is greater than 2, and the smallest possible value of b is greater than 3, so the smallest possible value of $a + b$ must be greater than $2 + 3 = 5$. Similarly, the largest values of a and b are less than 5 and 6, respectively, so the largest possible value of $a + b$ is less than 11. Therefore, the sum must be between 5 and 11. (419)

22. Choice D is correct. If the sides of the original square are each equal to s, then the area of the square is s^2, and the diagonal is $s\sqrt{2}$. Now, a new square, with an area of $2s^2$, must have a side of $s\sqrt{2}$. Thus, the diagonal is $2s$, which is $\sqrt{2}$ times the original length of the diagonal. (302, 303)

23. Choice D is correct. First place all of the variable terms on one side and all of the numerical terms on the other side. Subtracting $7.7y$ and adding 4 to both sides of the equation gives $1.1y = 11$. Now divide both sides by 1.1 to solve for $y = 10$. (406)

24. Choice E is correct. To determine whether an expression is a factor of another expression, give the variable a specific value in both expressions. An expression divided by its factor will be a whole number. If we give x the value 0, then the expression $2x^2 + 1$ has the value of 1. $x + 2$ then has the value of 2. 1 is not divisible by 2, so the first choice is not a factor. The next choice has the value of -2, also not a factor of 1. Similarly, $x + \sqrt{2}$ and $x - \sqrt{2}$ take on the values of $\sqrt{2}$ and $-\sqrt{2}$, respectively, when $x = 0$, and are not factors of $2x^2 + 1$. Therefore, the correct choice is (E). (409)

25. Choice C is correct. Let x equal the average salary of the employees. Then the employees receive a total of $10x$ dollars, and the businessman receives six times the average, or $6x$. Together, the eleven of them receive a total of $10x + 6x = 16x$, which equals $640,000. Thus, x equals $40,000, and the businessman's salary is $6x$, or $240,000. (406)

26. Choice A is correct. $6x + 3 = 15$; therefore $6x = 12$ and $x = 2$. Substituting $x = 2$ into the expression $12x - 3$ gives $24 - 3$ which equals 21. (406)

27. Choice D is correct. $2p + 7 > 3p - 5$. To both sides of the equation add 5 and subtract $2p$, obtaining $12 > p$. Thus, p is less than 12. (419, 426)

28. Choice A is correct. Substituting 1 for x in the given equation obtains $1 + q + 1 = 0$, or $q + 2 = 0$. This is solved only for $q = -2$. (406)

29. Choice B is correct.

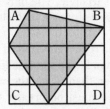

The area of the shaded figure can most easily be found by taking the area of the square surrounding it (25), and subtracting the areas of the four triangles marked A (1), B (2), C (3), and D (6), leaving an area of $25 - (1 + 2 + 3 + 6) = 13$ square units. (418)

30. Choice D is correct. If the number b is equal to zero, the quotient $\frac{a}{b}$ is not defined. For all other pairs, all five statements are true. (401–405)

31. Choice E is correct. If a product equals zero, one of the factors must be equal to zero also. Thus, either $x - 1 = 0$, or $x - 2 = 0$, or $x^2 - 4 = 0$. The possible solutions, therefore, are $x = 1$, $x = 2$, and $x = -2$. (408)

32. Choice D is correct. Solve the equation $P + Q = R$, for Q (the variable we wish to eliminate), to get $Q = R - P$. Substituting this for Q in the second equation yields $P + R = 2(R - P) = 2R - 2P$, or $3P = R$. Therefore, the ratio of P to R is $\frac{P}{R}$, or $\frac{1}{3}$. (406)

33. Choice B is correct. The fraction in question will equal zero if the numerator equals zero, and the denominator is nonzero. The expression $r^2 + 5r + 6$ can be factored into $(r + 2)(r + 3)$. As long as r is not equal to -2 the equation is defined, and $r + 2$ can be canceled in the original equation to yield $r + 3 = 0$, or $r = -3$. For r equals -2 the denominator is equal to zero, and the fraction in the original equation is not defined. (404, 409)

34. Choice E is correct. This problem can be shortened considerably by factoring the expression $a^2b + 4ab^2 + 4b^3$ into the product $(b)(a + 2b)^2$. Now, since $b = 5$, and $(a + 2b) = 25$, our product equals $5 \times 25 \times 25$, or 3,125. (409)

35. Choice E is correct. Subtract $m + 2n$ from both sides of the given equation and obtain the equivalent form, $2n = 7m$. Dividing this equation by $2m$ gives $\frac{n}{m} = \frac{7}{2}$, the ratio of n to m. (406)

36. Choice E is correct. The product will be positive in the case: a positive and b positive, or a negative and b negative; and the product will be negative in the case: a positive and b negative, or a negative and b positive. Thus, the positive products must be $(+2)(+1)$ and $(-5)(-7)$. The largest positive value is 35. Similarly, the negative products are $(-5)(+1)$ and $(+2)(-7)$; and the most negative value that can be obtained is -14. Thus, the product falls between -14 and 35. (419)

37. Choice A is correct. As can be seen from a diagram, this triangle must be a right triangle, since the line from $(-5,1)$ to $(-5,4)$ is vertical, and the line from $(-5,4)$ to $(2,4)$ is horizontal. The lengths of these two perpendicular sides are 3 and 7, respectively. Since the area of a right triangle is half the product of the perpendicular sides, the area is equal to $\frac{1}{2} \times 3 \times 7$, or 10.5. (410, 418)

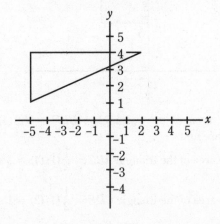

38. Choice E is correct. Solving the first equation for A gives $A = 12 - B$. Solving the second equation for C gives $C = 16 - B$. Thus, the sum $A + C$ is equal to $28 - 2B$. There is nothing to determine the value of B, so the sum of A and C is not determined from the information given. (406)

39. Choice D is correct. Factor $x^2 + 2x + 1$ to get $(x + 1)(x + 1) = 0$. Thus $x + 1 = 0$, so $x = -1$. (409)

40. Choice C is correct. If we graph the five choices we will get:

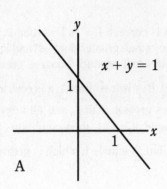

A

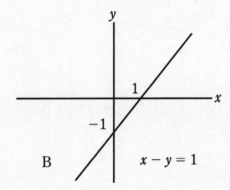

B

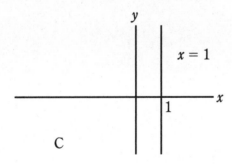

C

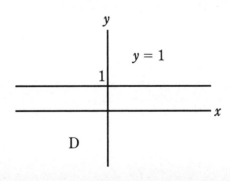

D

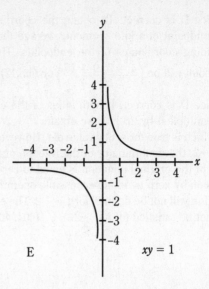

E

The only choice that is a vertical line is $x = 1$.

(413)

41. Choice C is correct. The factors of $x^2 + 3x + 2$ are $(x + 1)$ and $(x + 2)$. Either $x + 1 = 0$, or $x + 2 = 0$. x may equal either -1 or -2. (408)

42. Choice B is correct. $a + b = 12$ and $a - b = 6$. Rewrite these equations as $a = 12 - b$ and $a = 6 + b$. $12 - b$ and $6 + b$ are both equal to a. Or, $12 - b = 6 + b$. Thus, $6 = 2b$ and $b = 3$. (407)

43. Choice C is correct. Let $m^2 + 4 = 4m$. Subtracting $4m$ from both sides yields $m^2 - 4m + 4 = 0$. Factor to get the following equation: $(m - 2)^2 = 0$. Thus, $m = 2$ is the only solution. (408)

44. Choice B is correct. Substitute for the given values of x and y, obtaining: $(0)^2 (2)(z) + (3)(0)(z)^2 + (2)^2(z) + (3)(2) + (4)(0) = 0$. Perform the indicated multiplications, and combine terms. $0(z) + 0(z^2) + 4z + 6 + 0 = 4z + 6 = 0$. This equation has $z = -\dfrac{3}{2}$ as its only solution. (406)

45. Choice C is correct. $c + 4d = 3c - 2d$. Add $2d - c$ to each side and get $6d = 2c$. (Be especially careful about your signs here.) Dividing by $2d$: $\dfrac{c}{d} = \dfrac{6}{2} = \dfrac{3}{1}$. Thus, $c : d = 3 : 1$. (406)

46. Choice C is correct. x must be greater than 3, less than 7, greater than 2, and less than 6. These conditions can be reduced as follows: If x is less than 6 it is also less than 7. Similarly, x must be greater than 3, which automatically makes it greater than 2. Thus, x must be greater than 3 *and* less than 6.

(419)

47. Choice D is correct. To obtain the coordinates of the midpoint of a line segment, average the corresponding coordinates of the endpoints. Thus, the midpoint will be $\left(\dfrac{4+5}{2}, \dfrac{9+15}{2}\right)$ or (4.5,12). (412)

48. Choice D is correct. If both sides of the equation are multiplied by $2t + 4$, we obtain: $t^2 + 2t = t^2 + 2t$, which is true for every value of t. However, when $t = -2$, the denominator of the fraction on the left side of the original equation is equal to zero. Since division by zero is not a permissible operation, this fraction will not be defined for $t = -2$. The equation cannot be satisfied for $t = -2$.   (404, 406, 409)

49. Choice A is correct. If we subtract the second of our equations from the first, we will be left with the following: $(x + y) - (x + z) = 4 - 9$, or $y - z = -5$.
(402)

50. Choice A is correct. If x^2 is less than 9, then x may take on any value greater than -3 and less than $+3$; other values will produce squares greater than or equal to 9. If $\dfrac{1}{x}$ is less than $\dfrac{1}{3}$, x is restricted to positive values greater than 3, and all negative values. For example, if $x = 1$, then conditions I and II are satisfied, but $\dfrac{1}{x}$ equals 1, which is greater than $\dfrac{1}{3}$.
(419)

MATH REFRESHER
SESSION 5

Geometry Problems

Basic Definitions

500. *Plane geometry* deals with points and lines. A point has no dimensions and is generally represented by a dot (·). A line has no thickness, but it does have length. Lines can be straight or curved, but here it will be assumed that a line is straight unless otherwise indicated. All lines have infinite length. Part of a line that has a finite length is called a line segment.

> Remember that the **distance** between two parallel lines or from a point to a line always means the perpendicular distance. Thus, the distance between the two parallel lines pictured below in the diagram to the left is line *A*, as this is the only perpendicular line. Also, as shown in the diagram to the right, the distance from a line to a point is the perpendicular from the point to the line. Thus, *AB* is the distance from point *A* to the line segment *CBD*.

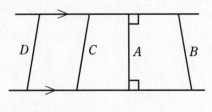

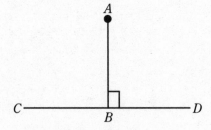

501. *Angles.* An angle is formed when two lines intersect at a point.

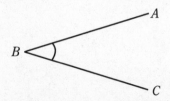

Angle *B*, angle *ABC*, ∠*B*, ∠*ABC* are all possible names for the angle shown.

The measure of the angle is given in degrees. If the sides of the angle form a straight line, then the angle is said to be a straight angle and has 180°. A circle has 360°, and a straight angle is a turning through a half circle. All other angles are either greater or less than 180°.

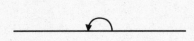
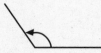
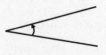

Angles are classified in different ways:
An *acute* angle has less than 90°.

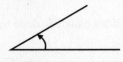

A *right* angle has exactly 90°.

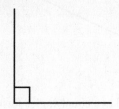

In the diagram, the small square in the corner of the angle indicates a right angle (90°).

An *obtuse* angle has between 90° and 180°.

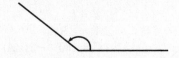

A *straight* angle has exactly 180°.

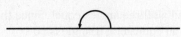

A *reflex* angle has between 180° and 360°.

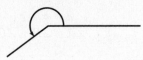

502. Two angles are *complementary* if their sum is 90°. For example, an angle of 30° and an angle of 60° are complementary. Two angles are *supplementary* if their sum is 180°. If one angle is 82°, then its supplement is 98°.

503. *Vertical angles.* These are pairs of opposite angles formed by the intersection of two straight lines. Vertical angles are always equal to each other.

   Example: In the diagram shown, angles *AEC* and *BED* are equal because they are vertical angles. For the same reason, angles *AED* and *BEC* are equal.

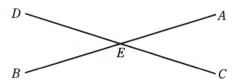

504. When two parallel lines are crossed by a third straight line (called a *transversal*), then all the acute angles formed are equal, and all of the obtuse angles are equal.

   Example: In the diagram below, angles 1, 4, 5, and 8 are all equal. Angles 2, 3, 6, and 7 are also equal.

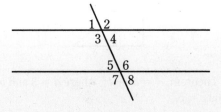

Triangles

505. *Triangles.* A triangle is a closed figure with three sides, each side being a line segment. The sum of the angles of a triangle is *always* 180°.

506. *Scalene triangles* are triangles with no two sides equal. Scalene triangles also have no two angles equal.

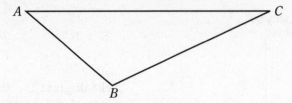

507. *Isosceles triangles* have two equal sides and two equal angles formed by the equal sides and the unequal side. See the figure below.

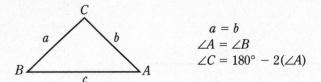

$$a = b$$
$$\angle A = \angle B$$
$$\angle C = 180° - 2(\angle A)$$

508. *Equilateral triangles* have all three sides and all three angles equal. Since the sum of the three angles of a triangle is 180°, each angle of an equilateral triangle is 60°.

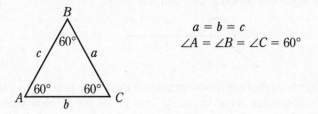

$$a = b = c$$
$$\angle A = \angle B = \angle C = 60°$$

509. A *right triangle* has one angle equal to a right angle (90°). The sum of the other two angles of a right triangle is, therefore, 90°. The most important relationship in a right triangle is the Pythagorean Theorem. It states that $c^2 = a^2 + b^2$, where c, the hypotenuse, is the length of the side opposite the right angle, and a and b are the lengths of the other two sides. Recall that this was discussed in Section 317.

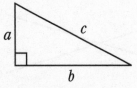

Example: If the two sides of a right triangle adjacent to the right angle are 3 inches and 4 inches respectively, find the length of the side opposite the right angle.

Solution:

Use the Pythagorean Theorem, $c^2 = a^2 + b^2$, where $a = 3$ and $b = 4$. Then, $c = 3^2 + 4^2$ or $c^2 = 9 + 16 = 25$. Thus $c = 5$.

Certain sets of integers will always fit the formula $c^2 = a^2 + b^2$. These integers can always represent the lengths of the sides of a right triangle. For example, a triangle whose sides are 3, 4, and 5 will always be a right triangle. Further examples are 5, 12, and 13, and 8, 15, and 17. Any multiples of these numbers also satisfy this formula. For example, 6, 8, and 10; 9, 12, and 15; 10, 24, and 26; 24, 45, and 51, etc.

Properties of Triangles

510. Two triangles are said to be *similar* (having the same shape) if their corresponding angles are equal. The sides of similar triangles are in the same proportion. The two triangles below are similar because they have the same corresponding angles.

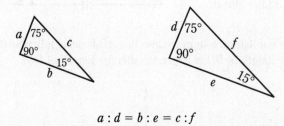

$$a : d = b : e = c : f$$

Example: Two triangles both have angles of 30°, 70°, and 80°. If the sides of the triangles are as indicated below, find the length of side x.

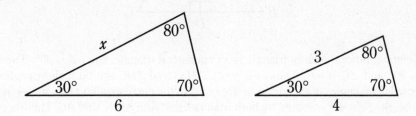

Solution: The two triangles are similar because they have the same corresponding angles. The corresponding sides of similar triangles are in proportion, so $x : 3 = 6 : 4$. This can be rewritten as $\frac{x}{3} = \frac{6}{4}$. Multiplying both sides by 3 gives $x = \frac{18}{4}$, or $x = 4\frac{1}{2}$.

511. Two triangles are *congruent* (*identical* in shape and size) if any one of the following conditions is met:

1. Each side of the first triangle equals the corresponding side of the second triangle.
2. Two sides of the first triangle equal the corresponding sides of the second triangle, and their included angles are equal. The included angle is formed by the two sides of the triangle.
3. Two angles of the first triangle equal the corresponding angles of the second triangle, and any pair of corresponding sides are equal.

Example: Triangles *ABC* and *DEF* in the following diagrams are congruent if any one of the following conditions can be met:

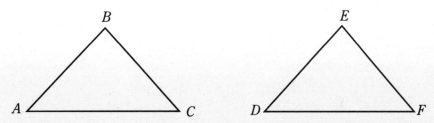

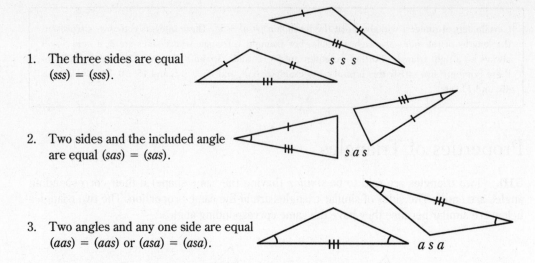

1. The three sides are equal
   (*sss*) = (*sss*).

2. Two sides and the included angle
   are equal (*sas*) = (*sas*).

3. Two angles and any one side are equal
   (*aas*) = (*aas*) or (*asa*) = (*asa*).

Example: In the equilateral triangle below, line *AD* is perpendicular (forms a right angle) to side *BC*. If the length of *BD* is 5 feet, what is the length of *DC*?

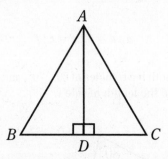

Solution: Since the large triangle is an equilateral triangle, each ∠ is 60°. Therefore ∠*B* is 60° and ∠*C* is 60°. Thus, ∠*B* = ∠*C*. *ADB* and *ADC* are both right angles and are equal. Two angles of each triangle are equal to the corresponding two angles of the other triangle. Side *AD* is shared by both triangles and side *AB* = side *AC*. Thus, according to condition 3 in Section 511, the two triangles are congruent. Then *BD* = *DC* and, since *BD* is 5 feet, *DC* is 5 feet.

512. The *medians* of a triangle are the lines drawn from each vertex to the midpoint of its opposite side. The medians of a triangle cross at a point that divides each median into two parts: one part of one-third the length of the median and the other part of two-thirds the length.

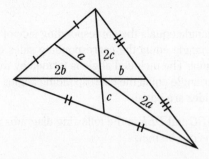

513. The *angle bisectors* of a triangle are the lines that divide each angle of the triangle into two equal parts. These lines meet in a point that is the center of a circle inscribed in the triangle.

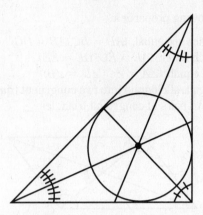

514. The *altitudes* of the triangle are lines drawn from the vertices perpendicular to the opposite sides. The lengths of these lines are useful in calculating the area of the triangle since the area of the triangle is $\frac{1}{2}$ (base) (height) and the height is identical to the altitude.

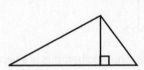 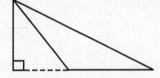

515. The *perpendicular bisectors* of the triangle are the lines that bisect and are perpendicular to each of the three sides. The point where these lines meet is the center of the circumscribed circle.

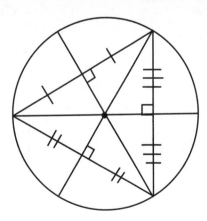

516. The sum of any two sides of a triangle is greater than the third side.

Example: If the three sides of a triangle are 4, 2, and x, then what is known about the value of x?

Solution: Since the sum of two sides of a triangle is always greater than the third side, then $4 + 2 > x$, $4 + x > 2$, and $2 + x > 4$. These three inequalities can be rewritten as $6 > x$, $x > -2$, and $x > 2$. For x to be greater than -2 and 2, it must be greater than 2. Thus, the values of x are $2 < x < 6$.

Four-Sided Figures

517. A *parallelogram* is a four-sided figure with each pair of opposite sides parallel.

A parallelogram has the following properties:

1. Each pair of opposite sides are equal. ($AD = BC, AB = DC$)
2. The diagonals bisect each other. ($AE = EC, DE = EB$)
3. The opposite angles are equal. ($\angle A = \angle C, \angle D = \angle B$)
4. One diagonal divides the parallelogram into two congruent triangles. Two diagonals divide the parallelogram into two pairs of congruent triangles.

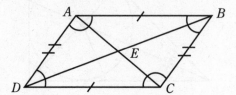

518. A *rectangle* is a parallelogram in which all the angles are right angles. Since a rectangle is a parallelogram, all of the laws that apply to a parallelogram apply to a rectangle. In addition, the diagonals of a rectangle are equal.

$AC = BD$

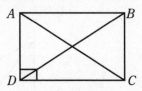

519. A *rhombus* is a parallelogram with four equal sides. Since a rhombus is a parallelogram, all of the laws that apply to a parallelogram apply to a rhombus. In addition, the diagonals of a rhombus are perpendicular to each other and bisect the vertex angles.

$\angle DAC = \angle BAC = \angle DCA = \angle BCA$
$\angle ADB = \angle CDB = \angle ABD = \angle CBD$
AC is perpendicular to DB

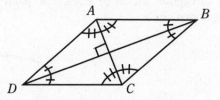

520. A *square* is a rectangular rhombus. Thus the square has the following properties:

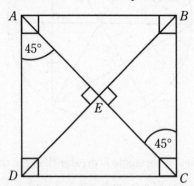

1. All four sides are equal. ($AB = BC = CD = DA$)
2. Opposite pairs of sides are parallel. ($AD \| BC, AB \| DC$)
3. Diagonals are equal, are perpendicular to each other, and bisect each other. ($AC = BD$, $AC \perp BD, AE = EC = DE = EB$)
4. All the angles are right angles (90°). ($\angle A = \angle B = \angle C = \angle D = 90°$)
5. Diagonals intersect the vertices at 45°. ($\angle DAC = \angle BAC = 45°$, and similarly for the other 3 vertices.)

Many-Sided Figures

521. A *polygon* is a closed plane figure whose sides are straight lines. The sum of the angles in any polygon is equal to $180(n - 2)°$, where n is the number of sides. Thus, in a polygon of 3 sides (a triangle), the sum of the angles is $180(3 - 2)°$, or $180°$.

522. A *regular polygon* is a polygon all of whose sides are equal and all of whose angles are equal. These polygons have special properties:

1. A regular polygon can be inscribed in a circle and can be circumscribed about another circle. For example, a hexagon is inscribed in a circle in the diagram below.

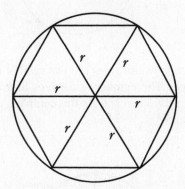

2. Each angle of a regular polygon is equal to the sum of the angles divided by the number of sides, $\dfrac{180(n - 2)°}{n}$. Thus, a square, which is a regular polygon of 4 sides, has each angle equal to $\dfrac{180(4 - 2)°}{4}$ or $90°$.

523. An important regular polygon is the *hexagon*. The diagonals of a regular hexagon divide it into 6 equilateral triangles, the sides of which are equal to the sides of the hexagon. If a hexagon is inscribed in a circle, the length of each side is equal to the length of the radius of the circle. (See diagram of hexagon above.)

Circles

524. A *circle* (also see Section 310) is a set of points equidistant from a given point, the *center*. The distance from the center to the circle is the *radius*. Any line that connects two points on the circle is a *chord*. A chord through the center of the circle is a *diameter*. On the circle below, O is the center, line segment OF is a radius, DE is a diameter, and AC is a chord.

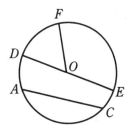

The length of the diameter of a circle is twice the length of the radius. The circumference (distance around circle) is 2π times the length of the radius. π is a constant approximately equal to $\dfrac{22}{7}$ or 3.14. The formula for the circumference of a circle is $C = 2\pi r$, where C = circumference and r = radius.

525. A *tangent* to a circle is a line that is perpendicular to a radius and that passes through only one point of the circle. In the diagram below, *AB* is a tangent.

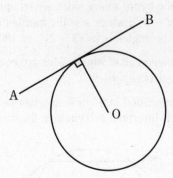

526. A *central angle* is an angle whose sides are two radii of the circle. The vertex of this angle is the center of the circle. The number of degrees in a central angle is equal to the amount of arc length that the radii intercept. As the complete circumference has 360°, any other arc lengths are less than 360°.

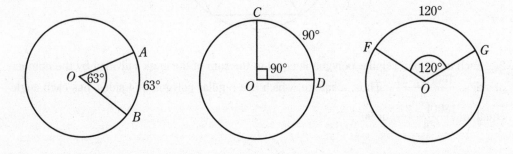

Angles *AOB*, *COD*, and *FOG* are all central angles.

527. An *inscribed angle* of a circle is an angle whose sides are two chords. The vertex of the angle lies on the circumference of the circle. The number of degrees in the inscribed angle is equal to one-half the intercepted arc.

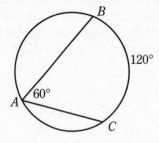

∠*BAC* is an inscribed angle.

528. An angle inscribed in a semicircle (one-half of a circle) is always a right angle. ∠*ABC* and ∠*ADC* are inscribed in semicircles *AOCB* and *AOCD*, respectively, and are thus right angles.

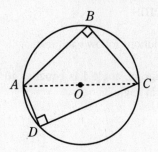

529. Two tangents to a circle from the same point outside of the circle are always equal.

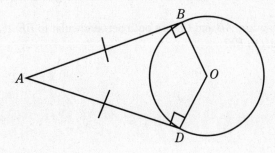

Tangents *AB* and *AD* are equal.

Practice Test 5

Geometry Problems

Correct answers and solutions follow each test.

1. In the following diagram, angle 1 is equal to 40°, and angle 2 is equal to 150°. What is the number of degrees in angle 3?

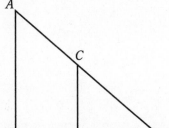

(A) 70°
(B) 90°
(C) 110°
(D) 190°
(E) The answer cannot be determined from the given information.

2. In this diagram, *AB* and *CD* are both perpendicular to *BE*. If *EC* = 5, and *CD* = 4, what is the ratio of *AB* to *BE*?

(A) 1 : 1
(B) 4 : 3
(C) 5 : 4
(D) 5 : 3
(E) None of these.

3. In triangle *PQR*, *PR* = 7.0, and *PQ* = 4.5. Which of the following cannot possibly represent the length of *QR*?

(A) 2.0
(B) 3.0
(C) 3.5
(D) 4.5
(E) 5.0

4. In this diagram, *AB* = *AC*, and *BD* = *CD*. Which of the following statements is true?

(A) *BE* = *EC*.
(B) *AD* is perpendicular to *BC*.
(C) Triangles *BDE* and *CDE* are congruent.
(D) Angle *ABD* equals angle *ACD*.
(E) All of these.

5. In the following diagram, if *BC* = *CD* = *BD* = 1, and angle *ADC* is a right angle, what is the perimeter of triangle *ABD*?

(A) 3
(B) 2 + √2
(C) 2 + √3
(D) 3 + √3
(E) 4

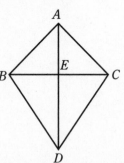

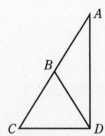

6. A B C D E

6. In this diagram, if *PQRS* is a parallelogram, which of the following can be deduced?

    I. $QT + PT = RT + ST$
    II. *QS* is perpendicular to *PR*
    III. The area of the shaded portion is exactly three times the area of triangle *QRT*.

(A) I only
(B) I and II only
(C) II only
(D) I and III only
(E) I, II, and III

7. A B C D E

7. James lives on the corner of a rectangular field that measures 120 yards by 160 yards. If he wants to walk to the opposite corner, he can either travel along the perimeter of the field or cut directly across in a straight line. How many yards does he save by taking the direct route? (Express to the nearest ten yards.)

(A) 40 yards
(B) 60 yards
(C) 80 yards
(D) 100 yards
(E) 110 yards

8. A B C D E

8. In a square, the perimeter is how many times the length of the diagonal?

(A) $\dfrac{\sqrt{2}}{2}$

(B) $\sqrt{2}$

(C) 2

(D) $2\sqrt{2}$

(E) 4

9. A B C D E

9. How many degrees are there in the angle formed by two adjacent sides of a regular nonagon (nine-sided polygon)?

(A) 40°
(B) 70°
(C) 105°
(D) 120°
(E) 140°

10. A B C D E

10. In the diagram below, $AB = CD$. From this we can deduce that:

(A) *AB* is parallel to *CD*.
(B) *AB* is perpendicular to *BD*.
(C) $AC = BD$.
(D) Angle *ABD* equals angle *BDC*.
(E) Triangle *ABD* is congruent to triangle *ACD*.

(Note: Figure is not drawn to scale.)

11. A B C D E

11. If two lines, *AB* and *CD*, intersect at a point *E*, which of the following statements is *not* true?

(A) Angle *AEB* equals angle *CED*.
(B) Angles *AEC* and *BEC* are complementary.
(C) Angle *CED* is a straight angle.
(D) Angle *AEC* equals angle *BED*.
(E) Angle *BED* plus angle *AED* equals 180 degrees.

12. A B C D E

12. In the following diagram, $AC = CE$ and $BD = DE$. Which of these statements is (are) true?

    I. *AB* is twice as long as *CD*.
    II. *AB* is parallel to *CD*.
    III. Triangle *AEB* is similar to triangle *CED*.

    (A) I only
    (B) II and III only
    (C) I and III only
    (D) I, II, and III
    (E) None of these.

13. A B C D E

13. In triangle *ABC,* angle *A* is obtuse, and angle *B* equals 30°. Which of the following statements *best* describes angle *C*?

    (A) Angle *C* must be less than 60°.
    (B) Angle *C* must be less than or equal to 60°.
    (C) Angle *C* must be equal to 60°.
    (D) Angle *C* must be greater than or equal to 60°.
    (E) Angle *C* must be greater than 60°.

14. A B C D E

14. In this diagram, *ABCD* is a parallelogram, and *BFDE* is a square. If $AB = 20$ and $CF = 16$, what is the perimeter of the parallelogram *ABCD*?

    (A) 72
    (B) 78
    (C) 86
    (D) 92
    (E) 96

15. A B C D E

15. The hypotenuse of a right triangle is exactly twice as long as the shorter leg. What is the number of degrees in the smallest angle of the triangle?

    (A) 30°
    (B) 45°
    (C) 60°
    (D) 90°
    (E) The answer cannot be determined from the given information.

16. A B C D E

16. The legs of an isosceles triangle are equal to 17 inches each. If the altitude to the base is 8 inches long, how long is the base of the triangle?

    (A) 15 inches
    (B) 20 inches
    (C) 24 inches
    (D) 25 inches
    (E) 30 inches

17. A B C D E

17. The perimeter of a right triangle is 18 inches. If the midpoints of the three sides are joined by line segments, they form another triangle. What is the perimeter of this new triangle?

    (A) 3 inches
    (B) 6 inches
    (C) 9 inches
    (D) 12 inches
    (E) The answer cannot be determined from the given information.

18. A B C D E

18. If the diagonals of a square divide it into four triangles, the triangles *cannot* be

(A) right triangles
(B) isosceles triangles
(C) similar triangles
(D) equilateral triangles
(E) equal in area

19. A B C D E

19. In the diagram below, *ABCDEF* is a regular hexagon. How many degrees are there in angle *ADC*?

(A) 45°
(B) 60°
(C) 75°
(D) 90°
(E) None of these.

20. A B C D E

20. This diagram depicts a rectangle inscribed in a circle. If the measurements of the rectangle are 10″ × 14″, what is the area of the circle?

(A) 74π
(B) 92π
(C) 144π
(D) 196π
(E) 296π

21. A B C D E

21. How many degrees are included between the hands of a clock at 5:00?

(A) 50°
(B) 60°
(C) 75°
(D) 120°
(E) 150°

22. A B C D E

22. *ABCD* is a square. If the midpoints of the four sides are joined to form a new square, the perimeter of the old square is how many times the perimeter of the new square?

(A) 1
(B) $\sqrt{2}$
(C) 2
(D) $2\sqrt{2}$
(E) 4

23. A B C D E

23. Angles *A* and *B* of triangle *ABC* are both acute angles. Which of the following *best* describes angle *C*?

(A) Angle *C* is between 0° and 180°.
(B) Angle *C* is between 0° and 90°.
(C) Angle *C* is between 60° and 180°.
(D) Angle *C* is between 60° and 120°.
(E) Angle *C* is between 60° and 90°.

24. A B C D E

24. The angles of a quadrilateral are in the ratio $1:2:3:4$. What is the number of degrees in the largest angle?

(A) 72
(B) 96
(C) 120
(D) 144
(E) 150

25. A B C D E

25. *ABCD* is a rectangle; the diagonals *AC* and *BD* intersect at *E*. Which of the following statements is *not necessarily true*?

(A) $AE = BE$
(B) Angle *AEB* equals angle *CED*.
(C) *AE* is perpendicular to *BD*.
(D) Triangles *AED* and *AEB* are equal in area.
(E) Angle *BAC* equals angle *BDC*.

26. A B C D E

26. City A is 200 miles from City B, and City B is 400 miles from City C. Which of the following best describes the distance between City A and City C? (Note: The cities A, B, and C do *not* all lie on a straight line.)

(A) It must be greater than zero.
(B) It must be greater than 200 miles.
(C) It must be less than 600 miles and greater than zero.
(D) It must be less than 600 miles and greater than 200.
(E) It must be exactly 400 miles.

27. A B C D E

27. At 7:30, how many degrees are included between the hands of a clock?

(A) $15°$
(B) $30°$
(C) $45°$
(D) $60°$
(E) $75°$

28. A B C D E

28. If a ship is sailing in a northerly direction and then turns to the right until it is sailing in a southwesterly direction, it has gone through a rotation of:

(A) $45°$
(B) $90°$
(C) $135°$
(D) $180°$
(E) $225°$

29. A B C D E

29. x, y, and z are the angles of a triangle. If $x = 2y$, and $y = z + 30°$, how many degrees are there in angle x?

(A) $22.5°$
(B) $37.5°$
(C) $52.5°$
(D) $90.0°$
(E) $105.0°$

30. A B C D E

30. In the diagram shown, *AB* is parallel to *CD*. Which of the following statements is *not necessarily true*?

(A) $\angle 1 + \angle 2 = 180°$
(B) $\angle 4 = \angle 7$
(C) $\angle 5 + \angle 8 + \angle 2 + \angle 4 = 360°$
(D) $\angle 2 + \angle 3 = 180°$
(E) $\angle 2 = \angle 6$

31. A B C D E

31. What is the ratio of the diagonal of a square to the hypotenuse of the isosceles right triangle having the same area?

(A) $1:2$
(B) $1:\sqrt{2}$
(C) $1:1$
(D) $\sqrt{2}:1$
(E) $2:1$

32. A B C D E

32. How many degrees are there between two adjacent sides of a regular ten-sided figure?

(A) $36°$
(B) $72°$
(C) $120°$
(D) $144°$
(E) $154°$

33. A B C D E

33. Which of the following sets of numbers *cannot* represent the lengths of the sides of a right triangle?

(A) 5, 12, 13
(B) 4.2, 5.6, 7
(C) 9, 28, 35
(D) 16, 30, 34
(E) 7.5, 18, 19.5

34. A B C D E

34. How many degrees are there in the angle that is its own supplement?

(A) $30°$
(B) $45°$
(C) $60°$
(D) $90°$
(E) $180°$

35. A B C D E

35. If a central angle of $45°$ intersects an arc 6 inches long on the circumference of a circle, what is the radius of the circle?

(A) $\dfrac{24}{\pi}$ inches

(B) $\dfrac{48}{\pi}$ inches

(C) 6π inches
(D) 24 inches
(E) 48 inches

36. A B C D E

36. What is the length of the line segment connecting the two most distant vertices of a 1-inch cube?

(A) 1 inch
(B) $\sqrt{2}$ inches
(C) $\sqrt{3}$ inches
(D) $\sqrt{5}$ inches
(E) $\sqrt{6}$ inches

37. A B C D E

37. Through how many degrees does the hour hand of a clock move in 70 minutes?

(A) $35°$
(B) $60°$
(C) $80°$
(D) $90°$
(E) $120°$

38. A B C D E

38. In the diagram pictured below, *AB* is tangent to circle *O* at point *A*. *CD* is perpendicular to *OA* at *C*. Which of the following statements is (are) true?

    I. Triangles *ODC* and *OBA* are similar.
   II. *OA* : *CD* = *OB* : *AB*
  III. *AB* is twice as long as *CD*.

  (A) I only
  (B) III only
  (C) I and II only
  (D) II and III only
  (E) None of the above combinations.

39. A B C D E

39. The three angles of triangle *ABC* are in the ratio 1 : 2 : 6. How many degrees are in the largest angle?

  (A) 45°
  (B) 90°
  (C) 120°
  (D) 135°
  (E) 160°

40. A B C D E

40. In this diagram, *AB* = *AC*, angle *A* = 40°, and *BD* is perpendicular to *AC* at *D*. How many degrees are there in angle *DBC* ?

  (A) 20°
  (B) 40°
  (C) 50°
  (D) 70°
  (E) None of these.

41. A B C D E

41. If the line *AB* intersects the line *CD* at point *E*, which of the following pairs of angles need *not* be equal?

  (A) ∠*AEB* and ∠*CED*
  (B) ∠*AEC* and ∠*BED*
  (C) ∠*AED* and ∠*CEA*
  (D) ∠*BEC* and ∠*DEA*
  (E) ∠*DEC* and ∠*BEA*

42. A B C D E

42. All right isosceles triangles must be

  (A) similar
  (B) congruent
  (C) equilateral
  (D) equal in area
  (E) None of these.

43. A B C D E

43. What is the area of a triangle whose sides are 10 inches, 13 inches, and 13 inches?

  (A) 39 square inches
  (B) 52 square inches
  (C) 60 square inches
  (D) 65 square inches
  (E) The answer cannot be determined from the given information.

44. If each side of an equilateral triangle is 2 inches long, what is the triangle's altitude?

(A) 1 inch

(B) $\sqrt{2}$ inches

(C) $\sqrt{3}$ inches

(D) 2 inches

(E) $\sqrt{5}$ inches

45. In the parallelogram ABCD, diagonals AC and BD intersect at E. Which of the following must be true?

(A) $\angle AED = \angle BEC$
(B) $AE = EC$
(C) $\angle BDC = \angle DBA$
(D) Two of the above must be true.
(E) All three of the statements must be true.

46. If ABCD is a square, and diagonals AC and BD intersect at point E, how many isosceles right triangles are there in the figure?

(A) 4
(B) 5
(C) 6
(D) 7
(E) 8

47. How many degrees are there in each angle of a regular hexagon?

(A) 60°
(B) 90°
(C) 108°
(D) 120°
(E) 144°

48. The radius of a circle is 1 inch. If an equilateral triangle is inscribed in the circle, what will be the length of one of the triangle's sides?

(A) 1 inch

(B) $\frac{\sqrt{2}}{2}$ inches

(C) $\sqrt{2}$ inches

(D) $\frac{\sqrt{3}}{2}$ inches

(E) $\sqrt{3}$ inches

49. If the angles of a triangle are in the ratio 2 : 3 : 4, how many degrees are there in the largest angle?

(A) 20°
(B) 40°
(C) 60°
(D) 80°
(E) 120°

50. A B C D E

50. Which of the following combinations may represent the lengths of the sides of a right triangle?

(A) 4, 6, 8
(B) 12, 16, 20
(C) 7, 17, 23
(D) 9, 20, 27
(E) None of these.

Answer Key for Practice Test 5

1. C	**14.** E	**27.** C	**39.** C
2. B	**15.** A	**28.** E	**40.** A
3. A	**16.** E	**29.** E	**41.** C
4. E	**17.** C	**30.** D	**42.** A
5. C	**18.** D	**31.** B	**43.** C
6. D	**19.** B	**32.** D	**44.** C
7. C	**20.** A	**33.** C	**45.** E
8. D	**21.** E	**34.** D	**46.** E
9. E	**22.** B	**35.** A	**47.** D
10. D	**23.** A	**36.** C	**48.** E
11. B	**24.** D	**37.** A	**49.** D
12. D	**25.** C	**38.** C	**50.** B
13. A	**26.** D		

Answers and Solutions
for Practice Test 5

1. Choice C is correct. In the problem it is given that $\angle 1 = 40°$ and $\angle 2 = 150°$. The diagram below makes it apparent that: (1) $\angle 1 = \angle 4$ and $\angle 3 = \angle 5$ (vertical angles); (2) $\angle 6 + \angle 2 = 180°$ (straight angle); (3) $\angle 4 + \angle 5 + \angle 6 = 180°$ (sum of angles in a triangle). To solve the problem, $\angle 3$ must be related through the above information to the known quantities in $\angle 1$ and $\angle 2$. Proceed as follows: $\angle 3 = \angle 5$, but $\angle 5 = 180° - \angle 4 - \angle 6$. $\angle 4 = \angle 1 = 40°$ and $\angle 6 = 180° - \angle 2 = 180° - 150° = 30°$. Therefore, $\angle 3 = 180° - 40° - 30° = 110°$.

(501, 503, 505)

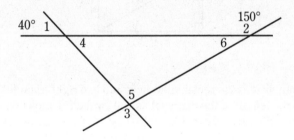

2. Choice B is correct. Since CD is perpendicular to DE, CDE is a right triangle, and using the Pythagorean Theorem yields $DE = 3$. Thus, the ratio of CD to DE is $4 : 3$. But triangle ABE is similar to triangle CDE. Therefore, $AB : BE = CD : DE = 4 : 3$. (509, 510)

3. Choice A is correct. In a triangle, it is impossible for one side to be longer than the sum of the other two (a straight line is the shortest distance between two points). Thus 2.0, 4.5, and 7.0 cannot be three sides of a triangle. (516)

4. Choice E is correct. $AB = AC$, $BD = CD$, and AD equal to itself is sufficient information (three sides) to prove triangles ABD and ACD congruent. Also, since $AB = AC$, $AE = AE$, and $\angle BAE = \angle CAE$ (by the previous congruence), triangles ABE and ACE are congruent. Since $BD = CD$, $ED = ED$, and angle BDE equals angle CDE (by initial congruence), triangles BDE and CDE are congruent. Through congruence of triangle ABE and triangle ACE, angles BEA and CEA are equal, and their sum is a straight angle (180°). They must both be right angles. Thus, from the given information, we can deduce all the properties given as choices. (511)

5. Choice C is correct. The perimeter of triangle *ABD* is *AB* + *BD* + *AD*. The length of *BD* is 1. Since *BC* = *CD* = *BD*, triangle *BCD* is an equilateral triangle. Therefore, angle *C* = 60° and angle *BDC* = 60°. Angle *A* + angle *C* = 90° (the sum of two acute angles in a right triangle is 90°), and angle *BDC* + angle *BDA* = 90° (these two angles form a right angle). Since angle *C* and angle *BDC* both equal 60°, angle *A* = angle *BDA* = 30°. Now two angles of triangle *ADB* are equal. Therefore, triangle *ADB* is an isosceles triangle with side *BD* = side *AB*. Since *BD* = 1, then *AB* = 1. *AD* is a leg of the right triangle, with side *CD* = 1 and hypotenuse *AC* = 2. (*AC* = *AB* + *BC* = 1 + 1.) Using the relationship $c^2 = a^2 + b^2$ gives us the length of *AD* as $\sqrt{3}$. Thus the perimeter is $1 + 1 + \sqrt{3}$, or $2 + \sqrt{3}$. (505, 507, 509)

6. Choice D is correct. (I) must be true, since the diagonals of a parallelogram bisect each other, so *QT* = *ST*, and *PT* = *RT*. Thus, since the sums of equals are equal, *QT* + *PT* = *RT* + *ST*.

(II) is not necessarily true and, in fact, can be true only if the parallelogram is also a rhombus (all four sides equal).

(III) is true, since the four small triangles each have the same area. The shaded portion contains three such triangles. This can be seen by noting that the altitudes from point *P* to the bases of triangles *PQT* and *PTS* are identical. We have already seen from part (I) that these bases (*QT* and *TS*) are also equal. Therefore, only I and III can be deduced from the given information. (514, 517)

7. Choice C is correct.

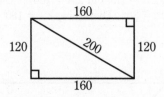

The diagonal path divides the rectangular field into two right triangles. The Pythagorean Theorem gives the length of the diagonal as 200 yards. If James takes the route around the perimeter, he will travel 120 + 160, or 280 yards. Thus, the shorter route saves him 80 yards. (509, 518)

8. Choice D is correct. Let one side of a square be *s*. Then the perimeter must be 4*s*. The diagonal of a square with side *s* is equal to $s\sqrt{2}$. Dividing the perimeter by the diagonal produces $2\sqrt{2}$. The perimeter is $2\sqrt{2}$ times the diagonal. (509, 520)

9. Choice E is correct. The sum of the angles of any polygon is equal to 180° (*n* − 2), where *n* is the number of sides. Thus the total number of degrees in a nonagon = 180° (9 − 2) = 180° × 7 = 1,260°. The number of degrees in each angle is $\dfrac{1{,}260°}{n} = \dfrac{1{,}260°}{9} = 140°$. (521, 522)

10. Choice D is correct. Since chord *AB* equals chord *CD*, it must be true that arc *AB* equals arc *CD*. By adding arc *AC* to arc *CD* and to arc *AB*, it is apparent that arc *ACD* is equal to arc *CAB*. These arcs are intersected by inscribed angles *ABD* and *BDC*. Therefore, the two inscribed angles must be equal. If we redraw the figure as shown below, the falseness of statements (A), (B), (C), and (E) becomes readily apparent. (527)

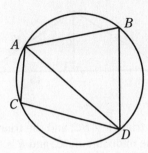

11. Choice B is correct. $\angle AEC + \angle BEC = \angle AEB$, a straight angle (180°). Thus, angles *AEC* and *BEC* are *supplementary*. (Complementary means that the two angles add up to a *right angle*, or 90°.) (501, 502)

12. Choice D is correct. Since $AC = CE$ and $BD = DE$, triangles *AEB* and *CED* are similar, and *AB* is twice as long as *CD*, since by proportionality, $AB : CD = AE : CE = 2 : 1$. From the similarity it is found that angle *ABE* equals angle *CDE*, and, therefore, that *AB* is parallel to *CD*. Thus, all three statements are true. (504, 510)

13. Choice A is correct. Angle *A* must be greater than 90°; angle *B* equals 30°. Thus, the sum of angles *A* and *B* must be greater than 120°. Since the sum of the three angles *A*, *B*, and *C* must be 180°, angle *C* must be *less than* 60°. (It cannot equal 60°, because then angle *A* would be a right angle instead of an obtuse angle.) (501, 505)

14. Choice E is correct. *CDF* is a right triangle with one side of 16 and a hypotenuse of 20. Thus, the third side, *DF*, equals 12. Since *BFDE* is a square, *BF* and *ED* are also equal to 12. Thus, $BC = 12 + 16 = 28$, and $CD = 20$. *ABCD* is a parallelogram, so $AB = CD$, $AD = BC$. The perimeter is $28 + 20 + 28 + 20 = 96$. (509, 517, 520)

15. Choice A is correct. Recognize that the sides of a 30°–60°–90° triangle are in the proportion $1 : \sqrt{3} : 2$, and the problem is solved. 30° is the smallest angle. (509)

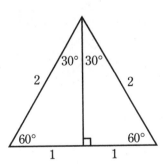

16. Choice E is correct. The altitude to the base of an isosceles triangle divides it into two congruent right triangles, each with one leg of 8 inches and a hypotenuse of 17 inches. By the Pythagorean Theorem, the third side of each right triangle must be 15 inches long. The base of the isosceles triangle is the sum of two such sides, totaling 30 inches.

(507, 509, 514)

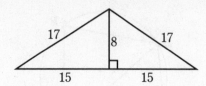

17. Choice C is correct. Call the triangle ABC, and the triangle of midpoints PQR, where P is the midpoint of BC, Q is the midpoint of AC, and R is the midpoint of AB. Then, PQ is equal to half the length of AB, $QR = \frac{1}{2}BC$, and $PR = \frac{1}{2}AC$. This has nothing to do with the fact that ABC is a right triangle. Thus, the perimeter of the small triangle is equal to $PQ + QR + PR = \frac{1}{2}(AB + BC + AC)$. The new perimeter is half the old perimeter, or 9 inches.

(509, 510, 512)

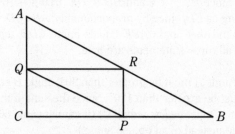

18. Choice D is correct. The diagonals of the square form four right triangles, each of which is isosceles because each has two 45° angles. The triangles are all identical in shape and size, so they all are similar and have the same area. The only choice left is equilateral, which cannot be true, since the sum of the angles at the intersection of the diagonals must be 360°. The sum of four 60° angles would be only 240°.

(520)

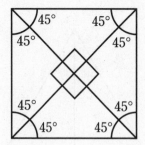

19. Choice B is correct. First, draw in the lines *CF* and *BE*. These intersect *AD* at its midpoint (also the midpoint of *CF* and *BE*) and divide the hexagon into six equilateral triangles. Since *ADC* is an angle of one of these equilateral triangles, it must be equal to 60°. (Another way to do this problem is to calculate the number of degrees in one angle of a regular hexagon and divide this by 2.) (508, 523)

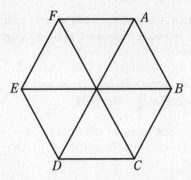

20. Choice A is correct. The diagonal of an inscribed rectangle is equal to the diameter of the circle. To find this length, use the Pythagorean Theorem on one of the two triangles formed by two of the sides of the rectangle and the diagonal. Thus, the square of the diagonal is equal to $10^2 + 14^2 = 100 + 196 = 296$. The area of the circle is equal to π times the square of the radius. The square of the radius of the circle is one-fourth of the diameter squared (since $d = 2r$, $d^2 = 4r^2$), or 74. Thus, the area is 74π. (509, 518, 524)

21. Choice E is correct. Each number (or hour marking) on a clock represents an angle of 30°, as 360° divided by 12 is 30° (a convenient fact to remember for other clock problems). Since the hands of the clock are on the 12 and the 5, there are five hour units between the hands; $5 \times 30° = 150°$. (501, 526)

22. Choice B is correct.

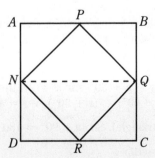

Let S represent the side of the large square. Then the perimeter is $4S$. Let s represent the side of the smaller square. Then the perimeter is $4s$. Line NQ is the diagonal of the smaller square, so the length of NQ is $\sqrt{2}s$. (The diagonal of a square is $\sqrt{2}$ times the side.) Now, NQ is equal to DC, or S, which is the side of the larger square. So now $S = \sqrt{2}s$. The perimeter of the large square equals $4S = 4\sqrt{2}s = \sqrt{2}(4s) = \sqrt{2} \times$ perimeter of the small square. (520)

23. Choice A is correct. Angles A and B are both greater than 0 degrees and less than 90 degrees, so their sum is between 0 degrees and 180 degrees. Then angle C must be between 0 and 180 degrees. (501, 505)

24. Choice D is correct. Let the four angles be x, $2x$, $3x$, and $4x$. The sum, $10x$, must equal $360°$. Thus, $x = 36°$, and the largest angle, $4x$, is $144°$. (505)

25. Choice C is correct. The diagonals of a rectangle are perpendicular only when the rectangle is a square. AE is part of the diagonal AC, so AE will not necessarily be perpendicular to BD. (518)

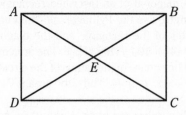

26. Choice D is correct.

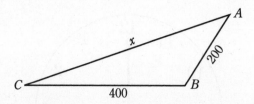

Draw the three cities as the vertices of a triangle. The length of side CB is 400 miles, the length of side AB is 200 miles, and x, the length of side AC, is unknown. The sum of any two sides of a triangle is greater than the third side, or in algebraic terms: $400 + 200 > x$, $400 + x > 200$, and $200 + x > 400$. These simplify to $600 > x$, $x > -200$, and $x > 200$. For x to be greater than 200 and -200, it must be greater than 200. Thus, the values of x are $200 < x < 600$. (506, 516)

27. Choice C is correct. At 7:30, the hour hand is *halfway between the 7 and the 8*, and the minute hand is on the 6. Thus, there are one and one-half "hour units," each equal to $30°$, so the whole angle is $45°$. (501, 526)

28. Choice E is correct. If a ship is facing north, a right turn of $90°$ will face it eastward. Another $90°$ turn will face it south, and an additional $45°$ turn will bring it to southwest. Thus, the total rotation is $90° + 90° + 45° = 225°$. (501)

29. Choice E is correct. Since $y = z + 30°$ and $x = 2y$, then $x = 2(z + 30°) = 2z + 60°$. Thus, $x + y + z$ equals $(2z + 60°) + (z + 30°) + z = 4z + 90°$. This must equal $180°$ (the sum of the angles of a triangle). So $4z + 90° = 180°$, and the solution is $z = 22\frac{1}{2}°$; $x = 2z + 60° = 45° + 60° = 105°$. (505)

30. Choice D is correct. Since *AB* is parallel to *CD*, angle 2 = angle 6, and angle 3 + angle 7 = 180°. If angle 2 + angle 3 equals 180°, then angle 2 = angle 7 = angle 6. However, since there is no evidence that angles 6 and 7 are equal, angle 2 + angle 3 does not necessarily equal 180°. Therefore, the answer is (D). (504)

31. Choice B is correct. Call the side of the square s. Then, the diagonal of the square is $\sqrt{2}s$ and the area is s^2. The area of an isosceles right triangle with leg r is $\frac{1}{2}r^2$. Now, the area of the triangle is equal to the area of the square, so $s^2 = \frac{1}{2}r^2$. Solving for r gives $r = \sqrt{2}s$. The hypotenuse of the triangle is $\sqrt{r^2 + r^2}$. Substituting $r = \sqrt{2}s$, the hypotenuse is $\sqrt{2s^2 + 2s^2}$ $= \sqrt{4s^2} = 2s$. Therefore, the ratio of the diagonal to the hypotenuse is $\sqrt{2}s : 2s$. Since $\sqrt{2}s$: $2s$ is $\frac{\sqrt{2s}}{2s}$ or $\frac{\sqrt{2}}{2}$, multiply by $\frac{\sqrt{2}}{\sqrt{2}}$, which has a value of 1. $\frac{\sqrt{2}}{2} \cdot \frac{\sqrt{2}}{\sqrt{2}} = \frac{2}{2\sqrt{2}} = \frac{1}{\sqrt{2}}$ or $1 : \sqrt{2}$, which is the final result. (507, 509, 520)

32. Choice D is correct. The formula for the number of degrees in the angles of a polygon is $180(n-2)$, where n is the number of sides. For a ten-sided figure this is $180°(10 - 2) = 180°(8) = 1440°$. Since the ten angles are equal, they must each equal 144°. (521, 522)

33. Choice C is correct. If three numbers represent the lengths of the sides of a right triangle, they must satisfy the Pythagorean Theorem: The squares of the smaller two must equal the square of the largest one. This condition is met in all the sets given except the set 9, 28, 35. There, $9^2 + 28^2 = 81 + 784 = 865$, but $35^2 = 1,225$. (509)

34. Choice D is correct. Let the angle be x. Since x is its own supplement, then $x + x = 180°$, or, since $2x = 180°$, $x = 90°$. (502)

35. Choice A is correct. The length of the arc intersected by a central angle of a circle is proportional to the number of degrees in the angle. Thus, if a 45° angle cuts off a 6-inch arc, a 360° angle intersects an arc eight times as long, or 48 inches. The length of the arc of a 360° angle is equal to the circle's circumference, or 2π times the radius. Thus, to obtain the radius, divide 48 inches by 2π. 48 inches $\div 2\pi = \frac{24}{\pi}$ inches. (524, 526)

36. Choice C is correct. Refer to the diagram pictured below. Calculate the distance from vertex 1 to vertex 2. This is simply the diagonal of a 1-inch square and equal to $\sqrt{2}$ inches. Now, vertices 1, 2, and 3 form a right triangle, with legs of 1 and $\sqrt{2}$. By the Pythagorean Theorem, the hypotenuse is $\sqrt{3}$. This is the distance from vertex 1 to vertex 3, the two most distant vertices. (509, 520)

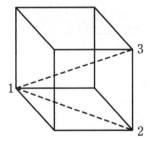

37. Choice A is correct. In one hour, the hour hand of a clock moves through an angle of 30° (one "hour unit"). 70 minutes equals $\frac{7}{6}$ hours, so during that time the hour hand will move through $\frac{7}{6} \times 30°$, or 35°. (501, 526)

38. Choice C is correct. In order to be similar, two triangles must have corresponding angles equal. This is true of triangles *ODC* and *OBA*, since angle *O* equals itself, and angles *OCD* and *OAB* are both right angles. (The third angles of these triangles must be equal, as the sum of the angles of a triangle is always 180°.) Since the triangles are similar, *OD* : *CD* = *OB* : *AB*. But *OD* and *OA* are radii of the same circle and are equal. Therefore, substitute *OA* for *OD* in the above proportion. Hence, *OA* : *CD* = *OB* : *AB*. There is, however, no information given on the relative sizes of any of the line segments, so statement III may or may not be true. (509, 510, 524)

39. Choice C is correct. Let the three angles equal x, $2x$, and $6x$. Then, $x + 2x + 6x = 9x = 180°$. Therefore, $x = 20°$ and $6x = 120°$. (505)

40. Choice A is correct. Since $AB = AC$, angle *ABC* must equal angle *ACB*. (Base angles of an isosceles triangle are equal.) As the sum of angles *BAC*, *ABC*, and *ACB* is 180°, and angle *BAC* equals 40°, angle *ABC* and angle *ACB* must each equal 70°. Now, *DBC* is a right triangle, with angle $BDC = 90°$ and angle $DCB = 70°$. (The three angles must add up to 180°.) Angle *DBC* must equal 20°. (507, 514)

41. Choice C is correct.

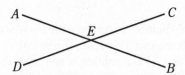

$\angle AEB$ and $\angle CED$ are both straight angles, and are equal; similarly, $\angle DEC$ and $\angle BEA$ are both straight angles. $\angle AEC$ and $\angle BED$ are vertical angles, as are $\angle BEC$ and $\angle DEA$, and are equal. $\angle AED$ and $\angle CEA$ are supplementary and need not be equal. (501, 502, 503)

42. Choice A is correct. All right isosceles triangles have angles of 45°, 45°, and 90°. Since all triangles with the same angles are similar, all right isosceles triangles are similar. (507, 509, 510)

43. Choice C is correct.

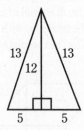

As the diagram shows, the altitude to the base of the isosceles triangle divides it into two congruent right triangles, each with 5–12–13 sides. Thus, the base is 10, the height is 12, and the area is $\frac{1}{2}(10)(12) = 60$. (505, 507, 509)

44. Choice C is correct. The altitude to any side divides the triangle into two congruent 30°–60°–90° right triangles, each with a hypotenuse of 2 inches and a leg of 1 inch. The other leg equals the altitude. By the Pythagorean Theorem, the altitude is equal to $\sqrt{3}$ inches. (The sides of a 30°–60°–90° right triangle are always in the proportion $1 : \sqrt{3} : 2$.)

(509, 514)

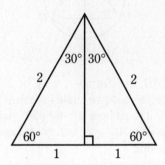

45. Choice E is correct.

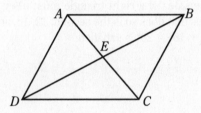

As the diagram illustrates, angles *AED* and *BEC* are vertical and, therefore, equal. *AE* = *EC*, because the diagonals of a parallelogram bisect each other. Angles *BDC* and *DBA* are equal because they are alternate interior angles of parallel lines (*AB*∥*CD*). (503, 517)

46. Choice E is correct. There are eight isosceles right triangles: *ABE, BCE, CDE, ADE, ABC, BCD, CDA*, and *ABD*. (520)

47. Choice D is correct. Recall that a regular hexagon may be broken up into six equilateral triangles.

Since the angles of each triangle are 60°, and two of these angles make up each angle of the hexagon, an angle of the hexagon must be 120°. (523)

48. Choice E is correct.

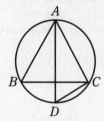

Since the radius equals 1″, *AD*, the diameter, must be 2″. Now, since *AD* is a diameter, *ACD* must be a right triangle, because an angle inscribed in a semicircle is a right angle. Thus, because $\angle DAC = 30°$, it must be a 30°–60°–90° right triangle. The sides will be in the proportion $1 : \sqrt{3} : 2$. As $AD : AC = 2 : \sqrt{3}$, so *AC*, one of the sides of the equilateral triangle, must be $\sqrt{3}$ inches long. (508, 524)

49. Choice D is correct. Let the angles be $2x$, $3x$, $4x$. Their sum, $9x = 180°$, and $x = 20°$. Thus, the largest angle, $4x$, is 80°. (505)

50. Choice B is correct. The sides of a right triangle must obey the Pythagorean Theorem. The only group of choices that does so is the second: 12, 16, and 20 are in the $3 : 4 : 5$ ratio, and the relationship $12^2 + 16^2 = 20^2$ is satisfied. (509)

MATH REFRESHER
SESSION 6

Miscellaneous Problems: Averages, Properties of Integers, Approximations, Combinations, Permutations, Probability, the Absolute Value Sign, and Functions

Averages, Medians, Modes, and Standard Deviation

601. *Averages.* The average of n numbers is merely their sum, divided by n.

Example: Find the average of: 20, 0, 80, and 12.

Solution: The average is the sum divided by the number of entries, or:

$$\frac{20 + 0 + 80 + 12}{4} = \frac{112}{4} = 28$$

A quick way of obtaining an average of a set of numbers that are close together is the following:

STEP 1. Choose any number that will approximately equal the average.

STEP 2. Subtract this approximate average from each of the numbers (this sum will give some positive and some negative results). Add the results.

STEP 3. Divide this sum by the number of entries.

STEP 4. Add the result of Step 3 to the approximate average chosen in Step 1. This will be the true average.

Example: Find the average of 92, 93, 93, 96, and 97.

Solution: Choose 95 as an approximate average. Subtracting 95 from 92, 93, 93, 96, and 97 gives -3, -2, -2, 1, and 2. The sum is -4. Divide -4 by 5 (the number of entries) to obtain -0.8. Add -0.8 to the original approximation of 95 to get the true average, $95 - 0.8$, or 94.2.

601a. *Medians.* The median of a set of numbers is that number which is in the *middle* of all the numbers.

Example: Find the median of 20, 0, 80, 12, and 30.

Solution: Arrange the numbers in increasing order:

$$0$$
$$12$$
$$20$$
$$30$$
$$80$$

The *middle* number is 20, so 20 is the *median*.

Note: If there is an *even* number of items, such as

$$
\begin{aligned}
&0\\
&12\\
&20\\
&24\\
&30\\
&80
\end{aligned}
$$

there is no *middle* number.

So in this case we take the average of the two middle numbers, 20 and 24, to get 22, which is the *median*.

In the above set of 6 numbers, if 24 was replaced by 22, the median would be 21 (just the average of 20 and 22).

601b.   *Modes.* The mode of a set of numbers is the number that occurs most frequently.

If we have numbers 0, 12, 20, 30, and 80, there is *no* mode, since no one number appears with the greatest frequency. But consider this:

Example: Find the mode of 0, 12, 12, 20, 30, 80.

Solution: 12 appears most frequently, so it is the mode.

Example: Find the mode of 0, 12, 12, 20, 30, 30, 80.

Solution: Here *both* 12 and 30 are modes.

602.   *Standard Deviation.* Let's consider what a standard deviation is with an example:

Consider a population consisting of the following eight values:

$$2, 4, 4, 4, 5, 5, 7, 9$$

The eight data points have a *mean* (or average) value of 5:

$$\frac{2+4+4+4+5+5+7+9}{8}=5$$

To calculate the population standard deviation, first compute the difference of each data point from the mean, and <u>square</u> the result of each:

$$
\begin{aligned}
(2-5)^2 = (-3)^2 = 9 \qquad & (5-5)^2 = 0^2 = 0\\
(4-5)^2 = (-1)^2 = 1 \qquad & (5-5)^2 = 0^2 = 0\\
(4-5)^2 = (-1)^2 = 1 \qquad & (7-5)^2 = 2^2 = 4\\
(4-5)^2 = (-1)^2 = 1 \qquad & (9-5)^2 = 4^2 = 16
\end{aligned}
$$

Next divide the sum of these values by the number of values and take the <u>square root</u> to give the standard deviation:

$$\sqrt{\frac{9+1+1+1+0+0+4+16}{8}}=2$$

Therefore, the above has a population standard deviation of 2.

So, in effect, to calculate the standard deviation of a set of numbers, subtract each number from the average of the numbers, then square the result for each of the numbers. Add all those results and then divide by how many numbers you originally had. Take the square root of that result. That then is your standard deviation.

Properties of Integers

603. *Even–Odd.* These are problems that deal with even and odd numbers. An even number is divisible by 2, and an odd number is not divisible by 2. All even numbers end in the digits 0, 2, 4, 6, or 8; odd numbers end in the digits 1, 3, 5, 7, or 9. For example, the numbers 358, 90, 18, 9,874, and 46 are even numbers. The numbers 67, 871, 475, and 89 are odd numbers. It is important to remember the following facts:

604. The sum of *two even* numbers is *even*, and the sum of *two odd* numbers is *even*, but the sum of an *odd* number *and* an *even* number is *odd*. For example, $4 + 8 = 12$, $5 + 3 = 8$, and $7 + 2 = 9$.

> **Example:** If m is any integer, is the number $6m + 3$ an even or odd number?
>
> *Solution:* $6m$ is even, since 6 is a multiple of 2. 3 is odd. Therefore $6m + 3$ is odd, since even + odd = odd.

605. The product of *two odd* numbers is *odd*, but the product of an *even* number and *any other* number is an *even* number. For example, $3 \times 5 = 15$ (odd); $4 \times 5 = 20$ (even); $4 \times 6 = 24$ (even).

> **Example:** If m is any integer, is the product $(2m + 3)(4m + 1)$ even or odd?
>
> *Solution:* Since $2m$ is even and 3 is odd, $2m + 3$ is odd. Likewise, since $4m$ is even and 1 is odd, $4m + 1$ is odd. Thus $(2m + 3)(4m + 1)$ is (odd $\times$ odd), which is odd.

606. Even numbers are expressed in the form $2k$, where k may be any integer. Odd numbers are expressed in the form of $2k + 1$ or $2k - 1$, where k may be any integer. For example, if $k = 17$, then $2k = 34$ and $2k + 1 = 35$. If $k = 6$, then we have $2k = 12$ and $2k + 1 = 13$.

> **Example:** Prove that the product of two odd numbers is odd.
>
> *Solution:* Let one of the odd numbers be represented as $2x + 1$. Let the other number be represented as $2y + 1$. Now multiply $(2x + 1)(2y + 1)$. We get $4xy + 2x + 2y + 1$. Since $4xy + 2x + 2y$ is even because it is a multiple of 2, that quantity is even. Since 1 is odd, $4xy + 2x + 2y + 1$ is odd, since even + odd = odd.

607. *Divisibility.* If an integer P is divided by an integer Q, and an integer is obtained as the quotient, then P is said to be divisible by Q. In other words, if P can be expressed as an integral multiple of Q, then P is said to be divisible by Q. For example, dividing 51 by 17 gives 3, an integer. 51 is divisible by 17, or 51 equals 17 times 3. On the other hand, dividing 8 by 3 gives $2\frac{2}{3}$, which is not an integer. 8 is not divisible by 3, and there is no way to express 8 as an integral multiple of 3. There are various tests to see whether an integer is divisible by certain numbers. These tests are listed below:

1. Any integer is divisible *by 2* if the last digit of the number is a 0, 2, 4, 6, or 8.

   > **Example:** We know the numbers 98, 6,534, 70, and 32 are divisible by 2 because they end in 8, 4, 0, and 2, respectively.

2. Any integer is divisible *by 3* if the sum of its digits is divisible by 3.

   > **Example:** Is the number 34,237,023 divisible by 3?
   >
   > *Solution:* Add the digits of the number. $3 + 4 + 2 + 3 + 7 + 0 + 2 + 3 = 24$. Now, 24 is divisible by 3 ($24 \div 3 = 8$), so the number 34,237,023 is also divisible by 3.

3. Any integer is divisible *by 4* if the last two digits of the number make a number that is divisible by 4.

   > **Example:** Which of the following numbers is divisible by 4?
   > 3,456; 6,787,612; 67,408; 7,877; 345; 98.
   >
   > *Solution:* Look at the last two digits of the numbers: 56, 12, 08, 77, 45, 98. Only 56, 12, and 08 are divisible by 4, so only the numbers 3,456; 6,787,612; and 67,408 are divisible by 4.

4. An integer is divisible *by 5* if the last digit is either a 0 or a 5.

Example: The numbers 780, 675, 9,000, and 15 are divisible by 5, while the numbers 786, 5,509, and 87 are not divisible by 5.

5. Any integer is divisible *by 6* if it is divisible by both 2 and 3.

   Example: Is the number 12,414 divisible by 6?

   Solution: Test whether 12,414 is divisible by 2 and 3. The last digit is a 4, so it is divisible by 2. Adding the digits yields $1 + 2 + 4 + 1 + 4 = 12$. 12 is divisible by 3, so the number 12,414 is divisible by 3. Since it is divisible by both 2 and 3, it is divisible by 6.

6. Any integer is divisible *by 8* if the last three digits are divisible by 8. (Since 1,000 is divisible by 8, you can ignore all multiples of 1,000 in applying this rule.)

   Example: Is the number 342,169,424 divisible by 8?

   Solution: $424 \div 8 = 53$, so 342,169,424 is divisible by 8.

7. Any integer is divisible *by 9* if the sum of its digits is divisible by 9.

   Example: Is the number 243,091,863 divisible by 9?

   Solution: Adding the digits yields $2 + 4 + 3 + 0 + 9 + 1 + 8 + 6 + 3 = 36$. 36 is divisible by 9, so the number 243,091,863 is divisible by 9.

8. Any integer is divisible *by 10* if the last digit is a 0.

   Example: We know the numbers 60, 8,900, 5,640, and 34,000 are all divisible by 10 because the last digit in each is a 0.

Note that if a number P is divisible by a number Q, then P is also divisible by all the factors of Q. For example, 60 is divisible by 12, so 60 is also divisible by 2, 3, 4, and 6, which are all factors of 12.

---

608. *Prime numbers.* A prime number is one that is divisible only by 1 and itself. The first few prime numbers are 2, 3, 5, 7, 11, 13, 17, 19, 23, 29, 31, 37. . . . Note that the number 1 is not considered a prime number. To determine if a number is prime, follow these steps:

STEP 1. Determine a very rough approximate square root of the number. Remember that the square root of a number is that number which, when multiplied by itself, gives the original number. For example, the square root of 25 is 5 because $5 \times 5 = 25$.

STEP 2. Divide the number by all of the primes that are less than the approximate square root. If the number is not divisible by any of these primes, then it is prime. If it is divisible by one of the primes, then it is not prime.

   Example: Is the number 97 prime?

   Solution: An approximate square root of 97 is 10. All of the primes less than 10 are 2, 3, 5, and 7. Divide 97 by 2, 3, 5, and 7. No integer results, so 97 is prime.

   Example: Is the number 161 prime?

   Solution: An approximate square root of 161 is 13. The primes less than 13 are 2, 3, 5, 7, and 11. Divide 161 by 2, 3, 5, 7, and 11. 161 is divisible by 7 ($161 \div 7 = 23$), so 161 is not prime.

Approximations

609. *Rounding off numbers with decimal points.* A number expressed to a certain number of places is rounded off when it is approximated as a number with fewer places of accuracy. For example, the number 8.987 is expressed more accurately than the number rounded off to 8.99. To round off to n places, look at the digit that is to the right of the nth digit. (The nth digit is found by counting n places to the right of the decimal point.) If this digit is less than 5, eliminate all of the digits to the right of the nth digit. If the digit to the right of the nth digit is 5 or more, then add 1 to the nth digit and eliminate all of the digits to the right of the nth digit.

Example: Round off 8.73 to the nearest tenth.

Solution: The digit to the right of the 7 (.7 is seven tenths) is 3. Since this is less than 5, eliminate it, and the rounded-off answer is 8.7.

Example: Round off 986 to the nearest tens place.

Solution: The number to the right of the tens place is 6. Since this is 5 or more, add 1 to the 8 and replace the 6 with a 0 to get 990.

610. *Approximating sums with decimal points.* When adding a small (10 or fewer) set of numbers and when the answer must have a given number of places of accuracy, follow the steps below.

STEP 1.   Round off each addend (number being added) to one less place than the number of places the answer is to have.

STEP 2.   Add the rounded addends.

STEP 3.   Round off the sum to the desired number of places of accuracy.

Example: What is the sum of 12.0775, 1.20163, and 121.303 correct to the nearest hundredth?

Solution: Round off the three numbers to the nearest thousandth (one less place than the accuracy of the sum): 12.078, 1.202, and 121.303. The sum of these is 134.583. Rounded off to the nearest hundredth, this is 134.58.

611. *Approximating products.* To multiply certain numbers and have an answer to the desired number of places of accuracy (significant digits), follow the steps below.

STEP 1.   Round off the numbers being multiplied to the number of places of accuracy (significant digits) desired in the answer.

STEP 2.   Multiply the rounded-off factors (numbers being multiplied).

STEP 3.   Round off the product to the desired number of places (significant digits).

Example: Find the product of 3,316 and 1,432 to the nearest thousandth.

Solution: First, round off 3,316 to 3 places, to obtain 3,320. Round off 1,432 to 2 places to give 1,430. The product of these two numbers is 4,747,600. Rounded off to 3 places, this is 4,748,000.

612. *Approximating square roots.* The square root of a number is that number which, when multiplied by itself, gives the original number. For example, 6 is the square root of 36. Often, on tests, a number with different choices for the square root is given. Follow this procedure to determine which is the best choice.

STEP 1.   Square all of the choices given.

STEP 2.   Select the closest choice that is too large and the closest choice that is too small (assuming that no choice is the exact square root). Find the average of these two *choices* (not of their squares).

STEP 3.   Square this average; if the square is greater than the original number, choose the lower of the two choices; if the square is lower than the original number, choose the higher.

Example: Which of the following is closest to the square root of 86: 9.0, 9.2, 9.4, 9.6, or 9.8?

Solution: The squares of the five numbers are: 81, 84.64, 88.36, 92.16, and 96.04, respectively. (Actually, it is not necessary to calculate the last two, since they are greater than the third square, which is already greater than 86.) The two closest choices are 9.2 and 9.4; their average is 9.3. The square of 9.3 is 86.49. Therefore, 9.3 is greater than the square root of 86. So, the square root must be closer to 9.2 than to 9.4.

Combinations

613. Suppose that a job has 2 different parts. There are *m* different ways of doing the first part, and there are *n* different ways of doing the second part. The problem is to find the number of ways of doing the entire job. For each way of doing the first part of the job, there are *n* ways of doing the second part. Since there are *m* ways of doing the first part, the total number of ways of doing the entire job is *m* × *n*. The formula that can be used is

$$\text{Number of ways} = m \times n$$

For any problem that involves 2 actions or 2 objects, each with a number of choices, and asks for the number of combinations, this formula can be used. For example: A man wants a sandwich and a drink for lunch. If a restaurant has 4 choices of sandwiches and 3 choices of drinks, how many different ways can he order his lunch?

Since there are 4 choices of sandwiches and 3 choices of drinks, use the formula

$$\text{Number of ways} = 4(3)$$
$$= 12$$

Therefore, the man can order his lunch 12 different ways.

If we have objects *a*, *b*, *c*, and *d*, and want to arrange them two at a time—that is, like *ab*, *bc*, *cd*, etc.—we have four combinations taken two at a time. This is denoted as $_4C_2$. The rule is that $_4C_2 = \dfrac{(4)(3)}{(2)(1)}$. In general, *n* combinations taken *r* at a time is represented by the formula:

$$_nC_r = \frac{(n)(n-1)(n-2)\ldots(n-r+1)}{(r)(r-1)(r-2)\ldots(1)}$$

$$\text{Examples: } _3C_2 = \frac{3 \times 2}{2 \times 1}; \quad _8C_3 = \frac{8 \times 7 \times 6}{3 \times 2 \times 1}$$

Suppose there are 24 people at a party and each person shakes another person's hand (only once). How many handshakes are there?

Solution: Represent the people at the party as *a*, *b*, *c*, *d*, etc.
The combinations of handshakes would be *ab*, *ac*, *bc*, *bd*, etc., or 24 combinations taken 2 at a time:

$$_{24}C_2 . \text{ This is } \frac{24 \times 23}{2 \times 1} = 276.$$

Permutations

613a. Permutations are like combinations except in permutations the order is important. As an example, if we want to find how many permutations there are of three objects taken 2 at a time, we would have for *a*, *b*, *c*, *ab*, *ba*, *ac*, *ca*, *bc*, *cb*. Thus as an example, *ba* would be one permutation and *ab* would be another. The permutations of 3 objects taken 2 at a time would be $_3P_2 = 3 \times 2$ and not $(3 \times 2)/(2 \times 1)$ as in combinations. The number of permutations of *n* objects taken *r* at a time would be

$$_nP_r = (n)(n-1)\ldots(n-r+1).$$

Example: How many permutations of the digits 142 are there, where the digits are taken two at a time?

Solution: You have 14, 41, 12, 21, 42, 24. That is, $_3P_2 = 3 \times 2 = 6$.

Probability

614. The probability that an event will occur equals the number of favorable ways divided by the total number of ways. If P is the probability, m is the number of favorable ways, and n is the total number of ways, then

$$P = \frac{m}{n}$$

For example: What is the probability that heads will turn up on a single throw of a penny?

The favorable number of ways is 1 (heads).

The total number of ways is 2 (heads and tails). Thus, the probability is $\frac{1}{2}$.

If a and b are two mutually exclusive events, then the probability that a or b will occur is the sum of the individual probabilities.

Suppose P_a is the probability that an event a occurs. Suppose that P_b is the probability that a second independent event b occurs. Then the probability that the first event a occurs *and* the second event b occurs subsequently is $P_a \times P_b$.

The Absolute Value Sign

615. The symbol $|\ |$ denotes absolute value. The absolute value of a number is the numerical value of the number without the plus or minus sign in front of it. Thus all absolute values are positive. For example, $|+3|$ is 3, and $|-2|$ is 2. Here's another example:

If x is positive and y is negative, $|x| + |y| = x - y$. Because y is negative, we must have $x - y$ to make the term positive.

Functions

616. Suppose we have a function of x. This is denoted as $f(x)$ (or $g(y)$ or $h(z)$, etc.). As an example, if $f(x) = x$ then $f(3) = 3$. In this example we substitute the value 3 wherever x appears in the function. Similarly $f(-2) = -2$.

Consider another example: If $f(y) = y^2 - y$, then $f(2) = 2^2 - 2 = 2$. $f(-2) = (-2)^2 - (-2) = 6$. $f(z) = z^2 - z$. $f(2z) = (2z)^2 - (2z) = 4z^2 - 2z$.

Let us consider still another example: Let $f(x) = x + 2$ and $g(y) = 2^y$. What is $f[g(-2)]$? Now $g(-2) = 2^{-2} = \frac{1}{4}$. Thus $f[g(-2)] = f\left(\frac{1}{4}\right)$. Since $f(x) = x + 2$, $f\left(\frac{1}{4}\right) = \frac{1}{4} + 2 = 2\frac{1}{4}$.

Practice Test 6

Miscellaneous Problems: Averages, Properties of Integers, Approximations, Combinations, Permutations, Probability, the Absolute Value Sign, and Functions

Correct answers and solutions follow each test.

1. A B C D E

1. If n is the first of five consecutive odd numbers, what is their average?

(A) n
(B) $n + 1$
(C) $n + 2$
(D) $n + 3$
(E) $n + 4$

2. A B C D E

2. What is the average of the following numbers: 35.5, 32.5, 34.0, 35.0, 34.5?

(A) 33.0
(B) 33.8
(C) 34.0
(D) 34.3
(E) 34.5

3. A B C D E

3. If P is an even number, and Q and R are both odd, which of the following *must* be true?

(A) $P \cdot Q$ is an odd number
(B) $Q - R$ is an even number
(C) $PQ - PR$ is an odd number
(D) $Q + R$ cannot equal P
(E) $P + Q$ cannot equal R

4. A B C D E

4. If a number is divisible by 102, then it is also divisible by:

(A) 23
(B) 11
(C) 103
(D) 5
(E) 2

5. A B C D E

5. Which of the following numbers is divisible by 36?

(A) 35,924
(B) 64,530
(C) 74,098
(D) 152,640
(E) 192,042

6. A B C D E

6. How many prime numbers are there between 45 and 72?

(A) 4
(B) 5
(C) 6
(D) 7
(E) 8

7. A B C D E

7. Which of the following represents the smallest possible value of $\left(M - \frac{1}{2}\right)^2$, if M is an integer?

(A) 0.00
(B) 0.25
(C) 0.50
(D) 0.75
(E) 1.00

8. A B C D E

8. Which of the following best approximates $\dfrac{7.40096 \times 10.0342}{.2001355}$?

(A) 0.3700
(B) 3.700
(C) 37.00
(D) 370.0
(E) 3700

9. A B C D E

9. In a class with 6 boys and 4 girls, the students all took the same test. The boys' scores were 74, 82, 84, 84, 88, and 95, while the girls' scores were 80, 82, 86, and 86. Which of the following statements is true?

(A) The boys' average was 0.1 higher than the average for the whole class.
(B) The girls' average was 0.1 lower than the boys' average.
(C) The class average was 1.0 higher than the boys' average.
(D) The boys' average was 1.0 higher than the class average.
(E) The girls' average was 1.0 lower than the boys' average.

10. A B C D E

10. Which of the following numbers *must* be odd?

(A) The sum of an odd number and an odd number.
(B) The product of an odd number and an even number.
(C) The sum of an odd number and an even number.
(D) The product of two even numbers.
(E) The sum of two even numbers.

11. A B C D E

11. Which of the following numbers is the best approximation of the length of one side of a square with an area of 12 square inches?

(A) 3.2 inches
(B) 3.3 inches
(C) 3.4 inches
(D) 3.5 inches
(E) 3.6 inches

12. A B C D E

12. If n is an odd number, then which of the following *best* describes the number represented by $n^2 + 2n + 1$?

(A) It can be odd or even.
(B) It must be odd.
(C) It must be divisible by four.
(D) It must be divisible by six.
(E) The answer cannot be determined from the given information.

13. A B C D E

13. What is the average of the following numbers: $3\frac{1}{2}, 4\frac{1}{4}, 2\frac{1}{4}, 3\frac{1}{4}, 4$?

(A) 3.25
(B) 3.35
(C) 3.45
(D) 3.50
(E) 3.60

14. A B C D E

14. Which of the following numbers is divisible by 24?

(A) 76,300
(B) 78,132
(C) 80,424
(D) 81,234
(E) 83,636

15. A B C D E

15. In order to graduate, a boy needs an average of 65 percent for his five major subjects. His first four grades were 55, 60, 65, and 65. What grade does he need in the fifth subject in order to graduate?

(A) 65
(B) 70
(C) 75
(D) 80
(E) 85

16. A B C D E

16. If t is any integer, which of the following represents an odd number?

(A) $2t$
(B) $2t + 3$
(C) $3t$
(D) $2t + 2$
(E) $t + 1$

17. A B C D E

17. If the average of five whole numbers is an even number, which of the following statements is *not true*?

(A) The sum of the five numbers must be divisible by 2.
(B) The sum of the five numbers must be divisible by 5.
(C) The sum of the five numbers must be divisible by 10.
(D) At least one of the five numbers must be even.
(E) All of the five numbers must be odd.

18. A B C D E

18. What is the product of 23 and 79 to one significant digit?

(A) 1,600
(B) 1,817
(C) 1,000
(D) 1,800
(E) 2,000

19. A B C D E

19. Which of the following is closest to the square root of $\frac{1}{2}$?

(A) 0.25
(B) 0.5
(C) 0.6
(D) 0.7
(E) 0.8

20. A B C D E

20. How many prime numbers are there between 56 and 100?

(A) 8
(B) 9
(C) 10
(D) 11
(E) None of the above.

21. A B C D E

21. If you multiply 1,200,176 by 520,204, and then divide the product by 1,000,000,000, your result will be closest to:

(A) 0.6
(B) 6
(C) 600
(D) 6,000
(E) 6,000,000

22. A B C D E

22. The number 89.999 rounded off to the nearest tenth is equal to which of the following?

(A) 90.0
(B) 89.0
(C) 89.9
(D) 89.99
(E) 89.90

23. A B C D E

23. a, b, c, d, and e are integers; M is their average; and S is their sum. What is the ratio of S to M?

(A) 1 : 5
(B) 5 : 1
(C) 1 : 1
(D) 2 : 1
(E) depends on the values of a, b, c, d, and e

24. A B C D E

24. The sum of five odd numbers is always:

(A) even
(B) divisible by three
(C) divisible by five
(D) a prime number
(E) None of the above.

25. A B C D E

25. If E is an even number, and F is divisible by three, then what is the *largest* number by which E^2F^3 *must* be divisible?

(A) 6
(B) 12
(C) 54
(D) 108
(E) 144

26. A B C D E

26. If the average of five consecutive even numbers is 8, which of the following is the smallest of the five numbers?

(A) 4
(B) 5
(C) 6
(D) 8
(E) None of the above.

27. A B C D E

27. If a number is divisible by 23, then it is also divisible by which of the following?

(A) 7
(B) 24
(C) 9
(D) 3
(E) None of the above.

28. A B C D E

28. What is the average (to the nearest tenth) of the following numbers: 91.4, 91.5, 91.6, 91.7, 91.7, 92.0, 92.1, 92.3, 92.3, 92.4?

(A) 91.9
(B) 92.0
(C) 92.1
(D) 92.2
(E) 92.3

29. A B C D E

29. Which of the following numbers is divisible by 11?

(A) 30,217
(B) 44,221
(C) 59,403
(D) 60,411
(E) None of the above.

30. A B C D E

30. Which of the following is the best approximation of the product $(1.005)(20.0025)(0.0102)$?

(A) 0.02
(B) 0.2
(C) 2.0
(D) 20
(E) 200

31. A B C D E

31. If a, b, and c are all divisible by 8, then their average must be

(A) divisible by 8
(B) divisible by 3
(C) divisible by 5
(D) divisible by 7
(E) None of the above.

32. A B C D E

32. Which of the following numbers is divisible by 24?

(A) 13,944
(B) 15,746
(C) 15,966
(D) 16,012
(E) None of the above.

33. A B C D E

33. Which of the following numbers is a prime?

(A) 147
(B) 149
(C) 153
(D) 155
(E) 161

34. A B C D E

34. The sum of four consecutive odd integers must be:

(A) even, but not necessarily divisible by 4
(B) divisible by 4, but not necessarily by 8
(C) divisible by 8, but not necessarily by 16
(D) divisible by 16
(E) None of the above.

35. A B C D E

35. Which of the following is closest to the square root of $\frac{3}{5}$?

(A) $\frac{1}{2}$

(B) $\frac{2}{3}$

(C) $\frac{3}{4}$

(D) $\frac{4}{5}$

(E) 1

36. A B C D E

36. The sum of an odd and an even number is

(A) a perfect square
(B) negative
(C) even
(D) odd
(E) None of the above.

Answer Key for Practice Test 6

1. E	10. C	19. D	28. A
2. D	11. D	20. B	29. A
3. B	12. C	21. C	30. B
4. E	13. C	22. A	31. E
5. D	14. C	23. B	32. A
6. C	15. D	24. E	33. B
7. B	16. B	25. D	34. C
8. D	17. E	26. A	35. C
9. E	18. E	27. E	36. D

Answers and Solutions for Practice Test 6

1. Choice E is correct. The five consecutive odd numbers must be n, $n + 2$, $n + 4$, $n + 6$, and $n + 8$. Their average is equal to their sum, $5n + 20$, divided by the number of addends, 5, which yields $n + 4$ as the average.   (601)

2. Choice D is correct. Choosing 34 as an approximate average results in the following addends: $+1.5$, -1.5, 0, $+1.0$, and $+0.5$. Their sum is $+1.5$. Now, divide by 5 to get $+0.3$ and add this to 34 to get 34.3. (To check this, add the five original numbers and divide by 5.)   (601)

3. Choice B is correct. Since Q is an odd number, it may be represented by $2m + 1$, where m is an integer. Similarly, call R $2n + 1$, where n is an integer. Thus, $Q - R$ is equal to $(2m + 1) - (2n + 1)$, $2m - 2n$, or $2(m - n)$. Now, since m and n are integers, $m - n$ will be some integer p. Thus, $Q - R = 2p$. Any number in the form of $2p$, where p is any integer, is an even number. Therefore, $Q - R$ *must* be even. (A) and (C) are wrong, because an even number multiplied by an odd is always even. (D) and (E) are only true for specific values of P, Q, and R.   (604)

4. Choice E is correct. If a number is divisible by 102, then it must be divisible by all of the factors of 102. The only choice that is a factor of 102 is 2.   (607)

5. Choice D is correct. To be divisible by 36, a number must be divisible by both 4 and 9. Only (A) and (D) are divisible by 4. (Recall that only the last two digits must be examined.) Of these, only (D) is divisible by 9. (The sum of the digits of (A) is 23, which is not divisible by 9; the sum of the digits of (D) is 18.)   (607)

6. Choice C is correct. The prime numbers between 45 and 72 are 47, 53, 59, 61, 67, and 71. All of the others have factors other than 1 and themselves.   (608)

7. Choice B is correct. Since M must be an *integer*, the closest value it can have to $\frac{1}{2}$ is either 1 or 0. In either case, $\left(M - \frac{1}{2}\right)^2$ is equal to $\frac{1}{4}$, or 0.25.   (409)

8. Choice D is correct. Approximate each of the numbers to only one significant digit (this is permissible, because the choices are so far apart; if they had been closer together, two or three significant digits should be used). After this approximation, the expression is: $\frac{7 \times 10}{0.2}$, which is equal to 350. This is closest to 370.   (609)

9. Choice E is correct. The average for the boys alone was $\frac{74 + 82 + 84 + 84 + 88 + 95}{6}$, or $507 \div 6 = 84.5$. The girls' average was $\frac{80 + 82 + 86 + 86}{4}$, or $334 \div 4 = 83.5$, which is 1.0 below the boys' average.   (601)

10. Choice C is correct. The sum of an odd number and an even number can be expressed as $(2n + 1) + (2m)$, where n and m are integers. ($2n + 1$ must be odd, and $2m$ must be even.) Their sum is equal to $2n + 2m + 1$, or $2(m + n) + 1$. Since $(m + n)$ is an integer, the quantity $2(m + n) + 1$ *must* represent an odd integer. (604, 605)

11. Choice D is correct. The actual length of one of the sides would be the square root of 12. Square each of the five choices to find that the square of 3.4 is 11.56, and the square of 3.5 is 12.25. The square root of 12 must lie between 3.4 and 3.5. Squaring 3.45 (halfway between the two choices) yields 11.9025, which is less than 12. Thus the square root of 12 must be greater than 3.45 and therefore closer to 3.5 than to 3.4. (612)

12. Choice C is correct. Factor $n^2 + 2n + 1$ to $(n + 1)(n + 1)$ or $(n + 1)^2$. Now, since n is an odd number, $n + 1$ must be even (the number after every odd number is even). Thus, representing $n + 1$ as $2k$, where k is an integer ($2k$ is the standard representation for an even number), yields the expression $(n + 1)^2 = (2k)^2$, or $4k^2$. Thus, $(n + 1)^2$ is a multiple of 4, and it must be divisible by 4. A number divisible by 4 must also be even, so (C) is the best choice. (604–607)

13. Choice C is correct. Convert to decimals. Then calculate the value of $\dfrac{3.50 + 4.25 + 2.25 + 3.25 + 4.00}{5}$. This equals $17.25 \div 5$, or 3.45. (601)

14. Choice C is correct. If a number is divisible by 24, it must be divisible by 3 and 8. Of the five choices given, only choice (C) is divisible by 8. Add the digits in 80,424 to get 18. As this is divisible by 3, the number is divisible by 3. The number, therefore, is divisible by 24. (607)

15. Choice D is correct. If the boy is to average 65 for five subjects, the total of his five grades must be five times 65, or 325. The sum of the first four grades is $55 + 60 + 65 + 65$, or 245. Therefore, the fifth mark must be $325 - 245$, or 80. (601)

16. Choice B is correct. If t is any integer, then $2t$ is an even number. Adding 3 to an even number always produces an odd number. Thus, $2t + 3$ is always odd. (606)

17. Choice E is correct. Call the five numbers a, b, c, d, and e. Then the average is $\dfrac{(a + b + c + d + e)}{5}$. Since this must be even, $\dfrac{(a + b + c + d + e)}{5} = 2k$, where k is an integer. Thus $a + b + c + d + e = 10k$. Therefore, the sum of the 5 numbers is divisible by 10, 2, and 5. Thus the first three choices are eliminated. If the five numbers were 1, 1, 1, 1, and 6, then the average would be 2. Thus, the average is even, but not all of the numbers are even. Thus, choice (D) can be true. If all the numbers were odd, the sum would have to be odd. This contradicts the statement that the average is even. Thus, choice (E) is the answer. (601, 607)

18. Choice E is correct. First, round off 23 and 79 to one significant digit. The numbers become 20 and 80. The product of these two numbers is 1,600, which rounded off to one significant digit is 2,000. (611)

19. Choice D is correct. 0.7 squared is 0.49. Squaring 0.8 yields 0.64. Thus, the square root of $\frac{1}{2}$ must lie between 0.7 and 0.8. Take the number halfway between these two, 0.75, and square it. This number, 0.5625, is more than $\frac{1}{2}$, so the square root must be closer to 0.7 than to 0.8. An easier way to do problems concerning the square roots of 2 and 3 and their multiples is to memorize the values of these two square roots. The square root of 2 is about 1.414 (remember fourteen-fourteen), and the square root of three is about 1.732 (remember that 1732 was the year of George Washington's birth). Apply these as follows: $\frac{1}{2} = \frac{1}{4} \times 2$. Thus, $\sqrt{\frac{1}{2}} = \sqrt{\frac{1}{4}} \times \sqrt{2} = \frac{1}{2} \times 1.414 = 0.707$, which is very close to 0.7. (612)

20. Choice B is correct. The prime numbers can be found by taking all the odd numbers between 56 and 100 (the even ones cannot be primes) and eliminating all the ones divisible by 3, by 5, or by 7. If a number under 100 is divisible by none of these, it must be prime. Thus, the only primes between 56 and 100 are 59, 61, 67, 71, 73, 79, 83, 89, and 97.   (608)

21. Choice C is correct. Since all the answer requires is an order-of-ten approximation, do not calculate the exact answer. Approximate the answer in the following manner: $\dfrac{1,000,000 \times 500,000}{1,000,000,000} = 500$. The only choice on the same order of magnitude is 600.   (609)

22. Choice A is correct. To round off 89.999, look at the number in the hundredths place. 9 is more than 5, so add 1 to the number in the tenths place and eliminate all of the digits to the right. Thus, we get 90.0.   (609)

23. Choice B is correct. The average of five numbers is found by dividing their sum by five. Thus, the sum is five times the average, so $S : M = 5 : 1$.   (601)

24. Choice E is correct. None of the first four choices is necessarily true. For example, the sum $5 + 7 + 9 + 13 + 15 = 49$ is not even, not divisible by 3, not divisible by 5, nor prime.   (604, 607, 608)

25. Choice D is correct. Any even number can be written as $2m$, and any number divisible by 3 can be written as $3n$, where m and n are integers. Thus, $E^2 F^3$ equals $(2m)^2 (3n)^3 = (4m^2)(27n^3) = 108(m^2 n^3)$, and 108 is the largest number by which $E^2 F^3$ must be divisible.   (607)

26. Choice A is correct. The five consecutive even numbers can be represented as n, $n + 2$, $n + 4$, $n + 6$, and $n + 8$. Taking the sum and dividing by five yields an average of $n + 4$. Thus, $n + 4 = 8$, the given average, and $n = 4$, the smallest number.   (601)

27. Choice E is correct. If a number is divisible by 23, then it is divisible by all of the factors of 23. But 23 is a prime with no factors except 1 and itself. Therefore, the correct choice is (E).   (607)

28. Choice A is correct. To find the average, it is convenient to choose 92.0 as an approximate average and then find the average of the differences between the actual numbers and 92.0. Thus, add up: $(-0.6) + (-0.5) + (-0.4) + (-0.3) + (-0.3) + (0.0) + 0.1 + 0.3 + 0.3 + 0.4 = -1.0$; divide this by 10 (the number of quantities to be averaged) to obtain -0.1. Finally, add this to the approximate average, 92.0, to obtain a final average of 91.9.   (601)

29. Choice A is correct. To determine if a number is divisible by 11, take each of the digits separately and, beginning with either end, subtract the second from the first, add the following digit, subtract the next one, add the one after that, etc. If this result is divisible by 11, the entire number is. Thus, because $3 - 0 + 2 - 1 + 7 = 11$, we know that 30,217 is divisible by 11. Using the same method, we find that the other four choices are not divisible by 11.   (607)

30. Choice B is correct. This is simply an order-of-ten approximation, so round off the numbers and work the following problem. $(1.0)(20.0)(0.01) = 0.20$. The actual answer is closest to 0.2.   (611)

31. Choice E is correct. Represent the three numbers as $8p$, $8q$, and $8r$, respectively. Thus, their sum is $8p + 8q + 8r$, and their average is $\dfrac{(8p + 8q + 8r)}{3}$. This need not even be a whole number. For example, the average of 8, 16, and 32 is $\dfrac{56}{3}$, or $18\dfrac{2}{3}$.   (601, 607)

32. Choice A is correct. To be divisible by 24, a number must be divisible by both 3 and 8. Only 13,944 and 15,966 are divisible by 3; of these, only 13,944 is divisible by 8 ($13,944 = 24 \times 581$).   (607)

33. Choice B is correct. The approximate square root of each of these numbers is 13. Merely divide each of these numbers by the primes up to 13, which are 2, 3, 5, 7, and 11. The only number not divisible by any of these primes is 149. (608, 612)

34. Choice C is correct. Call the first odd integer $2k + 1$. (This is the standard representation for an odd integer.) Thus, the next 3 odd integers are $2k + 3$, $2k + 5$, and $2k + 7$. (Each one is 2 more than the previous one.) The sum of these integers is $(2k + 1) + (2k + 3) + (2k + 5) + (2k + 7) = 8k + 16$. This can be written as $8(k + 2)$, which is divisible by 8, but not necessarily by 16. (606, 607)

35. Choice C is correct. By squaring the five choices, it is evident that the two closest choices are $\left(\frac{3}{4}\right)^2 = 0.5625$ and $\left(\frac{4}{5}\right)^2 = 0.64$. Squaring the number halfway between $\frac{3}{4}$ and $\frac{4}{5}$ gives $(0.775)^2 = 0.600625$. This is greater than $\frac{3}{5}$, so the square root of $\frac{3}{5}$ must be closer to $\frac{3}{4}$ than to $\frac{4}{5}$. (612)

36. Choice D is correct. Let the even number be $2k$, where k is an integer, and let the odd number be $2m + 1$, where m is an integer. Thus, the sum is $2k + (2m + 1)$, $2k + 2m + 1$, or $2(k + m) + 1$. Now $k + m$ is an integer, since k and m are integers. Call $k + m$ by another name, p. Thus, $2(k + m) + 1$ is $2p + 1$, which is the representation of an odd number. (604, 606)

MATH REFRESHER
SESSION 7

Tables, Charts, and Graphs

Charts and Graphs

701. Graphs and charts show the relationship of numbers and quantities in visual form. By looking at a graph, you can see at a glance the relationship between two or more sets of information. If such information were presented in written form, it would be hard to read and understand.

Here are some things to remember when doing problems based on graphs or charts:

1. Understand what you are being asked to do before you begin figuring.

2. Check the dates and types of information required. Be sure that you are looking in the proper columns, and on the proper lines, for the information you need.

3. Check the units required. Be sure that your answer is in thousands, millions, or whatever the question calls for.

4. In computing averages, be sure that you add the figures you need and no others, and that you divide by the correct number of years or other units.

5. Be careful in computing problems asking for percentages.
   (a) Remember that to convert a decimal into a percent you must multiply it by 100. For example, 0.04 is 4%.
   (b) Be sure that you can distinguish between such quantities as 1% (1 percent) and .01% (one one-hundredth of 1 percent), whether in numerals or in words.
   (c) Remember that if quantity X is greater than quantity Y, and the question asks what percent quantity X is of quantity Y, the answer must be greater than 100 percent.

Tables and Charts

702. A table or chart shows data in the form of a box of numbers or chart of numbers. Each line describes how the numbers are connected.

Example:

Test Score	Number of Students
90	2
85	1
80	1
60	3

Example: How many students took the test?

Solution: To find out the number of students that took the test, just add up the numbers in the column marked "Number of Students." That is, add $2 + 1 + 1 + 3 = 7$.

Example: What was the difference in score between the highest and the lowest score?

Solution: First look at the highest score: 90. Then look at the lowest score: 60. Now calculate the difference: $90 - 60 = 30$.

Example: What was the <u>median</u> score?

Solution: The median score means the score that is in the *middle* of all the scores. That is, there are just as many scores above the median as below it. So in this example, the scores are 90, 90 (there are two 90s) 85, 80, and 60, 60, 60 (there are three 60s). So we have:

$$90$$
$$90$$
$$85$$
$$80$$
$$60$$
$$60$$
$$60$$

80 is right in the middle. That is, there are three scores above it and three scores below it. So 80 is the median.

Example: What was the <u>mean</u> score?

Solution: The mean score is defined as the *average* score. That is, it is the

$$\frac{\text{sum of the scores}}{\text{total number of scores}}$$

The sum of the scores is $90 + 90 + 85 + 80 + 60 + 60 + 60 = 525$. The total number of scores is $2 + 1 + 1 + 3 = 7$, so divide 7 into 525 to get the average: 75.

Graphs

703. To read a graph, you must know what *scale* the graph has been drawn to. Somewhere on the face of the graph will be an explanation of what each division of the graph means. Sometimes the divisions will be labeled. At other times, this information will be given in a small box called a *scale* or *legend*. For instance, a map, which is a specialized kind of graph, will always carry a scale or legend on its face telling you such information as $1'' = 100$ miles or $\frac{1}{4}'' = 2$ miles.

Bar Graphs

704. The bar graph shows how information is compared by using broad lines, called bars, of varying lengths. Sometimes single lines are used as well. Bar graphs are good for showing a quick comparison of the information involved; however, the bars are difficult to read accurately unless the end of the bar falls exactly on one of the divisions of the scale. If the end of the bar falls between divisions of the scale, it is not easy to arrive at the precise figure represented by the bar. In bar graphs, the bars can run either vertically or horizontally. The sample bar graph following is a horizontal graph.

EXPENDITURES PER PUPIL—1990

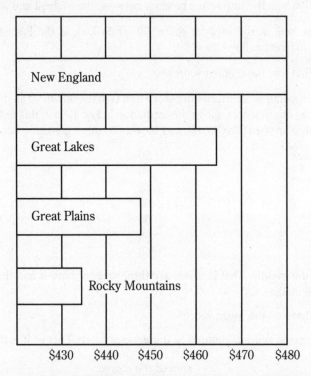

The individual bars in this kind of graph may carry a label within the bar, as in this example. The label may also appear alongside each bar. The scale used on the bars may appear along one axis, as in the example, or it may be noted somewhere on the face of the graph. Each numbered space on the *x*-axis (or horizontal axis) represents an expenditure of $10 per pupil. A wide variety of questions may be answered by a bar graph, such as:

(1) Which area of the country spends least per pupil? Rocky Mountains.

(2) How much does the New England area spend per pupil? $480.

(3) How much less does the Great Plains spend per pupil than the Great Lakes?
$464 − 447 = $17/pupil.

(4) How much more does New England spend on a pupil than the Rocky Mountain area?
$480 − 433 = $47/pupil.

Circle Graphs

705. A circle graph (or pie chart) shows how an entire quantity has been divided or apportioned. The circle represents 100 percent of the quantity; the different parts into which the whole has been divided are shown by sections, or wedges, of the circle. Circle graphs are good for showing how money is distributed or collected, and for this reason they are widely used in financial graphing. The information is usually presented on the face of each section, telling you exactly what the section stands for and the value of that section in comparison to the other parts of the graph.

SOURCES OF INCOME—PUBLIC COLLEGES OF THE U.S.

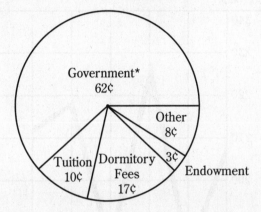

*Government refers to all levels of government—not exclusively the federal government.

The circle graph above indicates where the money originates that is used to maintain public colleges in the United States. The size of the sections tells you at a glance which source is most important (government) and which is least important (endowments). The sections total 100¢, or $1.00. This graph may be used to answer the following questions:

(1) What is the most important source of income to the public colleges? Government.

(2) What part of the revenue dollar comes from tuition? 10¢.

(3) Dormitory fees bring in how many times the money that endowments bring in? $5\frac{2}{3}$ times $\left(\frac{17}{3} = 5\frac{2}{3}\right)$.

(4) What is the least important source of revenue to public colleges? Endowments.

Line Graphs

706. Graphs that have information running both across (horizontally) and up and down (vertically) can be considered to be laid out on a grid having a *y*-axis and an *x*-axis. One of the two quantities being compared will be placed along the *y*-axis, and the other quantity will be placed along the *x*-axis. When we are asked to compare two values, we subtract the smaller from the larger.

SHARES OF STOCK SOLD
NEW YORK STOCK EXCHANGE DURING ONE SIX-MONTH PERIOD

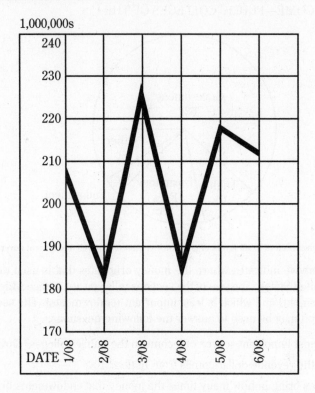

Our sample line graph represents the total shares of stock sold on the New York Stock Exchange between January and June. The months are placed along the *x*-axis, while the sales, in units of 1,000,000 shares, are placed along the *y*-axis.

(1) How many shares were sold in March? 225,000,000.

(2) What was the trend of stock sales between April and May? The volume of sales rose.

(3) Compare the share sales in January and February. 25,000,000 fewer shares were sold in February.

(4) During which months of the period was the increase in sales largest? February to March.

Practice Test 7 and Solutions

Tables, Charts, and Graphs

Correct answers and solutions follow each test.

TABLE CHART TEST

Questions 1–5 are based on this table chart.

The following chart is a record of the performance of a baseball team for the first seven weeks of the season.

	Games Won	Games Lost	Total No. of Games Played
First Week	5	3	8
Second Week	4	4	16
Third Week	5	2	23
Fourth Week	6	3	32
Fifth Week	4	2	38
Sixth Week	3	3	44
Seventh Week	2	4	50

1. How many games did the team win during the first seven weeks?

   (A) 32
   (B) 29
   (C) 25
   (D) 21
   (E) 50

2. What percent of the games did the team win?

   (A) 75%
   (B) 60%
   (C) 58%
   (D) 29%
   (E) 80%

3. According to the chart, which week was the worst for the team?

   (A) second week
   (B) fourth week
   (C) fifth week
   (D) sixth week
   (E) seventh week

4. Which week was the best week for the team?

   (A) first week
   (B) third week
   (C) fourth week
   (D) fifth week
   (E) sixth week

5. If there are fifty more games to play in the season, how many more games must the team win to end up winning 70% of the games?

   (A) 39
   (B) 35
   (C) 41
   (D) 34
   (E) 32

Solutions

1. Choice B is correct. To find the total number of games won, add the number of games won for all the weeks, $5 + 4 + 5 + 6 + 4 + 3 + 2 = 29$. (702)

2. Choice C is correct. The team won 29 out of 50 games, or 58%. (702)

3. Choice E is correct. The seventh week was the only week that the team lost more games than it won. (702)

4. Choice B is correct. During the third week, the team won 5 games and lost 2, or it won about 70% of the games that week. Compared with the winning percentages for other weeks, the third week's was the highest. (702)

5. Choice C is correct. To win 70% of all the games, the team must win 70 out of 100. Since it won 29 games out of the first 50 games, it must win $70 - 29$, or 41 games out of the next 50 games. (702)

PIE CHART TEST

Questions 1–5 are based on this pie chart.

POPULATION BY REGION, 1964

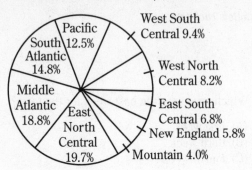

Total U.S. Population: 191.3 million = 100%

1. Which region was the most populated region in 1964?

   (A) East North Central
   (B) Middle Atlantic
   (C) South Atlantic
   (D) Pacific
   (E) New England

2. What part of the entire population lived in the Mountain region?

   (A) $\frac{1}{10}$

   (B) $\frac{1}{30}$

   (C) $\frac{1}{50}$

   (D) $\frac{1}{25}$

   (E) $\frac{1}{8}$

3. What was the approximate population in the Pacific region?

   (A) 20 million
   (B) 24 million
   (C) 30 million
   (D) 28 million
   (E) 15 million

4. Approximately how many more people lived in the Middle Atlantic region than in the South Atlantic?

   (A) 4.0 million
   (B) 7.7 million
   (C) 5.2 million
   (D) 9.3 million
   (E) 8.5 million

5. What was the total population in all the regions combined?

   (A) 73.3 million
   (B) 100.0 million
   (C) 191.3 million
   (D) 126.8 million
   (E) 98.5 million

Solutions

1. Choice A is correct. East North Central, with 19.7% of the total population, had the largest population. (705)

2. Choice D is correct. The Mountain region had 4.0% of the population. 4.0% is $\frac{1}{25}$. (705)

3. Choice B is correct. Pacific had 12.5% of the population. 12.5% of 191.3 million is .125 × 191.3, or about 24 million. (705)

4. Choice B is correct. Middle Atlantic had 18.8% and South Atlantic had 14.8% of the population. So, Middle Atlantic had 4.0% more. 4.0% of 191.3 million is .04 × 191.3, or about 7.7 million. (705)

5. Choice C is correct. All the regions combined had 100% of the population, or 191.3 million. (705)

LINE GRAPH TEST

Questions 1–5 are based on this line graph.

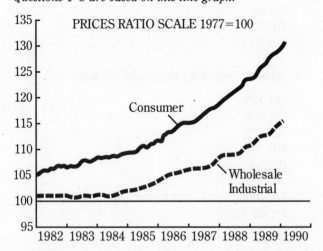

1. On the ratio scale, what were consumer prices recorded as at the end of 1985?

   (A) 95
   (B) 100
   (C) 105
   (D) 110
   (E) 115

2. During what year did consumer prices rise fastest?

(A) 1983
(B) 1985
(C) 1987
(D) 1988
(E) 1989

3. When wholesale and industrial prices were recorded as 110, consumer prices were recorded as

(A) between 125 and 120
(B) between 120 and 115
(C) between 115 and 110
(D) between 110 and 105
(E) between 105 and 100

4. For the eight years 1982–1989 inclusive, the average increase in consumer prices was

(A) 1 point
(B) 2 points
(C) 3 points
(D) 4 points
(E) 5 points

5. The percentage increase in wholesale and industrial prices between the beginning of 1982 and the end of 1989 was

(A) 1 percent
(B) 5 percent
(C) 10 percent
(D) 15 percent
(E) less than 1 percent

Solutions

1. Choice D is correct. Drawing a vertical line at the end of 1985, we reach the consumer price graph at about the 110 level. (706)

2. Choice E is correct. The slope of the consumer graph is clearly steepest in 1989. (706)

3. Choice A is correct. Wholesale and industrial prices were about 110 at the beginning of 1989, when consumer prices were between 120 and 125. (706)

4. Choice C is correct. At the beginning of 1982 consumer prices were about 105; at the end of 1989 they were about 130. The average increase is $\frac{130-105}{8} = \frac{25}{8}$, or about 3. (706)

5. Choice D is correct. At the beginning of 1982, wholesale prices were about 100; at the end of 1989, they were about 115. The percent increase is about

$$\frac{115-100}{100} \times 100\%, \text{ or } 15\%. \quad (706)$$

BAR GRAPH TEST

Questions 1–3 are based on this bar graph.

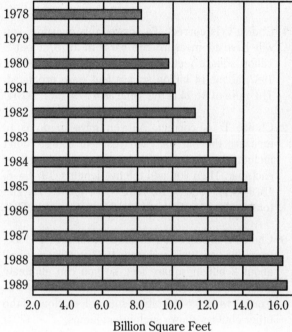

Softwood Plywood Shows Growth

1. What was the approximate ratio of soft plywood produced in 1978 as compared with that produced in 1987?

(A) 1 : 1
(B) 2 : 3
(C) 4 : 7
(D) 3 : 4
(E) 1 : 3

2. For the years 1978 through 1983, excluding 1982, how many billion square feet of plywood were produced altogether?

(A) 23.2
(B) 29.7
(C) 34.1
(D) 49.8
(E) 52.6

3. Between which consecutive odd years and between which consecutive even years was the plywood production jump greatest?

(A) 1985 and 1987; 1978 and 1980
(B) 1983 and 1985; 1984 and 1986
(C) 1979 and 1981; 1980 and 1982
(D) 1981 and 1983; 1980 and 1982
(E) 1983 and 1985; 1982 and 1984

Solutions

1. Choice C is correct. To answer this question, you will have to measure the bars. In 1978, about 8 billion square feet of plywood were produced. In 1987, about 14 billion square feet were produced. The ratio of 8 : 14 is the same as 4 : 7.   (704)

2. Choice D is correct. All you have to do is to measure the bar for each year—of course, don't include the 1982 bar—and estimate the length of each bar. Then you add the five lengths. 1978 = 8, 1979 = 10, 1980 = 10, 1981 = 10, 1983 = 12. The total is close to 50.   (704)

3. Choice E is correct. The jumps from 1981 to 1983, from 1983 to 1985, and from 1987 to 1989 were all about 2 billion square feet, so you can eliminate answers A and C. The jump from 1982 to 1984 was from 11 to 13.5 = 2.5 billion square feet. None of the other choices shows such broad jumps.   (704)

CUMULATIVE GRAPH TEST

Questions 1–5 are based on this cumulative graph.

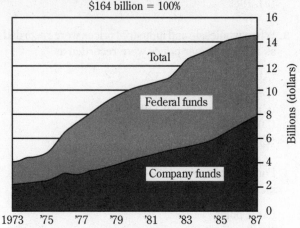

Spending for Research & Development
by Type of Research, 1987
$164 billion = 100%

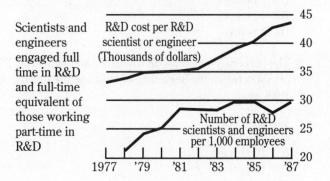

Scientists and engineers engaged full time in R&D and full-time equivalent of those working part-time in R&D

1. About how much in government funds was spent for research and development in 1987?

(A) $4 billion
(B) $6 billion
(C) $12 billion
(D) $16 billion
(E) $24 billion

2. In 1987, about what percent of the total spending in research and development were company funds?

(A) 25%

(B) 35%

(C) 45%

(D) 55%

(E) 65%

3. What was the change in the relative number of research and development scientists and engineers with respect to all employees from 1984 to 1985?

(A) 10%
(B) 5%
(C) 2%
(D) 3%
(E) 0%

4. What was the increase in company funds in research and development from 1973 to 1987?

(A) $12 billion
(B) $6 billion
(C) $8 billion
(D) $4 billion
(E) $14 billion

5. What was the percent of increase of the company funds spent in research and development from 1973 to 1987?

(A) 100%
(B) 50%
(C) 300%
(D) 400%
(E) 1,000%

Solutions

1. Choice B is correct. Total spending was about $14 billion, and company spending was about $8 billion. So, government spending was about $6 billion.

(706)

2. Choice D is correct. Company funds totaled about $8 billion, and the total funds were about $14 billion. So, company funds were $\frac{4}{7}$ of total funds, or 57%.

(706)

3. Choice E is correct. The graph showing the relative employment of research and development scientists and engineers was horizontal between 1984 and 1985. This means no change. (706)

4. Choice B is correct. Company funds totaled $8 billion in 1987 and $2 billion in 1973. The increase was $6 billion. (706)

5. Choice C is correct. Company funds totaled $2 billion in 1973, and the increase from 1973 to 1987 was $6 billion, or 300% of $2 billion. (706)

MATH REFRESHER
SESSION 8

Modern Math:
Sets, Relations, Solution
Sets, Axioms, Closed Sets,
and Mathematical Symbols

Sets

801. A set is a collection of anything: numbers, letters, objects, etc. The members, or elements of the set are written between braces like this: $\{1, 2, 3, 4, 5\}$. The elements of this set are simply the numbers 1, 2, 3, 4, and 5. Another example of a set is {apples, peaches, pears}. Two sets are equal if they have the same elements. The order in which the elements of the set are listed does not matter. Thus $\{1, 2, 3, 4, 5\} = \{5, 4, 3, 2, 1\}$. We can use one letter to stand for a whole set; for example, $A = \{1, 2, 3, 4, 5\}$.

802. To find the union of two sets:

Write down every member in one or both of the two sets. The union of two sets is a new set. The union of sets A and B is written $A \cup B$.

For example: If $A = \{1, 2, 3, 4\}$ and $B = \{2, 4, 6\}$, find $A \cup B$. All the elements in either A or B or both are 1, 2, 3, 4, and 6. Therefore $A \cup B = \{1, 2, 3, 4, 6\}$.

803. To find the intersection of two sets:

Write down every member that the two sets have in common. The intersection of the sets A and B is a set written $A \cap B$.

Example: If $A = \{1, 2, 3, 4\}$ and $B = \{2, 4, 6\}$, find $A \cap B$. The elements in both A and B are 2 and 4. Therefore $A \cap B = \{2, 4\}$.

> If two sets have no elements in common, then their intersection is the null or empty set, written as $\varnothing$.

Example: The intersection of $\{1, 3, 5, 7\}$ with $\{2, 4, 6, 8\}$ is $\varnothing$, since they have no members in common.

804. To perform several union and intersection operations, first operate on sets within parentheses.

Example: If $A = \{1, 2, 3\}$ and $B = \{2, 3, 4, 5, 6\}$ and $C = \{1, 4, 6\}$ find $A \cup (B \cap C)$.
First we find $B \cap C$ by listing all the elements in both B and C. $B \cap C = \{4, 6\}$.
Then $A \cup (B \cap C)$ is just the set of all members in at least one of the sets A and $\{4, 6\}$.
Therefore, $A \cup (B \cap C) = \{1, 2, 3, 4, 6\}$.

805. A subset of a set is a set, all of whose members are in the original set. Thus, $\{1, 2, 3\}$ is a subset of the set $\{1, 2, 3, 4, 5\}$. Note that the null set is a subset of every set, and also that every set is a subset of itself. In general, a set with n elements has 2^n subsets. For example: How many subsets does $\{x, y, z\}$ have? This set has 3 elements and therefore 2^3, or 8, subsets.

Relations

806. When the elements of a set are ordered pairs, then the set is called a relation. An ordered pair is written (x, y). The order of the two components of the ordered pair matters. Therefore the ordered pairs (x, y) and (y, x) are not equal.

> The domain of a relation is the set of the first components of the ordered pairs. The range of a relation is the set of the second components of the ordered pairs. A relation is a function if each element of the domain occurs only once as a first component.

Example: $R = \{(a, b), (a, c), (b, c), (c, d)\}$. Find the domain and range of R. Is the relation R a function?

The domain is the set of first components. These are a, a, b, and c, so that the domain is $\{a, b, c\}$. The range is the set of second components. These are b, c, c, and d. Thus the range is $\{b, c, d\}$. R is not a function, since the letter a occurs twice as a first component.

807. The inverse of a relation is the relation with all the ordered pairs reversed. Thus, the inverse of $R = \{(1, 2), (3, 4), (5, 6)\}$ is $\{(2, 1), (4, 3), (6, 5)\}$.

Example: Find the domain of the inverse of $\{(m, n), (p, q), (r, s)\}$.

The domain of the inverse is simply the range of the original relation. So, the domain of the inverse is $\{n, q, s\}$. Similarly, the range of the inverse is the domain of the original relation.

Solution Sets

808. Sets can be used to indicate solutions to equations or inequalities. These sets are called solution sets. A solution set is just the set of the solutions to an equation. We may also demand that the elements of the solution set meet another condition. Thus, the solution set for the equation $10x - 5 = 0$ is simply $\left\{\frac{1}{2}\right\}$, since only $x = \frac{1}{2}$ solves the equation. If we demanded that the solution set consist only of whole numbers, then the solution set would be $\varnothing$, since no whole number solves this equation.

The solution set in the positive integers (whole numbers greater than 0) for the inequality $x < 4$ is $\{1, 2, 3\}$, since these are the only positive integers less than 4.

> When finding a solution set, first solve the equation or inequality and then use only the solutions that satisfy the condition required.

Example: Find the solution set in the positive integers for the inequality $4x < x + 13$.

First, $4x < x + 13$ means $3x < 13$, or $x < 4\frac{1}{3}$. Since x must be a positive integer, the solution set is the set of positive integers less than $4\frac{1}{3}$, or $\{1, 2, 3, 4\}$.

Sometimes we use the following notation:

$$R = \{x : x \geq 10\}$$

This would be read as "the set of all x such that x is greater than or equal to 10."

Axioms

809. On your test, there may be a list of axioms, or rules, about arithmetical operations with numbers. The list will contain examples of the use of the axioms. Problems will then ask you to identify which axiom is used to make a specific statement. An example of these axioms is the distributive law. A problem may ask you: Which axiom is used to justify $3(4 + 1) = 3 \cdot 4 + 3 \cdot 1$? The distributive axiom is used to justify this statement.

Another axiom is the commutative axiom of addition and multiplication. The equations $5 + 3 = 3 + 5$ and $5 \cdot 3 = 3 \cdot 5$ illustrate this axiom.

The last two rules are the associative axioms of addition and multiplication. Examples of these operations are the equations $(3 + 5) + 6 = 3 + (5 + 6)$ and $(3 \cdot 5)6 = 3(5 \cdot 6)$.

Closed Sets

810. A set is called "closed" under an operation if, under the operation, any two members of the set constitute an element of the set. Consider, for example, the set $\{0, 1\}$. This set is closed under the operation of multiplication because $0 \times 0 = 0$, $1 \times 1 = 1$, and $0 \times 1 = 0$. Note that in order for the set to be closed, the product of the elements multiplied by themselves must also be an element of the set $\{0 \times 0 = 0 \text{ and } 1 \times 1 = 1\}$.

Mathematical Symbols

- $\cdot$ multiplication dot; as in $x \cdot y$
- $(\ )$ parentheses; used to group expressions
- $\%$ percent
- $\div$ division
- $:$ ratio
- $=$ equals
- $\neq$ does not equal
- $<$ less than
- $>$ greater than
- $\leq$ less than or equal to
- $\geq$ greater than or equal to
- $\sqrt{\ }$ square root
- π pi, the ratio between the circumference and diameter of a circle; approximately equal to $\frac{22}{7}$.
- $\angle$ angle
- $\parallel$ is parallel to
- $\perp$ is perpendicular to
- $\wedge$ and
- $\vee$ or
- $\sim$ approximately
- $\rightarrow$ implies
- $\in$ belongs to
- $\subset$ is a subset of

Practice Test 8 and Solutions

Modern Math: Sets, Relations, Solution Sets, Axioms, Closed Sets, and Mathematical Symbols

Correct answers and solutions follow each test.

Sets Test

1. Which set equals {1, 2, 3, 4}?

(A) {*a, b, c, d*}
(B) {4, 5, 6, 7}
(C) {1, 3, 5, 7, 9}
(D) {4, 3, 2, 1}
(E) None of the above.

2. *A* = {1, 2, 3, 4, 5}. *B* = {2, 4, 6, 8}. *A* ∩ *B* equals

(A) {1, 2, 3, 4, 5, 6, 7, 8}
(B) {2, 4}
(C) {1, 2, 3, 4, 5, 6, 8, 10}
(D) {9}
(E) {1, 2, 6, 8}

3. *C* = {*a, b, c, d*}. *D* = {3, 4, *b*}. *C* ∪ *D* equals

(A) {*a, b, c, d*, 3, 4}
(B) {*b*}
(C) {3, 4}
(D) {*b, d*, 4}
(E) {*a, c*, 3, 4}

4. *A* = {1, 2, 3}. *B* = {2, 3, 4}. *C* = {3, 4, 5}. (*A* ∩ *B*) ∩ *C* equals

(A) {1, 2, 3, 4, 5}
(B) {1, 3, 5}
(C) {2, 3, 4}
(D) {1}
(E) {3}

5. How many elements are there in the set of even integers between 2 through 10 inclusive?

(A) 3
(B) 5
(C) 7
(D) 9
(E) 10

6. How many subsets does {*a, b, c*} have?

(A) 6
(B) 7
(C) 8
(D) 9
(E) 10

Use the following information to answer Questions 7–10.

A = {1, 3, 2, 5}.   *B* = {2, 4, 6}.   *C* = {1, 3, 5}.

7. (*A* ∪ *B*) ∩ *C* equals

(A) {1, 2, 3}
(B) {2, 4, 5}
(C) {1, 2, 5}
(D) {1, 3, 5}
(E) {3, 4, 5}

8. (*A* ∩ *B*) ∪ *C* equals

(A) {1, 2, 3, 5}
(B) {4}
(C) {2, 4}
(D) {1, 3, 5}
(E) {1, 2, 3, 4, 5}

9. How many subsets does *A* ∪ (*B* ∪ *C*) have?

(A) 2
(B) 4
(C) 16
(D) 32
(E) 64

10. Which set is not a subset of *A* ∪ *C*?

(A) ∅
(B) *A*
(C) *C*
(D) {4}
(E) {1, 2, 5}

Answers and Solutions

1. **(D)** {4, 3, 2, 1} contains the same elements as {1, 2, 3, 4}. Since the order does not matter, the sets are equal. (801)

2. **(B)** $A \cap B$ means the set of elements in both A and B, or {2, 4}. (803)

3. **(A)** $C \cup D$ means the set of elements in at least one of C and D, or {a, b, c, d, 3, 4}. (802)

4. **(E)** $(A \cap B) \cap C$ is the set of elements in all three sets. Only 3 is a member of all three sets, so $(A \cap B) \cap C = \{3\}$. (803)

5. **(B)** The set of even integers from 2 through 10 inclusive is {2, 4, 6, 8, 10}, which has 5 elements. (801)

6. **(C)** {a, b, c} has 3 elements and therefore 2^3, or 8, subsets. (805)

7. **(D)** First $(A \cup B) = \{1, 2, 3, 4, 5, 6\}$. Then {1, 2, 3, 4, 5, 6} $\cap$ {1, 3, 5} = {1, 3, 5}. (804)

8. **(A)** First $(A \cap B) = \{2\}$. Then {2} $\cup$ {1, 3, 5} = {1, 2, 3, 5}. (804)

9. **(E)** $A \cup (B \cup C)$ is the set of elements in at least one of the three sets, or {1, 2, 3, 4, 5, 6}, which has 2^6, or 64, subsets. (805)

10. **(D)** $A \cup C = \{1, 2, 3, 5\}$. Since 4 is not an element of this set, {4} is not a subset of $A \cup C$. (802, 805)

Relations Test

1. Which of the following sets are relations?

   I. $\{(1, 2), (a, c)\}$
   II. $\{(3, 8), (8, 3)\}$
   III. $\{(1, a), (2, c)\}$

(A) I only
(B) II only
(C) III only
(D) I and III only
(E) II and III only

2. Which of the following relations equals the relation $\{(a, b), (1, 2), (x, y)\}$?

(A) $\{(a, b), (1, x), (2, y)\}$
(B) $\{(x, y), (a, b), (1, 2)\}$
(C) $\{(12, xy), (a, b)\}$
(D) $\{(b, a), (2, 1), (x, y)\}$
(E) None of the above.

3. What is the range of $\{(1, 2), (3, 4), (5, 6)\}$?

(A) $\{1, 2, 3, 4, 5, 6\}$
(B) $\{(1, 2)\}$
(C) $\{(1, 2), (3, 4), (5, 6)\}$
(D) $\{1, 3, 5\}$
(E) None of the above.

4. What is the domain of $\{(1, 2), (2, 1), (1, 5)\}$?

(A) $\{1, 2\}$
(B) $\{(1, 2)\}$
(C) $\{1, 2, 5\}$
(D) $\{8\}$
(E) $\{3\}$

5. Which relation is a function?

(A) $\{(1, 1), (2, 2), (3, 3)\}$
(B) $\{(1, 1), (1, 2), (1, 3)\}$
(C) $\{(a, b), (b, a), (b, b)\}$
(D) $\{(1, 3), (1, 5), (1, 7)\}$
(E) $\{(1, a), (2, b), (2, 1)\}$

6. What is the inverse of $\{(1, 2), (3, 6), (4, 2)\}$?

(A) $\{1, 2, 3, 4, 5, 6\}$
(B) $\{(1, 3), (1, 4), (1, 6)\}$
(C) $\{(2, 1), (6, 3), (2, 4)\}$
(D) $\{(3, 2), (6, 4), (4, 1)\}$
(E) None of the above.

7. Which relation equals its inverse?

(A) $\{(1, 2)\}$
(B) $\{(1, 2), (3, 3)\}$
(C) $\{(1, 2), (3, 3), (2, 1)\}$
(D) $\{(4, 4), (2, 3), (3, 4)\}$
(E) $\{(1, 2), (2, 3), (3, 1)\}$

8. What is the domain of the inverse of $\{(a, 1), (b, 3), (c, 5)\}$?

(A) $\{a, b, c\}$
(B) $\{1, 3, 5\}$
(C) $\{1, a, 2, b, 3, c\}$
(D) $\{a, 5\}$
(E) $\{(a, 5)\}$

9. The inverse of which of the following is a function?

(A) $\{(1, 1), (1, 2), (1, 3)\}$
(B) $\{(a, 0), (b, 0), (c, 0)\}$
(C) $\{(a, j), (r, j), (a, r)\}$
(D) $\{(1, 2), (2, 3), (3, 2)\}$
(E) $\{(u, v), (w, v), (y, x)\}$

10. What is the range of the inverse of $\{(P, Q), (R, S), (T, V)\}$?

(A) $\{1, 2, 3\}$
(B) $\{P, Q, R\}$
(C) $\{Q, S, V\}$
(D) $\{P, R, T\}$
(E) $\{P, Q, R, S, T, V\}$

Answers and Solutions

1. **(D)** A set is a relation if all its elements are ordered pairs; I and III meet this condition; II does not. (806)

2. **(B)** Two relations are equal if their elements are equal. Though it doesn't matter in what order the ordered pairs are listed, if the elements of the ordered pairs are switched, the relation is changed. (806)

3. **(E)** The range of a relation is the set of second elements of the ordered pairs. The range of {(1, 2), (3, 4), (5, 6)} is {2, 4, 6}. (806)

4. **(A)** The domain is the set of first elements of the ordered pairs. The domain of {(1, 2), (2, 1), (1, 5)} is {1, 2}. (806)

5. **(A)** To be a function, a relation must not repeat any of the first elements of its ordered pairs. The first elements of {(1, 1), (2, 2), (3, 3)} are all distinct. (806)

6. **(C)** To find the inverse, simply reverse all the ordered pairs. (807)

7. **(C)** Reversing (1, 2) we get (2, 1); reversing (3, 3) we get (3, 3); reversing (2, 1) we get (1, 2). Though they are in a different order, the ordered pairs of the inverse of (C) are the same as the ordered pairs of (C). (807)

8. **(B)** The domain of the inverse is the range of the relation, or {1, 3, 5}. (806, 807)

9. **(A)** If the inverse of the relation is to be a function, the second elements must be all distinct. The second elements of the ordered pairs of (A) are 1, 2, and 3, all distinct. (806, 807)

10. **(D)** The range of the inverse is the domain of the function, or {P, R, T}. (806, 807)

Solution Sets Test

Find the solution sets in Questions 1–3.

1. $2x - 4 = 0$

(A) $\{2\}$
(B) $\{4\}$
(C) $\{-4\}$
(D) $\{0\}$
(E) $\{2, -4\}$

2. $x + 9 = 3 - x$

(A) $\{-3\}$
(B) $\{9\}$
(C) $\{3\}$
(D) $\{-3, 9\}$
(E) $\varnothing$

3. $(x + 2)(x - 1) = 0$

(A) $\{-1\}$
(B) $\{-2, -1\}$
(C) $\{1\}$
(D) $\{-2, 1\}$
(E) $\{2, 1\}$

Find the solution sets in the positive integers for Questions 4–7.

4. $x + 7 = 9$

(A) $\{7\}$
(B) $\{9\}$
(C) $\{16\}$
(D) $\{2\}$
(E) $\{9, 7\}$

5. $x - 3 = -4$

(A) $\{-3\}$
(B) $\{-4\}$
(C) $\{1\}$
(D) $\{-1\}$
(E) $\varnothing$

6. $x > 2x - 4$

(A) $\{1\}$
(B) $\{2, 3\}$
(C) $\{1, 2, 3\}$
(D) $\{1, 2, 3, 4\}$
(E) $\varnothing$

7. $(x + 1)(x - 4) = 0$

(A) $\{4\}$
(B) $\{1, 4\}$
(C) $\{-1, 1, 4\}$
(D) $\{0\}$
(E) $\{-4\}$

Find the solution set in the negative integers for Questions 8–10.

8. $(x + 3)(x + 6) = 0$

(A) $\{3, 6\}$
(B) $\{-3, -6\}$
(C) $\{-3\}$
(D) $\{-6\}$
(E) $\varnothing$

9. $(2x + 7)(x - 3) = 0$

(A) $\{2, 7, -3\}$
(B) $\{-3\}$
(C) $\left\{-3\frac{1}{2}\right\}$
(D) $\{2\}$
(E) $\varnothing$

10. $10 + 2x > 0$

(A) $\{-1, -2\}$
(B) $\{-10, -8, -6\}$
(C) $\{-1, -2, -3, -4, -5\}$
(D) $\{-1, -2, -3, -4\}$
(E) $\{1, 2, 3, 4\}$

Answers and Solutions

1. **(A)** $2x - 4 = 0$. $x = 2$, so the solution set is $\{2\}$.
(808)

2. **(A)** $x + 9 = 3 - x$. $2x = -6$, or $x = -3$. The solution set is $\{-3\}$.
(808)

3. **(D)** $(x + 2)(x - 1) = 0$, so $x = -2$ or 1. The solution set is $\{-2, 1\}$.
(808)

4. **(D)** $x + 7 = 9$ or $x = 2$, which is a positive integer. The solution set is $\{2\}$.
(808)

5. **(E)** $x - 3 = -4$, or $x = -1$, which is not a positive integer. The solution set is $\varnothing$.
(808)

6. **(C)** $x > 2x - 4$, or $x < 4$. The positive integers less than 4 are 1, 2, and 3.
(808)

7. **(A)** $(x + 1)(x - 4) = 0$. $x = -1$ or 4. 4 is a positive integer but -1 is not, so the solution set is $\{4\}$.
(808)

8. **(B)** $(x + 3)(x + 6) = 0$. $x = -3$ or -6, both of which are negative integers, so the solution set is $\{-3, -6\}$.
(808)

9. **(E)** $(2x + 7)(x - 3) = 0$. $x = -3\frac{1}{2}$ or 3, neither of which is a negative integer. The solution set is $\varnothing$.
(808)

10. **(D)** $10 + 2x > 0$. $2x > -10$ or $x > -5$. The negative integers greater than -5 are -1, -2, -3, and -4.
(808)

Axioms Test

Use the following axioms to answer Questions 1–5.

I.   Commutative axiom for addition: $a + b = b + a$

II. Associative axiom for addition: $a + (b + c) = (a + b) + c$

III. Commutative axiom for multiplication: $ab = ba$

IV. Associative axiom for multiplication: $(ab)c = a(bc)$

V.   Distributive axiom: $a(b + c) = ab + ac$

In Questions 1–4, which axiom can be used to justify the given statements?

1. $3 \cdot 5 = 5 \cdot 3$

(A) I
(B) II
(C) III
(D) IV
(E) V

2. $(3 + 7) + 4 = 3 + (7 + 4)$

(A) I
(B) II
(C) III
(D) IV
(E) V

3. $(2 \cdot 5) \cdot 3 = (5 \cdot 2) \cdot 3$

(A) I
(B) II
(C) III
(D) IV
(E) V

4. $3(6 + 2) = 18 + 6$

(A) I
(B) II
(C) III
(D) IV
(E) V

5. Which two axioms can be used to justify the following:
$5(3 + 4) = 20 + 15$?

(A) I and II
(B) I and III
(C) III and V
(D) IV and V
(E) V and I

Answers and Solutions

1. **(C)** To go from 3 · 5 to 5 · 3, we switch the order of multiplication. The axiom that deals with order of multiplication is the commutative axiom for multiplication, III. (809)

2. **(B)** Switching parentheses in addition involves the associative axiom for addition, II. (809)

3. **(C)** To go from (2 · 5) · 3 to (5 · 2) · 3 we switch the order of multiplying inside the parentheses. This is justified by the commutative axiom for multiplication, III. (809)

4. **(E)** To go from 3(6 + 2) to 3 · 6 + 3 · 2, or 18 + 16, we use the distributive axiom, V. (809)

5. **(E)** To go from 5(3 + 4) to 5 · 3 + 5 · 4, or 15 + 20, we use the distributive axiom, V. To go from 15 + 20 to 20 + 15, we use the commutative axiom of addition, I. (809)

PART 7

VOCABULARY BUILDING THAT IS GUARANTEED TO RAISE YOUR GRE SCORE

Knowing Word Meanings Is Essential for a Higher GRE Score

Improving your vocabulary is essential if you want to get a high score on the Verbal Reasoning Section of the GRE.

The Verbal Reasoning Section part of the GRE consists of two different question types: Sentence Completions and Reading Comprehension. In this part, almost all GRE exam takers come across many "tough" words, whose meanings they do not know. These students thereby lose many points, because if they do not know the meanings of the words in the questions, they aren't able to answer the questions confidently—and so, they are likely to answer incorrectly.

Every additional correct answer on the GRE gives you approximately 10 additional points, or 1 additional point on the new GRE scale. The Sentence Completion questions contain quite a number of tough words whose meanings you will have to know in order to answer these questions correctly.

Several tough words show up in the Reading Comprehension passages of every GRE exam. Knowing the meanings of these difficult words will, of course, help you to understand the passages better. It follows that knowing what the passages are all about will help you correctly answer the Reading Comprehension questions that appear on the GRE—*and each additional correct answer nets you approximately 10 more points, or 1 more point on the new GRE scale.*

8 Steps to Word Power

1. Study vocabulary lists. This book has the list you need for GRE preparation. "The Gruber GRE 3,400-Word List" begins on page 377.

2. Take vocabulary tests. "100 Tests to Strengthen Your Vocabulary" begins on page 426.

3. Learn those Latin and Greek roots, prefixes, and suffixes that make up many English words. It has been estimated that more than half of all English words come from Latin and Greek. "The Gruber Prefix-Root-Suffix List" begins on page 366. Also learn the "Hot Prefixes and Roots" in Appendix A beginning on page 717.

4. Have a dictionary at home or look up meanings of words online. When you are on the move, you can use a dictionary app on your phone.

5. Read—read—read. By reading a great deal, you will encounter new and valuable words. You will learn the meanings of many of these words by context—that is, you will perceive a clear connection between a new word and the words that surround that word. In this way, you will learn the meaning of that new word.

6. Listen to what is worth listening to. Listen to good radio and TV programs. Listen to people who speak well. Go to selected movies and plays. Just as you will increase your vocabulary by reading widely, you will increase your vocabulary by listening to English that is spoken well.

7. Play word games like crossword puzzles, anagrams, and Scrabble.

8. Make sure you learn the Vocabulary Strategies beginning on page 168.

No One Can Dispute This Fact!

You will pile up GRE points by taking advantage of the valuable Vocabulary Building study and practice materials that are offered to you in the following pages of this chapter.

You Don't Have to Learn the Meaning of Every Word on the GRE 3,400-Word List

Go as far into the alphabetized groups as time permits. Use the Vocabulary Learning Steps listed on page 377. If you cannot learn the meanings of all the words in the 3,400-Word List, don't fret. Whatever words you have added to your vocabulary *before* you take the actual test will raise your GRE Verbal score substantially.

IMPORTANT NOTE: If you cannot spend time memorizing some of the words in the Gruber 3,400-Word List, I strongly suggest that you read through the Vocabulary Strategies in the Strategy Section beginning on page 168. Also make sure you study the roots and prefixes on pages 366 through 370, especially the checked ones. You may also want to study the Hot Prefixes and Roots in Appendix A beginning on page 717.

The Gruber Prefix-Root-Suffix List That Gives You the Meanings of More Than 150,000 Words

Word Building with Roots, Prefixes, and Suffixes

According to some linguistic studies, approximately 60 percent of our English words are derived from Latin and Greek. One reliable study has shown that a selected list of 20 prefixes and 14 root elements pertain to more than 100,000 words in an unabridged dictionary. Here we have done even better—we've given you a list of prefixes and roots that will give you meanings of more than 150,000 words! The following entries of Latin and Greek roots, prefixes, and suffixes frequently show up in some of the words in the GRE Verbal areas, Sentence Completions and Reading Comprehension. Learn these Latin and Greek word parts to increase your vocabulary immensely—and thus score well in the Verbal part of your GRE.

> The shortest and best way of learning a language is to know the roots of it; that is, those original primitive words from which other words are formed.
>
> —Lord Chesterfield

Lord Chesterfield is, in effect, saying that roots are used as important "building blocks" of many of our English words. As you study the following list of Latin and Greek roots, prefixes, and suffixes, have a dictionary by your side. Look up the meanings of the word examples that are given if you do not know their meanings.

Roots

A ROOT IS THE BASIC ELEMENT—FUNDAMENTAL OR ESSENTIAL PART—OF A WORD.

The checked roots are especially important.

ROOT	MEANING AND EXAMPLE*
✓ **ag, act**	do, act; as *agent, counteract*
agr	field; as *agriculture, agoraphobia*
alt	high; as *altitude, altar*
alter	other; as *altercation, alternative*
✓ **am**	friend, love; as *amity, amorous*
anim	mind, life spirit; as *animate, animal, animosity*
ann, annu, enni	year; as *annuity, annual, anniversary, perennial*
anthrop	man; as *philanthropy, anthropoid*
aper	open; as *aperture, aperient*
apt	fit; as *adapt, aptitude*
aqu	water; as *aqueous, aquacade*
arch	rule, govern; as *anarchy, matriarch*
aster, astr	star; as *asteroid, disaster, astronomy*
aud	hear; as *audible, audition*
aur	gold; as *auriferous*
✓ **bas**	low; as *debase, basement*
bell	war; as *bellicose, antebellum*
ben	good, well; as *benevolent, benefactor*
bibl	book; as *biblical, bibliography*
bio	life; as *biology, biopsy*
brev	short; as *brevity, abbreviation*
cad, cas, cid	fall; as *cadence, casualty, incident*
cand	white, shining; as *candid, candidate*
✓ **cap, capt, cept**	take, hold; as *capable, captive, intercept*
capit	head; as *capital, decapitate*
carn	flesh; as *carnal, carnivorous*
✓ **ced, cess**	yield, go; as *cede, procession*
celer	swift; as *celerity, accelerate*
cent	hundred; as *century, centipede*
chrom	color; as *chromium, chromatic*
chron	time; as *chronology, chronic*

ROOT	MEANING AND EXAMPLE
cid, cis	cut, kill; as *suicide, precision*
clin	lean, bend; as *inclination, recline*
clud, clus	close, shut; as *conclude, recluse*
cogn	know; as *incognito, cognizant*
cord	heart; as *cordial, accord*
corp	body; as *corpulent, corpse*
cosm	world; as *cosmic, cosmopolitan*
✓ **cred**	believe; as *incredible, credentials*
✓ **curr, curs**	run; as *current, cursory*
dec	ten; as *decimal, decade*
dem	people; as *democracy, demographic*
derm	skin; as *epidermis, dermatologist*
di	day; as *diary, sundial*
✓ **dic, dict**	speak, say; as *indicate, contradict*
dign	worthy; as *dignity, indignant*
domin	lord, master; as *dominate, indomitable*
dorm	sleep; as *dormant, dormitory*
✓ **duc, duct**	lead; as *induce, ductile*
ego	I; as *egotism, egomaniac*
equ	equal; as *equity, equanimity*
✓ **fac, fact, fect, fic**	make, do; as *facile, factory, infection, fiction*
✓ **fer**	bear, carry; as *fertile, confer*
fid	faith, trust; as *confide, infidelity*
fin	end; as *infinite, final*
flect, flex	bend; as *reflect, flexible*
form	shape; as *conform, reformation*
✓ **fort**	strong; as *fortitude, fortify*
frag, fract	break; as *fragile, fracture*
fug	flee; as *fugitive, refugee*
fus	pour; as *confuse, fusion*
✓ **gen**	kind, race, birth; as *generate, generic, generation*
gest	carry, bring; as *congestion, gestation*
grad, gress	step, go; as *graduate, digress*

* Refer to a dictionary for word meanings you don't know.

ROOT	MEANING AND EXAMPLE	ROOT	MEANING AND EXAMPLE
graph	write; as *autograph, graphic*	**pater, patri**	father; as *paternal, patriot*
grat	pleasing; as *gratitude, congratulate*	**ped, pod**	foot; as *impede, biped, tripod*
hydr	water; as *dehydrated, hydrant*	**ped**	child; as *pediatrics, pedagogue*
integr	entire, whole; as *integrate, integral*	**pel, puls**	drive; as *compel, expulsion*
✓ **ject**	throw; as *inject, projection*	**pend, pens**	hang; as *pendant, pension*
junct	join; as *conjunction, juncture*	**pet**	seek; as *impetus, petition*
lat	carry; as *translation, dilate*	**petr**	stone, rock; as *petrify*
leg, lig, lect	choose, gather; as *legible, eligible, collect*	**phil**	loving; as *philosophy*
liber	free; as *liberate, libertine*	**phob**	fear; as *claustrophobia*
✓ **loc**	place; as *dislocate, local*	**phon**	sound; as *phonic, phonetics*
log	word, study; as *catalogue, psychology*	✓ **plic**	fold, bend; as *complicate, implicate*
loqu, locut	speak, talk; as *loquacious, circumlocution*	✓ **pon, pos**	place, put; as *component, compose*
luc, lum	light; as *translucent, illuminate*	✓ **port**	carry, bring; as *porter, import*
magn	great; as *magnitude, magnificent*	**pot**	drink; as *potion, potable*
✓ **man**	hand; as *manufacture, manual*	**poten**	powerful; as *potentate, impotent*
mar	sea; as *marine, maritime*	**prehend, prehens**	take, grasp; as *apprehend, comprehension*
mater	mother; as *maternal, matrimony*	**prot**	first; as *protagonist, prototype*
mega	large; as *megaton, megaphone*	**psych**	mind; as *psychological, psychic*
ment	mind; as *mentality, mentally*	**quer, quir, quis, ques**	ask, seek; as *query, inquiry, inquisition, quest*
merg	plunge, sink; as *submerge, merger*	**reg, rig, rect**	rule, govern; as *regent, rigid, corrective*
meter	measure; as *chronometer, symmetry*	**rid, ris**	laugh; as *ridiculous, risible*
micro	small; as *microscope, microfilm*	**rupt**	break; as *rupture, erupt, interruption*
migr	wander; as *migrate, immigration*	**sacr**	holy; as *sacred, sacrificial*
mir	look; as *admire, mirror*	**sanct**	holy; as *sanction, sanctify*
✓ **mit, miss**	send; as *admit, submission*	**sci, scio**	know; as *science, conscious, omniscient*
mon	advise, remind; as *admonish, monument*	**scop**	watch; as *periscope, horoscope*
✓ **mort**	death; as *immortality, mortal*	✓ **scrib, script**	write; as *describe, prescription*
mot, mov	move; as *motor, motility, movable*	**sec, sect**	cut; as *secant, bisect*
✓ **mult**	many; as *multitude, multifarious*	**sed, sid, sess**	sit, seat; as *sedate, reside, session*
✓ **mut**	change; as *mutation, transmute, immutable*	**sent, sens**	feel, think; as *sentiment, sensible*
✓ **nat**	born; as *natal, innate*	✓ **sequ, secut**	follow; as *sequel, consecutive*
nav	ship; as *naval, navigate*	**serv**	keep; as *reserve, conservation*
neg	deny; as *negate, renege*	**sist**	place, stand; as *assist, resistance*
nomen	name; as *nominee, nomenclature, cognomen*	**solv, solu**	loosen; as *dissolve, absolution*
nov	new; as *novelty, novice, innovation*	**somn**	sleep; as *somnambulist, insomnia*
ocul	eye; as *oculist, binocular*	**soph**	wisdom; as *sophisticated, philosophy*
oper	work; as *cooperation, operate*		

ROOT	MEANING AND EXAMPLE	ROOT	MEANING AND EXAMPLE
✓ spec, spect, spic	look, appear; as *specimen, prospect, conspicuous*	trit	rub; as *trite, attrition*
spir	breathe; as *conspire, respiration*	trud, trus	thrust; as *intrude, abstruse*
✓ stat, stab	stand; as *status, stability*	umbra	shade; as *umbrella, umbrage*
string, strict	bind; as *stringent, stricture*	urb	city; as *suburb, urban*
stru, struct	build; as *construe, destructive*	vac	empty; as *vacate, evacuation*
sum, sumpt	take; as *assume, presumption*	vad, vas	go; as *evade, evasive*
tang, ting, tact, tig	touch; as *tangent, contingency, contact, contiguous*	val, vail	be strong; as *valid, prevail*
teg, tect	cover; as *tegument, detect*	✓ ven, vent	come; as *convene, prevention*
tele	distance; as *telescope, teletype*	✓ ver	true; as *veracity, aver*
tempor	time; as *temporary, extemporaneous*	verb	word; as *verbose, verbatim*
✓ ten, tain	hold, reach; as *tenant, tension, retain*	✓ vert, vers	turn; as *convert, reverse*
term	end; as *terminal, terminate*	vid, vis	see; as *evident, visible*
ter, terr	land, earth; as *inter, terrace*	vinc, vict	conquer; as *invincible, evict*
therm	heat; as *thermometer, thermos*	viv, vit	live; as *vivacity, vital*
tort, tors	twist; as *contort, torsion*	voc, vok	call; as in *vocation, revoke*
✓ tract	draw; as *attract, extract*	volv, volut	roll, turn; as in *involve, revolution*

Prefixes

A PREFIX IS PART OF A WORD THAT MAY BE PLACED BEFORE THE BASIC ELEMENT (ROOT) OF A WORD.

The checked prefixes are especially important.

PREFIX	MEANING AND EXAMPLE	PREFIX	MEANING AND EXAMPLE
✓ a, ab, abs	from, away; as *avert, abjure, absent*	✓ contra, contro, counter	against; as *contradict, controvert, counteract*
✓ ad	to; as *adhere*. By assimilation, *ad-* takes the forms of **a-, ac-, af-, al-, an-, ap-, as-, at-**; as *aspire, accord, affect, allude, annex, appeal, assume, attract*	✓ de	down, away from, about; as *descend, depart, describe*
ambi, amphi	around, both; as *ambidextrous, amphibious*	demi	half; as *demigod, demitasse*
		dia	across, through; as *diameter, diastole*
✓ ante, anti	before; as *antedate, anticipate*	✓ dis, di, dif	apart, not; as *dissension, division, diffident*
✓ anti	against; as *antidote, antislavery*	✓ equi	equal; as *equinox, equivalent*
arch	first, chief; as *archangel, archenemy*	✓ ex, e, ef	out of, from; as *extract, eject, efface*
auto	self; as *autobiography, automatic*	extra	out of, beyond; as *extraordinary, extraterrestrial*
ben	good, well; as *benediction, benefactor*		
✓ bi	two; as *bilateral, bisect*	✓ hyper	too much; as *hypercritical, hypersensitive*
✓ circum	around; as *circumnavigate, circumvent*	hypo	too little, under; as *hypochondriac, hypodermic*
✓ com, con, col, cor, co	together; as *commit, concord, collect, correct, coworker*		

PREFIX	MEANING AND EXAMPLE
✓ in, il, im, ir	into, in, on; as *invade, illustrate, immerse, irritate*
✓ in, il, im, ir	not; as *indistinct, illegal, impossible, irresponsible*
inter, intro	between, among; as *interpose, introduce*
✓ mal, mis	bad; as *malevolent, mistreat*
mono	one, single; as *monotone, monorail*
neo	new; as *neoplasm, neophyte*
✓ non	not; as *nonentity, nonconformist*
✓ ob, of, op	against; as *obviate, offend, oppose*
✓ omni	all; as *omniscient, omnipresent*
ortho	straight; as *orthodox, orthopedic*
pan	all; as *pantheism, Pan-American*
✓ peri	around; as *perimeter, periscope*
✓ poly	many; as *polygon, polygamy*
✓ post	after; as *postpone, postmortem*

PREFIX	MEANING AND EXAMPLE
✓ pre	before; as *predict, precursory*
✓ pro	forward, before; as *proceed, provide*
✓ re	back, again; as *recur, recede*
retro	backward; as *retrogress, retrospect*
se	apart, away; as *seduce, sedition*
semi	half; as *semicircle, semiconscious*
✓ sub	under; as *submarine, subversive*
✓ super	above, beyond; as *superpose, supernatural*
syn, sym	with, at the same time; as *synonymous, sympathetic*
✓ trans	across; as *transcontinental, transmit*
ultra	beyond; as *ultraliberal, ultramodern*
✓ un	not; as *unaware, uninformed*
✓ uni	one; as *unanimous, uniform*
vice	instead of; as *vice-chancellor, viceroy*

Suffixes

A SUFFIX IS PART OF A WORD THAT MAY FOLLOW THE BASIC ELEMENT (ROOT) OF A WORD.

The checked suffixes are especially important.

SUFFIX	MEANING AND EXAMPLE
✓ able, ible	able; as *pliable, returnable, comestible*
acious, cious	having the quality of; as *capacious, meretricious*
age	act, condition; as *courage, foliage*
al	belonging to; as *legal, regal*
✓ ance, ence	state of; as *abundance, indulgence*
✓ ate, ent, ant, ante	one who; as *candidate, advocate, resident, tenant, debutante*
ary, eer, er	one who, concerning; as *secretary, engineer, mariner*
✓ cy	state, position of; as *adequacy, presidency*
dom	state of; as *freedom, serfdom*
✓ ence	state of; as *presence, credence*
er, or	one who; as *player, actor, monitor, employer*
✓ escent	becoming; as *adolescent, putrescent*
✓ fy	make; as *beautify, sanctify*
hood	state of; as *knighthood, childhood*
ic, id	of, like; as *bucolic, acrid*

SUFFIX	MEANING AND EXAMPLE
✓ il, ile	capable of being; as *evil, servile*
✓ ion	act of; as *desperation, perspiration*
✓ ious	characterized by; as *spacious, illustrious*
✓ ish	like; as *boyish, foolish*
ism	belief in or practice of; as *idealism, capitalism*
ist	one who practices or is devoted to; as *anarchist, harpist*
✓ ive	relating to; as *abusive, plaintive*
mony	state of; as *harmony, matrimony*
✓ ness	quality of; as *willingness, shrewdness*
ory	a place for; as *factory, depository*
✓ ous, ose	full of; as *ponderous, verbose*
ship	state of, skill; as *friendship, gamesmanship*
✓ some	characteristic of; as *loathsome, fearsome*
tude	state of; as *lassitude, rectitude*
ward	in the direction of; as *windward, backward*
✓ y	full of; as *unruly, showy*

A List of Standardized Test Words Appearing More Than Once on Actual Standardized Exams Such as the GRE and SAT

We have made a computerized analysis of frequently occurring words on 47 complete standardized exams. (1,175 questions have been examined.) Following is a list of words or associated words appearing *more than once* on these 47 actual exams.

The definitions of these words have not been included here because we want you to *refer to a dictionary* to learn the meanings of these words, which have been repeated in subsequent question sections.

Note that after each word a numeral indicates the number of times that the word has appeared on the 47 actual exams.

Also note that certain pairs of words have a left-side bracket. The bracket indicates that the words are very closely allied in meaning—so if you learn the meaning of one of the two words in the pair, you will easily arrive at the meaning of the other word of the pair.

Learn the meanings of these words, as they are often repeated in questions of the test.

abolish 2	⌈ capitulate 1	⌈ daunt 3	⌈ expendable 1	⌈ leniency 1
abridge 2	⌊ capitulation 1	⌊ dauntless 1	⌊ expenditures 1	⌊ lenient 1
abstemious 2	capricious 4	debilitate 2	exclude 2	⌈ levity 1
⌈ accent 1	clemency 2	deplete 2	facilitate 2	⌊ levitate 1
⌊ accented 1	⌈ coalesce 2	discrepancy 3	fallow 2	listless 2
accolade 2	⌊ coalescence 1	disentangle 2	fertile 2	maladroit 2
acquiesce 2	⌈ cohere 1	⌈ disputatious 1	⌈ flourish 3	mitigate 2
affirmation 2	⌊ coherent 1	⌊ dispute 2	⌊ flower 1	mobile 2
amass 2	⌈ compress 1	⌈ distend 1	fraudulent 3	⌈ munificent 2
⌈ ambivalence 1	⌊ compression 1	⌊ distention 1	⌈ fruitful 1	⌊ munificence 1
⌊ ambivalent 1	⌈ confide 1	drawback 2	⌊ fruitless 1	myriad 2
ambulatory 2	⌊ confidential 1	efface 3	garner 2	nefarious 2
ameliorate 2	confound 2	⌈ effervesce 1	guile 2	⌈ obscure 1
amity 2	congeal 2	⌊ effervescent 1	hackneyed 2	⌊ obscurity 1
anchor 2	⌈ contaminant 1	enhance 2	hefty 2	⌈ opaque 1
antediluvian 2	⌊ contaminate 2	enigmatic 2	hideous 2	⌊ opacity 1
ascendancy 2	converge 2	ephemeral 3	hilarity 2	parsimony 2
atrophy 2	convivial 2	equilibrium 3	humane 2	paucity 2
⌈ bane 1	copious 2	⌈ euphonious 1	⌈ hypocrisy 1	penury 2
⌊ baneful 1	corroborate 2	⌊ euphony 1	⌊ hypocritical 1	⌈ peripheral 2
bizarre 2	corrugated 2	evacuate 2	innocuous 2	⌊ periphery 2
blunder 2	⌈ corrupt 1	evanescent 2	irascible 2	placate 2
bungle 2	⌊ corruption 1	⌈ expedite 1	jettison 2	⌈ precise 1
burgeon 2	cursory 2	⌊ expeditious 1	kindle 2	⌊ precision 1

premature 2
premeditated 2
prevalent 2
proclivity 2
[prodigal 1
[prodigious 2
[profuse 1
[profusion 2
[pulverize 1
[pulverized 1

rant 2
recalcitrant 2
recant 2
replete 2
rescind 2
reserve 2
ruffle 2
rupture 2
saccharine 2
salubrious 2

somber 4
[specify 1
[specificity 1
spurn 2
squander 2
stymie 2
subtle 2
summary 2
summon 3
sumptuous 2

[surreptitious 1
[surreptitiously 1
tantamount 2
[tenacious 1
[tenacity 1
[transience 1
[transient 1
turbulence 3
venturesome 3
viable 2

[vibrancy 1
[vibrant 1
vilification 2
[virulence 1
[virulent 1
whet 2
zany 2

The Most Important/Frequently Used GRE Words and Their Opposites

Following is a list of popular GRE words and their opposites. *Note:* These words fit into specific categories, and it may be a little easier memorizing the meaning of these important words knowing what category they fit into.

POSITIVE	NEGATIVE	POSITIVE	NEGATIVE
TO PRAISE	TO BELITTLE	TO CALM OR MAKE BETTER	TO MAKE WORSE OR RUFFLE
acclaim	admonish		
applaud	assail	abate	alienate
commend	berate	accede	antagonize
eulogize	calumniate	accommodate	contradict
exalt	castigate	allay	dispute
extol	censure	ameliorate	embitter
flatter	chastise	appease	estrange
hail	chide	assuage	incense
laud	decry	comply	infuriate
panegyrize	denigrate	concede	nettle
resound	denounce	conciliate	oppugn
tout	disparage	gratify	oppose
	excoriate	mitigate	repulse
	execrate	mollify	snub
	flay	pacify	
	lambaste	palliate	
	malign	placate	
	reprimand	propitiate	
	reproach	quell	
	scold	satiate	
	upbraid		
	vilify		

POSITIVE	NEGATIVE	POSITIVE	NEGATIVE
PLEASANT	**UNPLEASANT**	**YIELDING**	**NOT YIELDING**
affable	callous	accommodating	adamant
amiable	cantankerous	amenable	determinate
agreeable	captious	compliant	immutable
captivating	churlish	deferential	indomitable
congenial	contentious	docile	inflexible
cordial	gruff	flexible	intractable
courteous	irascible	hospitable	intransigent
decorous	ireful	inclined	recalcitrant
engaging	obstinate	malleable	relentless
gracious	ornery	obliging	resolute
obliging	peevish	pliant	steadfast
sportive	perverse	submissive	tenacious
unblemished	petulant	subservient	
undefiled	querulous	tractable	
	testy		
	vexing		
	wayward		
GENEROUS	**CHEAP**	**COURAGEOUS**	**TIMID**
altruistic	frugal	audacious	diffident
beneficent	miserly	dauntless	indisposed
benevolent	niggardly	gallant	laconic
charitable	paltry	intrepid	reserved
effusive	parsimonious	stalwart	reticent
hospitable	penurious	undaunted	subdued
humanitarian	skinflinty	valiant	timorous
magnanimous	spartan	valorous	
munificent	tight-fisted		
philanthropic	thrifty		
ABUNDANT OR RICH	**SCARCE OR POOR**	**LIVELY**	**BLEAK**
affluent	dearth	brisk	dejected
bounteous	deficit	dynamic	forlorn
copious	destitute	ebullient	lackluster
luxuriant	exiguous	exhilarating	lugubrious
multifarious	impecunious	exuberant	melancholy
multitudinous	impoverished	inspiring	muted
myriad	indigent	provocative	prostrate
opulent	insolvent	scintillating	somber
pecunious	meager	stimulating	tenebrous
plenteous	paltry	titillating	
plentiful	paucity		
plethoric	penurious		
profuse	scanty		
prosperous	scarcity		
superabundant	sparse		
teeming			
wealthy			

POSITIVE	NEGATIVE	POSITIVE	NEGATIVE
CAREFUL	CARELESS	HUMBLE	HAUGHTY
chary	culpable	demure	affected
circumspect	felonious	diffident	aristocratic
conscientious	indifferent	indisposed	arrogant
discreet	insouciant	introverted	audacious
exacting	lackadaisical	laconic	authoritarian
fastidious	lax	plebeian	autocratic
gingerly	negligent	reluctant	condescending
heedful	perfunctory	restrained	disdainful
judicious	rash	reticent	egotistical
meticulous	remiss	subdued	flagrant
provident	reprehensible	subservient	flippant
prudent	temerarious	taciturn	imperious
punctilious		timid	impertinent
scrupulous		timorous	impudent
scrutinous		unassuming	insolent
wary		unostentatious	ostentatious
		unpretentious	pompous
			proud
			supercilious
			vainglorious

Note: In many cases you can put the prefix *im-* or *un-* in front of the word to change its meaning to its opposite.

EXAMPLE: *Pecunious.* Opposite: *Impecunious*
Ostentatious. Opposite: *Unostentatious*

Practice Questions

1. Find the OPPOSITE of EXTOL:

   (A) oppose (B) restrain (C) enter
   (D) deviate (E) denigrate

2. ALLAY (opposite):

   (A) incense (B) drive (C) berate
   (D) signify (E) determine

3. DECOROUS (opposite):

   (A) scanty (B) irascible (C) musty
   (D) pliant (E) rigid

4. AMENABLE (opposite):

   (A) tiresome (B) uncultured (C) intransigent
   (D) soothing (E) careless

5. MUNIFICENT (opposite):

   (A) simple (B) pallid (C) crafty
   (D) penurious (E) stable

6. PLETHORIC (opposite):

   (A) impecunious (B) slothful (C) indifferent
   (D) reticent (E) sly

7. METICULOUS (opposite):

   (A) timid (B) plenteous (C) peevish
   (D) intractable (E) perfunctory

8. IMPERIOUS (opposite):

   (A) unostentatious (B) lackadaisical
   (C) insolvent (D) churlish (E) immutable

9. TIMOROUS (opposite):

   (A) judicious (B) intrepid (C) multifarious
   (D) benevolent (E) tenebrous

10. LUGUBRIOUS (opposite):

    (A) flexible (B) unblemished (C) ebullient
    (D) conciliatory (E) impertinent

Answers to Practice Questions

1. Choice E is correct. *Extol* fits into the category of TO PRAISE. *Denigrate* fits into the category TO BELITTLE—the opposite category.

2. Choice A is correct. *Allay* fits into the category of TO CALM. *Incense* fits into the opposite category—TO MAKE WORSE or TO RUFFLE.

3. Choice B is correct. *Decorous* fits into the category of PLEASANT. The opposite category is UNPLEASANT. *Irascible* fits into this category.

4. Choice C is correct. *Amenable* fits into the category of YIELDING. *Intransigent* fits into the opposite category—NOT YIELDING.

5. Choice D is correct. *Munificent* fits into the category of GENEROUS. *Penurious* fits into the category of CHEAP, the opposite category.

6. Choice A is correct. *Plethoric* fits into the category of ABUNDANT or RICH. *Impecunious* fits into the opposite category of SCARCE or POOR.

7. Choice E is correct. *Meticulous* fits into the category of CAREFUL. *Perfunctory* fits into the category of CARELESS (or mechanical).

8. Choice A is correct. *Imperious* fits into the category of HAUGHTY (high-brow). *Unostentatious* fits into the category of HUMBLE, the opposite category.

9. Choice B is correct. *Timorous* fits into the category of TIMID. *Intrepid* fits into the opposite category of COURAGEOUS.

10. Choice C is correct. *Lugubrious* fits into the category of BLEAK, or dismal. *Ebullient* fits into the opposite category of LIVELY.

The Gruber GRE
3,400-Word List

Every new word that you learn in this GRE word list can help you to add extra points to your GRE verbal score.

Vocabulary Learning Steps

1. Conceal each definition with a card as you go down the column.

2. *Jot down each word whose meaning you do not know.* Then prepare a flash card for each word you did not know. Write the synonym (word with a similar meaning) on the back of the card.

3. Study the flash cards that you have made up.

4. After you have studied the DID-NOT-KNOW flash cards, give yourself a flash card test. Put aside the flash cards for the words you did know.

5. For each word you still do not know, write a sentence that includes the word you still have not learned well.

6. Now test yourself again on the DID-NOT-KNOW flash cards referred to in Step 5. Put aside your flash cards for the words you did know.

7. Study the newly reduced pile of DID-NOT-KNOW flash cards.

8. Give yourself a flash card test on this newly reduced DID-NOT-KNOW pile.

9. Keep reducing your DID-NOT-KNOW flash card pile until you have no DID-NOT-KNOW words.

IMPORTANT

Do not throw your flash cards away. Keep the cards for reinforcement testing in the future.

In past exams, 70 to 80 percent of all test vocabulary words appeared on this list!

ABACK–AZURE

aback   (preceded by *taken*) surprised; startled

abandon   to leave; to give up; to discontinue

abase   to humiliate; to humble; to lower

abash   ashamed; embarrassed

abate   to lessen; to decrease

abdicate   to yield; to give up

abduct   to take away; to kidnap

aberration   abnormality; deviation

abet   to aid; to encourage

abeyance   a temporary postponement

abhor   to hate; to detest

abide   (*two meanings*) to remain; to put up with

abject   miserable; wretched

abjure   to give up (rights)

ablution   a washing; cleansing

abnegate   to deny; to reject

abolition   doing away with; putting an end to

abominate   to detest; to dislike strongly

aborigine   original inhabitant

abortive   unsuccessful

abound   to be large in number

aboveboard   honest; frank; open

abrade   to wear away

abridge   to shorten

abrogate   to abolish; to repeal

abscond   to leave secretly; to flee

absolve   to free from responsibility

abstemious   moderate or sparing in eating or drinking

abstinence   self-denial; resistance to temptation

abstract   (*two meanings*) a summary (*noun*); to remove (*verb*)

abstruse   hard to understand

absurd   ridiculous; unreasonable

abut   to touch; to rest on or against

abysmal   wretched; extremely bad

abyss   a bottomless pit; anything infinite

academic   (*two meanings*) pertaining to school; theoretical or unrealistic

accede   to agree to

accelerate   to speed up; to move faster

accessible   easy to approach; open

access   approach; admittance

accessory   something additional

acclaim   to greet with approval

acclimate   to adapt; to get used to

acclivity   upward slope

accolade   honor; award; approval

accommodate   to make fit; to help

accomplice   a partner in crime

accord   agreement

accost   to approach and speak to

accoutrement   equipment; outfit

accredit   to approve; to certify

accretion   an increase; an addition

accrue   to gather; to accumulate

acerbic   sharp or bitter in smell or taste; sharpness of temper or words

Achilles' heel   a weakness

acknowledge   to admit; to confess

acme   highest point; peak

acoustics   the branch of physics dealing with sound

acquiesce   to agree; to consent

acquit   to free of guilt; to clear

acrid   bitter to the taste or smell; sarcastic

acrimonious   harsh in speech or behavior

acronym   word formed from initials

acrophobia   fear of heights

actuate   to put into motion or action

acumen   mental keenness; shrewdness

acute   sharp; keen

ad infinitum   endlessly; forever

ad lib   to act or speak without preparation

adage   a familiar saying

adamant   stubborn; unyielding

adapt   to adjust; to change

addendum   something added as a supplement

addled   confused

adduce   to give an example in proving something

adept   highly skilled

adherent   (*two meanings*) sticking fast (*adjective*); a follower or a supporter (*noun*)

adipose   fatty

adjacent   near; close; adjoining

adjudicate   to judge

adjunct   a subordinate; an assistant

admonish   to warn

ado   fuss; trouble

Adonis   a very handsome man

adorn   to dress up; to decorate

adroit   skillful; clever

adulation   excessive praise or flattery

adulterate   to make impure

advent   an arrival; a coming

adventitious   accidental; nonessential

adversary   enemy; opponent

adversity   a misfortune; distress

advocate   to recommend; to defend

aegis   a shield; protection; sponsorship

aesthetic   pertaining to beauty

affable   friendly; agreeable

affectation   a phony attitude; insincerity

affiliate   to associate or to unite with

affinity   attraction to

affirmation   a statement that something is true

affix   to attach

affliction   great suffering; hardship

affluence   wealth

affront   an insult

aftermath   outcome; result

agape   open-mouthed; surprised

agenda   a list or program of things to be done

aggrandize   to enlarge or to expand

aggravate   to worsen an already bad situation; to intensify

aggregate   to collect; to gather together

aghast   shocked; terrified

agile   able to move quickly

agitate   to upset; to stir up

agnostic   one who doubts the existence of God

agoraphobia   fear of open places

agrarian   pertaining to farmers and agriculture

ague   a fever; plague

alacrity   liveliness; willingness

albatross   (*two meanings*) a seabird; a constant burden

albeit   although

alchemy   chemistry of the Middle Ages

alias   an assumed name

alien   strange; foreign

alienate   to make others unfriendly to you

alimentary   furnishing food or nourishment

allay   to relieve or to calm

alleged   so-called; supposed

allegory   a symbolic work of literature

allegro   rapid; quick

alleviate   to lessen; to relieve

allocate   to set aside for a specific purpose

allude   to hint at; to refer to indirectly

alluring   tempting; fascinating; charming

alluvial   pertaining to a deposit of sand formed by flowing water

aloft   up in the air; high

aloof   reserved; cool; indifferent

alter   to change

altercation   an argument; a disagreement

altruism   unselfishness; concern for others

amalgamate   to combine; to unite; to blend

amass   to accumulate; to collect

amazon   a big, strong, masculine woman

ambidextrous   equally skillful with either hand

ambient   surrounding; on all sides

ambiguous   unclear; open to more than one interpretation

ambivalence   conflicting feelings toward something or someone

ambrosial   pleasing to the taste or smell

ambulatory   moving about; capable of walking

ambuscade   hidden or secret attack

ameliorate   to improve; to make better

amenable   agreeable; responsive

amend   to change; to alter

amenities   courtesies; social graces; pleasantries

amiable   friendly; pleasant

amicable   friendly; agreeable

amiss   wrong; faulty; improper

amity   friendship

amnesty   official pardon for an offense

amoral   lacking a sense of right and wrong

amorous   loving

amorphous   shapeless

amphibious   able to live on both land and water

ample   roomy; abundant

amplify   to make larger or greater

amulet   a charm worn to keep evil away

anachronism   something out of place or time

analgesic   drug that relieves pain

analogy   similarity or comparison

anarchy   absence of government

anathema   a curse; a person or thing to be avoided

ancillary   helping; subordinate

anecdote   a short, entertaining story

anent   regarding; concerning

anguish   great suffering or grief

anhydrous   without water

animadversion   criticism; comment that opposes

animate   to give life to

animosity   hatred; hostility

animus   hostile feeling

annals   historical records

anneal   to heat and then cool; to toughen

annihilate   to totally destroy

annuity   specified income payable at stated intervals

annul   to cancel; to do away with

anomalous   abnormal; inconsistent

anon   soon

anoxia   lack of oxygen

antecedent   that which goes before something else

antediluvian   very old-fashioned; primitive

anterior   located in front or forward

anteroom   a lobby or waiting room

anthem   song of praise

anthology   collection of literary works

anthropoid   resembling man

anthropomorphic   attributing human form to objects, gods, etc.

antic   playful or silly act; prank

anticlimax   something unimportant coming after something important

antidote   a remedy; a counteractive

antipathy   intense dislike

antipodes   opposite sides (of the earth)

antiquated   ancient; extremely old

antithesis   an exact opposite

apathy   indifference; lack of feeling

ape   (*two meanings*) a monkey (*noun*); to imitate or to mimic (*verb*)

aperture   an opening; a gap

apex   the highest point; summit

aphasia   loss of the ability to speak

aphorism   brief saying; proverb

apiary   place where bees are kept

aplomb   self-confidence; poise

apocryphal   doubtful; not authentic

apogee   farthest point away from the earth

apoplexy   sudden loss of consciousness; paralysis

apostate   one who gives up his beliefs

apothecary   druggist

apothegm   brief instructive saying

apotheosis   glorification of a person to the rank of God

appall   to frighten; to cause loss of courage

apparel   clothing; attire

apparition   a ghost

appease   to soothe; to satisfy

appellation   a name

append   to attach; to add

apposite appropriate

apprehend (*two meanings*) to seize; to understand

apprehensive fearful; anxious

apprise to inform

approbation approval

appropriate to take possession of (*verb*); suitable (*adjective*)

appurtenance something added to another more important thing

apropos relevant; appropriate; fitting

aptitude ability

aquatic pertaining to water

aquiline like an eagle; curved or hooked

arable good for farming

arbiter a judge; an umpire

arbitrary partial; biased

arbor a shaded area

arcane mysterious

archaic outdated; old-fashioned

archaeology study of remains of past cultures

archetype original; first of its kind

archipelago group of islands

archives public records and documents

ardent intensely enthusiastic

arduous difficult; strenuous

aria a solo in an opera

arid dry

armistice a truce; suspension of hostilities

aromatic pleasant-smelling

arraign to accuse

arrant notorious; downright

array an orderly arrangement

arrears (preceded by *in*) in debt

arrogant proud; haughty

arroyo a deep ditch caused by running water

arson illegal burning of property

artful cunning; tricky; crafty

articulate to speak clearly

artifact a handmade object

artifice trick; deception

artisan one skilled in arts and crafts

ascendant rising

ascertain to find out; to determine

ascetic one who denies his body pleasure and comfort

ascribe to attribute; to credit as to a cause or source

aseptic without bacteria

asinine stupid; silly

askance (preceded by *to look*) sidewise; suspiciously

askew crooked; out of position

asperity harshness; roughness

aspersion a damaging remark

aspire to desire; to have an ambition

assail to attack; to assault

assay to test; to try

assent to agree; to accept

assertive confident; positive

assess to estimate the value of

assiduity diligence; care

assimilate to absorb

assuage to calm; to make less severe

asteroid a very small planet

astral pertaining to the stars

astray in the wrong direction

astringent substance that contracts blood vessels or shrinks tissues

astute shrewd; very smart

asunder into separate parts

asylum a safe place; a refuge

atavistic going back to behavior found in a remote ancestor

atheist one who denies God's existence

atlas book of maps

atone to make up for; to repent

atrocious cruel; brutal

atrophy to waste away; to become useless

attenuated decreased; weakened

attest to confirm; to declare to be correct

attribute (*two meanings*) to credit or assign to (*verb*); a characteristic or trait (*noun*)

attrition a wearing down or away; a decline

atypical abnormal; not usual

au courant up-to-date; fully informed

audacity boldness; daring

audible capable of being heard

audit to examine accounts

augment to increase; to make greater

augur to predict

august majestic; worthy of respect; impressive

aura a radiance; a glow

aural pertaining to the sense of hearing

auroral rosy; pertaining to the dawn

auspices approval; support

auspicious favorable

austere severe; stern; self-disciplined

authenticate to confirm; to make acceptable

authoritative dictatorial; having power

autocratic despotic; unlimited in authority

automaton self-operating machine; robot

autonomy self-rule

autumnal mature; declining

auxiliary giving assistance; subordinate

avarice greed

avenge to get even; to take revenge

aver to declare; to state firmly

averse reluctant; not willing

aversion intense dislike

avert to prevent; to turn away

aviary place where birds are kept

avid enthusiastic

avocation a hobby; not one's regular work

avoirdupois heaviness; weight

avow to declare openly

avuncular like an uncle

awe (*in awe of*) great admiration for or fear of

awry twisted to one side; in the wrong direction

axiom true statement; established principle

azure blue

BACCHANALIAN–BUTTRESS

---

bacchanalian wild with drunkenness

badger to nag; to annoy

badinage playful, teasing talk

baffle to confuse; to bewilder

bagatelle thing of little value; trifle

bait (*two meanings*) to entrap or to seduce (*verb*); a decoy (*noun*)

baleful harmful; menacing; pernicious

balk to stop short

balm something that calms or soothes

balmy (*two meanings*) mild and refreshing; mentally unstable (*slang*)

banal common; ordinary; trite

bandy to exchange (*as words*)

bane cause of ruin, harm, or distress

banter teasing; good-natured joking

barb a pointed part, as of an arrow or fishhook

barbarous uncultured; crude

bard a poet

bark a boat or sailing vessel

baroque overdecorated; showy

barrage heavy attack

barrister lawyer (*British*)

bask to lie in or be exposed to warmth

bastion a strong defense; a fort

bauble showy but useless thing; trinket

bawdy indecent; humorously obscene

bayou marshy body of water

beacon a light used for warning or guiding

beatitude state of bliss

bedlam (*two meanings*) a madhouse; a noisy uproar

befuddle to confuse; to perplex

beget   to produce

begrudge   to resent another's success or enjoyment

beguile   to deceive; to charm

behemoth   huge animal

beholden   obligated; indebted

belated   delayed or detained

beleaguer   to encircle (with an army); to annoy

belittle   to put down; to humiliate

belligerent   warlike; quarrelsome

bellow   to yell loudly

benediction   blessing

benefactor   one who helps or supports another

beneficiary   one who receives benefits or profits

benevolent   generous; kindly

benign   harmless; gentle

benignant   kindly; gentle

bequeath   to hand down; to pass on to

berate   to scold severely

bereave   to leave in a sad or lonely state; to deprive by force

berserk   frenzied; violently destructive

beseech   to beg; appeal to

beset   to attack

besiege   to overwhelm; to close in on

besmirch   to make dirty

bestial   savage; brutal

bestow   to give or present

bestride   to mount (a horse)

betrothed   engaged; pledged to marry

bevy   a large group

bewitch   to cast a spell on; to charm; to fascinate

bias   preference; prejudice

bibliophile   lover of books

bibulous   absorbent; fond of alcoholic beverages

bicker   to quarrel

bide   (*one's time*) to wait for a favorable opportunity

biennial   occurring every two years

bigot   a narrow-minded, prejudiced person

bilious   bad-tempered; cross

bilk   to cheat; to swindle

binge   a spree; wild party

biped   two-legged animal

bivouac   temporary shelter

bizarre   weird; strange

blanch   to whiten; to make pale

bland   mild; tasteless; dull

blandishment   flattery

blasé   bored with life; unexcited; indifferent

blasphemy   disrespect for holy places, people, or things; irreverence

blatant   annoyingly conspicuous; offensively noisy and loud

blazon   to display; to proclaim

bleak   unsheltered; gloomy

bleary   blurred; dimmed

blight   destruction; withering; disease

bliss   extreme happiness

blithe   carefree; lighthearted

bludgeon   a short, heavy club (*noun*); to bully or coerce (*verb*)

blunt   (*two meanings*) abrupt in speech or manner; having a dull edge

blurt   (*out*) to utter suddenly or indiscreetly

bluster   to speak noisily; to boast

bode   to indicate in advance, as an omen does

bog   (*two meanings*) a swamp (*noun*); to sink or become stuck in (*verb*)

bogus   false; fake

bolster   to prop up; to support

bolt   to dash out suddenly; to discontinue support of

bombastic   using impressive but meaningless language

bon mot   witty remark

bona fide   genuine; in good faith

bondage   slavery

boon   a benefit; a blessing; a favor

boor   a rude or impolite person

booty   stolen money or goods

boreal   northern

borne   carried; put up with

botch   to mess up; to perform clumsily

bountiful   plentiful; abundant

bounty   reward; generosity

bourgeoisie   middle class

bovine   pertaining to cows or cattle

bowdlerize   to censor; to remove offensive passages of a play, novel, etc.

braggart   one who boasts

brandish   to shake or wave a weapon aggressively

brash   offensively bold; rude

bravado   a show of courage; false bravery

brawn   muscular strength

brazen   shameless or impudent

breach   a violation; a gap

breadth   width

brethren   brothers

brevity   briefness

brigand   a robber

brine   salt water

brisk   lively; quick

bristling   showing irritation

broach   to introduce (a subject)

brochure   a pamphlet

bronchial   pertaining to the windpipe

browbeat   to bully; to intimidate

bruit   to spread the news

brunt   shock, force, or impact, as of a blow

brusque   abrupt in manner, blunt; rough

buccaneer   a pirate

bucolic   pertaining to the countryside; rural

buffoon   clown or fool

bugbear   something causing fear

bulbous   swollen; shaped like a bulb

bulwark   a strong defense

bumptious   conceited; arrogant

bungle   to do things clumsily or badly

buoy   (*two meanings*) a floating object (*noun*); to encourage (*verb*)

buoyant   (*two meanings*) able to float; lighthearted and lively

bureaucracy   system of government through departments

burgeon   to flourish; to grow rapidly

burlesque   a speech or action that treats a serious subject with ridicule

burly   muscular; husky

burnish   to polish

buttress   any prop or support

CABAL–CYNOSURE

cabal   a small, secret group

cache   a hiding place

cacophony   harsh or unpleasant sound

cadaverous   pale; ghastly; corpselike

cadence   rhythm; beat

caesura   pause

cajole   to coax; to persuade

calamitous   causing trouble or misery; disastrous

caliber   degree of worth

calligraphy   fancy handwriting

callous   unyielding; insensitive

callow   young and inexperienced

calumny   a false accusation; slander

camaraderie   loyalty; friendship

canard   a false story, report, or rumor

candor   honesty; openness; frankness

canine   pertaining to dogs

canny   shrewd

canon   rule; law; standard

cant   insincere statements usually made in a singsong tone

cantankerous   bad-tempered; quarrelsome

canter   smooth, easy pace; gallop

canvass   to make a survey

capacious   spacious; roomy

capitulate   to surrender

capricious   erratic; impulsive

captious   hard to please; faultfinding

captivate   to capture; to charm; to fascinate

carapace   shell; hard, protective covering

carcinogenic   causing cancer

cardinal   principal; chief

careen   to swerve; to dip to one side

caricature   an exaggerated portrayal

carnage   slaughter; massacre

carnal   sensual; sexual

carnivorous   flesh-eating

carouse   to engage in a noisy, drunken party

carp   (*two meanings*) a type of fish (*noun*); to complain (*verb*)

carrion   decaying flesh

carte blanche   freedom to use one's own judgment

cartel   association of business firms

cartographer   mapmaker

cascade   a waterfall

caste   social class

castigate   to punish

casualty   (*two meanings*) an accident; one who is hurt in an accident

cataclysm   a violent change

catacomb   underground burial place

catalyst   person or thing that speeds up a result

cataract   (*two meanings*) large waterfall; abnormality of the eye

catastrophe   disaster; calamity

cathartic   cleansing

catholic   universal; wide-ranging

caucus   a private meeting

caustic   sarcastic; severely critical; corrosive

cauterize   to burn

cavalcade   a procession; a sequence of events

cavalier   a haughty and casually indifferent person

caveat   a warning

cavil   to quibble; to argue

cavort   to leap about; to frolic

celerity   speed; swiftness

celestial   heavenly

celibate   unmarried

censure   to criticize sharply

centrifugal   moving away from the center

cerebration   thinking; using one's brain

certitude   sureness; certainty

cessation   a stopping; a discontinuance

chafe   to irritate; to annoy

chaff   worthless matter

chagrin   embarrassment; complete loss of courage

chameleon   (*two meanings*) a lizard able to change its skin color; a changeable or fickle person

champ   (*verb*) to bite impatiently; to show impatience (*to champ at the bit*)

chaos   complete disorder

charisma   great appeal or attraction

charlatan   a fake; a quack

charnel   cemetery; tomb

chary   (*of*) careful; cautious

chasm   a wide gap

chaste   pure; virtuous

chastise   to punish; to purify

chattel   slave

chauvinism   fanatical devotion to one's country, sex, religion, etc.

cherub   angel; an innocent person

chic   stylish; fashionable

chicanery   trickery; deception

chide   to scold

chimerical   imaginary; fantastic; unreal

chirography   the art of handwriting

chivalrous   courteous; courageous; loyal

choleric   easily angered

chronic   long-lasting

churlish   rude; ill-bred

cipher   person or thing of no value; zero

circuitous   roundabout; indirect

circumlocution   roundabout way of speaking

circumscribe   to encircle; to limit or confine

circumspect   cautious; careful

circumvent to surround or entrap; to go around or bypass

citadel a fortress

cite to quote a passage, book, author, etc.; to refer to an example

civility politeness

clairvoyant having great insight; keenly perceptive

clamber to climb with effort or difficulty

clamor noise

clandestine secretive; private

clangor harsh ringing sound

clarify to make clear

clarion clear and shrill

claustrophobia fear of enclosed spaces

cleave (*two meanings*) to split something apart; to stick or cling to something

cleft split; divided

clemency mercy; leniency

cliché a trite or worn-out expression

clientele customers

climax highest point

clime climate; region

clique a small, exclusive group

cloistered secluded; confined

clout (*colloquial*) power; influence

cloven divided; split

coadjutor assistant; helper

coalesce to blend; to merge; to fuse

coddle to treat tenderly

coerce to force

coffer a strongbox

cog a gear tooth; a minor part

cogent convincing

cogitate to think; to consider carefully

cognate related; relevant

cognizant aware

cognomen family name; last name

coherent logically connected; consistent

cohesive tending to stick

cohort colleague; associate; partner

coincide to occur simultaneously

collaborate to work together; to cooperate

collage collection of various bits and pieces (*usually artistic*)

collate to put together in order

collateral security for payment of a loan

colloquial informal

colloquy conversation

collusion conspiracy; agreement to commit a wrongful act

colossal huge; enormous

combative eager to fight; argumentative

combustible capable of catching fire easily

comely attractive

commemorative honoring; remembering

commence to begin

commendation praise

commensurate proportionate

commiserate to express pity for

commodious roomy; spacious

communal shared; pertaining to a group of people

compact (*two meanings*) firmly packed (*adjective*); a treaty (*noun*)

compassion pity; sympathy

compatible agreeable; harmonious

compel to force

compendium brief summary

compensatory paying back; making up for

complacent self-satisfied

complement (*note spelling, as* compliment *means to praise*) to make whole; to complete

compliant yielding; submissive

complicity partnership in a wrongful act

components ingredients; elements

composure calmness of mind or manner

compulsory required

compunction uneasiness; remorse

compute to calculate; to estimate

concave hollow; curved inward

concede to admit; to grant

concentrate (*two meanings*) to think deeply; to increase in strength or degree

concentric   having a common center

conception   (*two meanings*) a beginning; original idea or plan

concession   allowance; the act of yielding

conciliate   to soothe the anger of; to win over

concise   brief and to the point

conclave   secret meeting

concoct   to invent; to devise

concomitant   accompanying; attending

concord   agreement; harmony

concourse   a crowd; a wide street

concur   to agree

condescend   to lower oneself to an inferior's level

condign   deserved; suitable

condiment   seasoning; spices

condolence   expression of sorrow

condone   to excuse; to overlook

conducive   tending to or leading to

conduit   pipe or tube through which fluid or electricity passes

confidant   a close, trusted friend

configuration   shape; arrangement

confiscate   to seize by way of penalty

conflagration   a large and destructive fire

confluent   merging; flowing together

conformity   agreement; doing the same as others

confounded   confused; amazed

congeal   to freeze solid; to thicken

congenial   friendly; agreeable

congenital   existing at birth

conglomerate   mass; cluster; corporation

congregate   to gather; to assemble

congruent   in agreement

coniferous   bearing cones (*pertaining to trees*)

conjecture   to guess

conjugal   pertaining to marriage

conjure   to call upon or to command a devil or spirit to practice magic; cast a spell on

connivance   pretended ignorance of another's wrong-doing; conspiracy

connoisseur   an expert

connote   to suggest or imply

connubial   pertaining to marriage

consanguinity   close relationship, usually by blood

consecrate   to make holy

consensus   general agreement, especially of opinion

console   (*two meanings*) a musical panel or unit (*noun*); to comfort (*verb*)

consolidate   to combine; to make or become solid

consonant   in agreement or harmony

consort   (*two meanings*) a husband or wife (*noun*); to associate or join (*verb*)

consternation   sudden confusion; panic

constituents   voters; supporters

constraints   restrictions; limits

constrict   to shrink; to bind

construe   to analyze; to interpret

consummate   to complete (*verb*); perfect (*adjective*)

contagious   likely to spread; infectious

contaminant   substance that pollutes or infects

contemn   to regard with scorn or contempt

contemporary   happening in the same time period; current

contemptuous   scornful

contentious   ready to argue; quarrelsome

contest   (*three meanings*) a competitive game (*noun*); to dispute (*verb*); to compete (*verb*)

contiguous   nearby; neighboring

contingent   possible

contort   to twist; to distort

contraband   smuggled or stolen goods

contrary   opposite

contravene   to go against; to oppose

contretemps   an embarrassing occurrence

contrite   sorrowful; penitent

controversial   debatable; questionable

contumacious   disobedient; obstinate

contumely   rudeness

contusion   a bruise

conundrum   a riddle

convalesce   to recover from an illness

convene   to come together; to assemble

conventional   ordinary; usual

converge   to come together; to meet in a point or line

conversant   familiar with

converse   (*two meanings*) to talk to someone (*verb*); the opposite (*noun*)

convex   curving outward

conveyance   a vehicle

convivial   sociable; friendly

convoke   to call together

convoluted   twisted; coiled

cope   (*with*) to deal with; to contend with

copious   plentiful; abundant

coquetry   flirtation

cordial   friendly; courteous

cornucopia   horn of plenty; abundance

corollary   inference; deduction; consequence

corona   crown; bright circle

corporeal   pertaining to the body

corpulent   fat; fleshy

corroborate   to strengthen; to confirm

corrosive   eating away, as an acid

corrugated   wrinkled; ridged; furrowed

cortege   funereal procession; group of followers

cosmic   pertaining to the universe; vast

cosmopolitan   worldly-wise; universal

coterie   close circle of friends

countenance   (*two meanings*) the face (*noun*); to permit, tolerate, or approve (*verb*)

countermand   to cancel an order

counterpart   duplicate; copy

coup   a brilliant move; a successful and sudden attack

courier   messenger

covenant   an agreement; a contract

covert   hidden; secretive

covet   to desire

cower   to tremble in fear

coy   shy; modest

cozen   to trick

crafty   sly; tricky

crass   stupid; unrefined

crave   to desire strongly

craven   cowardly

credence   belief; trust

credible   believable

credulity   readiness to believe; gullibility

creed   a religious belief

crescendo   gradual increase in intensity or loudness

crestfallen   dejected; humbled

crevice   an opening; a crack

cringe   to shrink back, as in fear

criterion   measure of value; standard of judging

crone   hag; withered old woman

crony   close friend

crotchety   grouchy; eccentric

crucial   extremely important; decisive

crucible   a severe test or trial

crux   the essential part

cryptic   mysterious; secretive

crystallize   to settle; to take on a definite form

cubicle   small compartment

cudgel   club; thick stick

cue   a hint; a signal

cuisine   style of cooking

culinary   pertaining to cooking

cull   to select; to pick

culminate   to result in; to reach the highest point

culpable   blameworthy

cumbersome   heavy; hard to handle because of size or weight

cumulative   collected; accumulated

cupidity   greed

curb   to control; to check

curry   to try to win favor by flattery

cursive   running or flowing

cursory   superficial; hasty

curtail   to cut short

cynic   one who is critical; a fault-finder

cynosure   center of attention

DAIS–DYSPHASIA

dais   platform; speaker's stand

dale   valley

dally   to waste time

dank   chilly and wet

dappled   spotted

dastardly   sneaking and cowardly; shameful

daub   to smear; to cover over with paint, etc.

daunt   to discourage

dawdle   to waste time; to idle

de facto   in fact; in reality

deadlock   a standstill; a tie

dearth   a scarcity or lack

debacle   a complete failure; total collapse

debase   to lower in rank; to humiliate

debauch   to corrupt

debilitate   to weaken

debonair   pleasant; courteous; charming

debris   fragments; litter; rubble

debut   first public appearance

decadence   moral deterioration

decant   to pour off (a liquid)

decapitate   to behead

decelerate   to slow down

deciduous   not permanent; passing

decipher   decode; figure out the meaning of

declaim   to speak dramatically

declivity   downward slope

decompose   to decay; to break up into parts

decorum   appropriate social behavior

decoy   a person or thing that entices or lures, as into danger

decrepit   broken down by age or disease

decry   to speak out against

deduce   to reason out; to infer

deem   to think; to believe; to judge

defalcate   to misuse funds; to embezzle

defamatory   damaging another's reputation with false remarks

default   to fail to pay a debt or to perform a task

defection   desertion

defer   to postpone; to put off

deference   respect

defile   to pollute; to corrupt

definitive   comprehensive; complete

deflect   to turn aside; to bend

defoliate   to strip of leaves

defray   to pay the cost of

deft   skillful

defunct   no longer in existence; extinct

degrade   to lower in degree or quality

deify   to idolize; to make godlike

deign   to lower oneself before an inferior

delectable   delicious; very pleasing

delete   to leave out; to cross out

deleterious   harmful

delineate   to describe; to depict

delirium   condition of mental disturbance; wild excitement

delude   to deceive; to mislead

deluge   a flood; a rush

delve   to search; to investigate

demagogue   a popular leader who appeals to the emotions

demean   to degrade; to lower

demeanor   behavior

demented   deranged; insane

demigod   a person who is partly a god and partly human

demise   death; ending

demography   study of population trends

demolish   to tear down

demoralize   to discourage; to cause to lose spirit

demur   to object; to take exception to

demure   shy

denigrate   to ruin the reputation of; to blacken

denizen   occupant; inhabitant; resident

denomination   the name or designation for a class of persons, such as a religious group

denouement   outcome; result

denounce   to publicly condemn

depict   to portray; to represent

depilate   to remove hair from

deplete   to use up gradually (resources, strength, etc.)

deplore   to regret

deploy   to place troops in position

depose   to remove from office

depraved   sinful; immoral

deprecate   to disapprove of

depreciate   to lessen in value

deranged   insane

derelict   (*three meanings*) abandoned (*adjective*); negligent (*adjective*); a vagrant or bum (*noun*)

deride   to ridicule

derision   ridicule

dermatology   study of skin diseases

derogatory   belittling

descry   to discover

desecrate   to damage a holy place

desiccate   to dry up; to wither

desist   to cease or stop

desolate   lonely; deserted

despicable   contemptible; hateful

despise   to scorn; to regard with disgust

despoil   to rob; to plunder

despondent   depressed; dejected

despot   a dictator

destitute   poor; lacking

desuetude   condition of disuse; extinction

desultory   wandering from subject to subject; rambling

détente   a lessening of tension or hostility

deter   to discourage; to hinder

detergent   a cleansing agent

detonate   explode

detoxify   remove the poison from

detract   to take away; to diminish

detriment   harm; damage

devastate   to destroy; to overwhelm

deviate   to turn aside; to digress

devious   sly; underhand

devoid   completely without

devotee   an enthusiastic follower

devout   religious; pious; sincere

dexterity   skill; cleverness

diabolical   devilish; cruel

diadem   crown

dialectic   logical discussion

diaphanous   transparent; very sheer and light

diatribe   bitter criticism

dichotomy   division into two parts

dicker   to bargain; to argue over prices

diction   style of speaking

dictum   a positive statement

didactic   instructive; inclined to lecture others too much

diffident   shy; modest

diffuse   to spread; to scatter

digress   to wander off the subject

dilapidated   broken down; falling apart

dilate   to expand; to become wider

dilatory   slow or late in doing things

dilemma   a troubling situation

dilettante   a dabbler in the fine arts; one who is not an expert

diligent   hard-working; industrious

diminutive   small

dint   power; force

dipsomaniac   drunkard

dire   dreadful; causing disaster

dirge   a funeral song or hymn

disarray   disorder; confusion

disavow   to disown; to deny; to repudiate

disburse   to pay out

discern   to distinguish; to recognize; to perceive

disciple a follower

disclaimer denial; renunciation

disclose to reveal; to make known

discomfiture frustration; confusion

disconcert to upset; to embarrass

disconsolate without hope

discordant disagreeing; harsh-sounding

discount (*two meanings*) reduction (*noun*); to disregard (*verb*)

discountenance to disapprove of

discourse conversation; lecture

discredit to disgrace; to cast doubt on

discreet showing good judgment; cautious

discrepancy inconsistency; difference

discrete separate; not attached

discretion good judgment

discrimination (*two meanings*) prejudice; ability to distinguish

discursive rambling; wandering

disdain to scorn

disgruntled unhappy; discontented

dishearten to discourage; to depress

disheveled untidy

disinter to uncover; to dig up

disinterested impartial; not prejudiced

dismal gloomy; depressing

dismantle to take apart

dismember to cut or pull off limbs

disparage to belittle; to put down

disparity inequality; difference

dispassionate calm; impartial

dispel to drive away

disperse to scatter

disputatious fond of arguing

disreputable having a bad reputation

dissection cutting apart; analysis

dissemble to conceal; to pretend

disseminate to scatter; to spread

dissension disagreement; opposition

dissertation a written essay

dissident disagreeing

dissimulate to hide one's feelings

dissipate to waste; to scatter

dissociate to break ties with; to part company

dissolute immoral; unrestrained

dissonant out of harmony

dissuade to advise or urge against

distend to expand; to swell; to stretch out

distort to twist out of shape

distraught troubled

dither (preceded by *in a*) nervously excited or confused

diurnal daily

divergent varying; different

divers several

diverse different

divest to deprive

divination the act of foretelling the future

divulge to reveal; to make known

docile obedient; submissive

doddering shaky; senile

doff to throw off or away

doggedly stubbornly

dogmatic having a definite opinion; authoritative

doldrums low spirits

dole to distribute; to give out sparingly

doleful sorrowful

dolorous mournful; sad

dolt a dull, stupid person

domicile home; residence

donnybrook rough, rowdy fight

dormant asleep; inactive

dorsal pertaining to the back

dossier a complete group of documents containing detailed information

dotage feeblemindedness of old age

doughty courageous; worthy

dour gloomy

douse to put out (a fire); to extinguish

dowdy shabby; untidy

downtrodden trampled on; suppressed

doyen senior or eldest member

Draconian severe; cruel

dregs leftovers

drivel childish nonsense; stupid talk

droll amusing in an odd way

drone (*three meanings*) a male bee (*noun*); an idle person (*noun*); to talk on and on monotonously (*verb*)

dross waste matter

drudgery hard, tiresome work

dual consisting of two people, items, or parts

dubious doubtful; questionable

ductile capable of being molded or shaped

dudgeon anger, resentment

dulcet pleasing to the ear

dulcimer a type of zither

dupe to trick; to deceive

duplicity deceit; double-dealing; dishonesty

duress force

dutiful obedient

dwindle to shrink; to become smaller

dynamo a powerful person

dyspepsia poor digestion

dysphasia difficulty in speaking

EARNEST–EXULT

---

earnest sincere; serious

earthy realistic; coarse

ebb to slowly decrease

ebullient enthusiastic

eccentric odd; out of the ordinary

ecclesiastical pertaining to the church

echelon rank of authority; level of power

éclat brilliance; fame

eclectic selecting; choosing from various sources

eclipse to overshadow; to outshine

ecology study of the environment

ecstatic extremely happy

edifice structure; building

edify to improve someone morally; to instruct

educe to draw or bring out

eerie weird; mysterious

efface to erase; to wipe out

effectual effective; adequate

effeminate unmanly; womanly; soft and weak

effervescent bubbly; spirited

effete worn-out; barren

efficacy power to produce an effect

effigy a likeness; an image

efflorescent blossoming; flowering

effluent flowing out

effrontery shameful boldness

effulgent shining forth brilliantly; radiant

effusion a pouring out; an uncontrolled display of emotion

egalitarian pertaining to belief in the equality of all men

ego a feeling of self-importance

egotism selfishness; boasting about oneself

egregious remarkably bad; outrageous

egress exit (*noun and verb*)

ejaculation an exclamation

eject to throw out

elapse to pass; to slip away

elated overjoyed

electrify to thrill

elegy a sad or mournful poem

elicit to draw forth; to cause to be revealed

elite the choice or best of a group of persons

elixir remedy

ellipsis the omission in a sentence of a word or words

eloquent   convincing or forceful in speech

elucidate   to make clear

elude   to avoid; to escape notice

elusive   difficult to grasp

elysian   blissful; heavenly

emaciated   abnormally thin

emanate   to come forth; to send forth

emancipate   to set free

embark   (*on*) to begin a journey or an endeavor

embellish   to decorate

embezzle   to steal

embroil   to involve in trouble; to complicate

embryonic   undeveloped; in an early stage

emendation   correction

emetic   causing vomiting

eminent   famous; renowned

emissary   one sent on a special mission

emit   to send out; to give forth

emollient   something that soothes or softens

emolument   profit; gain

empathy   understanding another's feelings

empirical   based on experience rather than theory

emulate   to imitate

emulous   jealous; envious

enamored   (*of*) in love with

enclave   a country, or part of a country, surrounded by another country

encomium   an expression of high praise

encompass   to include; to surround

encore   a repeat performance

encroach   (*upon*) to trespass; to intrude

encumbrance   hindrance; obstruction

encyclopedic   filled with knowledge; comprehensive

endearment   an expression of affection

endemic   confined to a particular country or area

energize   to rouse into activity

enervate   to weaken

enfranchise   to give the right to vote

engender   to promote

engrossed   completely absorbed in

engulf   to overwhelm

enhance   to increase in value or beauty; to improve

enigma   a puzzling situation; dilemma

enigmatic   mysterious; puzzling

enlighten   to inform; to reveal truths

enmity   hostility; hatred

ennui   boredom

enormity   an outrageous and immoral act

enrapture   to delight beyond measure

ensconce   to hide; to conceal; to settle comfortably

ensue   to follow; to result from

enthrall   to charm; to captivate

entice   to attract; to tempt

entity   independent being

entomology   study of insects

entourage   a group of personal attendants

entranced   filled with delight or wonder

entreaty   a request; a plea

entrenched   firmly established; dug in

entrepreneur   successful businessman; promoter

enunciate   to pronounce words clearly

environs   surroundings

envisage   to imagine; to form a mental picture

envoy   messenger; agent

eon   extremely long period of time

ephemeral   temporary; short-lived

epic   a long poem about heroic occurrences

epicure   one who seeks pleasure in fine foods

epigram   witty saying

epilogue   closing part of a speech or literary work

epiphany   appearance of a deity (god); revelation

epistle   a letter

epitaph   inscription on a tomb

epithet   a descriptive word or phrase

epitome   a typical example; a summary or condensed account

epoch   particular period of history

equanimity   calmness; evenness of temperament

equestrian   a horseback rider

equilibrium   balance; stability

equine   pertaining to horses

equinox   the time when day and night are of equal length

equipoise   balance

equitable   fair; just

equity   fairness; justice; impartiality

equivocal   doubtful; ambiguous

equivocate   to confuse by speaking in ambiguous terms

eradicate   to erase; to wipe out

ergo   therefore

erode   to wear away

erotic   pertaining to sexual love

err   to make a mistake

errant   wandering (*in search of adventure*); straying from what is right

erratic   irregular; abnormal

erroneous   mistaken; wrong

ersatz   artificial; inferior substitute

erstwhile   formerly; in the past

erudite   scholarly; learned

escalate   to increase; to grow rapidly; to intensify

escapade   a reckless adventure

escarpment   steep cliff

eschew   to avoid; to keep away from

escrow   (preceded by *in*) money deposited with a third person pending fulfillment of a condition

esoteric   for a select few; not generally known

espionage   spying

espouse   to support (*a cause*)

essay   (*verb*) to try; to attempt; (*noun*) a short personal literary composition dealing with a single subject

estival   pertaining to summer

estranged   separated; alienated

ethereal   spiritual; airy

ethnic   pertaining to a particular race or culture

etymology   the origin and development of words

eugenics   science of improving the human race

eulogy   praise for a dead person

euphemism   substitution of a pleasant expression for an unpleasant one

euphonious   having a pleasant sound; harmonious

euphoria   a feeling of well-being

euthanasia   mercy killing

evanescent   temporary; fleeting

evasive   not straightforward; tricky

eventuate   to result; to happen finally

evict   to expel; to throw out

evince   to show clearly

evoke   to call forth; to produce

evolve   to develop gradually

exacerbate   to aggravate; to make more violent

exact   (*two meanings*) accurate (*adjective*); to demand or to require (*verb*)

exalt   to raise in position; to praise

exasperate   to irritate; to annoy extremely

excise   (*two meanings*) a tax on liquor, tobacco, etc. (*noun*); to cut out or off (*verb*)

excoriate   (*two meanings*) to scrape the skin off; to criticize sharply

excruciating   unbearably painful

exculpate   to free from blame; to vindicate

execrate   to curse

exemplary   worthy of imitation

exhilaration   liveliness; high spirits

exhort   to warn

exhume   to bring out of the earth; to reveal

exigent   urgent; critical

exiguous   scanty; small in quantity

exodus   a departure; a going out

exonerate   to free from guilt or blame

exorbitant   excessive; unreasonable

exorcise   to drive out an evil spirit

exotic   foreign; excitingly strange

expatiate   to enlarge upon; to speak or write at length

expatriate   a person who is banished from, or leaves, his native country

expectorate   to spit out

expedient   practical; advantageous

expedite   to speed up; to make easy

expendable   replaceable

expiate   to atone for

explicate   explain in detail; make clear

explicit   clear; unambiguous; direct

exploit to use for one's own advantage

expound to explain; to interpret

expressly especially; particularly

expunge to erase

expurgate to remove offensive passages; to cleanse

extant still in existence

extemporaneous offhand; done without preparation

extenuating less serious

extinct no longer in existence

extirpate to destroy; to remove completely

extol to praise

extort to obtain by force

extradite to give up a prisoner to another authority

extraneous unrelated; not essential

extrapolate to estimate; to infer

extricate to set free; to disentangle

extrinsic external; coming from outside

extrovert an outgoing person

exuberant full of enthusiasm

exude to discharge; to ooze

exult to rejoice

FABRICATE–FUTILE

---

fabricate (*two meanings*) to construct; to lie

fabulous incredible; imaginative

facade outward appearance

facet aspect

facetious joking; sarcastic

facile easy; effortless

facilitate to make easy

facsimile an exact copy; a duplicate

faction a minority within a larger group

factious causing disagreement

factitious artificial

factotum an employee who can do all kinds of work

faculty power; ability; skill

fallacious misleading; deceptive

fallible capable of error

fallow inactive; unproductive

falter to stumble; to hesitate

fanatic a person with uncontrolled enthusiasm

fanciful unreal; imaginative; unpredictable

fanfare noisy or showy display

farcical absurd; ridiculous

fastidious hard to please

fatal causing death

fatalistic believing that all things in life are inevitable

fathom (*two meanings*) nautical measure of 6 feet in depth (*noun*); to comprehend (*verb*)

fatuous foolish

fauna animals of a certain area

fawn (*two meanings*) a young deer (*noun*); to act slavishly submissive (*verb*)

faze to disturb; to discourage

fealty loyalty; devotion

feasible capable of being accomplished; suitable

feat deed or accomplishment

febrile feverish

fecund fertile; productive

feign to pretend

feint a false show; a pretended blow

feisty quick-tempered or quarrelsome

felicity happiness

feline pertaining to cats

fell (*two meanings*) to knock down (*verb*); fierce or cruel (*adjective*)

felon a criminal

felonious treacherous; base; villainous

ferment a state of agitation or excitement

ferret (*two meanings*) a small animal of the weasel family (*noun*); to search or drive out (*verb*)

fervent eager; earnest

fervid   very emotional

fester   to rot

festive   joyous; merry

fete   to honor; to entertain

fetid   foul-smelling

fetish   object with magical power; object that receives respect or devotion

fetter   to confine; to put into chains

fiasco   a total disaster

fiat   an official order

fickle   changeable in affections; unfaithful

fictitious   false; not genuine

fidelity   faithfulness

figment   something imagined

filch   to steal

filial   like a son or daughter

finale   the climax; end

finesse   diplomacy; tact

finicky   extremely particular; fussy

finite   limited; measurable

firebrand   one who stirs up a revolution

firmament   sky; heavens

fiscal   pertaining to finances

fissure   opening; groove; split

fitful   irregular; occurring in spurts

flabbergasted   astonished; made speechless

flaccid   flabby

flag   (*two meanings*) a banner (*noun*); to droop or to slow down (*verb*)

flagellate   to whip

flagrant   scandalous; shocking

flail   to strike freely and wildly

flair   a knack; a natural talent

flamboyant   showy; conspicuous

flaunt   to boast; to show off

flay   (*two meanings*) to strip the skin off; to criticize sharply

fledgling   a young, inexperienced person

fleece   (*two meanings*) wool of a lamb (*noun*); to swindle (*verb*)

flexible   bendable

flinch   to draw back; to cringe

flippant   treating serious matters lightly

flora   plant life of a certain area

florid   flowery; ornate

flotilla   small fleet of ships

flotsam   floating cargo or wreckage

flout   to mock; to ridicule

fluctuate   to move back and forth; to vary

fluent   flowing; able to speak and/or write easily and clearly

fluster   to upset; to confuse

fluvial   pertaining to a river

flux   state of continual change

foible   a weakness; minor fault

foil   (*two meanings*) to prevent the success of a plan (*verb*); a person who, by contrast, makes another person seem better (*noun*)

foist   (*on*) to pass off merchandise that is inferior

folderol   nonsense

folly   a foolish action

foment   to stir up; to instigate

foolhardy   foolish; reckless

fop   an excessively vain man

foray   a sudden attack

forbearance   patience; restraint

forebear   ancestor

foreboding   a warning; an omen

foregone   (*note spelling, as* forgone *means going or to abstain from something*) long past

forensic   pertaining to a formal discussion or debate

forerunner   ancestor; predecessor

foreshadow   to hint

forestall   to prevent by action in advance; to anticipate

forfeit   to give up

forgo   to do without; to give up

formidable   dreadful; discouraging

forte   strong point

forthright   direct; frank

fortitude   strength; courage

fortnight   two weeks; fourteen days

fortuitous   lucky; by chance

foster   to nourish; to encourage

fracas   a loud quarrel

fractious   irritable; quarrelsome; stubborn

fracture   to break or to crack

frailty   a weakness; a defect

franchise   special right or privilege

fraternal   brotherly

fraudulent   dishonest; cheating

fraught   (*with*) filled

fray   (*two meanings*) a noisy quarrel (*noun*); to unravel or to come apart (*verb*)

frenetic   frantic; wild

frenzy   madness; fury

freshet   a fresh water stream

fretful   worried; irritated

friction   (*two meanings*) a rubbing together (*noun*); conflict or disagreement (*noun*)

frigid   extremely cold

frivolous   trivial; silly

frowzy   dirty; unkempt

frugal   economical; thrifty

fruition   fulfillment; realization

fruitless   barren; yielding no results

frustrate   to prevent; to discourage

fugacious   pertaining to the passing of time

fulminate   to explode; to denounce

fulsome   disgusting; sickening; repulsive

furor   rage; frenzy; fury

furtive   stealthy; secretive

fusion   a union; merging

futile   useless

GADFLY–GYRATE

---

gadfly   a person who annoys others

gaff   a hook

gainsay   to deny; to contradict

gait   manner of walking

gala   festive

galaxy   a group of stars; any large and brilliant assemblage of persons

gall   bitterness

gallant   polite; noble

galvanize   to stimulate; to startle into sudden activity

gambit   strategy; an opening one uses to advantage

gambol   to frolic; to romp about

gamut   the whole range or extent

gape   to stare with open mouth

garble   to distort

gargantuan   gigantic; huge

garish   tastelessly gaudy

garland   a wreath of flowers

garner   to gather; to acquire

garnish   to decorate; to trim

garrulous   talkative

gauche   awkward; tactless

gaudy   flashy; showy

gaunt   thin and bony; bleak and barren

gazebo   an open structure with an enjoyable view

gazette   newspaper

gelid   very cold; frozen

genealogy   family history

generate   to produce; to originate

generic   general; not specific; pertaining to a class

genesis   origin; beginning

genial   warm; friendly

genocide   killing of a race of people

genre   an art form or class

genteel   polite; refined

gentry   upper-class people

genuflect   to kneel; to bend the knee

germane   relevant; fitting

gerontology   the study of older people and their problems

gesticulation   lively or excited gesture

ghastly   horrible; dreadful

ghoul   grave robber; ogre

gibberish   silly, unintelligible talk

gibbet   gallows from which criminals are hanged

gibe   to scoff; to ridicule

giddy   dizzy; flighty; whirling

gild   to cover with gold

gingerly   carefully; cautiously

gird   to encircle

gist   main point; essence

glazed   glassy; smooth; shiny

glean   to gather patiently and with great effort

glee   joy

glib   fluent; smooth

glissade   a skillful glide over snow or ice in descending a mountain

glitch   a malfunction; an error

gloaming   twilight; dusk

gloat   to look at or think about with great satisfaction

glower   to frown; to stare angrily at

glum   sad; gloomy

glutinous   gluey; sticky

glutton   one who eats or drinks too much

gnarled   knotty; twisted; roughened

gnome   a legendary dwarflike creature

goad   to encourage; to spur on

gorge   (*two meanings*) a deep valley with steep sides (*noun*); to eat or to swallow greedily (*verb*)

gory   bloody

gossamer   light; flimsy; fine

Gothic   medieval; mysterious

gouge   (*two meanings*) to dig out; to swindle or overcharge

gourmand   a glutton; a person who eats excessively

gourmet   an expert of fine food and drink

gradient   a slope; a ramp

granary   a storehouse for grain

grandiloquent   pretentious; speaking in a pompous style

grandiose   impressive; showy

graphic   giving a clear and effective picture

grapple   to grip and hold; to struggle

grate   (*two meanings*) to grind to shreds; to irritate

gratify   to please; to satisfy

gratis   without payment; free

gratuitous   free of cost; unnecessary

grave   serious; somber

gregarious   sociable; friendly

grievous   causing grief or sorrow; distressing

grim   fierce; stern

grimace   a distorted face; an expression of disapproval

grime   dirt

gripe   complaint

grisly   horrible; gruesome; ghastly

grit   stubborn courage

gross   extreme; vulgar

grotesque   absurd; distorted

grotto   a cave

grovel   to lower oneself to please another

grudging   resentful; reluctant

grueling   exhausting

gruff   rough or harsh in manner

guile   deceit; trickery

guileless   sincere

guise   a false appearance

gull   to trick; to deceive

gullible   easily deceived; too trusting

gumption   courage and initiative

gustatory   pertaining to the sense of taste

gusto   hearty enjoyment

gusty   windy; stormy

guttural   pertaining to the throat

gyrate   to rotate; to spin

HABITAT–HYPOTHESIS

habitat dwelling

hackneyed trite; commonplace; overused

haggard worn out from sleeplessness, grief, etc.

haggle to bargain over a price

halcyon calm

hale healthy

hallmark a symbol of high quality

hallow to make holy; to bless

hallucination illusion; a false notion

hamper to hinder; to keep someone from acting freely

haphazard dependent upon mere chance

hapless unlucky

harangue long speech

harass to annoy; to bother

harbinger an omen or sign

harbor (*two meanings*) a body of water providing ships with protection from winds, waves, etc. (*noun*); to conceal or hide (*verb*)

hardy courageous; sturdy

harlequin a clown

harpy a greedy, grasping person; a scolding, nagging, bad-tempered woman

harrowing upsetting; distressing

harry to worry; to torment

hart a male deer

haughty snobbish; arrogant

haunt to appear as a spirit or ghost; to visit frequently; to disturb or distress

haven a safe place

havoc great destruction

hazard risk; danger

headlong recklessly; impulsively

headstrong stubborn; willful

hearsay rumor; gossip

hearth fireplace

hector to bully

hedonist a pleasure-seeker

heedless careless; unmindful

hefty large and powerful; heavy

hegemony leadership or strong influence

hegira flight; escape

heinous hateful; abominable

hemophilia a blood defect in which the blood does not clot to close a wound

herald to announce; to usher in

herbivorous feeding on vegetation

herculean tremendous in size, strength, or difficulty

heresy rejection of a religious belief

hermetic airtight; tightly sealed

heterodox departing from acceptable beliefs

heterogeneous different; unlike; dissimilar

heyday period of success

hiatus pause or gap

hibernate to be inactive, especially during the winter

hierarchy a ranking, one above the other

hilarity gaiety; joy

hircine goat-like

hirsute hairy; bearded

histrionic theatrical; overly dramatic

hoard to store away; to accumulate

hoary white with age or frost

hoax a practical joke

hobgoblin a frightening apparition; something that causes fear

hodgepodge mixture

hogwash meaningless or insincere talk

hoi polloi common people; the masses

holocaust complete destruction

homage respect; honor

homily a sermon

homogeneous composed of parts all of the same kind

homophonic sounding alike

hone to sharpen

hoodwink to deceive

hoot to shout in disapproval

horde a crowd of people

horticulture   the science of gardening

hospice   shelter

hovel   a dirty, wretched living place

hover   to keep lingering about; to wait near at hand

hubris   excessive pride or self-confidence

hue   a color; a shade

humane   kind; compassionate

humbug   trick; hoax

humdrum   monotonous; routine

humid   moist

humility   lowliness; meekness

humus   black soil for fertilizing

hurtle   to dash; speed; run

husbandry   the science of raising crops; careful management

hybrid   mixed; assorted

hydrophobia   fear of water; rabies

hymeneal   pertaining to marriage

hyperbole   extreme exaggeration

hypercritical   overcritical; faultfinding

hypochondriac   a person with imaginary ailments

hypocrite   one who pretends to be someone or something he is not

hypothesis   an assumption; an unproven theory

ICHTHYOLOGY–ITINERANT

---

ichthyology   study of fish

icon   a statue or idol

iconoclast   a rebel; one who breaks with tradition

idealist   one with very high standards

idiosyncrasy   a peculiar personality trait

idolatry   excessive or blind adoration; worship of idols

idyllic   charmingly simple or poetic

igneous   pertaining to fire

ignoble   dishonorable

ignominious   shameful; disgraceful

ignoramus   a stupid person

ilk   type; sort; kind

illicit   unlawful; illegal

illiterate   uneducated

illumine   to brighten; to inspire

illusion   fake impression

illustrious   distinguished; bright

imbibe   to drink; to absorb

imbroglio   a difficult or confusing situation

imbue   to fill completely; to penetrate

immaculate   spotless; pure

imminent   likely to happen; threatening

immolate   to kill someone as a sacrificial victim, usually by fire

immortal   not subject to death

immunity   freedom from disease

immutable   unchangeable

impair   to weaken; to cause to become worse

impale   to pierce with a sharp stake through the body

impalpable   vague; not understandable

impartial   without prejudice

impasse   a dead end; a problem without a solution

impeach   to accuse

impeccable   flawless; without fault

impecunious   without money; penniless

impede   to hinder; to obstruct

impediment   a barrier; an obstruction

impel   push into motion; urge

impending   likely to happen soon

imperative   extremely necessary

imperious   domineering; haughty

impermeable   not permitting passage

impertinent   rude; disrespectful

imperturbable   steady; calm

impervious   not capable of being affected; hardened

impetuous   acting without thought; impulsive

impetus   a stimulus; a moving force

impinge   to strike; to collide; to encroach

impious   disrespectful toward God

implacable   unbending; inflexible; merciless

implausible   unbelievable

implement   (*two meanings*) a tool (*noun*); to carry out or put into practice (*verb*)

implication   an indirect indication; a statement that suggests something

implicit   suggested, but not plainly expressed

imply   to suggest

import   (*two meanings*) significance; meaning (*noun*); to bring in from a foreign country (*verb*)

importune   to persistently ask; to beg

impostor   a person who goes about under an assumed name or character

impotent   powerless; lacking strength

imprecation   a curse

impregnable   unconquerable

impromptu   without preparation; offhand

impropriety   pertaining to something that is not proper or suitable

improvident   wasteful

improvise   to do without preparation

impudent   disrespectful; shameless

impugn   to attack a person with words; to challenge a person in regard to motives

impunity   freedom from punishment

impute   to accuse a person of some wrongdoing; to attribute a fault or a crime to a person

inadvertent   unintentional

inalienable   not able to be transferred to another

inane   silly; meaningless

inanimate   lifeless; dull; dead

inarticulate   pertaining to speech that is not clear or understandable

incandescent   very bright; shining

incapacitated   disabled; unable to function

incarcerate   to imprison

incarnadine   blood-red; flesh-colored

incarnate   in human form

incendiary   causing fire; stirring up trouble

incense   to inflame; to enrage

incentive   something that incites to action

inception   beginning; start

incessant   continuous; without pause

inchoate   at an early stage; just beginning

incipient   beginning to exist or appear

incisive   sharp; keen

incite   to urge to action; to stir up

inclement   (*usually refers to weather*) harsh; unfavorable; severe

incognito   disguised

incoherent   rambling; not logically connected

incongruous   unsuited; inappropriate

inconsequential   unimportant

incontrovertible   certain; undeniable

incorrigible   bad beyond correction or reform

incredulous   skeptical; disbelieving

increment   an increase; a gain

incriminate   to charge with a crime; to connect or relate to a wrongdoing

incubus   nightmare

inculcate   (*in* or *upon*) to teach earnestly; to influence someone to accept an idea

incumbent   (*two meanings*) resting or lying down (*adjective*); one who holds a political office (*noun*)

incur   to bring upon oneself; to run into some undesirable consequence

incursion   a raid; an invasion

indefatigable   incapable of being tired out

indelible   incapable of being erased

indemnify   to insure; to repay

indicative   signifying; implying

indict   to charge with a crime; to accuse of a wrong-doing

indigenous   native to a particular area; inborn

indigent   extremely poor

indignant   angry as a result of unjust treatment

indisputable   unquestionable; without doubt

indissoluble   permanent

indoctrinate   to teach someone principles or beliefs

indolent   lazy

indomitable   unconquerable; unyielding

indubitable   unquestionable; certain

induce   to cause; to bring about

indulgence   gentle treatment; tolerance

inebriated   drunk

ineffable   not able to be described; unspeakable

ineluctable   inevitable; inescapable

inept   unfit; bungling; inefficient

inert   without power to move; inactive

inevitable   unavoidable; sure to happen

inexorable   unyielding

infallible   certain; without mistakes

infamous   having an extremely bad reputation; detestable

infantile   childish; immature

infectious   passing on a disease with germs; likely to spread; contagious

infer   to conclude; to derive by reasoning

infernal   hellish; fiendish; diabolical

infidel   unbeliever

infinitesimal   exceedingly small; minute (pronounced *my-newt*)

infirmity   weakness; feebleness

inflated   puffed up; swollen

influx   a flowing in

infraction   the breaking of a law or rule

infringe   (*on* or *upon*) to break a law; to violate; to trespass

ingenious   clever

ingenuous   simple; innocent; naïve

ingrate   ungrateful person

ingratiate   (*oneself*) to work one's way into another's favor

inherent   inborn

inhibition   restraint; reserve

inimical   harmful; unfriendly

inimitable   not able to be imitated or equaled

iniquity   wickedness

initiate   to begin

injunction   a command; an order

inkling   a hint

innate   inborn; existing from birth

innocuous   harmless

innovate   to introduce a new idea

innuendo   indirect remark; hint

inordinate   unusual; excessive

insatiable   unable to be satisfied

inscrutable   mysterious; difficult to understand

insidious   treacherous

insightful   having a penetrating understanding of things; mentally alert and sharp

insinuate   to hint; to suggest

insipid   tasteless; dull

insolent   boldly disrespectful

insolvent   bankrupt; unable to pay creditors

insomnia   sleeplessness

insouciant   carefree; happy-go-lucky

instigate   to provoke; to stir up

insubordinate   disobedient

insular   pertaining to an island; detached; isolated

insuperable   unconquerable

insurgence   rebellion; action against authority

insurrection   uprising; rebellion

intact   entire; left whole; sound

integral   essential; whole

integrate   to unify; to bring together into a whole

integrity   honesty; sincerity

intellectual   intelligent; having mental capacity to a high degree

intelligentsia   highly educated, cultured people

inter   to bury

interdict   to prohibit; to ban

interim   meantime; period of time between

interlocutor   one who takes part in a conversion

interloper   an intruder

interlude   a period of time between two events

interminable   endless

intermittent   starting and stopping; periodic

interpolate   to insert between; to estimate

interpose   to place between

interregnum   pause; interval; any period during which a nation is without a permanent ruler

interrogate   to question

interstellar   between or among stars

intervene   to come between

intimate   (*two meanings*) private or personal (*adjective*); to imply (*verb*)

intimidate   to make afraid; threaten

intolerant   bigoted; narrow-minded

intractable   hard to manage

intransigent   stubborn; refusing to give in

intrepid   fearless; courageous

intricate   complex; hard to understand

intrinsic   essential; pertaining to a necessary part of something

introspective   looking into oneself

introvert   a person who is concerned with his own thoughts or feelings

intuitive   insightful; knowing by a hidden sense

inundate   to fill to overflowing; to flood

inured   (*to*) accustomed to

invalidate   to deprive of legal value; to make null and void

invariably   constantly; uniformly; without changing

invective   strong verbal abuse

inveigh   (*against*) to make a bitter verbal attack

inveigle   to trick; lure; deceive

invert   to turn inside out or upside down

inveterate   firmly established; deep-rooted

invidious   causing resentment; offensive

invigorate   to fill with energy

invincible   not able to be defeated; unconquerable

invoke   to call upon

invulnerable   not able to be hurt; immune to attack

iota   a small quantity

irascible   easily angered

ire   anger; wrath

iridescent   displaying a wide range of colors like those of the rainbow

irksome   annoying; bothersome

ironic   contrary to what was expected

irrational   senseless; unreasonable

irreconcilable   unable to agree

irredeemable   hopeless; unable to be brought back

irremediable   unable to be corrected or cured

irreparable   beyond repair

irrepressible   unable to be controlled or restrained

irresolute   indecisive; doubtful; undecided

irreverent   disrespectful

irrevocable   final; unchangeable

itinerant   traveling from place to place

JADED–KNUCKLE

---

jaded   tired; worn out; dulled

jargon   vocabulary peculiar to a particular trade or group of people; meaningless talk; gibberish

jaundiced   (*two meanings*) pertaining to a yellowed skin; prejudiced

jaunt   short trip; excursion

jaunty   carefree; confident

jeer   to sneer; to mock

jeopardy   danger

jest   to joke; to make light of

jetsam   goods cast overboard to lighten a ship

jettison   to throw goods overboard

jilt   to reject; to cast off

jingoism   extreme patriotism

jinx   to bring bad luck to

jocose   joking; humorous

jocular   humorous

jostle   to bump; to push

jovial   jolly; good-natured

jubilation   celebration; rejoicing

judicious   wise; showing sound judgment

juggernaut   a terrible destructive force

jugular   pertaining to the throat or neck

juncture   a point of time; a crisis

junket   a pleasure trip; an excursion

junta   a small group ruling a country

jurisprudence   science of law

jut   to stick out; to project

juxtapose   to place side by side

kaleidoscopic   constantly changing

ken   range of knowledge

kindle   to set on fire; to excite

kindred   relative; family, tribe, or race

kinetic   pertaining to motion

kismet   destiny; fate

kleptomania   a compulsion to steal

knave   a tricky, deceitful person

knead   to work dough, clay, etc., into a uniform mixture

knell   the sound made by a bell rung slowly for a death or funeral

knoll   a small rounded hill

knuckle   (*under*) to yield; (*down*) to apply oneself vigorously

---

LABYRINTHINE–LUXURIANT

---

labyrinthine   complicated; intricate

lacerate   to tear (*flesh*) roughly; to mangle

lachrymose   tearful

lackadaisical   uninterested; listless

lackey   slavish follower

lackluster   lacking brilliance or liveliness; dull or vapid

laconic   using few words; concise

lactic   pertaining to milk

laden   burdened; loaded

laggard   a slow person; one who falls behind

laity   religious worshipers who are not clergy

lambent   softly bright or radiant; running or moving lightly over a surface

lament   to mourn

laminated   covered with thin sheets, often plastic

lampoon   a sharp, often harmful satire

languid   sluggish; drooping from weakness

languish   to become weak or feeble

lank   long and slender

lapidary   a dealer in precious stones

larceny   theft

largess   gifts that have been given generously

lascivious   lustful or lewd; inciting sexual desire

lassitude   a feeling of weakness and weariness

latent   present, but hidden

lateral   to the side; sideways

latitude   freedom; margin

laudable   praiseworthy

laureate   (*adjective*) worthy of praise or honor; (*noun*) an honored person

lave   to wash or bathe

lavish   very generous; extravagant

lax   careless or negligent

leeway   room for freedom of action; margin

legerdemain   sleight of hand; deception

lenient   mild; lax; permissive

leonine   lionlike; fierce; authoritative

lesion   an injury; a wound

lethal   deadly; fatal

lethargic   dull; slow-moving; sluggish

leviathan   anything vast or huge; a sea monster

levity   lightness of body or spirit; lack of seriousness

levy   to impose and collect taxes

lewd   pertaining to lust or sexual desire

lexicon   dictionary

liaison   a bond; a connection; an illicit relationship between a man and a woman

libation   a drink; a beverage

libel   a false statement in written form

liberal   giving freely; not strict

libertine   one who leads an immoral life

libretto   the words of an opera

licentious   lawless; immoral; lewd

liege   lord; master

lieu   (*in lieu of*) in place of; instead of

lilliputian   tiny; narrow-minded

limber   easily bent; flexible

limpid   clear, transparent

lineage   ancestry; descent

lineaments   facial features

linguistic   pertaining to language

lionize   to treat as a celebrity

liquidate   (*two meanings*) to get rid of by killing; to wind up the affairs of a business

lissome   moving gracefully; agile or active

listless   feeling no interest in anything; indifferent

literal   exact; precise; word for word

lithe   graceful; flexible

litigation   lawsuit

livid   darkened or discolored; pale from anger or embarrassment

loath   reluctant; unwilling

loathe   to hate; to feel disgust for

locus   place

lode   a rich source of supply such as a mineral deposit

lofty   very high; formal; proud

logistics   military operations dealing with the supply and maintenance of equipment

loiter   to linger; to hang around

loll   to lean or lounge about; to droop

longevity   a long life

lope   to move along with a swinging walk

loquacious   talkative

lot   fate

lout   an awkward, stupid person

lowly   humble; ordinary

lucent   giving off light; shining

lucid   clear; easy to understand; rational or sane

lucrative   profitable; producing wealth or riches

ludicrous   ridiculous

lugubrious   sad; mournful

lull   to soothe or calm

luminous   bright

lunacy   insanity; madness

lunar   pertaining to the moon

lupine   wolflike; fierce

lurch   to move suddenly forward

lurid   shocking; glowing; sensational

lurk   to lie concealed in waiting; to stay hidden

lush   abundant; rich

lustrous   shining; bright

luxuriant   rich; extravagant

MACABRE–MYTHICAL

macabre   horrible; gruesome

Machiavellian   deceitful; tricky

machination   evil design

macroscopic   visible to the naked eye

maelstrom   whirlpool

magnanimous   generous

magnate   important person in any field

magnitude   size; extent

maim   to cripple; to deprive of the use of some part of the body

maladroit   clumsy; unskillful; awkward

malady   disease; illness

malaise   discomfort; uneasiness

malapropism   word humorously misused

malcontent   one who is dissatisfied

malediction   curse

malefactor   wrongdoer; villain

malevolent   showing ill will or hatred; very dangerous, harmful

malfeasance   wrongdoing

malicious   spiteful; vengeful

malign   to speak badly of

malignant   evil; deadly

malingerer   one who pretends to be sick to avoid work

malleable   capable of being changed; adaptable

malodorous   bad-smelling; stinking

mammoth   huge; enormous

manacle   handcuff; restraint

mandarin   influential person

mandate   an order; a command

mandatory   required; obligatory

mangle   to cut, slash, or crush so as to disfigure

mangy   shabby; filthy

manifest   evident; obvious

manifold   many; varied

manipulate   (*two meanings*) to handle or manage with skill; to influence a person in a bad way

manumit   to set free

maraud   to raid; to plunder

marital   pertaining to marriage

maritime   pertaining to the sea

marquee   a rooflike shelter, such as glass, projecting above an outer door

martial   warlike

martinet   a strict disciplinarian

martyr   one who suffers for a cause

marvel   to be amazed; to wonder

masochist   one who enjoys his own pain and suffering

massive   huge; bulky

masticate   to chew

maternal   motherly

matriarchy   a social organization in which the mother is the head of the family

matrix   a place of origin

maudlin   excessively sentimental

maul   to injure; to handle roughly

mausoleum   large tomb for many bodies

maverick   a rebel; a nonconformist

mawkish   sickeningly sweet; overly sentimental

maxim   a proverb or saying

meager   inadequate; of poor quality

mean   (*three meanings*) nasty or offensive (*adjective*); inferior or low (*adjective*); an average (*noun*)

meander   to wander aimlessly

meddlesome   interfering; curious

mediate   to settle a dispute; to act as a go-between

mediocre   ordinary; average; neither good nor bad

meditate   to think deeply; to ponder

medley   a mixture; a musical selection combining parts from various sources

megalomania   false impression of one's own greatness; tendency to exaggerate

melancholy   sad; depressed

melee   noisy fight

mellifluous   smoothly flowing; sweet-sounding

melodramatic   overly emotional

memento   remembrance; a souvenir

menace   a threat; a danger

ménage   household; domestic establishment

menagerie   collection of wild or strange animals

mendacious   lying; false

mendicant   a beggar

menial   low; degrading

mentor   adviser

mercantile   pertaining to merchants; commercial

mercenary   motivated only by a desire for money

mercurial   changeable; fickle; erratic

meretricious   gaudy; showy; attractive in a cheap, flashy way

mesa   a flat-topped elevation of land with steep rock walls

mesmerize   to hypnotize

metamorphosis   a change; a transformation

metaphor   comparison (without *like* or *as*)

metaphysics   pertaining to beyond what is natural

mete   (*out*) to distribute in portions

meteoric   momentarily dazzling; swift

meteorology   study of weather and climate

meticulous   excessively careful; finicky

metropolis   large city

mettle   courage; spirit

miasma   pollution; poisonous environment

microcosm   a miniature world

mien   manner; bearing

migratory   wandering; moving from place to place

milieu   environment; setting

militant   ready and willing to fight

millennium   a thousand years

mimic   to imitate

minion   a devoted follower; a highly regarded person

minuscule   very small

minute   (*two meanings*) sixtieth part of an hour (pronounced *min-ut*); very small and insignificant (pronounced *my-newt*)

minutiae   insignificant details; trivia

mirage   an apparition or illusion

mire   (*two meanings*) wet, swampy ground (*noun*); to involve in difficulties (*verb*)

mirth   joy; amusement; laughter

misanthrope   hater of mankind

misapprehension   a misunderstanding

miscegenation   mixture of races, especially through marriage

mischance   unlucky accident; bad luck

misconstrue   misinterpret; misjudge

miscreant   a vicious person; a villain

misdemeanor   a criminal offense less serious than a felony

misgiving   doubt; suspicion

misnomer   an error in listing the name of a person

misogamy   hatred of marriage

misogynist   woman-hater

missive   letter

mitigate   to make less severe; to become milder

mnemonic   pertaining to memory

mobile   movable; flexible

mock   to ridicule; to insult; to lower in esteem

modicum   a small amount

modish   fashionable; stylish

modulate   to soften; to tone down

mogul   powerful person

molest   to disturb; to bother

mollify   to pacify; to calm; to appease

molt   to shed, such as feathers and skin

molten   melted

momentous   very important

monarchy   government by one ruler

monastic   pertaining to a monk; self-denying

monetary   pertaining to money

monitor   one who watches or warns

monograph   a paper, book, etc., written about a single subject

monolithic   unyielding; unified

monologue   long speech by one person

monotheism   belief in one god

monumental   great; important

moot   doubtful; debatable

moratorium   delay; postponement

morbid   depressing; gruesome

mordant   sarcastic; biting

mores   customs; traditions; morals

moribund   dying

morose   gloomy; ill-humored

mortal   destined to die; causing death

mortify   to embarrass; to humiliate

motif   theme; central idea

motley   diverse; assorted; having different colors

mottled   spotted; blotched; streaked

mountebank   a phony; a fraud; a charlatan

muddle   to confuse; to mix up

mulct   to punish with a fine; to obtain money by extortion

mull   (*over*) to study or think about

multifarious   varied; having many parts

mundane   worldly

munificent   generous

murky   dark; unclear; gloomy

muse   to think deeply

muster   to gather together

musty   stale; moldy

mute   silent

mutilate   to disfigure; to cripple

mutinous   rebellious

muzzle   to restrain; to gag

myopic   nearsighted; having a limited point of view

myriad   infinitely vast in number

myrmidon   an unquestioning follower

mythical   imaginary; fictitious

NABOB–NUTRIMENT

nabob   a very wealthy or powerful person

nadir   lowest point

naïve   simple; unsophisticated

narcissistic   conceited; vain

nascent   coming into being; being born

natation   the act or art of swimming

nativity   birth

naught   nothing

nautical   pertaining to ships, sailors, navigation

nebulous   hazy; vague; uncertain

necromancy   magic, especially that practiced by a witch

nefarious   wicked

negate   to deny; to make ineffective

negligent   careless

nemesis   something that a person cannot conquer or achieve

neologism   new use of a word or a new coinage of a word

neophyte   a beginner; a novice

nepotism   favoritism shown toward relatives

nether   lower; under

nettle   to irritate; to annoy

neutralize   to make ineffective; to counteract

nexus   connection, tie, or link among the units of a group

nicety   delicacy; subtlety

niche   recess or hollow in a wall

niggardly   stingy; miserly

niggle   to spend excessive time on unimportant details

nihilism   total rejection of established laws

nimble   quick and light in motion

nirvana   place of great peace or happiness

nocturnal   pertaining to night

nodule   a small, rounded mass or lump

noisome   foul-smelling; harmful or injurious

nomadic   wandering; homeless

nomenclature   a set of names or terms

nominal   in name only; not in fact

non sequitur   something that does not logically follow

nonage   a period of immaturity

nonchalant   unconcerned; casual

noncommittal   having no definite point of view

nonentity   person or thing of little importance

nonpareil   unequaled; unrivaled

nonplus   to confuse; to perplex

nostalgia   homesickness; longing for the past

nostrum   quack medicine; supposed cure-all

notorious   having a bad reputation; infamous

novice   a beginner

noxious   harmful

nuance   delicate variation in meaning, tone, color, etc.

nub   a lump or small piece

nubile   suitable for marriage, in regard to age and physical development

nugatory   worthless; invalid

nullify   to make useless or ineffective

numismatist   coin collector

nuptial   pertaining to marriage

nurture   to feed; to sustain

nutriment   food; nourishment

OAF–OVOID

oaf   a dunce or blockhead

oasis   a place that offers a pleasant relief

obdurate   stubborn; hard-hearted

obeisance   a bow or similar gesture expressing deep respect

obese   very fat

obfuscate   to confuse; to bewilder; to perplex

oblation   an offering for religious or charitable purposes

obligatory   required; mandatory

oblique   slanted; indirect

obliterate   to erase; to do away with

oblivious   forgetful; unmindful

obloquy   strong disapproval; bad reputation resulting from public criticism

obnoxious   objectionable; offensive

obscurant   a person who tries to prevent the spread of knowledge

obscure   dim; not clear; not easily understood

obsequious   excessively submissive; overly attentive

obsequy   a funeral rite or ceremony

obsess   to control the thoughts or feelings of a person

obsolescent   going out of use; becoming extinct

obstinate   stubborn

obstreperous   boisterous; unruly

obtrude   to push something toward or upon a person

obtuse   slow to comprehend

obviate   to prevent

occidental   western; opposite of oriental

occlude   to close; to shut; to block out

occult   hidden; secret; mysterious

ocular   pertaining to sight

odious   disgusting; hateful

odoriferous   giving off a displeasing or strong smell

odyssey   a long journey

offal   garbage; waste parts

officious   meddling; interfering

ogle   to look at with desire

ogre   monster; hideous being

olfactory   pertaining to smell

oligarchy   government in which power is in the hands of only a few individuals

Olympian   majestic

omen   an event that indicates the future

ominous   threatening; indicating evil or harm

omnifarious   of all kinds

omnipotent   all-powerful

omniscient   all-knowing

omnivorous   eating any kind of food; absorbing everything

onerous   burdensome; heavy

onslaught   a furious attack

onus   a burden; a responsibility

opaque   not transparent; not letting light pass through

opiate   narcotic; causing sleep or relief

opportunist   one who takes advantage of a situation

oppress   to rule harshly; tyrannize

opprobrious   shameful; disgraceful

opt   (*for*) to choose

optimist   one who sees the good side of things

optimum   the best; most favorable

opulent   rich; luxurious

oracular   mysterious; predicting

oration   a speech delivered on a special occasion

orbit   a curved path, such as a planet takes around the sun

ordain   to order; to establish; to arrange

ordeal   difficult or painful experience; a primitive form of trial

ordinance   law; regulation

organic   fundamental; essential; natural, not artificial; carbon-based

Orient, orient   (*two meanings*) an area of the Far East, such as Asia (*noun, capitalized*); to adjust or adapt to (*verb, lowercase*)

orifice   mouth; opening

ornate   showy; highly decorated

ornithology   study of birds

orthodox   accepting the usual or traditional beliefs

orthography   correct spelling

oscillate   to swing or move back and forth, like a pendulum

ossify   to change into bone; to become rigid

ostensible   apparent; conspicuous

ostentatious   showing off; boastful

ostracize   to banish; to exclude

oust   to drive out; to expel

outwit   to trick; to get the better of

overt   open; aboveboard; not hidden

ovine   of or like a sheep

ovoid   egg-shaped

PACIFY–PYRRHIC VICTORY

pacify   to calm down

pact   an agreement

paean   song of praise or joy

palatable   pleasant to the taste

palatial   magnificent

paleontology   study of prehistoric life

pall   (*two meanings*) something that covers or conceals (*noun*); to become wearisome or unpleasant (*verb*)

palliate   to ease; to lessen

pallid   pale; dull

palpable   obvious; capable of being touched or felt

palpitate   to beat rapidly; to tremble

palsy   muscle paralysis

paltry   trivial; worthless

panacea   a cure-all; an answer for all problems

panache   self-confidence; a showy manner

pandemic   general; widespread

pandemonium   wild disorder; confusion

panegyric   an expression of praise

pang   a sharp pain

panoply   suit of armor; any protective covering

panorama   unlimited view; comprehensive survey

parable   a simple story giving a moral or religious lesson

paradigm   a model; an example

paradox   a statement that seems contradictory, but is probably true

paragon   a model of excellence or perfection

parameter   boundary; limits

paramount   chief; supreme

paranoia   mental disorder characterized by a feeling of being persecuted

paraphernalia   personal belongings; equipment

paraphrase   to reword; to restate

parched   dried up; extremely thirsty

pariah   an outcast

parity   equality; similarity

parley   discussion; conference

parlous   dangerous

parochial   local; narrow; limited

parody   a work that imitates another in a ridiculous manner

paroxysm   a sudden outburst; a fit

parrot   to repeat or imitate without understanding

parry   to avoid something such as a thrust or blow

parsimonious   stingy; miserly

partisan   a strong supporter of a cause

passé   old fashioned; out-of-date

passive   submissive; unresisting

pastoral   pertaining to the country; rural

patent   (*two meanings*) a government protection for an inventor (*noun*); evident or obvious (*adjective*)

paternal   fatherly

pathogenic   causing disease

pathos   pity; deep feeling

patriarch   an early biblical person regarded as one of the fathers of the human race

patrician   aristocratic

patrimony   inherited right; heritage

patronage   the control of power to make appointments to government jobs

patronize   (*two meanings*) to be a customer; to talk down to

paucity   scarcity; lack

peccadillo   a minor offense

pectoral   pertaining to the chest

peculate   to steal; to embezzle

pecuniary   pertaining to money

pedagogue   a schoolteacher

pedantic   tending to show off one's learning

pedestrian   (*two meanings*) one who walks (*noun*); ordinary or dull (*adjective*)

pedigree   a record of ancestors; a line of descent

peer   (*two meanings*) an equal (*noun*); to look closely (*verb*)

peerless   without equal; unmatched

peevish   hard to please; irritable

pejorative   having a negative effect; insulting

pellucid   transparent; clear

pelt   (*two meanings*) skin of a fur-bearing animal (*noun*); to throw things at (*verb*)

penal   pertaining to punishment

penchant   a strong liking for; an inclination

pendant   anything that hangs or is suspended

penitent   expressing sorrow for sin or wrongdoing

pensive   dreamily thoughtful

penury   extreme poverty

peon   common worker

perceive   to observe

perceptible   observable; recognizable

perdition   damnation; ruin; hell

peregrinate   to travel from place to place

peremptory   decisive; final; not open to debate

perennial   lasting for a long time; perpetual

perfidious   deceitful; treacherous; unfaithful

perforce   of necessity

perfunctory   done without care; routine

perigee   point in an orbit nearest to the earth

perilous   dangerous; risky

periphery   outside boundary; unimportant aspects of a subject

periphrastic   said in a roundabout way

perjury   making a false statement while under oath

permeate   to spread throughout

pernicious   deadly; destructive

peroration   the concluding part of a speech

perpetrate   to do something evil; to be guilty of

perpetuate   to cause to continue

perplexity   confusion

perquisite   something additional to regular pay

persevere   to endure; to continue

personification   giving human qualities to a non-human being

perspicacity   keenness of judgment

perspicuity   clearness, as of a statement

pert   bold; saucy

pertinent   relevant; to the point

perturb   to unsettle; to disturb

peruse   to read carefully

pervade   to spread throughout; to pass through

perverse   contrary; cranky

pervert   to lead astray; to corrupt

pessimist   one who sees the worst in everything

petrify   to turn to rock; to paralyze with fear

petrology   study of rocks

petty   unimportant; minor

petulant   irritable; rude

phalanx   closely massed body of persons

phenomenon   extraordinary person, thing, or event

philander   to engage in various love affairs

philanthropy   a desire to help mankind; generosity

philately   stamp collecting

philippic   a bitter verbal attack

philistine   (*adjective*) uncultured; common; (*noun*) one who is uncultured or common

phlegmatic   unemotional; cool; not easily excited

phobia   intense fear

phoenix   a bird that symbolizes immortality

picaresque   pertaining to an adventurous wanderer

piddling   trifling; petty

piecemeal   bit by bit; gradually

pied   many-colored; variegated

piety   reverence; devotion

pigment   dye; coloring matter

pilgrimage   a journey to a holy place

pillage   to rob by violence

pillory   to expose to public ridicule or abuse

pinnacle   peak; highest point

pious   religious

piquant   stimulating to the taste; exciting interest

pique   to irritate or annoy

piscine   of or like a fish

pitfall   unexpected difficulty; a trap

pithy   concise; to the point

pittance   small share or amount

pivotal   central; crucial

placard   small poster

placate   to soothe; to calm

placebo   harmless, phony medicine; something said or done to soothe

placid   calm

plagiarism   the claiming of another's work as one's own

plague   (*two meanings*) a contagious disease (*noun*); to torment; to trouble (*verb*)

plaintive   sorrowful; sad

platitude   a dull or trite remark

platonic   spiritual; free from sensual desire

plaudit   applause; (*in the plural*) any expression of approval

plausible   apparently true, fair, or reasonable

plebeian   pertaining to a member of the lower classes

plenary   full; complete; absolute

plethora   abundance

pliant   easily bent; adaptable

plight   a sad or dangerous situation

ploy   a gimmick; a trick

pluck   (*two meanings*) to pull at (*verb*); courage (*noun*)

plumb   to test; to measure

plunder   to rob; to take by force

plutocracy   rule by the wealthy class

poach   to trespass or steal

podium   a platform

poignant   keenly distressing; affecting the emotions

polarize   to separate into opposing groups

polemic   a controversy or argument

politic   diplomatic; shrewd

poltroon   a coward

polychromatic   many-colored

polyglot   speaking or writing several languages

polymorphic   having many forms

polytheism   belief in many gods

pomp   brilliant show or display

ponder   to think deeply; to consider carefully

ponderous   heavy; burdensome

porcine   of or like a pig

portable   capable of being carried

portal   door; gate; entrance

portentous   warning; foreshadowing

portly   stout; large

posterity   future generations

posthumous   occurring after death

postulate   to assume without proof; to take for granted

potable   drinkable

potent   powerful; strong

potentate   ruler; monarch

potential   capacity for being or becoming something

potion   a drink

potpourri   a mixture

pragmatic   practical

prate   to talk extensively and pointlessly; to babble

precarious   uncertain; dangerous; risky

precede   to be, come, or go before

precedent   an act that may be used as an example in the future

precept   a rule of conduct

precipice   cliff

precipitate   to bring about an action suddenly

precipitous   extremely steep

précis   brief summary

preclude   to prevent; to shut out

precocious   prematurely developed

precursor   a forerunner; predecessor

predatory   living by plunder, exploitation, etc.

predicate   to declare; to assert

predilection   a liking; preference; inclination

predispose   to make susceptible

preeminent   standing out above all others

preen   to dress oneself carefully or smartly

prehensile   adapted for seizing or grasping something

prelude   an introduction

premeditate   to plan beforehand

premier   first in importance or time

premise   statement from which a conclusion is drawn

premonition   forewarning; hunch

preponderance   superiority in quantity or power; dominance

preposterous   absurd; ridiculous

prerogative   privilege or right

presage   to indicate or warn in advance

prescience   knowledge of things before they happen

presentiment   anticipation, especially of something evil

prestige   influence; importance

presumptuous   boldly assuming

pretentious   showy; putting on airs

preternatural   abnormal; beyond what is natural

pretext   a false reason or motive; an excuse

prevail   to succeed; to gain the advantage

prevaricate   to lie

prim   formal; proper

primary   first; chief

primeval   of the earliest times or ages

primogeniture   state of being the firstborn

primordial   first; original

primp   to dress up in a fussy way

prismatic   many-colored

pristine   uncorrupted; in its original state

privation   loss or lack of something essential

privy   (*to*) having knowledge of something private or secret

probe   to investigate; to examine

probity   honesty; integrity

proclivity   inclination; tendency

procrastinate   to postpone; to delay

procreate   to beget or produce

procrustean   designed to get conformity at any cost

procure   to obtain; to secure

prod   to urge; to poke or jab

prodigal   wasteful

prodigious   enormous; vast

profane   showing disrespect for sacred things

profess   to acknowledge; to admit frankly

proffer   to offer

proficiency   skill; competency

profligate   shamelessly immoral; extremely wasteful

profound   very deep

profuse   abundant

progeny   descendants

prognosticate   to predict; to foretell

projectile   a bullet, shell, grenade, etc., for firing from a gun

proletarian   one who belongs to the working class

proliferate   to expand; to increase

prolific   productive; fertile

prolix   tediously long and wordy

prologue   introduction

promenade   a stroll or a walk; an area used for walking

promiscuous   sexually loose

promontory   piece of land that juts out

promulgate   to announce; to advocate

prone   reclining; lying flat; inclined

propagate   to spread; to multiply

propensity   inclination; tendency

prophetic   predicting

propinquity   nearness; closeness

propitious   favorable

proponent   a person who supports a cause or doctrine

propriety   conformity; appropriateness

prosaic   dull; commonplace; unimaginative

proscribe   to denounce; exile

proselyte   a person who has changed from one religion to another; a convert

prospectus   a report describing a forthcoming project

prostrate   lying flat; thrown or fallen to the ground

protagonist   main character

protean   changeable; variable

protégé   one who has been guided or instructed by another

protocol   the etiquette observed by diplomats

prototype   the original; first of its kind; a model

protract   to draw out; to prolong

protrude   to stick out; to project

proverbial   well-known

provident   having foresight

provincial   countrified; narrow; limited

provisional   temporary

proviso   a condition; a stipulation

provoke   to anger; to irritate; to annoy

prowess   skill; strength; daring

proximity   nearness in place or time

proxy   one who acts in place of another

prude   an overly proper person

prudence   caution; good judgment

prune   to cut off or lop off, such as twigs, branches, or roots

prurient   lustful; obscene; lewd

pseudo   false; counterfeit

pseudonym   a fake or assumed name

psyche   the human soul or spirit

puerile   childish; immature

pugilist   a boxer

pugnacious   eager to fight; quarrelsome

puissant   powerful; strong

pulchritude   beauty

pulmonary   pertaining to the lungs

pulverize   to crush or grind into powder; totally destroy

pummel   to beat or thrash with the fists

pun   the humorous use of a word, or of different words sounding alike, so as to play on their various meanings

punctilious   very exact; precise

pundit   a learned man; an expert or authority

pungent   having a sharp taste or smell; severely critical or sarcastic

punitive   pertaining to punishment

puny   weak; inferior

purge   to cleanse; to purify

puritanical   strict; rigid; harsh

purloin   to steal

purport   to claim to be

purvey   to furnish; to supply

pusillanimous   cowardly; fearful

putative   supposed; believed

putrefy   to rot; to decay

pyre   a funeral fire in which the corpse is burned

pyretic   pertaining to fever

pyromaniac   one who likes to start fires; arsonist

Pyrrhic victory   success gained at too high a cost

QUACK–QUOTIDIAN

quack   an untrained doctor; a pretender to any skill

quadruped   a four-footed animal

quaff   to gulp; to drink in large quantities

quagmire   a swamp; a difficult situation

quail   to lose courage; to shrink with fear

quaint   strange or unusual in a pleasing or amusing way

qualm   a feeling of uneasiness

quandary   a puzzling situation; a dilemma

quarry   an animal that is being hunted down

quash   to cancel; to set aside (as an indictment)

quasi   resembling; seeming

quaver   to tremble; to shake

quay   a wharf

queasy   uneasy; nauseated

quell   to subdue; to calm down

querulous   complaining

query   a question

quest   a search

queue   a line of people waiting their turn

quibble   petty objection or argument

quiddity   essential quality

quidnunc   a gossip or busybody

quiescent   at rest; motionless

quietus   finishing stroke; anything that ends an activity

quintessence   the pure and concentrated essence of something

quip   a witty or sarcastic remark

quirk   a peculiar characteristic of a person; a sudden twist or turn

quiver   to tremble; to shake

quixotic   extremely idealistic; romantic; not practical

quizzical   odd; questioning; puzzled

quotidian   daily

RABBLE–RUTHLESS

rabble   mob; disorderly crowd

rabid   intense; furious or raging; mad

rack   to torment; to torture

raconteur   storyteller

radical   extreme; complete; violent

rail   (*at* or *against*) to complain bitterly

raillery   good-humored ridicule

raiment   clothing; garments

rakish   carefree; lively

rambunctious   restless; hard to control

ramification   a result; a consequence; a branch

rampant   widespread; raging

ramshackle   shaky; ready to fall apart

rancid   having a bad taste or smell; stale; repulsive

rancor   bitter resentment; hatred

rankle   to cause irritation; to fester

rant   to speak in a loud or violent manner

rapacious   taking by force; greedy

rapport   a close relationship; harmony

rapt   completely absorbed in; overcome with joy, love, etc.

rarefy   to make less dense; to refine

rash   (*two meanings*) a skin irritation (*noun*); reckless or daring (*adjective*)

raspy   harsh; grating

ratify   to officially approve of

ratiocinate   to reason

ration   a fixed portion; a share

rational   sensible; reasonable

rationalize   to make an excuse for

raucous   irritating or harsh in sound

ravage   to damage; ruin

ravenous   extremely hungry; greedy

raze   to destroy; to level to the ground

realm   kingdom; region

rebuff   to refuse; to snub

rebuke   to scold; to blame

rebuttal   contradiction; opposing argument

recalcitrant   disobedient; hard to manage

recant   to withdraw or disavow a statement or opinion

recapitulate   to summarize; repeat briefly

recede   to go or move back; to withdraw

recess   (*two meanings*) a cut or notch in something; a pause or rest

recidivist   a person who goes back to crime

recipient   one who receives

reciprocal   interchangeable; mutual

reciprocate   to give in return

recluse   hermit; one who shuts himself off from the world

recoil   to retreat; to draw back

reconcile   to bring into agreement or harmony

recondite   difficult to understand; profound

reconnoiter   to survey; to check out in advance

recount   to tell or relate, as a story

recreant   coward; traitor

recrimination   countercharge

rectify   to correct; to make right

rectitude   honesty; moral uprightness

recumbent   lying down; reclining

recuperate   to get well

recur   to happen again

redemption   deliverance from sin; a rescue

redolent   having a pleasant odor

redoubtable   formidable; commanding respect

redress   to set right; to remedy

redundant   repetitious; unnecessary

reek   to give off; emit

refractory   stubborn; hard to manage

refulgent   shining; glowing

refurbish   to make new; to freshen up

refute   to prove wrong, such as an opinion

regal   pertaining to a king; splendid

regale   to entertain

regenerate   to re-create; to reform morally; to replace a lost part of the body

regent   one who governs

regicide   the killing of a king

regime   a system of government

regimen   a regular system (of exercise, diet, etc.)

regressive   moving in a backward direction

regurgitate   to rush or surge back, as undigested food

rehabilitate   to restore to useful life

reimburse   to pay back

reiterate   to repeat

rejuvenate   to make young again

relegate   to banish; to assign to an inferior position

relentless   unyielding

relevant   significant; pertaining to the subject

relinquish   to give up; to let go

relish   to enjoy; to take delight in

remediable   capable of being corrected

remedial   intended to correct

reminisce   to remember

remiss   negligent

remission   a lessening; a forgiveness as of sins or offenses

remonstrate   to protest; to complain

remorse   regret for wrongdoing

remuneration   payment for a service

renaissance   rebirth; renewal; revival

renal   pertaining to the kidneys

rend   to split; to tear apart

rendezvous   a meeting; appointment

renegade   a deserter; a traitor

renege   to go back on one's word

renounce   to give up (a belief)

renovate   to make new; to repair

reparation   compensation; something done to make up for a wrong or injury done

repartee   a quick, witty reply

repast   a meal

repellent   something that drives away or wards off (insects, etc.)

repercussion   reaction; aftereffect

repertoire   special skills or talents one possesses; collection

repine   to complain; to fret

replenish   to fill up again

replete   well-filled

repose   (*verb*) to rest; to sleep; (*noun*) rest

reprehensible   deserving criticism or blame; shameful

repress   to control; to subdue

reprimand   to scold

reprisal   retaliation; revenge

reproach   to blame; to scold

reprobate   a wicked person

reproof   a rebuke

repudiate   to reject; to disown

repugnant   distasteful; disgusting

repulse   to drive back; to repel

reputed   supposed to be

requiem   funeral hymn; mass for the dead

requisite   required or necessary; indispensable

requite   to make a return or repayment

rescind   to cancel; to repeal

residue   that which remains

resilient   recovering quickly; elastic

resolute   very determined

resonance   fullness of sound

resourceful   able to deal effectively with problems

respite   a delay; rest

resplendent   shining brightly; dazzling

restitution   repayment; a giving back

restive   restless; uneasy; impatient

restrain   to hold back; to control

résumé   a summary

resurge   to rise again

resurrection   revival; rebirth

resuscitate   to revive from apparent death or from unconsciousness

retaliation   revenge; repayment for an evil act

retentive   having a good memory; remembering

reticent   silent or reserved in manner

retinue   body of attendants or followers

retort   a short, witty reply

retract   to take back (a statement); to withdraw

retrench   to cut down or reduce expenses

retribution   deserved punishment

retrieve   to get or bring back

retroactive   applying to a period before a certain law was passed

retrogressive   going backward; becoming worse

retrospect   (preceded by *in*) looking back on past events

revelation   something made known; a disclosure

revelry   noisy merrymaking

reverberate   to echo; to resound

revere   to honor; to respect

reverie   a daydream

revile   to abuse; to slander

rhetorical   concerned with mere style or effect

ribald   vulgar; indecent

rife   frequently occurring; widespread

rift   a break or split

righteous   behaving justly or morally

rigorous   strict

risible   laughable; funny

risqué   daring or indecent; not proper

rite   a religious ceremony; a solemn act

robust   strong; hearty

rogue   a dishonest person; a scoundrel

rollicking   jolly; carefree

roster   a list

rote   (preceded with *by*) from memory, without thought for meaning

rotund   round; fat

rout   overwhelming defeat

rudimentary   elementary; basic

rue   to regret; to be sorrowful

ruffian   hoodlum; lawless person

ruffle   (*two meanings*) a wrinkle or a ripple (*noun*); to irritate or to annoy (*verb*)

ruminate   to consider carefully; to meditate on

rupture   to break apart; to burst

ruse   a skillful trick or deception

rustic   pertaining to the country

rustle   (*two meanings*) to steal; to make a swishing sound

ruthless   cruel; merciless

SACCHARINE–SYNTHETIC

---

saccharine   overly sweet

sacrilege   the violation of anything sacred

sacrosanct   extremely holy

sadistic   deriving pleasure from inflicting pain on others

saga   a long story of adventure

sagacious   wise

sage   a wise person

salacious   obscene; lusty

salient   significant; conspicuous

saline   salty

sallow   sickly pale

salubrious   healthful

salutary   healthful; wholesome

salutatory   a welcoming address, as at a graduation

salvage   to rescue; to save from destruction

sanctimonious   hypocritical in regard to religious belief

sanction   to authorize; to give permission

sangfroid   calmness; composure

sanguinary   bloody

sanguine   cheerful; optimistic

sapient   wise

sardonic   mocking; scornful

sartorial   pertaining to clothes or tailoring

satiated   satisfied; filled up

satirical   sarcastic; ironic

saturate   to soak; to fill up

saturnine   gloomy; sluggish

saunter   to stroll; to walk leisurely

savant   a person of extensive learning

savoir faire   tact; knowledge of just what to do in any situation

savor   to enjoy, as by taste or smell

scant   inadequate in size or amount

scapegoat   one who takes the blame for others

scathing   extremely severe or harsh, such as a remark

schism   a split or break

scintilla   a tiny amount; a speck

scintillate   to sparkle; to twinkle

scion   an offspring; a descendant

scoff   to ridicule

scope   range; extent

scourge   a whip or a lash; a person or thing that punishes or destroys

scrupulous   honest; ethical; precise

scrutinize   to examine closely

scurrilous   coarsely abusive; vulgar

scurry   run about; to hurry

scuttle   to sink (a ship); to abandon

sear   to burn; to scorch

sebaceous   fatty

seclude   to keep apart; to isolate

secrete   to hide or conceal

secular   worldly; nonreligious

sedate   quiet; calm; serious

sedentary   sitting most of the time

sediment   material that settles on the bottom; residue

sedition   rebellion

sedulous   hard-working; industrious; diligent

seedy   run-down; shabby

seethe   to boil; to be violently agitated

seismic   pertaining to earthquakes

semblance   outward appearance

senile   pertaining to mental weakness due to old age

sensate   pertaining to feeling

sensual   pertaining to enjoyment of food and sex

sensuous   pertaining to enjoyment of art, music, etc.

sententious   concise; including proverbs and brief remarks

sentient   conscious; capable of feeling

sentinel   a guard

sepulcher   tomb; burial vault

sequel   an event or literary work that follows a previous one

sequester   to separate; to set aside

seraphic   angelic; pure

serendipity   a talent for making desirable discoveries by accident

serene   calm; peaceful

serpentine   winding

serrated   having toothlike edges

servile   like a slave

servitude   slavery; bondage

sever   to cut in two; to separate

shackle   to keep prisoner; to restrain

sham   a pretense

shambles   a slaughterhouse; great disorder

shard   a fragment

sheepish   embarrassed; bashful

shibboleth   a slogan; a password

shiftless   lazy; inefficient

shoal   a shallow place in the water; a reef

shortcomings   defects; deficiencies

shrew   a nagging, bad-tempered woman

shroud   a cloth or sheet in which a corpse is wrapped for burial

sibilant   hissing

sibling   a brother or sister

simian   pertaining to an ape or monkey

simile   a comparison using *like* or *as*

simony   the sin of buying or selling church benefits

simper   to smile in a silly way

simulacrum   an image; a likeness

simulate   to pretend; to imitate

simultaneous   occurring at the same time

sinecure   job with no responsibility

sinewy   tough; firm; strong

singular   extraordinary; remarkable; exceptional

sinister   threatening evil; ominous

sinuous   curving; winding

siren   an attractive but dangerous woman

skeptic   one who doubts

skinflint   stingy person; miser

skittish   restless; excitable; nervous

skulduggery   trickery; deception

skulk   to sneak around; to lie in hiding

slacken   become loose; to relax

slake   to lessen (thirst, desire, anger, etc.) by satisfying; to quench

slander   to make a false statement against someone

slattern   an untidy woman

sleazy   cheap; flimsy

sleek   smooth and shiny

slither   to slide or glide

slothful   lazy

slough   (*off*) to discard; to shed

slovenly   untidy; dirty; careless

smirk   to smile in an affected or offensive way

smite   to strike forcefully

smolder   to burn without flame; to keep feelings concealed

smug   self-satisfied

snare   to trap

sneer   to look at with contempt; to scorn; to deride

snicker   to laugh in a half-suppressed way

snippet   a small fragment

snivel   to whine; to complain

sober   not drunk; serious

sobriquet   nickname; assumed name

sodden   soaked; damp

sojourn   a brief stay or visit

solace   comfort

solar   pertaining to the sun

solecism   ungrammatical usage; an error or inconsistency in speech

solicit   to ask; to seek; to try to get an order in business

solicitude   concern; anxiety

soliloquy   act of talking to oneself

solipsistic   pertaining to the theory that only oneself exists or can be proved to exist

solitude   loneliness

solon   a wise man

solvent   (*two meanings*) having the ability to pay a debt (*adjective*); a substance that dissolves another (*noun*)

somber   dark; gloomy

somnambulate   walk in one's sleep

somniferous   causing sleep

somnolent   drowsy; sleepy

sonorous   producing a deep, rich sound

sophistry   a deceptive, tricky argument

sophomoric   immature; pretentious

soporific   causing sleep

sordid   dirty; filthy

sot   a drunkard

sobriquet   nickname; assumed name

sovereign   a monarch or other supreme ruler

spacious   roomy; convenient

Spartan   warlike; brave; disciplined

spasm   a sudden burst of energy

specious   not genuine; pleasing to the eye but deceptive

specter   a ghost; a phantom

speculate   (*two meanings*) to meditate; to participate in a risky business transaction

sphinx   person who is difficult to understand

splenetic   bad-tempered; irritable

sporadic   infrequent; irregular

spry   full of life; active

spume   foam

spurious deceitful; counterfeit

spurn to reject

squalid filthy; dirty

staccato made up of short, abrupt sounds

stagnant not flowing; stale; sluggish

staid sedate; settled

stalemate a deadlock; a draw

stalwart strong; sturdy

stamina endurance; resistance to fatigue

stance attitude; posture

stark complete; harsh; severe

static inactive; motionless

stationary standing still; not moving

statute law; rule

steadfast firm in purpose; dependable; constant

stench a foul smell

stentorian very loud

stereotyped not original; commonplace

sterling of high quality; excellent

stigma mark of disgrace

stilted artificially formal

stint to be sparing; to conserve

stipend salary

stipulate to specify; to arrange definitely

stoic showing no emotion; indifferent to pleasure or pain

stolid impassive; having little emotion

strait a position of difficulty; a narrow passage of water

stratagem a plan, scheme, or trick

strew to spread about; to scatter

striated striped; marked with lines

stricture negative criticism; a restriction

strident harsh-sounding; loud and shrill

stringent strict; tight

strut to walk in a proud manner; to show off

stultify to make absurd or ridiculous; to render worthless

stupefy to stun; to amaze

stygian dark; gloomy

stymie to hinder; to block

suave polished; sophisticated

sub rosa secretly; confidentially

subaqueous underwater

subjective not objective; personal

subjugate to conquer

sublimate to make a person act noble or moral

sublime majestic; elevated or lofty in thought

subliminal subconscious; unaware

submissive yielding; humbly obedient

subordinate of lower rank

suborn to hire for an unlawful act

subsequent following; occurring later

subservient submissive; helpful, in an inferior capacity

subside to become quiet; to settle down

subsidiary auxiliary; supplementary; serving to assist

substantiate to prove; to confirm; to support

subterfuge trickery; deceit

subterranean underground

subversive tending to overthrow or undermine

succinct concise; brief and to the point

succor assistance; help; relief

succulent juicy

succumb to yield; to give in

suffrage the right to vote

sullen gloomy; showing irritation

sully to soil, stain, or tarnish

sultry hot and moist

sumptuous luxurious; lavish; extravagant

sundry various; assorted

superannuated retired because of old age

supercilious proud; haughty

superficial on the surface; shallow

superfluous excessive; unnecessary

supernal heavenly

supernumerary extra; more than necessary

supersede to take the place of

supervene to take place or occur unexpectedly

supine lying on the back

supplant to replace

supple flexible

suppliant   begging; asking humbly

supplicate   to pray humbly; to beg

surfeit   an excessive amount

surly   rude; bad-tempered

surmise   to guess

surmount   to go beyond; to overcome

surreptitious   acting in a sneaky way

surrogate   substitute

surveillance   supervision; close watch

sustenance   nourishment

susurration   whispering; murmuring

suture   to join together, as with stitches

svelte   slender; graceful

swarthy   dark-complexioned

swathe   to wrap closely or fully

sybarite   one who is fond of luxuries and pleasure

sycophant   a flatterer; a parasite

sylvan   wooded; pertaining to the forest

symbiosis   mutual dependence between two different organisms

symmetrical   balanced; well-proportioned

synchronize   to happen at the same time

synthesis   a combination; a fusion

synthetic   not genuine; artificial

TABLEAU–TYRO

tableau   dramatic scene or picture

taboo   forbidden; unacceptable

tabulation   a systematic listing by columns or rows

tacit   silent; not expressed

taciturn   speaking very little

tactics   plan; method; strategy

tactile   pertaining to sense of touch

taint   to infect; to harm a person's reputation

talisman   a good-luck charm

tally   to count; to make a record of

tangent   touching

tangible   real; capable of being touched

tantalize   to tease or torment

tantamount   (followed by *to*) equivalent to

tarn   a small lake or pool

tarnish   to soil; to discolor; to stain

tarry   to linger; to delay

taunt   to ridicule; to tease

taurine   like a bull

taut   tight; tense

tawdry   cheap; showy; flashy

tawny   yellowish-brown

tedious   boring; monotonous

teeming   overfilled; pouring out

temerity   reckless boldness; rashness

temper   (*verb*) to moderate; to soften or tone down

temperate   not extreme; moderate

temporal   pertaining to time

temporize   to be indecisive; to be evasive; to delay an action

tenacious   holding on; persistent; stubborn

tendentious   biased; favoring a cause

tenet   a doctrine; a belief

tensile   capable of being stretched; elastic

tentative   for the time being; experimental

tenuous   slender; flimsy; without substance

tenure   the holding or possessing of anything

tepid   lukewarm

terminate   to put an end to; to conclude

terminus   a boundary; a limit

terpsichorean   pertaining to dancing

terrestrial   earthly; living on land

terse   brief; to the point

testy   irritable

thanatology   the study of death and dying

theocracy   government by religious leaders

therapeutic pertaining to the treatment and curing of disease

thermal pertaining to heat

thesaurus a book of synonyms and antonyms; a dictionary

thespian an actor

thrall a slave

threnody a funeral song

throes a violent struggle; pains (*of childbirth*); agony (*of death*)

throng a crowd

thwart to prevent or hinder

timorous fearful; cowardly

tinge a faint color; a trace

tirade a long angry speech; an outburst of bitter denunciation

titanic huge

titillate to tickle; to excite agreeably

titter to laugh in a self-conscious or nervous way

token (*two meanings*) sign or symbol (*noun*); slight or unimportant (*adjective*)

tome large, heavy book

toothsome tasty

topple to overturn; to fall over

torpid inactive; sluggish

torsion twisting; bending

torso the human body excluding the head and limbs

tortuous twisting; winding

torturous causing extreme pain

touchstone standard; a test or criterion for quality

toxic poisonous; harmful

tractable easy to manage

traduce to speak badly of; to slander

trait a characteristic; a quality

tranquil calm; peaceful

transcend to go beyond; to overcome

transcendental supernatural; going beyond ordinary experience or belief

transgression violation of a rule or law

transient temporary; passing

transitory lasting a short time; brief

translucent letting light pass through

transmute to change from one form to another; to transform

transparent easily seen through; clear

transpire to be revealed or become known; to occur

trappings articles of dress; equipment

trauma a shock; an aftereffect

travail very hard work; intense pain

travesty an absurd or inadequate imitation

treacherous dangerous; deceptive; disloyal

treatise a book or writing about some particular subject

treble three times as much

tremulous trembling; quivering

trenchant keen or incisive; vigorous; effective

trepidation fear; alarm

trespass to invade; to enter wrongfully

tribulation trouble

tributary a stream flowing into a river

tribute a gift; an acknowledgment to show admiration

trinity group of three

trite worn out; stale; commonplace

trivia matters or things that are very unimportant; trivialities

truckle (*to*) to submit; to yield

truculent savage; brutal; cruel

truism a self-evident, obvious truth

truncate to shorten; to cut off

truncheon a club

tryst a secret meeting

tumid swollen; bulging

tumult great noise and confusion

turbid muddy; unclear

turbulence wild disorder; violent motion

turgid swollen

turmoil confusion

turpitude baseness; shameful behavior

tussle a struggle; a fight

tutelage instruction

twain two

tycoon a wealthy businessman

tyro a beginner

UBIQUITOUS–UXORIOUS

ubiquitous   present everywhere

ulcerous   infected

ulterior   lying beyond; hidden

ultimatum   a final demand or proposal

umbrage   a feeling of resentment

unanimity   agreement; oneness

unassailable   unable to be attacked

uncanny   weird; strange

unconscionable   unreasonable; excessive

uncouth   crude; clumsy

unctuous   oily; excessively polite

undue   inappropriate; unreasonable

undulate   to move or sway in wavelike motion

unequivocal   clear; definite

unerring   accurate; not going astray or missing the mark

unfledged   not feathered; immature

unilateral   one-sided

unimpeachable   above suspicion; unquestionable

uninhibited   free; not restricted

unique   being the only one of its kind

unison   harmony; agreement

universal   broad; general; effective everywhere or in all cases

unkempt   untidy; sloppy

unmindful   unaware

unmitigated   absolute; not lessened

unobtrusive   inconspicuous; not noticeable

unruly   not manageable; disorderly

unsavory   unpleasant to taste or smell

unscathed   unharmed; uninjured

unseemly   not in good taste

untenable   unable to be defended or upheld

unwieldy   hard to manage because of size or weight

unwitting   unintentional; unaware

upbraid   to scold; to find fault with

uproarious   loud; outrageously funny

urbane   refined; suave; citified

urchin   a mischievous child

ursine   like a bear

usurp   to seize illegally

usury   excessive amount of money charged as interest

utilitarian   useful; practical

utopian   perfect; ideal

uxorious   overly fond of one's wife

VACILLATE–VULPINE

vacillate   to sway back and forth; to hesitate in making a decision

vagabond   a wanderer

vagary   an odd notion; an unpredictable action

vagrant   a homeless person; a wanderer

vain   conceited; excessively proud about one's appearance

vainglorious   boastfully proud

valedictory   saying farewell

valiant   courageous; brave

valid   true; logical; sound

validate   to approve; to confirm

valor   courage; bravery

vanguard   the front part

vanity   excessive pride; conceit

vanquish   to defeat

vapid   uninteresting; tasteless; tedious

variegated   having different colors; diversified

vaunt to brag or boast

veer to change direction

vegetate to lead a dull, inactive life

vehement forceful; furious

velocity speed

venal corrupt; able to be bribed

vendetta bitter quarrel or feud

veneer an outward show that misrepresents

venerable worthy of respect

venerate to regard with respect

venial excusable; minor

venomous poisonous; spiteful; malicious

vent to give release to; to be relieved of a feeling

venturesome daring; adventurous; risky

veracious truthful; honest

verbatim word for word

verbiage overabundance of words

verbose wordy

verdant green; flourishing

verisimilitude the appearance of truth

veritable true; actual; genuine

verity truth

vernacular native language; informal speech

vernal pertaining to spring

versatile good at many things; serving many purposes

vertex top; highest point

vertiginous whirling; dizzy; unstable

verve energy; enthusiasm

vestige a trace; visible evidence of something that is no longer present

veteran an experienced person

vex to irritate; to annoy

viable capable of living; workable; practicable

viaduct a bridge

viands various foods

vicarious taking the place of another person or thing; substituted

viceroy a representative; a deputy appointed by a sovereign to rule a province

vicissitudes unpredictable changes; ups and downs

victimize to make a victim of; to swindle or cheat

victuals food

vie to compete

vigilant watchful

vignette a short literary sketch; a decorative design

vilify to speak evil of; to defame

vindicate to clear of guilt or blame

vindictive spiteful; seeking revenge

vintage representative of the best (*especially of wines*)

viper (*two meanings*) a poisonous snake; a malignant or spiteful person

virago a loud, bad-tempered woman; a shrew

virile masculine; manly

virtuoso an expert; a skilled person

virulent deadly; poisonous; harmful

visage the face; appearance

visceral pertaining to instinctive rather than intellectual motivation

viscous sticky

vista a distant view

vitiate to weaken; to impair

vitreous of or like glass

vitriolic biting; sharp; bitter

vituperate to scold; to criticize

vivify to give life to; to enliven

vixen female fox; ill-tempered woman

vociferous loud; shouting

vogue fashion; style

volant capable of flying

volatile unstable; explosive

volition free will

voluble talkative; fluent

voluminous large; copious

voluptuous sensual; shapely

voracious extremely hungry; greedy

votary loyal follower

vouchsafe to grant; to allow or permit

vulgar showing poor taste or manners

vulnerable defenseless; open to attack

vulpine like a fox; clever

WAIF–ZEST

waif   a homeless person

waive   to give up (a right)

wallow   to indulge oneself; to roll around in

wan   pale; weak; tired

wane   to gradually decrease in size or intensity

wangle   to manipulate; to obtain by scheming or by underhand methods

wanton   reckless; immoral

warble   to sing melodiously

warp   to bend out of shape; to pervert

wary   cautious; watchful

wastrel   a spendthrift; one who wastes

waver   to sway; to be uncertain

wax   to grow in size or intensity

weighty   of utmost importance

wend   to direct one's way

wheedle   to coax or to persuade

whet   to stimulate; to make sharp

whimsical   unpredictable; changeable

wield   to handle (*a tool*); to exercise control (*over others*)

willful   contrary; stubborn

wily   tricky; sly

wince   to shrink, as in pain, fear, etc.; to flinch

windfall   unexpected good fortune

winsome   pleasing; charming

withal   in spite of all; nevertheless

wizened   withered; shriveled

woe   sorrow; grief

wolfish   ferocious

wont   (*to*) accustomed (*adjective*)

workaday   everyday; ordinary

wraith   a ghost; an apparition

wrangle   to quarrel

wrath   anger; rage

wrench   to twist; to pull

wrest   to take away by force

wroth   angry

wrought   produced or shaped

wry   produced by distorting the face (*a wry grin*); ironic (*wry humor*)

xenophobia   fear of foreigners or strangers

xyloid   pertaining to wood

yen   an intense desire; a longing

yoke   to join together; to link

zany   comical; clownishly crazy

zeal   great enthusiasm

zealot   a fanatic

zenith   the highest point

zephyr   a gentle, mild breeze

zest   hearty enjoyment

100 Tests to Strengthen Your Vocabulary

This vocabulary section consists of 100 Vocabulary Tests. Each test consists of 10 multiple-choice questions, including GRE-type words. Practically all the words whose meanings you are tested on in these 100 tests are among the 3,400 words in the GRE Word List beginning on page 377.

These 100 Vocabulary Tests provide you with an opportunity to make sure that you really know the meanings of the hundreds of words you are being tested on. Several of these words are likely to appear on your actual GRE.

We suggest that you use the following procedure while you are taking these 100 tests:

1. Take Vocabulary Test 1.

2. Turn to the Answer Keys beginning on page 469.

3. For each word that you got wrong, jot down the word on a "Special List" of your own.

4. Make up a sentence using each word that you got wrong on Vocabulary Test 1.

5. Repeat the previous procedure for Vocabulary Tests 2, 3, 4—right on through Vocabulary Test 100.

6. When you have finished taking the 100 Vocabulary Tests, go back to your "Special List." See whether you really know the meanings of these words by having someone else test you on them. For those words you still have trouble with, look up their meanings in a dictionary. Compose three sentences including each of these troublemakers.

Gentle reminder: Knowing the meanings of many of the words in these 100 tests is likely to raise your score in Sentence Completions and Reading Comprehension.

Directions for the 100 Vocabulary Tests

Each vocabulary question consists of a word in capital letters, followed by five lettered words or phrases. Choose the word or phrase that is most nearly the *same* in meaning as the word in capital letters. Since some of the questions require you to distinguish fine shades of meaning, consider all choices before deciding which is best.

Vocabulary Test 1

1. FILCH
   (A) hide
   (B) swindle
   (C) drop
   (D) steal
   (E) covet

2. URBANE
   (A) crowded
   (B) polished
   (C) rural
   (D) friendly
   (E) prominent

3. DECANT
   (A) bisect
   (B) speak wildly
   (C) bequeath
   (D) pour off
   (E) abuse verbally

4. ANTITHESIS
   (A) contrast
   (B) conclusion
   (C) resemblance
   (D) examination
   (E) dislike

5. HERETICAL
   (A) heathenish
   (B) impractical
   (C) quaint
   (D) rash
   (E) unorthodox

6. COALESCE
   (A) associate
   (B) combine
   (C) contact
   (D) conspire
   (E) cover

7. CHARLATAN
   (A) clown
   (B) philanthropist
   (C) jester
   (D) dressmaker
   (E) quack

8. GAUCHE
   (A) clumsy
   (B) stupid
   (C) feebleminded
   (D) impudent
   (E) foreign

9. REDUNDANT
   (A) necessary
   (B) plentiful
   (C) sufficient
   (D) diminishing
   (E) superfluous

10. ATROPHY
    (A) lose leaves
    (B) soften
    (C) waste away
    (D) grow
    (E) spread

Vocabulary Test 2

1. RESILIENCE
   (A) submission
   (B) elasticity
   (C) vigor
   (D) determination
   (E) recovery

2. ANALOGY
   (A) similarity
   (B) transposition
   (C) variety
   (D) distinction
   (E) appropriateness

3. FACETIOUS
   (A) obscene
   (B) shrewd
   (C) impolite
   (D) complimentary
   (E) witty

4. DIATRIBE
   (A) debate
   (B) monologue
   (C) oration
   (D) tirade
   (E) conversation

5. MALEDICTION
   (A) curse
   (B) mispronunciation
   (C) grammatical error
   (D) tactless remark
   (E) epitaph

6. AGGREGATE
   (A) result
   (B) difference
   (C) quotient
   (D) product
   (E) sum

7. APLOMB
   (A) caution
   (B) timidity
   (C) self-assurance
   (D) shortsightedness
   (E) self-restraint

8. THERAPEUTIC
   (A) curative
   (B) restful
   (C) warm
   (D) stimulating
   (E) professional

9. TRANSMUTE
   (A) remove
   (B) change
   (C) duplicate
   (D) carry
   (E) explain

10. ATTRITION
    (A) annihilation
    (B) encirclement
    (C) counterattack
    (D) appeasement
    (E) wearing down

Vocabulary Test 3

1. TRUNCATE
   (A) divide equally
   (B) end swiftly
   (C) cut off
   (D) act cruelly
   (E) cancel

2. OSCILLATE
   (A) confuse
   (B) kiss
   (C) turn
   (D) vibrate
   (E) whirl

3. INOCULATE
   (A) make harmless
   (B) infect
   (C) cure
   (D) overcome
   (E) darken

4. PERUSAL
   (A) approval
   (B) estimate
   (C) reading
   (D) translation
   (E) computation

5. QUERULOUS
(A) peculiar
(B) fretful
(C) inquisitive
(D) shivering
(E) annoying

6. AUTONOMY
(A) tyranny
(B) independence
(C) plebiscite
(D) minority
(E) dictatorship

7. MACHINATIONS
(A) inventions
(B) ideas
(C) mysteries
(D) plots
(E) alliances

8. SCHISM
(A) government
(B) religion
(C) division
(D) combination
(E) coalition

9. PUSILLANIMOUS
(A) cowardly
(B) extraordinary
(C) ailing
(D) evil-intentioned
(E) excitable

10. TERMINOLOGY
(A) technicality
(B) finality
(C) formality
(D) explanation
(E) nomenclature

Vocabulary Test 4

1. STIPEND
(A) increment
(B) bonus
(C) commission
(D) gift
(E) salary

2. LITIGATION
(A) publication
(B) argument
(C) endeavor
(D) lawsuit
(E) ceremony

3. FIASCO
(A) disappointment
(B) turning point
(C) loss
(D) celebration
(E) complete failure

4. VAGARY
(A) caprice
(B) confusion
(C) extravagance
(D) loss of memory
(E) shiftlessness

5. GRAPHIC
(A) serious
(B) concise
(C) short
(D) detailed
(E) vivid

6. CONNOTATION
(A) implication
(B) footnote
(C) derivation
(D) comment
(E) definition

7. TORTUOUS
(A) crooked
(B) difficult
(C) painful
(D) impassable
(E) slow

8. FULMINATING
(A) throbbing
(B) pointed
(C) wavelike
(D) thundering
(E) bubbling

9. CIRCUMVENT
(A) freshen
(B) change
(C) control
(D) harass
(E) frustrate

10. CARTEL
(A) rationing plan
(B) world government
(C) industrial pool
(D) skilled craft
(E) instrument of credit

Vocabulary Test 5

1. PROLIFIC
(A) meager
(B) obedient
(C) fertile
(D) hardy
(E) scanty

2. ASSUAGE
(A) create
(B) ease
(C) enlarge
(D) prohibit
(E) rub out

3. DECORUM
(A) wit
(B) charm
(C) adornment
(D) seemliness
(E) charity

4. PHLEGMATIC
(A) tolerant
(B) careless
(C) sensitive
(D) stolid
(E) sick

5. INTREPID
(A) quick-witted
(B) brutal
(C) fearless
(D) torrid
(E) hearty

6. ACTUATE
(A) frighten
(B) direct
(C) isolate
(D) dismay
(E) impel

7. MOUNTEBANK
(A) trickster
(B) courier
(C) scholar
(D) cashier
(E) pawnbroker

8. LACONIC
(A) terse
(B) informal
(C) convincing
(D) interesting
(E) tedious

9. BOORISH
(A) sporting
(B) tiresome
(C) argumentative
(D) monotonous
(E) rude

10. ERUDITE
(A) modest
(B) egotistical
(C) learned
(D) needless
(E) experienced

Vocabulary Test 6

1. ACRIMONIOUS
(A) repulsive
(B) enchanting
(C) stinging
(D) snobbish
(E) disgusting

2. EMBRYONIC
(A) hereditary
(B) arrested
(C) developed
(D) functioning
(E) rudimentary

3. INEXORABLE
(A) unfavorable
(B) permanent
(C) crude
(D) relentless
(E) incomplete

4. PROTRACTED
(A) boring
(B) condensed
(C) prolonged
(D) comprehensive
(E) measured

5. OBSEQUIOUS
(A) courteous
(B) fawning
(C) respectful
(D) overbearing
(E) inexperienced

6. LOQUACIOUS
(A) queer
(B) logical
(C) gracious
(D) rural
(E) voluble

7. PUGNACIOUS
(A) bold
(B) combative
(C) brawny
(D) pug-nosed
(E) valiant

8. ASTRINGENT
(A) bossy
(B) musty
(C) flexible
(D) corrosive
(E) contracting

9. ESCARPMENT
(A) threat
(B) limbo
(C) cliff
(D) behemoth
(E) blight

10. AMENITIES
(A) prayers
(B) ceremonies
(C) pageantries
(D) pleasantries
(E) social functions

Vocabulary Test 7

1. DEPLORE
(A) condone
(B) forget
(C) forgive
(D) deny
(E) regret

2. BANAL
(A) commonplace
(B) flippant
(C) pathetic
(D) new
(E) unexpected

3. ABACUS
(A) casserole
(B) blackboard
(C) slide rule
(D) adding device
(E) long spear

4. SEISMISM
(A) inundation
(B) tide
(C) volcano
(D) earthquake
(E) tornado

5. AMELIORATE
(A) favor
(B) improve
(C) interfere
(D) learn
(E) straddle

6. CHARY
(A) burned
(B) careful
(C) comfortable
(D) fascinating
(E) gay

7. CORPULENT
(A) dead
(B) fat
(C) full
(D) organized
(E) similar

8. ENIGMA
(A) ambition
(B) foreigner
(C) instrument
(D) officer
(E) riddle

9. INEPT
(A) awkward
(B) intelligent
(C) ticklish
(D) tawdry
(E) uninteresting

10. INVETERATE
(A) evil
(B) habitual
(C) inconsiderate
(D) reformed
(E) unintentional

Vocabulary Test 8

1. OBEISANCE
(A) salary
(B) justification
(C) conduct
(D) deference
(E) forethought

2. PEDANTIC
(A) stilted
(B) odd
(C) footworn
(D) selfish
(E) sincere

3. PETULANT
(A) lazy
(B) loving
(C) patient
(D) peevish
(E) wary

4. PROCLIVITY
(A) backwardness
(B) edict
(C) rainfall
(D) slope
(E) tendency

5. TRENCHANT
(A) keen
(B) good
(C) edible
(D) light
(E) subterranean

6. VAPID
(A) carefree
(B) crazy
(C) insipid
(D) spotty
(E) speedy

7. PROGNOSTICATE
(A) forecast
(B) ravish
(C) salute
(D) scoff
(E) succeed

8. PROPRIETY
(A) advancement
(B) atonement
(C) fitness
(D) sobriety
(E) use

9. PULCHRITUDE
(A) beauty
(B) character
(C) generosity
(D) intelligence
(E) wickedness

10. SCRUPULOUS
(A) drunken
(B) ill
(C) masterful
(D) exact
(E) stony

Vocabulary Test 9

1. INVARIABLE
(A) diverse
(B) eternal
(C) fleeting
(D) inescapable
(E) uniform

2. VORACIOUS
(A) excitable
(B) honest
(C) greedy
(D) inclusive
(E) circular

3. CONCENTRATE
(A) agitate
(B) protest
(C) debate
(D) harden
(E) consolidate

4. PLAGIARIZE
(A) annoy
(B) borrow
(C) steal ideas
(D) imitate poorly
(E) impede

5. CORTEGE
(A) advisers
(B) official papers
(C) slaves
(D) retinue
(E) personal effects

6. ANTIPATHY
(A) sympathy
(B) detachment
(C) aversion
(D) amazement
(E) opposition

7. DEMUR
(A) object
(B) agree
(C) murmur
(D) discard
(E) consider

8. PARAGON
(A) dummy
(B) lover
(C) image
(D) model
(E) favorite

9. FINITE
(A) impure
(B) firm
(C) minute
(D) limited
(E) unbounded

10. ANARCHY
(A) laissez-faire
(B) motor-mindedness
(C) pacifism
(D) lawless confusion
(E) self-sufficiency

Vocabulary Test 10

1. DISCRIMINATION
(A) acquittal
(B) insight
(C) caution
(D) indiscretion
(E) distortion

2. INVECTIVE
(A) richness
(B) goal
(C) solemn oath
(D) praise
(E) verbal abuse

3. ADROIT
(A) hostile
(B) serene
(C) pompous
(D) skillful
(E) allergic

4. DISTRESS
(A) injury
(B) contortion
(C) suffering
(D) convulsion
(E) aggravation

5. DILETTANTE
(A) epicure
(B) dabbler
(C) procrastinator
(D) literary genius
(E) playboy

6. PROVISIONAL
(A) military
(B) tentative
(C) absentee
(D) democratic
(E) appointed

7. CONDIMENT
(A) ledger
(B) ore
(C) telegraph device
(D) musical instrument
(E) spice

8. RECALCITRANT
(A) insincere
(B) obstinate
(C) crafty
(D) conservative
(E) reconcilable

9. BON MOT
(A) witticism
(B) pun
(C) praise
(D) last word
(E) exact meaning

10. ACCOUTREMENTS
(A) sealed orders
(B) equipment
(C) cartons
(D) correspondence
(E) financial records

Vocabulary Test 11

1. HYPOTHESIS
(A) assumption
(B) proof
(C) estimate
(D) random guess
(E) established truth

2. ALACRITY
(A) slowness
(B) indecision
(C) caution
(D) promptness
(E) fearlessness

3. JETTISON
(A) throw overboard
(B) dismantle
(C) scuttle
(D) unload cargo
(E) camouflage

4. VACILLATE
(A) glitter
(B) swerve
(C) surrender
(D) soften
(E) waver

5. ASTUTE
(A) shrewd
(B) futile
(C) potent
(D) provocative
(E) ruthless

6. PROVISO
(A) final treaty
(B) condition
(C) demand
(D) official document
(E) proclamation

7. MACABRE
(A) gruesome
(B) meager
(C) sordid
(D) fantastic
(E) cringing

8. AUGMENT
(A) curtail
(B) change
(C) restore
(D) conceal
(E) increase

9. INTEGRAL
(A) useful
(B) powerful
(C) essential
(D) mathematical
(E) indestructible

10. IMPUNITY
(A) shamelessness
(B) power of action
(C) self-reliance
(D) haughtiness
(E) exemption from punishment

Vocabulary Test 12

1. LATENT
(A) inherent
(B) lazy
(C) dormant
(D) crushed
(E) anticipated

2. OBDURATE
(A) patient
(B) stupid
(C) rude
(D) stubborn
(E) tolerant

3. BELLICOSE
(A) boastful
(B) warlike
(C) sluggish
(D) fantastic
(E) oriental

4. ARROYO
(A) cliff
(B) plain
(C) ranch
(D) gully
(E) cactus

5. AUGUR
(A) enrage
(B) foretell
(C) suggest
(D) evaluate
(E) minimize

6. CONTRITE
(A) infectious
(B) worried
(C) penitent
(D) sympathetic
(E) tolerant

7. PETULANT
(A) silly
(B) gay
(C) sarcastic
(D) officious
(E) quarrelsome

8. PAEAN
(A) prize
(B) song of praise
(C) decoration
(D) certificate
(E) story of heroism

9. EXOTIC
(A) romantic
(B) exciting
(C) wealthy
(D) strange
(E) tropical

10. ARCHIPELAGO
(A) slender isthmus
(B) long, narrow land mass
(C) string of lakes
(D) high, flat plain
(E) group of small islands

Vocabulary Test 13

1. PREVARICATE
(A) hesitate
(B) lie
(C) protest
(D) ramble
(E) remain silent

2. INCREDULOUS
(A) argumentative
(B) imaginative
(C) indifferent
(D) irreligious
(E) skeptical

3. PLACATE
(A) amuse
(B) appease
(C) embroil
(D) pity
(E) reject

4. COGNIZANT
(A) afraid
(B) aware
(C) capable
(D) ignorant
(E) optimistic

5. DISSONANCE
(A) disapproval
(B) disaster
(C) discord
(D) disparity
(E) dissimilarity

6. IMMINENT
(A) declining
(B) distinguished
(C) impending
(D) terrifying
(E) unlikely

7. TORSION
(A) bending
(B) compressing
(C) sliding
(D) stretching
(E) twisting

8. ACCRUED
(A) added
(B) incidental
(C) miscellaneous
(D) special
(E) unearned

9. EFFRONTERY
(A) bad taste
(B) conceit
(C) dishonesty
(D) impudence
(E) snobbishness

10. ACQUIESCENCE
(A) advice
(B) advocacy
(C) compliance
(D) friendliness
(E) opposition

Vocabulary Test 14

1. RETICENT
(A) fidgety
(B) repetitious
(C) reserved
(D) restful
(E) truthful

2. STIPULATE
(A) bargain
(B) instigate
(C) prefer
(D) request
(E) specify

3. PSEUDO
(A) deep
(B) obvious
(C) pretended
(D) provoking
(E) spiritual

4. FLOTSAM
(A) dark sand
(B) fleet
(C) life preserver
(D) shoreline
(E) wreckage

5. AWRY
(A) askew
(B) deplorable
(C) odd
(D) simple
(E) striking

6. NEFARIOUS
(A) clever
(B) necessary
(C) negligent
(D) short-sighted
(E) wicked

7. GLIB
(A) cheerful
(B) delightful
(C) dull
(D) fluent
(E) gloomy

8. PAUCITY
(A) abundance
(B) ease
(C) hardship
(D) lack
(E) stoppage

9. LUCRATIVE
(A) debasing
(B) fortunate
(C) influential
(D) monetary
(E) profitable

10. INDUBITABLE
(A) doubtful
(B) fraudulent
(C) honorable
(D) safe
(E) undeniable

Vocabulary Test 15

1. CONNIVANCE
(A) approval
(B) collusion
(C) conflict
(D) permission
(E) theft

2. SAVANT
(A) diplomat
(B) inventor
(C) learned person
(D) thrifty person
(E) wiseacre

3. INCIPIENT
(A) beginning
(B) dangerous
(C) hasty
(D) secret
(E) widespread

4. VIRILE
(A) honest
(B) loyal
(C) manly
(D) pugnacious
(E) virtuous

5. ASSIDUOUS
(A) courteous
(B) diligent
(C) discouraged
(D) frank
(E) slow

6. CATACLYSM
(A) blunder
(B) superstition
(C) treachery
(D) triumph
(E) upheaval

7. AUSPICIOUS
(A) condemnatory
(B) conspicuous
(C) favorable
(D) questionable
(E) spicy

8. SATIRE
(A) conversation
(B) criticism
(C) gossip
(D) irony
(E) jesting

9. VERNACULAR
(A) common speech
(B) correct usage
(C) long words
(D) oratory
(E) poetic style

10. EMOLUMENT
(A) capital
(B) compensation
(C) liabilities
(D) loss
(E) output

Vocabulary Test 16

1. TURGID
(A) dusty
(B) muddy
(C) rolling
(D) swollen
(E) tense

2. EXPUNGE
(A) clarify
(B) copy
(C) delete
(D) investigate
(E) underline

3. ETHNOLOGY
(A) causation
(B) morals
(C) social psychology
(D) study of races
(E) word analysis

4. DEDUCE
(A) diminish
(B) infer
(C) outline
(D) persuade
(E) subtract

5. PANORAMIC
(A) brilliant
(B) comprehensive
(C) pretty
(D) fluorescent
(E) unique

6. IGNOMINY
(A) disgrace
(B) isolation
(C) misfortune
(D) sorrow
(E) stupidity

7. RELEVANT
(A) ingenious
(B) inspiring
(C) obvious
(D) pertinent
(E) tentative

8. GAMUT
(A) game
(B) range
(C) risk
(D) organization
(E) plan

9. APPOSITE
(A) appropriate
(B) contrary
(C) different
(D) spontaneous
(E) tricky

10. AMBULATORY
(A) able to walk
(B) confined to bed
(C) injured
(D) quarantined
(E) suffering from disease

Vocabulary Test 17

1. DISPARAGE
(A) belittle
(B) upgrade
(C) erase
(D) reform
(E) scatter

2. LIMPID
(A) calm
(B) clear
(C) crippled
(D) delightful
(E) opaque

3. DERISIVE
(A) dividing
(B) furnishing
(C) reflecting
(D) expressing ridicule
(E) suggesting

4. DEBILITATE
(A) encourage
(B) insinuate
(C) prepare
(D) turn away
(E) weaken

5. OPULENT
(A) fearful
(B) free
(C) oversized
(D) trustful
(E) wealthy

6. BLANDISHMENT
(A) dislike
(B) flattery
(C) ostentation
(D) praise
(E) rejection

7. CRYPTIC
(A) appealing
(B) arched
(C) deathly
(D) hidden
(E) intricate

8. RAUCOUS
(A) harsh
(B) loud
(C) querulous
(D) rational
(E) violent

9. AVIDITY
(A) friendliness
(B) greediness
(C) resentment
(D) speed
(E) thirst

10. EPITOME
(A) conclusion
(B) effort
(C) letter
(D) summary
(E) summit

Vocabulary Test 18

1. HIATUS
(A) branch
(B) disease
(C) gaiety
(D) insect
(E) break

2. PLENARY
(A) easy
(B) empty
(C) full
(D) rewarding
(E) untrustworthy

3. CAPRICIOUS
(A) active
(B) fickle
(C) opposed
(D) sheeplike
(E) slippery

4. SPECIOUS
(A) frank
(B) particular
(C) deceptive
(D) suspicious
(E) vigorous

5. EXTIRPATE
(A) besmirch
(B) clean
(C) eradicate
(D) favor
(E) subdivide

6. EQUIVOCAL
(A) doubtful
(B) medium
(C) monotonous
(D) musical
(E) well-balanced

7. RECOMPENSE
(A) approval
(B) blessing
(C) gift
(D) prayer
(E) reward

8. BEATIFIC
(A) giving bliss
(B) eager
(C) hesitant
(D) lovely
(E) sad

9. SANGUINE
(A) limp
(B) mechanical
(C) muddy
(D) red
(E) stealthy

10. SURCEASE
(A) end
(B) hope
(C) resignation
(D) sleep
(E) sweetness

Vocabulary Test 19

1. SENTIENT
(A) very emotional
(B) capable of feeling
(C) hostile
(D) sympathetic
(E) wise

2. OBVIATE
(A) grasp
(B) reform
(C) simplify
(D) smooth
(E) make unnecessary

3. PERUSE
(A) endure
(B) perpetuate
(C) read
(D) undertake
(E) urge

4. RANCOR
(A) dignity
(B) fierceness
(C) odor
(D) spite
(E) suspicion

5. TRUNCHEON
(A) baton
(B) canopy
(C) dish
(D) gun
(E) rejected food

6. SEBACEOUS
(A) fatty
(B) fluid
(C) porous
(D) transparent
(E) watery

7. DILATORY
(A) hairy
(B) happy-go-lucky
(C) ruined
(D) tardy
(E) well-to-do

8. EBULLITION
(A) bathing
(B) boiling
(C) refilling
(D) retiring
(E) returning

9. RELEGATE
(A) banish
(B) deprive
(C) designate
(D) report
(E) request

10. RECONDITE
(A) brittle
(B) concealed
(C) explored
(D) exposed
(E) uninformed

Vocabulary Test 20

1. REDOLENT
(A) odorous
(B) quick
(C) refined
(D) repulsive
(E) supple

2. DISSIMULATE
(A) confound
(B) pretend
(C) question
(D) separate
(E) strain

3. SUBLIME
   (A) below par
   (B) highly praised
   (C) extreme
   (D) noble
   (E) settled

4. VIXEN
   (A) fever
   (B) quarrelsome woman
   (C) sea bird
   (D) sedative
   (E) squirrel

5. SEDULOUS
   (A) deceptive
   (B) diligent
   (C) grassy
   (D) hateful
   (E) sweet

6. VITIATE
   (A) contaminate
   (B) flavor
   (C) freshen
   (D) illuminate
   (E) refer

7. CURVET
   (A) come around
   (B) follow
   (C) leap
   (D) restrain
   (E) warp

8. ADVENTITIOUS
   (A) accidental
   (B) courageous
   (C) favorable
   (D) risk-taking
   (E) expected

9. ANIMUS
   (A) animosity
   (B) breath
   (C) faith
   (D) light
   (E) poison

10. DESCRIED
    (A) hailed
    (B) rebuffed
    (C) recalled
    (D) regretted
    (E) sighted

Vocabulary Test 21

1. ADULATION
   (A) approach
   (B) echo
   (C) flattery
   (D) gift
   (E) imitation

2. SUBSEQUENTLY
   (A) continually
   (B) factually
   (C) farther
   (D) incidentally
   (E) later

3. EXPURGATE
   (A) amplify
   (B) emphasize
   (C) offend
   (D) purify
   (E) renew

4. LIAISON
   (A) derivative
   (B) liability
   (C) link
   (D) malice
   (E) officer

5. SEDENTARY
   (A) careful
   (B) inactive
   (C) notched
   (D) pleasant
   (E) uneventful

6. LASSITUDE
   (A) childishness
   (B) energy
   (C) ignorance
   (D) languor
   (E) seriousness

7. ALTRUISTICALLY
   (A) egotistically
   (B) harmfully
   (C) harshly
   (D) highly
   (E) unselfishly

8. PERFIDIOUS
   (A) ambiguous
   (B) flawless
   (C) perforated
   (D) treacherous
   (E) trusting

9. CONSUMMATE
   (A) achieve
   (B) devour
   (C) effuse
   (D) ignite
   (E) take

10. MUNIFICENTLY
    (A) acutely
    (B) awkwardly
    (C) cruelly
    (D) generously
    (E) militarily

Vocabulary Test 22

1. LUGUBRIOUS
   (A) calm
   (B) doleful
   (C) tepid
   (D) wan
   (E) warm

2. DISCONSOLATE
   (A) desolate
   (B) emotional
   (C) incorrigible
   (D) gloomy
   (E) sad

3. COTERIE
   (A) clique
   (B) cure-all
   (C) expert judge
   (D) forerunner
   (E) society girl

4. CONDUIT
   (A) doorway
   (B) electric generator
   (C) power
   (D) screen
   (E) tube

5. SHIBBOLETH
   (A) a friend in need
   (B) lonely home
   (C) personal complaint
   (D) reason for action
   (E) watchword

6. EVANESCENT
   (A) colorful
   (B) consecrated
   (C) converted
   (D) empty
   (E) vanishing

7. PARSIMONIOUS
(A) cautious
(B) ecclesiastical
(C) luxurious
(D) stingy
(E) unique

8. MACHIAVELLIAN
(A) cunning
(B) humble
(C) kingly
(D) machinelike
(E) saintly

9. COMPENDIUM
(A) amplification
(B) appendix
(C) expansion
(D) paraphrase
(E) summary

10. MEGALOMANIA
(A) desire for beauty
(B) mania for sympathy
(C) miserliness
(D) passion for grandeur
(E) pity for the poor

Vocabulary Test 23

1. TORPOR
(A) cyclone
(B) frenzy
(C) sluggishness
(D) strain
(E) twisting

2. ESOTERIC
(A) clear
(B) external
(C) popular
(D) secret
(E) uncertain

3. SUPERCILIOUSLY
(A) critically
(B) haughtily
(C) hypersensitively
(D) naïvely
(E) softly

4. ABSTEMIOUS
(A) blatant
(B) exhilarating
(C) greedy
(D) temperate
(E) wasteful

5. KEN
(A) acceptance
(B) belief
(C) dune
(D) knowledge
(E) woody glen

6. GERMANE
(A) diseased
(B) foreign
(C) infected
(D) pertinent
(E) polished

7. VITUPERATION
(A) abuse
(B) appendectomy
(C) complication
(D) rejuvenation
(E) repeal

8. CHIMERICAL
(A) clever
(B) imaginary
(C) experimental
(D) foreign
(E) provisional

9. DULCIMER
(A) dolly
(B) doublet
(C) duenna
(D) gadget
(E) musical instrument

10. SARTORIAL
(A) disheveled
(B) frozen
(C) satirical
(D) tailored
(E) warm

Vocabulary Test 24

1. VERTIGO
(A) curiosity
(B) dizziness
(C) enlivenment
(D) greenness
(E) invigoration

2. DEBACLE
(A) ceremony
(B) collapse
(C) dance
(D) deficit
(E) dispute

3. CONDIGN
(A) deserved
(B) hidden
(C) perplexed
(D) pretended
(E) unworthy

4. EPHEMERALLY
(A) enduringly
(B) lightly
(C) openly
(D) suspiciously
(E) transiently

5. HISTRIONIC
(A) authentic
(B) hysterical
(C) reportorial
(D) sibilant
(E) theatrical

6. URBANITY
(A) aggressiveness
(B) mercenary
(C) municipality
(D) rustic
(E) suavity

7. TRUCULENT
(A) rambling
(B) relenting
(C) savage
(D) tranquil
(E) weary

8. INVEIGH
(A) allure
(B) entice
(C) guide cautiously
(D) originate
(E) speak bitterly

9. DESULTORY
(A) delaying
(B) disconnected
(C) flagrant
(D) insulting
(E) irritating

10. INGENUOUS
(A) clever
(B) naïve
(C) ignorant
(D) native
(E) unkind

Vocabulary Test 25

1. CUMULATIVE
   (A) additive
   (B) clumsy
   (C) cumbersome
   (D) incorrect
   (E) secretive

2. EPIGRAM
   (A) chemical term
   (B) exclamation
   (C) outer skin
   (D) pithy saying
   (E) tombstone

3. GESTICULATE
   (A) dance
   (B) digest easily
   (C) ridicule
   (D) travel
   (E) use gestures

4. BEGUILE
   (A) benefit
   (B) bind
   (C) deceive
   (D) envy
   (E) petition

5. AVID
   (A) eager
   (B) glowing
   (C) indifferent
   (D) lax
   (E) potent

6. LABYRINTH
   (A) laboratory
   (B) maze
   (C) path
   (D) portal
   (E) room

7. REGURGITATE
   (A) make new investments
   (B) obliterate
   (C) restore to solvency
   (D) slacken
   (E) surge back

8. PODIUM
   (A) chemical element
   (B) dais
   (C) foot specialist
   (D) magistrate
   (E) Roman infantryman

9. BEREFT
   (A) annoyed
   (B) awarded
   (C) deprived
   (D) enraged
   (E) insane

10. ELUCIDATE
    (A) condense
    (B) escape
    (C) evade
    (D) explain
    (E) shine through

Vocabulary Test 26

1. EMOLLIENT
   (A) comical
   (B) despicable
   (C) enthusiastic
   (D) raucous
   (E) soothing

2. NOSTALGIC
   (A) expressive
   (B) forgetful
   (C) homesick
   (D) inconstant
   (E) seasick

3. EXPIATE
   (A) atone for
   (B) die
   (C) hasten
   (D) imitate
   (E) make holy

4. PARADOX
   (A) accepted opinion
   (B) axiom
   (C) contradiction
   (D) enigma
   (E) pattern

5. ARCHETYPE
   (A) bowman
   (B) original model
   (C) public records
   (D) roguishness
   (E) star

6. MUNDANE
   (A) deformed
   (B) free
   (C) rough-shelled
   (D) tearful
   (E) worldly

7. PALLIATIVE
   (A) boring
   (B) callous
   (C) permanent
   (D) softening
   (E) unyielding

8. FOMENT
   (A) curb
   (B) explode
   (C) exclude
   (D) turn into wine
   (E) instigate

9. PREDACIOUS
   (A) beautiful
   (B) incongruous
   (C) peaceful
   (D) preying
   (E) valuable

10. RESILIENT
    (A) thrifty
    (B) elastic
    (C) timid
    (D) fragile
    (E) unsociable

Vocabulary Test 27

1. BLATANT
   (A) clamorous
   (B) conceited
   (C) prudish
   (D) reticent
   (E) unsuited

2. ADVERSITY
   (A) advertising
   (B) counsel
   (C) criticism
   (D) misfortune
   (E) proficiency

3. CADAVEROUS
   (A) cheerful
   (B) contemptible
   (C) ghastly
   (D) hungry
   (E) ill-bred

4. WRAITH
   (A) anger
   (B) apparition
   (C) figurine
   (D) mannequin
   (E) model

5. PERSPICACITY
   (A) clearness
   (B) dullness
   (C) keenness
   (D) vastness
   (E) wideness

6. EXTRANEOUS
   (A) derived
   (B) foreign
   (C) unsuitable
   (D) visible
   (E) wasteful

7. PAROXYSM
   (A) catastrophe
   (B) sudden outburst
   (C) illusion
   (D) lack of harmony
   (E) loss of all bodily movement

8. SAPIENT
   (A) discerning
   (B) foolish
   (C) mocking
   (D) soapy
   (E) youthful

9. FLACCID
   (A) flabby
   (B) golden
   (C) hard
   (D) strong
   (E) wiry

10. IMPECUNIOUS
   (A) frugal
   (B) guiltless
   (C) miserly
   (D) monied
   (E) poor

Vocabulary Test 28

1. ABDUCT
   (A) ruin
   (B) aid
   (C) fight
   (D) abolish
   (E) kidnap

2. DEMERIT
   (A) outcome
   (B) fault
   (C) prize
   (D) notice
   (E) belief

3. MUTINOUS
   (A) silent
   (B) oceangoing
   (C) rebellious
   (D) miserable
   (E) deaf

4. NEGLIGENT
   (A) lax
   (B) desperate
   (C) cowardly
   (D) ambitious
   (E) informal

5. CONTEST
   (A) disturb
   (B) dispute
   (C) detain
   (D) distrust
   (E) contain

6. QUERY
   (A) wait
   (B) lose
   (C) show
   (D) ask
   (E) demand

7. INSIDIOUS
   (A) treacherous
   (B) excitable
   (C) internal
   (D) distracting
   (E) secretive

8. PALPITATE
   (A) mash
   (B) stifle
   (C) creak
   (D) pace
   (E) throb

9. ANIMOSITY
   (A) hatred
   (B) interest
   (C) silliness
   (D) amusement
   (E) power

10. EGOTISM
   (A) sociability
   (B) aggressiveness
   (C) self-confidence
   (D) conceit
   (E) willingness

Vocabulary Test 29

1. CALLIGRAPHY
   (A) weaving
   (B) handwriting
   (C) drafting
   (D) mapmaking
   (E) graph making

2. SYNCHRONIZE
   (A) happen at the same time
   (B) follow immediately in time
   (C) alternate between events
   (D) postpone to a future time
   (E) have difficulty in hearing

3. SEMBLANCE
   (A) surface
   (B) diplomacy
   (C) replacement
   (D) appearance
   (E) confidence

4. WISTFUL
   (A) winding
   (B) mutual
   (C) exciting
   (D) rugged
   (E) yearning

5. CURTAIL
   (A) threaten
   (B) strengthen
   (C) lessen
   (D) hasten
   (E) collide

6. NOXIOUS
   (A) spicy
   (B) smelly
   (C) foreign
   (D) noisy
   (E) harmful

7. PAUCITY
   (A) fatigue
   (B) scarcity
   (C) nonsense
   (D) waste
   (E) motion

8. JEOPARDIZE
   (A) soothe
   (B) cleanse
   (C) enjoy
   (D) reward
   (E) endanger

9. INTREPID
(A) exhausted
(B) moderate
(C) anxious
(D) youthful
(E) fearless

10. TREACHEROUS
(A) ignorant
(B) envious
(C) disloyal
(D) cowardly
(E) inconsiderate

Vocabulary Test 30

1. UNSAVORY
(A) unfriendly
(B) joyless
(C) tactless
(D) colorless
(E) tasteless

2. HEARSAY
(A) testimony
(B) argument
(C) rumor
(D) accusation
(E) similarity

3. HAMPER
(A) restrain
(B) pack
(C) clarify
(D) grip
(E) err

4. BEDLAM
(A) inadequacy
(B) confusion
(C) translation
(D) courtesy
(E) curiosity

5. INFALLIBLE
(A) negative
(B) unfair
(C) essential
(D) certain
(E) weary

6. CONTEND
(A) solve
(B) observe
(C) outwit
(D) encourage
(E) compete

7. AMOROUS
(A) shapeless
(B) helpful
(C) familiar
(D) loving
(E) solemn

8. ALLEVIATE
(A) reject
(B) ease
(C) imitate
(D) consent
(E) elevate

9. NEOPHYTE
(A) participant
(B) officer
(C) beginner
(D) winner
(E) quarrel

10. SOLACE
(A) comfort
(B) weariness
(C) direction
(D) complaint
(E) respect

Vocabulary Test 31

1. ULTIMATUM
(A) shrewd plan
(B) final terms
(C) first defeat
(D) dominant leader
(E) electric motor

2. GIRD
(A) surround
(B) appeal
(C) request
(D) break
(E) glance

3. WANGLE
(A) moan
(B) mutilate
(C) exasperate
(D) manipulate
(E) triumph

4. PROCUREMENT
(A) acquisition
(B) resolution
(C) healing
(D) importance
(E) miracle

5. CULMINATION
(A) rebellion
(B) lighting system
(C) climax
(D) destruction
(E) mystery

6. INSUPERABLE
(A) incomprehensible
(B) elaborate
(C) unusual
(D) indigestible
(E) unconquerable

7. CLICHÉ
(A) summary argument
(B) new information
(C) new hat
(D) trite phrase
(E) lock device

8. CONCESSION
(A) nourishment
(B) plea
(C) restoration
(D) similarity
(E) acknowledgment

9. INSIPID
(A) disrespectful
(B) uninteresting
(C) persistent
(D) whole
(E) stimulating

10. REPRISAL
(A) retaliation
(B) drawing
(C) capture
(D) release
(E) suspicion

Vocabulary Test 32

1. DUBIOUS
(A) economical
(B) well-groomed
(C) boring
(D) discouraged
(E) uncertain

2. ATROCIOUS
(A) brutal
(B) innocent
(C) shrunken
(D) yellowish
(E) unsound

Vocabulary Test 33

3. PRESTIGE
   (A) speed
   (B) influence
   (C) omen
   (D) pride
   (E) excuse

4. VINDICATE
   (A) outrage
   (B) waver
   (C) enliven
   (D) justify
   (E) fuse

5. EXUDE
   (A) accuse
   (B) discharge
   (C) inflect
   (D) appropriate
   (E) distress

6. FACTION
   (A) clique
   (B) judgment
   (C) truth
   (D) type of architecture
   (E) health

7. INCLEMENT
   (A) merciful
   (B) sloping
   (C) harsh
   (D) disastrous
   (E) personal

8. SPURIOUS
   (A) concise
   (B) false
   (C) obstinate
   (D) sarcastic
   (E) severe

9. SUBSERVIENT
   (A) existing
   (B) obsequious
   (C) related
   (D) underlying
   (E) useful

10. IMPORTUNE
    (A) aggrandize
    (B) carry
    (C) exaggerate
    (D) prolong
    (E) urge

1. CONTROVERSIAL
   (A) faultfinding
   (B) pleasant
   (C) debatable
   (D) ugly
   (E) talkative

2. GHASTLY
   (A) hasty
   (B) furious
   (C) breathless
   (D) deathlike
   (E) spiritual

3. BELLIGERENT
   (A) worldly
   (B) warlike
   (C) loudmouthed
   (D) furious
   (E) artistic

4. PROFICIENCY
   (A) wisdom
   (B) oversupply
   (C) expertness
   (D) advancement
   (E) sincerity

5. COMPASSION
   (A) rage
   (B) strength of character
   (C) forcefulness
   (D) sympathy
   (E) uniformity

6. DISSENSION
   (A) treatise
   (B) pretense
   (C) fear
   (D) lineage
   (E) discord

7. INTIMATE
   (A) charm
   (B) hint
   (C) disguise
   (D) frighten
   (E) hum

8. BERATE
   (A) classify
   (B) scold
   (C) underestimate
   (D) take one's time
   (E) evaluate

9. DEARTH
   (A) scarcity
   (B) width
   (C) affection
   (D) wealth
   (E) warmth

10. MEDITATE
    (A) rest
    (B) stare
    (C) doze
    (D) make peace
    (E) reflect

Vocabulary Test 34

1. STAGNANT
   (A) inactive
   (B) alert
   (C) selfish
   (D) difficult
   (E) scornful

2. MANDATORY
   (A) insane
   (B) obligatory
   (C) evident
   (D) strategic
   (E) unequaled

3. INFERNAL
   (A) immodest
   (B) incomplete
   (C) domestic
   (D) second-rate
   (E) fiendish

4. EXONERATE
   (A) free from blame
   (B) warn
   (C) drive out
   (D) overcharge
   (E) plead

5. ARBITER
   (A) friend
   (B) judge
   (C) drug
   (D) tree surgeon
   (E) truant

6. ENMITY
   (A) boredom
   (B) puzzle
   (C) offensive language
   (D) ill will
   (E) entanglement

7. DISCRIMINATE
(A) fail
(B) delay
(C) accuse
(D) distinguish
(E) reject

8. DERISION
(A) disgust
(B) ridicule
(C) fear
(D) anger
(E) heredity

9. EXULTANT
(A) essential
(B) elated
(C) praiseworthy
(D) plentiful
(E) high-priced

10. OSTENSIBLE
(A) vibrating
(B) odd
(C) apparent
(D) standard
(E) ornate

Vocabulary Test 35

1. ABHOR
(A) hate
(B) admire
(C) taste
(D) skip
(E) resign

2. DUTIFUL
(A) lasting
(B) sluggish
(C) required
(D) soothing
(E) obedient

3. ZEALOT
(A) breeze
(B) enthusiast
(C) vault
(D) wild animal
(E) musical instrument

4. MAGNANIMOUS
(A) high-minded
(B) faithful
(C) concerned
(D) individual
(E) small

5. CITE
(A) protest
(B) depart
(C) quote
(D) agitate
(E) perform

6. OBLIVION
(A) hindrance
(B) accident
(C) courtesy
(D) forgetfulness
(E) old age

7. CARDINAL
(A) independent
(B) well-organized
(C) subordinate
(D) dignified
(E) chief

8. DEPLETE
(A) restrain
(B) corrupt
(C) despair
(D) exhaust
(E) spread out

9. SUPERSEDE
(A) retire
(B) replace
(C) overflow
(D) bless
(E) oversee

10. SPORADIC
(A) bad-tempered
(B) infrequent
(C) radical
(D) reckless
(E) humble

Vocabulary Test 36

1. NEUTRALIZE
(A) entangle
(B) strengthen
(C) counteract
(D) combat
(E) converse

2. INSINUATE
(A) destroy
(B) hint
(C) do wrong
(D) accuse
(E) release

3. DIMINUTIVE
(A) proud
(B) slow
(C) small
(D) watery
(E) puzzling

4. PLIGHT
(A) departure
(B) weight
(C) conspiracy
(D) predicament
(E) stamp

5. ILLICIT
(A) unlawful
(B) overpowering
(C) ill-advised
(D) small-scale
(E) unreadable

6. BENIGN
(A) contagious
(B) fatal
(C) ignorant
(D) kindly
(E) decorative

7. REVERIE
(A) abusive language
(B) love song
(C) backward step
(D) daydream
(E) holy man

8. APPREHENSIVE
(A) quiet
(B) firm
(C) curious
(D) sincere
(E) fearful

9. RECOIL
(A) shrink
(B) attract
(C) electrify
(D) adjust
(E) enroll

10. GUISE
(A) trickery
(B) request
(C) innocence
(D) misdeed
(E) appearance

Vocabulary Test 37

1. ACQUIT
(A) increase
(B) harden
(C) clear
(D) sharpen
(E) sentence

2. DEXTERITY
(A) conceit
(B) skill
(C) insistence
(D) embarrassment
(E) guidance

3. ASSIMILATE
(A) absorb
(B) imitate
(C) maintain
(D) outrun
(E) curb

4. DESPONDENCY
(A) relief
(B) gratitude
(C) dejection
(D) hatred
(E) poverty

5. BUOYANT
(A) conceited
(B) cautioning
(C) youthful
(D) musical
(E) cheerful

6. CULINARY
(A) having to do with cooking
(B) pertaining to dressmaking
(C) fond of eating
(D) loving money
(E) tending to be secretive

7. CAPRICE
(A) wisdom
(B) ornament
(C) pillar
(D) whim
(E) energy

8. DETERRENT
(A) restraining
(B) cleansing
(C) deciding
(D) concluding
(E) crumbling

9. PUGNACIOUS
(A) sticky
(B) cowardly
(C) precise
(D) vigorous
(E) quarrelsome

10. ABSCOND
(A) detest
(B) reduce
(C) swallow up
(D) dismiss
(E) flee

Vocabulary Test 38

1. BOUNTY
(A) limit
(B) boastfulness
(C) cheerfulness
(D) reward
(E) punishment

2. NOVICE
(A) storyteller
(B) iceberg
(C) adolescent
(D) mythical creature
(E) beginner

3. BOLSTER
(A) contradict
(B) insist
(C) defy
(D) sleep
(E) prop

4. MOBILE
(A) changeable
(B) scornful
(C) mechanical
(D) stylish
(E) solid

5. CREDULITY
(A) prize
(B) feebleness
(C) balance
(D) laziness
(E) belief

6. DOLDRUMS
(A) charity
(B) curing agents
(C) contagious disease
(D) low spirits
(E) places of safety

7. LOATH
(A) idle
(B) worried
(C) unwilling
(D) ready
(E) sad

8. INVENTIVE
(A) aimless
(B) clever
(C) moist
(D) false
(E) nearby

9. LITHE
(A) tough
(B) obstinate
(C) flexible
(D) damp
(E) gay

10. VACILLATE
(A) waver
(B) defeat
(C) favor
(D) endanger
(E) humiliate

Vocabulary Test 39

1. OBNOXIOUS
(A) dreamy
(B) visible
(C) angry
(D) daring
(E) objectionable

2. VERBATIM
(A) word for word
(B) at will
(C) without fail
(D) in secret
(E) in summary

3. ENTICE
(A) inform
(B) observe
(C) permit
(D) attract
(E) disobey

4. ACCLAIM
(A) discharge
(B) excel
(C) applaud
(D) divide
(E) speed

5. TURBULENCE
(A) treachery
(B) commotion
(C) fear
(D) triumph
(E) overflow

6. DEFER
(A) discourage
(B) postpone
(C) empty
(D) minimize
(E) estimate

7. ADAGE
(A) proverb
(B) supplement
(C) tool
(D) youth
(E) hardness

8. ENSUE
(A) compel
(B) remain
(C) absorb
(D) plead
(E) follow

9. ZENITH
(A) lowest point
(B) compass
(C) summit
(D) middle
(E) wind direction

10. HYPOTHETICAL
(A) magical
(B) visual
(C) two-faced
(D) theoretical
(E) excitable

Vocabulary Test 40

1. IMPROMPTU
(A) offhand
(B) laughable
(C) fascinating
(D) rehearsed
(E) deceptive

2. CHIVALROUS
(A) crude
(B) military
(C) handsome
(D) foreign
(E) courteous

3. HAVOC
(A) festival
(B) disease
(C) ruin
(D) sea battle
(E) luggage

4. REJUVENATE
(A) reply
(B) renew
(C) age
(D) judge
(E) reconsider

5. STILTED
(A) stiffly formal
(B) talking much
(C) secretive
(D) fashionable
(E) senseless

6. SOLILOQUY
(A) figure of speech
(B) historical incident
(C) monologue
(D) isolated position
(E) contradiction

7. AFFABLE
(A) monotonous
(B) affected
(C) wealthy
(D) sociable
(E) selfish

8. NEBULOUS
(A) subdued
(B) eternal
(C) dewy
(D) cloudy
(E) careless

9. STEREOTYPED
(A) lacking originality
(B) illuminating
(C) pictorial
(D) free from disease
(E) sparkling

10. STUPEFY
(A) lie
(B) talk nonsense
(C) bend
(D) make dull
(E) overeat

Vocabulary Test 41

1. SUPERFICIAL
(A) shallow
(B) unusually fine
(C) proud
(D) aged
(E) spiritual

2. DISPARAGE
(A) separate
(B) compare
(C) refuse
(D) belittle
(E) imitate

3. PROTAGONIST
(A) prophet
(B) explorer
(C) talented child
(D) convert
(E) leading character

4. LUDICROUS
(A) profitable
(B) excessive
(C) disordered
(D) ridiculous
(E) undesirable

5. INTREPID
(A) moist
(B) tolerant
(C) fearless
(D) rude
(E) gay

6. SAGE
(A) wise man
(B) tropical tree
(C) tale
(D) era
(E) fool

7. ADMONISH
(A) polish
(B) escape
(C) worship
(D) distribute
(E) caution

8. BESET
(A) plead
(B) perplex
(C) pertain to
(D) deny
(E) harass

9. FIGMENT
(A) ornamental openwork
(B) perfume
(C) undeveloped fruit
(D) statuette
(E) invention

10. GLIB
(A) dull
(B) thin
(C) weak
(D) fluent
(E) sharp

Vocabulary Test 42

1. FORTITUDE
(A) wealth
(B) courage
(C) honesty
(D) loudness
(E) luck

2. ABOLITION
(A) retirement
(B) disgust
(C) enslavement
(D) unrestricted power
(E) complete destruction

3. EPITOME
(A) pool
(B) summary
(C) formula
(D) monster
(E) song

4. MAIM
(A) heal
(B) disable
(C) outwit
(D) murder
(E) bury

5. CRESTFALLEN
(A) haughty
(B) dejected
(C) fatigued
(D) disfigured
(E) impolite

6. CUISINE
(A) headdress
(B) game of chance
(C) leisurely voyage
(D) artistry
(E) style of cooking

7. CENSURE
(A) erase
(B) build up
(C) criticize adversely
(D) charm
(E) help

8. DEVIATE
(A) destroy
(B) lower in value
(C) invent
(D) stray
(E) depress

9. SWARTHY
(A) dark-complexioned
(B) slender
(C) grass-covered
(D) springy
(E) rotating

10. MERCENARY
(A) poisonous
(B) unworthy
(C) serving only for pay
(D) luring by false charms
(E) showing pity

Vocabulary Test 43

1. ACUTE
(A) keen
(B) bitter
(C) brisk
(D) genuine
(E) certain

2. CLIENTELE
(A) legal body
(B) customers
(C) board of directors
(D) servants
(E) tenants

3. SUCCUMB
(A) follow
(B) help
(C) respond
(D) yield
(E) overthrow

4. SLOTH
(A) selfishness
(B) hatred
(C) laziness
(D) misery
(E) slipperiness

5. INFRINGE
(A) enrage
(B) expand
(C) disappoint
(D) weaken
(E) trespass

6. UNCANNY
(A) ill-humored
(B) immature
(C) weird
(D) unrestrained
(E) insincere

7. SUBMISSIVE
(A) unintelligent
(B) underhanded
(C) destructive
(D) enthusiastic
(E) meek

8. PEER
(A) ancestor
(B) teacher
(C) judge
(D) equal
(E) assistant

9. EULOGIZE
(A) kill
(B) apologize
(C) glorify
(D) soften
(E) imitate

10. INNOVATION
(A) change
(B) prayer
(C) hint
(D) restraint
(E) inquiry

Vocabulary Test 44

1. EXHILARATION
(A) animation
(B) withdrawal
(C) payment
(D) suffocation
(E) despair

2. RASPING
(A) irritating
(B) scolding
(C) fastening
(D) sighing
(E) plundering

3. PROPONENT
   (A) spendthrift
   (B) rival
   (C) distributor
   (D) advocate
   (E) neighbor

4. REDUNDANT
   (A) flooded
   (B) dreadful
   (C) aromatic
   (D) excessive
   (E) reclining

5. BEGRUDGING
   (A) humid
   (B) envious
   (C) living in seclusion
   (D) involving a choice
   (E) aimless

6. EMPATHIZE
   (A) cheapen
   (B) underestimate
   (C) charm
   (D) sympathize
   (E) forgive

7. PRUDENT
   (A) lighthearted
   (B) eager
   (C) cautious
   (D) insincere
   (E) fast-moving

8. OMNIVOROUS
   (A) devouring everything
   (B) many-sided
   (C) powerful
   (D) living on plants
   (E) all-knowing

9. APPEND
   (A) rely
   (B) recognize
   (C) arrest
   (D) divide
   (E) attach

10. STRATAGEM
    (A) sneak attack
    (B) military command
    (C) thin layer
    (D) deceptive device
    (E) narrow passage

Vocabulary Test 45

1. COLLABORATE
   (A) condense
   (B) converse
   (C) arrange in order
   (D) provide proof
   (E) act jointly

2. FUTILITY
   (A) uselessness
   (B) timelessness
   (C) stinginess
   (D) happiness
   (E) indistinctness

3. INTACT
   (A) blunt
   (B) fashionable
   (C) hidden
   (D) uninjured
   (E) attentive

4. FERVOR
   (A) originality
   (B) justice
   (C) zeal
   (D) productivity
   (E) corruption

5. UNERRING
   (A) modest
   (B) illogical
   (C) ghostly
   (D) matchless
   (E) unfailing

6. REFUTE
   (A) polish
   (B) disprove
   (C) throw away
   (D) break up
   (E) shut out

7. CONSENSUS
   (A) steadfastness of purpose
   (B) general agreement
   (C) lack of harmony
   (D) informal vote
   (E) impressive amount

8. COMPLIANT
   (A) tangled
   (B) grumbling
   (C) self-satisfied
   (D) treacherous
   (E) submissive

9. ACCESS
   (A) agreement
   (B) rapidity
   (C) welcome
   (D) approach
   (E) surplus

10. PRUDENT
    (A) wise
    (B) overcritical
    (C) famous
    (D) dull
    (E) early

Vocabulary Test 46

1. APPEASE
   (A) attack
   (B) soothe
   (C) pray for
   (D) estimate
   (E) confess

2. RUTHLESS
   (A) senseless
   (B) sinful
   (C) ruddy
   (D) pitiless
   (E) degrading

3. MUSTER
   (A) rebel
   (B) mask
   (C) gather
   (D) dampen
   (E) grumble

4. EXECRATE
   (A) embarrass
   (B) desert
   (C) omit
   (D) curse
   (E) resign

5. KNOLL
   (A) elf
   (B) mound
   (C) bell
   (D) development
   (E) technique

6. IRATE
   (A) evil
   (B) wandering
   (C) repetitious
   (D) colorful
   (E) angry

7. GRIMACE
(A) peril
(B) subtle suggestion
(C) signal
(D) wry face
(E) impurity

8. ACME
(A) layer
(B) summit
(C) edge
(D) pit
(E) interval

9. COVENANT
(A) solemn agreement
(B) formal invitation
(C) religious ceremony
(D) general pardon
(E) hiding place

10. APPALL
(A) honor
(B) decorate
(C) calm
(D) bore
(E) dismay

Vocabulary Test 47

1. INCUR
(A) take to heart
(B) anticipate
(C) bring down on oneself
(D) impress by repetition
(E) attack

2. CAUSTIC
(A) solemn
(B) puzzling
(C) biting
(D) influential
(E) attentive

3. DILATE
(A) retard
(B) fade
(C) wander
(D) expand
(E) startle

4. APATHY
(A) fixed dislike
(B) skill
(C) sorrow
(D) lack of feeling
(E) discontent

5. ELICIT
(A) draw forth
(B) cross out
(C) run away
(D) lengthen
(E) revise

6. JUDICIOUS
(A) wise
(B) dignified
(C) lighthearted
(D) confused
(E) respectful

7. UNSCATHED
(A) unashamed
(B) uninjured
(C) unskilled
(D) unsuccessful
(E) unconscious

8. CHIDE
(A) misbehave
(B) cool
(C) select
(D) conceal
(E) scold

9. CHARLATAN
(A) scholar
(B) acrobat
(C) quack
(D) faithful servant
(E) fast talker

10. DISBURSE
(A) remove forcibly
(B) twist
(C) amuse
(D) vary slightly
(E) pay out

Vocabulary Test 48

1. PARAMOUNT
(A) equal
(B) supreme
(C) well-known
(D) difficult
(E) ready

2. BROCHURE
(A) heavy shoe
(B) weapon
(C) pamphlet
(D) trite remark
(E) ornament

3. FIDELITY
(A) happiness
(B) bravery
(C) prosperity
(D) hardness
(E) loyalty

4. DIFFUSE
(A) explain
(B) scatter
(C) differ
(D) congeal
(E) dart

5. AGGRESSIVE
(A) disgusting
(B) impulsive
(C) shortsighted
(D) coarse-grained
(E) self-assertive

6. AMASS
(A) accumulate
(B) encourage
(C) comprehend
(D) blend
(E) astonish

7. DIABOLIC
(A) puzzling
(B) uneducated
(C) ornamental
(D) fiendish
(E) spinning

8. FORBEARANCE
(A) rejection
(B) forgetfulness
(C) sensitivity
(D) patience
(E) expectation

9. TAINT
(A) snarl
(B) infect
(C) unite
(D) annoy
(E) list

10. DISGRUNTLED
(A) untidy
(B) rambling
(C) disabled
(D) cheating
(E) displeased

Vocabulary Test 49

1. PLACID
   (A) apparent
   (B) peaceful
   (C) wicked
   (D) unusual
   (E) absent-minded

2. EVASIVE
   (A) emotional
   (B) effective
   (C) destructive
   (D) empty
   (E) shifty

3. CHAOS
   (A) complete disorder
   (B) deep gorge
   (C) challenge
   (D) sudden attack
   (E) rejoicing

4. DESPICABLE
   (A) insulting
   (B) ungrateful
   (C) contemptible
   (D) unbearable
   (E) jealous

5. DERIDE
   (A) question
   (B) ignore
   (C) mock
   (D) unseat
   (E) produce

6. ELUDE
   (A) gladden
   (B) fascinate
   (C) mention
   (D) escape
   (E) ignore

7. MUTABLE
   (A) colorless
   (B) harmful
   (C) uniform
   (D) changeable
   (E) invisible

8. INDICATIVE
   (A) suggestive
   (B) curious
   (C) active
   (D) angry
   (E) certain

9. LEVITY
   (A) cleanness
   (B) tastiness
   (C) deadliness
   (D) sluggishness
   (E) lightness

10. EXCRUCIATING
    (A) disciplinary
    (B) screaming
    (C) torturing
    (D) offensive
    (E) outpouring

Vocabulary Test 50

1. PRECEPT
   (A) rule
   (B) disguise
   (C) refinement
   (D) hasty decision
   (E) delaying action

2. HOMOGENEOUS
   (A) numerous
   (B) healthful
   (C) similar
   (D) assorted
   (E) educational

3. ARCHIVES
   (A) public records
   (B) models
   (C) supporting columns
   (D) tombs
   (E) large ships

4. INFAMY
   (A) anger
   (B) truth
   (C) disgrace
   (D) weakness
   (E) excitement

5. IMPINGE
   (A) swear
   (B) involve
   (C) erase
   (D) encroach
   (E) beg

6. DEPOSE
   (A) lay bare
   (B) deprive of office
   (C) empty
   (D) behead
   (E) blemish

7. OSTENTATIOUS
   (A) unruly
   (B) showy
   (C) varied
   (D) scandalous
   (E) probable

8. CONCLAVE
   (A) private meeting
   (B) covered passage
   (C) solemn vow
   (D) curved surface
   (E) ornamental vase

9. FRAY
   (A) combat
   (B) trickery
   (C) unreality
   (D) madness
   (E) freedom

10. OBSESS
    (A) fatten
    (B) beset
    (C) make dull
    (D) exaggerate
    (E) interfere

Vocabulary Test 51

1. CHAFE
   (A) pretend
   (B) joke
   (C) drink deeply
   (D) irritate
   (E) lose courage

2. MISCONSTRUE
   (A) hate
   (B) destroy
   (C) misbehave
   (D) misinterpret
   (E) misplace

3. PHILANTHROPIST
   (A) student of language
   (B) collector of stamps
   (C) lover of mankind
   (D) seeker of truth
   (E) enemy of culture

4. CASTE
   (A) feudal system
   (B) division of society
   (C) political theory
   (D) method of punishment
   (E) monetary system

5. CHASTEN
   (A) punish
   (B) engrave
   (C) attract
   (D) trick
   (E) laugh at

6. CONDUCIVE
   (A) pardonable
   (B) identical
   (C) incidental
   (D) helpful
   (E) exceptional

7. SUBORDINATE
   (A) hostile
   (B) inferior
   (C) separate
   (D) earlier
   (E) adaptable

8. SUPERFLUOUS
   (A) inexact
   (B) excessive
   (C) insincere
   (D) excellent
   (E) unreal

9. WIELD
   (A) protect
   (B) handle
   (C) postpone
   (D) resign
   (E) unite

10. GARISH
   (A) showy
   (B) talkative
   (C) sleepy
   (D) thin
   (E) vine-covered

Vocabulary Test 52

1. MEANDER
   (A) grumble
   (B) wander aimlessly
   (C) come between
   (D) weigh carefully
   (E) sing

2. DESTITUTION
   (A) trickery
   (B) fate
   (C) lack of practice
   (D) recovery
   (E) extreme poverty

3. MALIGN
   (A) slander
   (B) prophesy
   (C) entreat
   (D) approve
   (E) praise

4. IMPOTENT
   (A) unwise
   (B) lacking strength
   (C) free of sin
   (D) without shame
   (E) commanding

5. SNIVEL
   (A) crawl
   (B) cut short
   (C) whine
   (D) doze
   (E) giggle

6. SOJOURN
   (A) court order
   (B) nickname
   (C) temporary stay
   (D) slip of the tongue
   (E) makeshift

7. PLATITUDE
   (A) home remedy
   (B) trite remark
   (C) balance wheel
   (D) rare animal
   (E) protective film

8. CONCORD
   (A) brevity
   (B) blame
   (C) kindness
   (D) worry
   (E) agreement

9. ABOMINABLE
   (A) hateful
   (B) ridiculous
   (C) untamed
   (D) mysterious
   (E) boastful

10. QUALM
   (A) sudden misgiving
   (B) irritation
   (C) cooling drink
   (D) deceit
   (E) attention to detail

Vocabulary Test 53

1. EQUITABLE
   (A) charitable
   (B) even-tempered
   (C) two-faced
   (D) undecided
   (E) just

2. AFFRONT
   (A) quarrel
   (B) fright
   (C) denial
   (D) boast
   (E) insult

3. EPOCH
   (A) heroic deed
   (B) legend
   (C) witty saying
   (D) period of time
   (E) summary

4. RETRIBUTION
   (A) donation
   (B) jealousy
   (C) intense emotion
   (D) slow withdrawal
   (E) punishment

5. ABASE
   (A) forgive
   (B) degrade
   (C) attach
   (D) take leave
   (E) cut off

6. CAREEN
   (A) celebrate
   (B) mourn
   (C) ridicule
   (D) lurch
   (E) beckon

7. CONVIVIAL
   (A) formal
   (B) gay
   (C) rotating
   (D) well-informed
   (E) insulting

8. RAMPANT
   (A) playful
   (B) crumbling
   (C) roundabout
   (D) unchecked
   (E) defensive

9. DOCILE
(A) delicate
(B) positive
(C) dreary
(D) obedient
(E) melodious

10. VESTIGE
(A) bone
(B) test
(C) entrance
(D) cloak
(E) trace

Vocabulary Test 54

1. IMPEDIMENT
(A) foundation
(B) conceit
(C) hindrance
(D) luggage
(E) instrument

2. ADHERE
(A) pursue
(B) control
(C) arrive
(D) cling
(E) attend

3. COMPOSURE
(A) sensitiveness
(B) weariness
(C) stylishness
(D) hopefulness
(E) calmness

4. PROVOCATION
(A) sacred vow
(B) formal announcement
(C) cause of irritation
(D) careful management
(E) expression of disgust

5. SAVORY
(A) thrifty
(B) wise
(C) appetizing
(D) warm
(E) uncivilized

6. CANDID
(A) hidden
(B) shining
(C) straightforward
(D) critical
(E) warmhearted

7. ECLIPSE
(A) stretch
(B) obscure
(C) glow
(D) overlook
(E) insert

8. CORRELATE
(A) punish
(B) wrinkle
(C) conspire openly
(D) give additional proof
(E) connect systematically

9. INFIRMITY
(A) disgrace
(B) unhappiness
(C) rigidity
(D) hesitation
(E) weakness

10. PALPITATE
(A) faint
(B) harden
(C) throb
(D) soothe
(E) taste

Vocabulary Test 55

1. DEBRIS
(A) sadness
(B) decay
(C) ruins
(D) landslide
(E) hindrance

2. CONSOLIDATE
(A) show pity
(B) strengthen
(C) restrain
(D) infect
(E) use up

3. STAMINA
(A) flatness
(B) clearness
(C) hesitation
(D) vigor
(E) reliability

4. FACET
(A) phase
(B) humor
(C) story
(D) discharge
(E) assistance

5. INANIMATE
(A) emotional
(B) thoughtless
(C) lifeless
(D) inexact
(E) silly

6. CALLOUS
(A) frantic
(B) misinformed
(C) youthful
(D) impolite
(E) unfeeling

7. ENHANCE
(A) sympathize
(B) act out
(C) weaken
(D) make greater
(E) fascinate

8. DISREPUTABLE
(A) impolite
(B) bewildered
(C) debatable
(D) unavailable
(E) shameful

9. SEDATE
(A) sober
(B) seated
(C) buried
(D) drugged
(E) timid

10. LUCRATIVE
(A) lazy
(B) coarse
(C) profitable
(D) brilliant
(E) amusing

Vocabulary Test 56

1. IMPRUDENT
(A) reckless
(B) unexcitable
(C) poor
(D) domineering
(E) powerless

2. DISSENSION
(A) friction
(B) analysis
(C) swelling
(D) injury
(E) slyness

Vocabulary Test 57

3. DISCONCERT
   (A) separate
   (B) cripple
   (C) lessen
   (D) upset
   (E) dismiss

4. RUDIMENTARY
   (A) discourteous
   (B) brutal
   (C) displeasing
   (D) elementary
   (E) embarrassing

5. AUTONOMOUS
   (A) self-governing
   (B) self-important
   (C) self-educated
   (D) self-explanatory
   (E) self-conscious

6. ASCERTAIN
   (A) hold fast
   (B) long for
   (C) declare
   (D) find out
   (E) avoid

7. LITERAL
   (A) flowery
   (B) matter-of-fact
   (C) sidewise
   (D) well-educated
   (E) firsthand

8. OSCILLATE
   (A) please
   (B) swing
   (C) purify
   (D) saturate
   (E) harden

9. CONCISE
   (A) accurate
   (B) brief
   (C) sudden
   (D) similar
   (E) painful

10. CONSTERNATION
    (A) restraint
    (B) close attention
    (C) dismay
    (D) self-importance
    (E) acknowledgment

1. COLOSSAL
   (A) ancient
   (B) influential
   (C) destructive
   (D) dramatic
   (E) huge

2. EVICT
   (A) summon
   (B) excite
   (C) force out
   (D) prove
   (E) draw off

3. MISCHANCE
   (A) omission
   (B) ill luck
   (C) feeling of doubt
   (D) unlawful act
   (E) distrust

4. FELON
   (A) criminal
   (B) fugitive
   (C) traitor
   (D) coward
   (E) loafer

5. CENSURE
   (A) empty
   (B) criticize
   (C) spread out
   (D) take an oath
   (E) omit

6. IMPLICIT
   (A) implied
   (B) rude
   (C) relentless
   (D) sinful
   (E) daring

7. SLOVENLY
   (A) sleepy
   (B) tricky
   (C) untidy
   (D) moody
   (E) cowardly

8. EXTRANEOUS
   (A) familiar
   (B) unprepared
   (C) foreign
   (D) proper
   (E) utmost

9. IMPASSE
   (A) command
   (B) stubbornness
   (C) crisis
   (D) deadlock
   (E) failure

10. ABSOLVE
    (A) forgive
    (B) reduce
    (C) mix
    (D) deprive
    (E) detect

Vocabulary Test 58

1. CUMBERSOME
   (A) habitual
   (B) clumsy
   (C) hasty
   (D) blameworthy
   (E) uneducated

2. CAPTIVATE
   (A) charm
   (B) dictate terms
   (C) overturn
   (D) find fault
   (E) hesitate

3. ZEALOUS
   (A) serious
   (B) speedy
   (C) flawless
   (D) necessary
   (E) enthusiastic

4. AROMATIC
   (A) shining
   (B) precise
   (C) ancient
   (D) fragrant
   (E) dry

5. RETROSPECT
   (A) careful inspection
   (B) reversal of form
   (C) review of the past
   (D) respect for authority
   (E) special attention

6. WHET
   (A) bleach
   (B) exhaust
   (C) harden
   (D) stimulate
   (E) question

7. CONTUSION
(A) puzzle
(B) shrinkage
(C) bruise
(D) uncleanness
(E) fraud

8. COMPATIBLE
(A) eloquent
(B) adequate
(C) overfed
(D) comfortable
(E) harmonious

9. CALLOUS
(A) secretive
(B) unruly
(C) gloomy
(D) unfeeling
(E) hotheaded

10. REPUDIATE
(A) reject
(B) revalue
(C) repay
(D) forget
(E) forgive

Vocabulary Test 59

1. PROLETARIAT
(A) revolutionists
(B) intellectuals
(C) slaves
(D) laboring classes
(E) landowners

2. REQUISITE
(A) desirable
(B) ridiculous
(C) liberal
(D) necessary
(E) majestic

3. TENACIOUS
(A) violent
(B) given to arguing
(C) slender
(D) holding fast
(E) menacing

4. SCINTILLATE
(A) whirl
(B) wander
(C) scorch
(D) sharpen
(E) sparkle

5. PROPRIETY
(A) success
(B) cleverness
(C) nearness
(D) security
(E) suitability

6. UNWITTING
(A) undignified
(B) unintentional
(C) slack
(D) obstinate
(E) unaccustomed

7. ATTRIBUTE
(A) quality
(B) tax
(C) desire
(D) law
(E) final sum

8. SCRUPULOUS
(A) scornful
(B) clean
(C) frightening
(D) doubting
(E) conscientious

9. USURP
(A) lend money
(B) replace
(C) murder
(D) surrender
(E) seize by force

10. CESSATION
(A) witnessing
(B) stopping
(C) strain
(D) leave-taking
(E) unwillingness

Vocabulary Test 60

1. RESOLUTE
(A) determined
(B) vibrating
(C) irresistible
(D) elastic
(E) demanding

2. CRYSTALLIZE
(A) glitter
(B) give definite form to
(C) chill
(D) sweeten
(E) polish vigorously

3. REGIME
(A) ruler
(B) military unit
(C) form of government
(D) contagion
(E) guardian

4. LACERATED
(A) unconscious
(B) stitched
(C) slender
(D) raveled
(E) mangled

5. AMISS
(A) friendly
(B) faulty
(C) tardy
(D) central
(E) purposeless

6. INDOLENCE
(A) poverty
(B) laziness
(C) danger
(D) truth
(E) attention

7. PRECARIOUS
(A) trustful
(B) early
(C) previous
(D) cautious
(E) uncertain

8. CONNOISSEUR
(A) investigator
(B) government official
(C) pretender
(D) critical judge
(E) portrait artist

9. HILARITY
(A) wittiness
(B) disobedience
(C) mirth
(D) heedlessness
(E) contentment

10. EMIT
(A) overlook
(B) adorn
(C) discharge
(D) encourage
(E) stress

Vocabulary Test 61

1. DYNAMIC
   (A) specialized
   (B) active
   (C) fragile
   (D) magical
   (E) comparative

2. ACHILLES' HEEL
   (A) source of strength
   (B) critical test
   (C) hereditary curse
   (D) vulnerable point
   (E) base conduct

3. AD LIB
   (A) cheerfully
   (B) freely
   (C) carefully
   (D) literally
   (E) wisely

4. DECRY
   (A) baffle
   (B) weep
   (C) trap
   (D) belittle
   (E) imagine

5. RAVAGE
   (A) ruin
   (B) tangle
   (C) delight
   (D) scold
   (E) crave

6. RENDEZVOUS
   (A) surrender
   (B) appointment
   (C) souvenir
   (D) hiding place
   (E) mutual exchange

7. SKULK
   (A) trail
   (B) shadow
   (C) ambush
   (D) lurk
   (E) race

8. PLETHORA
   (A) formal farewell
   (B) exclusive group
   (C) abundance
   (D) conclusive argument
   (E) good taste

9. NUPTIAL
   (A) moonlike
   (B) blunted
   (C) ritualistic
   (D) matrimonial
   (E) blessed

10. BALKED
    (A) swindled
    (B) thwarted
    (C) enlarged
    (D) waved
    (E) punished

Vocabulary Test 62

1. AD INFINITUM
   (A) to a limit
   (B) from eternity
   (C) occasionally
   (D) endlessly
   (E) periodically

2. EXTRICATE
   (A) disentangle
   (B) die out
   (C) praise
   (D) purify
   (E) argue with

3. SQUALID
   (A) dirty
   (B) unresponsive
   (C) wasteful
   (D) stormy
   (E) congested

4. COERCE
   (A) coincide
   (B) strengthen
   (C) accompany
   (D) compel
   (E) seek out

5. INTER
   (A) bury
   (B) stab
   (C) change
   (D) make peace
   (E) emphasize

6. CRESCENDO
   (A) increasing volume
   (B) decreasing tempo
   (C) abrupt ending
   (D) discordant note
   (E) musical composition

7. INDISCREET
   (A) unpopular
   (B) embarrassing
   (C) disloyal
   (D) unwise
   (E) greatly upset

8. UNWIELDY
   (A) stubborn
   (B) unhealthy
   (C) monotonous
   (D) shameful
   (E) clumsy

9. ENVISAGE
   (A) plot
   (B) conceal
   (C) wrinkle
   (D) contemplate
   (E) sneer

10. INTERIM
    (A) go-between
    (B) meantime
    (C) mixture
    (D) hereafter
    (E) period of rest

Vocabulary Test 63

1. DISHEARTEN
   (A) shame
   (B) discourage
   (C) astound
   (D) disown
   (E) cripple

2. COMPONENT
   (A) memorial
   (B) pledge
   (C) convenience
   (D) ingredient
   (E) similarity

3. LURK
   (A) stagger
   (B) tempt
   (C) sneak
   (D) grin
   (E) rob

4. GRUDGING
   (A) impolite
   (B) dirty
   (C) hoarse
   (D) alarming
   (E) unwilling

5. SEMBLANCE
   (A) likeness
   (B) noise
   (C) foundation
   (D) glance
   (E) error

6. NETTLE
   (A) irritate
   (B) catch
   (C) accuse
   (D) make ill
   (E) fade away

7. TREMULOUS
   (A) slow
   (B) high-pitched
   (C) huge
   (D) shaking
   (E) spirited

8. TERSE
   (A) delicate
   (B) nervous
   (C) mild
   (D) numb
   (E) concise

9. AFFINITY
   (A) solemn declaration
   (B) indefinite amount
   (C) natural attraction
   (D) pain
   (E) wealth

10. VOLATILE
    (A) disobedient
    (B) changeable
    (C) forceful
    (D) willing
    (E) luxurious

Vocabulary Test 64

1. HOMAGE
   (A) welcome
   (B) honor
   (C) coziness
   (D) criticism
   (E) regret

2. DISPERSE
   (A) restore
   (B) spread
   (C) grumble
   (D) soak
   (E) spend

3. RATIONAL
   (A) resentful
   (B) overjoyed
   (C) sensible
   (D) reckless
   (E) apologetic

4. RECLUSE
   (A) schemer
   (B) criminal
   (C) miser
   (D) adventurer
   (E) hermit

5. COMPLACENCY
   (A) tenderness
   (B) admiration
   (C) dependence
   (D) unity
   (E) self-satisfaction

6. MENACE
   (A) kill
   (B) threaten
   (C) waste
   (D) indicate
   (E) tease

7. DUPE
   (A) combine
   (B) reproduce
   (C) fool
   (D) grab
   (E) follow

8. ABATE
   (A) surprise
   (B) desert
   (C) decrease
   (D) humiliate
   (E) pay for

9. CONGENITAL
   (A) existing at birth
   (B) displaying weakness
   (C) related by marriage
   (D) overcrowded
   (E) unintelligent

10. INSURGENT
    (A) impractical
    (B) unbearable
    (C) overhanging
    (D) rebellious
    (E) patriotic

Vocabulary Test 65

1. CONJECTURE
   (A) work
   (B) joke
   (C) initiate
   (D) add
   (E) guess

2. DAIS
   (A) platform
   (B) easy chair
   (C) waiting room
   (D) ornamental pin
   (E) figurehead

3. IMPETUS
   (A) deadlock
   (B) collision
   (C) warning
   (D) wickedness
   (E) stimulus

4. INTROSPECTIVE
   (A) lacking strength
   (B) practicing self-examination
   (C) highly critical
   (D) intrusive
   (E) lacking confidence

5. DEIFY
   (A) describe
   (B) disobey
   (C) make presentable
   (D) worship as a god
   (E) challenge

6. AGGREGATION
   (A) method
   (B) irritation
   (C) prize
   (D) collection
   (E) blessing

7. EXALTED
   (A) honored
   (B) underhanded
   (C) funny
   (D) conceited
   (E) secondary

8. POTENTATE
   (A) slave
   (B) soldier
   (C) adviser
   (D) informer
   (E) ruler

9. INTIMIDATE
(A) frighten
(B) suggest
(C) dare
(D) border upon
(E) befriend

10. SARDONIC
(A) decorative
(B) polished
(C) strange
(D) fashionable
(E) sarcastic

Vocabulary Test 66

1. ELECTRIFY
(A) punish
(B) improve
(C) thrill
(D) explain
(E) investigate

2. DISCRETION
(A) special privilege
(B) individual judgment
(C) unfair treatment
(D) disagreement
(E) embarrassment

3. GRAPPLE
(A) dive
(B) wrestle
(C) handle
(D) fit together
(E) fondle

4. LAUDABLE
(A) brave
(B) comical
(C) peaceful
(D) praiseworthy
(E) conspicuous

5. LONGEVITY
(A) wisdom
(B) length of life
(C) society
(D) system of measure
(E) loudness

6. BLANCH
(A) destroy
(B) drink
(C) whiten
(D) feel
(E) mend

7. SHREW
(A) moneylender
(B) fortune-teller
(C) chronic invalid
(D) unruly child
(E) scolding woman

8. STALWART
(A) diseased
(B) feeble
(C) needy
(D) sturdy
(E) truthful

9. APOGEE
(A) rate of ascent
(B) force of gravity
(C) measuring device
(D) expression of regret
(E) highest point

10. BANTER
(A) tease playfully
(B) strut boldly
(C) ruin
(D) bend slightly
(E) relieve

Vocabulary Test 67

1. REPRESS
(A) sharpen
(B) restrain
(C) repeat
(D) disgust
(E) grieve

2. BREACH
(A) obstruction
(B) violation
(C) anticipation
(D) accusation
(E) decoration

3. DILIGENT
(A) hesitant
(B) prosperous
(C) offensive
(D) industrious
(E) straightforward

4. CONCOCT
(A) devise
(B) link together
(C) harmonize
(D) meet privately
(E) sweeten

5. FLAMBOYANT
(A) scandalous
(B) showy
(C) nonsensical
(D) manly
(E) temporary

6. ECCENTRICITY
(A) overabundance
(B) self-consciousness
(C) adaptability
(D) publicity
(E) oddity

7. VINDICTIVE
(A) gloomy
(B) cowardly
(C) vengeful
(D) cheerful
(E) boastful

8. GRAPHIC
(A) vivid
(B) harsh-sounding
(C) free from error
(D) dignified
(E) pliable

9. PLACARD
(A) poster
(B) souvenir
(C) soothing medicine
(D) exact reproduction
(E) contemptuous remark

10. PUTREFY
(A) scour
(B) paralyze
(C) rot
(D) neglect
(E) argue

Vocabulary Test 68

1. GRANDIOSE
(A) selfish
(B) thankful
(C) quarrelsome
(D) elderly
(E) impressive

2. INCONGRUOUS
(A) indistinct
(B) unsuitable
(C) unimportant
(D) illegal
(E) inconvenient

3. PRONE
(A) disposed
(B) speechless
(C) tardy
(D) two-edged
(E) quick

4. EMISSARY
(A) rival
(B) secret agent
(C) master of ceremonies
(D) refugee
(E) clergyman

5. INVALIDATE
(A) turn inward
(B) deprive of force
(C) mistrust
(D) support with facts
(E) neglect

6. CLEMENCY
(A) purity
(B) timidity
(C) courage
(D) simplicity
(E) mildness

7. UNSCATHED
(A) uninterested
(B) unsettled
(C) unspoken
(D) unharmed
(E) unknown

8. RELINQUISH
(A) shrink from
(B) take pity on
(C) yield
(D) lessen
(E) recall

9. ALLAY
(A) offend
(B) suffer
(C) resemble
(D) assign
(E) calm

10. ANIMOSITY
(A) liveliness
(B) worry
(C) ill will
(D) regret
(E) sarcasm

Vocabulary Test 69

1. SOLICIT
(A) request
(B) worry
(C) command
(D) deny
(E) depend

2. PERTURB
(A) pierce
(B) filter
(C) calculate
(D) agitate
(E) disregard

3. JAUNTY
(A) bored
(B) envious
(C) quarrelsome
(D) chatty
(E) lively

4. DRIVEL
(A) shrill laughter
(B) foolish talk
(C) untidy dress
(D) waste matter
(E) quaint humor

5. FRUGAL
(A) sickly
(B) sparing
(C) slow
(D) chilled
(E) frightened

6. IOTA
(A) first step
(B) sacred picture
(C) ornamental scroll
(D) crystalline substance
(E) very small quantity

7. POACH
(A) squander
(B) trespass
(C) outwit
(D) bully
(E) borrow

8. DEFECTION
(A) delay
(B) slander
(C) respect
(D) desertion
(E) exemption

9. MASTICATE
(A) chew
(B) slaughter
(C) ripen
(D) enroll
(E) tangle

10. ANALOGY
(A) imitation
(B) research
(C) calendar
(D) similarity
(E) disagreement

Vocabulary Test 70

1. DILEMMA
(A) punishment
(B) division in ranks
(C) ability to detect
(D) perplexing choice
(E) word with two meanings

2. CELESTIAL
(A) musical
(B) heavenly
(C) stately
(D) unmarried
(E) aged

3. MILITANT
(A) political
(B) mighty
(C) aggressive
(D) peaceable
(E) illegal

4. EMINENT
(A) noted
(B) moral
(C) future
(D) low
(E) unwise

5. PERCEIVE
(A) resolve
(B) observe
(C) organize
(D) stick in
(E) copy down

6. IDIOSYNCRASY
(A) stupidity
(B) virtue
(C) personal peculiarity
(D) foreign dialect
(E) similarity

7. EDIFICE
(A) tool
(B) large building
(C) garden
(D) mushroom
(E) set of books

8. SEEDY
(A) dishonest
(B) helpless
(C) vague
(D) nervous
(E) shabby

9. SUPPLANT
(A) spend
(B) unite
(C) recall
(D) replace
(E) purpose

10. DESIST
(A) loiter
(B) stand
(C) hurry
(D) stumble
(E) stop

Vocabulary Test 71

1. GIRD
(A) stare
(B) thresh
(C) encircle
(D) complain
(E) perforate

2. BIZARRE
(A) charitable
(B) joyous
(C) flattering
(D) insane
(E) fantastic

3. PERENNIAL
(A) superior
(B) unceasing
(C) notable
(D) short-lived
(E) authoritative

4. PROGENITOR
(A) genius
(B) wastrel
(C) forefather
(D) magician
(E) publisher

5. EMBELLISH
(A) organize
(B) involve
(C) rob
(D) beautify
(E) correct

6. IMPLEMENT
(A) carry out
(B) fall apart
(C) give freely
(D) object strongly
(E) praise highly

7. INSUBORDINATE
(A) unreal
(B) disobedient
(C) inferior
(D) unfaithful
(E) unnecessary

8. ITINERANT
(A) small
(B) intensive
(C) repetitive
(D) wandering
(E) begging

9. ADVERSITY
(A) misfortune
(B) surprise
(C) economy
(D) publicity
(E) warning

10. DISSIPATE
(A) explain
(B) puzzle
(C) rearrange
(D) envy
(E) waste

Vocabulary Test 72

1. VALOR
(A) courage
(B) honesty
(C) beauty
(D) alertness
(E) modesty

2. DISSUADE
(A) offend
(B) lessen
(C) advise against
(D) spread out
(E) separate

3. ERRATIC
(A) unpredictable
(B) upright
(C) well-informed
(D) self-centered
(E) artificial

4. COVET
(A) take for granted
(B) keep secret
(C) disbelieve
(D) steal
(E) long for

5. VERBOSE
(A) forbidden
(B) expanding
(C) talented
(D) wordy
(E) opinionated

6. FLIPPANT
(A) fishlike
(B) anxious
(C) frivolous
(D) savage
(E) shy

7. ACCLAMATION
(A) seasoning
(B) applause
(C) slope
(D) harmony
(E) collection

8. INCITE
(A) include
(B) destroy
(C) withdraw
(D) arouse
(E) perceive

9. FINESSE
(A) end
(B) skill
(C) habit
(D) expense
(E) vanity

10. TANTALIZE
(A) prevent
(B) protect
(C) rob
(D) predict
(E) torment

Vocabulary Test 73

1. INSOMNIA
(A) boredom
(B) loss of memory
(C) seasickness
(D) sleeplessness
(E) lonesomeness

2. FEASIBLE
(A) enjoyable
(B) juicy
(C) regrettable
(D) responsible
(E) possible

3. BLURT
(A) brag
(B) utter impulsively
(C) challenge
(D) shout angrily
(E) weep noisily

4. ALIENATE
(A) advise
(B) entertain
(C) forgive
(D) sympathize with
(E) make unfriendly

5. STARK
(A) barely
(B) offensively
(C) uselessly
(D) completely
(E) artistically

6. NONCHALANCE
(A) refinement
(B) foresight
(C) air of indifference
(D) lack of knowledge
(E) lack of common sense

7. GRIT
(A) honesty
(B) reverence
(C) trustworthiness
(D) cheerfulness
(E) bravery

8. MEDIATE
(A) make changes
(B) argue earnestly
(C) consider carefully
(D) propose hesitantly
(E) reconcile differences

9. DE FACTO
(A) commercial
(B) economic
(C) in reality
(D) unnecessary
(E) the following

10. IRREVOCABLE
(A) unreliable
(B) disrespectful
(C) unforgivable
(D) unalterable
(E) heartless

Vocabulary Test 74

1. ABYSMAL
(A) bottomless
(B) ill
(C) forgetful
(D) unoccupied
(E) slight

2. PREROGATIVE
(A) forewarning
(B) formal investigation
(C) privilege
(D) reputation
(E) opening speech

3. ILLUSTRIOUS
(A) believable
(B) unrewarding
(C) cynical
(D) decorative
(E) famous

4. INTERMINABLE
(A) scanty
(B) secret
(C) open-faced
(D) endless
(E) stationary

5. FRANCHISE
(A) secrecy
(B) right to vote
(C) imprisonment
(D) free-for-all
(E) avoidable tragedy

6. LINEAGE
(A) brilliance
(B) ancestry
(C) narrowness
(D) straightness
(E) ceremony

7. RECIPROCATE
(A) reconsider
(B) refresh
(C) repay
(D) recall
(E) reclaim

8. REBUFF
(A) send back
(B) make over
(C) snub
(D) defend
(E) remind

9. CLANDESTINE
(A) unfriendly
(B) fateful
(C) unified
(D) secret
(E) argumentative

10. LETHARGY
(A) unnatural drowsiness
(B) excessive caution
(C) lack of consideration
(D) vice
(E) foolishness

Vocabulary Test 75

1. ACCREDITED
(A) obligated
(B) approved
(C) discharged
(D) quickened
(E) confessed

2. ADHERENT
(A) clergyman
(B) critic
(C) executive
(D) supporter
(E) journalist

3. WHEEDLE
(A) mourn
(B) coax
(C) revolve
(D) hesitate
(E) entertain

4. CIRCUITOUS
(A) electrical
(B) watery
(C) roundabout
(D) forbidding
(E) tender

5. DESPOT
   (A) murderer
   (B) impostor
   (C) invader
   (D) avenger
   (E) tyrant

6. DETER
   (A) hinder
   (B) mistake
   (C) neglect
   (D) injure
   (E) restore

7. UTILITARIAN
   (A) practical
   (B) widespread
   (C) inexpensive
   (D) praiseworthy
   (E) fortunate

8. INCREDULITY
   (A) forgetfulness
   (B) faithlessness
   (C) immaturity
   (D) disbelief
   (E) unreality

9. INTERDICT
   (A) lessen
   (B) separate
   (C) fatigue
   (D) permit
   (E) forbid

10. TIMOROUS
    (A) necessary
    (B) expected
    (C) afraid
    (D) wild
    (E) brief

Vocabulary Test 76

1. BRAWN
   (A) boldness
   (B) muscular strength
   (C) rustiness
   (D) unruliness
   (E) protective covering

2. STALEMATE
   (A) athletic contest
   (B) complete defeat
   (C) deadlock
   (D) storm
   (E) refusal to fight

3. KINDLE
   (A) relate
   (B) pass on
   (C) pretend
   (D) arouse
   (E) punish

4. POMP
   (A) splendor
   (B) illness
   (C) hopefulness
   (D) apple
   (E) posture

5. TINGE
   (A) mold
   (B) draw forth
   (C) color slightly
   (D) sketch
   (E) create

6. RECOIL
   (A) steer
   (B) link up
   (C) put down
   (D) scrape
   (E) shrink back

7. QUASH
   (A) creep
   (B) mix thoroughly
   (C) repeat
   (D) suppress completely
   (E) falsify

8. PALTRY
   (A) trivial
   (B) sacred
   (C) metallic
   (D) careless
   (E) positive

9. IMPETUOUS
   (A) controlled
   (B) hasty
   (C) vigorous
   (D) defamatory
   (E) vehement

10. HARANGUE
    (A) unintelligible prose
    (B) ranting speech
    (C) poetic imagery
    (D) anonymous letter
    (E) heavy overcoat

Vocabulary Test 77

1. APROPOS
   (A) witty
   (B) forceful
   (C) nearly correct
   (D) richly decorated
   (E) to the point

2. INIMICAL
   (A) speechless
   (B) unfriendly
   (C) unnecessarily rude
   (D) poor
   (E) hopelessly sad

3. SORDID
   (A) biting
   (B) filthy
   (C) mysterious
   (D) grief-stricken
   (E) sickly

4. CATACLYSM
   (A) severe criticism
   (B) gorge
   (C) launching device
   (D) unconsciousness
   (E) violent upheaval

5. FETTERED
   (A) stricken
   (B) scolded
   (C) commanded
   (D) confined
   (E) loosened

6. VERACITY
   (A) endurance
   (B) selfishness
   (C) truthfulness
   (D) courtesy
   (E) thoughtfulness

7. REPLETE
   (A) filled
   (B) tarnished
   (C) golden
   (D) economical
   (E) wrecked

8. TREED
   (A) met
   (B) cornered
   (C) followed
   (D) searched
   (E) scented

9. DERISIVE
(A) hereditary
(B) rebellious
(C) fragmentary
(D) scornful
(E) determined

10. TEMPER
(A) decorate
(B) annoy
(C) blame
(D) postpone
(E) moderate

Vocabulary Test 78

1. RESIDUE
(A) dwelling
(B) remainder
(C) debt
(D) sample
(E) storehouse

2. BUNGLE
(A) complain
(B) approach
(C) live in
(D) handle badly
(E) talk boastfully

3. ADVOCATE
(A) flatter
(B) caution
(C) recommend
(D) take an oath
(E) charge

4. CALAMITOUS
(A) disastrous
(B) inexperienced
(C) hard-hearted
(D) scheming
(E) slanderous

5. JILT
(A) fill in
(B) cast aside
(C) move about
(D) pick up
(E) help forward

6. FUTILE
(A) violent
(B) one-sided
(C) weary
(D) stingy
(E) useless

7. INCESSANT
(A) even
(B) illegal
(C) dirty
(D) continuous
(E) loud

8. PRATTLE
(A) sell
(B) storm
(C) babble
(D) explain
(E) keep

9. PERVERSE
(A) contrary
(B) rhythmic
(C) imaginary
(D) alert
(E) rich

10. QUARRY
(A) dispute
(B) prey
(C) initial
(D) request
(E) output

Vocabulary Test 79

1. PATERNAL
(A) generous
(B) aged
(C) fatherly
(D) thrifty
(E) narrow-minded

2. CALIBER
(A) gaiety
(B) quality
(C) hope
(D) similarity
(E) politeness

3. PARADOX
(A) virtuous man
(B) equal rights
(C) seeming contradiction
(D) complicated design
(E) geometric figure

4. DISPEL
(A) punish
(B) excite
(C) pay out
(D) drive away
(E) misunderstand

5. VERBATIM
(A) out loud
(B) word for word
(C) in set phrases
(D) elegantly expressed
(E) using too many words

6. GRUELING
(A) exhausting
(B) surprising
(C) insulting
(D) embarrassing
(E) boring

7. CREDIBILITY
(A) freedom from prejudice
(B) religious doctrine
(C) capacity for belief
(D) questioning attitude
(E) good judgment

8. APPROPRIATE
(A) betray
(B) compliment
(C) take possession of
(D) give thanks
(E) draw near to

9. EXONERATE
(A) overcharge
(B) lengthen
(C) leave out
(D) free from blame
(E) serve as a model

10. BLAND
(A) flattering
(B) foolish
(C) successful
(D) soothing
(E) sharp

Vocabulary Test 80

1. EFFIGY
(A) representation
(B) shadow
(C) parade
(D) ancestor
(E) present

2. ZEST
(A) operation
(B) mood
(C) great dismay
(D) keen enjoyment
(E) false alarm

Vocabulary Test 81

3. ASTUTE
   (A) shrewd
   (B) inflammable
   (C) defiant
   (D) out of tune
   (E) bitter

4. DISCREPANCY
   (A) variance
   (B) disbelief
   (C) feebleness
   (D) insult
   (E) forcefulness

5. COPIOUS
   (A) copyrighted
   (B) tricky
   (C) abundant
   (D) complete
   (E) sincere

6. ADVENT
   (A) approval
   (B) opportunity
   (C) welcome
   (D) recommendation
   (E) arrival

7. IMMINENT
   (A) about to occur
   (B) never-ending
   (C) up-to-date
   (D) inconvenient
   (E) youthful

8. RANKLE
   (A) spread around
   (B) seize quickly
   (C) crease
   (D) search
   (E) irritate deeply

9. INJUNCTION
   (A) exclamation
   (B) rebellion
   (C) directive
   (D) crisis
   (E) illegality

10. DEFT
    (A) critical
    (B) conceited
    (C) lighthearted
    (D) skillful
    (E) tactful

1. HEEDLESS
   (A) unfortunate
   (B) expensive
   (C) careless
   (D) happy
   (E) weather-beaten

2. IMPEDIMENT
   (A) obstacle
   (B) base
   (C) spice
   (D) mechanism
   (E) footstool

3. QUAVER
   (A) launch
   (B) quicken
   (C) sharpen
   (D) tremble
   (E) forget

4. SHACKLE
   (A) hide
   (B) glide
   (C) anger
   (D) quiet
   (E) hamper

5. LOWLY
   (A) idle
   (B) silent
   (C) humble
   (D) sorrowful
   (E) solitary

6. CUBICLE
   (A) wedge
   (B) puzzle
   (C) tiny amount
   (D) unit of measure
   (E) small compartment

7. ARRAIGN
   (A) debate
   (B) accuse
   (C) excite
   (D) cancel
   (E) protect

8. OBLIVIOUS
   (A) unwanted
   (B) disorderly
   (C) unaware
   (D) sickly
   (E) evident

9. PROFOUND
   (A) plentiful
   (B) beneficial
   (C) lengthy
   (D) religious
   (E) deep

10. WAN
    (A) pale
    (B) humorous
    (C) pleasing
    (D) watchful
    (E) lovesick

Vocabulary Test 82

1. HAUNT
   (A) contain
   (B) give up
   (C) expect
   (D) stay around
   (E) extend greatly

2. UNMINDFUL
   (A) unaware
   (B) illogical
   (C) unaccustomed
   (D) unchanging
   (E) inefficient

3. EMANCIPATE
   (A) change
   (B) overjoy
   (C) bring forward
   (D) raise up
   (E) set free

4. LOLL
   (A) find
   (B) respect
   (C) lounge
   (D) steal
   (E) trap

5. SUBSEQUENT
   (A) later
   (B) lower
   (C) thick
   (D) secret
   (E) light

6. CRUCIAL
   (A) reverent
   (B) decisive
   (C) tiresome
   (D) dangerous
   (E) rude

7. REBUKE
(A) prove
(B) dislike
(C) overwork
(D) swallow
(E) criticize

8. CLOISTERED
(A) uneasy
(B) agreeable
(C) sincere
(D) regretful
(E) confined

9. DRONE
(A) beggar
(B) nightmare
(C) queen bee
(D) humming sound
(E) delaying action

10. PEDESTRIAN
(A) clumsy
(B) senseless
(C) curious
(D) learned
(E) commonplace

Vocabulary Test 83

1. DAWDLE
(A) hang loosely
(B) waste time
(C) fondle
(D) splash
(E) paint

2. ANGUISH
(A) torment
(B) boredom
(C) resentment
(D) stubbornness
(E) clumsiness

3. IMPARTIAL
(A) unlawful
(B) incomplete
(C) unprejudiced
(D) unfaithful
(E) unimportant

4. FORESTALL
(A) press
(B) preserve
(C) prevent
(D) boil
(E) restore

5. EFFRONTERY
(A) boldness
(B) agitation
(C) brilliance
(D) toil
(E) talkativeness

6. EMBROIL
(A) explain
(B) entangle
(C) swindle
(D) greet
(E) imitate

7. INCANDESCENT
(A) insincere
(B) melodious
(C) electrical
(D) magical
(E) glowing

8. STENTORIAN
(A) extremely careful
(B) little known
(C) hardly capable
(D) rarely reliable
(E) very loud

9. RENEGADE
(A) retired soldier
(B) public speaker
(C) complainer
(D) traitor
(E) comedian

10. INTERMITTENT
(A) emphatic
(B) stormy
(C) hopeless
(D) innermost
(E) periodic

Vocabulary Test 84

1. INTERLOPER
(A) thief
(B) intruder
(C) translator
(D) inquirer
(E) representative

2. SCATHING
(A) bitterly severe
(B) hastily spoken
(C) unnecessary
(D) ill-advised
(E) easily misunderstood

3. ACRID
(A) abnormal
(B) gifted
(C) insincere
(D) drying
(E) irritating

4. TALISMAN
(A) peddler
(B) mechanic
(C) charm
(D) juryman
(E) metal key

5. DISPATCH
(A) stir up
(B) leave out
(C) glorify
(D) persuade
(E) send away

6. BOOTY
(A) navy
(B) arson
(C) police
(D) voyage
(E) spoils

7. DEMURE
(A) unforgiving
(B) out-of-date
(C) modest
(D) uncooperative
(E) overemotional

8. CRUX
(A) great disappointment
(B) supporting argument
(C) debatable issue
(D) critical point
(E) criminal act

9. AGGRANDIZE
(A) enlarge
(B) condense
(C) astonish
(D) interpret
(E) attack

10. SUMPTUOUS
(A) dictatorial
(B) topmost
(C) radiant
(D) luxurious
(E) additional

Vocabulary Test 85

1. VERSATILE
(A) lonesome
(B) backward
(C) talkative
(D) brave
(E) all-around

2. FORTHRIGHT
(A) frank
(B) joyful
(C) imaginary
(D) conscious
(E) preferred

3. TUSSLE
(A) meet
(B) struggle
(C) confuse
(D) murmur
(E) practice

4. CLARITY
(A) loudness
(B) certainty
(C) clearness
(D) glamour
(E) tenderness

5. ASSESSMENT
(A) appraisal
(B) revision
(C) property
(D) illness
(E) warning

6. CLIQUE
(A) social outcast
(B) ringing sound
(C) headdress
(D) exclusive group
(E) tangled web

7. NEGATE
(A) polish to a bright shine
(B) find quickly
(C) make ineffective
(D) file a protest
(E) take into consideration

8. IMPEL
(A) accuse
(B) force
(C) encourage
(D) prevent
(E) pierce

9. CONSTRAINTS
(A) group processes
(B) new laws
(C) doctrines
(D) current news
(E) limits

10. ORTHODOX
(A) accepted
(B) flawless
(C) contradictory
(D) dignified
(E) extraordinary

Vocabulary Test 86

1. COUNTERPART
(A) hindrance
(B) peace offering
(C) password
(D) balance of power
(E) duplicate

2. LOW-KEY
(A) official
(B) secret
(C) restrained
(D) unheard of
(E) complicated

3. STIPULATION
(A) imitation
(B) signal
(C) excitement
(D) agreement
(E) decoration

4. ANTITHESIS
(A) fixed dislike
(B) musical response
(C) lack of feeling
(D) direct opposite
(E) prior knowledge

5. TRANSITORY
(A) short-lived
(B) delayed
(C) idle
(D) unexpected
(E) clear

6. ENTRENCHED
(A) filled up
(B) bordered by
(C) followed by
(D) kept down
(E) dug in

7. LOT
(A) name
(B) right
(C) folly
(D) fate
(E) oath

8. APPREHENSION
(A) gratitude
(B) requirement
(C) apology
(D) dread
(E) punishment

9. AMENABLE
(A) religious
(B) masculine
(C) proud
(D) brave
(E) agreeable

10. AFFLUENT
(A) neutral
(B) sentimental
(C) wealthy
(D) handsome
(E) evil

Vocabulary Test 87

1. VELOCITY
(A) willingness
(B) swiftness
(C) truthfulness
(D) smoothness
(E) skillfulness

2. ENVOY
(A) messenger
(B) assistant
(C) planner
(D) expert
(E) leader

3. AUXILIARY
(A) reliable
(B) mechanical
(C) sociable
(D) supporting
(E) protective

4. PINNACLE
(A) topmost point
(B) feather
(C) fastener
(D) card game
(E) small boat

5. BOORISH
   (A) shy
   (B) rude
   (C) thieving
   (D) cunning
   (E) foreign

6. ENCOMPASS
   (A) include
   (B) measure
   (C) attempt
   (D) direct
   (E) border on

7. LURCH
   (A) trap
   (B) brake
   (C) stagger
   (D) waste time
   (E) laugh noisily

8. EFFACE
   (A) rub out
   (B) paint red
   (C) build upon
   (D) stay in front
   (E) bring about

9. ABOUND
   (A) do good
   (B) store up
   (C) run away
   (D) stand firm
   (E) be plentiful

10. THWART
    (A) avoid
    (B) accuse
    (C) suffer
    (D) block
    (E) serve

Vocabulary Test 88

1. PRUNE
   (A) cut off
   (B) expect
   (C) put away
   (D) lay waste
   (E) remind

2. AMIABLE
   (A) active
   (B) good-natured
   (C) religious
   (D) changeable
   (E) absentminded

3. IMPROVISE
   (A) object loudly
   (B) predict
   (C) refuse support
   (D) prepare offhand
   (E) translate

4. CONNIVE
   (A) cooperate secretly
   (B) enter quickly
   (C) pause slightly
   (D) push unexpectedly
   (E) need greatly

5. GAIT
   (A) turning over and over
   (B) passing in review
   (C) manner of walking
   (D) fundamental attitude
   (E) crowd of spectators

6. BOTCH
   (A) weep
   (B) rebel
   (C) resent
   (D) blunder
   (E) complain

7. DEVOID OF
   (A) accompanied by
   (B) in the care of
   (C) without
   (D) behind
   (E) despite

8. PANG
   (A) feeling of indifference
   (B) sense of duty
   (C) fatal disease
   (D) universal remedy
   (E) spasm of pain

9. TEDIUM
   (A) bad temper
   (B) boredom
   (C) warmth
   (D) abundance
   (E) musical form

10. INTIMATE
    (A) hospitable
    (B) well-behaved
    (C) familiar
    (D) plainly seen
    (E) forgiving

Vocabulary Test 89

1. DELVE
   (A) hope for
   (B) believe in
   (C) set upon
   (D) take into account
   (E) dig into

2. SHROUDED
   (A) found
   (B) torn
   (C) stoned
   (D) wrapped
   (E) rewarded

3. EXPLOIT
   (A) annoy
   (B) join
   (C) use
   (D) mix up
   (E) set free

4. RUT
   (A) fixed practice
   (B) honest labor
   (C) useless regret
   (D) happy home
   (E) vain hope

5. CONSTITUENTS
   (A) tradesmen
   (B) students
   (C) voters
   (D) judges
   (E) ministers

6. REPREHENSIBLE
   (A) distracting
   (B) blameworthy
   (C) glowing
   (D) frightening
   (E) truthful

7. HAZARD
   (A) confuse
   (B) avoid
   (C) resign
   (D) chance
   (E) overlook

8. ROBUST
   (A) bragging
   (B) huge
   (C) sincere
   (D) upright
   (E) sturdy

9. PIECEMEAL
   (A) on the spur of the moment
   (B) bit by bit
   (C) over and over
   (D) as a matter of course
   (E) from first to last

10. INSCRUTABLE
    (A) disorderly
    (B) shallow
    (C) unwritten
    (D) painful
    (E) mysterious

Vocabulary Test 90

1. NEEDLE
   (A) join
   (B) prod
   (C) discuss
   (D) give
   (E) command

2. TENTATIVE
   (A) forgotten
   (B) fabricated
   (C) sunny
   (D) temporary
   (E) absentee

3. HUMDRUM
   (A) false
   (B) ugly
   (C) uninteresting
   (D) mournful
   (E) disappointing

4. RATIFY
   (A) create
   (B) revive
   (C) deny
   (D) confirm
   (E) displease

5. HORDE
   (A) crowd
   (B) framework
   (C) nonbeliever
   (D) choir
   (E) warrior

6. RELENTLESS
   (A) unwise
   (B) fearless
   (C) straightforward
   (D) unappetizing
   (E) unyielding

7. MUDDLE
   (A) saucy remark
   (B) confused mess
   (C) delaying tactics
   (D) simple truth
   (E) great outcry

8. ADULTERATE
   (A) grow up
   (B) push ahead
   (C) make impure
   (D) send away
   (E) die off

9. CONCEDE
   (A) gain
   (B) join
   (C) force
   (D) struggle
   (E) admit

10. PLIGHT
    (A) final decision
    (B) spy system
    (C) plant disease
    (D) bad situation
    (E) listening post

Vocabulary Test 91

1. BURLY
   (A) useless
   (B) wild
   (C) strong
   (D) easy
   (E) medical

2. DEBASE
   (A) call to mind
   (B) send from home
   (C) rely upon
   (D) take part in
   (E) reduce the value of

3. STANCE
   (A) performance
   (B) defense
   (C) length
   (D) posture
   (E) concentration

4. EXACT
   (A) fall
   (B) appeal
   (C) strain
   (D) loosen
   (E) demand

5. DANK
   (A) moist
   (B) unhealthy
   (C) smoky
   (D) frozen
   (E) cloudy

6. EXPRESSLY
   (A) definitely
   (B) regularly
   (C) quickly
   (D) safely
   (E) loudly

7. DISCOUNT
   (A) discover
   (B) disgrace
   (C) disregard
   (D) dislike
   (E) display

8. TOKEN
   (A) timely
   (B) minimal
   (C) stiff
   (D) imaginary
   (E) enforced

9. DECADENCE
   (A) false reasoning
   (B) hasty retreat
   (C) self-assurance
   (D) period of decline
   (E) fraud

10. ALACRITY
    (A) eagerness
    (B) joy
    (C) criticism
    (D) milkiness
    (E) fullness

Vocabulary Test 92

1. CLAMOR
   (A) magic spell
   (B) loose garment
   (C) poisoned arrow
   (D) loud noise
   (E) deep-sea fisherman

2. CONVENTIONAL
   (A) inexperienced
   (B) close
   (C) foolish
   (D) kindly
   (E) usual

Vocabulary Test 93

3. INDISPUTABLE
   (A) unjust
   (B) undeniable
   (C) indelicate
   (D) indescribable
   (E) unconcerned

4. PUNY
   (A) weak
   (B) humorous
   (C) quarrelsome
   (D) studious
   (E) innocent

5. FACILITATE
   (A) make angry
   (B) copy
   (C) make easier
   (D) joke about
   (E) decorate

6. REPULSE
   (A) force
   (B) disown
   (C) restore
   (D) repel
   (E) indicate

7. CHARISMA
   (A) happy feeling
   (B) quality of leadership
   (C) Greek letter
   (D) deep hole
   (E) contrary view

8. RIGOR
   (A) padding
   (B) mold
   (C) liner
   (D) building
   (E) strictness

9. NOXIOUS
   (A) harmful
   (B) lively
   (C) uncertain
   (D) unprepared
   (E) calming

10. ENLIGHTEN
    (A) please
    (B) put away
    (C) instruct
    (D) reduce
    (E) criticize

1. INTANGIBLE
   (A) incomplete
   (B) individual
   (C) vagile
   (D) uninjured
   (E) careless

2. COMPLIANT
   (A) yielding
   (B) standing
   (C) admiring
   (D) trusting
   (E) grabbing

3. ERADICATE
   (A) exclaim
   (B) heat up
   (C) break out
   (D) plant
   (E) eliminate

4. ABYSS
   (A) great ignorance
   (B) evil man
   (C) bottomless pit
   (D) wide sea
   (E) religious sign

5. CRITERION
   (A) standard
   (B) award
   (C) achievement
   (D) objection
   (E) claim

6. IRREVERENT
   (A) illogical
   (B) unimportant
   (C) violent
   (D) disrespectful
   (E) unafraid

7. SALLOW
   (A) temporary
   (B) animal-like
   (C) stupid
   (D) clean
   (E) yellowish

8. RENOUNCE
   (A) proclaim
   (B) approve
   (C) give up
   (D) guarantee
   (E) speak plainly

9. ASSIMILATE
   (A) pretend
   (B) absorb
   (C) poke
   (D) copy
   (E) expect

10. EXHORT
    (A) annoy
    (B) deduct
    (C) enlarge quickly
    (D) urge strongly
    (E) stick out

Vocabulary Test 94

1. JEST
   (A) spout
   (B) trot
   (C) joke
   (D) judge
   (E) leap

2. MOLEST
   (A) disturb
   (B) reduce
   (C) submit
   (D) delight
   (E) urge

3. TURMOIL
   (A) conclusion
   (B) reversal
   (C) meanness
   (D) confusion
   (E) mistake

4. ORDINANCE
   (A) trial
   (B) law
   (C) right
   (D) fault
   (E) property

5. LATERAL
   (A) financial
   (B) lingering
   (C) of the past
   (D) from the beginning
   (E) to the side

6. PIGMENT
   (A) light
   (B) pillar
   (C) dye
   (D) weed
   (E) book

7. CONCEPT
(A) desire
(B) thought
(C) solution
(D) method
(E) experiment

8. ORNATE
(A) elaborate
(B) original
(C) systematic
(D) unbecoming
(E) obsolete

9. BEGRUDGE
(A) roar mightily
(B) walk swiftly
(C) give reluctantly
(D) await eagerly
(E) seek desperately

10. REPOSE
(A) task
(B) calm
(C) strain
(D) fact
(E) surprise

Vocabulary Test 95

1. BOLSTER
(A) reinforce
(B) thicken
(C) uncover
(D) quote
(E) bother

2. INFRINGEMENT
(A) old age
(B) added benefit
(C) protection
(D) violation
(E) fireproofing

3. AGILE
(A) colored
(B) healthy
(C) dull
(D) false
(E) nimble

4. DIVERSIFY
(A) fix
(B) vary
(C) correct
(D) relieve
(E) explain

5. RUSTLE
(A) steal
(B) instruct
(C) strive
(D) bend
(E) tax

6. HAPLESS
(A) optimistic
(B) uncounted
(C) unfortunate
(D) simple
(E) unyielding

7. UNPRETENTIOUS
(A) loyal
(B) virtuous
(C) modest
(D) fair
(E) extravagant

8. BUOY
(A) wet
(B) dry up
(C) rescue
(D) sustain
(E) direct

9. PARAGON
(A) weak pun
(B) even distribution
(C) geometric figure
(D) moralistic story
(E) model of excellence

10. INDIGENOUS
(A) confused
(B) native
(C) poor
(D) unconcerned
(E) wrathful

Vocabulary Test 96

1. PROLOGUE
(A) stairway
(B) introduction
(C) conversation
(D) reading
(E) extension

2. ACKNOWLEDGE
(A) propose
(B) strangle
(C) convict
(D) advance
(E) admit

3. INDICTMENT
(A) accusation
(B) publisher
(C) announcer
(D) conviction
(E) trial

4. LACKLUSTER
(A) sparkling
(B) tender
(C) misty
(D) uninspired
(E) disobedient

5. CONDOMINIUM
(A) new type of metal
(B) noisy celebration
(C) individually owned
apartment
(D) important decision
(E) group meeting

6. INCUMBENT
(A) office holder
(B) lawyer
(C) politician
(D) green vegetable
(E) sacred honor

7. POLARIZATION
(A) performance in cold
weather
(B) point of view
(C) change in opinion
(D) division into opposites
(E) cultural bias

8. GENESIS
(A) wisdom
(B) origin
(C) classification
(D) humor
(E) night

9. DIMINUTION
(A) devotion
(B) difference
(C) difficulty
(D) decision
(E) decrease

10. WARY
(A) sorrowful
(B) lazy
(C) unfriendly
(D) cautious
(E) hopeful

Vocabulary Test 97

1. SLEEK
   (A) smooth
   (B) moldy
   (C) loose
   (D) small
   (E) delicate

2. SUCCULENT
   (A) literal
   (B) tardy
   (C) yielding
   (D) sportsmanlike
   (E) juicy

3. LACERATED
   (A) bright
   (B) gaunt
   (C) punishable
   (D) torn
   (E) tied

4. SUBSIDE
   (A) pay in full
   (B) become quiet
   (C) return soon
   (D) rush around
   (E) send forth

5. ACQUITTAL
   (A) setting free
   (B) agreeing with
   (C) holding forth
   (D) getting up steam
   (E) appealing to higher authority

6. APPREHEND
   (A) inform
   (B) resound
   (C) frighten
   (D) squeeze
   (E) seize

7. IMPERATIVE
   (A) unbiased
   (B) obscure
   (C) repetitious
   (D) compulsory
   (E) unworthy

8. SUBSTANTIATE
   (A) verify
   (B) replace
   (C) influence
   (D) condemn
   (E) accept

9. RANCID
   (A) illegal
   (B) rotten
   (C) ashen
   (D) flimsy
   (E) mean

10. OUST
    (A) nag
    (B) evict
    (C) excel
    (D) defy
    (E) emerge

Vocabulary Test 98

1. TOPPLE
   (A) drink
   (B) choose
   (C) stray
   (D) stumble
   (E) overturn

2. PREVAIL
   (A) preview
   (B) question
   (C) relax
   (D) triumph
   (E) restore

3. CREDENCE
   (A) cowardice
   (B) size
   (C) belief
   (D) variety
   (E) nobility

4. DIVULGE
   (A) send
   (B) shrink
   (C) despair
   (D) separate
   (E) reveal

5. MISGIVINGS
   (A) cheap gifts
   (B) feelings of doubt
   (C) added treats
   (D) false promises
   (E) slips of the tongue

6. ACCLAIM
   (A) find
   (B) restore
   (C) praise
   (D) judge
   (E) demand

7. HALLOWED
   (A) sacred
   (B) noisy
   (C) deep
   (D) permitted
   (E) costumed

8. GUISE
   (A) ability
   (B) direction
   (C) guilt
   (D) appearance
   (E) mistake

9. TUMULT
   (A) vacation
   (B) reversal
   (C) swelling
   (D) suffering
   (E) commotion

10. REMINISCENT
    (A) amazed by
    (B) obligated to
    (C) suggestive of
    (D) under the control of
    (E) careless with

Vocabulary Test 99

1. REMIT
   (A) promise
   (B) injure
   (C) send
   (D) profit
   (E) menace

2. PANDEMONIUM
   (A) wild uproar
   (B) diseased state
   (C) contempt
   (D) luxury
   (E) gloom

3. EJECT
   (A) expose
   (B) exceed
   (C) extend
   (D) expel
   (E) excite

4. TALLY
   (A) load
   (B) record
   (C) hunt
   (D) play
   (E) move

Vocabulary Test 100

5. DEVASTATE
   (A) cough
   (B) ruin
   (C) chop
   (D) point
   (E) swell

6. MAUL
   (A) trap
   (B) cuddle
   (C) carve
   (D) throw
   (E) beat

7. ANIMATION
   (A) liveliness
   (B) automation
   (C) carelessness
   (D) dispute
   (E) exchange

8. SMOLDER
   (A) show suppressed anger
   (B) grow up quickly
   (C) find easily
   (D) report back
   (E) become weary

9. PROTRUDE
   (A) make a fool of
   (B) fall into
   (C) put down
   (D) thrust out
   (E) steer clear of

10. BENEVOLENT
    (A) profitable
    (B) sociable
    (C) wealthy
    (D) receptive
    (E) charitable

1. UNOBTRUSIVE
   (A) annoying
   (B) unquestionable
   (C) inconspicuous
   (D) united
   (E) healthy

2. SCRUTINY
   (A) signal
   (B) plot
   (C) delay
   (D) investigation
   (E) announcement

3. HEINOUS
   (A) evil
   (B) permanent
   (C) unreasonable
   (D) open
   (E) timid

4. GARRULOUS
   (A) confused
   (B) eager
   (C) panting
   (D) talkative
   (E) informal

5. CONVERSE
   (A) junction
   (B) poetry
   (C) ancestor
   (D) follower
   (E) opposite

6. MALEFACTOR
   (A) fugitive
   (B) joker
   (C) show-off
   (D) evildoer
   (E) daydreamer

7. MARTIAL
   (A) heavenly
   (B) keen
   (C) warlike
   (D) tremendous
   (E) masculine

8. RETORT
   (A) answer
   (B) jot
   (C) retire
   (D) recall
   (E) decay

9. VIGILANCE
   (A) lawlessness
   (B) funeral
   (C) watchfulness
   (D) processional
   (E) strength

10. LESION
    (A) dream
    (B) group
    (C) justice
    (D) style
    (E) injury

Answers to Vocabulary Tests

Test 1	Test 5	Test 9	Test 13	Test 17	Test 21	Test 25	Test 29
1. D	1. C	1. E	1. B	1. A	1. C	1. A	1. B
2. B	2. B	2. C	2. E	2. B	2. E	2. D	2. A
3. D	3. D	3. E	3. B	3. D	3. D	3. E	3. D
4. A	4. D	4. C	4. B	4. E	4. C	4. C	4. E
5. E	5. C	5. D	5. C	5. E	5. B	5. A	5. C
6. B	6. E	6. C	6. C	6. B	6. D	6. B	6. E
7. E	7. A	7. A	7. E	7. D	7. E	7. E	7. B
8. A	8. A	8. D	8. A	8. A	8. D	8. B	8. E
9. E	9. E	9. D	9. D	9. B	9. A	9. C	9. E
10. C	10. C	10. D	10. C	10. D	10. D	10. D	10. C

Test 2	Test 6	Test 10	Test 14	Test 18	Test 22	Test 26	Test 30
1. B	1. C	1. B	1. C	1. E	1. B	1. E	1. E
2. A	2. E	2. E	2. E	2. C	2. D	2. C	2. C
3. E	3. D	3. D	3. C	3. B	3. A	3. A	3. A
4. D	4. C	4. C	4. E	4. C	4. E	4. C	4. B
5. A	5. B	5. B	5. A	5. C	5. E	5. B	5. D
6. E	6. E	6. B	6. E	6. A	6. E	6. E	6. E
7. C	7. B	7. E	7. D	7. E	7. D	7. D	7. D
8. A	8. E	8. B	8. D	8. A	8. A	8. E	8. B
9. B	9. C	9. A	9. E	9. D	9. E	9. D	9. C
10. E	10. D	10. B	10. E	10. A	10. D	10. B	10. A

Test 3	Test 7	Test 11	Test 15	Test 19	Test 23	Test 27	Test 31
1. C	1. E	1. A	1. B	1. B	1. C	1. A	1. B
2. D	2. A	2. D	2. C	2. E	2. D	2. D	2. A
3. B	3. D	3. A	3. A	3. C	3. B	3. C	3. D
4. C	4. D	4. E	4. C	4. D	4. D	4. B	4. A
5. B	5. B	5. A	5. B	5. A	5. D	5. C	5. C
6. B	6. B	6. B	6. E	6. A	6. D	6. B	6. E
7. D	7. B	7. A	7. C	7. D	7. A	7. B	7. D
8. C	8. E	8. E	8. D	8. B	8. B	8. A	8. E
9. A	9. A	9. C	9. A	9. A	9. E	9. A	9. B
10. E	10. B	10. E	10. B	10. B	10. D	10. E	10. A

Test 4	Test 8	Test 12	Test 16	Test 20	Test 24	Test 28	Test 32
1. E	1. D	1. C	1. D	1. A	1. B	1. E	1. E
2. D	2. A	2. D	2. C	2. B	2. B	2. B	2. A
3. E	3. D	3. B	3. D	3. D	3. A	3. C	3. B
4. A	4. E	4. D	4. B	4. B	4. E	4. A	4. D
5. E	5. A	5. B	5. B	5. B	5. E	5. B	5. B
6. A	6. C	6. C	6. A	6. A	6. E	6. D	6. A
7. A	7. A	7. E	7. D	7. C	7. C	7. A	7. C
8. D	8. C	8. B	8. B	8. A	8. E	8. E	8. B
9. E	9. A	9. D	9. A	9. A	9. B	9. A	9. B
10. C	10. D	10. E	10. A	10. E	10. B	10. D	10. E

Test 33	Test 37	Test 41	Test 45	Test 49	Test 53	Test 57	Test 61
1. C	1. C	1. A	1. E	1. B	1. E	1. E	1. B
2. D	2. B	2. D	2. A	2. E	2. E	2. C	2. D
3. B	3. A	3. E	3. D	3. A	3. D	3. B	3. B
4. C	4. C	4. D	4. C	4. C	4. E	4. A	4. D
5. D	5. E	5. C	5. E	5. C	5. B	5. B	5. A
6. E	6. A	6. A	6. B	6. D	6. D	6. A	6. B
7. B	7. D	7. E	7. B	7. D	7. B	7. C	7. D
8. B	8. A	8. B	8. E	8. A	8. D	8. C	8. C
9. A	9. E	9. E	9. D	9. E	9. D	9. D	9. D
10. E	10. E	10. D	10. A	10. C	10. E	10. A	10. B

Test 34	Test 38	Test 42	Test 46	Test 50	Test 54	Test 58	Test 62
1. A	1. D	1. B	1. B	1. A	1. C	1. B	1. D
2. B	2. E	2. E	2. D	2. C	2. D	2. A	2. A
3. E	3. E	3. B	3. C	3. A	3. E	3. E	3. A
4. A	4. A	4. B	4. D	4. C	4. C	4. D	4. D
5. B	5. E	5. B	5. B	5. D	5. C	5. C	5. A
6. D	6. D	6. E	6. E	6. B	6. C	6. D	6. A
7. D	7. C	7. C	7. D	7. B	7. B	7. C	7. D
8. B	8. B	8. D	8. B	8. A	8. E	8. E	8. E
9. B	9. C	9. A	9. A	9. A	9. E	9. D	9. D
10. C	10. A	10. C	10. E	10. B	10. C	10. A	10. B

Test 35	Test 39	Test 43	Test 47	Test 51	Test 55	Test 59	Test 63
1. A	1. E	1. A	1. C	1. D	1. C	1. D	1. B
2. E	2. A	2. B	2. C	2. D	2. B	2. D	2. D
3. B	3. D	3. D	3. D	3. C	3. D	3. D	3. C
4. A	4. C	4. C	4. D	4. B	4. A	4. E	4. E
5. C	5. B	5. E	5. A	5. A	5. C	5. E	5. A
6. D	6. B	6. C	6. A	6. D	6. E	6. B	6. A
7. E	7. A	7. E	7. B	7. B	7. D	7. A	7. D
8. D	8. E	8. D	8. E	8. B	8. E	8. E	8. E
9. B	9. C	9. C	9. C	9. B	9. A	9. E	9. C
10. B	10. D	10. A	10. E	10. A	10. C	10. B	10. B

Test 36	Test 40	Test 44	Test 48	Test 52	Test 56	Test 60	Test 64
1. C	1. A	1. A	1. B	1. B	1. A	1. A	1. B
2. B	2. E	2. A	2. C	2. E	2. A	2. B	2. B
3. C	3. C	3. D	3. E	3. A	3. D	3. C	3. C
4. D	4. B	4. D	4. B	4. B	4. D	4. E	4. E
5. A	5. A	5. B	5. E	5. C	5. A	5. B	5. E
6. D	6. C	6. D	6. A	6. C	6. D	6. B	6. B
7. D	7. D	7. C	7. D	7. B	7. B	7. E	7. C
8. E	8. D	8. A	8. D	8. E	8. B	8. D	8. C
9. A	9. A	9. E	9. B	9. A	9. B	9. C	9. A
10. E	10. D	10. D	10. E	10. A	10. C	10. C	10. D

Test 65	Test 69	Test 73	Test 77	Test 81	Test 85	Test 89	Test 93	Test 97
1. E	1. A	1. D	1. E	1. C	1. E	1. E	1. C	1. A
2. A	2. D	2. E	2. B	2. A	2. A	2. D	2. A	2. E
3. E	3. E	3. B	3. B	3. D	3. B	3. C	3. E	3. D
4. B	4. B	4. E	4. E	4. E	4. C	4. A	4. C	4. B
5. D	5. B	5. D	5. D	5. C	5. A	5. C	5. A	5. A
6. D	6. E	6. C	6. C	6. E	6. D	6. B	6. D	6. E
7. A	7. B	7. E	7. A	7. B	7. C	7. D	7. E	7. D
8. E	8. D	8. E	8. B	8. C	8. B	8. E	8. C	8. A
9. A	9. A	9. C	9. D	9. E	9. E	9. B	9. B	9. B
10. E	10. D	10. D	10. E	10. A	10. A	10. E	10. D	10. B

Test 66	Test 70	Test 74	Test 78	Test 82	Test 86	Test 90	Test 94	Test 98
1. C	1. D	1. A	1. B	1. D	1. E	1. B	1. C	1. E
2. B	2. B	2. C	2. D	2. A	2. C	2. D	2. A	2. D
3. B	3. C	3. E	3. C	3. E	3. D	3. C	3. D	3. C
4. D	4. A	4. D	4. A	4. C	4. D	4. D	4. B	4. E
5. B	5. B	5. B	5. B	5. A	5. A	5. A	5. E	5. B
6. C	6. C	6. B	6. E	6. B	6. E	6. E	6. C	6. C
7. E	7. B	7. C	7. D	7. E	7. D	7. B	7. B	7. A
8. D	8. E	8. C	8. C	8. E	8. D	8. C	8. A	8. D
9. E	9. D	9. D	9. A	9. D	9. E	9. E	9. C	9. E
10. A	10. E	10. A	10. B	10. E	10. C	10. D	10. B	10. C

Test 67	Test 71	Test 75	Test 79	Test 83	Test 87	Test 91	Test 95	Test 99
1. B	1. C	1. B	1. C	1. B	1. B	1. C	1. A	1. C
2. B	2. E	2. D	2. B	2. A	2. A	2. E	2. D	2. A
3. D	3. B	3. B	3. C	3. C	3. D	3. D	3. E	3. D
4. A	4. C	4. C	4. D	4. C	4. A	4. E	4. B	4. B
5. B	5. D	5. E	5. B	5. A	5. B	5. A	5. A	5. B
6. E	6. A	6. A	6. A	6. B	6. A	6. A	6. C	6. E
7. C	7. B	7. A	7. C	7. E	7. C	7. C	7. C	7. A
8. A	8. D	8. D	8. C	8. E	8. A	8. B	8. D	8. A
9. A	9. A	9. E	9. D	9. D	9. E	9. D	9. E	9. D
10. C	10. E	10. C	10. D	10. E	10. D	10. A	10. B	10. E

Test 68	Test 72	Test 76	Test 80	Test 84	Test 88	Test 92	Test 96	Test 100
1. E	1. A	1. B	1. A	1. B	1. A	1. D	1. B	1. C
2. B	2. C	2. C	2. D	2. A	2. B	2. E	2. E	2. D
3. A	3. A	3. D	3. A	3. E	3. D	3. B	3. A	3. A
4. B	4. E	4. A	4. A	4. C	4. A	4. A	4. D	4. D
5. B	5. D	5. C	5. C	5. E	5. C	5. C	5. C	5. E
6. E	6. C	6. E	6. E	6. E	6. D	6. D	6. A	6. D
7. D	7. B	7. D	7. A	7. C	7. C	7. B	7. D	7. C
8. C	8. D	8. A	8. E	8. D	8. E	8. E	8. B	8. A
9. E	9. B	9. E	9. C	9. A	9. B	9. A	9. E	9. C
10. C	10. E	10. B	10. D	10. D	10. C	10. C	10. D	10. E

PART 8

ANALYTICAL WRITING SECTION

There are two sections on the GRE that require you to write an essay.

The first is called **Analyze an Issue**, which requires you to write a response in which you have to discuss the extent to which you agree or disagree with a statement given, citing examples and addressing compelling reasons that could be used to challenge your position.

The second is called **Analyze an Argument**. Each argument consists of a passage that presents an argument followed by specific task instructions that describe how to analyze the argument. You are to write a response to the argument that would explain and support it, weaken it, or describe which assumptions in the argument are unwarranted.

Here are directions for the **Analyze an Issue** part, with an example.

Analytical Writing 1 Test— Analyze an Issue

ANALYZE AN ISSUE

Time—30 minutes

You have 30 minutes to plan and compose a response to the following issue. A response to any other issue will receive a score of zero. Make sure that you respond according to the specific instructions and support your position on the issue with reasons and examples drawn from such areas as your reading, experience, observations, and/or academic studies.

> The best test of an argument is the argument's ability to convince someone with an opposing viewpoint.
>
> Write a response in which you discuss the extent to which you agree or disagree with the statement and explain your reasoning for the position you take. In developing and supporting your position, you should consider ways in which the statement might or might not hold true and explain how these considerations shape your position.

Trained GRE readers will evaluate your response for its overall quality based on how well you:

- Respond to the specific task instructions
- Consider the complexities of the issue
- Organize, develop, and express your ideas
- Support your ideas with relevant reasons and/or examples
- Control the elements of standard written English

Before you begin writing, you may want to think for a few minutes about the issue and the specific task instructions and then plan your response. **Use the next page to plan your response, then write your response starting on the first lined page that follows. A total of four lined pages are provided for your response.** Be sure to develop your position fully and organize it coherently, but leave time to reread what you have written and make any revisions you think are necessary.

Write your response within the boxed area on the pages provided. Any text outside the boxed area will not be scored.

Here are three more examples:

> No field of study can advance significantly unless it incorporates knowledge and experience from outside that field.

Write a response in which you discuss the extent to which you agree or disagree with the statement, and explain your reasoning for the position you take. In developing and supporting your position, you should consider ways in which the statement might or might not hold true and explain how these considerations shape your position.

Claim: When planning courses, educators should take into account the interests and suggestions of their students. Reason: Students are more motivated to learn when they are interested in what they are studying.

Write a response in which you discuss the extent to which you agree or disagree with the claim and the reason on which that claim is based.

There is little justification for society to make extraordinary efforts—especially at a great cost in money and jobs—to save endangered animal or plant species.

Write a response in which you discuss the extent to which you agree or disagree with the statement, and explain your reasoning for the position you take. In developing and supporting your position, you should consider ways in which the statement might or might not hold true and explain how these considerations shape your position.

Scoring the "Analyze an Issue" Analytical Writing 1 Section

GRE Scoring Guide: Analyze an Issue

Score 6

In addressing the specific task directions, a 6 response presents a cogent, well-articulated analysis of the issue and conveys meaning skillfully.

A typical response in this category:

- articulates a clear and insightful position on the issue in accordance with the assigned task
- develops the position fully with compelling reasons and/or persuasive examples
- sustains a well-focused, well-organized analysis, connecting ideas logically
- conveys ideas fluently and precisely, using effective vocabulary and sentence variety
- demonstrates facility with the conventions of standard written English (i.e., grammar, usage, and mechanics) but may have minor errors

Score 5

In addressing the specific task directions, a 5 response presents a generally thoughtful, well-developed analysis of the issue and conveys meaning clearly.

A typical response in this category:

- presents a clear and well-considered position on the issue in accordance with the assigned task
- develops the position with logically sound reasons and/or well-chosen examples
- is focused and generally well organized, connecting ideas appropriately
- conveys ideas clearly and well, using appropriate vocabulary and sentence variety
- demonstrates facility with the conventions of standard written English but may have minor errors

Score 4

In addressing the specific task directions, a 4 response presents a competent analysis of the issue and conveys meaning with acceptable clarity.

A typical response in this category:

- presents a clear position on the issue in accordance with the assigned task
- develops the position with relevant reasons and/or examples
- is adequately focused and organized
- demonstrates sufficient control of language to express ideas with reasonable clarity
- generally demonstrates control of the conventions of standard written English but may have some errors

Score 3

A 3 response demonstrates some competence in addressing the specific task directions, in analyzing the issue, and in conveying meaning but is obviously flawed.

A typical response in this category exhibits ONE OR MORE of the following characteristics:

- is vague or limited in addressing the specific task directions and/or in presenting or developing a position on the issue
- is weak in the use of relevant reasons or examples or relies largely on unsupported claims
- is poorly focused and/or poorly organized
- has problems in language and sentence structure that result in a lack of clarity
- contains occasional major errors or frequent minor errors in grammar, usage, or mechanics that can interfere with meaning

GRE Scoring Guide: Analyze an Issue (continued)

Score 2

A 2 response largely disregards the specific task directions and/or demonstrates serious weaknesses in analytical writing.

A typical response in this category exhibits ONE OR MORE of the following characteristics:

- is unclear or seriously limited in addressing the specific task directions and/or in presenting or developing a position on the issue
- provides few, if any, relevant reasons or examples in support of its claims
- is unfocused and/or disorganized
- has serious problems in language and sentence structure that frequently interfere with meaning
- contains serious errors in grammar, usage, or mechanics that frequently obscure meaning

Score 1

A 1 response demonstrates fundamental deficiencies in analytical writing.

A typical response in this category exhibits ONE OR MORE of the following characteristics:

- provides little or no evidence of understanding the issue
- provides little evidence of the ability to develop an organized response (i.e., is extremely disorganized and/or extremely brief)
- has severe problems in language and sentence structure that persistently interfere with meaning
- contains pervasive errors in grammar, usage, or mechanics that result in incoherence

Score 0

A typical response in this category is off topic (i.e., provides no evidence of an attempt to respond to the assigned topic), is in a foreign language, merely copies the topic, consists of only keystroke characters, or is illegible or nonverbal.

Sample Analytical Writing Topics, Scored Sample Essay Responses, and Reader Commentary

Issue Essay Responses and Reader Commentary

Sample Issue Task

> As people rely more and more on technology to solve problems, the ability of humans to think for themselves will surely deteriorate.

Discuss the extent to which you agree or disagree with the statement and explain your reasoning for the position you take. In developing and supporting your position, you should consider ways in which the statement might or might not hold true and explain how these considerations shape your position.

NOTE: All responses are reproduced exactly as written, including errors, misspellings, etc., if any.

Essay Response—Score 6

The statement linking technology negatively with free thinking plays on recent human experience over the past century. Surely there has been no time in history where the lived lives of people have changed more dramatically. A quick reflection on a typical day reveals how technology has revolutionized the world. Most people commute to work in an automobile that runs on an internal combustion engine. During the workday, chances are high that the employee will interact with a computer that processes information on silicon bridges that are .09 microns wide. Upon leaving home, family members will be reached through wireless networks that utilize satellites orbiting the earth. Each of these common occurrences could have been inconceivable at the turn of the 19th century.

The statement attempts to bridge these dramatic changes to a reduction in the ability for humans to think for themselves. The assumption is that an increased reliance on technology negates the need for people to think creatively to solve previous quandaries. Looking back at the introduction, one could argue that without a car, computer, or mobile phone, the hypothetical worker would need to find alternate methods of transport, information processing and communication. Technology short circuits this thinking by making the problems obsolete.

However, this reliance on technology does not necessarily preclude the creativity that marks the human species. The prior examples reveal that technology allows for convenience. The car, computer and phone all release additional time for people to live more efficiently. This efficiency does not preclude the need for humans to think for themselves. In fact, technology frees humanity to not only tackle new problems, but may itself create new issues that did not exist without technology. For example, the proliferation of automobiles has introduced a need for fuel conservation on a global scale. With increasing energy demands from emerging markets, global warming becomes a concern inconceivable to the horse-and-buggy generation. Likewise dependence on oil has created nation-states that are not dependent on taxation, allowing ruling parties to oppress minority groups such as women. Solutions to these complex problems require the unfettered imaginations of maverick scientists and politicians.

In contrast to the statement, we can even see how technology frees the human imagination. Consider how the digital revolution and the advent of the internet has allowed for an unprecedented exchange of ideas. WebMD, a popular internet portal for medical information, permits patients to self research symptoms for a more informed doctor visit. This exercise opens pathways of thinking that were previously closed off to the medical layman. With increased interdisciplinary interactions, inspiration can arrive from the most surprising corners. Jeffrey Sachs, one of the architects of the UN Millenium Development Goals, based his ideas on emergency care triage techniques. The unlikely marriage of economics and medicine has healed tense, hyperinflation environments from South America to Eastern Europe.

This last example provides the most hope in how technology actually provides hope to the future of humanity. By increasing our reliance on technology, impossible goals can now be achieved. Consider how the late 20th century witnessed the complete elimination of smallpox. This disease had ravaged the human race since prehistorical days, and yet with the technology of vaccines, free thinking humans dared to imagine a world free of smallpox. Using technology, battle plans were drawn out, and smallpox was systematically targeted and eradicated.

Technology will always mark the human experience, from the discovery of fire to the implementation of nanotechnology. Given the history of the human race, there will be no limit to the number of problems, both new and old, for us to tackle. There is no need to retreat to a Luddite attitude to new things, but rather embrace a hopeful posture to the possibilities that technology provides for new avenues of human imagination.

Reader Commentary for Essay Response—Score 6

The author of this essay stakes out a clear and insightful position on the issue and follows the specific instructions by presenting reasons to support that position. The essay cogently argues that technology does not decrease our ability to think for ourselves but merely provides "additional time for people to live more efficiently." In fact, the problems that have developed alongside the growth of technology (pollution, political unrest in oil-producing nations) actually call for more creative thinking, not less.

In further examples, the essay shows how technology allows for the linking of ideas that may never have been connected in the past (like medicine and economic models), pushing people to think in new ways. Examples are persuasive and fully developed; reasoning is logically sound and well supported.

Ideas in the essay are connected logically, with effective transitions used both between paragraphs ("However" or "In contrast to the statement") and within paragraphs. Sentence structure is varied and complex, and the essay clearly demonstrates facility with the "conventions of standard written English (i.e., grammar, usage, and mechanics)" with only minor errors appearing. Thus, this essay meets all the requirements for receiving a top score, a 6.

Essay Response—Score 5

Surely many of us have expressed the following sentiment, or some variation on it, during our daily commutes to work: "People are getting so stupid these days!" Surrounded as we are by striding and strident automatons with cell phones glued to their ears, PDA's gripped in their palms, and omniscient, omnipresent CNN gleaming in their eyeballs, it's tempting to believe that technology has isolated and infantilized us, essentially transforming us into dependent, conformist morons best equipped to sideswip one another in our SUV's.

Furthermore, hanging around with the younger, pre-commute generation, whom tech-savviness seems to have rendered lethal, is even less reassuring. With "Teen People" style trends shooting through the air from tiger-striped PDA to zebra-striped PDA, and with the latest starlet gossip zipping from juicy Blackberry to teeny, turbo-charged cell phone, technology seems to support young people's worst tendencies to follow the crowd. Indeed, they have seemingly evolved into intergalactic conformity police. After all, today's tech-aided teens are, courtesy of authentic, hands-on video games, literally trained to kill; courtesy of chat and instant text messaging, they have their own language; they even have tiny cameras to efficiently photodocument your fashion blunders! Is this adolescence, or paparazzi terrorist training camp?

With all this evidence, it's easy to believe that tech trends and the incorporation of technological wizardry into our everyday lives have served mostly to enforce conformity, promote dependence, heighten comsumerism and materialism, and generally create a culture that values self-absorption and personal entitlement over cooperation and collaboration. However, I argue that we are merely in the inchoate stages of learning to live with technology while still loving one another. After all, even given the examples provided earlier in this essay, it seems clear that technology hasn't impaired our thinking and problem-solving capacities. Certainly it has incapacitated our behavior and manners; certainly our values have taken a severe blow. However, we are inarguably more efficient in our badness these days. We're effective worker bees of ineffectiveness!

If technology has so increased our senses of self-efficacy that we can become veritable agents of the awful, virtual CEO's of selfishness, certainly it can be beneficial. Harnessed correctly, technology can improve our ability to think and act for ourselves. The first challenge is to figure out how to provide technology users with some direly-needed direction.

Reader Commentary for Essay Response—Score 5

The language of this essay clearly illustrates both its strengths and weaknesses. The flowery and sometimes uncannily keen descriptions are often used to powerful effect, but at other times this descriptive language results in errors in syntax. See, for example, the problems of parallelism in the second-to-last sentence of paragraph 2 ("After all, today's tech-aided teens…").

There is consistent evidence of facility with syntax and complex vocabulary ("Surrounded as we are by striding and strident automatons with cell phones glued to their ears, PDA's gripped in their palms, and omniscient, omnipresent CNN gleaming in their eyeballs, it's tempting to believe…"). However, such lucid prose is often countered by an overreliance on abstractions and tangential reasoning. For example, what does the fact that video games "literally train [teens] to kill" have to do with the use or deterioration of thinking abilities?

Because this essay takes a complex approach to the issue (arguing, in effect, that technology neither enhances nor reduces our ability to think for ourselves but can do one or the other, depending on the user) and because the author makes use of "appropriate vocabulary and sentence variety," a score of 5 is appropriate.

Essay Response—Score 4

In all actuality, I think it is more probable that our bodies will surely deteriorate long before our minds do in any significant amount. Who can't say that technology has made us lazier, but that's the key word, lazy, not stupid. The ever increasing amount of technology that we incorporate into our daily lives makes people think and learn every day, possibly more than ever before. Our abilities to think, learn, philosophize, etc. may even reach limits never dreamed of before by average people. Using technology to solve problems will continue to help us realize our potential as a human race.

If you think about it, using technology to solve more complicating problems gives humans a chance to expand their thinking and learning, opening up whole new worlds for many people. Many of these people are glad for the chance to expand their horizons by learning more, going to new places, and trying new things. If it wasn't for the invention of new technological devices, I wouldn't be sitting at this computer trying to philosophize about technology. It would be extremely hard for children in much poorer countries to learn and think for themselves with out the invention of the internet. Think what an impact the printing press, a technologically superior machine at the time, had on the ability of the human race to learn and think.

Right now we are seeing a golden age of technology, using it all the time during our every day lives. When we get up there's instant coffee and the microwave and all these great things that help us get ready for our day. But we aren't allowing our minds to deteriorate by using them, we are only making things easier for ourselves and saving time for other important things in our days. Going off to school or work in our cars instead of a horse and buggy. Think of the brain power and genius that was used to come up with that single invention that has changed the way we move across this globe.

Using technology to solve our continually more complicated problems as a human race is definately a good thing. Our ability to think for ourselves isn't deteriorating, it's continuing to grow, moving on to higher though functions and more ingenious ideas. The ability to use what technology we have is an example.

Reader Commentary for Essay Response—Score 4

This essay meets all the criteria of a level-4 essay. The writer develops a clear position ("Using technology to solve problems will continue to help us realize our potential as a human race"). The position is then developed with relevant reasons ("using technology to solve more complicat[ed] problems gives humans a chance to expand their thinking and learning" and "we are seeing a golden age of technology").

Point 1, "using technology," is supported with the simple but relevant notion that technology allows us access to information and abilities to which we would not normally have access. Similarly, point 2, the "golden age," is supported by the basic description of our technologically saturated social condition. Though the overall development and organization of the essay does suffer from an occasional misdirection (see paragraph 3's abrupt progression from coffeepots to the benefits of technology to cars), the essay as a whole flows smoothly and logically from one idea to the next.

It is useful to compare this essay to the level-3 essay presented next. Though both essays entail some surface-level discussion and often fail to probe deeply

into the issue, this writer does take the analysis a step further. In paragraph 2, the distinction between this essay and the next one (the level-3 response) can most clearly be seen. To support the notion that advances in technology actually help increase thinking ability, the writer draws a clever parallel between the promise of modern, sophisticated technology (computer) and the actual impact of equally promising and pervasive technologies of the past (printing press).

Like the analysis, the language in this essay clearly meets the requirements for a score of 4. The writer displays sufficient control of language and the conventions of standard written English. The preponderance of mistakes is of a cosmetic nature ("trying to solve more complicating problems"). There is a sentence fragment ("Going off…") along with a comma splice ("Our ability…isn't deteriorating, it's continuing to grow…") in paragraph 4. However, these errors are minor and do not interfere with the clarity of the ideas being presented.

Essay Response—Score 3

There is no current proof that advancing technology will deteriorate the ability of humans to think. On the contrary, advancements in technology had advanced our vast knowledge in many fields, opening opportunities for further understanding and achievement. For example, the problem of dibilitating illnesses and diseases such as alzheimer's disease is slowing being solved by the technological advancements in stem cell research. The future ability of growing new brain cells and the possibility to reverse the onset of alzheimer's is now becoming a reality. This shows our initiative as humans to better our health demonstrates greater ability of humans to think.

One aspect where the ability of humans may initially be seen as an example of deteriorating minds is the use of internet and cell phones. In the past humans had to seek out information in many different enviroments and aspects of life. Now humans can sit in a chair and type anything into a computer and get an answer. Our reliance on this type of technology can be detrimental if not regulated and regularily substituted for other information sources such as human interactions and hands on learning. I think if humans understand that we should not have such a reliance on computer technology, that we as a species will advance further by utilizing the opportunity of computer technology as well as the other sources of information outside of a computer. Supplementing our knowledge with internet access is surely a way for technology to solve problems while continually advancing the human race.

Reader Commentary for Essay Response—Score 3

This essay never moves beyond a superficial discussion of the issue. The writer attempts to develop two points: that advancements in technology have advanced our knowledge in many fields and that supplementing rather than relying on technology is "surely a way for technology to solve problems while continually advancing the human race." Each point, then, is developed with relevant but insufficient evidence. In discussing the potential of technology to advance knowledge in many fields (a broad subject, rife with possible examples), the writer uses only one limited and very brief example from a specific field (medicine and stem cell research).

Development of the second point is hindered by a lack of specificity and organization. The writer creates what might be best described as an outline. The writer cites a need for regulation/supplementation and warns of the detriment of overreliance upon technology. However, the explanation of both the problem and solution is vague and limited ("Our reliance...can be detrimental...If humans understand that we should not have such a reliance...we...will advance further"). There is neither explanation of consequences nor clarification of what is meant by "supplementing." This second paragraph is a series of generalizations that are loosely connected and lack a much-needed grounding.

In the essay, there are some minor language errors and a few more serious flaws (e.g., "The future ability of growing new brain cells" or "One aspect where the ability of humans may initially be seen as an example of deteriorating minds"). Despite the accumulation of such flaws, the writer's meaning is generally clear. Because of its limited development, however, this essay earns a score of 3.

Essay Response—Score 2

In recent centuries, humans have developed the technology very rapidly, and you may accept some merit of it, and you may see a distortion in society occured by it. To be lazy for human in some meaning is one of the fashion issues in thesedays. There are many symptoms and resons of it. However, I can not agree with the statement that the technology make humans to be reluctant to thinkng thoroughly.

Of course, you can see the phenomena of human laziness along with developed technology in some place. However, they would happen in specific condition, not general. What makes human to be laze of thinking is not merely technology, but the the tendency of human that they treat them as a magic stick and a black box. Not understanding the aims and theory of them couses the disapproval problems.

The most important thing to use the thechnology, regardless the new or old, is to comprehend the fundamental idea of them, and to adapt suit tech to tasks in need. Even if you recognize a method as a all-mighty and it is extremely over-spec to your needs, you cannot see the result you want. In this procedure, humans have to consider as long as possible to acquire adequate functions. Therefore, humans can not escape from using their brain.

In addition, the technology as it is do not vain automatically, the is created by humans. Thus, the more developed tech and the more you want a convenient life, the more you think and emmit your creativity to breakthrough some banal method sarcastically.

Consequently, if you are not passive to the new tech, but offensive to it, you would not lose your ability to think deeply. Furthermore, you may improve the ability by adopting it.

Reader Commentary for Essay Response—Score 2

The language of this essay is what most clearly links it to the score of 2. Amid sporadic moments of clarity, this essay is marred by serious errors in grammar, usage, and mechanics that often interfere with meaning. It is unclear what the writer means when he/she states, "To be lazy for human in some meaning is one of the fashion issues in thesedays," or "to adapt suit tech to tasks in need."

Despite such severe flaws, the writer has made an obvious attempt to respond to the prompt ("I can not agree with the statement that the technology make humans to be reluctant to thinking thoroughly") as well as an unclear attempt to support such an assertion ("Not understanding the aims and theory of them [technology] couses the disapproval problems" and "The most important thing to use the thechnology...is to comprehend the fundamental idea of them"). On the whole, the essay displays a seriously flawed but not fundamentally deficient attempt to develop and support its claims.

(NOTE: In this specific case, the analysis is tied directly to the language. As the language falters, so too does the analysis.)

Essay Response—Score 1

Humans have invented machines but they have forgot it and have started everything technically so clearly their thinking process is deterioating.

Reader Commentary for Essay Response—Score 1

The essay is clearly on topic, as evidenced by the writer's usage of the more significant terms from the prompt: "technically" (technologically), "humans," "thinking" (think), and "deterio[r]ating" (deteriorate). Such usage is the only clear evidence of understanding. Meaning aside, the brevity of the essay (one sentence) clearly indicates the writer's inability to develop a response that follows the specific instructions given ("Discuss the extent to which you agree or disagree with the statement and explain your reasoning for the position you take").

The language, too, is clearly level 1, as the sentence fails to achieve coherence. The coherent phrases in this one-sentence response are those tied to the prompt: "Humans have invented machines" and "their thinking process is deterio[r]ating." Otherwise, the point being made is unclear.

Here are directions for the **Analyze an Argument** part with an example.

Analytical Writing 2 Test— Analyze an Argument

ANALYZE AN ARGUMENT

Time—30 minutes

You have 30 minutes to plan and compose a response in which you evaluate the argument passage that appears below. A response to any other argument will receive a score of zero. Make sure that you respond according to the specific instructions and support your evaluation with relevant reasons and/or examples.

Note that you are NOT being asked to present your own views on the subject.

> The following appeared in an article in the *Grandview Beacon*.
>
> "For many years the city of Grandview has provided annual funding for the Grandview Symphony. Last year, however, private contributions to the symphony increased by 200 percent and attendance at the symphony's concerts-in-the-park series doubled. The symphony has announced an increase in ticket prices for next year. Given such developments, some city commissioners argue that the symphony can now be fully self-supporting, and they recommend that funding for the symphony be eliminated from next year's budget."

Write a response in which you discuss what questions would need to be answered in order to decide whether the recommendations and argument on which it is based are reasonable. Be sure to explain how the answers to these questions would help to evaluate the recommendation.

Trained GRE readers will evaluate your response for its overall quality based on how well you:

- Respond to the specific task instructions
- Consider the complexities of the issue
- Organize, develop, and express your ideas
- Support your ideas with relevant reasons and/or examples
- Control the elements of standard written English

Before you begin writing, you may want to think for a few minutes about the issue and the specific task instructions and then plan your response. **Use the next page to plan your response, then write your response starting on the first lined page that follows. A total of four lined pages are provided for your response.** Be sure to develop your position fully and organize it coherently, but leave time to reread what you have written and make any revisions you think are necessary.

Write your response within the boxed area on the pages provided. Any text outside the boxed area will not be scored.

Here are three more examples:

The following appeared in a health magazine published in Corpora.

"Medical experts say that only one-quarter of Corpora's citizens meet the current standards for adequate physical fitness, even though twenty years ago, one-half of all of Corpora's citizens met the standards as then defined. But these experts are mistaken when they suggest that spending too much time using computers has caused a decline in fitness. Since overall fitness levels are highest in the regions of Corpora where levels of computer ownership are also highest, it is clear that using computers has not made citizens less physically fit. Instead, as shown by this year's unusually low expenditures on fitness-related products and services, the recent decline in the economy is most likely the cause, and fitness levels will improve when the economy does."

Write a response in which you examine the stated and/or unstated assumptions of the argument. Be sure to explain how the argument depends on these assumptions and what the implications are for the argument if the assumptions prove unwarranted.

The following is a memorandum from the business manager of a television station.

"Over the past year, our late-night news program has devoted increased time to national news and less time to weather and local news. During this time period, most of the complaints received from viewers were concerned with our station's coverage of weather and local news. In addition, local businesses that used to advertise during our late-night news program have just canceled their advertising contracts with us. Therefore, in order to attract more viewers to the program and to avoid losing any further advertising revenue, we should restore the time devoted to weather and local news to its former level."

Write a response in which you discuss what specific evidence is needed to evaluate the argument and explain how the evidence would weaken or strengthen the argument.

The following appeared in a memo from the vice president of a food distribution company with food storage warehouses in several cities.

"Recently, we signed a contract with the Fly-Away Pest Control Company to provide pest control services at our fast-food warehouse in Palm City, but last month we discovered that over $20,000 worth of food there had been destroyed by pest damage. Meanwhile, the Buzzoff Pest Control Company, which we have used for many years, continued to service our warehouse in Wintervale, and last month only $10,000 worth of the food stored there had been destroyed by pest damage. Even though the price charged by Fly-Away is considerably lower, our best means of saving money is to return to Buzzoff for all our pest control services."

Write a response in which you discuss what specific evidence is needed to evaluate the argument and explain how the evidence would weaken or strengthen the argument.

Scoring the "Analyze an Argument" Analytical Writing 2 Section

GRE Scoring Guide: Analyze an Argument

Score 6

In addressing the specific task directions, a 6 response presents a cogent, well-articulated examination of the argument and conveys meaning skillfully.

A typical response in this category:

- clearly identifies aspects of the argument relevant to the assigned task and examines them insightfully
- develops ideas cogently, organizes them logically, and connects them with clear transitions
- provides compelling and thorough support for its main points
- conveys ideas fluently and precisely, using effective vocabulary and sentence variety
- demonstrates facility with the conventions of standard written English (i.e., grammar, usage, and mechanics) but may have minor errors

Score 5

In addressing the specific task directions, a 5 response presents a generally thoughtful, well-developed examination of the argument and conveys meaning clearly.

A typical response in this category:

- clearly identifies aspects of the argument relevant to the assigned task and examines them in a generally perceptive way
- develops ideas clearly, organizes them logically, and connects them with appropriate transitions
- offers generally thoughtful and thorough support for its main points
- conveys ideas clearly and well, using appropriate vocabulary and sentence variety
- demonstrates facility with the conventions of standard written English but may have minor errors

Score 4

In addressing the specific task directions, a 4 response presents a competent examination of the argument and conveys meaning with acceptable clarity.

A typical response in this category:

- identifies and examines aspects of the argument relevant to the assigned task but may also discuss some extraneous points
- develops and organizes ideas satisfactorily, but may not connect them with transitions
- supports its main points adequately but may be uneven in its support
- demonstrates sufficient control of language to convey ideas with reasonable clarity
- generally demonstrates control of the conventions of standard written English but may have some errors

Score 3

A 3 response demonstrates some competence in addressing the specific task directions, in examining the argument, and in conveying meaning but is obviously flawed.

A typical response in this category exhibits ONE OR MORE of the following characteristics:

- does not identify or examine most of the aspects of the argument relevant to the assigned task, although some relevant examination of the argument is present
- mainly discusses tangential or irrelevant matters or reasons poorly
- is limited in the logical development and organization of ideas
- offers support of little relevance and value for its main points
- has problems in language and sentence structure that result in a lack of clarity
- contains occasional major errors or frequent minor errors in grammar, usage, or mechanics that can interfere with meaning

GRE Scoring Guide: Analyze an Argument (continued)

Score 2

A 2 response largely disregards the specific task directions and/or demonstrates serious weaknesses in analytical writing.

A typical response in this category exhibits ONE OR MORE of the following characteristics:

- does not present an examination based on logical analysis but may instead present the writer's own views on the subject; does not follow the directions for the assigned task
- does not develop ideas or is poorly organized and illogical
- provides little, if any, relevant or reasonable support for its main points
- has serious problems in language and sentence structure that frequently interfere with meaning
- contains serious errors in grammar, usage, or mechanics that frequently obscure meaning

Score 1

A 1 response demonstrates fundamental deficiencies in analytical writing.

A typical response in this category exhibits ONE OR MORE of the following characteristics:

- provides little or no evidence of understanding the argument
- provides little evidence of the ability to develop an organized response (i.e., is extremely disorganized and/or extremely brief)
- has severe problems in language and sentence structure that persistently interfere with meaning
- contains pervasive errors in grammar, usage, or mechanics that result in incoherence

Score 0

A typical response in this category is off topic (i.e., provides no evidence of an attempt to respond to the assigned topic), is in a foreign language, merely copies the topic, consists of only keystroke characters, or is illegible or nonverbal.

Analytical Writing Score Level Descriptions

Although the GRE Analytical Writing measure contains two discrete analytical writing tasks, a single combined score is reported, because it is more reliable than a score for either task alone. The reported score, the average of the scores for the two tasks, ranges from 0 to 6, in half-point increments.

The following statements describe, for each score level, the overall quality of analytical writing demonstrated across both the Issue and Argument tasks. Because the test assesses "analytical writing," critical thinking skills (the ability to reason, to assemble evidence to develop a position, and to communicate complex ideas) weigh more heavily than the writer's control of fine points of grammar or the mechanics of writing (e.g., spelling).

SCORES 6 and 5.5: Sustains insightful, in-depth analysis of complex ideas; develops and supports main points with logically compelling reasons and/or highly persuasive examples; is well focused and well organized; skillfully uses sentence variety and precise vocabulary to convey meaning effectively; demonstrates superior facility with sentence structure and language usage but may have minor errors that do not interfere with meaning.

SCORES 5 and 4.5: Provides generally thoughtful analysis of complex ideas; develops and supports main points with logically sound reasons and/or well-chosen examples; is generally focused and well organized; uses sentence variety and vocabulary to convey meaning clearly; demonstrates good control of sentence structure and language usage but may have minor errors that do not interfere with meaning.

SCORES 4 and 3.5: Provides competent analysis of ideas; develops and supports main points with relevant reasons and/or examples; is adequately organized; conveys meaning with reasonable clarity; demonstrates satisfactory control of sentence structure and language usage but may have some errors that affect clarity.

SCORES 3 and 2.5: Displays some competence in analytical writing, although the writing is flawed in at least one of the following ways: limited analysis or development; weak organization; weak control of sentence structure or language usage, with errors that often result in vagueness or lack of clarity.

SCORES 2 and 1.5: Displays serious weaknesses in analytical writing. The writing is seriously flawed in at least one of the following ways: serious lack of analysis or development; lack of organization; serious and frequent problems in sentence structure or language usage, with errors that obscure meaning.

SCORES 1 and 0.5: Displays fundamental deficiencies in analytical writing. The writing is fundamentally flawed in at least one of the following ways: content that is extremely confusing or mostly irrelevant to the assigned tasks; little or no development; severe and pervasive errors that result in incoherence.

SCORE 0: The examinee's analytical writing skills cannot be evaluated because the responses do not address any part of the assigned tasks, are merely attempts to copy the assignments, are in a foreign language, or display only indecipherable text.

SCORE "NS": The examinee produced no text whatsoever.

Sample Argument Essay Responses and Reader Commentary

Sample Argument Task

> In surveys, Mason City residents rank water sports (swimming, boating, and fishing) among their favorite recreational activities. The Mason River flowing through the city is rarely used for these pursuits, however, and the city park department devotes little of its budget to maintaining riverside recreational facilities. For years there have been complaints from residents about the quality of the river's water and the river's smell. In response, the state has recently announced plans to clean up Mason River. Use of the river for water sports is therefore sure to increase. The city government should for that reason devote more money in this year's budget to riverside recreational facilities.
>
> Write a response in which you examine the stated and/or unstated assumptions of the argument. Be sure to explain how the argument depends on the assumptions and what the implications are if these assumptions prove unwarranted.

NOTE: All responses are reproduced exactly as written, including errors, misspellings, etc., if any.

Essay Response—Score 6

While it may be true that the Mason City government ought to devote more money to riverside recreational facilities, this author's argument does not make a cogent case for increased resources based on river use. It is easy to understand why city residents would want a cleaner river, but this argument is rife with holes and assumptions, and thus, not strong enough to lead to increased funding.

Citing surveys of city residents, the author reports city resident's love of water sports. It is not clear, however, the scope and validity of that survey. For example, the survey could have asked residents if they prefer using the river for water sports or would like to see a hydroelectric dam built, which may have swayed residents toward river sports. The sample may not have been representative of city residents, asking only those residents who live upon the river. The survey may have been 10 pages long, with 2 questions dedicated to river sports. We just do not know. Unless the survey is fully representative, valid, and reliable, it can not be used to effectively back the author's argument.

Additionally, the author implies that residents do not use the river for swimming, boating, and fishing, despite their professed interest, because the water is polluted and smelly. While a polluted, smelly river would likely cut down on river sports, a concrete connection between the resident's lack of river use and the river's current state is not effectively made. Though there have been complaints, we do not know if there have been numerous complaints from a wide range of people, or perhaps from one or two individuals who made numerous complaints. To strengthen his/her argument, the author would benefit from implementing a normed survey asking a wide range of residents why they do not currently use the river.

Building upon the implication that residents do not use the river due to the quality of the river's water and the smell, the author suggests that a river clean up will result in increased river usage. If the river's water quality and smell result from problems which can be cleaned, this may be true. For example, if the decreased water quality and aroma is caused by pollution by factories along the river, this conceivably could be remedied. But if the quality and aroma results from the natural mineral deposits in the water or surrounding rock, this may not be true. There are some bodies of water which emit a strong smell of sulphur due to the geography of the area. This is not something likely to be afffected by a clean-up. Consequently, a river clean up may have no impact upon river usage. Regardless of whether the river's quality is able to be improved or not, the author does not effectively show a connection between water quality and river usage.

A clean, beautiful, safe river often adds to a city's property values, leads to increased tourism and revenue from those who come to take advantage of the river, and a better overall quality of life for residents. For these reasons, city government may decide to invest in improving riverside recreational facilities. However, this author's argument is not likely significantly persuade the city goverment to allocate increased funding.

Reader Commentary for Essay Response—Score 6

This insightful response identifies important assumptions and thoroughly examines their implications. The proposal to spend more on riverside recreational facilities rests on several questionable assumptions, namely:

- that the survey provides a reliable basis for budget planning
- that the river's pollution and odor are the only reasons for its limited recreational use
- that efforts to clean the water and remove the odor will be successful

By showing that each assumption is highly suspect, this essay demonstrates the weakness of the entire argument. For example, paragraph 2 points out that the survey might not have used a representative sample, might have offered limited choices, and might have contained very few questions on water sports.

Paragraph 3 examines the tenuous connection between complaints and limited use of the river for recreation. Complaints about water quality and odor may be coming from only a few people and, even if such complaints are numerous, other completely different factors may be much more significant in reducing river usage. Finally, paragraph 4 explains that certain geologic features may prevent effective river cleanup. Details such as these provide compelling support.

In addition, careful organization ensures that each new point builds upon the previous ones. For example, note the clear transitions at the beginning of paragraphs 3 and 4, as well as the logical sequence of sentences within paragraphs (specifically paragraph 4).

Although this essay does contain minor errors, it still conveys ideas fluently. Note the effective word choices (e.g., "rife with...assumptions" and "may have swayed residents"). In addition, sentences are not merely varied; they also display skillful embedding of subordinate elements. For example, note the sustained parallelism in the first sentence of the concluding paragraph.

Since this response offers cogent examination of the argument and conveys meaning skillfully, it earns a score of 6.

Essay Response—Score 5

The author of this proposal to increase the budget for Mason City riverside recreational facilities offers an interesting argument but to move forward on the proposal would definitely require more information and thought. While the correlations stated are logical and probable, there may be hidden factors that prevent the City from diverting resources to this project.

For example, consider the survey rankings among Mason City residents. The thought is that such high regard for water sports will translate into usage. But, survey responses can hardly be used as indicators of actual behavior. Many surveys conducted after the winter holidays reveal people who list exercise and weight loss as a top priority. Yet every profession does not equal a new gym membership. Even the wording of the survey results remain ambiguous and vague. While water sports may be among the residents' favorite activities, this allows for many other favorites. What remains unknown is the priorities of the general public. Do they favor these water sports above a softball field or soccer field? Are they willing to sacrifice the municipal golf course for better riverside facilities? Indeed the survey hardly provides enough information to discern future use of improved facilities.

Closely linked to the surveys is the bold assumption that a cleaner river will result in increased usage. While it is not illogical to expect some increase, at what level will people begin to use the river? The answer to this question requires a survey to find out the reasons our residents use or do not use the river. Is river water quality the primary limiting factor to usage or the lack of docks and piers? Are people more interested in water sports than the recreational activities that they are already engaged in? These questions will help the city government forecast how much river usage will increase and to assign a proportional increase to the budget.

Likewise, the author is optimistic regarding the state promise to clean the river. We need to hear the source of the voices and consider any ulterior motives. Is this a campaign year and the plans a campaign promise from the state representative? What is the timeline for the clean-up effort? Will the state fully fund this project? We can imagine the misuse of funds in renovating the riverside facilities only to watch the new buildings fall into dilapidation while the state drags the river cleanup.

Last, the author does not consider where these additional funds will be diverted from. The current budget situation must be assessed to determine if this increase can be afforded. In a sense, the City may not be willing to draw money away from other key projects from road improvements to schools and education. The author naïvely assumes that the money can simply appear without forethought on where it will come from.

Examining all the various angles and factors involved with improving riverside recreational facilities, the argument does not justify increasing the budget. While the proposal does highlight a possibility, more information is required to warrant any action.

Reader Commentary for Essay Response—Score 5

Each paragraph in the body of this perceptive essay identifies and examines an unstated assumption that is crucial to the argument. The major assumptions discussed are:

- that a survey can accurately predict behavior
- that cleaning the river will, in itself, increase recreational usage
- that state plans to clean the river will actually be realized
- that Mason City can afford to spend more on riverside recreational facilities

Support within each paragraph is both thoughtful and thorough. For example, paragraph 2 points out vagueness in the wording of the survey: Even if water sports rank *among* the favorite recreational activities of Mason City residents, other sports may still be much more popular. Thus, if the first assumption proves unwarranted, the argument to fund riverside facilities—rather than soccer fields or golf courses—becomes much weaker. Paragraph 4 considers several reasons why river cleanup plans may not be successful (the plans may be nothing more than campaign promises, or funding may not be adequate). Thus, the weakness of the third assumption undermines the argument that river recreation will increase and riverside improvements will be needed at all.

Instead of dismissing each assumption in isolation, this response places them in a logical order and considers their connections. Note the appropriate transitions between and within paragraphs, clarifying the links among the assumptions (e.g., "Closely linked to the surveys…" or "The answer to this question requires…").

Along with strong development, this response also displays facility with language. Minor errors in punctuation are present, but word choices are apt and sentences suitably varied in pattern and length. The response uses a number of rhetorical questions, but the implied answers are always clear enough to support the points being made.

Thus, the response satisfies all requirements for a score of 5, but its development is not thorough or compelling enough for a 6.

Essay Response—Score 4

The problem with the arguement is the assumption that if the Mason River were cleaned up, that people would use it for water sports and recreation. This is not necessarily true, as people may rank water sports among their favorite recreational activities, but that does not mean that those same people have the financial ability, time or equipment to pursue those interests.

However, even if the writer of the arguement is correct in assuming that the Mason River will be used more by the city's residents, the arguement does not say why the recreational facilities need more money. If recreational facilities already exist along the Mason River, why should the city allot more money to fund them? If the recreational facilities already in existence will be used more in the coming years, then they will be making more money for themselves, eliminating the need for the city government to devote more money to them.

According to the arguement, the reason people are not using the Mason River for water sports is because of the smell and the quality of water, not because the recreational facilities are unacceptable.

If the city government alloted more money to the recreational facilities, then the budget is being cut from some other important city project. Also, if the assumptions proved unwarranted, and more people did not use the river for recreation, then much money has been wasted, not only the money for the recreational facilities, but also the money that was used to clean up the river to attract more people in the first place.

Reader Commentary for Essay Response—Score 4

This competent response identifies some important unstated assumptions:

- that cleaning up the Mason River will lead to increased recreational use
- that existing facilities along the river need more funding

Paragraph 1 offers reasons why the first assumption is questionable (e.g., residents may not have the necessary time or money for water sports). Similarly, paragraphs 2 and 3 explain that riverside recreational facilities may already be adequate and may, in fact, produce additional income if usage increases. Thus, the response is adequately developed and satisfactorily organized to show how the argument depends on questionable assumptions.

However, this essay does not rise to a score of 5 because it fails to consider several other unstated assumptions (e.g., that the survey is reliable or that the efforts to clean the river will be successful). Furthermore, the final paragraph makes some extraneous, unsupported assertions of its own. Mason City may actually have a budget surplus so that cuts to other projects will not be necessary, and cleaning the river may provide other real benefits even if it is not used more for water sports.

This response is generally free of errors in grammar and usage and displays sufficient control of language to support a score of 4.

Essay Response—Score 3

Surveys are created to speak for the people; however, surveys do not always speak for the whole community. A survey completed by Mason City residents concluded that the residents enjoy water sports as a form of recreation. If that is so evident, why has the river not been used? The blame can not be soley be placed on the city park department. The city park department can only do as much as they observe. The real issue is not the residents use of the river, but their desire for a more pleasant smell and a more pleasant sight. If the city government cleans the river, it might take years for the smell to go away. If the budget is changed to accomodate the clean up of the Mason River, other problems will arise. The residents will then begin to complain about other issues in their city that will be ignored because of the great emphasis being placed on Mason River. If more money is taken out of the budget to clean the river an assumption can be made. This assumption is that the budget for another part of city maintenance or building will be tapped into to. In addition, to the budget being used to clean up Mason River, it will also be allocated in increasing riverside recreational facilites. The government is trying to appease its residents, and one can warrant that the role of the government is to please the people. There are many assumptions being made; however, the government can not make the assumption that people want the river to be cleaned so that they can use it for recreational water activities. The government has to realize the long term effects that their decision will have on the monetary value of their budget.

Reader Commentary for Essay Response—Score 3

Even though much of this essay is tangential, it offers some relevant examination of the argument's assumptions. The early sentences mention a questionable assumption (that the survey results are reliable) but do not explain how the survey might have been flawed. Then the response drifts to irrelevant matters—a defense of the city park department, a prediction of budget problems, and the problem of pleasing city residents.

Some statements even introduce unwarranted assumptions that are not part of the original argument (e.g., "The residents will then begin to complain about other issues" and "This assumption is that the budget for another part of city maintenance or building will be tapped into"). Near the end, the response does correctly note that city government should not assume that residents want to use the river for recreation. Hence, the proposal to increase funding for riverside recreational facilities may not be justified.

In summary, the language in this response is reasonably clear, but its examination of unstated assumptions remains limited and therefore the essay earns a score of 3.

Essay Response—Score 2

This statement looks like logical, but there are some wrong sentences in it which is not logical.

First, this statement mentions raking water sports as their favorite recreational activities at the first sentence. However, it seems to have a ralation between the first sentence and the setence which mentions that increase the quality of the river's water and the river's smell. This is a wrong cause and result to solve the problem.

Second, as a reponse to the complaints from residents, the state plan to clean up the river. As a result,

the state expects that water sports will increase. When you look at two sentences, the result is not appropriate for the cause.

Third, the last statement is the conclusion. However, even though residents rank water sports, the city government might devote the budget to another issue. This statement is also a wrong cause and result.

In summary, the statement is not logical because there are some errors in it. The supporting setences are not strong enough to support this issue.

Reader Commentary for Essay Response—Score 2

Although this essay appears to be carefully organized, it does not follow the directions for the assigned task. In his/her vague references to causal fallacies, the writer attempts logical analysis but never refers to any unstated assumptions. Furthermore, several errors in grammar and sentence structure interfere with meaning (e.g., "This statement looks like logical, but there are some wrong sentences in it which is not logical").

Because this response "does not follow the directions for the assigned task" and contains errors in sentence structure and logical development, it earns a score of 2.

Essay Response—Score 1

The statement assumes that everyone in Mason City enjoys some sort of recreational activity, which may not be necessarily true. They statement also assumes that if the state cleans up the river, the use of the river for water sports will definitely increase.

Reader Commentary for Essay Response—Score 1

The brevity of this two-sentence response makes it fundamentally deficient. Sentence 1 states an assumption that is actually not present in the argument, and sentence 2 correctly states an assumption but provides no discussion of its implications. Although the response may begin to address the assigned task, it offers no development. As such, it clearly "provides little evidence of the ability to develop an organized response and is extremely brief" and should earn a score of 1.

Important Tips on How to Write the Best Essay

Making Your Sentences Effective

What Is Style?

Many good ideas are lost because they are expressed in a dull, wordy, involved way. We often have difficulty following—we may even ignore—instructions that are hard to read. Yet we find other instructions written in such a clear and simple way that a child could easily follow them. This way of writing—the words we choose and the way we use them—is called style.

No two people write exactly alike. Even when writing about the same thing, they probably will express ideas differently. Some will say what they think more effectively than others; what they say will be more easily read and understood. But there is seldom any one best way to say something. Rather, there are usually several equally good ways. This flexibility is what makes English such a rich language.

Style can't be taught; each person's style is like personality—it is unique to him or her. But we can each improve our styles. Let us consider how we can improve our writing styles by improving our sentences.

How to Write Effective Sentences

We speak in sentences; we write in sentences. A single word or phrase sometimes carries a complete thought, but sentences are more often the real units of thought communication.

Writing good sentences takes concentration, patience, and practice. It involves much more than just stringing words together, one after another, as they tumble from our minds. If writers aren't careful, their sentences may not mean to the reader what they want them to mean; they may mean what they didn't want them to—or they may mean nothing at all.

This section discusses five things writers can do to write better sentences—or improve sentences already written:

1. Create interest
2. Make your meaning clear
3. Keep your sentences brief
4. Make every word count
5. Vary your sentence patterns

Let's consider interest first.

1. Create Interest

We can make our writing more interesting by writing in an informal, conversational style. This style also makes our writing easier to understand and our readers more receptive to our thoughts.

Listen to two men meeting in the coffee shop. One tells the other, "Let me know when you need more paper clips." But how would he have written it? Probably as follows:

> Request this office be notified when your activity's supply of paper clips, wire, steel gem pattern, large type 1, stock No. 7510-634-6516, falls below 30-day level prescribed in AFR 67-1, Vol. II, Section IV, subject: Office Supplies. Requisition will be submitted as expeditiously as possible to preclude noncompliance with appropriate directives.

Judging from the formal, academic style of much of our writing, we want to *impress* rather than *express*. There seems to be something about writing that brings out our biggest words, our most complex sentences, and our most formal style. Obviously this is not effective writing. We wouldn't dare say it aloud this formally for fear someone would laugh at us, but we will write it.

WRITE TO EXPRESS

One of the best ways to make our writing more interesting to the reader and, hence, more effective, is to write as we talk. Of course we can't write exactly as we talk, and we shouldn't want to. We usually straighten out the sentence structure, make our sentences complete rather than fragmentary or run-on, substitute for obvious slang words, and so on. But we can come close to our conversational style without being folksy, ungrammatical, or wordy. This informal style is far more appropriate for the kind of writing we do and for the kind of readers we have than the old formal style. And it certainly makes better reading.

BE DEFINITE, SPECIFIC, AND CONCRETE

Another way—and one of the surest—to arouse and hold the interest and attention of readers is to be definite, specific, and concrete.

2. Make Your Meaning Clear

You do not need to be a grammarian to recognize a good sentence. After all, the first requirement of grammar is that you focus your reader's attention on the meaning you wish to convey. If you take care to make your meaning clear, your grammar will usually take care of itself. You can, however, do three things to make your meaning clearer to your reader: (1) emphasize your main ideas, (2) avoid wandering sentences, and (3) avoid ambiguity.

EMPHASIZE THE MAIN IDEAS

When we talk, we use gestures, voice changes, pauses, smiles, frowns, and so on to emphasize our main ideas. In writing, we have to use different methods for emphasis. Some are purely mechanical; others are structural.

Mechanical devices include capital letters, underlining or italics, punctuation, and headings. Printers used to capitalize the first letter of a word they wanted to emphasize. We still occasionally capitalize or use a heavier type to emphasize words, phrases, or whole sentences. Sometimes we underline or italicize words that we want to stand out. Often we label or head main sections or subdivisions, as we have done in this book. This effectively separates main ideas and makes them stand out so that the reader doesn't have to search for them.

But mechanical devices for emphasizing an idea—capitalization, particularly—are often overused. The best way to emphasize an idea is to place it effectively in the sentence. The most emphatic position is at the end of the sentence. The next most emphatic position is at the beginning of the sentence. The place of least importance is anywhere in the middle. Remember, therefore, to put the important clause, phrase, name, or idea at the beginning or at the end of your sentences, and never hide the main idea in a subordinate clause or have it so buried in the middle of the sentence that the reader has to dig it out or miss it altogether.

| *Unemphatic:* | People drive on the left side instead of the right side in England. |
| *Better:* | Instead of driving on the right side, people in England drive on the left. |

AVOID WANDERING SENTENCES

All parts of a sentence should contribute to one clear idea or impression. Long, straggling sentences usually contain a hodgepodge of unrelated ideas. You should either break long sentences up into shorter sentences or put the subordinate thoughts into subordinate form. Look at this sentence:

> The sergeant, an irritable fellow who had been a truck driver, born and brought up in the corn belt of Iowa, strong as an ox and six feet tall, fixed an angry eye on the recruit.

You can see that the main idea is "The sergeant fixed an angry eye on the recruit." That he was an irritable fellow, strong as an ox, and six feet tall adds to the main idea. But the facts that he had been a truck driver and had been born in Iowa add nothing to the main thought, and the sentence is better without them.

> The sergeant, an irritable fellow who was strong as an ox and six feet tall, fixed an angry eye on the recruit.

AVOID AMBIGUITY

If a sentence can be misunderstood, it will be misunderstood. A sentence that says, "The truck followed the jeep until its tire blew out," may be perfectly clear to the writer, but it will mean nothing to the reader until the pronoun *its* is identified.

MAKE SURE THAT YOUR MODIFIERS SAY WHAT YOU MEAN

"While eating oats, the farmer took the horse out of the stable." This sentence provides little more than a laugh until you add to the first part of the sentence a logical subject ("the horse"): "While the horse was eating oats, the farmer took him out of the stable." Sometimes simple misplacement of modifiers in sentences leads to misunderstanding: "The young lady went to the dance with her boyfriend wearing a low-cut gown." You can clarify this sentence by simply rearranging it: "Wearing a low-cut gown, the young lady went to the dance with her boyfriend."

3. Keep Your Sentences Brief

Sentences written like 10-word advertisements are hard to read. You cannot get the kind of brevity you want by leaving out the articles (*a*, *an*, and *the*). You can get brevity by dividing complex ideas into bite-size sentences and by avoiding unnecessary words and phrases and needless repetition and elaboration. Here are some suggestions that will help you to write short, straightforward sentences.

USE VERBS THAT WORK

The verb—the action word—is the most important word in a sentence. It is the power plant that supplies the energy, vitality, and motion in the sentence. So, use strong verbs, verbs that really *work* in your sentences.

USE THE ACTIVE VOICE

Sentences written in the basic subject-verb-object pattern are said to be written in the *active voice*. In such sentences, someone or something *does* something to the object—there is a forward movement of the idea. In sentences written in the *passive voice*, the subject merely receives the action—it has something done to it by someone or something, and there is no feeling of forward movement of the idea.

The active voice, in general, is preferable to the passive voice because it helps to give writing a sense of energy, vitality, and motion. When we use the passive voice predominantly, our writing doesn't seem to have much life, the actor in the sentences is not allowed to act, and verbs become weak. So don't rob your writing of its power by using the passive voice when you can use the active voice. Nine out of ten sentences will be both shorter (up to 25 percent shorter) and stronger in the active voice.

Let's compare the two voices:

Active: The pilot flew the aircraft.
       (Actor) *(action)* *(acted upon)*

Passive: The aircraft was flown by the pilot.
       (Acted upon) *(action)* *(actor)*

Now let's see some typical passive examples:

The committee will be appointed by the principal.
Reports have been received…
Provisions will be made by the manager in case of a subway strike.

Aren't these familiar? In most of these, we should be emphasizing the actor rather than leaving out or subordinating him or her.

See how much more effective those sentences are when they are written in the active voice.

The principal will appoint the committee.
We have received reports…
The manager will make provisions in case of a subway strike.

AVOID USING THE PASSIVE VOICE

The passive voice always takes more words to say what could be said just as well (and probably better) in the active voice. In the passive voice, the subject also becomes less personal and may seem less important, and the motion of the sentence grinds to a halt.

There are times, of course, when the passive voice is useful and justified—as when the person or thing doing the action is unknown or unimportant.

When we use the lifeless passive voice indiscriminately, we make our writing weak, ineffective, and dull. Remember that the normal English word order is subject-verb-object. There may be occasions in your writing when you feel that the passive voice is preferable. But should such an occasion arise, think twice before you write; the passive voice rarely improves your style. Before using a passive construction, make certain that you have a specific reason. After using it, check to see that your sentence is not misleading.

TAKE A DIRECT APPROACH

Closely related to passive voice construction is indirect phrasing.

It is requested…
It is recommended…
It has been brought to the attention of…
It is the opinion of…

Again, this is so familiar to us that we don't even question it. But who requested? Who recommended? Who knows? Who believes? No one knows from reading such sentences!

This indirect way of writing, this use of the passive voice and the indirect phrase, is perhaps the most characteristic feature of the formal style of the past. There are many explanations for it. A psychiatrist might say the writer was afraid to take the responsibility for what he or she was writing or was merely passing the buck. The writer may unjustifiably believe this style makes him or her anonymous or makes him or her sound less dogmatic and authoritarian.

Express your ideas immediately and directly. Unnecessary expressions like *it is, there is,* and *there are* weaken sentences and delay comprehension. They also tend to place part of the sentence in the passive voice. *It is the recommendation of the sales manager that the report be forwarded immediately* is more directly expressed as *The sales manager recommends that we send the report immediately.*

Change Long Modifiers to Shorter Ones

Mr. Barnes, who is president of the board, will preside.

Mr. Barnes, the board president, will preside.

Vehicles that are defective are...

Defective vehicles are...

They gave us a month for accomplishment of the task.

They gave us a month to do the job.

Break Up Long Sentences

There is not enough time available for the average executive to do everything that might be done and so it is necessary for him to determine wisely the essentials and do them first, then spend the remaining time on things that are "nice to do."

The average executive lacks time to do everything that might be done. Consequently, he must decide what is essential and do it first. Then he can spend the remaining time on things that are "nice to do."

4. Make Every Word Count

Don't cheat your readers. They are looking for ideas—for meaning—when they read your letter, report, or directive. If they have to read several words that have little to do with the real meaning of a sentence or if they have to read a number of sentences to get just a little meaning, you are cheating them. Much of their time and effort is wasted because they aren't getting full benefit. They expected something that you didn't deliver.

MAKE EACH WORD ADVANCE YOUR THOUGHT

Each word in a sentence should advance the thought of that sentence. To leave a word out would destroy the meaning you are trying to convey.

"Naturally," you say. "Of course!" But reread the last letter you wrote. Aren't some of your sentences rather wordy? Couldn't you have said the same thing in fewer words? And finally, how many times did you use a whole phrase to say what could have been said in one word, or a whole clause for what could have been expressed in a short phrase? In short, try tightening up a sentence like this:

The reason that prices rose was that the demand was increasing at the same time that the production was decreasing.

Rewritten:
Prices rose because the demand increased while production decreased.

Doesn't our rewrite say the same thing as the original? Yet we have saved the reader some effort by squeezing the unnecessary words out of a wordy sentence.

Now try this one:

Wordy: The following statistics serve to give a good idea of the cost of production.
Improved: The following statistics give a good idea of the production costs.

or

These statistics show production costs.

And this one:

Wordy: I have a production supervisor who likes to talk a great deal.

Improved: I have a talkative production supervisor.

In all of those rewritten sentences, we have saved our reader some time. The same thing has been said in fewer words.

Of course you can be *too* concise. If your writing is too brief or terse, it may sound rude and abrupt, and you may lose more than you gain. You need, then, to be politely concise. What you are writing, what you are writing about, and whom you are writing for will help you decide just where to draw the line. However, the general rule, make every word count, still stands. Say what you have to say in as few words as clarity and tact will allow.

CONSOLIDATE IDEAS

A second way to save the reader's effort is to consolidate ideas whenever possible. Pack as much meaning as possible into each sentence *without making the sentence structure too complicated.*

Each sentence is by definition an idea, a unit of thought. Each time the readers read one of these units, they should get as much meaning as possible. It takes just about as much effort to read a sentence with a simple thought as it does to read one with a strong idea or with two or three strong ideas.

There are several things we can do to pack meaning into a sentence. In general, they all have to do with summarizing, combining, and consolidating ideas.

Some people write sentences that are weak and insignificant, both in structure and thought. Ordinarily several such sentences can be summarized and the thought put into one good, mature sentence. Take the following as an example:

> We left Wisconsin the next morning. I remember watching three aircraft. They were F-4s. They were flying very low. I felt sure they were going to crash over a half a dozen times. The F-4 is new to me. I hadn't seen one before.

Rewritten:

> When we left Wisconsin the next morning, I remember watching three F-4s, a type of aircraft I had never seen before. They were flying so low that over a half dozen times I felt sure they were going to crash.

When summarizing like this, be sure to emphasize the main action. Notice in the next example how we have kept the main action as our verb and made the other actions subordinate by changing them to verbals.

Poor: It *was* in 1959 that he *retired* from teaching and he *devoted* his time to *writing* his autobiography. (three verbs, one verbal)

Improved: In 1959 he *retired* from teaching to *devote* his time to *writing* his autobiography. (one verb, two verbals)

Here is an example similar to ones we might find in a directive:

Poor: The evaluation forms will be picked up from your respective personnel office. You should have these completed by 1700 hours, 18 May. They will be delivered immediately to the security section.

Notice that in the above instructions all of the actions are to be performed by the reader, or "you." Now let's put these into one sentence, placing the things to be done in a series and using a single subject.

Improved: Pick up the evaluation forms from your personnel office; complete and deliver them to the security section by 1700 hours, 18 May. (The subject [you] is understood.)

The same thing can be done with subjects or predicates:

Poor: Horror stories shown on television appear to contribute to juvenile delinquency. Comic books with their horror stories seem to have the same effect. Even the reports of criminal activities which appear in our newspapers seem to contribute to juvenile delinquency.

Improved: Television, comic books, and newspapers seem to contribute to juvenile delinquency by emphasizing stories of horror and crime.

There is one more thing we can do to make our sentences better. We can vary their length and complexity. The following paragraphs suggest ways to do this.

5. *Vary Your Sentence Patterns*

We should, as a general rule, write predominantly short sentences. Similarly, we should keep our sentences simple enough for our readers to understand them easily and quickly.

But most people soon get tired of nothing but simple, straightforward sentences. So, give your reader an occasional change of pace. Vary both the length and the construction of your sentences.

VARY SENTENCE LENGTH

Some writers use nothing but short, choppy sentences ("The road ended in a wrecked village. The lines were up beyond. There was much artillery around."). In the hands of Hemingway, from whom this example is taken, short sentences can give an effect of purity and simplicity; in the hands of a less skillful writer, choppy sentences are usually only monotonous.

The other extreme, of course, is just as bad. The writer who always writes heavy sentences of 20 to 30 words soon loses the reader. Some great writers use long sentences effectively, but most writers do not.

The readability experts suggest that, for the most effective *communication*, a sentence should rarely exceed 20 words. Their suggestion is a good rule of thumb, but sentence length should vary. And an occasional long sentence is not hard to read if it is followed by shorter ones. A fair goal for most letter writers is an average of 21 words per sentence or fewer. For longer types of writing, such as regulations and manuals, sentences should average 15 words or fewer. The sentences in opening paragraphs and in short letters may run a little longer than the average.

VARY SENTENCE CONSTRUCTION

Just as important as varied sentence length is variety of construction. Four common sentence categories are simple, compound, complex, and compound-complex.

A *simple sentence* consists of only one main (independent) clause:

> Rain came down in torrents.
> Rain and hail started falling. (Simple sentence with compound subject)
> The storm began and soon grew in intensity. (Simple sentence with compound predicate)

A *compound sentence* has two or more main clauses:

> Rain started falling, and all work stopped.
> The storm began; all work stopped.
> The storm began, the workers found shelter, and all work stopped.

A *complex sentence* has one main clause and at least one subordinate (dependent) clause. (Subordinate clauses are underlined in the following sentences.)

> They were just starting their work <u>when the rain started.</u>
> <u>Before they had made any progress,</u> the rain started falling.
> The storm, <u>which grew rapidly in intensity,</u> stopped all work.

A *compound-complex sentence* has two or more main clauses and at least one subordinate clause. (Subordinate clauses are underlined in the following sentences.)

Rain started falling, and all work stopped <u>before they had made any progress.</u>
<u>Although the workers were eager to finish the job,</u> the storm forced them to stop, and they quickly found shelter.
They had made some progress <u>before the storm began,</u> but <u>when it started,</u> all work stopped.

The names of the categories are really not important, except to remind you to vary your sentence construction when you write. But remember that sentence variety is not just a mechanical chore to perform after your draft is complete. Good sentence variety comes naturally as the result of proper coordination and subordination when you write.

The following are some examples.

If two or more short sentences have the same subject, combine them into one simple sentence with a compound verb:

The men were hot. They were tired, too. They were also angry.
The men were hot and tired and angry.

If you have two ideas of equal weight or parallel thought, write them as two clauses in a compound sentence:

The day was hot and humid. The men had worked hard.
The men had worked hard, and the day was hot and humid.
The day was hot and humid, but the men had worked hard.

If one idea is more important than others, put it in the main clause of a complex sentence:

Poor: The men were tired, and they had worked hard, and the day was hot.

Better: The men were tired because they had worked hard on a hot day.
        or
    Although the day was hot and the men were tired, they worked hard.

If the adverbial modifier is the least important part of a complex sentence, put it first and keep the end position for the more important main clause:

Instead of: The men finished the job in record time, even though the day was hot and humid and they were tired.
Better: Even though the day was hot and humid and the men were tired, they finished the job in record time.

But be careful about having long, involved subordinate clauses come before the main clause. The reader may get lost or confused before getting to your main point or give up before getting to it. Also beware of letting too many modifying words, phrases, or clauses come between the subject and the verb. This is torture for the reader. The subject and the verb are usually the most important elements of a sentence; keep them close together whenever possible.

PART 9

A BRIEF REVIEW OF ENGLISH GRAMMAR

Frequent Grammatical Problems

Split Infinitive. By the 17th century, English had developed a two-word infinitive—*to go, to run, to talk*, etc. The word *to* was coupled with the verb and stood next to it. Since the Latin infinitive was always treated as one word, scholars decided that the infinitive in English must also be treated as one word. It was considered an error to split these two words by inserting an adverb between them.

But English isn't Latin, so people went on splitting the infinitive whenever it suited their purpose. And we've been doing it ever since.

It isn't necessary to split the infinitive deliberately, of course, but if it sounds better or seems more natural or will add emphasis, then do so. The following sentence is an example of a permissible split infinitive: "After they had won the baseball trophy, they went to the party *to proudly display* their prize." (*Proudly to display* or *to display proudly* makes the sentence stiff. And *they went proudly to the party to display their prize* changes the original meaning.)

Ending a Sentence with a Preposition. The old "rule" that you should never end a sentence with a preposition was another attempt to force Latin on English, and it also is fading out. Often, to avoid this "error," we have to write a much longer and more awkward sentence. Which sounds better?

> This is a rule up with which I will not put.
> This is a rule I won't put up with.

Distinction Between "Shall" and "Will." Formal usage required *shall* in the first person and *will* in the second and third persons when forming the simple future. For the emphatic future, these were reversed. Today most of us use *will* in all persons for both simple and emphatic future.

"It Is I." This question of which pronoun to use probably causes more uncertainty than any other problem in grammar. We do not change the form of a noun, whether we use it as a subject or as an object. But we do have different forms for our pronouns.

For example, *I, you, he, they, we,* etc., are the nominative forms and are used as subjects. *Me, you, him, them, us,* etc., are the objective forms. Normally we use the objective form after a verb, but after the *be* verbs (*am, is, are, was, will be,* etc.) we have traditionally used the nominative form; thus, *it is I* rather than *it is me.*

Usage, however, is divided on this. In informal conversation we often say, "It's me," just as the French do—"*C'est moi.*" The argument for this usage is pretty sound. The predicate is thought of as object territory, and it feels strange to us to use the nominative form here. Still, the traditional use of this form has come to be regarded as a sign of the well-educated individual. So, until "it is me" has become more widely accepted, we should continue to use "it is I."

Examples of the nominative forms for other pronouns may prove helpful:

> It was he (not *it was him*)
> This is she (not *this is her*)
> Had it been they (not *had it been them*)

There should be no question about using the objective case of the pronoun after other verbs. "The chairman appointed *him* and *me*" is considered correct, not "The chairman appointed *he* and *I*." But often, in trying to avoid this decision, we make an even worse error. Instead of the objective form, we use the reflective—*myself, himself,* etc. "He appointed John and myself" is definitely wrong.

"Who" versus "Whom." The pronoun *who* is used for the subject, and *whom* is used for the object.

> Give the letter to *whoever* answers the door. (not to *whomever*...) The pronoun *whoever* is the subject of its clause.
> Tell me *whom* you borrowed the money from. (not *who...from*) The pronoun *whomever* is the object of the preposition *from.*

The pronoun *who* used as the subject of a verb is not affected by a parenthetical expression such as *I think, he believes, they say* intervening between the subject and the verb.

He is the person *who* I think is best qualified.

Mr. Jameson is the attorney *who* we suppose will prepare the brief.

Adverbs and Adjectives. We seem to have more trouble with adverbs than with adjectives. A simple guide is this: An *adverb* may modify a verb, another adverb, or an adjective; an *adjective* may modify only a noun or a pronoun.

Our biggest problem comes in confusing adjectives and adverbs. For example, we may use the adjective *good* when we should use the adverb *well*:

Poor: The engines are running *good*.

Proper: The engines are running *well*.

Note: Both *good* and *well* may be used after a linking verb as predicate adjectives. For example, "I feel good" indicates a state of well-being, but "I feel well" indicates either that you are not sick or that your ability to use your sense of touch is above average.

Common Errors in Grammar

Most of us do not have too much trouble writing grammatically acceptable sentences. We just habitually follow the basic word order. But sometimes we get careless or we fall into bad habits. When we do, we can interfere with the meaning and with the movement of our sentences.

Here are some common grammatical errors that may confuse a reader. The errors may be so simple that the reader quickly sees the error, revises the sentence in his mind, and gets the proper message. But too often the reader won't catch the error and will get the wrong idea about what the writer is trying to say.

Misplaced Modifiers

1. Avoid dangling modifiers. When a word or phrase seems to modify another word that it cannot logically modify, we say it has been left dangling. Usually it will be a phrase beginning the sentence. From its position, we expect it to modify the subject. But the connection is illogical.

Confusing: Approaching the flight line from the east side, the operations building can be easily seen. (The operations building obviously does not approach the flight line.)

Improved: A person approaching the flight line from the east side can easily see the operations building.

Confusing: To make a climbing turn, the throttle is opened wider.

Improved: To make a climbing turn, open the throttle wider. (The subject *you* is understood.)

2. Keep your modifiers close to the words they modify. Sometimes we widely separate a modifier from its modified word and end up confusing the reader.

Confusing: It was impossible to find the book I had been reading in the dark.

Improved: It was impossible in the dark to find the book I had been reading.

Confusing: He had marked on the map the places where we were to watch for turns in red ink.

Improved: He marked on the map in red ink the places where we were to watch for turns.

3. Avoid using "squinting" modifiers that may refer to either of two parts of a sentence. A squinting modifier is so placed in a sentence that it could logically modify either the words that came before it or the words that follow it; it "squints" both ways. This may confuse the reader, who may not realize the ambiguity and may misinterpret the intended meaning.

Confusing: Personnel who drive their cars to work *only occasionally* can count on finding a parking space.

Improved: Only *occasionally* can personnel who drive their cars to work count on finding a parking space.

Confusing:	The electrician said Wednesday he would repair the light. (Did he make the statement on Wednesday, or did he say that he would repair the light on Wednesday?)
Improved:	Wednesday the electrician said he would repair the light.

or

The electrician said that he would repair the light on Wednesday.

By misplacing modifiers, we make it easy for the reader to misunderstand the meaning of our sentences, sometimes with dire results. We can eliminate such errors by reading and revising our writing before we release it. Don't confuse your reader or make him do your work. Keep your modifiers close to the words they modify.

Confusing Pronouns and Other Reference Words

1. Make sure that a pronoun agrees in number with the noun it refers to.

Confusing:	Though there may be different teacher unions, the policy of *its* delegates should be similar.
Improved:	Though there may be different teacher unions, the policy of *their* delegates should be similar.

2. Make sure a pronoun or other reference word has a definite and clearly understood antecedent. We often use words or pronouns such as *which, the latter, the former, this, it,* etc., to refer to something we have previously mentioned. This reference must be clear to the reader.

Confusing:	A piece of thread dangled over his belt that was at least 8 inches long.
Improved:	A piece of thread that was at least 8 inches long dangled over his belt.
Confusing:	The president told the executive he would handle all personnel assignments.
Improved:	The president told the executive to handle all personnel assignments.

or

The president told the executive that he, the president, would handle all personnel assignments.

Nonparallel Structure

Express parallel ideas in words with parallel grammatical construction. Nothing sounds quite so disorganized in writing as structure that is not parallel.

Not Parallel:	Briefly, the functions of a staff are to advise the general manager, transmit his instructions, and the supervision of the execution of his decisions.
Parallel:	Briefly, the functions of a staff are to advise the general manager, transmit his instructions, and supervise the execution of his decisions.
Not Parallel:	I have learned three things: that one should not argue about legalisms, never expect miracles, and the impropriety of using a singular verb with a compound subject.
Parallel:	I have learned three things: never argue about legalisms, never expect miracles, and never use a singular verb with a compound subject.

Some Basic Grammatical Terms

Parts of Speech

Nouns: names of people, things, qualities, acts, ideas, relationships: *General Smith, Texas, aircraft, confusion, running, predestination, grandfather.*

Pronouns: words that refer indirectly to nouns: *he, she, which, it, someone.*

Adjectives: words that point out or indicate a quality of nouns or pronouns: *big, lowest, cold, hard.*

Prepositions: words that link nouns and pronouns to other words by showing the relationship between them: *to, by, between, above, behind, about, of, in, on, from.*

Conjunctions: words used to join other words, phrases, and clauses: *and, but, however, because, although.*

Verbs: words that express action or indicate a state, feeling, or simply existence: *go, hate, fly, feel, is.*

Adverbs: words that tell how, where, when, or to what degree acts were performed, or indicate a degree of quality: *slowly, well, today, much, very.* Adverbs modify verbs, adjectives, and adverbs.

Don runs *slowly.* (modifies verb)
Emily is an *extremely* gifted pianist. (modifies adjective)
Eric skates *incredibly* well. (modifies adverb)

Note: Many of our words can serve as more than one part of speech. Some words may be used as nouns, adjectives, and verbs without any change in spelling: *Drinking* coffee is a popular pastime (noun); He broke the *drinking* glass (adjective); The boy *is drinking* a glass of milk (verb). Often words may be both adjectives and adverbs: *better, well, fast.* Ordinarily we add *-ly* to words to form adverbs, while adjectives may be formed by adding *-able, -ly, -ing, -al, -ese, -ful, -ish, -ous, -y,* etc. But these endings are not always necessary: *college* (noun); *college boy* (noun used as an adjective to modify the noun *boy*).

Other Grammatical Terms

Subject: a noun or pronoun (or word or phrase used as a noun) that names the actor in a sentence. The term may be used in a broader sense to include all of the words that are related to the actor.

Predicate: the verb with its modifiers and its object or complement.

Predicate complement: a noun completing the meaning of a linking verb and modifying the subject.

Jones is *chief* (noun). He was *pale* (adjective).

Linking verb: a verb with little or no meaning of its own that usually indicates a state of being or condition. It functions chiefly to connect the subject with an adjective or noun in the predicate. The most common linking verb is the verb *to be* (*am, are, is, was, were, had been*), but there are others.

He *feels* nervous.
He *acts* old.
He *seems* tired.

Clause: an element that is part of a complex or compound sentence and has a subject, a verb, and often an object. "Nero killed Agrippina" is a clause but is not ordinarily called one because it is a complete sentence. In the compound sentence *"Nero killed Agrippina, but he paid the penalty,"* each italicized group of words is an independent clause. In the complex sentence *"Because he killed Agrippina,* Nero paid the penalty," the italicized clause is made dependent or subordinate by the word *because;* it depends upon the rest of the sentence for the complete meaning.

Phrase: two or more words without a subject and predicate that function as a grammatical unit in a clause or sentence. A phrase may modify another word or may be used as a noun or verb. For example, *beside the radiator, approaching the pier, to fly a kite.*

Verbals: words made from verbs but used as other parts of speech:

Gerund: a verb used as a noun:
Swimming was his favorite sport.

Participle: a verb used as an adjective:
The aircraft *piloted* by Colonel Jones has crashed.

Infinitive: a verb used as a noun, adjective, or adverb:

> *To travel* is my greatest pleasure. (infinitive used as a noun)
> We have four days *to spend* at home. (infinitive used as an adjective)
> Bruce was glad *to have joined.* (infinitive used as an adverb)

Superlative degree: indicates the quality described by the adverb, which exists in the greatest or least degree for one person or thing.

> Ben works *most carefully* when someone is watching.

Common Grammar Errors Classified by Part of Speech

I. NOUNS	CORRECTION
Incorrect form to express plural number:	
He shot two deers.	He shot two *deer.*
Incorrect form to express masculine or feminine gender:	
She was an actor.	She was *an actress.*
Incorrect form of the possessive case:	
Two boy's heads and two sheeps' heads.	Two *boys'* heads and two *sheep's* heads.
Use of the objective case for the possessive:	
I was sorry to hear of John doing wrong.	I was sorry to hear of *John's* doing wrong.
II. PRONOUNS	
Pronoun *I* placed incorrectly:	
I and my sister will attend the concert.	My sister and *I* will attend the concert.
Use of compound personal pronoun for simple personal pronoun:	
Sam and myself will do it.	Sam and *I* will do it.
Incorrect choice of relative pronoun:	
I have a dog who barks at night.	I have a dog *which* barks at night. (Or, I have a dog *that* barks at night.)
This is the person which did the wrong.	This is the person *who* did the wrong.
This is the house what Jack built.	This is the house *which* Jack built. (Or, This is the house *that* Jack built.)
Columbus, that discovered America, was an Italian.	Columbus, *who* discovered America, was an Italian.
Lack of agreement between pronoun and antecedent:	
Every one of the pupils lost their books.	Every one of the pupils lost *his or her* book.
Incorrect form:	
The book is your's or his'.	The book is *yours* or *his.*
I recognize it's cover.	I recognize *its* cover.
Use of nominative case for objective:	
Give it to Kate and I.	Give it to Kate and *me.*
I knew it to be she.	I knew it to be *her.*
Use of objective case for nominative:	
Him and me are brothers.	*He* and *I* are brothers.
Whom do you suppose she is?	*Who* do you suppose she is?
It was her.	It was *she.*

Use of objective case for possessive:
There is no chance of me being chosen.   There is no chance of *my* being chosen.

Redundant use:
John, he tried, and then Mary, she tried.   John *tried*, and then Mary *tried*.

Ambiguous use:
The man told his son to take his coat to the tailor.   The man told his son to take *his (the man's)* coat to the tailor.

III. Verbs and Verbals

Use of the indicative mood for the subjunctive:
I wish I was you.   I wish I *were* you.

Use of the subjunctive mood for the indicative:
If the cavern were of artificial construction, considerable pains had been taken to make it look natural.   If the cavern *was* of artificial construction, considerable pains had been taken to make it look natural.

Use of incorrect form to express tense:
I done it.   I *did* it.
He seen it.   He *saw* it.
She come late yesterday.   She *came* late yesterday.
I see him last week.   I *saw* him last week.
The boy has went home.   The boy *has gone* home.
My hands were froze.   My hands were *frozen*.
He teached me all I know.   He *taught* me all I know.
I ain't seen it.   I *haven't seen* it.

Error in sequence of tenses:
I meant, when first I came, to have bought all the parts.   I meant, when first I came, *to buy* all the parts.
He did not know that mercury was a metal.   He did not know that mercury *is* a metal.

Lack of agreement between verb and subject:
Was you glad to see us?   *Were* you glad to see us?
Neither he nor she have ever been there.   Neither he nor she *has* ever been there.
It don't cost much.   It *doesn't* cost much.

Use of incorrect forms of principal parts of certain verbs; e.g., *sit* and *lie*:
The hen sets on the eggs.   The hen *sits* on the eggs.
The book lays on the table.   The book *lies* on the table.
It laid there yesterday.   It *lay* there yesterday.
It has laid there all week.   It *has lain* there all week.

Use of adjective participle without modified word:
Coming into the room, a great noise was heard.   *Coming* into the room, *I* heard a great noise.

IV. Adjectives

Omission of article:
The noun and pronoun are inflected.   The noun and *the* pronoun are inflected.

Use of superfluous article:
I do not like this kind of a story.   I do not like this *kind of* story.

Use of *a* for *an* and *an* for *a*:
This is an universal custom.   This is *a* universal custom.
I should like a apple.   I should like *an* apple.

Use of adverb for predicate adjective:
She looks nicely.   She looks *nice*.

Lack of agreement between certain adjectives and the words they modify:
I do not like these kind of grapes.   I do not like *this kind* of grapes.

Incorrect forms of comparison:
His ways have become eviler.   His ways have become *more evil*.

Use of comparative form not accompanied by certain necessary words:
He is shorter than any boy in his class.   He is shorter than any *other* boy in his class.

Use of superlative form accompanied by certain superfluous words:
This is of all others the most important.   This is the most important.

Use of double comparative or superlative form:
She is more kinder than you.   She is *kinder* than you.

Incorrect placing of adjective phrases and clauses:
The mariner shot the bird with an unfeeling heart.   *With an unfeeling heart,* the mariner shot the bird.

V. Adverbs

Use of adjective for adverb:
She sings real well.   She sings *really* well.

Incorrect use of double negatives:
I cannot go no faster.   I cannot go *any* faster.

Incorrect placing of adverbs and of adverbial phrases and clauses:
I only came yesterday, and I go today.   I came *only* yesterday, and I go today.

VI. Prepositions

Incorrect choice of prepositions:
I walked from the hall in the room.   I walked from the hall *into* the room.
Divide this between the three boys.   Divide this *among* the three boys.
I was to New York today.   I was *in* New York today.

Omission of preposition:
She is an example of what a person in good health is capable.   She is an example of what a person in good health is capable *of*.

Use of a superfluous preposition:
The book in which the story appears in is mine.   The book in which the story appears is mine.

VII. Conjunctions

Incorrect choice of words as conjunctions, especially *like* for *as* and *as* for *whether*:
I cannot write like you do.   I cannot write *as* you do.
I don't know as I can go.   I don't know *whether* I can go.

Incorrect choice of correlatives:
Neither this or that will do.   Neither this *nor* that will do.

Use of a superfluous conjunction:
I have no doubt but that he will come.   I have no doubt *that* he will come.
This is a fine picture and which all will admire.   This is a fine picture, *which* all will admire.

Incorrect placing of correlatives:
He is neither disposed to sanction bloodshed nor deceit.   He is disposed to sanction *neither* bloodshed nor deceit.

PART 10

3 GRE PRACTICE TESTS

5 Important Reasons for Taking These Practice Tests

Each of the 3 Practice GREs in the final part of this book is modeled very closely after the actual GRE. You will find that each of these Practice Tests has

a) the same level of difficulty as the actual GRE

and

b) the same question formats that the actual GRE questions have.

Accordingly, *taking each of the following tests is like taking the actual GRE.* There are 5 important reasons for taking each of these Practice GREs:

1. To find out which areas of the GRE you still need to work on.

2. To know just where to concentrate your efforts to eliminate weaknesses.

3. To reinforce the Critical Thinking Skills—25 Math Strategies and 17 Verbal Strategies— that you learned in Part 4 of this book, the Strategy Section. As we advised you at the beginning of Part 4, the diligent study of these strategies will result in a sharp rise in your GRE Math and Verbal scores.

4. To strengthen your basic Math skills that might still be a bit rusty. We hope that Part 6, the Complete GRE Math Refresher, helped you to polish up your skills.

5. To strengthen your writing skills. Look at Part 8, the Analytical Writing Section.

These 5 reasons for taking the 3 Practice Tests in this section of the book tie up closely with a very important educational principle:

WE LEARN BY DOING!

9 Tips for Taking the Practice Tests

1. Observe the time limits exactly as given.

2. Allow no interruptions.

3. Permit no talking by anyone in the "test area."

4. Mark all your answers on the answer choices or answer bubbles on the test.

5. Use scratch paper to figure things out. (On your actual GRE, you are permitted to use the test book for scratchwork.)

6. Omit a question when you start "struggling" with it. Go back to that question later if you have time to do so.

7. Don't get upset if you can't answer several of the questions. You can still get a high score on the test. Even if only 40 to 60 percent of the questions you answer are correct, you will get an average or above-average score.

8. You get the same credit for answering an easy question correctly as you do for answering a tough question correctly.

9. It is advisable to guess, since nothing is subtracted if you get the answer wrong.

Guidelines to See How You Would Do on a GRE and What You Should Do to Improve

This GRE Test is very much like the actual GRE. It follows the genuine GRE very closely. Taking this test is like taking the actual GRE. The following is the purpose of taking this test:

1. To find out what you are *weak* in and what you are *strong* in

2. To know where to concentrate your efforts in order to be fully prepared for the actual test

Taking this test will prove to be a very valuable TIME SAVER for you. Why waste time studying what you already know? Spend your time profitably by studying what you *don't* know. That is what this test will tell you.

In this book, we do not waste precious pages. We get right down to the business of helping you to increase your GRE scores.

Other GRE preparation books place their emphasis on drill, drill, drill. We do not believe that drill work is of primary importance in preparing for the GRE. Drill work has its place. In fact, this book contains a great variety of drill material—2,000 GRE-type multiple-choice questions (Verbal and Quantitative Reasoning), all of which have explanatory answers. But drill work must be coordinated with learning Critical Thinking Skills. These skills will help you to think clearly and critically so that you will be able to answer many more GRE questions correctly.

Ready? Start taking the test. It's just like the real thing.

GRE PRACTICE
TEST 1

Analytical Writing 1

ANALYZE AN ISSUE

Time—30 Minutes

You have 30 minutes to plan and compose a response to the following issue. A response to any other issue will receive a score of zero. Make sure that you respond according to the specific instructions and support your position on the issue with reasons and examples drawn from such areas as your reading, experience, observations, and/or academic studies.

> Knowing about the past cannot help people to make important decisions today.
>
> Write a response in which you discuss the extent to which you agree or disagree with the statement and explain your reasoning for the position you take. In developing and supporting your position, you should consider ways in which the statement might or might not hold true and explain how these considerations shape your position.

Trained GRE readers will evaluate your response for its overall quality based on how well you:

- Respond to the specific task instructions
- Consider the complexities of the issue
- Organize, develop, and express your ideas
- Support your ideas with relevant reasons and/or examples
- Control the elements of standard written English

Before you begin writing, you may want to think for a few minutes about the issue and the specific task instructions and then plan your response. **Use the next page to plan your response, then write your response starting on the first lined page that follows. A total of four lined pages are provided for your response.** Be sure to develop your position fully and organize it coherently, but leave time to reread what you have written and make any revisions you think are necessary.

Write your response within the boxed area on the pages provided. Any text outside the boxed area will not be scored.

GO ON TO THE NEXT PAGE

Plan Your Response Here. Begin Writing Your Essay on the Following Page.

This page will not be scored.

GO ON TO THE NEXT PAGE

Note: On the computerized test, you will type your response and you will be able to correct mistakes through a word processor.

ANALYZE AN ISSUE RESPONSE (Page 1 of 4)

_____
_____
_____
_____
_____
_____
_____
_____
_____
_____
_____
_____
_____
_____
_____
_____
_____
_____
_____
_____
_____
_____
_____
_____
_____
_____
_____
_____
_____
_____
_____

GO ON TO THE NEXT PAGE

ANALYZE AN ISSUE RESPONSE (Page 2 of 4)

GO ON TO THE NEXT PAGE

ANALYZE AN ISSUE RESPONSE (Page 3 of 4)

GO ON TO THE NEXT PAGE

ANALYZE AN ISSUE RESPONSE (Page 4 of 4)

STOP

If you finish before time is called, you may check your work on this section only.
Do not turn to any other section in the test.

Analytical Writing 2

ANALYZE AN ARGUMENT

Time—30 Minutes

You have 30 minutes to plan and compose a response in which you evaluate the following argument passage. A response to any other argument will receive a score of zero. Make sure that you respond according to the specific instructions and support your evaluation with relevant reasons and/or examples.

Note that you are NOT being asked to present your own views on the subject.

The following is taken from a memo from the advertising director of the Super Screen Movie Production Company.

"According to a recent report from our marketing department, during the past year, fewer people attended Super Screen–produced movies than in any other year. And yet the percentage of positive reviews by movie reviewers about specific Super Screen movies actually increased during the past year. Clearly, the contents of these reviews are not reaching enough of our prospective viewers. Thus, the problem lies not with the quality of our movies but with the public's lack of awareness that movies of good quality are available. Super Screen should therefore allocate a greater share of its budget next year to reaching the public through advertising."

Write a response in which you discuss what questions would need to be answered in order to decide whether the recommendation and the argument on which it is based are reasonable. Be sure to explain how the answers to these questions would help to evaluate the recommendation.

Trained GRE readers will evaluate your response for its overall quality based on how well you:

- Respond to the specific task instructions
- Consider the complexities of the issue
- Organize, develop, and express your ideas
- Support your ideas with relevant reasons and/or examples
- Control the elements of standard written English

Before you begin writing, you may want to think for a few minutes about the issue and the specific task instructions and then plan your response. **Use the next page to plan your response, then write your response starting on the first lined page that follows. A total of four lined pages are provided for your response.** Be sure to develop your position fully and organize it coherently, but leave time to reread what you have written and make any revisions you think are necessary.

Write your response within the boxed area on the pages provided. Any text outside the boxed area will not be scored.

GO ON TO THE NEXT PAGE

Plan Your Response Here. Begin Writing Your Essay on the Following Page.

This page will not be scored.

GO ON TO THE NEXT PAGE

Note: On the computerized test, you will type your response and you will be able to correct mistakes through a word processor.

ANALYZE AN ARGUMENT RESPONSE (Page 1 of 4)

GO ON TO THE NEXT PAGE

ANALYZE AN ARGUMENT RESPONSE (Page 2 of 4)

GO ON TO THE NEXT PAGE

ANALYZE AN ARGUMENT RESPONSE (Page 3 of 4)

GO ON TO THE NEXT PAGE

ANALYZE AN ARGUMENT RESPONSE (Page 4 of 4)

_____
_____
_____
_____
_____
_____
_____
_____
_____
_____
_____
_____
_____
_____
_____
_____
_____
_____
_____
_____
_____
_____
_____
_____
_____
_____
_____
_____
_____
_____
_____
_____
_____

STOP

If you finish before time is called, you may check your work on this section only.
Do not turn to any other section in the test.

Instructions for Verbal Reasoning and Quantitative Reasoning Sections

Important Notes

Your scores for these sections will be determined by the number of questions you answer correctly. Nothing is subtracted from your score if you answer a question incorrectly. Therefore, to maximize your scores it is better for you to guess at an answer than not to respond at all. Work as rapidly as you can without losing accuracy. Do not spend too much time on questions that are too difficult for you. Go on to the other questions and come back to the difficult ones later.

Some or all of the passages in this test have been adapted from published material to provide the examinee with significant problems for analysis and evaluation. To make the passages suitable for testing purposes, the style, content, or point of view of the original may have been altered.

You may use a calculator in the Quantitative Reasoning sections only. You will be provided with a calculator and cannot use any other calculator.

Marking Your Answers

All answers must be marked in this test book. When filling in the circles that accompany each question, BE SURE THAT EACH MARK IS DARK AND COMPLETELY FILLS THE CIRCLE.

Correct		Incorrect		
Ⓐ	Ⓧ	Ⓐ	Ⓐ	Ⓐ
●	Ⓑ	Ⓧ	Ⓑ	Ⓑ
Ⓒ	Ⓒ	Ⓒ	Ⓒ	ⓒ
Ⓓ	Ⓓ	Ⓓ	◑	Ⓓ

Be careful to erase any stray marks that lie in or near a circle. If you change an answer, be sure that all previous marks are erased completely. Stray marks and incomplete erasures may be read as intended answers. Scratch paper will not be provided. You may work out your answers in the blank areas of the test book, but do not work out answers near the circles.

Question Formats

The questions in these sections have several different formats. A brief description of these formats and instructions for entering your answer choices are given below.

Multiple-Choice Questions—Select One Answer Choice

These standard multiple-choice questions require you to select just one answer choice from a list of options. You will receive credit only if you mark the **single** correct answer choice and no other.

Example: What city is the capital of France?

- Ⓐ Rome
- ● Paris
- ⓒ London
- Ⓓ Cairo

Multiple-Choice Questions—Select One or More Answer Choices

Some of these questions specify how many answer choices to select; others require you to select all that apply. In either case, to receive credit you must mark all of the correct answer choices and no others. These questions are distinguished by the use of a square box.

Example: Select all that apply.

Which of the following countries are in Africa?

■ Chad

Ⓑ China

Ⓒ France

■ Kenya

Column Format Questions

This question type presents the answer choices in columns. You must select one answer choice from each column. You will receive credit only if you mark the correct answer choice **in each column**.

Example: Complete the following sentence,

(i) _____ is the capital of (ii) _____.

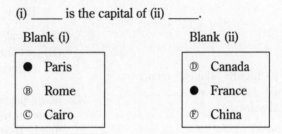

Blank (i)

● Paris

Ⓑ Rome

Ⓒ Cairo

Blank (ii)

Ⓓ Canada

● France

Ⓕ China

Numeric Entry Questions

To answer these questions, enter a number by filling in circles in a grid. Complete instructions for doing so will be found in the Quantitative Reasoning sections.

Section 1: Verbal Reasoning

Time—35 Minutes
25 Questions

For each question, indicate the best answer, using the directions given.

For each of Questions 1–8, select <u>one</u> entry for each blank from the corresponding column of choices. Fill all blanks in the way that best completes the text.

1. Having written 140 books to date, he may well be considered one of the most _____ novelists of the century.

    (A) eccentric
    (B) controversial
    (C) easygoing
    (D) unheralded
    (E) prolific

2. Though he was a highly skilled computer programmer, he had little or no _____ in designing educational software.

    (A) emotion
    (B) opportunity
    (C) structure
    (D) competition
    (E) creativity

3. Though Socrates was _____ by his students who found truth in his teachings, his philosophy constituted a threat to the existing government. Consequently, with the extreme position of completely destroying Socrates' position and philosophy, angry officials had sought to _____ the value of Socrates' premises.

Blank 1	Blank 2
(A) revered	(D) challenge
(B) slighted	(E) undermine
(C) vilified	(F) acknowledge

4. Before the inflation _____, one could have had a complete meal in a restaurant for five dollars, including the tip, whereas today, a hot dog, coffee, and dessert would _____ add up to two or three times that much.

Blank 1	Blank 2
(A) spiral	(D) incorrigibly
(B) promulgation	(E) indubitably
(C) criteria	(F) conditionally

5. Some psychologists and educators were adamant about the teaching procedures used at institutions of higher learning. For example, the renowned behaviorist B. F. Skinner believed that those colleges set up to train teachers should _____ change their training philosophy, or else be _____.

Blank 1	Blank 2
(A) voluntarily	(D) investigated
(B) drastically	(E) induced
(C) conditionally	(F) abolished

GO ON TO THE NEXT PAGE

6. The renowned psychologist B. F. Skinner's particular brand of behaviorism, which he called "Radical" behaviorism, unlike less austere behaviorisms, did not accept private events such as thinking, personal perceptions, and unobservable _____ in a casual account of an organism's _____, presumably a self-aware one reporting such _____ as an observer of itself.

Blank 1	Blank 2	Blank 3
(A) emotions	(D) structure	(G) characteristics
(B) conditions	(E) behavior	(H) notions
(C) premises	(F) criterion	(I) states

7. The president is _____ to grant federal pardons and reprieves, and to convene and adjourn either or both houses of Congress under extraordinary circumstances. Since the founding of the United States, the power of the president and the federal government have substantially grown, and each modern president, despite possessing no formal legislative powers beyond signing or vetoing congressionally passed bills, is largely responsible for _____ the legislative agenda of his party and the foreign and domestic policy of the United States. The president is frequently described as the most _____ person in the world.

Blank 1	Blank 2	Blank 3
(A) elected	(D) supporting	(G) important
(B) empowered	(E) dictating	(H) powerful
(C) chosen	(F) developing	(I) visible

8. The Classical Age of Greek culture ended with the defeat of Athens and Sparta; the _____ effect of the long war was the weakening and _____ of the Greek spirit, and the _____ of the creativity of the prominent artists.

Blank 1	Blank 2	Blank 3
(A) immediate	(D) rebuilding	(G) development
(B) ironic	(E) corrosion	(H) ingenuity
(C) cumulative	(F) separation	(I) stifling

For each of Questions 9–14, select <u>one</u> answer choice unless otherwise directed.

Questions 9–11 are based on this passage.

1   Classical music is termed "classical" because it can be heard over and over again without the listener tiring of the music. A symphony of Brahms can be heard and heard again with the same or even heightened enjoyment a few
5   months later. It is unfortunate that the Compact Disc (CD) sales of classical music are dismal compared to other types of music. Perhaps this is because many people in our generation were not exposed to classical music at an early age and therefore did not get to know the music.
10   In contrast to classical music, contemporary nonclassical music has a high impact on the listener but unfortunately is not evergreen. Its enjoyment lasts only as long as there is current interest in the topic or emotion that the music portrays, and that only lasts for three months or so until
15   other music replaces it, especially when another bestselling song comes out. The reason why the impact of this type of music is not as great when it first comes out is thought to be because technically the intricacy of the music is not high and not sophisticated, although many critics believe it is
20   because the music elicits a particular emotional feeling that gradually becomes worn out in time.

GO ON TO THE NEXT PAGE

9. According to the passage, it can be assumed that the majority of younger people do not like classical music because they

(A) buy only the bestselling CDs
(B) do not have the sophistication of a true music lover
(C) grow tired of classical music
(D) did not hear that type of music in their youth
(E) are more restless than the older generation

10. The reason the enjoyment of a particular piece of contemporary music may not last as long as a piece of classical music is the

(A) emotion of a person, which is thought to change in time
(B) high sophistication of the classical music and its technical intricacy
(C) fact that there is always another piece of contemporary music that replaces the one before it
(D) youth desiring something new
(E) economy and marketing of the CDs

11. The term "evergreen" in line 12 most nearly means

(A) colorful
(B) lasting
(C) current
(D) likeable
(E) encompassing

Questions 12–13 are based on this passage.

1   Fortunately it is as yet only through fantasy that we can see what the destruction of the scholarly and scientific disciplines would mean to mankind. From history we can learn what their existence has meant. The sheer power of
5 disciplined thought is revealed in practically all the great intellectual and technological advances that the human race has made. The ability of the man of disciplined mind to direct this power effectively upon problems for which he was not specifically trained is proved by examples without
10 number. The real evidence for the value of liberal education lies in history and in the biographies of men who have met the valid criteria of greatness. These support overwhelmingly the claim of liberal education that it can equip a man with fundamental powers of decision and action, applicable
15 not only to relationships, to tinkering hobbies, or to choosing the family dentist, but to all the great and varied concerns of human life—not least, those that are unforeseen.

For the following questions, consider each of the choices separately and select all that apply.

---

12. The author indicates that the person with a liberal education has the ability to

(A) read with more discernment than others
(B) apply general principles
(C) be active and not passive

13. In this passage, the author stresses the importance of

(A) broad-minded learning
(B) education for living
(C) satisfying the desire for security

Questions 14 is based on this passage.

1   The composition and density of the atmosphere and the altitude of the aurora determine the possible light emissions. **When an excited atom or molecule returns to the ground state, it sends out a photon with a specific**
5 **energy. This energy depends on the type of atom and on the level of excitement, and we perceive the energy of a photon as color.** The upper atmosphere consists of air just like the air we breathe. At very high altitudes there is atomic oxygen in addition to normal air, which is made up of
10 molecular nitrogen and molecular oxygen. **The energetic electrons in aurora are strong enough to occasionally split the molecules of the air into nitrogen and oxygen atoms.** The photons that come out of aurora have therefore the signature colors of nitrogen and oxygen molecules and
15 atoms. Oxygen atoms, for example, strongly emit photons in two typical colors: green and red. The red is a brownish red that is at the limit of what the human eye can see, and although the red auroral emission is often very bright, we can barely see it.

14. In the argument above, the two portions in **boldface** play which of the following roles?

(A) The first states the conclusion of the argument as a whole; the second provides support for that conclusion.
(B) The first provides support for the conclusion of the argument as a whole; the second provides evidence that supports an objection to that conclusion.
(C) The first provides support for an intermediate conclusion that supports a further conclusion stated in the argument; the second states that intermediate conclusion.
(D) The first serves as an intermediate conclusion that supports a further conclusion stated in the argument; the second states the position that the argument as a whole opposes.
(E) The first states the position that the argument as a whole opposes; the second supports the conclusion of the argument.

GO ON TO THE NEXT PAGE

For each of Questions 15–19, select the <u>two</u> answer choices that, when used to complete the sentence blank, fit the meaning of the sentence as a whole <u>and</u> produce completed sentences that are alike in meaning.

15. Because the people of India were _____ under British rule, many went over to the Japanese side during World War II.

   (A) employed
   (B) reviled
   (C) deported
   (D) abused
   (E) satisfied
   (F) educated

16. The author told the publisher that the royalty payment specified in the contract was _____ because the research costs, including traveling for writing the book, were far more than the royalties projected for a year.

   (A) rational
   (B) precarious
   (C) payable
   (D) insufficient
   (E) unrealistic
   (F) incomprehensible

17. Although the physical setup of the school's lunchroom seems rundown in many respects, it was enlarged and _____ quite recently.

   (A) relegated
   (B) examined
   (C) occupied
   (D) renovated
   (E) criticized
   (F) reinforced

18. The two performers taking the parts of shy, romantic teenagers were quite _____ in their roles even though they were in their forties.

   (A) convincing
   (B) flippant
   (C) amateurish
   (D) comfortable
   (E) personable
   (F) boring

19. Nature's brute strength is never more _____ than during a major earthquake, when the earth shifts with a sickening sway.

   (A) frightening
   (B) effective
   (C) unnerving
   (D) replaceable
   (E) placating
   (F) complete

For each of Questions 20–25, select <u>one</u> answer choice unless otherwise directed.

Questions 20–22 are based on this passage.

1   The modern biographer's task becomes one of discovering the "dynamics" of the personality he is studying rather than allowing the reader to deduce that personality from documents. If he achieves a reasonable likeness, he need
5   not fear too much that the unearthing of still more material will alter the picture he has drawn: it should add dimension to it, but not change its lineaments appreciably. After all, he has had more than enough material to permit him to reach conclusions and to paint his portrait. With this abundance
10 of material he can select moments of high drama and find episodes to illustrate character and make for vividness. In any event, biographers, I think, must recognize that the writing of a life may not be as "scientific" or as "definitive" as we have pretended. Biography partakes of a large part of the
15 subjective side of man; and we must remember that those who walked abroad in our time may have one appearance for us—but will seem quite different to posterity.

20. According to the author, which is the real task of the modern biographer?

   (A) interpreting the character revealed to him by study of the presently available data
   (B) viewing the life of the subject in the biographer's own image
   (C) leaving to the reader the task of interpreting the character from contradictory evidence
   (D) collecting facts and setting them down in chronological order
   (E) being willing to wait until all the facts on his subject have been uncovered

21. The author apparently thinks of biographers as

   (A) debunkers of history
   (B) creative artists
   (C) objective scientists
   (D) literary critics
   (E) mere collectors of facts

GO ON TO THE NEXT PAGE

22. In the context in which it appears, "definitive" (line 13) most nearly means

   (A) dynamical
   (B) pinpointed
   (C) conclusive
   (D) subjective
   (E) episodal

24. In the context in which it appears, "extenuate" (line 7) most nearly means

   (A) interpret
   (B) exaggerate
   (C) emphasize
   (D) excuse
   (E) condemn

Questions 23–24 are based on this passage.

1   Plutarch admired those who could use life for grand purposes and depart from it as grandly, but he would not pass over weaknesses and vices that marred the grandeur. His hero of heroes is Alexander the Great; he admires
5 him above all other men, while his abomination of abominations is bad faith, dishonorable action. Nevertheless he tells with no attempt to extenuate how Alexander promised a safe conduct to a brave Persian army if they surrendered, and then, "even as they were marching away he fell upon
10 them and put them all to the sword," "a breach of his word," Plutarch says sadly, "which is a lasting blemish to his achievements." He adds piteously, "but the only one." He hated to tell that story.

23. Which of the following conclusions is *least* justified by the passage?

   (A) Plutarch considered Alexander basically a great man.
   (B) The Persians believed that Alexander was acting in good faith.
   (C) The Persians withdrew from the battlefield in orderly array.
   (D) The author is familiar with Plutarch's writing.
   (E) The author considers Plutarch unfair to Alexander.

Question 25 is based on this passage.

1   A visual learner is one who approaches learning and solves problems from a visual point of view. For example, a visual learner will appreciate and excel in geometry more than in algebra, which is different from geometry. This is
5 because geometry deals for the most part with diagrams and figures, which are visual in nature, whereas algebra deals with numbers and variables, which are conceptual rather than visual.

25. Which of the following, if true, helps to explain why some people who are visual are able to excel in algebra?

   (A) Those people can formulate an algebraic problem into something visual.
   (B) Those people have developed an interest and appreciation in nonvisual applications.
   (C) Those people can solve many geometric problems by different methods and approaches.
   (D) Those people can solve the most difficult geometric problems without much effort.
   (E) Those people have taken many algebra courses before having taken geometry.

STOP

If you finish before time is called, you may check your work on this section only.
Do not turn to any other section in the test.

Section 2: Verbal Reasoning

Time—35 Minutes
25 Questions

For each question, indicate the best answer, using the directions given.

For each of Questions 1–8, select <u>one</u> entry for each blank from the corresponding column of choices.
Fill all blanks in the way that best completes the text.

1. Their married life was not _____ since it was fraught with bitter fighting and arguments.

   (A) nubile
   (B) tranquil
   (C) obvious
   (D) cogent
   (E) imminent

2. The activities that interested Jack were those that provided him with _____ pleasure, like dancing, feasting, and partying.

   (A) questionable
   (B) distant
   (C) immediate
   (D) limited
   (E) delayed

3. Although Sir Isaac Newton was acclaimed as the forerunner of the development of a viable concept of the law of gravity, Leonardo da Vinci _____ the law of gravity two centuries before Newton and also made the first complete _____ charts of the human body.

Blank 1	Blank 2
(A) examined	(D) anatomical
(B) perused	(E) judicious
(C) anticipated	(F) scintillating

4. The salesmen in that clothing store are so _____ that it is impossible to even look at a garment without being _____ by their efforts to convince you to purchase the item.

Blank 1	Blank 2
(A) impecunious	(D) harassed
(B) parsimonious	(E) subdued
(C) persistent	(F) berated

5. In a previous historical and unexpected event, President Anwar el-Sadat of Egypt, disregarding _____ criticism in the Arab world and in his own government, _____ had accepted Prime Minister Menachem Begin's invitation to visit Israel in order to address the Israeli Knesset.

Blank 1	Blank 2
(A) acrimonious	(D) audaciously
(B) categorical	(E) plaintively
(C) plethoric	(F) formally

6. The mayor's endorsement of the new judge _____ the immediate _____ of city officials even though some of them had _____ about the contender's stance on many issues that opposed the stances of the other candidates.

Blank 1	Blank 2	Blank 3
(A) provided for	(D) repercussion	(G) information
(B) won	(E) stature	(H) preconceptions
(C) created	(F) acclaim	(I) reservations

GO ON TO THE NEXT PAGE >

7. Some teachers can get influenced by the seemingly persuasive tactics used by their students. If a teacher is a truly objective person, he or she will allow neither _____ attempts to please nor open _____ on the part of the teacher's students to _____ a judgment of a student's work.

Blank 1	Blank 2	Blank 3
(A) unwarranted	(D) defiance	(G) conjure up
(B) condescending	(E) reliance	(H) diminish
(C) hypocritical	(F) understanding	(I) influence

8. Can there be any work of Beethoven's that confirms all this to a higher degree than his indescribably _____ symphony in C minor? How this wonderful composition, in a climax that climbs on and on, leads the listener imperiously forward into the world of _____. No doubt the whole rushes like an ingenious rhapsody past many a man, but the soul of each thoughtful listener is assuredly stirred, deeply and intimately, by a feeling that is none other than that unutterable _____ longing, and until the final chord—indeed, even in the moments that follow it—he will be powerless to step out of that wondrous spirit realm where grief and joy embrace him in the form of sound.

Blank 1	Blank 2	Blank 3
(A) meticulous	(D) complexity	(G) portentous
(B) profound	(E) the infinite	(H) anxious
(C) sensitive	(F) the harmonious	(I) devastating

For each of Questions 9–15, select one answer choice unless otherwise directed.

Questions 9–10 are based on this passage.

1   Windstorms have recently established a record that meteorologists hope will not be equaled for many years to come. Disastrous tornadoes along with devastating typhoons and hurricanes have cost thousands of lives
5   and left property damage totaling far into the millions. The prominence these storms have held in the news has led many people to ask about the difference between the three. Is a typhoon the same as a hurricane? Is a tornado the same as a typhoon? Basically, there is no difference.
10   All three consist of wind rotating counterclockwise (in the Northern Hemisphere) at a tremendous velocity around a low-pressure center. However, each type does have its own definite characteristics. Of the three the tornado is certainly the most treacherous. The Weather Bureau can, with some
15   degree of accuracy, forecast the typhoon and the hurricane; however, it is impossible to determine where or when the tornado will strike. And out of the three, if one had a choice, perhaps it would be safer to choose to withstand the hurricane.

For the following two Questions (9 and 10), consider each of the choices separately and select all that apply.

9. Which is common to all of the storms mentioned in the passage?

   (A) fairly accurate forecasting
   (B) violently rotating wind
   (C) high property damage

10. The author indicates that

   (A) hurricanes are less destructive than tornadoes
   (B) the Southern Hemisphere is free from hurricanes
   (C) tornadoes occur around a low pressure center

GO ON TO THE NEXT PAGE

Question 11 is based on this passage.

1   If the authority to which a professor is subject resides in the college of which he himself is a member, and in which the greater part of the other members are, like himself, persons who either are, or ought to be teachers, then
5 they are likely to make a common cause and to be all very indulgent to one another, and each man is likely to consent that his neighbor may neglect his duty, provided he himself is allowed to neglect his own. In the University of Oxford, the greater part of the professors have for many years given
10 up altogether even the pretense of teaching.

11. This argument would be weakened if it were established that

(A) people are generally unselfish
(B) professors are likely to band together
(C) professors earn large salaries
(D) colleges maintain small teaching staffs
(E) teaching is a very difficult profession

Questions 12–15 are based on this passage.

1   Siddhartha was now pleased with himself. He could have dwelt for a long time yet in that soft, well-upholstered hell, if this had not happened, this moment of complete hopelessness and despair and the tense moment when he
5 was ready to commit suicide. Was it not his Self, his small, fearful and proud Self, with which he had wrestled for many years, which had always conquered him again and again, which robbed him of happiness and filled him with fear?
    Siddhartha now realized why he had struggled in vain
10 with this Self when he was a Brahmin and an ascetic. Too much knowledge had hindered him; too many holy verses, too many sacrificial rites, too much mortification of the flesh, too much doing and striving. He had been full of arrogance; he had always been the cleverest, the most eager—always a
15 step ahead of the others, always the learned and intellectual one, always the priest or the sage. His Self had crawled into his priesthood, into this arrogance, into this intellectuality. It sat there tightly and grew, while he thought he was destroying it by fasting and penitence. Now he understood
20 it and realized that the inward voice had been right, that no teacher could have brought him salvation. That was why he had to go into the world, to lose himself in power, women, and money; that was why he had to be a merchant, a dice player, a drinker, and a man of property, until the priest and
25 Samana in him were dead. That was why he had to undergo those horrible years, suffer nausea, learn the lesson of the madness of an empty, futile life till the end, till he reached bitter despair, so that Siddhartha the pleasure-monger and Siddhartha the man of property could die. He had died
30 and a new Siddhartha had awakened from his sleep. He also would grow old and die. Siddhartha was transitory, all forms were transitory, but today he was young, he was a child—the new Siddhartha—and he was very happy.

    These thoughts passed through his mind. Smiling, he
35 listened thankfully to a humming bee. Happily he looked into the flowing river. Never had a river attracted him as much as this one. Never had he found the voice and appearance of flowing water so beautiful. It seemed to him as if the river had something special to tell him, something
40 which he did not know, something which still awaited him. The new Siddhartha felt a deep love for this flowing water and decided that he would not leave it again so quickly.

12. The "soft, well-upholstered hell" (lines 2–3) is a reference by the speaker to

(A) an attractive yet uncomfortable dwelling where he resided
(B) his lifestyle, which made him an unhappy person
(C) a place to which he went when he wished to be completely by himself
(D) his abode in a previous life not referred to in the passage
(E) a figment of his imagination that used to haunt him

13. Which of the following best describes the relation between the second and third paragraphs?

(A) Paragraph 3 shows how much happier one can be by living alone than in living with others, as brought out in paragraph 2.
(B) Paragraph 3 discusses the advantages of a simple life as opposed to the more complicated lifestyle discussed in paragraph 2.
(C) Paragraph 3 contrasts the life of a person without wealth and a formal religion with a person who has wealth and a formal religion, as in paragraph 2.
(D) Paragraph 3 demonstrates the happiness that can come as a result of giving up the power and the worldly pleasures referred to in paragraph 2.
(E) Paragraph 3 generalizes about the specific points made in paragraph 2.

14. Which of the following questions does the passage answer?

(A) What is the meaning of a Brahmin?
(B) Why did Siddhartha decide to commit suicide?
(C) Where did Siddhartha own property?
(D) For how many years was Siddhartha a member of the priesthood?
(E) Where did Siddhartha go to school?

GO ON TO THE NEXT PAGE

15. The word "transitory" in line 31 most likely means

    (A) quick on one's feet
    (B) invisible
    (C) short-lived
    (D) going from one place to another
    (E) frozen

For each of Questions 16–19, select the <u>two</u> answer choices that, when used to complete the sentence blank, fit the meaning of the sentence as a whole <u>and</u> produce completed sentences that are alike in meaning.

---

16. The police commissioner insisted on severity in dealing with the demonstrators rather than the _____ approach that his advisers suggested.

    (A) arrogant
    (B) defeatist
    (C) violent
    (D) conciliatory
    (E) placating
    (F) retaliatory

17. Feeling no particular affection for either of his two acquaintances, he was able to judge their dispute _____.

    (A) impartially
    (B) accurately
    (C) unemotionally
    (D) immaculately
    (E) heatedly
    (F) judiciously

18. Britain's seizure of American ships and _____ our sailors to serve in the British Navy were two major causes of the War of 1812.

    (A) compelling
    (B) recruiting
    (C) bribing
    (D) coercing
    (E) enlisting
    (F) deriding

19. Since he had not worked very hard on his project, the student was quite _____ upon learning that he had won the contest.

    (A) annoyed
    (B) apathetic
    (C) ecstatic
    (D) rebuffed
    (E) dismayed
    (F) elated

For each of Questions 20–25, select <u>one</u> answer choice unless otherwise directed.

Question 20 is based on this passage.

1   A steak dinner at a high-class restaurant on Main Street costs $70.00. A similarly delectable dinner on Wharf Street at Joe's Bar and Grill costs $25.00. Joe's Bar and Grill has a greater net profit than the Main Street restaurant. The only
5 explanation for this is that the restaurant on Main Street is poorly managed.

20. The author's argument would be *weakened* if attention were drawn to the fact that

    (A) the owners of the Main Street restaurant are known to be very greedy
    (B) Joe takes a loss on every steak dinner he sells
    (C) there is a much higher overhead at the Main Street restaurant
    (D) Joe uses low-quality meats
    (E) at Joe's Bar, two drinks are included in the price of the meal

Questions 21–22 are based on this passage.

1   Observe the dilemma of the fungus: it is a plant, but it possesses no chlorophyll. While all other plants can put the sun's energy to work for them combining the nutrients of ground and air into body structure, the chlorophyll-less
5 fungus must look elsewhere for an energy source. It finds it in those other plants that, having received their energy free from the sun, relinquish it at some point in their cycle either to other animals (like us humans) or to fungi.

    In this search for energy, the fungus has become the
10 earth's major source of rot and decay. Wherever you see mold forming on a piece of bread, or a pile of leaves turning to compost, or a blown-down tree becoming pulp on the ground, you are watching a fungus eating. Without fungus action the earth would be piled high with the dead plant life
15 of past centuries. In fact, certain plants that contain resins that are toxic to fungi will last indefinitely; specimens of the redwood, for instance, can still be found resting on the forest floor centuries after having been blown down.

GO ON TO THE NEXT PAGE >

For the following questions, consider each of the choices separately and select all that apply.

21. Which of the following statements is supported by the passage?

    (A) Fungi cannot live completely apart from other plants
    (B) Fungi can survive indefinitely under favorable conditions
    (C) It is necessary to have fungi to maintain the earth's surface appearance

22. The passage provides information on each of the following EXCEPT

    (A) an example of a plant containing resins toxic to fungi
    (B) the cause of the earth's rot and decay
    (C) where plants other than fungus plants get their energy
    (D) examples of what fungi thrive on
    (E) the procedure for destroying fungi

The passage below is followed by questions based on its content. Answer the questions on the basis of what is <u>stated</u> or <u>implied</u> in the passage and in any introductory material that may be provided.

Questions 23–25 are based on this passage.

1   In the South American rain forest abide the greatest acrobats on earth. The monkeys of the Old World, agile as they are, cannot hang by their tails. It is only the monkeys of America that possess this skill. They are called ceboids,
5   and their unique group includes marmosets, owl monkeys, sakis, spider monkeys, squirrel monkeys, and howlers. Among these the star gymnast is the skinny, intelligent spider monkey. Hanging head down like a trapeze artist from the loop of a liana, he may suddenly give a short
10 swing, launch himself into space and, soaring outward and downward across a 50-foot void of air, lightly catch a bough on which he spied a shining berry. Owl monkeys cannot match his leap, for their arms are shorter, their tails untalented. The marmosets, smallest of the tribe, tough noisy
15 hoodlums that travel in gangs, are also capable of leaps into space, but their landings are rough: smack against a tree trunk with arms and legs spread wide.

23. Which of the following titles best express the ideas of this selection?

    (A) The Star Gymnast
    (B) Monkeys and Trees
    (C) Travelers in Space
    (D) The Uniqueness of Monkeys
    (E) Ceboid Acrobats

24. Compared to monkeys of the Old World, American monkeys are

    (A) smaller
    (B) quieter
    (C) more dexterous
    (D) more protective of their young
    (E) less at home in their surroundings

25. In the context in which it appears, "untalented" (lines 13–14) most nearly means

    (A) curtailed
    (B) not agile
    (C) discolored
    (D) hard
    (E) developed

STOP

**If you finish before time is called, you may check your work on this section only.
Do not turn to any other section in the test.**

Section 3: Quantitative Reasoning

Time—40 Minutes
25 Questions

For each question, indicate the best answer, using the directions given.

Notes: All numbers used are real numbers.

All figures are assumed to lie in a plane unless otherwise indicated.

Geometric figures, such as lines, circles, triangles, and quadrilaterals, **are not necessarily** drawn to scale. That is, you should **not** assume that quantities such as lengths and angle measures are as they appear in a figure. You should assume, however, that lines shown as straight are actually straight, points on a line are in the order shown, and more generally, all geometric objects are in the relative positions shown. For questions with geometric figures, you should base your answers on geometric reasoning, not on estimating or comparing quantities by sight or by measurement.

Coordinate systems, such as xy planes and number lines, **are** drawn to scale; therefore, you can read, estimate, or compare quantities in such figures by sight or by measurement.

Graphical data presentations, such as bar graphs, circles graphs, and line graphs, **are** drawn to scale; therefore, you can read, estimate, or compare data values by sight or by measurement.

For each of Questions 1–9, compare Quantity A and Quantity B, using additional information centered above the two quantities if such information is given. Select one of the following four answer choices and fill in the corresponding circle to the right of the question.

(A) **Quantity A is greater.**
(B) **Quantity B is greater.**
(C) **The two quantities are equal.**
(D) **The relationship cannot be determined from the information given.**

A symbol that appears more than once in a question has the same meaning throughout the question.

Quantity A	Quantity B	Correct Answer
Example 1: (2)(6)	2 + 6	Ⓐ Ⓑ Ⓒ Ⓓ

$$\triangle PQR \text{ with } Q \text{ at top}, P \text{ lower left}, R \text{ lower right}, S \text{ on } PR$$

Quantity A	Quantity B	Correct Answer
Example 2: *PS*	*SR*	Ⓐ Ⓑ Ⓒ Ⓓ

(since equal lengths cannot be assumed, even though *PS* and *SR* appear equal)

SUMMARY DIRECTIONS FOR COMPARISON QUESTIONS

<u>Answer:</u>   A   if the quantity in Quantity A is greater;
B   if the quantity in Quantity B is greater;
C   if the two quantities are equal;
D   if the relationship cannot be determined from the information given.

GO ON TO THE NEXT PAGE

1

Quantity A	Quantity B	
The remainder when 14 is divided by 5	The remainder when 14 is divided by 3	Ⓐ Ⓑ Ⓒ Ⓓ

2

$$4a > 3b$$

Quantity A	Quantity B	
a	b	Ⓐ Ⓑ Ⓒ Ⓓ

3 John flips a quarter coin twice.

Quantity A	Quantity B	
The chances of John getting 2 tails	The chances of John getting no tails	Ⓐ Ⓑ Ⓒ Ⓓ

4

Quantity A	Quantity B	
The standard deviation of 4 different integers, each of which is between 0 and 7	The standard deviation of 4 different integers, each of which is between 7 and 14	Ⓐ Ⓑ Ⓒ Ⓓ

5 The regular price of a car is p dollars.

Quantity A	Quantity B	
The price of the car after a 20 percent discount	$0.80p$ dollars	Ⓐ Ⓑ Ⓒ Ⓓ

6

$$y^2 - 11y + 30 = 0$$

Quantity A	Quantity B	
y	7	Ⓐ Ⓑ Ⓒ Ⓓ

7 There are x boys in high school A. The number of girls in high school A is 8 less than 4 times the number of boys

Quantity A	Quantity B	
The number of girls in high school A	$4x - 8$	Ⓐ Ⓑ Ⓒ Ⓓ

8

Quantity A	Quantity B	
180	$x + y$	Ⓐ Ⓑ Ⓒ Ⓓ

Diagram not drawn to scale.

9

a and b are positive.
$$b > a$$

Quantity A	Quantity B	
$\boxed{b^2 - a}$	$\boxed{b^2 - a^2}$	Ⓐ Ⓑ Ⓒ Ⓓ

GO ON TO THE NEXT PAGE

Questions 10–25 have several different formats. Unless otherwise directed, select a single answer choice. For Numeric Entry questions, follow the instructions below.

Numeric Entry Questions

To answer these questions, enter a number by filling in circles in a grid.

- Your answer may be an integer, a decimal, or a fraction, and it may be negative.

- Equivalent forms of the correct answer, such as 2.5 and 2.50, are all correct. Although fractions do not need to be reduced to lowest terms, they may need to be reduced to fit in the grid.

- Enter the exact answer unless the question asks you to round your answer.

- If a question asks for a fraction, the grid will have a built-in division slash (/). Otherwise, the grid will have a decimal point.

- Start your answer in any column, space permitting. Fill in no more than one circle in any column of the grid. Columns not needed should be left blank.

- Write your answer in the boxes at the top of the grid and fill in the corresponding circles. **You will receive credit only if the circles are filled in correctly, regardless of the number written in the boxes at the top.**

Examples of acceptable ways to use the grid:

Integer answer: 502 (either position is correct)

Decimal answer: −4.13

Fraction answer: $-\frac{2}{10}$

10. The ratio of Sue's age to Bob's age is 3 to 7. The ratio of Sue's age to Joe's is 4 to 9. The ratio of Bob's age to Joe's is

(A) 28 to 27
(B) 7 to 9
(C) 27 to 28
(D) 10 to 13
(E) 13 to 10

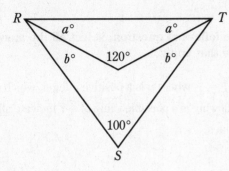

Note: Figure is not drawn to scale.

11. Given $\triangle RST$ above, what is the value of b?

(A) 50
(B) 40
(C) 30
(D) 20
(E) 10

For the following two questions, select all the answer choices that apply.

Box Number	Height of Box (in millimeters)
A	1,700
B	2,450
C	2,735
D	1,928
E	2,130

12. Which of the boxes listed in the table above are more than 20 decimeters high? (1 decimeter = 100 millimeters) Indicate <u>all</u> such boxes.

(A) A
(B) B
(C) C
(D) D
(E) E

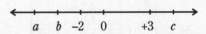

13. In the above number line, a, b, and c are real numbers. Which statement is true? Indicate <u>all</u> such statements.

(A) $b > -1$
(B) $|b| < 2$
(C) $-|c| = c$
(D) $|b| > |a|$
(E) $|a| > |b|$
(F) $c > 2$
(G) $a < -1$
(H) $a < b$

GO ON TO THE NEXT PAGE

14. Paul's average (arithmetic mean) for 3 tests was 85. The average of his scores for the first 2 tests was also 85. What was his score for the third test?

(A) 80
(B) 85
(C) 90
(D) 95
(E) It cannot be determined from the information given.

For the following question, use the grid to enter your answer.

15. If $x^2 + 2xy + y^2 = 25$, $x + y > 0$ and $x - y = 1$, then find the value of x.

List A: 25, 22, 30, 21, 17

List B: 15, 20, 19, 30, 14

16. What is the difference in the median of the numbers in List A from the median of the numbers in List B?

(A) 2
(B) 3
(C) 4
(D) 5
(E) 7

For the following question, select all the answer choices that apply.

17. If $\frac{a}{b} = \frac{1}{4}$, where a is a positive integer, which of the following is a possible value of $\frac{a^2}{b}$? Indicate <u>all</u> such values.

(A) $\frac{1}{4}$

(B) $\frac{1}{2}$

(C) 1

GO ON TO THE NEXT PAGE

Questions 18–21 are based on the following data.

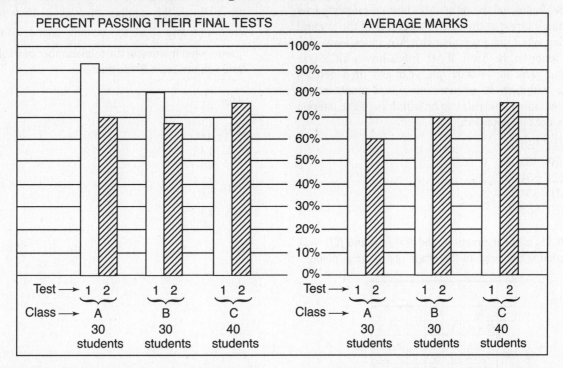

For the following, if there are no choices, use the grid to enter your answer.

18. What was the average score overall for test 1?

19. Which class, or classes, must have had at least one pupil who scored 75% or higher on test 2?

   (A) Class A only
   (B) Class B only
   (C) Class C only
   (D) More than one class
   (E) Cannot be determined from the given information

20. Which of the following statements is *true*?

   (A) 10% of Class A failed both tests.
   (B) 21 students in Class B passed test 2.
   (C) The average overall score on test 2 was 72.
   (D) More students from Class C passed test 1 than from Class B.
   (E) None of the above statements is true.

21. In which class or classes is it possible that 70% of the students passed both tests?

   (A) A only
   (B) A and C only
   (C) B and C only
   (D) A, B, and C
   (E) none of these

GO ON TO THE NEXT PAGE

22. Mr. Jones deposited $50 in a savings bank at the beginning of the year. Mr. Jones's money earns him interest at the rate of 8 percent of the amount deposited, for each year that Mr. Jones leaves his money in the bank. If Mr. Jones leaves his $50 in the bank for exactly one year and then decides to withdraw all of his money, how much money (including interest) can he withdraw? (The interest is not compounded.)

(A) $50.04
(B) $50.08
(C) $54.00
(D) $54.08
(E) $58.00

23. If f is a linear function, and $f(5) = 6$ and $f(7) = 8$, what is the slope of the graph of f in the xy plane?

24. If an ant runs randomly through an enclosed circular field of radius 2 feet with an inner circle of radius 1 foot, what is the probability that the ant will be in the inner circle at any one time?

(A) $\frac{1}{8}$

(B) $\frac{1}{6}$

(C) $\frac{1}{4}$

(D) $\frac{1}{2}$

(E) 1

25. At a certain college, the number of freshmen is three times the number of seniors. If $\frac{1}{4}$ of the freshmen and $\frac{1}{3}$ of the seniors attend a football game, what fraction of the total number of freshmen and seniors attends the game?

(A) $\frac{5}{24}$

(B) $\frac{13}{48}$

(C) $\frac{17}{48}$

(D) $\frac{11}{24}$

(E) $\frac{23}{48}$

STOP

If you finish before time is called, you may check your work on this section only.
Do not turn to any other section in the test.

Section 4: Quantitative Reasoning

Time—40 Minutes
25 Questions

For each question, indicate the best answer, using the directions given.

Notes: All numbers used are real numbers.

All figures are assumed to lie in a plane unless otherwise indicated.

Geometric figures, such as lines, circles, triangles, and quadrilaterals, **are not necessarily** drawn to scale. That is, you should **not** assume that quantities such as lengths and angle measures are as they appear in a figure. You should assume, however, that lines shown as straight are actually straight, points on a line are in the order shown, and more generally, all geometric objects are in the relative positions shown. For questions with geometric figures, you should base your answers on geometric reasoning, not on estimating or comparing quantities by sight or by measurement.

Coordinate systems, such as xy planes and number lines, **are** drawn to scale; therefore, you can read, estimate, or compare quantities in such figures by sight or by measurement.

Graphical data presentations, such as bar graphs, circles graphs, and line graphs, **are** drawn to scale; therefore, you can read, estimate, or compare data values by sight or by measurement.

For each of Questions 1–9, compare Quantity A and Quantity B, using additional information centered above the two quantities if such information is given. Select one of the following four answer choices and fill in the corresponding circle to the right of the question.

(A) **Quantity A is greater.**
(B) **Quantity B is greater.**
(C) **The two quantities are equal.**
(D) **The relationship cannot be determined from the information given.**

A symbol that appears more than once in a question has the same meaning throughout the question.

	Quantity A	Quantity B	Correct Answer
Example 1:	(2) (6)	2 + 6	● Ⓑ Ⓒ Ⓓ

	Quantity A	Quantity B	Correct Answer
Example 2:	*PS*	*SR*	Ⓐ Ⓑ Ⓒ ●

(since equal lengths cannot be assumed, even though *PS* and *SR* appear equal)

GO ON TO THE NEXT PAGE ⟩

SUMMARY DIRECTIONS FOR COMPARISON QUESTIONS

Answer: A if the quantity in Quantity A is greater;
            B if the quantity in Quantity B is greater;
            C if the two quantities are equal;
            D if the relationship cannot be determined from the information given.

1 y is a positive integer.

Quantity A	Quantity B	
y^3	3^y	Ⓐ Ⓑ Ⓒ Ⓓ

2 $\dfrac{3}{a} = 2$ and $\dfrac{5}{b} = 2$

Quantity A	Quantity B	
a	b	Ⓐ Ⓑ Ⓒ Ⓓ

3 $3y - 2 < 0$

Quantity A	Quantity B	
$3y$	-2	Ⓐ Ⓑ Ⓒ Ⓓ

4

Quantity A	Quantity B	
Units digit of the product of the first 7 positive integers	Units digit of the product $8 \cdot 9 \cdot 10 \cdot 11 \cdot 12 \cdot 13 \cdot 14$	Ⓐ Ⓑ Ⓒ Ⓓ

5 x is any nonnegative integer.

Quantity A	Quantity B	
The minimum value of $4x^2 + 1$	The minimum value of $5x^2 + 1$	Ⓐ Ⓑ Ⓒ Ⓓ

6 $\dfrac{4}{a} = \dfrac{b}{4}$

Quantity A	Quantity B	
a	b	Ⓐ Ⓑ Ⓒ Ⓓ

7

Quantity A	Quantity B	
$xy + 7$	$x(y + 7)$	Ⓐ Ⓑ Ⓒ Ⓓ

GO ON TO THE NEXT PAGE →

$$-4 \qquad\qquad\qquad 0$$

$$|\longleftarrow b \longrightarrow||\longleftarrow a \longrightarrow|$$

8   *a* and *b* are each lengths of segments on the number line shown above.

Quantity A	Quantity B	
$4 - a$	b	Ⓐ Ⓑ Ⓒ Ⓓ

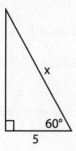

9

Quantity A	Quantity B	
x	8	Ⓐ Ⓑ Ⓒ Ⓓ

Questions 10–25 have several different formats. Unless otherwise directed, select a single answer choice. For Numeric Entry questions, follow the instructions below.

Numeric Entry Questions

To answer these questions, enter a number by filling in circles in a grid.

- Your answer may be an integer, a decimal, or a fraction, and it may be negative.

- Equivalent forms of the correct answer, such as 2.5 and 2.50, are all correct. Although fractions do not need to be reduced to lowest terms, they may need to be reduced to fit in the grid.

- Enter the exact answer unless the question asks you to round your answer.

- If a question asks for a fraction, the grid will have a built-in division slash (/). Otherwise, the grid will have a decimal point.

- Start your answer in any column, space permitting. Fill in no more than one circle in any column of the grid. Columns not needed should be left blank.

- Write your answer in the boxes at the top of the grid and fill in the corresponding circles. **You will receive credit only if the circles are filled in correctly, regardless of the number written in the boxes at the top.**

Examples of acceptable ways to use the grid:

Integer answer: 502 (either position is correct)

Decimal answer: −4.13

Fraction answer: $-\frac{2}{10}$

GO ON TO THE NEXT PAGE

For the following question, select all the answer choices that apply.

10. If x is a positive integer, which of the following must be an even integer? Indicate <u>all</u> such integers.

    (A) $x + 2$
    (B) $2x + 1$
    (C) $2x^2 + 4x + 6$
    (D) $x^2 + x + 1$
    (E) $x^2 + x + 2$

For the following question, use the grid to enter your answer.

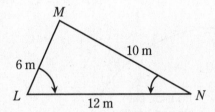

11. In the figure above, if sides LM and NM are cut apart from each other at point M, creating 2 free-swinging segments, and each is folded down to LN in the directions shown by the arrows, what will be the length, in meters, of the overlap of the 2 segments? (Disregard the thickness of the segments.)

12. At Jones College, there are a total of 100 students. If 30 of the students have cars on campus, and 50 have bicycles, and 20 have both cars and bicycles, then how many students have neither a car nor a bicycle on campus?

    (A) 80
    (B) 60
    (C) 40
    (D) 20
    (E) 0

13. The half-life of a certain radioactive substance is 6 hours. In other words, if you start with 8 grams of the substance, 6 hours later you will have 4 grams. If a sample of this substance contains x grams, how many grams remain after 24 hours?

    (A) $\dfrac{x}{32}$
    (B) $\dfrac{x}{16}$
    (C) $\dfrac{x}{8}$
    (D) $2x$
    (E) $4x$

14. The price of a car is reduced by 30 percent. The resulting price is reduced 40 percent. The two reductions are equal to one reduction of

    (A) 28%
    (B) 42%
    (C) 50%
    (D) 58%
    (E) 70%

15. A certain printer can print at the rate of 80 characters per second, and there is an average (arithmetic mean) of 2,400 characters per page. If the printer continued to print at this rate, how many *minutes* would it take to print an *M*-page report?

    (A) $\dfrac{M}{30}$
    (B) $\dfrac{M}{60}$
    (C) $\dfrac{M}{2}$
    (D) $\dfrac{2}{M}$
    (E) $\dfrac{60}{M}$

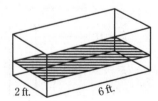

16. The figure above shows water in a tank whose base is 2 feet by 6 feet. If a rectangular solid whose dimensions are 1 foot by 1 foot by 2 feet is totally immersed in the water, how many *inches* will the water rise?

    (A) $\dfrac{1}{6}$
    (B) 1
    (C) 2
    (D) 3
    (E) 12

GO ON TO THE NEXT PAGE

17. A certain store is selling an $80 radio for $64. If a different radio had a list price of $200 and was discounted at $1\frac{1}{2}$ times the percent discount on the $80 model, what would its selling price be?

(A) $90
(B) $105
(C) $120
(D) $140
(E) $160

Questions 18–21 are based on the following graphs.

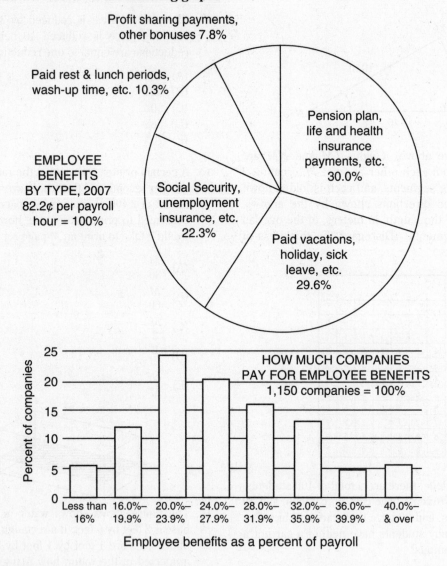

Profit sharing payments, other bonuses 7.8%

Paid rest & lunch periods, wash-up time, etc. 10.3%

EMPLOYEE BENEFITS BY TYPE, 2007
82.2¢ per payroll hour = 100%

Social Security, unemployment insurance, etc. 22.3%

Pension plan, life and health insurance payments, etc. 30.0%

Paid vacations, holiday, sick leave, etc. 29.6%

HOW MUCH COMPANIES PAY FOR EMPLOYEE BENEFITS
1,150 companies = 100%

Percent of companies

Less than 16% | 16.0%–19.9% | 20.0%–23.9% | 24.0%–27.9% | 28.0%–31.9% | 32.0%–35.9% | 36.0%–39.9% | 40.0% & over

Employee benefits as a percent of payroll

18. How many companies studied paid 40% or more of the payroll as employee benefits?

(A) 24
(B) 46
(C) 57
(D) 120
(E) 142

GO ON TO THE NEXT PAGE

For the following question, use the grid to enter your answer.

19. In how many ways can you add two sectors of the circle graph and have the sum equal to more than half the circle?

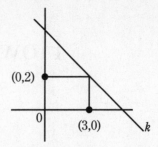

23. In the above figure, if line k has slope of -1, what is the y-intercept of k?

    (A) 4
    (B) 5
    (C) 6
    (D) 7
    (E) 8

For the following question, use the grid to enter your answer.

20. How many more of the companies studied have employee benefits as 24.0%–27.9% of the payroll than have the benefits as 16.0%–19.9% of the payroll?

    (A) 92
    (B) 180
    (C) 35
    (D) 75
    (E) 210

24. A lawn covers 108.6 square feet. Russ mowed all of the lawn in three evenings. He mowed $\frac{2}{9}$ of the lawn during the first evening. He mowed twice that amount on the second evening. On the third and final evening he mowed the remaining lawn. How many square feet were mowed the third evening?

21. If Social Security and Unemployment Insurance were abolished and this extra benefit money were distributed evenly among the other four categories, how many cents per payroll hour would be used for "Paid Vacations, Holiday, Sick Leave, etc."?

    (A) 28.9
    (B) 15.7
    (C) 45.0
    (D) 63.4
    (E) 33.4

9 9 9 9 7 7 7 7 13 13 13 x

For the following question, select all the answer choices that apply.

22. Given that ax is an integer and bx is an integer, which of the following must also be an integer? Indicate all such quantities.

    (A) a and b
    (B) x
    (C) $(a + b)x$

25. The numbers above represent the ages in years of twelve children. What is the median age of the twelve children in years?

    (A) 7
    (B) 9
    (C) 11
    (D) 13
    (E) This number cannot be determined.

STOP

**If you finish before time is called, you may check your work on this section only.
Do not turn to any other section in the test.**

How Did You Do on This Test?

Step 1. Go to the Answer Key on pages 557–560.

Step 2. For your "raw score," calculate it using the directions on page 561.

Step 3. Get your "scaled score" for the test by referring to the GRE Score Conversion Table on page 562.

THERE'S ALWAYS ROOM FOR IMPROVEMENT!

ANSWER KEY FOR PRACTICE TEST 1

Analytical Writing 1
and Analytical Writing 2
See Part 8, Page 473
for Scoring on These Parts

Answer Key for Practice Test 1

Verbal Reasoning

Verbal Reasoning

	Section 1 Correct Answer		Section 2 Correct Answer
1	E	1	B
2	E	2	C
3	A, E	3	C, D
4	A, E	4	C, D
5	B, F	5	A, F
6	A, E, I	6	B, F, I
7	B, E, H	7	C, D, I
8	C, E, I	8	B, E, G
9	D	9	B, C
10	A	10	A, C
11	B	11	A
12	B, C	12	B
13	A, B	13	D
14	C	14	B
15	B, D	15	C
16	D, E	16	D, E
17	D, F	17	A, C
18	A, D	18	A, D
19	A, C	19	C, F
20	A	20	C
21	B	21	A, C
22	C	22	E
23	E	23	E
24	D	24	C
25	A	25	B

Number correct   Number correct

Answer Key for Practice Test 1

Quantitative Reasoning

Section 3	Correct Answer		Section 4	Correct Answer
1	A		1	D
2	D		2	B
3	C		3	D
4	D		4	C
5	C		5	C
6	B		6	D
7	C		7	D
8	D		8	C
9	D		9	A
10	A		10	C, E
11	E		11	4
12	B, C, E		12	C
13	E, F, G, H		13	B
14	B		14	D
15	3		15	C
16	B		16	C
17	A, B, C		17	D
18	73		18	C
19	C		19	3
20	D		20	A
21	B		21	A
22	C		22	C
23	1, 1.0, etc.		23	B
24	C		24	36.2
25	B		25	B

Number correct   Number correct

Scoring the GRE Practice Test

Check your responses with the correct answers on the previous pages. Fill in the blanks below and do the calculations to get your Math and Verbal raw scores. Use the table to find your Math and Verbal scaled scores.

Get Your Verbal Reasoning Score

How many Verbal questions did you get **right**?

Section 1: Questions 1–25 _____

Section 2: Questions 1–25 + _____

Total = _____

Use the Score Conversion Table to find your Verbal Reasoning scaled score.

_____

Get Your Quantitative Reasoning Score

How many Math questions did you get **right**?

Section 3: Questions 1–25 _____

Section 4: Questions 1–25 + _____

Total = _____

Use the Score Conversion Table to find your Quantitative Reasoning scaled score.

_____

GRE Score Conversion Table

Raw Score	Verbal Reasoning Scaled Score		Quantitative Reasoning Scaled Score	
	130–170 Point Scale	200–800 Point Scale	130–170 Point Scale	200–800 Point Scale
50	170	800	170	800
49		790		790
48		780		790
47		770		780
46	167	760		780
45		750		770
44		740		770
43		730		770
42		710		760
41	163	700	167	750
40		670		740
39		660		730
38	160	650		720
37		640	163	700
36		620		690
35	157	600		680
34		590		670
33		570	160	650
32	153	550		640
31		540		630
30		530	157	600
29		520		590
28		510		570
27	150	500		570
26		490	153	550
25		470		530
24		460		510
23	147	450	150	500
22		440		480
21		430	147	450
20		420		440
19		410		430
18	143	400	143	400
17		380		390
16		370		380
15		360	140	350
14	140	350		340
13		340		330
12		330		310
11	137	300	137	300
10		290		280
9		280		260
8		260	133	250
7		260		230
6	133	250		210
5		230		200
4		220		200
3		200		200
2		200		200
1		200		200
0	130	200	130	200

Chart for Self-Appraisal Based on the Practice Test You Have Just Taken

Percent of Examinees Scoring Lower Than Selected Scale Scores (Percentile Rank) on the Verbal and Quantitative Reasoning Measures

Scaled Score	Verbal Reasoning	Quantitative Reasoning
800		94
790		91
780		89
770		87
760		84
750		82
740		80
730	99	77
720	98	75
710	98	72
700	97	70
690	97	68
680	96	66
670	95	63
660	94	61
650	93	59
640	92	56
630	91	54
620	89	52
610	88	49
600	86	47
590	84	45
580	82	43
570	80	40
560	78	38
550	75	36
540	73	34
530	70	32
520	68	30
510	65	28
500	63	27
490	60	25
480	57	23
470	55	22
460	52	20
450	49	19
440	46	17
430	43	16
420	41	15
410	38	14
400	35	12
390	32	11
380	29	10
370	27	9

Continued on next page.

Percent of Examinees Scoring Lower Than Selected Scale Scores (Percentile Rank) on the Verbal and Quantitative Reasoning Measures (cont'd)

Scaled Score	Verbal Reasoning	Quantitative Reasoning
360	24	8
350	21	8
340	19	7
330	16	6
320	13	5
310	10	5
300	8	4
290	6	3
280	5	3
270	3	2
260	2	2
250	1	2
240		1
230		
220		
210		
200		

Explanatory Answers for GRE Practice Test 1

Section 1: Verbal Reasoning

As you read these Explanatory Answers, you are advised to refer to "17 Verbal (Reading) Strategies" (beginning on page 136) whenever a specific Strategy is referred to in the answer. Of particular importance are the following Master Verbal Strategies:

Sentence Completion Master Strategy 1—page 137.
Sentence Completion Master Strategy 3—page 140.
Reading Comprehension Master Strategy 2—page 155.

Note: All Reading questions use Reading Comprehension Strategies 1, 2, and 3 (pages 152–157) as well as other strategies indicated.

1. Choice E is correct. See **Sentence Completion Strategy 1**. The world *prolific* (meaning "producing abundant works or results") completes the sentence so that it makes good sense. The other choices do *not* do that.

2. Choice E is correct. See **Sentence Completion Strategy 3**. The first word, "Though," is an *opposition indicator*. The beginning of the sentence speaks positively about the computer programmer. We must find a word that gives us a negative idea about him. Choice E, *creatively*, is the appropriate word. The other choices are incorrect because their words are not appropriate to that opposite feeling.

3. Choices A and E are correct. See **Sentence Completion Strategy 3**. Watch for key words like "consequently" and "extreme." In light of this, Choice D, *challenge*, is too weak, and Choice F, *acknowledge*, is the opposite of what the official

would do. For Choices A, B, or C you can see that *revered*, which means "very well admired," fits.

4. Choices A and E are correct. See **Sentence Completion Strategy 3**. Look at the contrasting clauses of the sentence—"five dollars" to "two or three times as much." A *spiral* would get things out of control and up and up. The second part has to indicate something that had to happen—like something with no doubt—*indubitably*.

5. Choices B and F are correct. Use **Sentence Completion Strategies 3 and 1**. Here we are looking at an extreme situation because of the word "adamant" in the first sentence. Choice B, *drastically*, certainly fits, and Choice F, *abolished*, also links with the tone here.

6. Choices A, E, and I are correct. Use **Sentence Completion Strategies 4, 3, and 1**. Look for key words that create a link in the sentence:

Behaviorism, unlike, and *observer.* The second blank must deal with *behavior* because of the previous references to the word *behavior.* This would imply that the third blank be very specific as in Choice I, *states.* Now we can see that the word in the remaining blank must deal with the word *emotions,* Choice A.

7. Choices B, E, and H are correct. Use **Sentence Completion Strategies 4, 3, and 1**. Look for key words that create a link in the sentence. "Power" is one of them. The flavor of the sentence deals with this *power* aspect. So the first blank would be *empowered,* Choice B; the second blank would be *dictating,* Choice E; and the third blank would be *powerful,* Choice H.

8. Choices C, E, and I are correct. Use Sentence **Completion Strategies 4, 3, and 1**. Look for key words that create a link in the sentence. "Weakening" and "creativity" are some. You can see that *cumulative* (meaning "additive"), Choice C, and *corrosion,* Choice E, will fit the first and second blanks. In light of this, *stifling,* Choice I, would be a good choice.

9. Choice D is correct. See lines 7–9, where it states that many people in our generation were not exposed to classical music. Don't be lured into the distractor Choice A, even though there was mention of sales.

10. Choice A is correct. See lines 19–21, where it mentions that the emotional feeling gradually wears out in time.

11. Choice B is correct. Since the next sentence after the word "evergreen" qualifies that enjoyment lasts only for a short time, "lasting" would be an appropriate definition of "evergreen" in this context. Be careful of the distractor choice "colorful."

12. Choices B and C are correct. Lines 7–10 confirm this: "The ability of the man of disciplined mind to direct this power effectively upon problems for which he was not specifically trained is proved by examples without number." Also, see lines 13–17: "...liberal education...can equip a man with fundamental powers of decision and action, applicable... to all the great and varied concerns of human life..." For C, see line 14: "decision and action."

13. Choices A and B are correct. See lines 13–16: "...liberal education can equip a man with fundamental powers of decision and action, applicable not only to boy-girl relationships, to tinkering hobbies, or to choosing the family dentist...."

14. Choice C is correct. The portion "...it sends out a photon with specific energy. The energy depends on the type...and we perceive the photon as color," provides support for the intermediate conclusion: "The energetic electrons...are strong enough to occasionally split the molecules of the air into nitrogen and oxygen atoms." This last statement supports the further conclusions (lines 13–15): "The photons that come out of aurora have therefore the signature colors of nitrogen and oxygen molecules and atoms."

15. Choices B and D are correct. **See Sentence Completion Strategy 1**. The beginning word "because" is a *result indicator.* We may expect, then, a reason in the first part of the sentence for the Indian people to escape from British rule and join the Japanese. The word *reviled* (Choice B) or *abused* (Choice D) provides the reason. The words in the other choices do not make sense.

16. Choices D and E are correct. See **Sentence Completion Strategy 1**. The author is obviously not satisfied with the royalty payment specified, as the sentence refers to the high research costs necessary for writing the book. Accordingly, Choices A, B, C, and F are incorrect.

17. Choices D and F are correct. See **Sentence Completion Strategy 3**. The word "Although" at the beginning of the sentence is an opposition indicator. As a contrast to the rundown condition of the school, the words *renovated* and *reinforced* are the acceptable choices.

18. Choices A and D are correct. See **Sentence Completion Strategy 3**. The opposition indicator "even though" should lead us to the correct Choice A with the fill-in word *convincing* and Choice D, *comfortable.*

19. Choices A and C are correct. See **Sentence Completion Strategy 3**. The word "when" is a *support indicator* in this sentence. As we try each choice, we find that *frightening* and *unnerving* are the only words that fit in this sentence. The fact that "the earth shifts with a sickening sway" reinforces the initial idea that "nature's brute strength is never more frightening or unnerving."

20. Choice A is correct. See lines 1–4 as related to the rest of the passage.

21. Choice B is correct. From the essence of the passage, it should be seen that the author believes that biographers are creative artists. Also see lines 7–9.

22. Choice C is correct. From the passage and the word "subjective" in line 15, *definitive* would seem to mean "conclusive." See **Reading Comprehension Strategy 5**.

23. Choice E is correct. See lines 5–6 and lines 10–12.

24. Choice D is correct. In the context you can see that "extenuate" means to excuse. See **Reading Comprehension Strategy 5**.

25. Choice A is correct. The only choice that appears logical is Choice A. If one can use his or her visual talents and formulate an algebraic problem with something visual, it would seem that he or she can solve the algebraic problem. Choices C and D are incorrect because they relate only to geometry. Choice B is weak—developing interest does not mean you will excel in the area. Choice E is incorrect. Taking algebra courses before taking geometry courses does not imply that you excel in algebra.

Explanatory Answers for GRE Practice Test 1 (continued)

Section 2: Verbal Reasoning

> As you read these Explanatory Answers, you are advised to refer to "17 Verbal (Reading) Strategies" (beginning on page 136) whenever a specific strategy is referred to in the answer. Of particular importance are the following Master Verbal Strategies:
>
> Sentence Completion Master Strategy 1—page 137.
> Sentence Completion Master Strategy 3—page 140.
> Reading Comprehension Master Strategy 2—page 155.

Note: All Reading questions use Reading Comprehension Strategies 1, 2, and 3 (pages 152–157) as well as other strategies indicated.

1. Choice B is correct. See **Sentence Completion Strategies 1 and 3**. Try each choice, being aware that "since" is a *result indicator*. Their married life was not *smooth and content*.

2. Choice C is correct. The word *immediate* is the only one that makes sense in the blank. **Sentence Completion Strategy 1**.

3. Choices C and D are correct. See **Sentence Completion Strategy 3**. Watch for key words like "although." Because we are talking about a period of time ("forerunner"), the word *anticipated* is more appropriate than *examined* or *perused*. Concerning Choices D, E, or F, a specific type of chart would be appropriate, thus *anatomical*.

4. Choices C and D are correct. Use **Sentence Completion Strategies 3 and 1**. Here you are looking for a *result indicator*. Facing someone so *persistent* would make you *harassed*.

5. Choices A and F are correct. Use **Sentence Completion Strategy 3**. Look for words like *disregarding* and *had accepted*. Anwar el-Sadat had not regarded the sharp (*acrimonious*) criticism but because he didn't want to antagonize his constituents, he formally accepted the invitation.

6. Choices B, F, and I are correct. Use Sentence **Completion Strategies 4, 3, and 1**. Look for key words and phrases that create a link in the sentence. *Even though* is one of them. Therefore the words in the first two blanks must be in contrast to the word in the third blank. You can see that Choice B, *won*, Choice F, *acclaim*, and Choice I, *reservations* fit the bill.

7. Choices C, D, and I are correct. Use **Sentence Completion Strategies 4, 3, and 1**. Look for key words that create a link in the sentence. "If," "will allow neither," and "nor" are key words. Look at the first sentence and beginning of the

second sentence. The strongest choices for the first two blanks would be Choice C, *hypocritical*, and Choice D, *defiance*. This would make the third choice, Choice I, *influence*.

8. Choices B, E, and G are correct. Use Sentence **Completion Strategies 4, 3, and 1**. Look for key words that create a link in the sentence and the flavor of the passage in general. "Wonderful," "none other than," "climbs on and on," and "imperiously forward" are some. From the words "wonderful" and "climbs on and on" in the second sentence, we can see that Choice B, *profound*, fits in the first blank. By the flavor of the passage and by the words "wonderful" and "imperiously forward" in the second sentence, it would look like *infinite*, Choice E, would fit well in the second blank. By the flavor of the passage, the third blank would be something like *amazing* or *ominous*; therefore, *portentous*, Choice G.

9. Choices B and C are correct. See lines 10–12: "All three consist of wind <u>rotating</u> counterclockwise (in the Northern Hemisphere) at a <u>tremendous velocity</u> around a low pressure center." And see lines 3–5: "Disastrous <u>tornadoes along with devastating typhoons and hurricanes</u> have cost thousands of lives and left <u>property damage totaling far into the millions.</u>"

10. Choices A and C are correct. See lines 10–12: "<u>All three</u>...at a tremendous velocity <u>around a low pressure center.</u>" And lines 13–14: "Of the three, <u>the tornado is certainly the most treacherous.</u>"

11. Choice A is correct. A basic unspoken presupposition of the author's argument is that people are motivated selfishly to seek their own ease. Thus, if it could be established that people are generally unselfish, and perform their duty even when not forced to, the argument would clearly be undermined. Choice B is actually one of the author's own premises. Choice C is irrelevant, since the salary of a professor might not be linked to the performance of his duty. Choice D would make it all the more likely that each professor could and would shirk his duty; and so would Choice E. **See Reading Comprehension Strategy 10.**

12. Choice B is correct. See lines 25–29: "That was why...till he reached bitter despair...the man of property could die." The "well-upholstered hell" constituted the lifestyle that almost caused him to commit suicide. The passage shows no justification for Choices A, C, D, or E. Accordingly, these are incorrect choices.

13. Choice D is correct. Throughout paragraph 3, we see the evidence of the speaker's happiness as a result of his renouncing the "power, women, and money" (lines 22–23) as well as the arrogance and intellectuality referred to in line 17. Choices A, B, and C are incorrect because, though the passage discusses these choices, they do not really pinpoint the relation between the third and fourth paragraphs. Choice E is incorrect because paragraph 3 does not generalize about the specific points made in paragraph 2.

14. Choice B is correct. His "complete hopelessness and despair" (lines 3–4) led to Siddhartha's decision to commit suicide. The passage does not answer the questions expressed in Choices A, C, D, and E. Therefore, these choices are incorrect.

15. Choice C is correct. From the context of the sentence and the one preceding it, we can see that the word "transitory" means "short-lived." (We are dealing with time.) See also **Reading Comprehension Strategy 5**.

16. Choices D and E are correct. See **Sentence Completion Strategies 2 and 3**. The key words "rather than" tell us that a word opposite to "severity" is needed to fill in the blank space. If you used the strategy of trying to complete the sentence *before* looking at the five choices, you might have chosen for your blank fill-in one of these appropriate words: *easy, friendly, diplomatic, pleasing, soothing*. Each of these words has a meaning much like that of the word *conciliatory* or *placating*. The words of the other four choices are *not* appropriate in the sentence. Therefore, these choices are incorrect.

17. Choices A and C are correct. See **Sentence Completion Strategy 1**. Try each choice. He would be able to be *impartial*, or *unbiased*, only as a result of not being emotionally attached to either acquaintance; he would not necessarily be able to be *accurate* (Choice B) or *judicious* (Choice F).

18. Choices A and D are correct. See **Sentence Completion Strategy 2**. This strategy suggests that you try to complete the sentence *before* looking at the six choices. Doing this, you might have come up with any of the following words that indicate an additional type of force or injury besides "seizure": *coercing, forcing, pressuring, compelling*. These words all come close to the meaning of Choice A, *compelling*. Therefore, Choices B, C, or E are incorrect.

19. Choices C and F are correct. See **Sentence Completion Strategy 3**. We have an opposition indicator here—the student's not working hard and his winning the contest. We, therefore, look for a definitely positive word as our choice to contrast with the negative thought embodied

in his not working hard. Those positive words are *elated* (Choice F), which means "delighted beyond measure," and *ecstatic* (Choice C), which means "overjoyed." Accordingly, A, B, D, and E are incorrect.

20. Choice C is correct. The author's argument leads us to the conclusion that the restaurant on Main Street is poorly managed. However, if we can find a reason why the restaurant charges more for a steak dinner but still has a smaller net profit than the Bar and Grill, we can weaken the author's argument. Of the five choices, only Choice C explains the restaurant's high prices but small net profit. Choice E strengthens the author's conclusion, as does Choice B. Choice D is contradicted by the passage, which states that the meals are similarly delectable. Choice A is irrelevant. **See Reading Comprehension Strategy 10.**

21. Choices A and C are correct. For (A), see lines 4–16: "...the chlorophyll-less fungus must look elsewhere for an energy source. It finds it in those other plants..." For (C), see lines 13–14: "Without fungus action the earth..." **See Reading Comprehension Strategy 10.**

22. Choice E is correct. For Choice A see lines 15–18. For Choice B see lines 9–10. For Choice C see lines 2–5. For Choice D see lines 10–13. Choice E, the procedure for destroying fungi, is not addressed. **See Reading Comprehension Strategy 10.**

23. Choice E is correct. See the beginning sentence, which states "the greatest acrobats on earth," introducing the monkeys, which in line 4 are called "ceboids." The whole passage is about the "ceboid acrobats."

24. Choice C is correct. See lines 12–17, where the comparisons are made.

25. Choice B is correct. Since it is stated, "can match his leap, for their arms are shorter, their tails untalented," we could assume that "untalented" has to do with dexterity or agility. See **Reading Comprehension Strategy 5.**

Explanatory Answers for Practice Test 1 (continued)

Section 3: Quantitative Reasoning

> As you read these solutions, you are advised to do two things if you answered the math question incorrectly:
>
> 1. When a specific Strategy is referred to in the solution, study that strategy, which you will find in "25 Math Strategies" (beginning on page 72).
>
> 2. When the solution directs you to the "Math Refresher" (beginning on page 185)—for example, Math Refresher #305—study the 305 Math principle to get a clear idea of the math operation that was necessary for you to know in order to answer the question correctly.

1. Choice A is correct.

Quantity A	Quantity B
The remainder when 14 is divided by 5	The remainder when 14 is divided by 3
$\frac{14}{5} = 2$ remainder 4	$\frac{14}{3} = 4$ remainder 3

(Math Refresher #101)

2. Choice D is correct.

Given: 4a > 3b $\qquad$ $\boxed{1}$

(Use Strategy C: Use numerics if it appears that the answer can't be determined.)

Let $a = 1$ and $b = 1$.
Then $4a = 4(1) = 4$ and $3b = 3(1) = 3$ and $\boxed{1}$ is satisfied. $\qquad$ $\boxed{2}$

Let $a = 2$ and $b = 1$.
Then $4a = 4(2) = 8$ and $3b = 3(1) = 3$ and $\boxed{1}$ is satisfied. $\qquad$ $\boxed{3}$

From $\boxed{2}$ and $\boxed{3}$ we see that two different relationships are possible. Thus, the answer can't be determined from the given information.

(Math Refresher #431)

3. Choice C is correct.

Given: John flips a quarter coin twice $\qquad$ $\boxed{1}$

Quantity A	Quantity B
The chances of John getting 2 tails	The chances of John getting no tails

(Use Strategy 17: Use the given information effectively.) Applying $\boxed{1}$, we get

$$\text{Chances of a tail} = \frac{1}{2} \qquad \boxed{2}$$

$$\text{Chances of no tail} = \frac{1}{2} \qquad \boxed{3}$$

Using $\boxed{2}$ and $\boxed{3}$, the columns become

Quantity A	Quantity B
$\left(\frac{1}{2}\right)\left(\frac{1}{2}\right)$	$\left(\frac{1}{2}\right)\left(\frac{1}{2}\right)$

(Math Refresher #614)

4. Choice D is correct. Quantity A: Let's choose four different integers between 0 and 7. Let's say 1, 2, 3, 6. The average of those integers is $(1 + 2 + 3 + 6)/4 = 3$ The standard deviation is

$$\sqrt{\frac{(1-3)^2 + (2-3)^2 + (3-3)^2 + (6-3)^2}{4}}$$

$$= \sqrt{\frac{14}{4}}$$

Quantity B: Let's choose four different integers between 7 and 14. Let's say 8, 9, 10, 13. The average of those integers is $(8 + 9 + 10 + 13)/4 = 40/4 = 10$. The standard deviation is

$$\sqrt{\frac{(8-10)^2 + (9-10)^2 + (10-10)^2 + (13-10)^2}{4}}$$

$$= \sqrt{14/4}$$

Thus Quantity A = Quantity B.

Use Math Strategy C. Now try a quantity that makes the columns unequal.
Choose, for Quantity B, numbers 9, 10, 11, 12.

The average is
$(9 + 10 + 11 + 12)/4 = 42/4 = 10\frac{1}{2}$

The standard deviation is

$$\sqrt{\frac{(9-10\frac{1}{2})^2 + (10-10\frac{1}{2})^2 + (11-10\frac{1}{2})^2 + (12-10\frac{1}{2})^2}{4}}$$

$$\neq \sqrt{14/4}$$

Thus Quantity A ≠ Quantity B.
In one case the quantities are equal, and in another they are not. Thus Choice D is correct.

(Math Refresher #602)

5. Choice C is correct.

   Given: The regular price of a car is p dollars.

   (Use Strategy 2: Know how to find a percent less than a given amount.)

Quantity A	Quantity B
The price of the car after a 20 percent discount	0.80p dollars

$= p - \left(\frac{20}{100}\right)p$

$= p - .20p$

$= 0.80p$ dollars   0.80p dollars

(Math Refresher #114 and #119)

6. Choice B is correct.
   Given: $y^2 - 11y + 30 = 0$ ⬜1

   (Use Strategy 17: Use the given information effectively.) Factoring ⬜1, we have

   $(y - 6)(y - 5) = 0$
   $y = 6$ or $y = 5$ ⬜2

Quantity A	Quantity B	
y	7	⬜3

Substituting each value from ⬜2 into ⬜3, we have

5	7
or	
6	7

In both cases, Quantity B is larger.

(Math Refresher #409)

7. Choice C is correct. **(Use Strategy 2: Translate from words to algebra.)**

   Given: x = number of boys in high school A

   The number of girls = $4x - 8$ ⬜1

Quantity A	Quantity B	
The number of girls in high school A	$4x - 8$	⬜2

Substituting ⬜1 into ⬜2, the columns become

$4x - 8$ $4x - 8$

(Math Refresher #406)

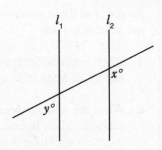

8. Choice D is correct.

   (Use Strategy C: Use numerical examples when it appears that a comparison cannot be determined.)

   We are given no information about the relationship between l_1, l_2 and the third line. l_1 may be parallel to l_2 or may not be.

   Choose x and y so that $x + y > 180$, and $x + y < 180$.

   If $x = 120$ and $y = 50$, then $x + y = 170$ ⬜1
   If $x = 130$ and $y = 70$, then $x + y = 200$ ⬜2

   Since two different results are possible, we cannot determine a specific relationship.

(Math Refresher #504 and #501)

9. Choice D is correct.

   Given: a and b are positive ⬜1
   $b > a$ ⬜2

   (Use Strategy A: Cancel expressions common to both columns by subtraction.)

Cancel b^2 from both columns:

Quantity A	Quantity B
$\cancel{b^2} - a$	$\cancel{b^2} - a^2$

(Use Strategy D: To make a comparison simpler, divide both columns by the same quantity, making sure that quantity is not negative or 0.)

Divide by a:

Quantity A	Quantity B
$\dfrac{-a}{a}$	$\dfrac{-a^2}{a}$
-1	$-a$

(Use Strategy C: Use numbers in place of variables.)

Let $a = 1$: Quantity A = Quantity B

Now let $a = 2$: Quantity A > Quantity B

Two different results are possible, so Choice D is correct.

(Math Refresher #429 and #431)

10. Choice A is correct.

(Use Strategy 2: Translate from words to algebra.)

The ratio of Sue's age to Bob's age is 3 to 7, which becomes

$$\frac{\text{Sue's age } (S)}{\text{Bob's age } (B)} = \frac{3}{7}$$

or $\qquad \dfrac{S}{B} = \dfrac{3}{7}$ $\boxed{1}$

The ratio of Sue's age to Joe's age is 4 to 9, which becomes

$$\frac{S}{J} = \frac{4}{9} \qquad \boxed{2}$$

Cross-multiplying $\boxed{1}$, we have $7S = 3B$

or $\quad \dfrac{7S}{3} = B$ $\boxed{3}$

Cross-multiplying $\boxed{2}$, we have $9S = 4J$

or $\quad \dfrac{9S}{4} = J$ $\boxed{4}$

We need the ratio of Bob's age to Joe's age. $\boxed{5}$

Substituting $\boxed{3}$ and $\boxed{4}$ into $\boxed{5}$, we get

$$\frac{\text{Bob's age}}{\text{Joe's age}} = \frac{\dfrac{7S}{3}}{\dfrac{9S}{4}}$$

$$= \frac{7S}{3} \div \frac{9S}{4}$$

$$= \frac{7S}{3} \times \frac{4}{9S}$$

$$\frac{\text{Bob's age}}{\text{Joe's age}} = \frac{28}{27}$$

(Math Refresher #200, #120, and #112)

11. Choice E is correct. **(Use Strategy 3: The whole equals the sum of its parts.)**

The sum of the angles in a $\Delta = 180$. For the small triangle we have

$$\begin{aligned} 120 + a + a &= 180 \\ 120 + 2a &= 180 \\ 2a &= 60 \\ a &= 30 \qquad \boxed{1} \end{aligned}$$

For $\Delta\, RST$, we have

$$100 + m\angle SRT + m\angle STR = 180 \qquad \boxed{2}$$

From the diagram, we get

$$\begin{aligned} m\angle SRT &= a + b \qquad \boxed{3} \\ m\angle STR &= a + b \qquad \boxed{4} \end{aligned}$$

Substituting $\boxed{3}$ and $\boxed{4}$ into $\boxed{2}$, we get

$$\begin{aligned} 100 + a + b + a + b &= 180 \\ 100 + 2a + 2b &= 180 \\ 2a + 2b &= 80 \qquad \boxed{5} \end{aligned}$$

Substituting $\boxed{1}$ into $\boxed{5}$, we get

$$\begin{aligned} 2(30) + 2b &= 80 \\ 60 + 2b &= 80 \\ 2b &= 20 \\ b &= 10 \end{aligned}$$

(Math Refresher #505 and #406)

12. Choices B, C, and E are correct.

(Use Strategy 17: Use the given information effectively.)

We are told that 1 decimeter = 100 millimeters.

Therefore, 20 decimeters = 2,000 millimeters, and choices E, C, and B are greater than 2,000 millimeters.

Thus choices B, C, and E are greater than 20.

(Math Refresher #121)

13. Choices E, F, G, and H are correct. Choice A is incorrect: On the number line, b is to the left of -2, so this implies that b is less than -2 (written as $b < -2$). Since $b < -2$, b is certainly less than -1 (written as $b < -1$). Thus Choice A is incorrect. Choice B is false because if $b < -2$, the absolute value of b (denoted as $|b|$) must be greater than 2. Choice C is false: c is positive ($c > +3 > 0$) so $c \neq -|c|$, since $-|c|$ is negative. Choice D is false: Since a and b are negative numbers and since $a < b$, $|a| > |b|$. Choice E is correct. You can see that Choices F, G, and H are all correct.

(Math Refresher #419, #615, #410, #129)

14. Choice B is correct.

Given: Paul's average on 3 tests = 85   1
       Paul's average on first 2 tests = 85   2

(**Use Strategy 5:**

$$\text{Average} = \frac{\textbf{Sum of values}}{\textbf{Total number of values}})$$

We know $\text{Average} = \dfrac{\text{Sum of values}}{\text{Total number of values}}$ 3

Let x be the first test score   4
     y be the second test score   5
     z be the third test score   6

Substituting 1, 4, 5 and 6 into 3, we have

$$85 = \frac{x + y + z}{3} \qquad 7$$

(**Use Strategy 13: Find unknowns by multiplying.**)

Multiply 7 by 3. We get

$$3(85) = \left(\frac{x + y + z}{3}\right)3 \qquad 8$$
$$255 = x + y + z$$

Substituting 2, 4 and 5 into 3, we have

$$85 = \frac{x + y}{2} \qquad 9$$

Multiply 9 by 2, we get

$$2(85) = \left(\frac{x + y}{2}\right)2$$
$$170 = x + y \qquad 10$$

Substituting 10 into 8, we get

$$225 = 170 + z$$
$$85 = z$$

(Math Refresher #601, #431, and #406)

15. 3 (**Use Strategy 4: Remember classic expressions.**)

$$x^2 + 2xy + y^2 = (x + y)^2 \qquad 1$$
$$Given: x^2 + 2xy + y^2 = 25 \qquad 2$$

Substitute 1 into 2, giving

$$(x + y)^2 = 25$$
$$x + y = \pm 5 \qquad 3$$

$Given: x + y > 0$ 4

Using 3 and 4 together, we conclude that

$$x + y = +5 \qquad 5$$
$$Given: \; x - y = 1 \qquad 6$$

(**Use Strategy 13: Find an unknown by adding equations.**)

Adding 5 and 6, we have

$$2x = 6$$
$$x = 3$$

(Math Refresher #409 and #407)

16. Choice B is correct. Arrange the numbers of each list in ascending order.
List A: 17, 21, 22, 25, 30. The median is the middle number, and this is 22.
Now arrange the numbers in List B in ascending order.
List B: 14, 15, 19, 20, 30.
The median again is the middle number, which is 19.
$22 - 19 = 3$.

(Math Refresher #601a)

17. Choices A, B, and C are correct.

$Given: \dfrac{a}{b} = \dfrac{1}{4}$ 1

(**Use Strategy 13: Find unknowns by multiplying.**) Cross-multiply 1. We have

$$4a = b \qquad 2$$

Substituting $4a = b$ in the given $\dfrac{a^2}{b}$, we get

$$\frac{a^2}{b} = \frac{a^2}{4a} = \frac{a}{4} \qquad 3$$

(**Use Strategy 7: Use numerics to help find the answer.**) If $a = 1$ is substituted into 3 we have

$$\frac{a^2}{b} = \frac{a}{4} = \frac{1}{4}$$

Thus, Choice A is satisfied. If $a = 2$ is substituted into 3, we get

$$\frac{a^2}{b} = \frac{a}{4} = \frac{2}{4} = \frac{1}{2}$$

Thus, Choice B is satisfied. If $a = 4$ is substituted into 3, we have

$$\frac{a^2}{b} = \frac{a}{4} = \frac{4}{4} = 1$$

Thus, Choice C is satisfied.

(Math Refresher #111 and #112)

18. 73. For the 100 students, the total is $(30)(80) + (30)(70) + (40)(70) = 7300$, so the average is $7300 \div 100 = 73$.

(Math Refresher #601 and #704)

19. Choice C is correct. Since Class C averaged 75% on test 2, it is impossible for them all to be below 75%; at least one of them must have scored 75% or higher.

(Math Refresher #601 and #704)

20. Choice D is correct. 28 students passed test 1 from class C. 24 students passed test 1 from class B.

(Math Refresher #601 and #704)

21. Choice B is correct. Since 70% passed one test, and more than 70% passed the other, in both classes A and C, it is possible that the same 70% in each class passed both tests. In class B, 35% failed test 2, so it is impossible that 70% passed *both* tests.

(Math Refresher #601 and #704)

22. Choice C is correct. **(Use Strategy 10: Know how to use units.)**

$$\text{Interest} = \text{rate} \times \text{time} \times \text{amount deposited}$$
$$= \frac{8\%}{\text{year}} \times 1 \text{ year} \times \$50$$
$$= .08 \times 1 \times \$50$$
$$= \$4$$

(Use Strategy 3: The whole equals the sum of its parts.)

$$\text{Total amount} = \text{Deposit} + \text{Interest}$$
$$= \$50 + \$4$$
$$= \$54$$

(Math Refresher #113, #114, and #121)

23. **1, 1.0, etc.** This means that when $x = 5$, $y = 6$ and when $x = 7$, $y = 8$.

The slope is $(y_2 - y_1)/(x_2 - x_1)$. Thus $(y_2 - y_1)/(x_2 - x_1) = (8 - 6)/(7 - 5) = 1/1$.
See diagram below:

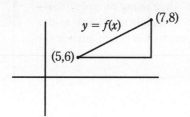

(Math Refresher #616 and #416)

24. Choice C is correct. The probability is the number of favorable outcomes divided by the number of total outcomes. The total outcomes is the number of points in the large circle of radius 2 feet. We can look at that as the area of the large circle, which is $\pi r^2 = 2 \times 2\pi = 4\pi$. The favorable outcomes are the number of points in the inner circle, which we can look at as the area of that circle, which is $\pi r^2 = 1 \times 1\pi = 1\pi$. Thus the probability is $1\pi/4\pi = \frac{1}{4}$.

(Math Refresher #614)

25. Choice B is correct. **(Use Strategy 2: Translate from words to algebra.)**

$$\text{Let } f = \text{Number of freshmen}$$
$$s = \text{Number of seniors}$$

We are given $f = 3s$ $\boxed{1}$

$\frac{1}{4}$ of the freshmen $= \frac{1}{4}f$ $\boxed{2}$

$\frac{1}{3}$ of the seniors $= \frac{1}{3}s$ $\boxed{3}$

Total number of freshmen
and seniors $= f + s$ $\boxed{4}$

(Use Strategy 17: Use the given information effectively.)

The desired fraction uses $\boxed{2}$, $\boxed{3}$ and $\boxed{4}$ as follows:

$$\frac{\frac{1}{4}f + \frac{1}{3}s}{f + s} \quad \boxed{4}$$

Substituting $\boxed{1}$ in $\boxed{5}$, we get

$$\frac{\frac{1}{4}(3s) + \frac{1}{3}s}{3s + s} = \frac{\frac{3}{4}s + \frac{1}{3}s}{4s} \quad \boxed{6}$$

Multiplying $\boxed{6}$, numerator and denominator, by 12, we get:

$$\left(\frac{12}{12}\right)\frac{\frac{3}{4}s + \frac{1}{3}s}{4s} =$$

$$\frac{9s + 4s}{48s} =$$

$$\frac{13\cancel{s}}{48\cancel{s}} =$$

$$\frac{13}{48}$$

(Math Refresher #200 and #402)

Explanatory Answers for Practice Test 1 (continued)

Section 4: Quantitative Reasoning

As you read these solutions, you are advised to do two things if you answered the math question incorrectly:

1. When a specific Strategy is referred to in the solution, study that strategy, which you will find in "25 Math Strategies" (beginning on page 72).

2. When the solution directs you to the "Math Refresher" (beginning on page 185)— for example, Math Refresher #305—study the 305 Math principle to get a clear idea of the math operation that was necessary for you to know in order to answer the question correctly.

1. Choice D is correct. **(Use Strategy C: Use numerical examples when it appears that a comparison cannot be determined.)**

Let $y = 1$, then
$$y^3 = 1^3 = 1 \qquad 3^y = 3^1 = 3$$
$$1 < 3$$
Let $y = 3$, then
$$y^3 = 3^3 = 27 \qquad 3^y = 3^3 = 27$$
$$27 = 27$$

There are two different possibilities, so you cannot determine which is the correct answer.

(Math Refresher #431)

2. Choice B is correct.

Given: $\dfrac{3}{a} = 2$ $\qquad$ $\boxed{1}$

$$\dfrac{5}{b} = 2 \qquad \boxed{2}$$

(Use Strategy 13: Find unknowns by multiplication.)

Multiplying $\boxed{1}$ by a, we get

$$a\left(\dfrac{3}{a}\right) = a\,(2)$$
$$3 = 2a$$
$$\dfrac{3}{2} = a \qquad \boxed{3}$$

Multiplying $\boxed{2}$ by a, we get

$$b\left(\dfrac{5}{b}\right) = b\,(2)$$
$$5 = 2b$$
$$\dfrac{5}{2} = b \qquad \boxed{4}$$

Comparing $\boxed{3}$ and $\boxed{4}$, we get $b > a$

(Math Refresher #406)

3. Choice D is correct. **(Use Strategy 6: Know how to work with inequalities.)**

Given: $3y - 2 < 0$ $\qquad$ $\boxed{1}$
Add 2 to both sides of $\boxed{1}$. We get $3y < 2$ $\qquad$ $\boxed{2}$

Now look at the two columns.

(Use Strategy C: Use numerical examples when it appears that a comparison cannot be determined.)

$3y$ could $= 1$ ③

This satisfies ②

$3y$ could $= -3$ ④

This satisfies ②

From ③, $1 > -2$ ⑤

From ④, $-3 < -2$ ⑥

Since there are 2 possible relations, we cannot determine a definite relationship for the columns.

(Math Refresher #419 and #431)

---

4. Choice C is correct.

Quantity A	Quantity B
Translates to the units digit of $1 \cdot 2 \cdot 3 \cdot 4 \cdot 5 \cdot 6 \cdot 7$	The units digit of $8 \cdot 9 \cdot 10 \cdot 11 \cdot 12 \cdot 13 \cdot 14$

(Use Strategy 17: Use the given information effectively.)

Seeing in Quantity A that $4 \cdot 5 = 20$, we know that any product of integers with 20 will have a units digit of 0.   ①

Seeing in Quantity B that 10 is one of the factors, we know that any product of integers with 10 will have a units digit of 0.   ②

Since ① and ②, we know that Choice C is correct.

(Use Strategy 12: Do not make tedious calculations. No tedious calculations were necessary!)

(Math Refresher #200)

---

5. Choice C is correct.

Given: x is any nonnegative integer, gives

x as 0, 1, 2, 3, 4, etc.

(Use Strategy C: Use numerical examples when it appears that a comparison cannot be determined.)

Quantity A	Quantity B
The minimum value of $4x^2 + 1$	The minimum value of $5x^2 + 1$

Let $x = 0$, we have

$4(0)^2 + 1$	$5(0)^2 + 1$
$0 + 1$	$0 + 1$
1 =	1

(Math Refresher #431)

---

6. Choice D is correct.

Given: $\dfrac{4}{a} = \dfrac{b}{4}$

Multiplying means and extremes (cross-multiplying), we get

$ab = 16$ ①

(Use Strategy C: Use numerical examples when it appears that a comparison cannot be determined.)

If $a = 16$ and $b = 1$, then $ab = 16$ as in ①

If $b = 16$ and $a = 1$, then $ab = 16$ as in ①

$a > b$ or $b > a$

Since there are two possible answers, we cannot determine which is the correct answer.

(Math Refresher #120 and #431)

---

7. Choice D is correct.

	Quantity A	Quantity B
Given:	$xy + 7$	$x(y + 7)$

Distribute in Column B, to get

$xy + 7$	$xy + 7x$

(Use Strategy A: Cancel equal quantities from both sides by subtracting.)

Subtract xy from both sides.
We then have

7	$7x$

(Use Strategy C: Use numerical examples when it appears that a comparison cannot be determined.)

$7x$ in Quantity B depends on the specific value of x, which we don't know.

If $x = 0$, then $7x = 0$ and Quantity A $>$ Quantity B

If $x = 1$, then $7x = 7$ and Quantity A $=$ Quantity B

Thus, we cannot determine which is the correct answer.

(Math Refresher #431)

---

8. Choice C is correct.

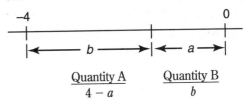

Quantity A	Quantity B
$4 - a$	b

(Use Strategy D: Make comparison simpler by adding.) Add a to both columns:

Quantity A	Quantity B
$4 - a + a$	$b + a$
4	$b + a$

Use Strategy 3: The whole equals the sum of its parts.) From the number line we see that $b + a = 4$. (The distance from 0 to -4 is 4 units.)

(Math Refresher #410)

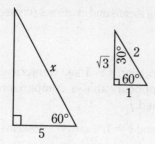

9. Choice A is correct. **(Use Strategy 18: Remember special right triangles.)**

The given triangle, at the left, is similar to the standard 30–60–90 triangle, at right. Thus, corresponding sides are in proportion.

$$\frac{x}{2} = \frac{5}{1}$$
$$x = 2 \times 5$$
$$x = 10$$

Clearly, 10 is greater than 8.

(Math Refresher #509 and #510)

10. Choices C and E are correct.

Choice E is $x^2 + x + 2$.

(Use Strategy 7: Use specific number examples.)

Let $x = 3$ (an odd positive integer)

Then $x^2 + x + 2 =$
$$3^2 + 3 + 2 =$$
$$9 + 3 + 2 =$$
$$14 = \text{(an even result)}$$

Now let $x = 2$ (an even positive integer).

Then $x^2 + x + 2 =$
$$2^2 + 2 + 2 =$$
$$4 + 2 + 2 =$$
$$8 = \text{(an even result)}$$

Whether x is odd or even, Choice E is even.

For Choice C, notice that this quantity is factorable by 2. That is, $2x^2 + 4x + 6$
$$= 2(x^2 + 2x + 3), \text{ which is even.}$$

(Math Refresher #431)

For Choice E, the more sophisticated way of doing this is to use **Strategy 4: Factor quantities.**

Choice E is $x^2 + x + 2$.

Now factor: $x^2 + x + 2 = x(x + 1) + 2$.

Note that since x is an integer, $x(x + 1)$ is always the product of an even integer multiplied by an odd integer. So $x(x + 1)$ is even and thus 2 times an integer. $+2$ is even, so $x(x + 1) + 2$ is even. And since $x(x + 1) + 2 = x^2 + x + 2$, $x^2 + x + 2$ is even.

(Math Refresher #409)

11. **4 (Use Strategy 17: Use the given information effectively.)**

Remembering that the sum of 2 sides of a triangle is greater than the third side, we know that

$$LM + MN > LN$$
or $$6 + 10 > 12$$
$$16 > 12$$

The difference between 16 and 12: $16 - 12 = 4$ is the amount of overlap.

Method 2: **(Use Strategy 14: Draw lines when appropriate.)**

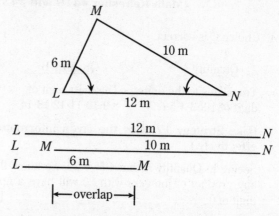

In the figure above, the segments have been redrawn so that the result can be easily discovered.

In $\boxed{2}$, the distance $LM = 12 \text{ m} - 10 \text{ m} = 2 \text{ m}$ $\boxed{4}$

Subtracting $\boxed{4}$ from the distance LM in $\boxed{3}$, we get $6 \text{ m} - 2 \text{ m} = 4 \text{ m}$ overlap.

(Math Refresher #419)

12. Choice C is correct. **(Use Strategy 2: Translate from words to algebra.)** Set up a Venn diagram:

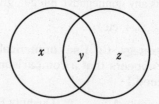

x = number of students with *only* a car
z = number of students with *only* a bicycle
y = number of students having a car and a bicycle

Total students = 100 $\qquad \boxed{1}$
We are given: $x + y = 30$ $\qquad \boxed{2}$
$z + y = 50$ $\qquad \boxed{3}$
$y = 20$ $\qquad \boxed{4}$

Substituting $\boxed{4}$ into $\boxed{2}$ and into $\boxed{3}$, we get

$x = 10, z = 30$ $\qquad \boxed{5}$

Using $\boxed{4}$ and $\boxed{5}$, we have:

The sum of $x + y + z =$
$$10 + 20 + 30 = 60 \qquad \boxed{6}$$

This is the number of students who have either a car, a bicycle, or both.

Using $\boxed{1}$ and $\boxed{6}$, we get $100 - 60 = 40$ as the number who have neither a car nor a bicycle nor both.

(Math Refresher #200 and #406)

13. Choice B is correct. **(Use Strategy 11: Use new definitions carefully.)**

After 6 hours, $\frac{x}{2}$ grams remain.

After 12 hours, $\frac{1}{2}\left(\frac{x}{2}\right)$ grams remain.

After 18 hours, $\frac{1}{2}\left(\frac{1}{2}\right)\left(\frac{x}{2}\right)$ grams remain.

After 24 hours, $\frac{1}{2}\left(\frac{1}{2}\right)\left(\frac{1}{2}\right)\left(\frac{x}{2}\right) = \frac{x}{16}$ grams remain.

(Math Refresher #431)

14. Choice D is correct. **(Use Strategy 2: Know how to find percent of a number.)**

$$\text{Let } x = \text{price of car} \qquad \boxed{1}$$
$$\text{Given: 1st reduction} = 30\% \qquad \boxed{2}$$
$$\text{2nd reduction} = 40\% \qquad \boxed{3}$$

We know amount of discount
$$= \text{percent} \times \text{price} \qquad \boxed{4}$$

Using $\boxed{1}$, $\boxed{2}$, and $\boxed{4}$, we get

$$\text{Amount of first discount} = 30\% \times x$$
$$= .30x \qquad \boxed{5}$$

(Use Strategy 13: Find unknowns by subtraction.) Subtracting $\boxed{5}$ from $\boxed{1}$, we have

$$\text{Reduced price} = x - .30x$$
$$= .70x \qquad \boxed{6}$$

Using $\boxed{3}$, $\boxed{6}$, and $\boxed{4}$, we get

$$\text{Amount of second discount} = 40\% \times .70x$$
$$= .40 \times .70x$$
$$= .28x \qquad \boxed{7}$$

Subtracting $\boxed{7}$ from $\boxed{6}$, we have

$$\text{Price after second reduction} = .70x - .28x$$
$$= .42x \qquad \boxed{8}$$

(Use Strategy 16: The obvious may be tricky!)

Since $\boxed{8} = .42x$, it is 42% of the original price of x. This is *not* the answer to the question.

Since $\boxed{8}$ is 42% of the original, it is the result of a 58% discount.

The answer is 58%.

(Math Refresher #200 and #114)

15. Choice C is correct.

$$\text{Given:} \quad \text{Print rate} = \frac{80 \text{ characters}}{\text{second}} \qquad \boxed{1}$$

$$\frac{\text{Number of characters}}{\text{page}} = 2,400 \qquad \boxed{2}$$

(Use Strategy 13: Find unknowns by division.)
Dividing $\boxed{2}$ by $\boxed{1}$, we have

$$\frac{2,400 \text{ characters}}{\text{page}} \div \frac{80 \text{ characters}}{\text{second}} =$$

$$\frac{2,400 \text{ characters}}{\text{page}} \times \frac{\text{second}}{80 \text{ characters}} =$$

$$\frac{2,400 \text{ seconds}}{80 \text{ pages}}$$

$$= \frac{30 \text{ seconds}}{\text{page}} \qquad \boxed{3}$$

The time for an M-page report will be

$$\frac{30 \text{ seconds}}{\text{page}} \times M \text{ pages} =$$

$$\text{Time for } M\text{-page report} = 30M \text{ seconds} \qquad \boxed{4}$$

(Use Strategy 10: Know how to use units.)

To change time from seconds to minutes, we multiply by

$$\frac{1 \text{ minute}}{60 \text{ seconds}} \cdot \qquad \boxed{5}$$

Applying $\boxed{5}$ to $\boxed{4}$, we get

$$\text{Time for } M\text{-page report, in minutes} = 30M \text{ seconds} \times \frac{1 \text{ minute}}{60 \text{ seconds}}$$

$$= \frac{30M \text{ minutes}}{60}$$

$$= \frac{M}{2} \text{ minutes}$$

(Math Refresher #201 and #121)

16. Choice C is correct.

The volume of the rectangular solid to be immersed is:

$$V = (1 \text{ ft})(1 \text{ ft})(2 \text{ ft}) = 2 \text{ cu. ft.} \qquad \boxed{1}$$

When the solid is immersed, the volume of the displaced water will be:

$$(2 \text{ ft.})(6 \text{ ft.})(x \text{ ft.}) = 12x \text{ cu. ft.} \qquad \boxed{2}$$

where x represents the height of the displaced water. $\boxed{1}$ and $\boxed{2}$ must be equal. So

$$2 \text{ cu. ft.} = 12x \text{ cu. ft.}$$

$$\frac{1}{6} \text{ ft} = x$$

(Use Strategy 10: Know how to use units.)

$$\left(\frac{1}{6} \text{ ft}\right)\left(\frac{12 \text{ inches}}{\text{foot}}\right) = \frac{12}{6} = 2 \text{ inches that the displaced}$$
water will rise.

(Math Refresher #312 and #121)

17. Choice D is correct.

Given: Selling price of radio = $64 $\boxed{1}$
               Regular price of radio = $80 $\boxed{2}$

(Use Strategy 2: Remember how to find percent discount.)

$$\text{Percent discount} = \frac{\text{amount off}}{\text{original price}} \times 100 \quad \boxed{3}$$

Subtracting $\boxed{1}$ from $\boxed{2}$, we get

Amount off = $80 − $64 = $16 $\boxed{4}$

Substituting $\boxed{2}$ and $\boxed{4}$ into $\boxed{3}$, we have

$$\text{Percent discount} = \frac{\$16}{\$80} \times 100$$

$$= \frac{\$16 \times 100}{\$80} \quad \boxed{5}$$

(Use Strategy 19: Factor and reduce.)

$$\text{Percent discount} = \frac{\$16 \times 5 \times 20}{\$16 \times 5}$$

$$\text{Percent discount} = 20 \quad \boxed{6}$$

Given: Regular price of different radio = $200 $\boxed{7}$

New percent discount

$$= 1\frac{1}{2} \times \text{Other radio's percent discount} \quad \boxed{8}$$

Using $\boxed{6}$ and $\boxed{8}$, we have

$$\text{New percent discount} = 1\frac{1}{2} \times 20 =$$

$$= \frac{3}{2} \times 20$$

$$= 30 \quad \boxed{9}$$

(Use Strategy 2: Remember how to find percent of a number.)

We know percent of a number =

percent × number. $\boxed{10}$

Substituting $\boxed{7}$ and $\boxed{9}$ into $\boxed{10}$, we have

Amount of discount = 30% × $200

$$= \frac{30}{100} \times \$200$$

Amount of discount = $60 $\boxed{11}$

(Use Strategy 13: Find unknowns by subtraction.)

Subtracting $\boxed{11}$ from $\boxed{7}$, we have

Selling price of different radio

= $200 − $60

= $140

(Math Refresher #200 and #114)

18. Choice C is correct. The bar graph tells us that about 5% of the companies are in this group. The total number of companies is 1,150. 5% of 1,150 = 0.05 × 1,150 = 57.5. But the percentage was only approximate, so 57 is the closest.

(Math Refresher #704)

19. 3. There are three ways to add sectors:
The 30.0% sector plus the 29.6% sector;
The 30.0% sector plus the 22.3% sector;
The 29.6% sector plus the 22.3% sector.

(Math Refresher #705)

20. Choice A is correct. The percent of companies in the 24.0%–27.9% bracket is 20. Only about 12% of the companies are in the 16.0%–19.9% bracket. This is a difference of 8% of the companies. There are 1,150 companies altogether. 8% of 1,150 is about 92.

(Math Refresher #704)

21. Choice A is correct. Social Security and Unemployment Insurance contribute 22.3% to the benefit money. This is split into four parts, each ¼ of 22.3%, and added to each sector. ¼ of 22.3% is about 5.6%. The new percentage of Paid Vacations, etc. is 29.6% + 5.6% = 35.2%. The total benefit money is 82.24¢ per payroll hour. 35.2% of 82.2 is 82.2 × .352, or about 28.9.

(Math Refresher #705)

22. Choice C is correct. **(Use Strategy 7: Use number examples.)**

$$\text{If } a = \frac{2}{3}, b = \frac{4}{3}, \text{ and } x = \frac{3}{2} \quad \boxed{1}$$

Then, substituting from $\boxed{1}$, we get

$$ax = \frac{2}{3}\left(\frac{3}{2}\right) \qquad bx = \frac{4}{3}\left(\frac{3}{2}\right) = \frac{4}{2}$$

$$ax = 1 \qquad\qquad bx = 2$$

Neither a nor b nor x are integers, but both ax and bx are integers.

Thus, Choices A and B are eliminated.

(Use Strategy 13: Find unknown expressions by addition of equations.)

Adding ax to bx, we get

$$ax + bx =$$
$$(a + b)x \quad \boxed{2}$$

Since ax and bx are integers, $\boxed{2}$ is an integer. Thus, Choice C is correct.

(Math Refresher #431)

23. Choice B is correct. Use $y = mx + b$ for representation of line k. m is the slope of the line and b is the y-intercept (that is, the value of y when $x = 0$). You can see that a point on the graph is at $x = 3$ and $y = 2$ from the points $(0,2)$ and $(3,0)$. Thus substituting $x = 3$ and $y = 2$ into $y = mx + b$, we get $2 = m(3) + b$. Since m is the slope of the graph and is equal to -1, we get

$$2 = (-1)(3) + b.$$

$$2 = -3 + b$$

and so $5 = b$.

(Math Refresher #415 and #416)

24. **36.2 (Use Strategy 2: Translate from words to algebra.)**

Fraction mowed during evening 1 $= \dfrac{2}{9}$ $\boxed{1}$

Fraction mowed during evening 2 $= 2\left(\dfrac{2}{9}\right) = \dfrac{4}{9}$ $\boxed{2}$

Adding $\boxed{1}$ and $\boxed{2}$, we get

Total fraction mowed during
first two evenings $= \dfrac{2}{9} + \dfrac{4}{9}$

$$= \dfrac{6}{9}$$

Total fraction mowed during
first two evenings $= \dfrac{2}{3}$

(Use Strategy 3: The whole equals the sum of its parts.)

Amount left for evening 3 $=$

1 whole lawn $- \dfrac{2}{3}$ already mowed $\boxed{3}$

Amount left for evening 3 $= \dfrac{1}{3}$ $\boxed{4}$

Given: Lawn area $= 108.6$ square feet

Multiplying $\boxed{3}$ by $\boxed{4}$, we get

Amount left for evening 3 $= \dfrac{1}{3} \times 108.6$ square feet

Amount left for evening 3 $= 36.2$ square feet

(Math Refresher #200 and #109)

25. Choice B is correct. First write the numbers in *ascending* order without the x.

7 7 7 7 9 9 9 9 13 13 13

Suppose $x \neq 9$. Then x would appear either after the 9 or before the 9. Examples would be like this.

7 7 7 7 9 9 9 9 x 13 13 13

or perhaps

7 7 7 7 9 9 9 9 13 13 13 x

Or perhaps like this:

7 7 7 7 x 9 9 9 9 13 13 13

or perhaps

x 7 7 7 7 9 9 9 9 13 13 13

No matter where the y appears, the middle numbers (note that the amount of numbers are even) are 9 and 9. The average is 9, which is the median.

Now suppose $x = 9$. Then we would have:

7 7 7 7 9 9 9 9 9 13 13 13

The middle numbers are still 9 and 9, so the average is still 9, which is the median.

(Math Refresher #601a)

What You Must Do Now to Raise Your GRE Score

1. Follow the directions on page 562 to determine your scaled score for the GRE Test you've just taken. These results will give you a good idea about how hard you'll need to study in order to achieve a certain score on the actual GRE.

2. Eliminate your weaknesses in each of the GRE test areas by taking the following Giant Steps toward GRE success:

Sentence Completion and Reading Part

Giant Step 1

Take advantage of the Sentence Completion and Reading Strategies that begin on page 136. Read again the Explanatory Answer for each of the Sentence Completion and Reading questions that you got wrong. Refer to the Reading Strategy that applies to each of your incorrect answers. Learn each of these strategies thoroughly. These strategies are crucial if you want to raise your GRE Verbal score substantially.

Giant Step 2

You can improve your vocabulary by doing the following:

1) Study the GRE 3,400-Word List beginning on page 377.

2) Take the 100 Tests to Strengthen Your Vocabulary beginning on page 426.

3) Study the Gruber Prefix-Root-Suffix List beginning on page 366.

4) Learn the Hot Prefixes and Roots beginning on page 717.

5) Read through the List of Standardized Test Words Appearing More Than Once beginning on page 371.

6) Look through the Most Important/Frequently Used GRE Words and Their Opposites beginning on page 373.

7) Learn the 3 Vocabulary Strategies beginning on page 168.

8) Read as widely as possible—not only novels. Nonfiction is important too…and don't forget to read newspapers and magazines.

9) Listen to people who speak well. Tune in to worthwhile TV programs.

10) Use the dictionary frequently and extensively—at home, on the bus, at work, etc.

11) Play word games—for example, crossword puzzles, anagrams, and Scrabble. Another game is to compose your own Sentence Completion questions. Try them on your friends.

Math Part

Giant Step 3

Make good use of the 25 Math Strategies that begin on page 72. Read again the solutions for each Math question that you answered incorrectly. Refer to the Math Strategy that applies to each of your incorrect answers. Learn each of these Math Strategies thoroughly. We repeat that these strategies are crucial if you want to raise your GRE Math score substantially.

Giant Step 4

You may want to take the **101 Most Important Math Questions You Need to Know How to Solve** test beginning on page 40 and follow the directions after the test for a basic Math skills diagnosis.

For each Math question that you got wrong in the test, note the reference to the Math Refresher section beginning on page 185. This reference will explain clearly the mathematical principle involved in the solution of the question you answered incorrectly. Learn that particular mathematical principle thoroughly.

For Both the Math and Reading Parts

Giant Step 5

You may want to take the **Strategy Diagnostic Test** beginning on page 1 to assess whether you're using the best strategies for the questions.

For the Writing Part

Giant Step 6

Take a look at Part 8, the Analytical Writing Section, which describes the various types of tasks in the Writing Section. Also make use of the Brief Review of English Grammar—Part 9.

3. After you have done some of the tasks you have been advised to do in the previous suggestions, proceed to Practice Test 2 beginning on page 584.

After taking Practice Test 2, concentrate on the weaknesses that still remain.

If you do the job *right* and follow the steps listed earlier, you are likely to raise your GRE score substantially on each of the Verbal, Math, and Writing parts of the test.

I am the master of my fate:
I am the captain of my soul.

—From the poem "Invictus"
by William Ernest Henley

GRE PRACTICE
TEST 2

Analytical Writing 1

ANALYZE AN ISSUE

Time—30 Minutes

You have 30 minutes to plan and compose a response to the following issue. A response to any other issue will receive a score of zero. Make sure that you respond according to the specific instructions and support your position on the issue with reasons and examples drawn from such areas as your reading, experience, observations, and/or academic studies.

> College students should be encouraged to pursue subjects that interest them rather than the courses that seem most likely to lead to jobs.

Write a response in which you discuss the extent to which you agree or disagree with the recommendation and explain your reasoning for the position you take. In developing and supporting your position, describe specific circumstances in which adopting the recommendation would or would not be advantageous and explain how these examples shape your position.

Trained GRE readers will evaluate your response for its overall quality based on how well you:

- Respond to the specific task instructions
- Consider the complexities of the issue
- Organize, develop, and express your ideas
- Support your ideas with relevant reasons and/or examples
- Control the elements of standard written English

Before you begin writing, you may want to think for a few minutes about the issue and the specific task instructions and then plan your response. **Use the next page to plan your response, then write your response starting on the first lined page that follows. A total of four lined pages are provided for your response.** Be sure to develop your position fully and organize it coherently, but leave time to reread what you have written and make any revisions you think are necessary.

Write your response within the boxed area on the pages provided. Any text outside the boxed area will not be scored.

GO ON TO THE NEXT PAGE

Plan Your Response Here. Begin Writing Your Essay on the Following Page.

This page will not be scored.

GO ON TO THE NEXT PAGE

Note: On the computerized test, you will type your response and you will be able to correct mistakes through a word processor.

ANALYZE AN ISSUE RESPONSE (Page 1 of 4)

GO ON TO THE NEXT PAGE

ANALYZE AN ISSUE RESPONSE (Page 2 of 4)

_____
_____
_____
_____
_____
_____
_____
_____
_____
_____
_____
_____
_____
_____
_____
_____
_____
_____
_____
_____
_____
_____
_____
_____
_____
_____
_____
_____

GO ON TO THE NEXT PAGE

ANALYZE AN ISSUE RESPONSE (Page 3 of 4)

GO ON TO THE NEXT PAGE

ANALYZE AN ISSUE RESPONSE (Page 4 of 4)

_____

_____

_____

_____

_____

_____

_____

_____

_____

_____

_____

_____

_____

_____

_____

_____

_____

_____

_____

_____

_____

_____

_____

_____

_____

_____

_____

_____

STOP

If you finish before time is called, you may check your work on this section only.
Do not turn to any other section in the test.

Analytical Writing 2

ANALYZE AN ARGUMENT

Time—30 Minutes

You have 30 minutes to plan and compose a response in which you evaluate the following argument passage. A response to any other argument will receive a score of zero. Make sure that you respond according to the specific instructions and support your evaluation with relevant reasons and/or examples.

Note that you are NOT being asked to present your own views on the subject.

The following appeared in a memo from a vice president of Quiot Manufacturing.

"During the past year, Quiot Manufacturing had 30 percent more on-the-job accidents than at the nearby Panoply Industries plant, where the work shifts are one hour shorter than ours. Experts say that significant contributing factors in many on-the-job accidents are fatigue and sleep deprivation among workers. Therefore, to reduce the number of on-the-job accidents at Quiot and thereby increase productivity, we should shorten each of our three work shifts by one hour so that employees will get adequate amounts of sleep."

Write a response in which you examine the stated and/or unstated assumptions of the argument. Be sure to explain how the argument depends on these assumptions and what the implications are for the argument if the assumptions prove unwarranted.

Trained GRE readers will evaluate your response for its overall quality based on how well you:

- Respond to the specific task instructions
- Consider the complexities of the issue
- Organize, develop, and express your ideas
- Support your ideas with relevant reasons and/or examples
- Control the elements of standard written English

Before you begin writing, you may want to think for a few minutes about the issue and the specific task instructions and then plan your response. **Use the next page to plan your response, then write your response starting on the first lined page that follows. A total of four lined pages are provided for your response.** Be sure to develop your position fully and organize it coherently, but leave time to reread what you have written and make any revisions you think are necessary.

Write your response within the boxed area on the pages provided. Any text outside the boxed area will not be scored.

GO ON TO THE NEXT PAGE

Plan Your Response Here. Begin Writing Your Essay on the Following Page.

This page will not be scored.

Note: On the computerized test, you will type your response and you will be able to correct mistakes through a word processor.

ANALYZE AN ARGUMENT RESPONSE (Page 1 of 4)

GO ON TO THE NEXT PAGE

ANALYZE AN ARGUMENT RESPONSE (Page 2 of 4)

GO ON TO THE NEXT PAGE

ANALYZE AN ARGUMENT RESPONSE (Page 3 of 4)

GO ON TO THE NEXT PAGE

ANALYZE AN ARGUMENT RESPONSE (Page 4 of 4)

STOP

If you finish before time is called, you may check your work on this section only.
Do not turn to any other section in the test.

Instructions for Verbal Reasoning and Quantitative Reasoning Sections

Important Notes

Your scores for these sections will be determined by the number of questions you answer correctly. Nothing is subtracted from your score if you answer a question incorrectly. Therefore, to maximize your scores it is better for you to guess at an answer than not to respond at all. Work as rapidly as you can without losing accuracy. Do not spend too much time on questions that are too difficult for you. Go on to the other questions and come back to the difficult ones later.

Some or all of the passages in this test have been adapted from published material to provide the examinee with significant problems for analysis and evaluation. To make the passages suitable for testing purposes, the style, content, or point of view of the original may have been altered.

You may use a calculator in the Quantitative Reasoning sections only. You will be provided with a calculator and cannot use any other calculator.

Marking Your Answers

All answers must be marked in this test book. When filling in the circles that accompany each question, BE SURE THAT EACH MARK IS DARK AND COMPLETELY FILLS THE CIRCLE.

Correct		Incorrect		
Ⓐ	Ⓧ	Ⓐ	Ⓐ	Ⓐ
●	Ⓧ	Ⓑ	Ⓑ	Ⓑ
Ⓒ	Ⓒ	Ⓒ	Ⓒ	Ⓒ
Ⓓ	Ⓓ	Ⓓ	Ⓓ	Ⓓ

Be careful to erase any stray marks that lie in or near a circle. If you change an answer, be sure that all previous marks are erased completely. Stray marks and incomplete erasures may be read as intended answers. Scratch paper will not be provided. You may work out your answers in the blank areas of the test book, but do not work out answers near the circles.

Question Formats

The questions in these sections have several different formats. A brief description of these formats and instructions for entering your answer choices are given below.

Multiple-Choice Questions—Select One Answer Choice

These standard multiple-choice questions require you to select just one answer choice from a list of options. You will receive credit only if you mark the **single** correct answer choice and no other.

Example: What city is the capital of France?

Ⓐ Rome

● Paris

Ⓒ London

Ⓓ Cairo

Multiple-Choice Questions—Select One or More Answer Choices

Some of these questions specify how many answer choices to select; others require you to select all that apply. In either case, to receive credit you must mark all of the correct answer choices and no others. These questions are distinguished by the use of a square box.

Example: Select all that apply.

Which of the following countries are in Africa?

- ■ Chad
- Ⓑ China
- Ⓒ France
- ■ Kenya

Column Format Questions

This question type presents the answer choices in columns. You must select one answer choice from each column. You will receive credit only if you mark the correct answer choice **in each column**.

Example: Complete the following sentence,

(i) _____ is the capital of (ii) _____.

Blank (i)   Blank (ii)

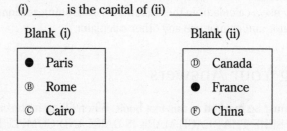

Numeric Entry Questions

To answer these questions, enter a number by filling in circles in a grid. Complete instructions for doing so will be found in the Quantitative Reasoning sections.

Section 1: Verbal Reasoning

Time—35 Minutes
25 Questions

For each question, indicate the best answer, using the directions given.

For each of Questions 1–8, select <u>one</u> entry for each blank from the corresponding column of choices.
Fill all blanks in the way that best completes the text.

1. He was _____ about a rise in the value of the stocks he had recently purchased and was eager to make a change in his investment portfolio.

   (A) fearful
   (B) unconcerned
   (C) hesitant
   (D) amused
   (E) dubious

2. Because the subject matter was so technical, the instructor made every effort to use _____ terms to describe it.

   (A) candid
   (B) simplified
   (C) discreet
   (D) specialized
   (E) involved

3. Although there was considerable _____ among the members of the panel as to the qualities essential for a champion, Sugar Ray Robinson was _____ voted the greatest fighter of all time.

Blank 1	Blank 2
(A) discourse	(D) characteristically
(B) disagreement	(E) overwhelmingly
(C) research	(F) presumably

4. The long-time philosophy professor displayed extreme stubbornness; not only did he _____ the logic of the student's argument, but he _____ to acknowledge that the textbook conclusion was correct.

Blank 1	Blank 2
(A) justify	(D) refused
(B) denigrate	(E) consented
(C) reject	(F) presumed

5. Many contenders argue that a sense of fairness _____ that the punishment should fit the crime; however, it is noted that in actual practice, judicial decisions _____ greatly for the same type of criminal offense.

Blank 1	Blank 2
(A) relegates	(D) deviate
(B) dictates	(E) emanate
(C) presupposes	(F) coincide

6. Governor Edwards combined _____ politics with administrative skills to dominate the state; in addition to his abilities, he was also _____ and possessed an air of _____.

Blank 1	Blank 2	Blank 3
(A) inept	(D) charismatic	(G) elegance
(B) corrupt	(E) lavish	(H) haughtiness
(C) astute	(F) creative	(I) subtleness

7. More and more people are not spending their _____ time at the cinema. With the film rental business and the retail sales of DVDs _____, one can watch not only _____ movies but also films that were made during the last fifty years in the peacefulness of one's own home.

Blank 1	Blank 2	Blank 3
(A) precious	(D) coordinating	(G) stylistic
(B) leisure	(E) leveling	(H) profound
(C) limited	(F) booming	(I) contemporary

GO ON TO THE NEXT PAGE

8. Athens was ruled not by kings and emperors as was common among other _____ at the time, but by a citizenry, which _____ fully in the affairs of the city. It was argued that the conditions and lifestyle in Athens were more _____ to the population by this type of government.

Blank 1	Blank 2	Blank 3
(A) popula-tions	(D) cooperated	(G) alien
(B) societies	(E) participated	(H) detrimental
(C) cities	(F) engaged	(I) advanta-geous

For each of Questions 9–14, select <u>one</u> answer choice unless otherwise directed.

Questions 9–11 are based on this passage.

1　　The wealthy hunting societies of late glacial Europe might have maintained or even enriched their culture, or allowed it to stagnate and decline: they could hardly have advanced it to a higher form of civilization, for the
5　environment forbade it. But their future was not left in their own hands. Inexorably, although no doubt to them imperceptibly, the climate changed: Summers grew longer and warmer, ice-sheets shrank, and glaciers retreated. Enslaved to climate, plant and animal life had to change also.
10　The mammoth, rhinoceros, and reindeer in turn disappeared from western Europe, their going perhaps accelerated by the inroads of the human hunters themselves. On what had been open grassland or tundra with a scrub of dwarf birch and willow, forest spread, stocked with the appropriate
15　forest animals: red deer, aurochs, and wild pig. With the withdrawal or extinction of the great herds on which they had preyed, the economic basis of the hunting societies was cut away and their carefully adjusted culture made obsolete. This was one of the moments when early man was able to
20　prove the full advantage of his self-made equipment over the biological specialization of the beasts: the reindeer found his coat intolerably hot and had to quit; man merely took his off and readjusted his habits.

9. The disappearance of certain animals from western Europe was

(A) probably hastened by man, the hunter
(B) disastrous to primitive man
(C) the direct result of man's self-made equipment
(D) the immediate result of a more advanced culture
(E) caused by the movement of glaciers

10. The primitive hunting societies were forced to change their way of life because

(A) they were the victims of their biological specialization
(B) they were incapable of enriching their lives
(C) they were stagnating
(D) the animals that they hunted disappeared
(E) their culture was allowed to decline

11. In the context in which it appears, "specialization" (line 21) most nearly means

(A) something unique
(B) a part of the beast's anatomy
(C) the concentration in a special branch or study
(D) the habits of the beasts
(E) the enormity of the animals

Questions 12–13 are based on this passage.

1　Most people want to know how things are made. They frankly admit, however, that they feel completely at sea when it comes to understanding how a piece of music is made. Where a composer begins, how he manages to keep
5　going—in fact, how and where he learns his trade—all are shrouded in impenetrable darkness. The composer, in short, is a man of mystery, and the composer's workshop an unapproachable ivory tower.
　　　One of the first things the layperson wants to hear
10　about is the part inspiration plays in composing. He finds it difficult to believe that composers are not much preoccupied with that question, that composing is as natural for the composer as eating or sleeping. Composing is something that the composer happens to have been born to do; and
15　because of that, it loses the character of a special virtue in the composer's eyes.
　　　The composer, therefore, does not say to himself: "Do I feel inspired?" He says to himself: "Do I feel like composing today?" And if he feels like composing, he does. It is more
20　or less like saying to himself: "Do I feel sleepy?" If you feel sleepy, you go to sleep. If you don't feel sleepy, you stay up. If the composer doesn't feel like composing, he doesn't compose. It's as simple as that.

For the following question, consider each of the choices separately and select all that apply.

---

12. The author of the passage indicates that creating music is an activity that is

(A) instinctive
(B) not necessarily inspirational
(C) fraught with anxiety

GO ON TO THE NEXT PAGE

For the following question, consider each of the choices separately and select all that apply.

13. When considering the work involved in composing music, the layperson often

    (A) exaggerates the difficulties of the composer in commencing work
    (B) minimizes the mental turmoil that the composer undergoes
    (C) has a preconceived notion of what is motivating the composer

Question 14 is based on this passage.

1 The editor ventures on too thin ice by trying to interpret Mozart's markings, perhaps using a dot for a fairly soft, "round" staccato, and the stroke for a sharper, more ener-getic one. In this case he will certainly have, at times, to
5 weight philological arguments (based on Mozart's inten-tion) against musical ones, and choose subjectively. For there are many cases in which the outward appearance of a sign in Mozart's manuscript clashes with its musical significance, for the simple reason that he happened to be
10 using a faulty quill whose points had spread.

14. Which of the following statements may be assumed from the paragraph?

    I. One ought to follow the exact wishes of the composer in playing his music.
    II. It is futile to attempt to edit Mozart's writings.
    III. More than one way to play staccato is possible.

    (A) I only
    (B) II only
    (C) III only
    (D) I and II only
    (E) I and III only

For each of Questions 15–19, select the two answer choices that, when used to complete the sentence blank, fit the meaning of the sentence as a whole <u>and</u> produce completed sentences that are alike in meaning.

15. In spite of David's tremendous intelligence, he was frequently _____ when confronted with practical matters.

    (A) coherent
    (B) baffled
    (C) cautious
    (D) philosophical
    (E) flustered
    (F) pensive

16. The photographs of Ethiopia's starving children demonstrate the _____ of drought, poor land use, and overpopulation.

    (A) consequences
    (B) prejudices
    (C) inequities
    (D) indications
    (E) mortalities
    (F) effects

17. The scientist averred that a nuclear war could _____ enough smoke and dust to blot out the sin and freeze the earth.

    (A) accentuate
    (B) extinguish
    (C) generate
    (D) elucidate
    (E) perpetrate
    (F) create

18. Until his death he remained _____ in the belief that the world was conspiring against him.

    (A) ignominious
    (B) taciturn
    (C) tantamount
    (D) obdurate
    (E) reticent
    (F) obstinate

19. Some illnesses, such as malaria, that have been virtually eliminated in the United States are still _____ in many places abroad.

    (A) discussed
    (B) prevalent
    (C) prevaricated
    (D) plentiful
    (E) unknown
    (F) hospitalized

For each of Questions 20–25, select <u>one</u> answer choice unless otherwise directed.

Questions 20–22 are based on this passage.

1   The wandering microscopic vegetables of the sea, of which the diatoms are most important, make the mineral wealth of the water available to the animals. Feeding directly on the diatoms and other groups of minute unicellular algae
5 are the marine protozoa, many crustaceans, the young of crabs, barnacles, sea worms, and fishes. Hordes of the

GO ON TO THE NEXT PAGE

small carnivores, the first link in the chain of flesh eaters, move among these peaceful grazers. There are fierce little dragons half an inch long, the sharp-jawed arrowworms.
10 There are gooseberrylike comb jellies, armed with grasping tentacles, and there are the shrimplike euphausiids that strain food from the water with their bristly appendages. They meander, with no power or will to oppose that of the sea. This strange community of creatures and the marine
15 plants that sustain them are called plankton.

20. Which characteristic of diatoms does the passage emphasize?

   (A) size
   (B) feeding habits
   (C) activeness
   (D) numerousness
   (E) cellular structure

21. According to the passage, which prey on other sea creatures?

   (A) sea worms
   (B) young crabs
   (C) barnacles
   (D) euphausiids
   (E) marine protozoa

22. In the context of the passage as a whole, "meander" (line 13) most nearly means

   (A) stay
   (B) destroy
   (C) feast
   (D) ramble
   (E) produce

Questions 23–24 are based on this passage.

1   Nevertheless there is such a voluble hue and cry about the abysmal state of culture in the United States by well-meaning, sincere critics that I would like to present some evidence to the contrary. One is tempted to remind
5 these critics that no country has ever achieved the complete integration of *haute culture* into the warp and woof of its everyday life. In the wishful memories of those who moon over the past glories of Shakespeare's England, it is seldom called to mind that bearbaiting was far more popular
10 than any of Master Shakespeare's presentations. Who cares to remember that the same Rome that found a Juvenal proclaiming *mens sana in corpore sano* could also watch an Emperor Trajan celebrate his victory over Decebalus of Dacia in 106 A.D. with no fewer than 5,000 pairs of gladiators
15 matched to the death? And this in the name of amusement!

23. The paragraph preceding this passage most probably discussed

   (A) the increased interest of Americans in public affairs
   (B) the popularity of Shakespeare during his lifetime
   (C) the interest of Americans in the arts
   (D) the duties of a literary critic
   (E) Juvenal's contributions to poetry

24. In the context in which it appears, "voluble hue and cry" (line 1) most nearly means:

   (A) interest
   (B) belief
   (C) predominance
   (D) shouting
   (E) sincerity

Question 25 is based on this passage.

1   For the past twenty years, there have been many improvements and innovations in bicycle equipment. These innovations and improvements have created a safer and more satisfying experience for bicyclists. However, even
5 with these improvements and innovations, bicycle-related injuries have climbed in the past twenty years.

25. Which of the following statements, if true, best accounts for the reason that bicycle injuries have risen even though bicycles were made safer?

   (A) Weather conditions caused some bicycle injuries.

   (B) Many bicyclists attempted bicycle feats above their ability.

   (C) There have been improvements and innovations in bicycle riding techniques as well as in bicycle equipment.

   (D) People who have never ridden bicycles are riding them now.

   (E) Because of the improvements and innovations in bicycle equipment, it is more complicated to ride a bicycle.

STOP

If you finish before time is called, you may check your work on this section only.
Do not turn to any other section in the test.

Section 2: Verbal Reasoning

Time—35 Minutes
25 Questions

For each question, indicate the best answer, using the directions given.

For each of Questions 1–8, select <u>one</u> entry for each blank from the corresponding column of choices.
Fill all blanks in the way that best completes the text.

1. The Prime Minister had stated that Spain would
   _____ to its decision to bar the United States jet
   fighters from Spanish soil, despite strong pressure
   from allies on behalf of our nation.

   (A) yield
   (B) return
   (C) refer
   (D) succumb
   (E) adhere

2. Steffi Graf, as a West German teenager, _____
   her hold on the Number 1 ranking, indicating that
   she was considered the world's best female tennis
   player.

   (A) confined
   (B) solidified
   (C) gladdened
   (D) appreciated
   (E) forfeited

3. The social-cultural trends of the 1960s _____ not
   only the relative affluence of the postwar period but
   also the coming to maturity of a generation that
   was the product of that _____.

Blank 1	Blank 2
(A) accentuated	(D) prosperity
(B) reflected	(E) revolution
(C) dominated	(F) movement

4. A survey depicted that some people are quite
   _____ about having a guest remove his shoes
   before he entered their house; yet the majority of
   rooms in the houses of those people were found
   to be _____ at the time the guests visited those
   houses.

Blank 1	Blank 2
(A) indifferent	(D) deranged
(B) perplexed	(E) professional
(C) adamant	(F) disorderly

5. The rights of citizens include the following: the
   right to life, liberty, the pursuit of happiness, and
   the free exercise of worship. _____ in these
   rights is the _____ to preserve and defend them
   to the best of the citizens' ability.

Blank 1	Blank 2
(A) Precluded	(D) principle
(B) Implicit	(E) opportunity
(C) Inherent	(F) responsibility

6. The discouragement and _____ that so often
   plague perfectionists can lead to decreases in
   _____ and production, also often _____ the
   quality and quantity of the material that is produced.

Blank 1	Blank 2	Blank 3
(A) frugality	(D) creativity	(G) affecting
(B) pressure	(E) development	(H) determining
(C) purpose-fulness	(F) promotion	(I) exacting

7. Originally conceived as a work in progress for a
   _____ film, *Utopia* has _____ into a one-of-
   a-kind show that threads together a century's
   worth of dizzying sounds and images into a
   deeply moving meditation on our world's _____
   shrinking idealism.

Blank 1	Blank 2	Blank 3
(A) magnani-mous	(D) transformed	(G) understand-ably
(B) still un-completed	(E) positioned itself	(H) ironically
(C) captivat-ing	(F) evolved	(I) seemingly

GO ON TO THE NEXT PAGE

8. Television is watched so frequently that intellectuals who detest the "tube" are _____, as they believe that because the medium creates _____ among the viewers, many of the viewers get into a mode in their life and work of relying on _____ means of stimulation and entertainment rather than using internal means of attaining knowledge and enjoyment.

Blank 1	Blank 2	Blank 3
(A) perplexed	(D) fervor	(G) external
(B) disillu-sioned	(E) an encouragement	(H) subtle
(C) infuriated	(F) a passivity	(I) superficial

For each of Questions 9–15, select one answer choice unless otherwise directed.

Questions 9–10 are based on this passage.

1 The person who reads well is the person who thinks well, who has a background for opinions and a touchstone for judgment. He or she may be a Lincoln who derives wisdom from a few books or a Roosevelt who ranges from Icelandic
5 sagas to *Penrod*. But reading makes him or her a full person, and out of that fullness he or she draws that example and precept that stand him or her in good stead when confronted with problems that beset a chaotic universe. Mere reading, of course, is nothing. It is but the veneer of education. But
10 wise reading is a help to action. American versatility is too frequently dilettantism, but reinforced by knowledge it becomes motive power. "Learning," as James L. Mursell says, "cashes the blank check of native versatility." And learning is a process not to be concluded with the formal
15 teaching of schooldays or to be enriched only by the active experience of later years, but to be broadened and deepened by persistent and judicious reading. "The true University of these days is a Collection of Books," said Carlyle. If that is not the whole of the truth it is enough of it for every young
20 person to hug to his or her bosom.

For the following two Questions (Questions 9 and 10), consider each of the choices separately and select all that apply.

9. What advice would the author of this passage most likely give to young people?

   (A) Develop a personal reading program.
   (B) Never stop learning.
   (C) You don't need to learn to read more rapidly and accurately, but more wisely.

10. The author apparently believes that

   (A) America can overcome her dilettantism by broader reading programs for her citizens
   (B) it is not the number of books one reads that is important, but the type of books one reads
   (C) people with wide reading backgrounds are likely to find right courses of action

Question 11 is based on this passage.

1 Researchers, conducting a long-term study of drug abusers who initially demonstrated no serious psychiatric illnesses, observed that after six years a significant number of amphetamine abusers had become schizophrenic, whereas
5 many of those using depressants suffered from severe depression. The researchers concluded that particular drugs, if abused, cause specific psychiatric illnesses.

11. Which of the following, if true, weakens the researchers' conclusion?

   (A) Preexisting undetected personality disorders lead drug abusers to choose particular drugs.
   (B) Regular use of drugs that are typically abused hastens the development of psychiatric disorders.
   (C) Constant tampering with the brain's chemistry causes permanent as well as temporary changes.
   (D) The use of drugs other than amphetamines and depressants may mask a number of underlying psychiatric problems.
   (E) Persons used to taking a particular kind of drug involuntarily change their behavior to mimic the effect of that drug.

GO ON TO THE NEXT PAGE

Questions 12–15 are based on this passage.

1   As in the case of so many words used by the biologist and the physiologist, the word *acclimatization* is hard to define. With increase in knowledge and understanding, meanings of words change. Originally, the term *acclimatiza-*
5   *tion* was taken to mean only the ability of human beings or animals or plants to accustom themselves to new and strange climatic conditions, primarily altered temperature. A person or a wolf moves to a hot climate and is uncomfortable there, but after a time is better able to withstand the heat. But
10   aside from temperature, there are other aspects of climate. A person or an animal may become adjusted to living at higher altitudes than those it was originally accustomed to. At really high altitudes, such as that which aviators may be exposed to, the low atmospheric pressure becomes a factor
15   of primary importance. In changing to a new environment, a person may, therefore, meet new conditions of temperature or pressure, and in addition may have to contend with different chemical surroundings. On high mountains, the amount of oxygen in the atmosphere may be relatively
20   small; in crowded cities, a person may become exposed to relatively high concentrations of carbon dioxide or even carbon monoxide; and in various areas may be exposed to conditions in which the water content of the atmosphere is extremely high or extremely low. Thus in the case of
25   humans, animals, and even plants, the concept of acclimatization includes the phenomena of increased toleration of high or low temperature, of altered pressure, and of changes in the chemical environment.
      Let us define acclimatization, therefore, as the process
30   by which an organism or a part of an organism becomes inured to an environment that is normally unsuitable to it or lethal for it. By and large, acclimatization is a relatively slow process. The term should not be taken to include relatively rapid adjustments such as those our sense organs
35   are constantly making. This type of adjustment is commonly referred to by physiologists as "adaptation." Thus our touch sense soon becomes accustomed to the pressure of our clothes and we do not feel them; we soon fail to hear the ticking of a clock; obnoxious odors after a time fail to make
40   much impression on us, and our eyes in strong light rapidly become insensitive.
      The fundamental fact about acclimatization is that all animals and plants have some capacity to adjust themselves to changes in their environment. This is one of the most
45   remarkable characteristics of living organisms, a characteristic for which it is extremely difficult to find explanations.

12. It can be inferred from the reading selection that

    (A) every change in the environment requires acclimatization by living things.
    (B) plants and animals are more alike than they are different.
    (C) biologists and physiologists study essentially the same things.
    (D) the explanation of acclimatization is specific to each plant and animal.
    (E) as science develops, the connotation of terms may change.

13. According to the reading selection, acclimatization

    (A) is similar to adaptation.
    (B) is more important today than it formerly was.
    (C) involves positive as well as negative adjustment.
    (D) may be involved with a part of an organism but not with the whole organism.
    (E) is more difficult to explain with the more complex present-day environment than formerly.

14. By inference from the reading selection, which one of the following would *not* require the process of acclimatization?

    (A) an ocean fish placed in a lake
    (B) a skin diver making a deep dive
    (C) an airplane pilot making a high-altitude flight
    (D) a person going from daylight into a darkened room
    (E) a businessman moving from Denver, Colorado, to New Orleans, Louisiana

15. According to the passage, a major distinction between acclimatization and adaptation is that acclimatization

    (A) is more important than adaptation
    (B) is relatively slow and adaptation is relatively rapid
    (C) applies to adjustments while adaptation does not apply to adjustments
    (D) applies to terrestrial animals and adaptation to aquatic animals
    (E) is applicable to all animals and plants and adaptation only to higher animals and man

GO ON TO THE NEXT PAGE

For each of Questions 16–19, select the two answer choices that, when used to complete the sentence blank, fit the meaning of the sentence as a whole and produce completed sentences that are alike in meaning.

16. The Forest Service warned that the spring forest fire season was in full swing and urged that _____ caution be exercised in wooded areas.

(A) unprecedented
(B) scant
(C) radical
(D) customary
(E) extreme
(F) reasonable

17. The plan turned out to be _____ because it would have required more financial backing than was available.

(A) intractable
(B) chaotic
(C) irreversible
(D) untenable
(E) superfluous
(F) infeasible

18. Thinking nothing can be done, many victims of arthritis ignore or delay _____ countermeasures, thus aggravating the problem.

(A) tardy
(B) injurious
(C) operative
(D) characteristic
(E) deleterious
(F) effective

19. Samuel Clemens chose the _____ Mark Twain as a result of his knowledge of riverboat piloting.

(A) protagonist
(B) pseudonym
(C) mountebank
(D) hallucination
(E) misanthrope
(F) pen name

For each of Questions 20–25, select one answer choice unless otherwise directed.

Question 20 is based on this passage.

1   You always knew there could be cars that deliver luxury, engineering, styling, and performance. Now your long wait is over. Now there is Lancelot. Years of Lancelot racing experience culminate in a superb driving experience.
5 It's your alternative to average and overpriced automobiles.

20. The argument above is most weakened by its failure to

(A) stress qualities in which car buyers are interested
(B) mention why people should buy the Lancelot
(C) appeal to status-conscious buyers
(D) provide adequate factual information about the Lancelot
(E) define technical terms used to describe the Lancelot

Questions 21–22 are based on this passage.

1   History has long made a point of the fact that the magnificent flowering of ancient civilization rested upon the institution of slavery, which released opportunity at the top for the art and literature that became the glory of antiq-
5 uity. In a way, the mechanization of the present-day world produces the condition of the ancient in that the enormous development of labor-saving devices and of contrivances that amplify the capacities of mankind affords the base for the leisure necessary to widespread cultural pursuits.
10 Mechanization is the present-day slave power, with the difference that in the mechanized society there is no group of the community that does not share in the benefits of its inventions.

For the following question, consider each of the choices separately and select all that apply.

21. Which of the following statements is supported by the passage?

(A) All people benefit from mechanized inventions.
(B) Mechanization primarily enabled cultural development.
(C) Specific examples of mechanization are not discussed.

GO ON TO THE NEXT PAGE

22. The passage provides information on each of the following EXCEPT

  (A) the effects of mechanization on society
  (B) the types of culture that mechanization enabled
  (C) the range of labor-saving devices
  (D) the time period in which mechanization developed
  (E) the relationship between mechanization and humans

Questions 23–25 are based on this passage.

1   A legendary island in the Atlantic Ocean beyond the Pillars of Hercules was first mentioned by Plato in the *Timaeus*. Atlantis was a fabulously beautiful and prosperous land, the seat of an empire nine thousand years before
5 Solon. Its inhabitants overran parts of Europe and Africa, Athens alone being able to defy them. Because of the impiety of its people, the island was destroyed by an earthquake and inundation. The legend may have existed before Plato and may have sprung from the concept of Homer's
10 Elysium. The possibility that such an island once existed has caused much speculation, resulting in a theory that pre-Columbian civilizations in America were established by colonists from the lost island.

23. According to the passage, we may most safely conclude that the inhabitants of Atlantis

  (A) were known personally to Homer
  (B) were ruled by Plato
  (C) were a religious and superstitious people
  (D) used the name Columbia for America
  (E) left no recorded evidence of their existence

24. According to the legend, Atlantis was destroyed because the inhabitants

  (A) failed to obtain an adequate food supply
  (B) failed to conquer Greece
  (C) failed to respect their gods
  (D) believed in Homer's Elysium
  (E) had become too prosperous

25. In the context in which it appears, "impiety" (line 7) most nearly means

  (A) unwillingness
  (B) uncooperativeness
  (C) disrespect
  (D) simplicity
  (E) steadfastness

STOP

If you finish before time is called, you may check your work on this section only.
Do not turn to any other section in the test.

Section 3: Quantitative Reasoning

Time—40 Minutes
25 Questions

For each question, indicate the best answer, using the directions given.

Notes: All numbers used are real numbers.

All figures are assumed to lie in a plane unless otherwise indicated.

Geometric figures, such as lines, circles, triangles, and quadrilaterals, **are not necessarily** drawn to scale. That is, you should **not** assume that quantities such as lengths and angle measures are as they appear in a figure. You should assume, however, that lines shown as straight are actually straight, points on a line are in the order shown, and more generally, all geometric objects are in the relative positions shown. For questions with geometric figures, you should base your answers on geometric reasoning, not on estimating or comparing quantities by sight or by measurement.

Coordinate systems, such as *xy* planes and number lines, **are** drawn to scale; therefore, you can read, estimate, or compare quantities in such figures by sight or by measurement.

Graphical data presentations, such as bar graphs, circles graphs, and line graphs, **are** drawn to scale; therefore, you can read, estimate, or compare data values by sight or by measurement.

For each of Questions 1–9, compare Quantity A and Quantity B, using additional information centered above the two quantities if such information is given. Select one of the following four answer choices and fill in the corresponding circle to the right of the question.

(A) **Quantity A is greater.**
(B) **Quantity B is greater.**
(C) **The two quantities are equal.**
(D) **The relationship cannot be determined from the information given.**

A symbol that appears more than once in a question has the same meaning throughout the question.

Quantity A	Quantity B	Correct Answer
Example 1: (2) (6)	2 + 6	● Ⓑ Ⓒ Ⓓ

Q

P S R

	Quantity A	Quantity B	Correct Answer
Example 2:	*PS*	*SR*	Ⓐ Ⓑ Ⓒ ●

(since equal lengths cannot be assumed, even though *PS* and *SR* appear equal)

GO ON TO THE NEXT PAGE

SUMMARY DIRECTIONS FOR COMPARISON QUESTIONS

<u>Answer:</u> A if the quantity in Quantity A is greater;
B if the quantity in Quantity B is greater;
C if the two quantities are equal;
D if the relationship cannot be determined from the information given.

1

Quantity A	Quantity B
$8 + 8n$	$9n$

Ⓐ Ⓑ Ⓒ Ⓓ

---

2 Of 54 people in a group, two-thirds were found to be Democrats, while the remaining individuals were Republicans.

Quantity A	Quantity B
17	Number of Republicans

Ⓐ Ⓑ Ⓒ Ⓓ

---

3 $(y - 4)^2 > 0$

Quantity A	Quantity B
y	4

Ⓐ Ⓑ Ⓒ Ⓓ

---

4 The volume of a cone with radius r and height h is found by the formula $V = \frac{1}{3}\pi r^2 h$.

Quantity A	Quantity B
Volume of a cone with radius 6 and height 3	Volume of a cone with radius 3 and height 6

Ⓐ Ⓑ Ⓒ Ⓓ

---

5 $\frac{a}{b} = \frac{2}{3}$ and $\frac{b}{c} = \frac{5}{8}$

Quantity A	Quantity B
$\frac{a}{c}$	$\frac{5}{6}$

Ⓐ Ⓑ Ⓒ Ⓓ

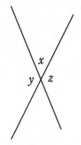

6 $x + 2y + z = 5y$

Quantity A	Quantity B
$\frac{3}{2}z$	x

Ⓐ Ⓑ Ⓒ Ⓓ

GO ON TO THE NEXT PAGE

7 An athlete pedals his bicycle 48 miles in $1\frac{1}{2}$ hours.

Quantity A	Quantity B	
The average speed that the athlete pedaled at (in miles per hour)	36 miles per hour	Ⓐ Ⓑ Ⓒ Ⓓ

8

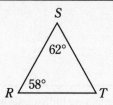

Quantity A	Quantity B	
Length of *ST*	Length of *RT*	Ⓐ Ⓑ Ⓒ Ⓓ

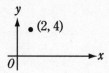

9

Quantity A	Quantity B	
The distance from point (2,4) to the origin	The distance from point (2,4) to point (*p*,0) where *p* > 0	Ⓐ Ⓑ Ⓒ Ⓓ

Questions 10–25 have several different formats. Unless otherwise directed, select a single answer choice. For Numeric Entry questions, follow the instructions below.

Numeric Entry Questions

To answer these questions, enter a number by filling in circles in a grid.

- Your answer may be an integer, a decimal, or a fraction, and it may be negative.

- Equivalent forms of the correct answer, such as 2.5 and 2.50, are all correct. Although fractions do not need to be reduced to lowest terms, they may need to be reduced to fit in the grid.

- Enter the exact answer unless the question asks you to round your answer.

- If a question asks for a fraction, the grid will have a built-in division slash (/). Otherwise, the grid will have a decimal point.

- Start your answer in any column, space permitting. Fill in no more than one circle in any column of the grid. Columns not needed should be left blank.

- Write your answer in the boxes at the top of the grid and fill in the corresponding circles. **You will receive credit only if the circles are filled in correctly, regardless of the number written in the boxes at the top.**

Examples of acceptable ways to use the grid:

Integer answer: 502 (either position is correct)

Decimal answer: -4.13

Fraction answer: $-\dfrac{2}{10}$

10. Given $8r + 3s = 12$ and $7r + 2s = 9$, find the value of $5(r + s)$.

    (A) 5
    (B) 10
    (C) 15
    (D) 20
    (E) 25

11. The degree measures of the four angles of a quadrilateral are w, x, y, and z respectively. If w is the average (arithmetic mean) of x, y, and z, then $x + y + z =$

    (A) 45°
    (B) 90°
    (C) 120°
    (D) 180°
    (E) 270°

12. If r and s are negative numbers, then which of the following must be positive? Choose all that apply.

    (A) $\dfrac{r}{s}$
    (B) rs
    (C) $(rs)^2$
    (D) $r + s$
    (E) $-r - s$

Question 16

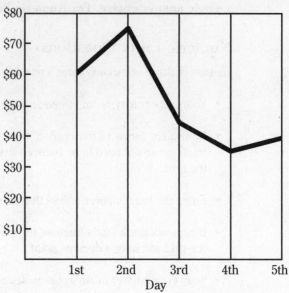

13. John works for 5 days. His daily earnings are displayed on the above graph. If John earned $35 on the sixth day, what would be the difference between the median and the mode of the wages for the six days?

    (A) $5.5
    (B) $6.5
    (C) $7.5
    (D) $8.5
    (E) $9.5

For the following question, use the grid to enter your answer.

14. To make enough paste to hang 6 rolls of wallpaper, a $\frac{1}{4}$-pound package of powder is mixed with $2\frac{1}{2}$ quarts of water. How many pounds of powder are needed to make enough of the same mixture of paste to hang 21 rolls of paper?

GO ON TO THE NEXT PAGE

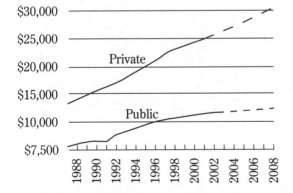

15. The length and width of a rectangle are $3w$ and w respectively. The length of the hypotenuse of a right triangle, one of whose acute angles is 30°, is $2w$. What is the ratio of the area of the rectangle to that of the triangle?

(A) $2\sqrt{3} : 1$
(B) $\sqrt{3} : 1$
(C) $1 : \sqrt{3}$
(D) $1 : 2\sqrt{3}$
(E) $1 : 6$

$$A = \left\{\frac{3}{8}, 2, \frac{3}{2}, 6, \frac{13}{2}, 8\right\}$$
$$B = \left\{\frac{3}{8}, \frac{8}{3}, 6, 8\right\}$$

16. If n is a member of both the sets A and B above, which of the following must be true?

   I. n is an integer
  II. $8n$ is an integer
 III. $n = 6$

(A) None
(B) I only
(C) II only
(D) III only
(E) I and II only

Questions 17–20
Average Charges for College Tuition, Room and Board

17. In the period 1995–96, the average private-school cost was closest to what percent of the average public-school cost?

(A) 50%
(B) 87.5%
(C) 100%
(D) 200%
(E) 250%

18. During which of the following time periods did the average cost for public schools increase most slowly?

(A) 1987–1989
(B) 1989–1991
(C) 1991–1993
(D) 1993–1995
(E) 1995–1997

19. If the expected rate of increase of costs for private schools were to continue past 2008, what would you expect the costs for private schools to be in 2016?

(A) $32,000
(B) $42,000
(C) $40,000
(D) $35,000
(E) $38,000

20. During which time period did costs for public schools increase at a rate greater than that at which costs for private schools increased?

(A) 1988–1989
(B) 1991–1992
(C) 1996–1997
(D) 1997–1998
(E) No such period exists.

21. The number of men in a certain class exceeds the number of women by 7. If the number of men is $\frac{5}{4}$ of the number of women, how many men are there in the class?

(A) 21
(B) 28
(C) 35
(D) 42
(E) 63

22. In 2006, the population of Smithdale was 900. Every year, the population of Smithdale had a net increase of 100. For example, in 2007, the population of Smithdale was 1,000. In which of the following periods was the percent increase in population of Smithdale the greatest?

(A) 2006–2007
(B) 2007–2008
(C) 2008–2009
(D) 2009–2010
(E) The answer cannot be determined from the information given.

GO ON TO THE NEXT PAGE

23. At Lincoln County College, 36 students are taking either calculus or physics or both, and 10 students are taking both calculus and physics. If there are 31 students in the calculus class, how many students are in the physics class?

(A) 14
(B) 15
(C) 16
(D) 17
(E) 18

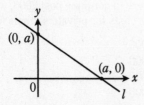

Note: Figure is not drawn to scale.

For the following question, select all the answer choices that apply.

24. In the rectangular coordinate system above, which of the following statements is true about line *l*? Indicate all such statements.

(A) the slope is −1
(B) the distance from point (0,*a*) to point (*a*,0) is equal to $a\sqrt{2}$
(C) the acute angle that line *l* makes with the *x*-axis is 45°

For the following question, use the grid to enter your answer.

$$
\begin{array}{r}
N\,5 \\
\times\ LM \\
\hline
3\,8\,5 \\
3\,8\,5 \\
\hline
4{,}2\,3\,5
\end{array}
$$

25. In the multiplication problem above, *L*, *M*, and *N* each represent one of the digits 0 through 9. If the problem is computed correctly, find *N*.

STOP

If you finish before time is called, you may check your work on this section only.
Do not turn to any other section in the test.

Section 4: Quantitative Reasoning

Time—40 Minutes
25 Questions

For each question, indicate the best answer, using the directions given.

Notes: All numbers used are real numbers.

All figures are assumed to lie in a plane unless otherwise indicated.

Geometric figures, such as lines, circles, triangles, and quadrilaterals, **are not necessarily** drawn to scale. That is, you should **not** assume that quantities such as lengths and angle measures are as they appear in a figure. You should assume, however, that lines shown as straight are actually straight, points on a line are in the order shown, and more generally, all geometric objects are in the relative positions shown. For questions with geometric figures, you should base your answers on geometric reasoning, not on estimating or comparing quantities by sight or by measurement.

Coordinate systems, such as xy planes and number lines, **are** drawn to scale; therefore, you can read, estimate, or compare quantities in such figures by sight or by measurement.

Graphical data presentations, such as bar graphs, circles graphs, and line graphs, **are** drawn to scale; therefore, you can read, estimate, or compare data values by sight or by measurement.

For each of Questions 1–9, compare Quantity A and Quantity B, using additional information centered above the two quantities if such information is given. Select one of the following four answer choices and fill in the corresponding circle to the right of the question.

(A) **Quantity A is greater.**
(B) **Quantity B is greater.**
(C) **The two quantities are equal.**
(D) **The relationship cannot be determined from the information given.**

A symbol that appears more than once in a question has the same meaning throughout the question.

	Quantity A	Quantity B	Correct Answer
Example 1:	$(2)(6)$	$2 + 6$	Ⓐ Ⓑ Ⓒ Ⓓ

	Quantity A	Quantity B	Correct Answer
Example 2:	PS	SR	Ⓐ Ⓑ Ⓒ Ⓓ

(since equal lengths cannot be assumed, even though PS and SR appear equal)

GO ON TO THE NEXT PAGE

SUMMARY DIRECTIONS FOR COMPARISON QUESTIONS

<u>Answer:</u>   A   if the quantity in Quantity A is greater;
B   if the quantity in Quantity B is greater;
C   if the two quantities are equal;
D   if the relationship cannot be determined from the information given.

1

$$\frac{a}{18} = \frac{2}{9}$$

$$\frac{b}{28} = \frac{1}{7}$$

Quantity A	Quantity B	
a	b	Ⓐ Ⓑ Ⓒ Ⓓ

2 r is an even integer and $5 < r < 8$

Quantity A	Quantity B	
$r + 1$	7	Ⓐ Ⓑ Ⓒ Ⓓ

3

Quantity A	Quantity B	
The number of hours in w days	v hours	Ⓐ Ⓑ Ⓒ Ⓓ

4 Darrin is older than Stephanie and Jimmy is older than Stephanie.

Quantity A	Quantity B	
Darrin's age	Jimmy's age	Ⓐ Ⓑ Ⓒ Ⓓ

5 $m - n > p - q$

Quantity A	Quantity B	
n	p	Ⓐ Ⓑ Ⓒ Ⓓ

6 On a certain test, 9 students received a 95 and one student received less than a 95.

Quantity A	Quantity B	
average (arithmetic mean) of test scores	95	Ⓐ Ⓑ Ⓒ Ⓓ

7 $\frac{2}{3} + \frac{r}{s} = \frac{5}{3}$

Quantity A	Quantity B	
r	s	Ⓐ Ⓑ Ⓒ Ⓓ

GO ON TO THE NEXT PAGE

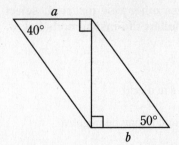

Note: Figure is not drawn to scale.

8	Quantity A	Quantity B	
	a	*b*	Ⓐ Ⓑ Ⓒ Ⓓ

9

Note: Figure is not drawn to scale.
Line *l* ∥ Line *m*. Line segments AC and EC intersect
Line *l* at B and D, respectively.

Quantity A	Quantity B	
The length of BC	The length of DC	Ⓐ Ⓑ Ⓒ Ⓓ

Questions 10–25 have several different formats. Unless otherwise directed, select a single answer choice. For Numeric Entry questions, follow the instructions below.

Numeric Entry Questions

To answer these questions, enter a number by filling in circles in a grid.

- Your answer may be an integer, a decimal, or a fraction, and it may be negative.

- Equivalent forms of the correct answer, such as 2.5 and 2.50, are all correct. Although fractions do not need to be reduced to lowest terms, they may need to be reduced to fit in the grid.

- Enter the exact answer unless the question asks you to round your answer.

- If a question asks for a fraction, the grid will have a built-in division slash (/). Otherwise, the grid will have a decimal point.

- Start your answer in any column, space permitting. Fill in no more than one circle in any column of the grid. Columns not needed should be left blank.

- Write your answer in the boxes at the top of the grid and fill in the corresponding circles. **You will receive credit only if the circles are filled in correctly, regardless of the number written in the boxes at the top.**

Examples of acceptable ways to use the grid:

Integer answer: 502 (either position is correct)

Decimal answer: −4.13

Fraction answer: $-\dfrac{2}{10}$

GO ON TO THE NEXT PAGE

10. If 9 and 12 each divide Q without remainder, which of the following must Q divide without remainder?

(A) 1
(B) 3
(C) 36
(D) 72
(E) The answer cannot be determined from the given information.

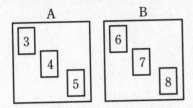

11. Box A contains 3 cards, numbered 3, 4, and 5. Box B contains 3 cards, numbered 6, 7, and 8. If one card is drawn from each box and their sum is calculated, how many different numerical results are possible?

(A) eight
(B) seven
(C) six
(D) five
(E) four

For the following question, use the grid to enter your answer.

12. During a party attended by 3 females and 3 males, 3 people at random enter a previously empty room. What is the probability that there are exactly 2 males in the room?

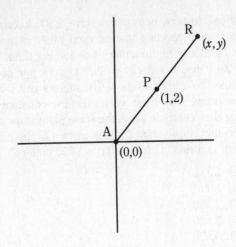

13. If points $(1, 2)$ and (x, y) are on the line represented in the above diagram, which of the following could represent the value of x and y?

(A) $x = 3, y = 5$
(B) $x = 4, y = 8$
(C) $x = 5, y = 11$
(D) $x = 6, y = 15$
(E) $x = 7, y = 17$

14. Over the first few weeks of the baseball season, the league's five leading pitchers had the following won–lost records. (All games ended in a win or loss for that pitcher.)

	Won	Lost
Pitcher A	4	2
Pitcher B	3	2
Pitcher C	4	1
Pitcher D	2	2
Pitcher E	3	1

At the time these statistics were compiled, which pitcher was leading the league in winning percentage? (That is, which pitcher had won the greatest percentage of his games?)

(A) Pitcher A
(B) Pitcher B
(C) Pitcher C
(D) Pitcher D
(E) Pitcher E

GO ON TO THE NEXT PAGE

15. At one instant, two meteors are 2,500 kilometers apart and traveling toward each other in straight paths along the imaginary line joining them. One meteor has a velocity of 300 meters per second while the other travels at 700 meters per second. Assuming that their velocities are constant and that they continue along the same paths, how many seconds elapse from the first instant to the time of their collision? (1 kilometer = 1,000 meters)

   (A) 250
   (B) 500
   (C) 1,250
   (D) 2,500
   (E) 5,000

16. The volume of a cube is less than 25, and the length of one of its edges is a positive integer. What is the largest possible value for the total area of the six faces?

   (A) 1
   (B) 6
   (C) 24
   (D) 54
   (E) 150

For the following question, select all the answer choices that apply.

17. Which are true statements of the graphs $y = 2x^2$ and $y = -2x^2$? Indicate all such statements.

   (A) They have only one point in common.
   (B) The shapes of both are the same but one is right side up and the other is upside down.
   (C) They both represent linear functions.

Questions 18–21 are based on the following data.

U.S. EXPORTS CONSTRUCTION MACHINERY THROUGHOUT THE WORLD

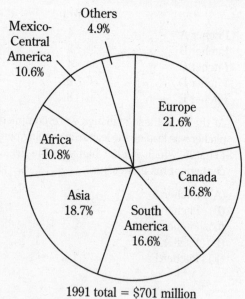

Others 4.9%
Mexico-Central America 10.6%
Africa 10.8%
Asia 18.7%
South America 16.6%
Canada 16.8%
Europe 21.6%

1991 total = $701 million

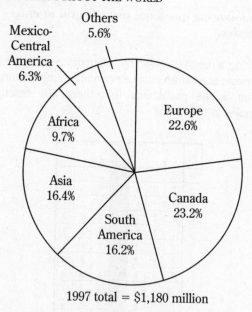

Others 5.6%
Mexico-Central America 6.3%
Africa 9.7%
Asia 16.4%
South America 16.2%
Canada 23.2%
Europe 22.6%

1997 total = $1,180 million

18. By what percent did Canada's share of American exports increase between 1991 and 1997?

   (A) 16.8%
   (B) 6.4%
   (C) 2.3%
   (D) .6%
   (E) 3.3%

19. What was the approximate average annual increase in U.S. exports between 1991 and 1997?

   (A) $30 million
   (B) $50 million
   (C) $60 million
   (D) $70 million
   (E) $80 million

GO ON TO THE NEXT PAGE

20. About what percent of its 1991 share did Europe get in 1997?

(A) 22.6%
(B) 1%
(C) 77.4%
(D) 140%
(E) 105%

For the following question, use the grid to enter your answer.

21. If the trends in market share on the table continue, when will South America have only 15% of the market?

For the following question, use the grid to enter your answer.

22. On a mathematics test, the average score for a certain class was 90. If 40 percent of the class scored 100, and 10 percent scored 80, what was the average score for the remainder of the class?

For the following question, select all the answer choices that apply.

23. If $f(x) = |x| - x$, which of the following statements is true? Indicate all such statements.

(A) $f(x) = f(-x)$
(B) $f(2x) = 2f(x)$
(C) $f(x + y) = f(x) + f(y)$
(D) $f(x) = -f(-x)$
(E) $f(x - y) = 0$
(F) $f(-1) = 2$
(G) $f(1) = 1$
(H) $f(-2) = 2$

For the following question, select all the answer choices that apply.

$$\begin{array}{r} AB \\ +BA \\ \hline CDC \end{array}$$

24. If each of the four letters in the sum above represents a *different* digit, which of the following *could* be a value of A? Indicate all such values.

(A) 6
(B) 5
(C) 4
(D) 3
(E) 2

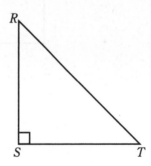

25. In $\triangle RST$ above, RS and ST have lengths equal to the same integer. All of the following could be the area of triangle RST *except*

(A) $\frac{1}{2}$

(B) 2

(C) $4\frac{1}{2}$

(D) $12\frac{1}{2}$

(E) 20

STOP

If you finish before time is called, you may check your work on this section only.
Do not turn to any other section in the test.

How Did You Do on This Test?

Step 1. Go to the Answer Key on pages 623–626.

Step 2. For your "raw score," calculate it using the directions on page 627.

Step 3. Get your "scaled score" for the test by referring to the GRE Score Conversion Table on page 628.

THERE'S ALWAYS ROOM FOR IMPROVEMENT!

ANSWER KEY FOR PRACTICE TEST 2

624

Analytical Writing 1
and Analytical Writing 2
See Part 8, Page 473
for Scoring on These Parts

Answer Key for Practice Test 2

Verbal Reasoning

Verbal Reasoning

Section 1		Section 2	
	Correct Answer		Correct Answer
1	E	1	E
2	B	2	B
3	B, E	3	B, D
4	C, D	4	C, F
5	B, D	5	B, F
6	C, D, G	6	B, D, G
7	B, F, I	7	B, F, I
8	B, E, I	8	C, F, G
9	E	9	A, B, C
10	D	10	B, C
11	C	11	A
12	A, B	12	E
13	A, C	13	A
14	E	14	D
15	B, E	15	B
16	A, F	16	C, E
17	C, F	17	D, F
18	D, F	18	C, F
19	B, D	19	B, F
20	A	20	D
21	D	21	A, B, C
22	D	22	C
23	C	23	E
24	D	24	C
25	B	25	C

Number correct   Number correct

Answer Key for Practice Test 2

Quantitative Reasoning

Section 3	Correct Answer
1	D
2	B
3	D
4	A
5	B
6	B
7	B
8	B
9	D
10	C
11	E
12	A, B, C, E
13	C
14	7/8
15	A
16	C
17	D
18	B
19	D
20	B
21	C
22	A
23	B
24	A, B, C
25	5

Number correct

Section 4	Correct Answer
1	C
2	C
3	D
4	D
5	D
6	B
7	C
8	A
9	D
10	E
11	D
12	9/20
13	B
14	C
15	D
16	C
17	A, B
18	B
19	E
20	E
21	2015
22	84
23	B, F
24	A, B, C, D
25	E

Number correct

Scoring the GRE Practice Test

Check your responses with the correct answers on the previous pages. Fill in the blanks below and do the calculations to get your Math and Verbal raw scores. Use the table to find your Math and Verbal scaled scores.

Get Your Verbal Reasoning Score

How many Verbal questions did you get **right**?

Section 1: Questions 1–25 _____

Section 2: Questions 1–25   + _____

Total = _____

_____

Use the Score Conversion Table to find your Verbal Reasoning scaled score.

_____

Get Your Quantitative Reasoning Score

How many Math questions did you get **right**?

Section 3: Questions 1–25 _____

Section 4: Questions 1–25   + _____

Total = _____

_____

Use the Score Conversion Table to find your Quantitative Reasoning scaled score.

_____

GRE Score Conversion Table

Raw Score	Verbal Reasoning Scaled Score		Quantitative Reasoning Scaled Score	
	130–170 Point Scale	200–800 Point Scale	130–170 Point Scale	200–800 Point Scale
50	170	800	170	800
49		790		790
48		780		790
47		770		780
46	167	760		780
45		750		770
44		740		770
43		730		770
42		710		760
41	163	700	167	750
40		670		740
39		660		730
38	160	650		720
37		640	163	700
36		620		690
35	157	600		680
34		590		670
33		570	160	650
32	153	550		640
31		540		630
30		530	157	600
29		520		590
28		510		570
27	150	500		570
26		490	153	550
25		470		530
24		460		510
23	147	450	150	500
22		440		480
21		430	147	450
20		420		440
19		410		430
18	143	400	143	400
17		380		390
16		370		380
15		360	140	350
14	140	350		340
13		340		330
12		330		310
11	137	300	137	300
10		290		280
9		280		260
8		260	133	250
7		260		230
6	133	250		210
5		230		200
4		220		200
3		200		200
2		200		200
1		200		200
0	130	200	130	200

Chart for Self-Appraisal Based on the Practice Test You Have Just Taken

Percent of Examinees Scoring Lower Than Selected Scale Scores (Percentile Rank) on the Verbal and Quantitative Reasoning Measures

Scaled Score	Verbal Reasoning	Quantitative Reasoning
800		94
790		91
780		89
770		87
760		84
750		82
740		80
730	99	77
720	98	75
710	98	72
700	97	70
690	97	68
680	96	66
670	95	63
660	94	61
650	93	59
640	92	56
630	91	54
620	89	52
610	88	49
600	86	47
590	84	45
580	82	43
570	80	40
560	78	38
550	75	36
540	73	34
530	70	32
520	68	30
510	65	28
500	63	27
490	60	25
480	57	23
470	55	22
460	52	20
450	49	19
440	46	17
430	43	16
420	41	15
410	38	14
400	35	12
390	32	11
380	29	10
370	27	9

Continued on next page.

Percent of Examinees Scoring Lower Than Selected Scale Scores (Percentile Rank) on the Verbal and Quantitative Reasoning Measures (cont'd)

Scaled Score	Verbal Reasoning	Quantitative Reasoning
360	24	8
350	21	8
340	19	7
330	16	6
320	13	5
310	10	5
300	8	4
290	6	3
280	5	3
270	3	2
260	2	2
250	1	2
240		1
230		
220		
210		
200		

Explanatory Answers for GRE Practice Test 2

Section 1: Verbal Reasoning

> As you read these Explanatory Answers, you are advised to refer to "17 Verbal (Critical Reading) Strategies" (beginning on page 136) whenever a specific strategy is referred to in the answer. Of particular importance are the following Master Verbal Strategies:
>
> Sentence Completion Master Strategy 1—page 137.
> Sentence Completion Master Strategy 3—page 140.
> Reading Comprehension Master Strategy 2—page 155.

Note: All Reading questions use Reading Comprehension Strategies 1, 2, and 3 (pages 152–157) as well as other strategies indicated.

1. Choice E is correct. The fact that the investor was eager to make an investment change points to his being "dubious" about his current investment—the stocks he had recently purchased. **See Sentence Strategy 1**.

2. Choice B is correct. **See Sentence Completion Strategy 2**. If you used this strategy of trying to complete the sentence *before* looking at the five choices, you might have come up with any of the following words:

simple	*ordinary*
understandable	*common*
easy-to-understand	

   These words all mean about the same as the correct Choice B, *simplified*. Therefore, Choices A, C, D, and E are incorrect.

3. Choices B and E are correct. Use **Sentence Completion Strategy 3**. Watch for an *opposition*

   indicator. "Although" is one of them. Opposites would be Choice B, *disagreement*, and Choice E, *overwhelmingly*.

4. Choices C and D are correct. Use **Sentence Completion Strategy 3**. Watch for a *support indicator. Not only* is one of them. The professor *rejected* the logic and on top of that *refused* to accept the textbook's conclusion, which was apparently the same as the student's.

5. Choices B and D are correct. Use **Sentence Completion Strategies 3 and 1**. Watch for an *opposition indicator.* "However" is one of them. If you say a sense of fairness *dictates* that the punishment should fit the crime, the opposite (because of the word "yet") would indicate that there are different punishments for the same crime. That is, the punishments (or judgments) *vary* or *deviate* greatly. Choice A, *relegates*, means to banish or assign to a lower position. This would really not make sense. And Choice C, *presupposes*, is too

weak in this sentence. Note that even if you chose Choice A or C, you'd still need to choose Choice D because of the *opposition indicator* "however."

6. Choices C, D, and G are correct. Use **Sentence Completion Strategies 4, 3, and 1**. Look for key words that create a link in the sentence. "In addition to" is an important set of words. So because of this, the words in the blanks must be associated with one another. It would seem that Choice A, *astute*, Choice D, *charismatic*, and Choice G, *elegance*, all match.

7. Choices B, F, and I are correct. Use **Sentence Completion Strategies 4, 3, 2, and 1**. Look for key words that create a link in the sentence. "More and more...not," "not only, but...," "made during the last fifty years," are important key words. Look at the last part of the second sentence. The word in the third blank must contrast with films made during the last fifty years. That word would be *present* or *contemporary*, Choice I. Now look at the link between the first and second sentences. It would seem that a good combination of the blank words would be *leisure*, Choice B, and *booming* (becoming very large), Choice F. Note that Choice A, *precious*, and Choice C, *limited*, may be true but would contradict the fact that the people are still watching movies in their home.

8. Choices B, E, and I are correct. Use **Sentence Completion Strategies 4, 3, and 1**. Look for key words that create a link in the sentence. "Was not ruled...but" is an important set of words. Because of the word "citizenry," it would seem that *societies*, Choice B, would be better than *populations*, and certainly better than *cities*, Choice C. The second blank indicates some sort of working with others or participation, Choice E. Since the first sentence uses the words "common among other...," the word *advantageous*, Choice I, would seem best, and we can rule out *alien*, Choice G, and *detrimental*, Choice H.

9. Choice E is correct. See lines 8–11: "...ice-sheets shrank and glaciers retreated. Enslaved to climate, plant and animal life had to change also. The mammoth, rhinoceros, and reindeer in turn disappeared from western Europe..."

10. Choice D is correct. See lines 15–18: "With the withdrawal or extinction of the great herds on which they had preyed, the economic basis of the hunting societies was cut away and their carefully adjusted culture made obsolete."

11. Choice C is correct. Based on the context in the passage and the words "basis of the hunting societies" and "carefully adjusted culture" (lines 17–18),

"biological specialization" would deal with a special branch or study. See **Reading Comprehension Strategy 5**.

12. Choices A and B are correct. See lines 9–18.

13. Choices A and C are correct. See lines 9–16.

14. Choice E is correct. The author admits, by implication, that if it were only possible to ascertain Mozart's wishes in playing staccato, one would be obligated to follow them; the problem is only that his wishes cannot be determined. Also, Statement III is presupposed by the passage since, if there were only one way to play staccato, the problem of interpretation would not arise. But the author does not say anywhere generally that it is futile to attempt to edit Mozart's writings (Statement II) —merely that there is a special problem in one particular case, that of the staccato markings.

15. Choices B and E are correct. **See Sentence Completion Strategy 3**. The words "in spite of" constitute an opposition indicator. We can then expect an opposing idea to complete the sentence. The word *baffled* means "puzzled" or "unable to comprehend." Choice B gives us the word that brings out the opposition thought we expect in the sentence. Choice E, *flustered*, also works. Choices A, C, D, and F do not give us a sentence that makes sense.

16. Choices A and F are correct. **See Sentence Completion Strategy 1 and 3**. Photographs of starving children must demonstrate something. If you tried to complete the sentence before looking at the six choices, you might have come up with words like "results" or "effects." Therefore, Choices A and F are correct. The other choices are incorrect because they do not make sense in the sentence.

17. Choices C and F are correct. **See Sentence Completion Strategy 1**. The words *generate* and *create* (meaning "to produce") complete the sentence so that it makes good sense. The other choices don't do that.

18. Choices D and F are correct. **See Sentence Completion Strategy 1**. Try each choice. The sentence implies that he retained the belief until his death; hence he was *stubborn* or unchanging (*obstinate* or *obdurate*) in his belief.

19. Choices B and D are correct. **See Sentence Completion Strategy 1**. The word *prevalent* (meaning "widely or commonly occurring") completes the sentence so that it makes good sense. Also, Choice D, *plentiful*, is good. The other choices don't work.

20. Choice A is correct. Note words like "microscopic" (line 1), "minute" (line 4), and "half an inch long" (line 9). Size is therefore emphasized.

21. Choice D is correct. See lines 11–12.

22. Choice D is correct. From line 1, these creatures are described as *wandering* or *rambling*. **See Reading Comprehension Strategy 5**.

23. Choice C is correct. The introductory word "Nevertheless" in line 1 means "in spite of that." Therefore, one can presume that the preceding paragraph discussed the evidences of culture in the United States today.

24. Choice D is correct. In the context of the first sentence together with the rest of the passage, *voluble hue* as associated with "cry" would relate to *shouting*. See **Reading Comprehension Strategy 5**.

25. Choice B is correct. Because bicyclists thought the bicycles were safer, they may have attempted dangerous feats, thus causing accidents and injuries. Choice A is incorrect. The fact that bicycles were made safer should reduce weather-related bicycle injuries. Choice C is incorrect. If anything, this should create fewer injuries. Choice D is incorrect. People who have never ridden bicycles would in fact benefit from the increased safety of the bicycle. Choice E is incorrect. It would seem that even if it were more complicated to ride a bicycle, the bicycle was made safer, not more complicated.

Explanatory Answers for
GRE Practice Test 2
(continued)

Section 2: Verbal Reasoning

As you read these Explanatory Answers, you are advised to refer to "17 Verbal (Critical Reading) Strategies" (beginning on page 136) whenever a specific strategy is referred to in the answer. Of particular importance are the following Master Verbal Strategies:

Sentence Completion Master Strategy 1—page 137.
Sentence Completion Master Strategy 3—page 140.
Reading Comprehension Master Strategy 2—page 155.

Note: All Reading questions use Reading Comprehension Strategies 1, 2, and 3 (pages 152–157) as well as other strategies indicated.

1. Choice E is correct. See **Sentence Completion Strategies 3 and 1**. Note that the last part of the sentence contains an *opposition indicator* ("Despite"). The word *adhere* in Choice E means "to stick" or "to cling." The Prime Minister's decision is in opposition to what the United States and its allies desire—that is, continuing to have United States jet fighters on Spanish soil. Choices A, B, C, and D are incorrect because they do not contain the opposition idea expressed in the sentence.

2. Choice B is correct. See **Sentence Completion Strategy 1**. The word *solidified* means "strengthened," which makes good sense in this sentence. The other choices do not fit into the context of the sentence.

3. Choices B and D are correct. Use **Sentence Completion Strategy 3**. Watch for a *support indicator*. "Not only" and "but also" are two of them. *Affluence* means "wealth," so the second word in the blank must be *prosperity* (Choice D). Choice B, *reflected*, then fits the first blank in the sentence.

4. Choices C and F are correct. Use **Sentence Completion Strategies 3 and 1**. Watch for an *opposition* indicator. "Yet" is one of them. Let's try Choice C, *adamant*, first. Choice F, *disorderly*, would seem to fit best for this contrast. Note that Choice D, *deranged*, is too strong.

5. Choices B and F are correct. Use **Sentence Completion Strategy 1**. Try the choices: You should spot Choice B, *implicit*, meaning "implied," which would link to Choice F, *responsibility*.

6. Choices B, D, and G are correct. Use **Sentence Completion Strategies 4, 3, and 1**. Look for key words that create a link in the sentence. Key words are "discouragement," "decreases," and "also often." Discouragement and *pressure* would involve decreases in *creativity*. This would *affect* the quality and quantity.

7. Choices B, F, and I are correct. Use **Sentence Completion Strategies 4, 3, and 1**. Look for key words that create a link in the sentence. "Originally" and "a work in progress" are an important set of words. Choice B, *still uncompleted*, would link with Choice F, *evolved*, and Choice I, *seemingly*, satisfies the flavor of the sentence.

8. Choices C, F, and G are correct. Use **Sentence Completion Strategies 4, 3, and 1**. Look for key words that create a link in the sentence. "Detest," "because," "relying on," and "rather than" are some. The second blank must link directly with the third blank due to the word "because." Therefore Choice F, *a passivity* (inactivity, submissiveness) and Choice G, *external* (outside—letting something else do the work) are correct. Based on Choices F and G, you can see that the word in the first blank must be a strong word: *infuriated*, Choice C.

9. Choice A is correct. See lines 9–17. Choice B is correct. See lines 13–15. Choice C is correct. See line 9.

10. Choice B is correct. See lines 3–5. Choice C is correct. See lines 9–17.

11. Choice A is correct. If there were preexisting disorders that were not detected, that led drug users to choose specific drugs, it would not be the current drugs that caused the illness. A striking example would be the following: Suppose there is some genetic problem that causes cancer. And suppose the same genetic problem causes one to smoke. It would not be true then that smoking causes cancer. Of course, that is probably not the case. See **Reading Comprehension Strategy 10**.

12. Choice E is correct. See lines 4–7: "Originally the term *acclimatization*...altered temperature." Also see lines 9–12: "But aside from temperature... originally accustomed to." Choices A, B, C, and D are incorrect because one *cannot* infer from the passage what any of these choices state.

13. Choice A is correct. Acclimatization and adaptation are both forms of adjustment. Accordingly, these two processes are similar. The difference between the two terms, however, is brought out in lines 32–36: "By and large...as adaptation." Choice D is incorrect because the passage does not indicate what is expressed in Choice D. See lines 29–32: "Let us define acclimatization...lethal for it." Choices B, C, and E are incorrect because the passage does not indicate that any of these choices are true.

14. Choice D is correct. A person going from daylight into a darkened room is an example of adaptation—not acclimatization. See lines 32–36: "By and large...as 'adaptation.'" Choices A, B, C, and E all require the process of acclimatization. Therefore, they are incorrect choices. An ocean fish placed in a lake (Choice A) is a chemical change. Choices B, C, and E are all pressure changes. Acclimatization, by definition, deals with chemical and pressure changes.

15. Choice B is correct. See lines 33–36: "The term [acclimatization] should not be taken...as 'adaptation.'" Choices A, D, and E are incorrect because the passage does not indicate that these choices are true. Choice C is partially correct in that acclimatization does apply to adjustments, but the choice is incorrect because adaptation also applies to adjustments. See lines 35–36: "This type of adjustment... as 'adaptation.'"

16. Choices C and E are correct. See **Sentence Completion Strategies 1 and 3**. The words *extreme* and *radical* are the most appropriate among the six choices because the forest fire season is in *full swing*. The other choices are not appropriate.

17. Choices D and F are correct. See **Sentence Completion Strategies 1 and 3**. The plan turned out to be impractical, unable to be logically supported. Note the root *ten*, "to hold," so *untenable* means "not holding." *Infeasible* means "not possible to do easily." Also note that the word "because" in the sentence is a *result indicator*.

18. Choices C and F are correct. See **Sentence Completion Strategy 1**. The word *effective* (meaning "serving the purpose" or "producing a result") makes good sense in the sentence. *Operative* would also work. The other choices don't. Note that Choice B, *injurious*, and Choice E, *deleterious*, are synonyms but they don't fit in the sentences.

19. Choices B and F are correct. See **Sentence Completion Strategies 1 and 3**. Try each choice, being aware that "result" is, of course, a *result indicator*. Samuel Clemens chose the *pen name*, or *pseudonym*, Mark Twain.

20. Choice D is correct. Here we have no backup claims of luxury, engineering, styling, and performance. See **Reading Comprehension Strategy 10**.

21. Choices A, B, and C are correct. For A, see lines 10–13. For B, see lines 6–9. For C, it is indeed interesting that nowhere in the passage are specific examples of mechanization mentioned. See **Reading Comprehension Strategy 10.**

22. Choice C is correct. For A, see lines 5–9. For B, see lines 2–5. For D, see lines 1–4 and 10–13. For E, see line 3 ("institution of slavery") and line 10 ("present-day slave power"). Choice C, the range of labor-saving devices, is not addressed. See **Reading Comprehension Strategy 10.**

23. Choice E is correct. Throughout the passage there was no evidence for the existence of the inhabitants of Atlantis. There was only a theory that was discussed in lines 11–13.

24. Choice C is correct. See lines 6–7, "because of the impiety of its people…"

25. Choice C is correct. It can be seen from the context in the passage that the people had disrespect for authority. See **Reading Comprehension Strategy 5.**

Explanatory Answers for Practice Test 2 (continued)

Section 3: Quantitative Reasoning

> As you read these solutions, you are advised to do two things if you answered the Math question incorrectly:
>
> 1. When a specific Strategy is referred to in the solution, study that strategy, which you will find in "25 Math Strategies" (beginning on page 72).
>
> 2. When the solution directs you to the "Math Refresher" (beginning on page 185)—for example, Math Refresher #305—study the 305 Math principle to get a clear idea of the math operation that was necessary for you to know in order to answer the question correctly.

1. Choice D is correct. **(Use Strategy C: Use numbers instead of variables.)**

   Try $n = 1$: Quantity A = 16, Column B = 9
   Try $n = 10$: Quantity A = 88, Column B = 90

   Depending on whether $n < 8$, $n = 8$, or $n > 8$, $8 + 8n$ will be greater than, equal to, or less than $9n$, respectively. Thus, the relationship cannot be determined.

   (Math Refresher #431)

2. Choice B is correct. **(Use Strategy 2: Translate from words to algebra.)**

   Given: $\frac{2}{3} \times 54$ = number of Democrats

   $$\frac{2}{\cancel{3}} \times \frac{18 \times \cancel{3}}{1} =$$

   36 = number of Democrats
   Thus, $54 - 36 = 18$ Republicans
   $18 > 17$

   (Math Refresher #200)

3. Choice D is correct. **(Use Strategy C: Use numbers instead of variables.)**

   Any real nonzero number, when squared, is greater than zero. Therefore, all we know from

   $$(y - 4)^2 > 0$$

   is that $y \neq 4$, else $(y - 4)^2 = 0$.

   However, we do not know whether y is less than or greater than 4.

   (Math Refresher #419 and #431)

4. Choice A is correct.

Quantity A	Quantity B
$r = 6$	$r = 3$
$h = 3$	$h = 6$

Do not be intimidated by the complex formula. Merely substitute the given into the formula for the volume of a cone.

$$V = \frac{1}{3}\pi(6)^2(3) \qquad\qquad V = \frac{1}{3}\pi(3)^2(6)$$

(Use Strategy A: Cancel numbers common to both columns.)

$$V = \frac{1}{\cancel{3}}\cancel{\pi}(36)(3) \qquad\qquad V = \frac{1}{\cancel{3}}\cancel{\pi}(9)(6)$$

$$V = 108 \qquad\qquad V = 54$$

(Math Refresher #200, #429, and #431)

5. Choice B is correct. **(Use Strategy E: Try to get the columns and the given to look similar.)**

We need to find $\frac{a}{c}$.

Given: $\qquad\qquad \frac{a}{b} = \frac{2}{3}$ $\qquad$ ☐1

$\qquad\qquad\qquad \frac{b}{c} = \frac{5}{8}$ $\qquad$ ☐2

(Use Strategy 13: Find unknowns by multiplying equations.) Multiply ☐1 by ☐2:

$$\frac{a}{\cancel{b}} \cdot \frac{\cancel{b}}{c} = \frac{\cancel{2}}{3} \cdot \frac{5}{\cancel{8}4}$$

$$\frac{a}{c} = \frac{5}{12}$$

$$\frac{5}{12} < \frac{5}{6}$$

(Math Refresher #101, #111, and #419)

6. Choice B is correct. **(Use Strategy 17: Use the given information effectively.)**

Given: $\qquad x + 2y + z = 5y$ $\qquad$ ☐1

From the diagram and basic geometry,

$$y = z \qquad\qquad ☐2$$

(Remember vertical angles?)

Substituting ☐2 into ☐1,

$$x + 2z + z = 5z$$
$$\text{or} \qquad x = 2z \qquad\qquad ☐3$$

Using ☐3, the columns become

Quantity	Quantity
$\frac{3}{2}z$	$2z$

and the answer is clear.

(Math Refresher #503 and #406)

7. Choice B is correct. **(Use Strategy 9: Know the rate, time, and distance relationship.)**

Remember the formula:

Average speed

$$= \frac{\text{total distance traveled}}{\text{total time elapsed}}$$

$$= \frac{48 \text{ miles}}{1\frac{1}{2} \text{ hours}}$$

$$= \frac{48}{\frac{3}{2}} = 48 \times \frac{2}{3} = 16 \times 3 \times \frac{2}{3}$$

$$= 32 \text{ miles per hour}$$

(Math Refresher #201 and #202)

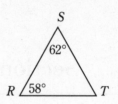

8. Choice B is correct.

Quantity A	Quantity B
Length ST	Length RT

(Use Strategy 18: Remember triangle facts.)
We know that in a triangle, the side opposite the larger angle is the larger side. Thus, $RT > ST$.

(Triangle inequalities)

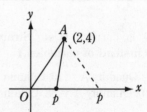

9. Choice D is correct.
See figure above. **(Use Strategy 14: Draw lines and label.)** For Column A, draw a line connecting the origin O with the point $(2,4)$. For Column B, label "p" on the x-axis. **(Use Strategy 18: Know about relations of sides and angles of triangles.)** I can draw $\angle ApO > \angle AOp$ and so line $AO >$ line Ap. I can also draw $\angle ApO < \angle AOp$, so line $AO <$ line Ap. Thus a definite relation cannot be determined.

(Math Refresher #410)

10. Choice C is correct.

$$Given:\ 8r + 3s = 12 \qquad \boxed{1}$$
$$7r + 2s = 9 \qquad \boxed{2}$$

(Use Strategy 13: Find unknowns by subtracting.)

Subtracting $\boxed{2}$ from $\boxed{1}$, we get

$$r + s = 3 \qquad \boxed{3}$$

Multiplying $\boxed{3}$ by 5, we get

$$5(r + s) = (3)5$$
$$5(r + s) = 15$$

(Math Refresher #406 and #407)

11. Choice E is correct. **(Use Strategy 2: Translate from words to algebra.)** The sum of the degree measures of the 4 angles of any quadrilateral is always 360. Therefore,

$$w + x + y + z = 360° \qquad \boxed{1}$$

(Use Strategy 5: Average =
$$\mathbf{\frac{Sum\ of\ values}{Total\ number\ of\ values}}\Big)$$

If w is the average (arithmetic mean) of x, y, and z, then

$$w = \frac{x + y + z}{3}$$

Multiplying both sides of the above equation by 3, we have

$$3w = x + y + z \qquad \boxed{2}$$

Substituting equation $\boxed{2}$ into equation $\boxed{1}$, we get

$$w + 3w = 360°$$
or $\qquad 4w = 360°$
or $\qquad w = 90°$

From equation $\boxed{2}$, we conclude that
$x + y + z = 3w = 3(90) = 270°$

(Math Refresher #521, #601, and #406)

12. Choices A, B, C, and E are correct.

Method 1: By inspection, Choice D is the sum of two negatives, which must be negative. The rest are positive.

Method 2: **(Use Strategy 7: Try numerics to help find the answer.)**

Let $r = -1, s = -2$

Choice E is $-r - s = -(-1)-(-2)$
$\qquad\qquad\quad = 1 + 2$
$\qquad\qquad\quad = 3$

Choice D is $r + s = -1 + (-2) = -3$
Similarly Choice C is $[(-1)(-2)]^2 = +2^2$
Choice B: $(-1)(-2) = +2$, Choice A $= \frac{-1}{-2} = +\frac{1}{2}$

(Math Refresher #431)

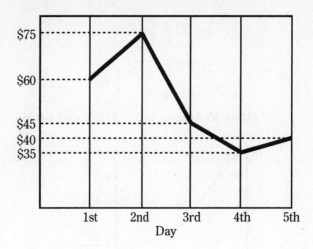

13. Choice C is correct. In ascending order, the wages for the six days are:

35
35
40
45
60
75

The median is the middle number. But wait! There is no middle number. So we average the two middle numbers, 40 and 45, to get 42.5.

The mode is the number appearing most frequently, that is, 35. So $42.5 - 35 = 7.5$.

(Math Refresher #601a, #601b)

14. $\dfrac{7}{8}$

(Use Strategy 17: Use the given information effectively.)

Given: 6 rolls uses $\frac{1}{4}$ pound of powder $\qquad \boxed{1}$

6 rolls uses $2\frac{1}{2}$ quarts of water $\qquad \boxed{2}$

Number $\boxed{2}$ is not necessary to solve the problem!

We need to know how much powder is needed for the same mixture for 21 rolls. Let x = number of pounds for 21 rolls. We set up a proportion:

$$\frac{6\ rolls}{\frac{1}{4}\ pound} = \frac{21\ rolls}{x}$$

(Use Strategy 10: Know how to use units.)

$$(6\ rolls)x = (21\ rolls) \times \left(\frac{1}{4}\ pound\right)$$
$$6x = 21 \times \frac{1}{4}\ pound \qquad \boxed{3}$$

(Use Strategy 13: Find unknowns by multiplication.) Multiply $\boxed{3}$ by $\frac{1}{6}$. We get

$$\frac{1}{6}\Big(6x\Big) = \frac{1}{6}\Big(21 \times \frac{1}{4}\ pound\Big)$$

$x = \frac{1}{6} \times 21 \times \frac{1}{4}$ pound

$x = \frac{21}{24}$ pound

$x = \frac{7}{8}$ of a pound

(Math Refresher #200, #120, and #406)

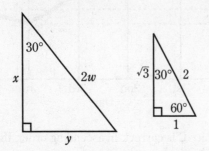

15. Choice A is correct. **(Use Strategy 18: Remember special right triangles.)** The triangle at left (given) is similar to the triangle at right, which is one of the standard triangles.

Corresponding sides of similar triangles are proportional. Thus,

$$\frac{2w}{2} = \frac{y}{1} \text{ and } \frac{2w}{2} = \frac{x}{\sqrt{3}}$$

or $\quad y = w$ and $x = w\sqrt{3}$

Area of triangle $= \frac{1}{2}$ (base) (height)

$= \frac{1}{2}(y)(x)$

$= \frac{1}{2}(w)(w\sqrt{3})$

Area of triangle $= \frac{\sqrt{3}}{2}w^2$ ☐1

Area of rectangle $= (3w)(w) = 3w^2$ ☐2

Using ☐1 and ☐2, we have

$$\frac{\text{Area of rectangle}}{\text{Area of triangle}} = \frac{3w^2}{\frac{\sqrt{3}}{2}w^2}$$

$$= \frac{3}{\frac{\sqrt{3}}{2}} = 3 \times \frac{2}{\sqrt{3}}$$

$$= \frac{6}{\sqrt{3}} = \frac{6\sqrt{3}}{3} = 2\sqrt{3}$$

or $2\sqrt{3} : 1$ (*Answer*)

(Math Refresher #510, #509, #306, and #304)

16. Choice C is correct. $n = \frac{3}{8}$ is a member of both sets. Note that n is not an integer in this case, and certainly in this case n is not equal to 6. Thus I and III are not true for this case. Members of both sets are $\frac{3}{8}$, 6, and 8. So for any of these members, $8n$ is an integer. Thus II is always true.

(Math Refresher #801)

17. Choice D is correct. The graph shows us that in the stated period average public-school cost was about $10,000 and average private-school cost was about $20,000. $20,000 is 200% of $10,000.

(Math Refresher #706)

18. Choice B is correct. The rate of increase of college costs can be inferred from the slope of the line on the graph. When the slope is the least, that is, the rate of climb is slowest, then the costs were increasing at the slowest pace. The slope of the graph is the least during the period 1989–1991.

19. Choice D is correct. Between 2000 and 2008 the costs for private schools rose from about $25,000 to about $30,000. Eight years after 2008, in 2016, we would expect the costs to have risen another $5,000 to $35,000.

(Math Refresher #706)

20. Choice B is correct. The rate of increase of costs can be seen by looking at the slope of the line on the graph. During the period 1991–1992, the line for public schools was steeper than the line for private schools.

(Math Refresher #706)

21. Choice C is correct. **(Use Strategy 2: Translate from words to algebra.)**

Let b = number of men
g = number of women

We are given

$b = g + 7$ ☐1

$b = \frac{5}{4}g$ ☐2

(Use Strategy 13: Find unknowns by multiplication.) Multiplying ☐2 by $\frac{4}{5}$,

$\frac{4}{5}b = g$ ☐3

Substituting ☐3 into ☐1,

$b = \frac{4}{5}b + 7$ ☐4

Multiplying ☐4 by 5,

$5b = 4b + 35$

or $\quad b = 35$

(Math Refresher #200 and #406)

22. Choice A is correct. **(Use Strategy 2: Translate words to algebra—see translation table for percent increase.)**

Percent increase $= \dfrac{\text{Amount of increase}}{\text{Original amount}}$ ☐1

Amount of increase is given as 100 per year ☐2

Substituting ☐2 into ☐1, we get

$$\% \text{ increase} = \frac{100}{\text{Original amount}} \qquad \boxed{3}$$

(Use Strategy 12: Try not to make tedious calculations.) The greatest % increase will occur when the original amount is least.

Since the population is increasing by 100 every year, it is least at the beginning, in 2006.

Thus ☐3 will be greatest from 2006–2007.

(Math Refresher #114 and #118)

23. Choice B is correct. **(Use Strategy 2: Translate from words to algebra.)** This problem tests the concepts of set union and set intersection. We can solve these types of problems with a diagram.

Thus, draw the diagram:

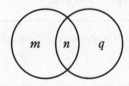

Where

m = number of students taking *only* calculus

q = number of students taking *only* physics

n = number of students taking *both* calculus and physics

Thus,

$m + n$ = number of students in calculus class
$n + q$ = number of students in physics class
$m + n + q$ = number of students taking either calculus or physics or both

We are given that

$$m + n + q = 36 \qquad \boxed{1}$$
$$n = 10 \qquad \boxed{2}$$
$$m + n = 31 \qquad \boxed{3}$$

We want to find

$$n + q \qquad \boxed{4}$$

(Use Strategy 13: Find unknowns by subtracting equations.) Subtract equation ☐2 from equation ☐3 to get

$$m = 21 \qquad \boxed{5}$$

Now subtract equation ☐5 from equation ☐1 to get

$$n + q = 15$$

(Math Refresher #406)

24. Choices A, B, and C are correct.

A: Slope is defined as $\frac{y_2 - y_1}{x_2 - x_1}$ where (x_1, y_1) and (x_2, y_2) are points on the line. Thus here $0 = x_1$, $a = y_1$, $a = x_2$, and $0 = y_2$

Thus $\frac{y_2 - y_1}{x_2 - x_1} = \frac{0 - a}{a - 0} = -1$: A is therefore true.

B: The triangle created above is an isosceles right triangle with sides a, a, $a\sqrt{2}$. Thus B is true.
C: In an isosceles right triangle, the interior angles of the triangle are 90-45-45 degrees. Thus C is true.

(Math Refresher #416, #411, #509)

25. 5

$$\begin{array}{r} N5 \\ \times\ LM \\ \hline 385 \\ \times\ 385 \\ \hline 4235 \end{array}$$

(Use Strategy 17: Use the given information effectively.) From the given problem we see that

$$N5 \times M = 385$$

(Use Strategy 7: Use numerical examples.)

Try $N = 1$

$$15 \times M = 385$$

M must be greater than 10, which is incorrect.

Try $N = 2$

$$25 \times M = 385$$

M must be greater than 10, which is incorrect.

Try $N = 3$

$$35 \times M = 385$$

M must be greater than 10, which is incorrect.

Try $N = 4$

$$45 \times M = 385$$

M is not an integer.

Try $N = 5$

$$55 \times M = 385. \text{ Thus, } M = 7$$

Therefore, L can be equal to 7 to give:

$$\begin{array}{r} 55 \\ \times\ 77 \\ \hline 385 \\ +\ 385 \\ \hline 4235 \end{array}$$

Explanatory Answers for Practice Test 2
(continued)

Section 4: Quantitative Reasoning

> As you read these solutions, you are advised to do two things if you answered the math question incorrectly:
>
> 1. When a specific Strategy is referred to in the solution, study that strategy, which you will find in "25 Math Strategies" (beginning on page 72).
>
> 2. When the solution directs you to the "Math Refresher" (beginning on page 185)—for example, Math Refresher #305—study the 305 Math principle to get a clear idea of the math operation that was necessary for you to know in order to answer the question correctly.

1. Choice C is correct.

Given: $\dfrac{a}{18} = \dfrac{2}{9}$ $\boxed{1}$

$\dfrac{b}{28} = \dfrac{1}{7}$ $\boxed{2}$

(Use Strategy 13: Find unknowns by multiplication.) Multiply $\boxed{1}$ by 18. We get

$$18\,\frac{a}{18} = 18\left(\frac{2}{9}\right)$$

$$a = 4$$

Multiply $\boxed{2}$ by 28. We get

$$28\,\frac{b}{28} = 28\,\frac{1}{7}$$

$$b = 4$$

(Math Refresher #406)

2. Choice C is correct.

Given: r is an even integer $\boxed{1}$
$5 < r < 8$ $\boxed{2}$

(Use Strategy 6: Know how to manipulate inequalities.) Using $\boxed{1}$ and $\boxed{2}$ together, the only even integer value of r between 5 and 8 is $r = 6$. $\boxed{3}$

Quantity A	Quantity B	
$r + 1$	7	$\boxed{4}$

Substituting $\boxed{3}$ into $\boxed{4}$, the columns become

$6 + 1 = 7$	7

(Math Refresher #603 and #419)

3. Choice D is correct.

Quantity A	Quantity B
The number of hours in w days	v hours

(Use Strategy C: Use numerics if it appears that the answer cannot be determined.) Let $w = 1$ and $v = 30$. The columns become

The number of hours in 1 day = 24 hours	30 hours

Quantity B is larger.

Now, let $w = 1$ and $v = 1$, the columns become

The number of hours in   1 hour
1 day = 24 hours

Quantity A is larger.

Since two different answers are possible, the answer cannot be determined from the information given.

(Math Refresher #431)

4. Choice D is correct.

    Given: Darrin is older than Stephanie. $\boxed{1}$
               Jimmy is older than Stephanie. $\boxed{2}$

(Use Strategy C: Use numerics if it appears that a unique comparison cannot be made.)

Let Darrin = 15, Jimmy = 13, Stephanie = 10. Darrin's age is greater than Jimmy's age.

Now, let Darrin = 15, Jimmy = 17, Stephanie = 10. Darrin's age is less than Jimmy's age.

Since two different results are possible, the answer cannot be determined.

(Math Refresher #431 and Logical Reasoning)

5. Choice D is correct. **(Use Strategy C: When a comparison is difficult, use numbers instead of variables.)**

    Given: $m - n > p - q$ $\boxed{1}$

Choose specific values of m, n, p, q that satisfy $\boxed{1}$.

EXAMPLE 1

$$m = 0, n = -1, p = 0, q = 0$$

The columns become

Quantity A	Quantity B
−1	0

and the quantity in Quantity B is greater.

EXAMPLE 2

$$m = 3, n = 0, p = 0, q = 1$$

The columns become

Quantity A	Quantity B
0	0

and the two quantities are equal. Thus, the answer depends on specific values of $m, n, p,$ and q.

(Math Refresher #431)

6. Choice B is correct.
(**Use Strategy 5:**

$$\text{Average} = \frac{\textbf{Sum of values}}{\textbf{Total number of values}})$$

If all 10 students received a 95, then the average would be 95. Since one student received a grade less than 95, the average of the ten test scores is less than 95.

Quantity A	Quantity B
Some number less than 95	95

So the answer is clear.

(Math Refresher #601)

7. Choice C is correct. **(Use Strategy 17: Use the given information effectively.)**

    Given: $\dfrac{2}{3} + \dfrac{r}{s} = \dfrac{5}{3}$ $\boxed{1}$

Subtract $\dfrac{2}{3}$ from both sides of $\boxed{1}$, giving

$$\frac{r}{s} = \frac{3}{3}$$

$$\frac{r}{s} = 1$$

Thus, $r = s$.

(Math Refresher #406)

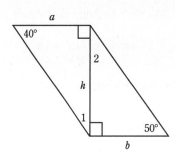

8. Choice A is correct. **(Use Strategy 18: Remember right triangle facts.)**

In a right triangle, the sum of the 2 acute angles is 90°. $\boxed{1}$

In the left-hand triangle, using $\boxed{1}$, we have
$$40 + \angle 1 = 90$$
$$\angle 1 = 50 \qquad \boxed{2}$$

In the right-hand triangle, using $\boxed{2}$, we have
$$50 + \angle 2 = 90$$
$$\angle 2 = 40 \qquad \boxed{3}$$

From $\boxed{1}$, $\boxed{2}$ and $\boxed{3}$ we see that each triangle has a 40°, a 50°, and a 90° angle.

METHOD 1

(Use Strategy 14: Label unknown quantities.) Label diagonal as shown. In the left-hand triangle, $a > h$ because side a lies opposite the larger angle of 50°, whereas side h lies opposite the smaller angle of 40°. In the right-hand triangle, $h > b$, because side h lies opposite the larger angle 50°, and side b lies opposite the smaller angle of 40°. So we get $a > h$ and $h > b$, which means $a > b$. **(See Strategy 6, Statement 5: How to Manipulate Inequalities.)**

(Math Refresher #509)

METHOD 2

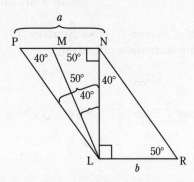

(Use Strategy 14: Draw lines to make the problem easier.) Draw LM, making a 50° angle with a.

$\triangle MNL \cong \triangle RLN$ by Angle-Side-Angle

Therefore, $MN = LR$
$$MN = b \qquad \boxed{4}$$

From the diagram, we know that
$$PN = a \qquad \boxed{5}$$

It is obvious that $PN > MN$. $\qquad \boxed{6}$

Substituting $\boxed{4}$ and $\boxed{5}$ into $\boxed{6}$, we get
$$a > b$$

(Math Refresher #501 and #511)

9. Choice D is correct.

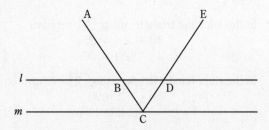

Given: $l \parallel m$

No information is supplied regarding the angle that AC or EC makes with m. **(Use Strategy 14: Draw lines to help solve the problem.)** Redraw AC at a different angle.

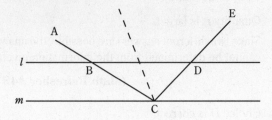

In the above diagram $BC > CD$. $\qquad \boxed{1}$
Redraw EC at a different angle.

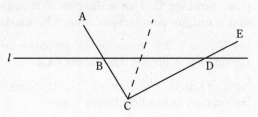

In the above diagram $CD > BC$. $\qquad \boxed{1}$

Since two different results are possible, a comparison can't be determined from the information given.

(Math Refresher #504)

10. Choice E is correct. The only restriction is that 9 and 12 must each divide Q without a remainder.
$\qquad \boxed{1}$

(Use Strategy 7: Use numerics to help find the answer.)

Choose specific values for Q that satisfy $\boxed{1}$.

EXAMPLE 1
$$Q = 36$$

Then, Q will divide 36 and 72.

EXAMPLE 2
$$Q = 108$$

Then, Q will divide neither 36 nor 72. Clearly, the answer to this question depends on the specific value of Q.

(Math Refresher #431)

11. Choice D is correct. **(Use Strategy 11: Use new definitions carefully.)** The smallest sum occurs when we choose 3 from A and 6 from B.

Therefore, the minimum sum = 3 + 6 = 9

The largest sum occurs when we choose 5 from A and 8 from B.

Therefore, the maximum sum = 5 + 8 = 13

All numbers from 9 to 13 inclusive can be sums.

Thus, there are 5 different sums possible.

(Math Refresher #431)

12. $\dfrac{9}{20}$

Label the females F_1, F_2, and F_3 and the males M_1, M_2, and M_3. The total number of combinations of three people (such as F_1–F_2–M_1 or F_1–M_2–M_3) is 6 combinations taken 3 at a time, or $_6C_3$, which is equal to $(6 \times 5 \times 4)/(3 \times 2 \times 1) = 20$. There are 9 favorable combinations (trios that include exactly two men): M_1–M_2–F_1, M_1–M_2–F_2, M_1–M_2–F_3, M_1–M_3–F_1, M_1–M_3–F_2, M_1–M_3–F_3, M_2–M_3–F_1, M_2–M_3–F_2, and M_2–M_3–F_3. The probability of exactly two males in the room is:

$$\frac{\text{Favorable combinations}}{\text{Total combinations}} = \frac{9}{20}$$

(Math Refresher #613 and #614)

13. Choice B is correct. Since the slope of the line is constant, the *ratio* of the *difference* in y-coordinates to the *difference* in x-coordinates must be constant for any two points on the line. For points P and A, this ratio is

$$\frac{2-0}{1-0} = 2$$

The only choice of x and y which gives the ratio 2 for point R and point A is Choice B, since if $x = 4$ and $y = 8$,

$$\frac{8-0}{4-0} = 2.$$

All the other choices give a different ratio from 2.

(Math Refresher #416)

14. Choice C is correct. **(Use Strategy 2: Remember how to calculate percent.)**

Winning percentage =

$$\frac{\text{\# of games won}}{\text{Total \# of games played}} \times 100$$

For example,

Winning % for pitcher A

$$= \frac{4}{4+2} \times 100 = \frac{4}{6} \times 100$$

$$= \frac{2 \times 2}{2 \times 3} \times 100$$

$$= \frac{200}{3} = 66\frac{2}{3}\%$$

For each pitcher, we have

Pitcher	Winning Percentage
A	$66\frac{2}{3}\%$
B	60%
C	80%
D	50%
E	75%

Pitcher C has the highest winning percentage.

(Math Refresher #106)

15. Choice D is correct.
Given:

Meteor 1 travels at 300 meters/second $\boxed{1}$
Meteor 2 travels at 700 meters/second $\boxed{2}$

Draw a diagram:

Let t be the time it takes meteors to meet. Call x the distance Meteor 1 travels. Then $2500 - x$ is the distance Meteor 2 travels.

(Use Strategy 9: Know Rate, Time, and Distance relationships.)

Rate $\times$ Time = Distance
300 m/sec $\times t = x$ $\boxed{3}$
700 m/sec $\times t = 2500 - x$ $\boxed{4}$

(Use Strategy 13: Find unknowns by addition.)

Add $\boxed{3}$ and $\boxed{4}$

(300 m/sec)t + (700 m/sec)t = 2500 km
           (1000 m/sec)t = 2500 km $\boxed{5}$

(Use Strategy 10: Know how to use units.)

1 km = 1000 m $\boxed{6}$

Substitute $\boxed{6}$ in $\boxed{5}$:

(1000 m/sec)t = 2500(1000) m $\boxed{7}$

Divide $\boxed{7}$ by 1000 m:

t/sec = 2500
t = 2500 sec

(Math Refresher #121, #201, and #202)

16. Choice C is correct. **(Use Strategy 2: Translate from words to algebra.)**
We know that the volume of a cube = e^3
We are told that $e^3 < 25$

(Use Strategy 17: Use the given information effectively.)

Since e is a positive integer (which was given),

$$e \text{ can be: } 1 \rightarrow 1^3 = 1$$
$$2 \rightarrow 2^3 = 8$$
$$3 \rightarrow 3^3 = 27$$
$$\text{etc.}$$

For $e = 2$, the volume is 8, which is < 25
Any larger e will have a volume < 25
Thus, area of one face $= e^2 = 2^2 = 4$
Total area $= 6(4) = 24$

(Math Refresher #202 and #313)

17. Choices A and B are correct. The graphs are represented as follows: Plot $x = 0$, $y = 0$.

For $y = 2x^2$, when $x = \pm 1$, $y = 2$; when $x = \pm 2$; $y = 8$. For $y = -2x^2$, when $x = \pm 1$, $y = -2$; when $x = \pm 2$; $y = -8$.
The graphs are represented as follows:

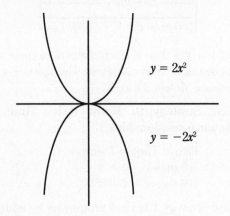

$y = 2x^2$

$y = -2x^2$

Thus, A and B are true. C is false. A linear function is of the form $y = mx + b$.

(Math Refresher #410)

18. Choice B is correct. Canada's 1991 share was 16.8%, and its 1997 share was 23.2%; the difference is 6.4%.

(Math Refresher #705)

19. Choice E is correct. 1180 – 701 is about $480 million. $480 million divided into 6 years gives an average gain of $80 million per year.

(Math Refresher #705)

20. Choice E is correct. Europe's 1997 share was 22.6%, while its 1991 share was 21.6%. 22.6 is about 105% of 21.6.

(Math Refresher #705)

21. 2015. South America lost .4% of the share in the six years on the table. To reach 15%, it must lose another 1.2% or 3(.4%). This will take 3 × 6, or 18 years. 1997 + 18 = 2015.

(Math Refresher #705)

22. **84**
(Use Strategy 5:

$$\text{Average} = \frac{\text{Sum of values}}{\text{Total number of values}})$$

Method 1: The simplest math and the quickest solution:

Suppose there are 10 students in the class. Since 40% of the class scored 100, 4 students scored 100. Since 10% of the class scored 80, 1 student scored 80.

That leaves us with 50% of the class, or 5 students, who scored an average of d.

The overall average was 90, so

$$90 = \frac{(4 \times 100) + (1 \times 80) + (5 \times d)}{10}$$

$$90 = \frac{400 + 80 + 5d}{10}$$

$$900 = 400 + 80 + 5d = 480 + 5d$$

$$420 = 5d$$

$$d = 84$$

Method 2: How a mathematician would solve this?

Let N be the number of students.
Then $0.4N =$ Number of students scoring 100
$0.1N =$ Number of students scoring 80

(Use Strategy 3: The whole equals the sum of its parts.)

We know that 50% of the class has been accounted for, so

$0.5N =$ Number of students remaining

Let d be the average score for the remaining students.

The overall average was 90, so

$$90 = \frac{(0.4N \times 100) + (0.1N \times 80) + (0.5N \times d)}{N}$$

$$= \frac{40N + 8N + (0.5N \times d)}{N}$$

$$= \frac{48N + (0.5N \times d)}{N}$$

$$90 = 48 + (.5 \times d) = 48 + \frac{d}{2}$$

$$42 = \frac{d}{2}$$

$$d = 84$$

(Math Refresher #601, #114, and #406)

23. Choices B and F are correct. $f(2x) = |2x| - 2x = 2(|x| - x) = 2f(x)$. $f(-1) = |-1| - (-1) = 1 + 1 = 2$.

(Math Refresher #616 and #615)

24. Choice A, B, C, and D are correct.

$$\begin{array}{r} AB \\ + \ BA \\ \hline CDC \end{array}$$

Given: A, B, C, and D are different digits. $\boxed{1}$

Let's get a range of possible digits so we don't have to work with so many combinations.

The largest possible AB is 98. Thus,

$$\begin{array}{r} 98 \\ + \ 89 \\ \hline 187 \end{array}$$

Thus, the only possible value for C is 1. $\boxed{2}$

(It cannot be greater than 1, since we used the largest value of AB.)

Using $\boxed{2}$, the problem becomes

$$\begin{array}{r} AB \\ + \ BA \\ \hline 1D1 \end{array}$$ $\boxed{3}$

We know that the sum of $B + A$ must end in a 1. $\boxed{4}$

Using $\boxed{4}$ and $\boxed{1}$ we know $B + A = 11$ $\boxed{5}$

(Use Strategy 8: When testing all choices, start with Choice E.)

If $A = 2$, we know (from $\boxed{5}$) that $B = 9$. Plug in these values for A and B.

$$\begin{array}{r} 29 \\ + \ 92 \\ \hline 121 \end{array}$$

But that would mean $D = 2$, the same digit as A, and the question stated that each letter represents a *different* digit. Thus A cannot be 2. You can see that $A = 3, 4, 5, 6$ will produce a sum of 121. Thus Choices A, B, C, and D are correct.

25. Choice E is correct. **(Use Strategy 17: Use the given information effectively.)**

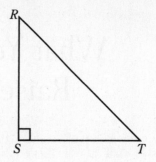

We know that Area of $\triangle = \frac{1}{2} \times$ base $\times$ height. $\boxed{1}$

We are given that $RS = ST =$ an integer. $\boxed{2}$

Substituting $\boxed{2}$ into $\boxed{1}$, we get

Area $\triangle RST = \frac{1}{2} \times$ (an integer) $\times$ (same integer)

Area $\triangle RST = \frac{1}{2} \times$ (an integer)^2 $\boxed{3}$

Multiplying $\boxed{3}$ by 2, we have

$2($Area $\triangle RST) =$ (an integer)^2 $\boxed{4}$

(Use Strategy 8: When all choices must be tested, start with E and work backward.)

Substituting Choice E, 20, into $\boxed{4}$, we get

$2(20) =$ (an integer)^2
$40 =$ (an integer)^2 $\boxed{5}$
$\boxed{5}$ is *not* possible, since
40 isn't the square of an integer.

(Math Refresher #307, #406, and #431)

What You Must Do Now to Raise Your GRE Score

1. Follow the directions on page 627 to determine your scaled score for the GRE Test you've just taken. These results will give you a good idea about how hard you'll need to study in order to achieve a certain score on the actual GRE.

2. Eliminate your weaknesses in each of the GRE test areas by taking the following Giant Steps toward GRE success:

Sentence Completion and Reading Part

Giant Step 1

Take advantage of the Sentence Completion and Reading Strategies that begin on page 136. Read again the Explanatory Answer for each of the Sentence Completion and Reading questions that you got wrong. Refer to the Reading Strategy that applies to each of your incorrect answers. Learn each of these strategies thoroughly. These strategies are crucial if you want to raise your GRE Verbal score substantially.

Giant Step 2

You can improve your vocabulary by doing the following:

1) Study the GRE 3,400-Word List beginning on page 377.

2) Take the 100 Tests to Strengthen Your Vocabulary beginning on page 426.

3) Study the Gruber Prefix-Root-Suffix List beginning on page 366.

4) Learn the Hot Prefixes and Roots beginning on page 717.

5) Read through the List of Standardized Test Words Appearing More Than Once beginning on page 371.

6) Look through the Most Important/Frequently Used GRE Words and Their Opposites beginning on page 373.

7) Learn the 3 Vocabulary Strategies beginning on page 168.

8) Read as widely as possible—not only novels. Nonfiction is important too…and don't forget to read newspapers and magazines.

9) Listen to people who speak well. Tune in to worthwhile TV programs.

10) Use the dictionary frequently and extensively—at home, on the bus, at work, etc.

11) Play word games—for example, crossword puzzles, anagrams, and Scrabble. Another game is to compose your own Sentence Completion questions. Try them on your friends.

Math Part

Giant Step 3

Make good use of the 25 Math Strategies that begin on page 72. Read again the solutions for each Math question that you answered incorrectly. Refer to the Math Strategy that applies to each of your incorrect answers. Learn each of these Math Strategies thoroughly. We repeat that these strategies are crucial if you want to raise your GRE Math score substantially.

Giant Step 4

You may want to take the **101 Most Important Math Questions You Need to Know How to Solve** test beginning on page 40 and follow the directions after the test for a basic Math skills diagnosis.

For each Math question that you got wrong in the test, note the reference to the Math Refresher section beginning on page 185. This reference will explain clearly the mathematical principle involved in the solution of the question you answered incorrectly. Learn that particular mathematical principle thoroughly.

For Both the Math and Reading Parts

Giant Step 5

You may want to take the **Strategy Diagnostic Test** beginning on page 1 to assess whether you're using the best strategies for the questions.

For the Writing Part

Giant Step 6

Take a look at Part 8, the Analytical Writing Section, which describes the various types of tasks in the Writing Section. Also make use of the Brief Review of English Grammar—Part 9.

3. After you have done some of the tasks you have been advised to do in the previous suggestions, proceed to Practice Test 3 beginning on page 650.

After taking Practice Test 3, concentrate on the weaknesses that still remain.

If you do the job *right* and follow the steps listed earlier, you are likely to raise your GRE score substantially on each of the Verbal, Math, and Writing parts of the test.

I am the master of my fate:
I am the captain of my soul.

—From the poem "Invictus"
by William Ernest Henley

GRE PRACTICE
TEST 3

Analytical Writing 1

ANALYZE AN ISSUE

Time—30 Minutes

You have 30 minutes to plan and compose a response to the following issue. A response to any other issue will receive a score of zero. Make sure that you respond according to the specific instructions and support your position on the issue with reasons and examples drawn from such areas as your reading, experience, observations, and/or academic studies.

Claim: Imagination is a more valuable asset than experience.

Reason: People who lack experience are free to imagine what is possible without the constraints of established habits and attitudes.

Write a response in which you discuss the extent to which you agree or disagree with the claim and the reason on which that claim is based.

Trained GRE readers will evaluate your response for its overall quality based on how well you:

- Respond to the specific task instructions
- Consider the complexities of the issue
- Organize, develop, and express your ideas
- Support your ideas with relevant reasons and/or examples
- Control the elements of standard written English

Before you begin writing, you may want to think for a few minutes about the issue and the specific task instructions and then plan your response. **Use the next page to plan your response, then write your response starting on the first lined page that follows. A total of four lined pages are provided for your response.** Be sure to develop your position fully and organize it coherently, but leave time to reread what you have written and make any revisions you think are necessary.

Write your response within the boxed area on the pages provided. Any text outside the boxed area will not be scored.

GO ON TO THE NEXT PAGE ⇒

Plan Your Response Here. Begin Writing Your Essay on the Following Page.

This page will not be scored.

GO ON TO THE NEXT PAGE

Note: On the computerized test, you will type your response and you will be able to correct mistakes through a word processor.

ANALYZE AN ISSUE RESPONSE (Page 1 of 4)

GO ON TO THE NEXT PAGE

ANALYZE AN ISSUE RESPONSE (Page 2 of 4)

GO ON TO THE NEXT PAGE

ANALYZE AN ISSUE RESPONSE (Page 3 of 4)

GO ON TO THE NEXT PAGE

ANALYZE AN ISSUE RESPONSE (Page 4 of 4)

_____
_____
_____
_____
_____
_____
_____
_____
_____
_____
_____
_____
_____
_____
_____
_____
_____
_____
_____
_____
_____
_____
_____
_____
_____
_____
_____
_____
_____
_____
_____
_____

STOP

If you finish before time is called, you may check your work on this section only.
Do not turn to any other section in the test.

Analytical Writing 2

ANALYZE AN ARGUMENT

Time—30 Minutes

You have 30 minutes to plan and compose a response in which you evaluate the following argument passage. A response to any other argument will receive a score of zero. Make sure that you respond according to the specific instructions and support your evaluation with relevant reasons and/or examples.

Note that you are NOT being asked to present your own views on the subject.

The following appeared in a letter from a firm providing investment advice for a client.

"Most homes in the northeastern United States, where winters are typically cold, have traditionally used oil as their major fuel for heating. Last heating season that region experienced 90 days with below-normal temperatures, and climate forecasters predict that this weather pattern will continue for several more years. Furthermore, many new homes are being built in the region in response to recent population growth. Because of these trends, we predict an increased demand for heating oil and recommend investment in Consolidated Industries, one of whose major business operations is the retail sale of home heating oil."

Write a response in which you examine the stated and/or unstated assumptions of the argument. Be sure to explain how the argument depends on these assumptions and what the implications are for the argument if the assumptions prove unwarranted.

Trained GRE readers will evaluate your response for its overall quality based on how well you:

- Respond to the specific task instructions
- Consider the complexities of the issue
- Organize, develop, and express your ideas
- Support your ideas with relevant reasons and/or examples
- Control the elements of standard written English

Before you begin writing, you may want to think for a few minutes about the issue and the specific task instructions and then plan your response. **Use the next page to plan your response, then write your response starting on the first lined page that follows. A total of four lined pages are provided for your response.** Be sure to develop your position fully and organize it coherently, but leave time to reread what you have written and make any revisions you think are necessary.

Write your response within the boxed area on the pages provided. Any text outside the boxed area will not be scored.

GO ON TO THE NEXT PAGE ⟩

Plan Your Response Here. Begin Writing Your Essay on the Following Page.

This page will not be scored.

GO ON TO THE NEXT PAGE

Note: On the computerized test, you will type your response and you will be able to correct mistakes through a word processor.

ANALYZE AN ARGUMENT RESPONSE (Page 1 of 4)

GO ON TO THE NEXT PAGE

ANALYZE AN ARGUMENT RESPONSE (Page 2 of 4)

GO ON TO THE NEXT PAGE

ANALYZE AN ARGUMENT RESPONSE (Page 3 of 4)

_____
_____
_____
_____
_____
_____
_____
_____
_____
_____
_____
_____
_____
_____
_____
_____
_____
_____
_____
_____
_____
_____
_____
_____
_____
_____
_____
_____
_____
_____
_____
_____

GO ON TO THE NEXT PAGE

ANALYZE AN ARGUMENT RESPONSE (Page 4 of 4)

_____
_____
_____
_____
_____
_____
_____
_____
_____
_____
_____
_____
_____
_____
_____
_____
_____
_____
_____
_____
_____
_____
_____
_____
_____
_____
_____
_____
_____

STOP

If you finish before time is called, you may check your work on this section only.
Do not turn to any other section in the test.

Instructions for Verbal Reasoning and Quantitative Reasoning Sections

Important Notes

Your scores for these sections will be determined by the number of questions you answer correctly. Nothing is subtracted from your score if you answer a question incorrectly. Therefore, to maximize your scores it is better for you to guess at an answer than not to respond at all. Work as rapidly as you can without losing accuracy. Do not spend too much time on questions that are too difficult for you. Go on to the other questions and come back to the difficult ones later.

Some or all of the passages in this test have been adapted from published material to provide the examinee with significant problems for analysis and evaluation. To make the passages suitable for testing purposes, the style, content, or point of view of the original may have been altered.

You may use a calculator in the Quantitative Reasoning sections only. You will be provided with a calculator and cannot use any other calculator.

Marking Your Answers

All answers must be marked in this test book. When filling in the circles that accompany each question, BE SURE THAT EACH MARK IS DARK AND COMPLETELY FILLS THE CIRCLE.

Be careful to erase any stray marks that lie in or near a circle. If you change an answer, be sure that all previous marks are erased completely. Stray marks and incomplete erasures may be read as intended answers. Scratch paper will not be provided. You may work out your answers in the blank areas of the test book, but do not work out answers near the circles.

Question Formats

The questions in these sections have several different formats. A brief description of these formats and instructions for entering your answer choices are given below.

Multiple-Choice Questions—Select One Answer Choice

These standard multiple-choice questions require you to select just one answer choice from a list of options. You will receive credit only if you mark the **single** correct answer choice and no other.

Example: What city is the capital of France?

- Ⓐ Rome
- ● Paris
- © London
- Ⓓ Cairo

Multiple-Choice Questions—Select One or More Answer Choices

Some of these questions specify how many answer choices to select; others require you to select all that apply. In either case, to receive credit you must mark all of the correct answer choices and no others. These questions are distinguished by the use of a square box.

Example: Select all that apply.

Which of the following countries are in Africa?

- ■ Chad
- Ⓑ China
- Ⓒ France
- ■ Kenya

Column-Format Questions

This question type presents the answer choices in columns. You must select one answer choice from each column. You will receive credit only if you mark the correct answer choice **in each column.**

Example: Complete the following sentence,

(i) _____ is the capital of (ii) _____.

Blank (i)	Blank (ii)
● Paris	Ⓓ Canada
Ⓑ Rome	● France
Ⓒ Cairo	Ⓕ China

Numeric Entry Questions

To answer these questions, enter a number by filling in circles in a grid. Complete instructions for doing so will be found in the Quantitative Reasoning sections.

Section 1: Verbal Reasoning

Time—35 Minutes
25 Questions

For each question, indicate the best answer, using the directions given.

For each of Questions 1–8, select <u>one</u> entry for each blank from the corresponding column of choices.
Fill all blanks in the way that best completes the text.

1. Because the majority of the evening cable TV programs available dealt with violence and sex, the parents decided that the programs were too _____ for the children to watch.

   (A) exclusive
   (B) acceptable
   (C) instructive
   (D) inappropriate
   (E) unnecessary

2. Although the death of his dog had saddened him markedly, his computer designing skills remained completely _____.

   (A) twisted
   (B) unaffected
   (C) incapable
   (D) repaired
   (E) demolished

3. During the postwar period, _____ firms met with great difficulty in maintaining their business as soon as the standard brands of _____ companies became generally available.

Blank 1	Blank 2
(A) contemporary	(D) enterprising
(B) manufacturing	(E) established
(C) specialized	(F) agricultural

4. Much research has shown that one of the mistakes in our educational jargon is the common fault of stressing the interests of _____ and eliding over the interests of the _____.

Blank 1	Blank 2
(A) the community	(D) individual
(B) society	(E) partisans
(C) the aristocracy	(F) oligarchy

5. The student of human nature knows that its components are, for the most part, _____; but the student is also aware that events—pleasant or unpleasant—do play a part in bringing to the fore at one time or another certain _____.

Blank 1	Blank 2
(A) multifarious	(D) reactions
(B) ephemeral	(E) characteristics
(C) immutable	(F) instincts

6. Even his most _____ backers expressed a feeling of _____ and _____ because of his current inability to complete his assignments in a timely and efficient manner.

Blank 1	Blank 2	Blank 3
(A) fervent	(D) surprise	(G) solidarity
(B) trusted	(E) disappoint-ment	(H) disillusion-ment
(C) proficient	(F) awe	(I) remorse

7. The dictator's slow and easy manner and his air of gentility _____ his firm intention to ensure no opposition to his planned _____ policies, and his _____ in carrying out these policies sustained them while he was in office for a long time to come.

Blank 1	Blank 2	Blank 3
(A) revealed	(D) unique	(G) determina-tion
(B) supported	(E) drastic	(H) manner
(C) belied	(F) revolutionary	(I) craft

GO ON TO THE NEXT PAGE ⇒

8. The profession of a major league baseball player involves more than _____ in these times when astronomical salaries and _____ contract bargaining is commonplace; many excellent players now need _____ agents to represent them, whereas many years ago, the players could make the major leagues and succeed on their own.

Blank 1	Blank 2	Blank 3
(A) playing skill	(D) efficient	(G) private
(B) practice	(E) astute	(H) seasoned
(C) enthu-siasm	(F) devious	(I) audacious

For each of Questions 9–14, select one answer choice unless otherwise directed.

Questions 9–11 are based on this passage.

1   Let's be honest right at the start. Physics is neither particularly easy to comprehend nor easy to love, but then again, *what*—or for that matter, *who*—is? For most of us it is a new vision, a different way of understanding with its
5   own scales, rhythms, and forms. And yet, as with *Macbeth*, *Mona Lisa*, or *La Traviata*, physics has its rewards. Surely you have already somehow prejudged this science. It's all too easy to compartmentalize our human experience: science in one box, music, art, and literature in other boxes.
10   The Western mind delights in little boxes—life is easier to analyze when it's presented in small pieces in small compartments (we call it specialization). It is our traditional way of seeing the trees and missing the forest. The label on the box for physics too often reads "Caution:
15   Not for Common Consumption" or "Free from Sentiment." If you can, please tear off that label and discard the box or we will certainly, sooner or later, bore each other to death. There is nothing more tedious than the endless debate between humanist and scientist on whose vision is truer;
20   each of us is less for what we lack of the other.
     It is pointless and even worse to separate physics from the body of all creative work, to pluck it out from history, to shear it from philosophy, and then to present it pristine, pure, all-knowing, and infallible. We know nothing of what
25   will be with absolute certainty. There is no scientific tome of unassailable, immutable truth. Yet what little we do know about physics reveals an inspiring grandeur and intricate beauty.

9. According to the author, what does the label on the box for physics suggest about physics?

(A) It is a dangerous area of study.
(B) It is a cause for great excitement.
(C) It is uninteresting to the ordinary person.
(D) It is difficult to understand because it is completely subjective.
(E) It is a subject that should be elective but not required.

10. What statement does the author make about physics?

(A) It should be recognized for its unique beauty.
(B) It is a boring course of study.
(C) It appeals only to the Western mind.
(D) It is superior to music, art, and literature.
(E) It is unpopular with people who are romantic.

11. In line 13, the phrase "seeing the trees and missing the forest" means

(A) putting experiences into categories
(B) viewing the world too narrowly
(C) analyzing scientific discoveries
(D) making judgments too hastily
(E) ignoring the beauty of natural surroundings

Questions 12–13 are based on this passage.

1   We still have, in short, all the weapons in the arsenal of satire: the rapier of wit, the broadsword of invective, the stiletto of parody, the Damoclean swords of sarcasm and irony. Their cutting edges are bright and sharp; they
5   glisten with barbs guaranteed to stick and stay stuck in the thickest hide, or stab the most inflated Polonius in the arras. Yet though they hang well-oiled and ready to our hands, we tend to use them separately and gingerly. We are afraid of hurting someone's feelings or of being hurt
10   in a return bout. We tremble at the prospect of treading on someone's moral corns. We are too full of the milque-toast of human kindness. We always see the Other Side of the Case, always remember that our Victim may have a Mom who loves him, always fear that we may be setting him back
15   a few hundred hours in his psychiatric progress toward the Terrestrial City of Perfect Readjustment. Oh, yes. We poke and pry a bit. We pin an errant butterfly to a board or two. But for real lessons in the ungentlest of the arts we must turn back to the older masters.

For the following two questions, Questions 12 and 13, consider each of the choices separately and select all that apply.

12. Which device does the author *not* use in the passage?

(A) literary allusions
(B) anecdotes
(C) sarcasm

GO ON TO THE NEXT PAGE

13. The passage suggest that modern man chiefly aspires to

    (A) a sense of security
    (B) a superficial sense of kindness
    (C) protection from satire

Question 14 is based on this passage.

1   I cannot think it effectual for determining truth to examine the several ways by which phenomena may be explained, unless where there can be a perfect enumeration of all those ways. You know, the proper method for
5   inquiring after the properties of things is to deduce them from experiments. And I told you that the theory that I propounded was evinced to me, not by inferring *'tis thus because not otherwise*, that is, not by deducing it only from a confutation of contrary suppositions, but by deriving it from
10 experiments concluding positively and directly.

14. Which of the following statements may be assumed from the paragraph?

    I.   Nature behaves in a lawful manner.
    II. Only direct establishment of scientific theory in the laboratory could conceivably establish truth.
    III. Scientific truth can always be established experimentally.

    (A) I only
    (B) II only
    (C) III only
    (D) I and III only
    (E) I and II only

> For each of Questions 15–19, select the <u>two</u> answer choices that, when used to complete the sentence blank, fit the meaning of the sentence as a whole <u>and</u> produce completed sentences that are alike in meaning.

15. For years a vocalist of spirituals, Marian Anderson was finally recognized as _____ singer when the Metropolitan Opera House engaged her.

    (A) a capable
    (B) an unusual
    (C) an attractive
    (D) a unique
    (E) a mediocre
    (F) a competent

16. As long as learning is made continually repugnant, so long will there be a predisposition to _____ it when one is free from the authority of parents and teachers.

    (A) master
    (B) reject
    (C) undermine
    (D) minimize
    (E) inculcate
    (F) enjoy

17. The industrialists in the East feared that migration would make workers scarce and wages high, and regarded the abundance of land open to settlement as _____ to themselves.

    (A) a challenge
    (B) a menace
    (C) an advantage
    (D) a guide
    (E) a directive
    (F) a threat

18. Many citizens objected vigorously to the _____ of the county offices, which, for the most part, could not be reached without traveling considerable distances.

    (A) inaccessibility
    (B) lack
    (C) inefficiency
    (D) unapproachability
    (E) corruption
    (F) layout

19. Most estimates of the incidence of chicken pox in communities are _____, not because of poor statistical techniques but because the disease is not well reported.

    (A) unnecessary
    (B) heartening
    (C) unreliable
    (D) variable
    (E) superfluous
    (F) ineffectual

GO ON TO THE NEXT PAGE

For each of Questions 20–25, select <u>one</u> answer choice unless otherwise directed.

Questions 20–22 are based on this passage.

1   For though the terms are often confused, obscurity is not at all the same thing as unintelligibility. Obscurity is what happens when a writer undertakes a theme and method for which the reader is not sufficiently prepared.
5 Unintelligibility is what happens when the writer undertakes a theme and method for which he himself is not sufficiently prepared.

    A good creation is an enlarging experience, and the act of enlargement must require the reader to extend
10 himself. Only the thoroughly familiar—which is to say, the already encompassed—may reasonably be expected to be immediately clear. True, the surface of a poem may seem deceptively clear, thus leading the careless reader to settle for an easy first-response as the true total. But even in work
15 of such surface clarity as Frost's, it will be a foolish reader indeed who permits himself the illusion that one easy reading will reveal all of the poem. In this sense, indeed, there can be no great poetry without obscurity.

20. The author defines obscurity and unintelligibility in order to

  (A) show his knowledge of literature
  (B) please the reader
  (C) set the stage for what follows
  (D) clarify his own thinking
  (E) defend unintelligibility

21. Which quality would the author of this passage expect in a poet?

  (A) sense of humor
  (B) skill in rhyming
  (C) use of the direct approach
  (D) surface clarity
  (E) knowledge of subject

22. In the context in which it appears, "encompassed" (line 11) most nearly means

  (A) guided
  (B) expected
  (C) encountered
  (D) described
  (E) revised

Questions 23–24 are based on the following passage.

1   A critic of politics finds himself driven to deprecate the power of words, while using them copiously in warning against their influence. It is indeed in politics that their influence is most dangerous, so that one is almost tempted
5 to wish that they did not exist, and that society might be managed silently, by instinct, habit, and ocular perception, without this supervening Babel of reports, arguments, and slogans.

23. The author implies that critics of misused language

  (A) become fanatical on this subject
  (B) are guilty of what they criticize in others
  (C) are clever in contriving slogans
  (D) tell the story of the Tower of Babel
  (E) rely too strongly on instincts

24. In the context of the passage as a whole, "Babel" (line 7) most nearly means

  (A) tyranny
  (B) kingdom
  (C) compilation
  (D) a confusion of voices
  (E) conflict

Question 25 is based on this passage.

1   The complete man does not confuse generic distinctions, nor does he accept as demonstrated truths what are only hypotheses. But he also does not compartmentalize or fragment his personality, so that on the one hand he limits
5 himself to observing, reasoning, and verifying, and on the other is content to believe in values that engage and direct him without his being able to understand them.

25. Which of the following statements may be assumed from the paragraph?

  I. Science is never value-free.
  II. Judgments of value generally are only hypotheses.
  III. Men should think about their values.

  (A) I only
  (B) II only
  (C) III only
  (D) I and II only
  (E) I, II, and III

STOP

If you finish before time is called, you may check your work on this section only.

Do not turn to any other section in the test.

Section 2: Verbal Reasoning

Time—35 Minutes
25 Questions

For each question, indicate the best answer, using the direction given.

For each of Questions 1–8, select <u>one</u> entry for each blank from the corresponding column of choices. Fill all blanks in the way that best completes the text.

---

1. Volkswagen, the first foreign automobile company to build cars in the United States, had at one time announced that because of _____ sales, it had decided to close several of its plants in the United States.

   (A) exclusive
   (B) indescribable
   (C) astounding
   (D) interesting
   (E) sluggish

2. Van Gogh's painting *Irises*, which was auctioned off for $53 million, failed to create _____ among several art critics when it was first shown in Paris a hundred years ago.

   (A) animosity
   (B) disparity
   (C) enthusiasm
   (D) ambiguity
   (E) indifference

3. When he saw his brother approach, he _____; he was sorry to have made such a show of his true feelings. He would have given much to have been able to suppress the _____ at the same moment.

Blank 1	Blank 2
(A) grimaced	(D) fervor
(B) exulted	(E) deliverance
(C) beckoned	(F) action

4. At the trial, the defendant maintained a manner that could be best described as _____; but the revelations concerning his actions in the commission of the crime portrayed a personality that could only be described as _____.

Blank 1	Blank 2
(A) sanctimonious	(D) impassioned
(B) impassive	(E) imperious
(C) continent	(F) jocose

5. Although some politicians believe that crime is decreasing, the government indicated after unbiased research that the crime rate in the United States remains _____ and that one in every three households _____ some form of major crime in any year.

Blank 1	Blank 2
(A) bountiful	(D) initiates
(B) incredible	(E) experiences
(C) stagnant	(F) anticipates

6. You can turn on a television and on a news program you can _____ view some piece of news that deals with a crime. In fact, violent crime has become so _____ in our cities throughout the country that hardly a day goes by when we are not made aware of some _____ act on our local news broadcasts.

Blank 1	Blank 2	Blank 3
(A) possibly	(D) prevalent	(G) destructive
(B) no doubt	(E) spectacular	(H) heinous
(C) probably	(F) vicious	(I) well carried out

GO ON TO THE NEXT PAGE

7. Education had been different many years ago. Now, in a rising tide of _____ in public education, there are some people that are examples of informed and _____ teachers—a blessing to children and _____ to education.

Blank 1	Blank 2	Blank 3
(A) specialization	(D) knowledgeable	(G) an asset
(B) superfluousness	(E) sophisticated	(H) a detriment
(C) mediocrity	(F) dedicated	(I) a revelation

8. The Gestalt school of psychology emphasizes that the mind tends to _____ and organize activities in _____ wholes. The best example of this is experiencing a single _____ and not simply a mass of blue points when you look at an unbroken expanse in the sky.

Blank 1	Blank 2	Blank 3
(A) perceive	(D) integrated	(G) point
(B) structure	(E) secular	(H) impression
(C) envelop	(F) exact	(I) relationship

For each of Questions 9–15, select one answer choice unless otherwise directed.

Questions 9–10 are based on this passage.

1   It is no longer needful to labor Dickens's power as a portrayer of modern society nor the seriousness of his "criticism of life." But we are still learning to appreciate his supreme attainment as an artist. Richness of
5 poetic imagery, modulations of emotional tone, subtleties of implication, complex unities of structure, intensities of psychological insight, a panoply of achievement, mount up to overwhelming triumph. Though contemporary readers perhaps still feel somewhat queasy about Dickens's senti-
10 ment, his comedy and his drama sweep all before them. Even his elaborate and multistranded plots are now seen as great symphonic compositions driving forward through theme and variation to the resolving chords on which they close.

For the following two questions, Questions 9 and 10, consider each of the choices separately and select all that apply.

9. According to the passage, readers most recently have begun to appreciate Dickens's

   (A) creative development
   (B) subtle synthesis
   (C) literary craftsmanship

10. According to the passage, the endings of Dickens's works are most probably characterized by

   (A) a lack of sense of completion
   (B) dramatic power
   (C) different takes in the development

Question 11 is based on this passage.

1   Some ecologists predict that a global heat wave will result from our increasing use of fossil fuels. They point out that the consumption of these fuels produces carbon dioxide, which locks solar heat into the atmosphere through
5 the "greenhouse effect." If there is a general increase in the temperature of the atmosphere in the next decades, we will be able to conclude that the ecologists' prediction was correct.

11. The most serious weakness of the argument above is that the author

   (A) does not adequately link carbon dioxide to the use of fossil fuels
   (B) associates a general increase in the temperature of the atmosphere with a global heat wave
   (C) assumes that an increase in atmospheric temperature can be caused only by an increased use of fossil fuels
   (D) fails to define the greenhouse effect and its relation to the production of carbon dioxide gases
   (E) gives no evidence that our use of fossil fuels has increased

GO ON TO THE NEXT PAGE

Questions 12–15 are based on this passage.

1   The discoveries made by scientific geniuses, from Archimedes through Einstein, have repeatedly revolutionized both our world and the way we see it. Yet no one really knows how the mind of a genius works. Most people think
5 that a very high IQ sets the great scientist apart. They assume that flashes of profound insight like Einstein's are the product of mental processes so arcane that they must be inaccessible to more ordinary minds.

    But a growing number of researchers in psychology,
10 psychiatry, and the history of science are investigating the way geniuses think. The researchers are beginning to give us tantalizing glimpses of the mental universe that can produce the discoveries of an Einstein, an Edison, a da Vinci—or any Nobel Prize winner.

15   Surprisingly, most researchers agree that the important variable in genius is not the IQ but creativity. Testers start with 135 as the beginning of the "genius" category, but the researchers seem to feel that, while an IQ above a certain point—about 120—is very helpful for a scientist,
20 having an IQ that goes much higher is not crucial for producing a work of genius. All human beings have at least four types of intelligence. The great scientist possesses the ability to move back and forth among them—the logical-mathematical; the spatial, which includes visual perception;
25 the linguistic; and the bodily-kinesthetic.

    Some corroboration of these categories comes from the reports of scientists who describe thought processes centered around images, sensations, or words. Einstein reported a special "feeling at the tips of the fingers" that
30 told him which path to take through a problem. The idea for a self-starting electric motor came to Nikola Tesla one evening as he was reciting a poem by Goethe and watching a sunset. Suddenly he imagined a magnetic field rapidly rotating inside a circle of electromagnets.

35   Some IQ tests predict fairly accurately how well a person will do in school and how quickly he or she will master knowledge, but genius involves more than knowledge. The genius has the capacity to leap significantly beyond his present knowledge and produce something
40 new. To do this, he sees the relationship between facts or pieces of information in a new or unusual way.

    The scientist solves a problem by shifting from one intelligence to another, although the logical-mathematical intelligence is dominant. Creative individuals seem to be
45 marked by a special fluidity of mind. They may be able to think of a problem verbally, logically, and also spatially.

    Paradoxically, fluid thinking may be connected to another generally agreed-upon trait of the scientific genius— persistence, or unusually strong motivation to work on a
50 problem. Persistence kept Einstein looking for the solution to the question of the relationship between the law of gravity and his special theory of relativity. Yet surely creative fluidity enabled him to come up with a whole new field that included both special relativity and gravitation.

55   Many scientists have the ability to stick with a problem even when they appear not to be working on it. Werner Heisenberg discovered quantum mechanics one night

during a vacation he had taken to recuperate from the mental jumble he had fallen into trying to solve the atomic-
60 spectra problem.

12. Which statement is true, according to the passage?

(A) The law of gravity followed the publication of Einstein's theory of relativity.
(B) Nikola Tesla learned about magnets from his research of the works of Goethe.
(C) Archimedes and Einstein lived in the same century.
(D) Most scientists have IQ scores above 120.
(E) We ought to refer to intelligences rather than to intelligence.

13. The author believes that, among the four intelligences he cites, the most important one for the scientist is

(A) spatial
(B) bodily-kinesthetic
(C) linguistic
(D) logical-mathematical
(E) not singled out

14. The author focuses on the circumstances surrounding the work of great scientists in order to show that

(A) scientific geniuses are usually eccentric in their behavior
(B) the various types of intelligence have come into play during their work
(C) scientists often give the impression that they are relaxing when they are really working on a problem
(D) scientists must be happy to do their best work
(E) great scientific discoveries are almost always accidental

15. The passage can best be described as

(A) a comparison of how the average individual and the great scientist think
(B) an account of the unexpected things that led to great discoveries by scientists
(C) an explanation of the way scientific geniuses really think
(D) a criticism of intelligence tests as they are given today
(E) a lesson clarifying scientific concepts such as quantum mechanics and relativity

GO ON TO THE NEXT PAGE

For each of Questions 16–19, select the two answer choices that, when used to complete the sentence blank, fit the meaning of the sentence as a whole and produce completed sentences that are alike in meaning.

16. Newton's picture of the universe was not one in which there was _____, and, in accordance with his teaching, the universe might very likely have been created out of one piece.

    (A) examination
    (B) synthesis
    (C) verification
    (D) inevitability
    (E) development
    (F) uniformity

17. There are stories and highly _____ suppositions that the Hyksos built a considerable empire in Egypt, although there are few written records or definite evidences of their conquests.

    (A) plausible
    (B) peculiar
    (C) superseded
    (D) regarded
    (E) improbable
    (F) unique

18. The typist made no effort to be _____; she double-spaced the first and third letter, then single-spaced the second, fourth, and fifth letters.

    (A) consistent
    (B) prompt
    (C) orderly
    (D) disputatious
    (E) contentious
    (F) considerate

19. Since the judge feels that the defendant's offense is _____, he will, probably, give him a light sentence.

    (A) vindictive
    (B) venal
    (C) egregious
    (D) venial
    (E) heinous
    (F) pardonable

For each of Questions 20–25, select one answer choice unless otherwise directed.

Question 20 is based on this passage.

1   Some lawyers argue that the perception of the intrinsic qualities of *pornography* in any work depends on literary criticism and is, therefore, a matter of opinion. It seems odd, though, that in a legal context, serious critics them-
5 selves often behave as though they believed criticism to be a matter of opinion. Why be a critic—and teach in universities—if criticism involves no more than uttering *capricious* and *arbitrary* opinions?

20. The argument can be *weakened* by pointing out that

    (A) literary critics, in fact, agree that nothing is pornographic
    (B) lawyers say that perception of the qualities of pornography is a matter of opinion because the literary critics do not agree
    (C) literary critics are not legal authorities
    (D) it is not the job of the literary critics to say what is pornographic
    (E) literary critics teach at universities only for the money

GO ON TO THE NEXT PAGE

Questions 21–22 are based on this passage.

1   The theory of agricultural primacy in the origins of cities says agriculture first, cities later. Behind it lies the idea that in pre-Neolithic times hunting peoples lived only in small, economically self-sufficient groups. Not until
5   some of them learned to cultivate grain and raise livestock did settled and stable villages emerge. And not until after the villages were built did complex divisions of labor, large economic projects, and intricate social organization become possible. These advances, coupled with a surplus
10   of agricultural food, made cities possible.

For the following question, consider each of the answer choices separately and select all that apply.

21. Which of the following statements is supported by the passage?

   (A) In pre-Neolithic times, people learned to cultivate grain and raise animals.
   (B) Cities were formed by a large number of factors.
   (C) Economy and work specialization played an important role in the development of cities.

22. The passage provides information on each of the following EXCEPT

   (A) how cities were formed
   (B) the size of the group that was important in the future development of the cities
   (C) the specific work people did for the villages to develop
   (D) the specific factors that eventually created the cities
   (E) the mechanics of social organization

Questions 23–25 are based on this passage.

1   The ancient Egyptians believed strongly in life after death. They also believed that a person would need his body to exist in this afterlife. Therefore, they carefully preserved the body by treating it with spices and oils and wrapping it
5   in linen cloth. The wrapped body was then placed in a tomb. A body that is treated in this way is called a mummy.
     Egyptian kings and nobles wanted to be certain that their mummies would be kept in safe places forever. They had great tombs built for themselves and their families.
10   Many kings were buried in secret tombs carved out of solid rock in a place near Thebes called the Valley of the Kings.
     About eighty kings built towering pyramid-shaped stone tombs. These pyramids have become famous as one of the Seven Wonders of the Ancient World.
15   One of the most amazing things about these pyramids is that they were constructed without using wheels or heavy equipment to move or raise the rocks. Egypt did not learn about the wheel until long after the pyramids were built. Workmen used levers to get large blocks of stone on and off
20   sledges and hauled them into place over long ramps built around the pyramids.

23. In the context in which it appears, the term "mummy" (line 6) was used to describe

   (A) kings of ancient Egypt
   (B) ancient Egyptian nobles
   (C) the place where Egyptian kings were buried
   (D) the preserved body of a dead person
   (E) one of the Seven Wonders of the Ancient World

24. The pyramids were built

   (A) before the Egyptians developed a sophisticated technology
   (B) after the Egyptians developed a sophisticated technology
   (C) to house the tombs of all ancient Egyptian kings and nobles
   (D) with the use of spices, oils, and linen cloth
   (E) to always protect the mummies

25. Which of the following practices is most closely associated with ancient Egyptian belief in an afterlife?

   (A) placing the dead in tombs carved out of solid rock
   (B) building pyramids to house the bodies of dead kings
   (C) preserving dead bodies with oils and spices
   (D) creating the Valley of the Kings near Thebes
   (E) constructing tombs without the use of wheels or heavy equipment

STOP
If you finish before time is called, you may check your work on this section only.
Do not turn to any other section in the test.

Section 3: Quantitative Reasoning

Time—40 Minutes
25 Questions

For each question, indicate the best answer, using the directions given.

Notes: All numbers used are real numbers.

All figures are assumed to lie in a plane unless otherwise indicated.

Geometric figures, such as lines, circles, triangles, and quadrilaterals, **are not necessarily** drawn to scale. That is, you should **not** assume that quantities such as lengths and angle measures are as they appear in a figure. You should assume, however, that lines shown as straight are actually straight, points on a line are in the order shown, and more generally, all geometric objects are in the relative positions shown. For questions with geometric figures, you should base your answers on geometric reasoning, not on estimating or comparing quantities by sight or by measurement.

Coordinate systems, such as *xy* planes and number lines, **are** drawn to scale; therefore, you can read, estimate, or compare quantities in such figures by sight or by measurement.

Graphical data presentations, such as bar graphs, circles graphs, and line graphs, **are** drawn to scale; therefore, you can read, estimate, or compare data values by sight or by measurement.

For each of Questions 1–9, compare Quantity A and Quantity B, using additional information centered above the two quantities if such information is given. Select one of the following four answer choices and fill in the corresponding circle to the right of the question.

(A) Quantity A is greater.
(B) Quantity B is greater.
(C) The two quantities are equal.
(D) The relationship cannot be determined from the information given.

A symbol that appears more than once in a question has the same meaning throughout the question.

Quantity A	Quantity B	Correct Answer
Example 1: $(2)(6)$	$2 + 6$	Ⓐ Ⓑ Ⓒ Ⓓ

Example 2: *PS*	*SR*	Ⓐ Ⓑ Ⓒ Ⓓ

(since equal lengths cannot
be assumed, even though
PS and *SR* appear equal)

GO ON TO THE NEXT PAGE

SUMMARY DIRECTIONS FOR COMPARISON QUESTIONS

Answer: A if the quantity in Quantity A is greater;

B if the quantity in Quantity B is greater;

C if the two quantities are equal;

D if the relationship cannot be determined from the information given.

1

$$7x + 21 = 35$$

Quantity A	Quantity B	
$4x + 12$	21	Ⓐ Ⓑ Ⓒ Ⓓ

2

Quantity A	Quantity B	
$(-2)^{88}$	$(-2)^{97}$	Ⓐ Ⓑ Ⓒ Ⓓ

3

$$-5 < y < 5$$

Quantity A	Quantity B	
$-y$	6	Ⓐ Ⓑ Ⓒ Ⓓ

4

$\triangle RST$ is scalene.

Quantity A	Quantity B	
Length of altitude to side RT	Length of side SR	Ⓐ Ⓑ Ⓒ Ⓓ

5

$$a - b = 5$$
$$a + b = -1$$

Quantity A	Quantity B	
a	b	Ⓐ Ⓑ Ⓒ Ⓓ

6

m is an integer > 0
$$0 < y < 1$$

Quantity A	Quantity B	
$\dfrac{m}{y}$	m	Ⓐ Ⓑ Ⓒ Ⓓ

7

$$-\frac{1}{3}y = \frac{1}{3}y$$

Quantity A	Quantity B	
$-y$	$-\dfrac{2}{3}$	Ⓐ Ⓑ Ⓒ Ⓓ

GO ON TO THE NEXT PAGE

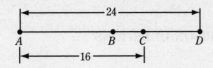

8 | Quantity A | Quantity B | |
| --- | --- | --- |
| Length of *BD* | 8 | Ⓐ Ⓑ Ⓒ Ⓓ |

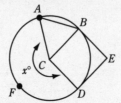

9 Equilateral triangle *ABC* and square *BCDE* have side $\overline{BC}$ in common. *C* is the center of the circle.

Quantity A	Quantity B	
x	200	Ⓐ Ⓑ Ⓒ Ⓓ

Questions 10–25 have several different formats. Unless otherwise directed, select a single answer choice. For Numeric Entry questions, follow the instructions below.

Numeric Entry Questions

To answer these questions, enter a number by filling in circles in a grid.

- Your answer may be an integer, a decimal, or a fraction, and it may be negative.

- Equivalent forms of the correct answer, such as 2.5 and 2.50, are all correct. Although fractions do not need to be reduced to lowest terms, they may need to be reduced to fit in the grid.

- Enter the exact answer unless the question asks you to round your answer.

- If a question asks for a fraction, the grid will have a built-in division slash (/). Otherwise, the grid will have a decimal point.

- Start your answer in any column, space permitting. Fill in no more than one circle in any column of the grid. Columns not needed should be left blank.

- Write your answer in the boxes at the top of the grid and fill in the corresponding circles. **You will receive credit only if the circles are filled in correctly, regardless of the number written in the boxes at the top.**

Examples of acceptable ways to use the grid:

Integer answer: 502 (either position is correct)   Decimal answer: −4.13   Fraction answer: $-\frac{2}{10}$

GO ON TO THE NEXT PAGE

10. If x and y are integers such that $1<|x|<5$ and $2<|y|<7$, what is the least possible value of $x + y$?

   (A) -10
   (B) -8
   (C) -5
   (D) 5
   (E) 10

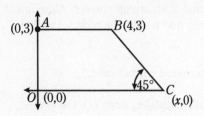

11. What is the area of quadrilateral $ABCO$ in the figure above?

   (A) 10.5
   (B) 14.5
   (C) 16.5
   (D) 21.0
   (E) The answer cannot be determined from the information given.

12. The difference between the sum of two numbers and the difference of the two numbers is 6. Find the larger of the two numbers if their product is 15.

   (A) 3
   (B) 5
   (C) 17
   (D) 20
   (E) 23

Question 13 refers to the figure above, where W, X, Y, and Z are four distinct digits from 0 to 9, inclusive, and $W + X + Y = 5Z$ (where $5Z$ is the product of 5 and Z).

For the following question, select all answer choices that apply.

13. Under the given conditions, which of the following could be values of Z? Indicate all such values.

   (A) 1
   (B) 2
   (C) 3
   (D) 4
   (E) 5

x	$f(x)$
0	3
1	4
2	2
3	5
4	8

14. According to the table above, for what value of x does $f(x) = x + 2$?

   (A) 0
   (B) 1
   (C) 2
   (D) 3
   (E) 4

For the following question, use the grid to enter your answer.

15. If the average (arithmetic mean) of 4 numbers is 8,000 and the average (arithmetic mean) of 3 of the 4 numbers is 7,500, then what must the fourth number be?

16. In a certain school, special programs in French and Spanish are available. If there are N students enrolled in the French program, and M students in the Spanish program, including P students who enrolled in both programs, how many students are taking only one (but not both) of the language programs?

   (A) $N + M$
   (B) $N + M - P$
   (C) $N + M + P$
   (D) $N + M - 2P$
   (E) $N + M + 2P$

GO ON TO THE NEXT PAGE

17. At a certain small town, p gallons of gasoline are needed per month for each car in town. At this rate, if there are r cars in town, how long, in months, will q gallons last?

(A) $\dfrac{pq}{r}$

(B) $\dfrac{qr}{p}$

(C) $\dfrac{r}{pq}$

(D) $\dfrac{q}{pr}$

(E) pqr

Questions 18–21 are based on the following data.

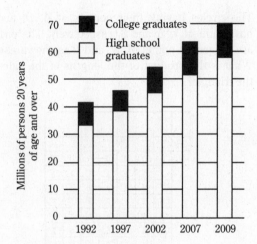

18. The ratio between the number of college graduates in 1992 and in 2009 is closest to

(A) 1:10
(B) 1:8
(C) 1:6
(D) 1:4
(E) 1:2

19. In 2002 the high school graduates outnumbered the college graduates by a number closest to

(A) 28 million
(B) 32 million
(C) 36 million
(D) 40 million
(E) 44 million

20. The graph shows, in a general way, that the number of college graduates and high school graduates combined, from one period to the next,

(A) has progressed arithmetically
(B) has progressed geometrically
(C) has doubled
(D) has tripled
(E) has quadrupled

For the following question, use the grid to enter your answer.

21. For which year did the total number of graduates (high school and college) exceed 50 million but did not exceed 60 million?

22. A box contains exactly 24 coins—nickels, dimes, and quarters. The probability of selecting a nickel by reaching into the box without looking is $\dfrac{3}{8}$. The probability of selecting a dime by reaching into the box without looking is $\dfrac{1}{8}$. How many quarters are in the box?

(A) 6
(B) 8
(C) 12
(D) 14
(E) 16

For the following question, select all answer choices that apply.

23. If p and q are positive integers, x and y are negative integers, and if $p > q$ and $x > y$, which of the following must be less than zero? Indicate all such quantities.

(A) $q - p$
(B) qy
(C) $p + x$

GO ON TO THE NEXT PAGE

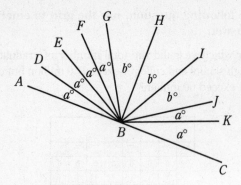

Note: Figure is not drawn to scale.

For the following question, select all answer choices that apply.

24. In the figure above, *AC* is a straight line segment. Line segments are drawn from *B* to *D, E, F, G, H, I, J,* and *K*, respectively. Which of the following angles has a degree measure that can be found? Indicate all such angles.

    (A) ∠*FBH*
    (B) ∠*EBG*
    (C) ∠*IBC*
    (D) ∠*GBI*
    (E) ∠*GBJ*
    (F) ∠*ABI*
    (G) ∠*ABC*
    (H) ∠*HBC*

For the following question, use the grid to enter your answer.

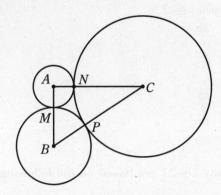

25. The circles having their centers at *A, B,* and *C* have radii of 1, 2, and 3, respectively. The circles are tangent at points *M, N,* and *P* as shown above. What is the product of the lengths of the sides of the triangle?

⊖						
	⊘	⊘	⊘	⊘	⊘	⊘
⓪	⓪	⓪	⓪	⓪	⓪	⓪
①	①	①	①	①	①	①
②	②	②	②	②	②	②
③	③	③	③	③	③	③
④	④	④	④	④	④	④
⑤	⑤	⑤	⑤	⑤	⑤	⑤
⑥	⑥	⑥	⑥	⑥	⑥	⑥
⑦	⑦	⑦	⑦	⑦	⑦	⑦
⑧	⑧	⑧	⑧	⑧	⑧	⑧
⑨	⑨	⑨	⑨	⑨	⑨	⑨

STOP

**If you finish before time is called, you may check your work on this section only.
Do not turn to any other section in the test.**

Section 4: Quantitative Reasoning

Time—40 Minutes
25 Questions

For each question, indicate the best answer, using the directions given.

Notes: All numbers used are real numbers.

All figures are assumed to lie in a plane unless otherwise indicated.

Geometric figures, such as lines, circles, triangles, and quadrilaterals, **are not necessarily** drawn to scale. That is, you should **not** assume that quantities such as lengths and angle measures are as they appear in a figure. You should assume, however, that lines shown as straight are actually straight, points on a line are in the order shown, and more generally, all geometric objects are in the relative positions shown. For questions with geometric figures, you should base your answers on geometric reasoning, not on estimating or comparing quantities by sight or by measurement.

Coordinate systems, such as *xy* planes and number lines, **are** drawn to scale; therefore, you can read, estimate, or compare quantities in such figures by sight or by measurement.

Graphical data presentations, such as bar graphs, circles graphs, and line graphs, **are** drawn to scale; therefore, you can read, estimate, or compare data values by sight or by measurement.

For each of Questions 1–9, compare Quantity A and Quantity B, using additional information centered above the two quantities if such information is given. Select one of the following four answer choices and fill in the corresponding circle to the right of the question.

(A) Quantity A is greater.
(B) Quantity B is greater.
(C) The two quantities are equal.
(D) The relationship cannot be determined from the information given.

A symbol that appears more than once in a question has the same meaning throughout the question.

	Quantity A	Quantity B	Correct Answer
Example 1:	(2)(6)	2 + 6	Ⓐ Ⓑ Ⓒ Ⓓ

	Quantity A	Quantity B	Correct Answer
Example 2:	*PS*	*SR*	Ⓐ Ⓑ Ⓒ Ⓓ

(since equal lengths cannot be assumed, even though *PS* and *SR* appear equal)

GO ON TO THE NEXT PAGE

SUMMARY DIRECTIONS FOR COMPARISON QUESTIONS

Answer: A   if the quantity in Quantity A is greater;
B   if the quantity in Quantity B is greater;
C   if the two quantities are equal;
D   if the relationship cannot be determined from the information given.

1

$$x > 0 > y$$

Quantity A	Quantity B
$y - x$	$x - y$

Ⓐ Ⓑ Ⓒ Ⓓ

2

$$w < 60$$
$$x < 60$$

Quantity A	Quantity B
80	$w + x$

Ⓐ Ⓑ Ⓒ Ⓓ

---

3 The average (arithmetic mean) of a and b is 8.

$$a - b + 4 = 0$$

Quantity A	Quantity B
a	6

Ⓐ Ⓑ Ⓒ Ⓓ

4

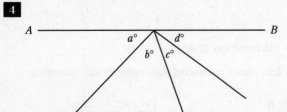

AB is a straight line.

$$a = c = d \text{ and } \frac{c}{b} = \frac{1}{3}$$

Quantity A	Quantity B
b	80

Ⓐ Ⓑ Ⓒ Ⓓ

GO ON TO THE NEXT PAGE

5

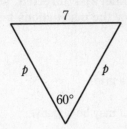

Quantity A	Quantity B
21	3p

Ⓐ Ⓑ Ⓒ Ⓓ

Questions 6–7 are based on the following chart.

Population of City A and City B from 1987 to 1993

Year	Population of City A (*in thousands of persons*)	Population of City B (*in thousands of persons*)
1987	106	128
1988	110	124
1989	113	118
1990	115	109
1991	122	108
1992	119	112
1993	127	105

6

Quantity A	Quantity B
Greatest one-year change in the population of City A	Greatest one-year change in the population of City B

Ⓐ Ⓑ Ⓒ Ⓓ

7

Quantity A	Quantity B
The difference between the population of City A in 1992 and the population of City B in 1988	5,000

Ⓐ Ⓑ Ⓒ Ⓓ

8

Quantity A	Quantity B
25% of 90	$\frac{1}{2}$ of 45

Ⓐ Ⓑ Ⓒ Ⓓ

9

$$x \neq 0$$

Quantity A	Quantity B
x	x^{-1}

Ⓐ Ⓑ Ⓒ Ⓓ

Questions 10–25 have several different formats. Unless otherwise directed, select a single answer choice. For Numeric Entry questions, follow the instructions below.

Numeric Entry Questions

To answer these questions, enter a number by filling in circles in a grid.

- Your answer may be an integer, a decimal, or a fraction, and it may be negative.

- Equivalent forms of the correct answer, such as 2.5 and 2.50, are all correct. Although fractions do not need to be reduced to lowest terms, they may need to be reduced to fit in the grid.

- Enter the exact answer unless the question asks you to round your answer.

- If a question asks for a fraction, the grid will have a built-in division slash (/). Otherwise, the grid will have a decimal point.

- Start your answer in any column, space permitting. Fill in no more than one circle in any column of the grid. Columns not needed should be left blank.

- Write your answer in the boxes at the top of the grid and fill in the corresponding circles. **You will receive credit only if the circles are filled in correctly, regardless of the number written in the boxes at the top.**

Examples of acceptable ways to use the grid:

Integer answer: 502 (either position is correct)   Decimal answer: −4.13   Fraction answer: $-\frac{2}{10}$

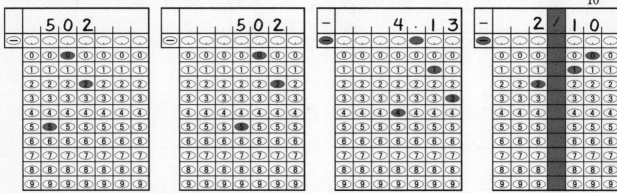

GO ON TO THE NEXT PAGE

10. There are 16 pages in a booklet. Last night, Ron read $\frac{1}{4}$ of the booklet. This morning, Ron read $\frac{1}{4}$ of the remaining pages. How many pages does Ron still have left to read?

   (A) 7
   (B) 8
   (C) 9
   (D) 10
   (E) 11

For the following question, select all answer choices that apply.

11. If $x < 0$ and $y < 0$, which of the following must always be positive? Indicate all such quantities.

   (A) $x \times y$
   (B) $x + y$
   (C) $x - y$
   (D) x^y
   (E) $\frac{x}{y}$

12. Given three positive integers, a, b, and 4, if their average (arithmetic mean) is 6, which of the following could *not* be the value of the product ab?

   (A) 13
   (B) 14
   (C) 40
   (D) 48
   (E) 49

Number of pounds of force	Height object is raised
3	6 feet
6	12 feet
9	18 feet

13. In a certain pulley system, the height an object is raised is equal to a constant c times the number of pounds of force exerted. The table above shows some pounds of force and the corresponding height raised. If a particular object is raised 15 feet, how many pounds of force were exerted?

   (A) $3\frac{3}{4}$
   (B) 7
   (C) $7\frac{1}{2}$
   (D) 8
   (E) 11

$$C = md + t$$

14. The cost, C, of a business trip is represented by the equation above, where m is a constant, d is the number of days of the complete trip and t is the cost of transportation, which does not change. If the business trip was increased by 5 days, how much more did the business trip cost than the original planned trip?

   (A) $5d$
   (B) $5m$
   (C) $5t$
   (D) $d(m - 3)$
   (E) $m(d - 3)$

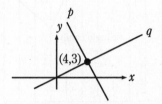

15. In the xy-coordinate system above, the lines q and p are perpendicular. The point $(3,a)$ is on line p. What is the value of a?

   (A) 3
   (B) 4
   (C) $4\frac{1}{3}$
   (D) $4\frac{2}{3}$
   (E) $5\frac{1}{3}$

For the following question, use the grid to enter your answer.

16. If p is $\frac{3}{5}$ of m and if q is $\frac{9}{10}$ of m, then, when $q \neq 0$, the ratio $\frac{p}{q}$ is equal to what value?

GO ON TO THE NEXT PAGE

Questions 17–20 are based on the following data.

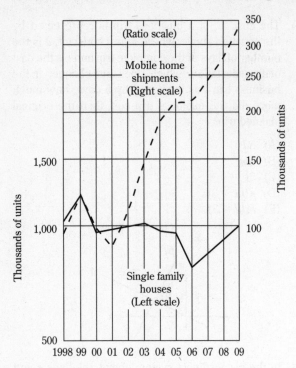

17. Which statement is true?

 (A) There have been more increases in single family houses, year by year, than mobile home shipment increases.
 (B) The greatest three-years-in-a-row increase for single family houses was from 2000 to 2003.
 (C) The longest chronological span of uninterrupted increases for mobile home shipments was from 2001–2004.
 (D) The increase in mobile home shipments has been relatively more consistent than the increase in single family houses.
 (E) The unit increase from 1998 to 1999 and the unit decrease from 1999 to 2000 was about the same for mobile home shipments and single family houses.

18. The ratio of mobile home shipments to single family houses in 2009 was closest to

 (A) 35:1
 (B) 1:35
 (C) 3:1
 (D) 1:3
 (E) 10:1

19. There were closest to 10 times as many single family houses as mobile home shipments in

 (A) 1999
 (B) 2003
 (C) 2005
 (D) 2007
 (E) 2009

20. If, for the four years 2006–2009, we total mobile home shipments and single family houses, we find that mobile home shipments constitute closest to what percent of the grand total for these years?

 (A) 18%
 (B) 23%
 (C) 30%
 (D) 62%
 (E) 78%

For the following question, select all answer choices that apply.

21. Which of the following is not always true for real numbers a, b, and c? Indicate all such quantities.

 (A) $\sqrt{a + b} = \sqrt{a} + \sqrt{b}$
 (B) $a^2 + b^2 = (a + b)^2$
 (C) $a^b + a^c = a^{(b + c)}$

22. A rectangular floor 8 feet long and 6 feet wide is to be completely covered with tiles. Each tile is a square with a perimeter of 2 feet. What is the least number of such tiles necessary to cover the floor?

 (A) 7
 (B) 12
 (C) 24
 (D) 48
 (E) 192

GO ON TO THE NEXT PAGE

For the following question, use the grid to enter your answer.

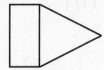

	First Place (6 points)	Second Place (4 points)	Third Place (2 points)
Game 1			
Game 2		Bob	
Game 3			Bob

23. In the figure above, the perimeter of the equilateral triangle is 39 inches and the area of the rectangle is 65 square inches. What is the perimeter of the rectangle in inches?

24. The figure above is a partially filled-in score card for a video game contest. Alan, Bob, and Carl each played in all of the three games. There were no ties. What is the *minimum* possible score for Carl in this tournament?

   (A) 2
   (B) 6
   (C) 8
   (D) 12
   (E) The answer cannot be determined from the information given.

25. In order to obtain admission into a special school program, all applicants must take a special exam, which is passed by three out of every five applicants. Of those who pass the exam, one-fourth are finally accepted. What is the percentage of all applicants who *fail* to gain admission into the program?

   (A) 55
   (B) 60
   (C) 75
   (D) 85
   (E) 90

STOP

If you finish before time is called, you may check your work on this section only.
Do not turn to any other section in the test.

How Did You Do on This Test?

Step 1. Go to the Answer Key on pages 689–692.

Step 2. For your "raw score," calculate it using the directions on page 693.

Step 3. Get your "scaled score" for the test by referring to the GRE Score Conversion Table on page 694.

THERE'S ALWAYS ROOM FOR IMPROVEMENT!

ANSWER KEY FOR PRACTICE TEST 3

Analytical Writing 1
and Analytical Writing 2
See Part 8, Page 473
for Scoring on These Parts

Answer Key for Practice Test 3

Verbal Reasoning

Section 1		Section 2	
	Correct Answer		Correct Answer
1	D	1	E
2	B	2	C
3	A, E	3	A, F
4	B, D	4	B, D
5	C, E	5	A, E
6	A, E, H	6	C, D, H
7	C, E, I	7	C, F, G
8	A, E, H	8	A, D, H
9	C	9	A, B, C
10	A	10	B, C
11	B	11	C
12	B	12	E
13	A, B	13	D
14	A	14	B
15	A, F	15	C
16	B, C	16	B, E
17	B, F	17	A, D
18	A, D	18	A, C
19	C, F	19	D, F
20	C	20	B
21	E	21	B, C
22	C	22	E
23	B	23	D
24	D	24	E
25	B	25	C

Number correct   Number correct

Answer Key for Practice Test 3

Quantitative Reasoning

<table>
<tr><td>Section 3</td><td></td><td>Section 4</td><td></td></tr>
<tr><td></td><td>Correct
Answer</td><td></td><td>Correct
Answer</td></tr>
<tr><td>1</td><td>B</td><td>1</td><td>B</td></tr>
<tr><td>2</td><td>A</td><td>2</td><td>D</td></tr>
<tr><td>3</td><td>B</td><td>3</td><td>C</td></tr>
<tr><td>4</td><td>B</td><td>4</td><td>A</td></tr>
<tr><td>5</td><td>A</td><td>5</td><td>C</td></tr>
<tr><td>6</td><td>A</td><td>6</td><td>B</td></tr>
<tr><td>7</td><td>A</td><td>7</td><td>C</td></tr>
<tr><td>8</td><td>A</td><td>8</td><td>C</td></tr>
<tr><td>9</td><td>A</td><td>9</td><td>D</td></tr>
<tr><td>10</td><td>A</td><td>10</td><td>C</td></tr>
<tr><td>11</td><td>C</td><td>11</td><td>A, E</td></tr>
<tr><td>12</td><td>B</td><td>12</td><td>B</td></tr>
<tr><td>13</td><td>A, B, C, D</td><td>13</td><td>C</td></tr>
<tr><td>14</td><td>D</td><td>14</td><td>B</td></tr>
<tr><td>15</td><td>9,500</td><td>15</td><td>C</td></tr>
<tr><td>16</td><td>D</td><td>16</td><td>2/3</td></tr>
<tr><td>17</td><td>D</td><td>17</td><td>D</td></tr>
<tr><td>18</td><td>E</td><td>18</td><td>D</td></tr>
<tr><td>19</td><td>C</td><td>19</td><td>A</td></tr>
<tr><td>20</td><td>A</td><td>20</td><td>B</td></tr>
<tr><td>21</td><td>2002</td><td>21</td><td>A, B, C</td></tr>
<tr><td>22</td><td>C</td><td>22</td><td>E</td></tr>
<tr><td>23</td><td>A, B</td><td>23</td><td>36</td></tr>
<tr><td>24</td><td>C, F, G</td><td>24</td><td>C</td></tr>
<tr><td>25</td><td>60</td><td>25</td><td>D</td></tr>
</table>

Number correct   **Number correct**

Scoring the GRE Practice Test

Check your responses with the correct answers on the previous pages. Fill in the blanks below and do the calculations to get your Math and Verbal raw scores. Use the table to find your Math and Verbal scaled scores.

Get Your Verbal Reasoning Score

How many Verbal questions did you get **right**?

Section 1: Questions 1–25 _____

Section 2: Questions 1–25 + _____

Total = _____

Use the Score Conversion Table to find your Verbal Reasoning scaled score.

_____

Get Your Quantitative Reasoning Score

How many Math questions did you get **right**?

Section 3: Questions 1–25 _____

Section 4: Questions 1–25 + _____

Total = _____

Use the Score Conversion Table to find your Quantitative Reasoning scaled score.

_____

GRE Score Conversion Table

Raw Score	Verbal Reasoning Scaled Score		Quantitative Reasoning Scaled Score	
	130–170 Point Scale	200–800 Point Scale	130–170 Point Scale	200–800 Point Scale
50	170	800	170	800
49		790		790
48		780		790
47		770		780
46	167	760		780
45		750		770
44		740		770
43		730		770
42		710		760
41	163	700	167	750
40		670		740
39		660		730
38	160	650		720
37		640	163	700
36		620		690
35	157	600		680
34		590		670
33		570	160	650
32	153	550		640
31		540		630
30		530	157	600
29		520		590
28		510		570
27	150	500		570
26		490	153	550
25		470		530
24		460		510
23	147	450	150	500
22		440		480
21		430	147	450
20		420		440
19		410		430
18	143	400	143	400
17		380		390
16		370		380
15		360	140	350
14	140	350		340
13		340		330
12		330		310
11	137	300	137	300
10		290		280
9		280		260
8		260	133	250
7		260		230
6	133	250		210
5		230		200
4		220		200
3		200		200
2		200		200
1		200		200
0	130	200	130	200

Chart for Self-Appraisal Based on the Practice Test You Have Just Taken

Percent of Examinees Scoring Lower Than Selected Scale Scores (Percentile Rank) on the Verbal and Quantitative Reasoning Measures

Scaled Score	Verbal Reasoning	Quantitative Reasoning
800		94
790		91
780		89
770		87
760		84
750		82
740		80
730	99	77
720	98	75
710	98	72
700	97	70
690	97	68
680	96	66
670	95	63
660	94	61
650	93	59
640	92	56
630	91	54
620	89	52
610	88	49
600	86	47
590	84	45
580	82	43
570	80	40
560	78	38
550	75	36
540	73	34
530	70	32
520	68	30
510	65	28
500	63	27
490	60	25
480	57	23
470	55	22
460	52	20
450	49	19
440	46	17
430	43	16
420	41	15
410	38	14
400	35	12
390	32	11
380	29	10
370	27	9

Continued on next page.

Percent of Examinees Scoring Lower Than Selected Scale Scores (Percentile Rank) on the Verbal and Quantitative Reasoning Measures (cont'd)

Scaled Score	Verbal Reasoning	Quantitative Reasoning
360	24	8
350	21	8
340	19	7
330	16	6
320	13	5
310	10	5
300	8	4
290	6	3
280	5	3
270	3	2
260	2	2
250	1	2
240		1
230		
220		
210		
200		

Explanatory Answers for GRE Practice Test 3

Section 1: Verbal Reasoning

> As you read these Explanatory Answers, you are advised to refer to "17 Verbal (Critical Reading) Strategies" (beginning on page 136) whenever a specific Strategy is referred to in the answer. Of particular importance are the following Master Verbal Strategies:
>
> Sentence Completion Master Strategy 1—page 137.
> Sentence Completion Master Strategy 3—page 140.
> Reading Comprehension Master Strategy 2—page 155.

Note: All Reading questions use Reading Comprehension Strategies 1, 2, and 3 (pages 152–157) as well as other strategies indicated.

1. Choice D is correct. See **Sentence Completion Strategy 3**. The first word, "because," is a *result indicator*. We can then expect some action to take place after the information about what the evening cable TV programs deal with. The expected action is that parents will consider such programs "inappropriate." Accordingly, only Choice D is correct.

2. Choice B is correct. See **Sentence Completion Strategy 3**. The first word, "although," is an *opposition indicator*. After the subordinate clause "although...markedly," we can expect an opposing idea in the main clause that follows and completes the sentence. Choice B, *unaffected*, gives us the word that brings out the opposition that we expect in the sentence. Choices A, C, D, and E do not give us a sentence that makes sense.

3. Choices A and E are correct. Use **Sentence Completion Strategies 2 and 3**. The key words are "as soon as." Try your own words for the blanks. You may try for the first blank, *newer*, and for the second, *existent*. You can see that choice A, *contemporary*, and Choice E, *established*, would fit.

4. Choices B and D are correct. Use **Sentence Completion 1**. Here we are comparing the interests of the individual and of society. You should be aware that *eliding* means "passing over." Note that the word *society*, Choice B, is better than *the community*, Choice A, because *society* refers to a more general concept and *community* is associated with individuals.

5. Choices C and E are correct. Use **Sentence Completion Strategies 3 and 1**. Note the *opposition* or *contrast indicator*, "but." *Immutable* means "not susceptible to change." So it would seem that Choice C, *immutable*, and Choice E, *characteristics*, would fit.

6. Choices A, E, and H are correct. Use **Sentence Completion Strategies 4 and 3**. Notice that "backers" must be positive, so the key word "even" would indicate an opposite feeling. So the choices in the second and third blanks must be of negative connotation. Choice E, *disappointment*, and Choice H, *disillusionment*, would fit. Choice A, *fervent*, meaning "devoted or earnest," is better than Choice B, *trusted*, because trust does not go as well with *disappointment* and *disillusionment*.

7. Choices C, E, and I are correct. Use **Sentence Completion Strategies 4, 3, and 2**. "Ensuring no opposition" would not indicate an "air of gentility." So the word in the first blank would be something like *misrepresented*, which means "belied." It would seem that in the second blank, Choice E, *drastic*, would also contrast with the dictator's "slow and easy manner and his air of gentility." For the third blank, Choice I, *craft*, is a more direct and meaningful word to use than the other choices.

8. Choices A, E, and H are correct. Use **Sentence Completion Strategies 4, 3 and 2**. Look for key words that create a link in the sentence. "Astronomical salaries" would link to *sharp* or *astute* contract bargaining. So the second blank would be Choice E, *astute*. As a result, players would need very *experienced* or *seasoned* agents to represent them. Thus the third blank is Choice H. Now you can see that the first blank has to deal with *skill*, so Choice A would be correct.

9. Choice C is correct. The two labels (lines 14–15) obviously have negative implications about the value of physics and thus indicate that physics is uninteresting and pointless to the ordinary person. Accordingly, Choice C is correct. It follows, then, that Choice B—which states that physics "is a cause for great excitement"—is incorrect. Choices A, D, and E are incorrect because none of these choices is stated or implied in the passage.

10. Choice A is correct. See lines 26–28: "Yet what little we do know…grandeur and intricate beauty." Choices B, C, D, and E are incorrect because none of these choices is brought up in the passage.

11. Choice B is correct. The author is, in effect, saying that one must appreciate the forest as a whole—not merely certain individual trees. He therefore implies that we should not separate physics from the body of all creative work. See lines 21–22: "It is pointless…all creative work…" Choices A, C, D, and E are incorrect because they are not justified by the content of the passage.

12. Choice B is correct. For literary allusions, see lines 6 and 11–12: "Polonius" (*Hamlet*) and the "…milque-toast of human kindness," (*Macbeth*). For sarcasm, see lines 12–16: "We…always fear that we may be setting him back a few hundred hours in his psychiatric progress toward the Terrestrial City of Perfect Readjustment." The author does not use anecdotes.

13. Choices A and B are correct. For A see lines 8–10: "We are afraid of hurting someone's feelings or of being hurt in a return bout. We tremble at the prospect of treading of someone's moral corns." For B, see lines 11–12: "…milque-toast of human kindness."

14. Choice A is correct. Without the lawful behavior of nature, one could not rely on the results of experiments. Statement II does not underlie this paragraph, since the author admits that under certain circumstances, the truth might be established indirectly (where one can enumerate all possible explanations). Further, the author does not presuppose Statement III, since he nowhere states that we can always establish scientific truth.

15. Choices A and F are correct. See **Sentence Completion Strategy 1**. The word *capable* (Choice A) means "skilled" or "competent." Choice F, *a competent*, also works. Clearly, choices A and F are correct.

16. Choices B and C are correct. See **Sentence Completion Strategy 1**. One would *reject*, or *undermine*, something that is repugnant when one is able to.

17. Choices B and F are correct. See **Sentence Completion Strategy 1**. The tone is that of fear. Thus the appropriate choice is *threat*, or *menace*.

18. Choices A and D are correct. See **Sentence Completion Strategy 1**. Choices A and D are consistent with the rest of the sentence.

19. Choices C and F are correct. Use **Sentence Completion Strategies 1 and 2**. The best words are *unreliable* and *ineffectual*.

20. Choice C is correct. See lines 8–12. What is discussed here is based on what is presented in lines 1–7.

21. Choice E is correct. See lines 8–12.

22. Choice C is correct. See line 10: "Only the thoroughly familiar…." This would relate to something encountered or seen before.

23. Choice B is correct. See lines 1–3. Note that even if you didn't know the meaning of "deprecate," you could figure that the word imparted a negative

connotation since the prefix *de-* means "away from" and is negative. Also, don't get lured into Choice D just because "Babel" was mentioned.

24. Choice D is correct. See lines 7–8. In the context of the sentence, where we have words like *arguments*, *slogans*, it would appear that Babel would relate to confusion of people's thought and ideas. See **Reading Comprehension Strategy 5**.

25. Choice B is correct. Statement I is just jargon. Statement II is clearly accepted by the author, since judgments of value would not be problematic if they were demonstrated truths. Statement III is a probable conclusion of the author's if it is supposed that to be a "complete man" is desirable. But it is not an assumption basic to the paragraph.

Explanatory Answers for
GRE Practice Test 3
(continued)

Section 2: Verbal Reasoning

As you read these Explanatory Answers, you are advised to refer to "17 Verbal (Critical Reading) Strategies" (beginning on page 136) whenever a specific Strategy is referred to in the answer. Of particular importance are the following Master Verbal Strategies:

Sentence Completion Master Strategy 1—page 137.
Sentence Completion Master Strategy 3—page 140.
Reading Comprehension Master Strategy 2—page 155.

Note: All Reading questions use Reading Comprehension Strategies 1, 2, and 3 (pages 152–157) as well as other strategies indicated.

1. Choice E is correct. See **Sentence Completion Strategy 1**. The word *sluggish* means "moving slowly," which completes the sentence satisfactorily. The other four choices do not fit into the context of the sentence.

2. Choice C is correct. See **Sentence Completion Strategy 1**. The word *enthusiasm* (Choice C) makes good sense in the sentence because the painting sold for $53 million, and yet it was not appreciated wholeheartedly a hundred years ago.

3. Choices A and F are correct. Use **Sentence Completion Strategies 3 and 1**. Note key words "he was sorry." So he did something that hurt his brother. Choice A, *grimaced*, and Choice F, *action*, fit best.

4. Choices B and D are correct. Use **Sentence Completion Strategies 3 and 1**. Note the opposition indicator, "but." Look for opposites in the choices. Choice B, *impassive* (emotionless), and Choice D, *impassioned* (filled with emotion), work.

5. Choices A and E are correct. Watch for key words such as "although." Use **Sentence Completion Strategies 3 and 1**. "One in three households" is a lot of households. So the first choices must represent a large number. *Incredible* is too strong, so I would choose *bountiful*—a large number. *Experiences* will fit the second blank then.

6. Choices C, D, and H are correct. Use **Sentence Completion Strategies 4, 3, and either 2 or 1**. Look for key words that create a link in the sentence. "So" and "hardly a day" are some. The second blank would seem to indicate a word like *common* or *prevalent*, Choice D. Then that would imply that the third blank would be something terrible like *heinous*, Choice H. Because of Choice D in Blank 2, the first blank should be Choice C, *probably*.

7. Choices C, F, and G are correct. Use **Sentence Completion Strategies 4, 3, and either 2 or 1**. Look for key words that create a link in the sentence. "A blessing to children," "informed," and "rising tide" are some. The second blank would seem to indicate a word like *interested in the students' learning*, or *dedicated*, Choice F. Note Choice D, *knowledgeable*, is too close to *informed*. The third blank would be something that's good for education, like an *asset*, Choice G. It would then seem that the first blank would be something negative: *mediocrity*, Choice C.

8. Choices A, D, and H are correct. Use **Sentence Completion Strategies 4, 3, and 1**. Look for key words that create a link in the sentence. *A single and not simply a mass of...points*. It would appear that the third blank would be Choice H, *impression*. The second blank would then be Choice D, *integrated*. The first blank, because of the word *experiencing* in the second sentence, would be Choice A, *perceive*.

9. Choices A, B, and C are correct. See lines 4–8, "Richness of poetic imagery...," and lines 11–14, "Even his elaborate and multistranded plots..."

10. Choices B and C are correct. Choice B is correct. See lines 11–14, which describe the forcefulness and power up to the closing. Choice C is correct. See lines 13–14.

11. Choice C is correct. The fault with the reasoning here is that it is assumed that an increase in temperature is due only to an increase in fossil fuels. There may be other causes of an increase in temperature. See **Reading Comprehension Strategy 10**.

12. Choice E is correct. See lines 21–22: "All human beings have at least four types of intelligence." Choice A is incorrect. See lines 50–52: "Persistence kept Einstein looking for the solution to the question of the relationship between the law of gravity and his special theory of relativity." Isaac Newton (1642–1727) formulated the law of gravitation. Choice B is incorrect. The passage simply states: "The idea for a self-starting electric motor came to Nikola Tesla one evening as he was reciting a poem by Goethe and watching a sunset" (lines 30–33). Choice C is incorrect. The author indicates a span of time when he states, "The discoveries made by scientific geniuses, from Archimedes through Einstein..." (lines 1–2). Archimedes was an ancient Greek mathematician, physicist, and inventor (287–212 BC), whereas Einstein was, of course, a modern scientist (1879–1955). Choice D is incorrect. The passage states, "...while an IQ above a certain point—about 120—is very helpful for a scientist,...[it] is not crucial

for producing a work of genius" (lines 18–21). The passage does not specifically say that most scientists have IQ scores above 120.

13. Choice D is correct. See lines 42–44: "The scientist solves a problem by shifting from one intelligence to another, although the logical-mathematical intelligence is dominant." Accordingly, Choices A, B, C, and E are incorrect.

14. Choice B is correct. When the author describes the work experiences of Einstein and Tesla, he refers to their use of one or more of the four types of intelligence. Moreover, lines 26–28 state, "Some corroboration of these [four intelligence] categories comes from the reports of scientists who describe thought processes centered around images, sensations, or words." Choices A, C, D, and E are incorrect because the author does not refer to these choices in the passage.

15. Choice C is correct. The author indicates that great scientists use to advantage four intelligences—logical-mathematical, spatial, linguistic, and bodily-kinesthetic. See lines 22–25: "The great scientist possesses the ability to move back and forth among them—the logical-mathematical; the spatial, which includes visual perception; the linguistic; and the bodily-kinesthetic." Choices B and D are brought out in the passage but not at any length. Therefore, Choices B and D are incorrect. Choice A is incorrect because the author nowhere compares the thinking of the average individual and that of the great scientist. Choice E is incorrect because though the concepts are mentioned, they are certainly not clarified in the passage.

16. Choices B and E are correct. See **Sentence Completion Strategies 1, 2, and 3**. In accordance with Newton's teaching, the universe might be very likely to have been created out of one piece. Thus, Newton's picture of the universe was probably not one in which there was *development* or *synthesis*.

17. Choices A and D are correct. See **Sentence Completion Strategy 1**. The suppositions were highly *plausible* (likely, or apparently valid) or highly *regarded* (accepted).

18. Choices A and C are correct. See **Sentence Completion Strategy 1**. The typist's inconsistency or disorder is obvious in the manner in which she typed the five letters. Choices B, D, E, and F are incorrect because they do not make good sense in the sentence.

19. Choices D and F are correct. See **Sentence Completion Strategies 1, 2, and 3**. The judge feels that the defendant's offense is small,

forgivable (*venial*), or *pardonable*, so he will probably give him a light sentence.

20. Choice B is correct. Choice A would not weaken the argument, since the author does not presuppose that literary critics believe that some works are pornographic. Choice C is irrelevant; the critics are not being asked to decide a legal question, since pornography is a matter of literary criticism. Choice D is irrelevant, since the literary critic could still be asked for his opinion even if he is not paid for giving it. Choice B weakens the argument, since the author ignores the problem of evaluating differences of opinion among literary critics. It is because of these differences that lawyers conclude that pornography is a matter of opinion. Note that Choice E does not weaken the argument because we are not addressing the financial motives of the critics. See **Reading Comprehension Strategy 10**.

21. Choices B and C are correct. For (A), see lines 4–6. Where it says, "Not until some of them learned…," this was *after* pre-Neolithic times. For (B), see lines 4–10. For (C), see lines 7–8: "divisions of labor, large economic projects." **See Reading Comprehension Strategy 10**.

22. Choice E is correct. For Choice A, see lines 9–10. For Choice B, see lines 3–4: "…only in small, economically self-sufficient groups." This would imply that after, there were larger groups and "size" would be a factor. For Choice C, see line 5: "learned to cultivate grain and raise livestock." For Choice D see lines 4–10. For Choice E, although "intricate social organization" is cited, the actual workings or mechanism of the social organization is not addressed. **See Reading Comprehension Strategy 10**.

23. Choice D is correct. See lines 3–6. The last sentence defines "mummy." **See Reading Comprehension Strategy 5**.

24. Choice E is correct. See lines 7–9 and line 12, where it discusses pyramids and why they were built.

25. Choice C is correct. See lines 1–5.

Explanatory Answers for
Practice Test 3
(continued)

Section 3: Quantitative Reasoning

> As you read these solutions, you are advised to do two things if you answered the math question incorrectly:
>
> 1. When a specific Strategy is referred to in the solution, study that strategy, which you will find in "25 Math Strategies" (beginning on page 72).
>
> 2. When the solution directs you to the "Math Refresher" (beginning on page 185)—for example, Math Refresher #305—study the 305 Math principle to get a clear idea of the math operation that was necessary for you to know in order to answer the question correctly.

1. Choice B is correct. **(Use Strategy 13: Find unknowns by multiplication.)**

Method 1: $7x + 21 = 35$ $\boxed{1}$

Multiplying $\boxed{1}$ by $\frac{4}{7}$,

$$4x + 12 = 20$$

Thus, the columns become

Quantity A	Quantity B
20	21

and the answer is clear.

Method 2:

Given: $7x + 21 = 35$

Solve to get x:

$$7x = 14$$
$$x = 2 \qquad \boxed{1}$$

Substitute $\boxed{1}$ into $4x + 12$
$$4(2) + 12 = 8 + 12$$
$$= 20$$

Clearly $20 < 21$.

(Math Refresher #406 and #431)

2. Choice A is correct.

Method 1: $(-2)^{88}$ is a positive number [a negative number raised to an even power is always positive]

$(-2)^{97}$ is a negative number [a negative number raised to an odd power is always negative]

Any positive is larger than any negative. Thus, $(-2)^{88}$ is larger than $(-2)^{97}$.

Method 2: $(-2)^{97} = (-2)^{88}(-2)^9$

Thus, the columns become

Quantity A	Quantity B
$(-2)^{88}$	$(-2)^{88}(-2)^9$

(Use Strategy B: Cancel equal, positive things from both sides by division.)

Dividing both columns by $(-2)^{88}$, we get

Quantity A	Quantity B
1	$(-2)^9 =$ negative

Thus, Quantity A is larger.

(Math Refresher #428 and #429)

3. Choice B is correct. (**Use Strategy 6: Know how to manipulate inequalities.**)

We are told

$$-5 < y \qquad \boxed{1}$$
$$y < 5 \qquad \boxed{2}$$

Multiplying $\boxed{1}$ by -1,

$$5 > -y \qquad \boxed{3}$$

It is always true that $6 > 5$ $\qquad \boxed{4}$

Comparing $\boxed{3}$ and $\boxed{4}$, we have

$$6 > -y$$

(Math Refresher #423)

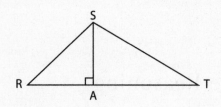

4. Choice B is correct. (**Use Strategy 18: Remember triangle facts.**)

SA is the altitude to side RT.
By definition, $SA \perp RT$.

The shortest distance from a point to a line is the length of $\perp$ segment from the point to the line. Thus, SA is the shortest distance from S to RT.
Thus,

$$SA < SR$$

(Math Refresher #514)

5. Choice A is correct.

Given: $\qquad a - b = 5 \qquad \boxed{1}$
$$a + b = -1 \qquad \boxed{2}$$

(**Use Strategy 17: Use the given information effectively.**)

Fast Method: Add b to both sides of $\boxed{1}$.

$$a = b + 5 \qquad \boxed{3}$$

From $\boxed{3}$, we can say right away that

$$a > b$$

Slow Method: Substitute $\boxed{3}$ into $\boxed{2}$.

$$b + 5 + b = -1$$
or $\qquad 2b + 5 = -1$
or $\qquad 2b = -6$
or $\qquad b = -3 \qquad \boxed{4}$

Substituting $\boxed{4}$ into $\boxed{3}$,

$$a = 2 \qquad \boxed{5}$$

Comparing $\boxed{4}$ and $\boxed{5}$, we see that

$$a > b$$

(Math Refresher #406 and #407)

6. Choice A is correct.

Method 1

Given: $\qquad m$ is an integer $> 0 \qquad \boxed{1}$
$$0 < y < 1 \qquad \boxed{2}$$

Quantity A	Quantity B
$\dfrac{m}{y}$	m

(**Use Strategy 6: Know how to manipulate inequalities.**) From $\boxed{2}$, since $y < 1$, we know that

$$\frac{1}{y} > 1 \qquad \boxed{3}$$

(**Use Strategy 13: Find unknowns by multiplication.**) (**Use Strategy E: Try to get the columns and given to look similar.**) Multiply $\boxed{3}$ by m, remembering, from $\boxed{1}$, that $m > 0$. We get

$$m\left(\frac{1}{y}\right) > (1)\,m$$
$$\frac{m}{y} > m$$

Method 2

$$m > 0$$
$$0 < y < 1$$

Quantity A	Quantity B
$\dfrac{m}{y}$	m

(**Use Strategy B: Cancel numbers by division.**) Cancel m, and we get

Quantity A	Quantity B
$\dfrac{1}{y}$	1

(**Use Strategy D: Multiply both columns by y.**) We get

Quantity A	Quantity B
1	y

From the given, $y < 1$. Therefore, Quantity A > Quantity B.

(Math Refresher #419 and #422)

7. Choice A is correct.

Given: $\qquad -\dfrac{1}{3}y = \dfrac{1}{3}y \qquad \boxed{1}$

(**Use Strategy 13: Find unknowns by multiplication.**) Multiply $\boxed{1}$ by 3. We get

$$3\left(-\frac{1}{3}y\right) = \left(\frac{1}{3}y\right)3$$
$$-y = y$$
$$0 = 2y$$
$$0 = y \qquad \boxed{2}$$

Quantity A	Quantity B
$-y$	$-\dfrac{2}{3}$

Substituting $\boxed{2}$ in $\boxed{3}$, the columns become

$$-(0) \qquad\qquad -\frac{2}{3}$$

(Math Refresher #406)

8. Choice A is correct. **(Use Strategy 3: Know how to find unknown quantities from known quantities.)**

From the diagram,

$$AC + CD = AD \qquad\qquad \boxed{1}$$
$$\text{Given:} \quad AC = 16, AD = 24 \qquad \boxed{2}$$

Substituting $\boxed{2}$ into $\boxed{1}$, we have

$$16 + CD = 24$$
$$CD = 8 \qquad\qquad \boxed{3}$$

From the diagram, $BD > CD$ $\qquad\qquad \boxed{4}$

Substituting $\boxed{3}$ into $\boxed{4}$, we get

$$BD > 8$$

(Math Refresher #431)

9. Choice A is correct. **(Use Strategy 3: The whole equals the sum of its parts.)** Each angle in an equilateral triangle has a measure of 60°. Each one in a square has a measure of 90°. Thus, $m\angle\text{ACD} = 60 + 90 = 150$.

Hence, $x = 360 - 150 = 210$ and $210 > 200$.

(Math Refresher #508, #520, and #526)

10. Choice A is correct. The least possible value of $x + y$ is when x is least and y is least. You can see that the smallest value of x is -4 (not 2 or -2) in the inequality $1 < |x| < 5$. The smallest value of y is -6 (not 3 or -3) in the inequality $2 < |y| < 7$. Thus the smallest value of $x + y = -10$.

(Math Refresher #615 and #419)

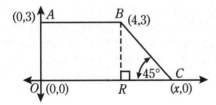

11. Choice C is correct.

Method 1: **(Use Strategy 17: Use the given information effectively.)**

The above figure has AB parallel to the x-axis. (Both A and B have y-coordinates of 3.) Thus, the figure is a trapezoid.

Its height (OA) is 3 $\qquad\qquad \boxed{1}$
Its top base is 4 $\qquad\qquad \boxed{2}$

(Use Strategy 14: Draw lines when appropriate.)

Draw BR perpendicular to the x-axis.
$$BR = OA = 3 \text{ and } AB = OR = 4$$

(Use Strategy 18: Remember isosceles triangle facts.)

Triangle BRC is an isosceles right triangle.
Thus, $BR = RC = 3$

The bottom base of the trapezoid

$$= OC = OR + RC = 4 + 3 = 7 \qquad \boxed{3}$$

The area of a trapezoid

$$=\frac{1}{2}h(\text{base 1} + \text{base 2}) \qquad\qquad \boxed{4}$$

Substituting $\boxed{1}$, $\boxed{2}$, and $\boxed{3}$ into $\boxed{4}$, we have

Area of trapezoid $= \frac{1}{2}(3)(4 + 7) = \frac{1}{2}(3)(11)$

$$= 16.5$$

Method 2: **(Use Strategy 14: Draw lines when appropriate.)**

Draw BR perpendicular to the x-axis.

$ABRO$ is a rectangle and BRC is an isosceles triangle.

Area $ABRO = (\text{base}) \times (\text{height})$

$$= 4 \times 3$$
$$= 12 \qquad\qquad \boxed{1}$$

Area $BRC = \frac{1}{2} \times (\text{base}) \times (\text{height})$

$$= \frac{1}{2} \times 3 \times 3$$
$$= 4.5 \qquad\qquad \boxed{2}$$

(Use Strategy 3: The whole equals the sum of its parts.)

Using $\boxed{1}$ and $\boxed{2}$, the total area of figure $ABCO$

$$= \text{Area of } ABRO + \text{Area of } BRC$$
$$= 12 + 4.5$$
$$= 16.5$$

(Math Refresher #410, #304, #306, #309, and #431)

12. Choice B is correct. **(Use Strategy 2: Translate from words to algebra.)**

Let $x + y = $ sum of the 2 numbers $\qquad \boxed{1}$

$x - y = $ difference of the 2 numbers $\qquad \boxed{2}$

$xy = $ product of the 2 numbers $\qquad \boxed{3}$

We are told that the difference between their sum and their difference is 6. $\qquad \boxed{4}$

Substituting $\boxed{1}$ and $\boxed{2}$ into $\boxed{4}$, we have

$$x + y - (x - y) = 6$$
$$x + y - x + y = 6$$
$$2y = 6$$
$$y = 3 \qquad\qquad \boxed{5}$$

Substituting $\boxed{5}$ into $\boxed{3}$, we get

$$x(3) = 15$$
$$x = 5$$

Clearly, 5 is the larger number.

(Math Refresher #200 and #406)

13. Choices A, B, C, D are correct. **(Use Strategy 8: When all choices must be tested, start with Choice E and work backward.)** In Choice E, if $Z = 5$, then $5Z = 25$. Thus $W + X + Y = 25$. Note that even if you used the highest ("distinct," which means "different") values of W, X, and Y, we would get $7 + 8 + 9 = 24$ as a maximum value. So Choice E could not be correct. Now go to Choice D: If $Z = 4$, then $5Z = 20$, and you would have $W + X + Y = 20$. An example that would work in that equation is $W = 9$, $X = 8$, and $Y = 3$. You can also see that for Choices C, B, and A, $W + X + Y$ could equal 5×3, or 5×2, or 5×1, by easily adjusting the values of W, X, and Y. Don't forget, you can use 0 for any one (but just one) of the variables W, X, or Y.

(Math Refresher #431)

14. Choice D is correct. You want to find a value of x such that $f(x) = x + 2$, so you look for a value of x in the x-column that makes $f(x)$ in the $f(x)$ column, $x + 2$. You can see that $x = 3$ corresponds to $f(x) = 5$, which is just $x + 2$ (or $3 + 2$).

(Math Refresher #616, #702)

15. **9,500**

$\left(\text{Use Strategy 5:}\right.$

$$\text{Average} = \left.\frac{\textbf{Sum of values}}{\textbf{Total number of values}}\right)$$

We are given:

$$\frac{x + y + z + w}{4} = 8,000 \qquad \boxed{1}$$

(Use Strategy 13: Find unknowns by multiplication.) Multiplying $\boxed{1}$ by 4, we get

$$x + y + z + w = 32,000 \qquad \boxed{2}$$

We are given that any 3 have an average of 7,500, so using x, y and z as the 3, we get

$$\frac{x + y + z}{3} = 7,500 \qquad \boxed{3}$$

Multiplying $\boxed{3}$ by 3, we get

$$x + y + z = 22,500 \qquad \boxed{4}$$

Substituting $\boxed{4}$ into $\boxed{2}$, we get

$$22,500 + w = 32,000$$
or $\qquad w = 9,500$

(Math Refresher #601 and #406)

16. Choice D is correct. Of the N French students, P are in both programs, so only $(N - P)$ are in the French program *alone*; similarly, $(M - P)$ students are in the Spanish program *only*. Thus, the number of students in only one language program is equal to $(N - P) + (M - P)$, which equals $N + M - 2P$. (*Note*: The following diagram may help you to visualize the answer better.)

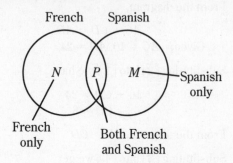

(Math Refresher #613)

17. Choice D is correct. **(Use Strategy 10: Know how to use units.)**

$$\left(\frac{p \text{ gallons}}{\text{car}}\right) \times (r \text{ cars}) = pr \text{ gallons for each month}$$

$$\frac{q \text{ gallons}}{pr \frac{\text{gallons}}{\text{months}}} = \frac{q}{pr} \text{ months}$$

(Math Refresher #121)

18. Choice E is correct. Estimate is approximate. There were 7 million college graduates in 1992 and 12 million in 2009. $\frac{7}{12}$ is about $\frac{6}{12}$, which is equal to $\frac{1}{2}$.

(Math Refresher #704)

19. Choice C is correct. In 2002 the number of high school graduates was 45 million. The number of college graduates was 9 million. So the difference was 45 million − 9 million = 36 million.

(Math Refresher #704)

20. Choice A is correct. Estimate is approximate. The combined number of college graduates and high school graduates for each period follows: 1992, 41 million; 1997, 45 million; 2002, 54 million; 2007, 63 million; 2009, 70 million. The increase has been generally arithmetical.

(Math Refresher #704)

21. 2002. From the graph given, we can see that only in 2002 was there more than a total of 50 million graduates and less than a total of 60 million graduates.

(Math Refresher #704)

22. Choice C is correct. Probability is defined as

$$\frac{\text{number of favorable ways (coins)}}{\text{total number of ways (coins)}} = \frac{F}{N}$$

If the probability of selecting a nickel is $\frac{3}{8}$, then for nickels, $\frac{F}{N} = \frac{3}{8}$. But N (the total number of ways [or coins]) is 24.

So $\frac{F}{N} = \frac{3}{8} = \frac{F}{24}$; $F = 9$ (nickels)

The probability of selecting a dime is $\frac{1}{8}$, so for a dime, $\frac{F}{N} = \frac{1}{8} = \frac{F}{24}$; $F = 3$ (dimes)

Since there are 24 coins and there are 9 nickels and 3 dimes, $24 - 3 - 9 = 12$ quarters. **(Use Strategy 3: Subtract whole from parts.)**

(Math Refresher #614)

23. Choices A and B are correct. **(Use Strategy 2: Translate from words to algebra.)** We are given

$$p > 0 \qquad \boxed{1}$$
$$q > 0 \qquad \boxed{2}$$
$$x < 0 \qquad \boxed{3}$$
$$y < 0 \qquad \boxed{4}$$

(Use Strategy 6: Know how to manipulate inequalities.)

$$p > q \text{ or } q < p \qquad \boxed{5}$$
$$x > y \text{ or } y < x \qquad \boxed{6}$$

For A: Add $-p$ to both sides of inequality $\boxed{5}$:

$$q - p < 0$$

Thus, A is less than zero.

For B: From inequalities $\boxed{2}$ and $\boxed{4}$, $qy < 0$, and B is less than zero.

For C: The value of p and x depends on specific values of p and x.

(Use Strategy 7: Use numerics to help decide the answer.)

EXAMPLE 1

$$p = 3 \text{ and } x = -5$$

Thus, $\qquad\qquad p + x < 0$

EXAMPLE 2

$$p = 5 \text{ and } x = -3$$

Thus, $\qquad\qquad p + x > 0$

Thus, C is not always less than zero. Choices A and B are correct.

(Math Refresher #420, #421, and #431)

24. Choices C, F, and G are correct.

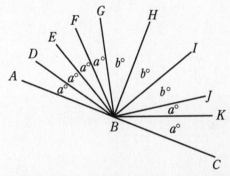

(Use Strategy 3: The whole equals the sum of its parts.) The whole straight angle ABC is equal to the sum of the individual angles.

Thus, $m \angle ABC = a + a + a + a + b +$
$$b + b + a + a$$
$$m \angle ABC = 6a + 3b \qquad \boxed{1}$$

We know $m \angle ABC = 180°$ $\qquad \boxed{2}$

Substituting $\boxed{2}$ into $\boxed{1}$, we get
$$180° = 6a + 3b \qquad \boxed{3}$$

(Use Strategy 13: Find an unknown expression by dividing.) Dividing both sides of $\boxed{3}$ by 3, we have

$$60° = 2a + b \qquad \boxed{4}$$

Choice C, $m \angle IBC = 2a + b$, so its measure can be determined. It is 60° (from $\boxed{4}$).

We also have $120 = 4a + 2b$ which is Choice F. From $\boxed{2}$ we see that $\angle ABC = 180°$, so Choice G is correct.

(Math Refresher #501 and #406)

25. 60

Since we are given the radii of the circles, we have

$$AN = AM = 1 \qquad \boxed{1}$$
$$BM = BP = 2 \qquad \boxed{2}$$
$$CN = CP = 3 \qquad \boxed{3}$$

We want to find

$$(AB)(BC)(AC) \qquad \boxed{4}$$

(Use Strategy 3: The whole equals the sum of its parts.) From the diagram, we see that

$$AB = AM + BM \qquad \boxed{5}$$
$$BC = BP + CP \qquad \boxed{6}$$

$$AC = AN + CN \qquad \boxed{7}$$

Substituting $\boxed{1}$, $\boxed{2}$, $\boxed{3}$ into $\boxed{5}$, $\boxed{6}$, $\boxed{7}$ we have

$$AB = 3$$
$$BC = 5$$
$$AC = 4$$

Thus,

$$(AB)(BC)(AC) = (3)(5)(4)$$
$$= 60$$

(Math Refresher #524)

Explanatory Answers for
Practice Test 3
(continued)

Section 4: Quantitative Reasoning

> As you read these solutions, you are advised to do two things if you answered the math question incorrectly:
>
> 1. When a specific Strategy is referred to in the solution, study that strategy, which you will find in "25 Math Strategies" (beginning on page 72).
>
> 2. When the solution directs you to the "Math Refresher" (beginning on page 185)—for example, Math Refresher #305—study the 305 Math principle to get a clear idea of the math operation that was necessary for you to know in order to answer the question correctly.

1. Choice B is correct. **(Use Strategy D: Add a quantity to both columns to get rid of minus signs.)**

Quantity A	Quantity B
	$x > 0 > y$
$y - x$	$x - y$
Add x: $\quad y - x + x$	$x - y + x$
y	$2x - y$
Add y: $\quad y + y$	$2x - y + y$
$2y$	$2x$
Divide by 2: $\quad y$	x

Since $x > 0 > y$, $x > y$

(Math Refresher #421)

2. Choice D is correct.

$$\text{Given:} \quad w < 60$$
$$x < 60$$

(Use Strategy C: Use numerical examples when it appears that a comparison cannot be determined.)

First: Let $w = 50$
$$x = 50$$
Then $w + x = 100$ $\qquad\boxed{1}$
which is > 80
Second: $w = 30$
$$x = 20$$
Then $w + x = 50$ $\qquad\boxed{2}$
which is < 80

From $\boxed{1}$ and $\boxed{2}$ we see that two different comparisons are possible. Therefore, we cannot determine a unique comparison.

(Math Refresher #122)

3. Choice C is correct.

Given:
The average (arithmetic mean) of a and b is 8. $\boxed{1}$

$$a - b + 4 = 0 \qquad\boxed{2}$$

Quantity A	Quantity B
a	6

$\Big($ **Use Strategy 5:**
$$\text{Average} = \frac{\text{Sum of values}}{\text{Total number of values}}\Big)$$

From $\boxed{1}$, we get

$$\frac{a+b}{2} = 8 \qquad \boxed{3}$$

Multiply $\boxed{3}$ by 2. We get

$$\cancel{2}\left(\frac{a+b}{\cancel{2}}\right) = (8)2$$

$$a + b = 16 \qquad \boxed{4}$$

From $\boxed{2}$, $a - b + 4 = 0$, we get

$$a - b = -4 \qquad \boxed{5}$$

(Use Strategy 13: Find unknowns by addition.)

Adding $\boxed{4}$ and $\boxed{5}$, we have

$$2a = 12$$
$$a = 6 \qquad \boxed{6}$$

Using $\boxed{6}$, the columns become

Quantity A	Quantity B
$a = 6$	6

(Math Refresher #601, #406, and #407)

4. Choice A is correct.

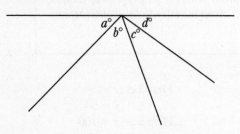

$$\text{Given: } a = c = d \qquad \boxed{1}$$

$$\frac{c}{b} = \frac{1}{3} \qquad \boxed{2}$$

(Use Strategy 13: Find unknowns by multiplication.) Multiply $\boxed{2}$ by b. We get

$$\cancel{b}\left(\frac{c}{\cancel{b}}\right) = b\left(\frac{1}{3}\right)$$

$$c = \frac{b}{3} \qquad \boxed{3}$$

Substituting $\boxed{3}$ into $\boxed{1}$, we have

$$a = \frac{b}{3}, \quad d = \frac{b}{3} \qquad \boxed{4}$$

(Use Strategy 3: The whole equals the sum of its parts.) From the diagram we see that

$$a + b + c + d = 180° \qquad \boxed{5}$$

Substituting $\boxed{3}$ and $\boxed{4}$ into $\boxed{5}$, we get

$$\frac{b}{3} + b + \frac{b}{3} + \frac{b}{3} = 180° \qquad \boxed{6}$$

(Use Strategy 13: Find unknowns by multiplication.) Multiply $\boxed{6}$ by 3. We get

$$b + 3b + b + b = 540°$$
$$6b = 540°$$
$$b = 90° \qquad \boxed{7}$$

Quantity A	Quantity B
b	80

Substituting $\boxed{7}$ into $\boxed{8}$, the columns become

90	80

(Math Refresher #111, #406, and #501)

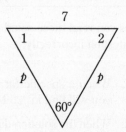

5. Choice C is correct. **(Use Strategy 18: Know equilateral and isosceles triangles.)**

Since the triangle has 2 equal sides, the angles opposite these sides are equal. Thus,

$$\angle 1 = \angle 2 \qquad \boxed{1}$$

(Use Strategy 3: The whole equals the sum of its parts.)
We know that the sum of the angles of a triangle = 180°

Thus, $\angle 1 + \angle 2 + 60° = 180°$ $\qquad \boxed{2}$

Substituting $\boxed{1}$ into $\boxed{2}$, we get
$$\angle 1 + \angle 1 + 60° = 180°$$
$$2(\angle 1) + 60 = 180°$$
$$2(\angle 1) = 120°$$
$$\angle 1 = 60° \qquad \boxed{3}$$

Substituting $\boxed{3}$ into $\boxed{1}$, we have
$$\angle 1 = \angle 2 = 60°$$

Thus, all three angles each = 60°, and the triangle is equilateral.
Therefore all three sides are equal. $\qquad \boxed{4}$

From $\boxed{4}$ and the diagram, we get $p = 7$. $\qquad \boxed{5}$

Quantity A	Quantity B	
21	$3p$	$\boxed{6}$

Substituting $\boxed{5}$ into $\boxed{6}$, we get

21	$3p =$
	$3(7) =$
21	21

(Math Refresher #507, #508, and #505)

6. Choice B is correct. **(Use Strategy 2: Translate words into math.)** The greatest one-year change in City A's population is 8,000. This occurred in 1992–93, when the population went from 119,000 to 127,000. The greatest one-year change in City B's population came in 1989–90, when the population went from 118,000 to 109,000. This was a change of 9,000.

(Math Refresher #702)

7. Choice C is correct. **(Use Strategy 2: Translate words into math.)** The population of City A in 1992 was 119,000. The population of City B in 1988 was 124,000. Thus, the difference is 5,000.

(Math Refresher #702)

8. Choice C is correct. **(Use Strategy 12: Try not to make tedious calculations, since there is usually an easier way.)**

Quantity A	Quantity B
25% of 90	$\frac{1}{2}$ of 45
$= \frac{1}{4} \times 90$	$= \frac{1}{2} \times 45$
$= \frac{90}{4}$	$= \frac{45}{2}$
$= \frac{45}{2}$	

Thus, Choice C is correct because the two quantities are equal.

(Math Refresher #107, #108, and #111)

9. Choice D is correct. **(Use Strategy C: Try numerics if it appears that a definite relationship of the columns can't be determined.)**

Choose numeric values of x.

EXAMPLE 1

$$x = 1$$

The columns then become

Quantity A	Quantity B
1	1

and the two quantities are equal.

EXAMPLE 2

$$x = 2$$

The columns then become

Quantity A	Quantity B
2	$\frac{1}{2}$

and the quantity in Column A is greater. Thus, a definite comparison cannot be made.

(Math Refresher #431)

10. Choice C is correct. **(Use Strategy 2: Translate from words to algebra.)**

Number of pages Ron read last night

$$= \frac{1}{4} \times 16 = 4$$

(Use Strategy 3: The whole equals the sum of its parts.)

Number of pages remaining immediately after Ron finished reading last night $= 16 - 4 = 12$

Number of pages read this morning $= \frac{1}{4} \times 12 = 3$

Pages still not read

$= $ Remaining pages $-$ pages read this morning
$= 12 - 3$

Pages still not read $= 9$

(Math Refresher #200)

11. Choices A and E are correct.

Given: $x < 0$		$\boxed{1}$
$y < 0$		$\boxed{2}$

(Use Strategy 6: Know how to manipulate inequalities.)

Multiplying $\boxed{1}$ by $\boxed{2}$, we get

$$x \cdot y > 0 \qquad \boxed{3}$$

Thus A is always positive.

Adding $\boxed{1}$ and $\boxed{2}$, we get

$$x + y < 0 \qquad \boxed{4}$$

Thus B is not positive.

(Use Strategy 7: Use numerics to help find the answer.)

Let $x = -2, y = -3$

$$C \text{ becomes } x - y = -2 - (-3)$$
$$= -2 + 3$$
$$= 1 \qquad \boxed{5}$$

Now let $x = -3, y = -2$

$$C \text{ becomes } x - y = -3 - (-2)$$
$$= -3 + 2$$
$$= -1 \qquad \boxed{6}$$

From $\boxed{5}$ and $\boxed{6}$ we see that C is not always positive.

For D, choose $x = -1$ and
$$y = -2$$

Thus

$$x^y = (-1)^{-2} = \frac{1}{(-1)^2} = +1$$

Now choose $x = -1$
and $y = -3$

$$x^y = (-1)^{-3} = \frac{1}{(-1)^3} = \frac{1}{-1} = -1$$

So D is not always positive.
For E,
If x is negative
and y is negative,
Then

$$\frac{x}{y} = \frac{\text{negative}}{\text{negative}} = \text{positive}$$

So E is positive.

(Math Refresher #419, #420, and #424)

12. Choice B is correct.

Given: a, b are integers $\boxed{1}$
         Average of a, b, and 4 is 6 $\boxed{2}$

$\left(\text{**Use Strategy 5:**}\right.$

$$\text{Average} = \frac{\text{Sum of values}}{\text{Total number of values}}\Big)$$

Using $\boxed{2}$, we have

$$\frac{a + b + 4}{3} = 6 \qquad \boxed{3}$$

(Use Strategy 13: Find unknowns by multiplication.)

Multiply $\boxed{3}$ by 3. We get

$$3\left(\frac{a + b + 4}{3}\right) = (6)3$$

$$a + b + 4 = 18$$
$$a + b = 14 \qquad \boxed{4}$$

Using $\boxed{1}$ and $\boxed{4}$, the possibilities are:

$a + b$	ab	
$1 + 13$	13	Choice A
$2 + 12$	24	
$3 + 11$	33	
$4 + 10$	40	Choice C
$5 + 9$	45	
$6 + 8$	48	Choice D
$7 + 7$	49	Choice E

Checking all the choices, we find that only Choice B, 14, is not a possible value of ab.

(Math Refresher #601 and #406)

13. Choice C is correct.

Number of pounds of force	Height object is raised	
3	6 feet	$\boxed{1}$
6	12 feet	
9	18 feet	

(Use Strategy 2: Translate from words to algebra.)

We are given that:

height raised $= c$ (force exerted) $\boxed{2}$

Substituting the numbers from the first row of $\boxed{1}$ into $\boxed{2}$, we get

$$6 = c(3)$$
$$2 = c \qquad \boxed{3}$$

Given: Height object is raised = 15 feet $\boxed{4}$

Substituting $\boxed{3}$ and $\boxed{4}$ into $\boxed{2}$, we have

$$15 = 2(\text{force exerted})$$
$$7\frac{1}{2} = \text{force exerted}$$

(Math Refresher #200 and #406)

14. Choice B is correct. **(Use Strategy 13: Subtract Equations)** Using $C = md + t$, if the business trip were increased by 5 days, $C' = m(d + 5) + t$. Subtracting equations, $C' - C = m(d + 5) + t - (md + t) = md + 5m + t - md - t = 5m$.

(Math Refresher #122)

15. Choice C is correct. For line q, $y = mx + b_1$. Since the line q crosses the origin where $x = 0$ and $y = 0$, b_1 must $= 0$. Thus for line q, $y = mx$. Now since $(4,3)$ is on line q, this means when $x = 4$, $y = 3$, so if $y = mx$, $3 = m(4)$ and $m = 3/4$.

Now let's look at line p. For this line, $y = Mx + b$. Since the lines p and q are perpendicular, the slope of one is the *negative reciprocal* of the other. Thus $m = -1/M$. Since $m = 3/4$, $3/4 = -1/M$, and so $M = -4/3$. Thus for line p, $y = -(4/3)x + b$. The point $(4,3)$ is also on line p, so substituting $x = 4$ and $y = 3$ in the equation $y = -(4/3)x + b$, we get $3 = -(4/3)(4) + b$.

From that we get $3 = -16/3 + b$, and thus $3 + 16/3 = b$ and $b = 25/3$. Thus for line p, $y = -(4/3)x + 25/3$. If $(3,a)$ is on line p, then substituting $x = 3$ and $y = a$, we get $a = -(4/3)3 + 25/3 = -4 + 25/3 = 13/3 = 4\frac{1}{3}$.

(Math Refresher #414)

16. $\dfrac{2}{3}$

(Use Strategy 2: Translate from words to algebra.)

$$p = \frac{3}{5}m \qquad \boxed{1}$$

$$q = \frac{9}{10}m \qquad \boxed{2}$$

(Use Strategy 13: Find unknowns by division of equations.)

$$Thus, \frac{p}{q} = \frac{\frac{3}{5}m}{\frac{9}{10}m}$$

$$= \frac{\frac{3}{5}}{\frac{9}{10}}$$

$$= \frac{3}{5} \times \frac{10}{9} = \frac{\overset{1}{\cancel{3}}}{\cancel{5}} \times \frac{\overset{2}{\cancel{10}}}{\underset{3}{\cancel{9}}}$$

$$\frac{p}{q} = \frac{2}{3}$$

(Math Refresher #200 and #112)

17. Choice D is correct. Note the relatively steady increase of mobile home shipments from 2001 to 2009.

(Math Refresher #706)

18. Choice D is correct. In 1969, there were about 340,000 mobile home shipments (Right Scale) and about 1,000,000 single family houses (Left Scale), Therefore, we have a 1:3 ratio.

(Math Refresher #706)

19. Choice A is correct. The graph shows that there were about 1,250,000 single family houses and 125,000 mobile home shipments in 1999.

(Math Refresher #706)

20. Choice B is correct. Figures are approximate. Mobile home shipments were as follows: 2006 = 215,000; 2007 = 245,000; 2008 = 275,000; 2009 = 340,000. Total of mobile home shipments for the four years = 1,075,000. Single family houses were as follows: 2006 = 800,000; 2007 = 850,000; 2008 = 950,000; 2009 = 1,000,000. Total of single family houses for the four years = 3,600,000, When we add the two totals, we get 4,675,000 as a grand total. 1,075,000 is about 23% of 4,675,000.

(Math Refresher #706)

21. Choices A, B, C are correct. **(Use Strategy 7: Use specific numerical examples to prove or disprove your guess.)**

$$\sqrt{2 + 2} \neq \sqrt{2} + \sqrt{2}$$

$$2^2 + 2^2 \neq (2 + 2)^2$$

$$2^1 + 2^2 \neq 2^{1+2}$$

Therefore, neither A, B, nor C is generally true.

(Math Refresher #429 and #430)

22. Choice E is correct. **(Use Strategy 2: Translate from words to algebra.)**

Each tile is a square with perimeter = 2 feet

Each side of the tile is $\frac{1}{4}$(2 feet) = $\frac{1}{2}$ foot $\boxed{1}$

The area of each tile is (side)^2.

Using $\boxed{1}$, we get the area of each tile

$$= \left(\frac{1}{2}\right)^2 \text{ square foot} = \frac{1}{4} \text{ square foot} \qquad \boxed{2}$$

The area of the floor is $b \times h =$
8 feet $\times$ 6 feet =
48 square feet $\qquad \boxed{3}$

(Use Strategy 17: Use the given information effectively.)

The number of tiles necessary, at minimum, to cover the floor

$$= \frac{\text{Area of floor}}{\text{Area of 1 tile}} \qquad \boxed{4}$$

Substituting $\boxed{2}$ and $\boxed{3}$ into $\boxed{4}$, we get:

$$= \frac{48}{\frac{1}{4}} = 48 \times \frac{4}{1}$$

$$= 192$$

(Math Refresher #200 and #303)

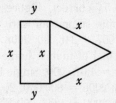

23. 36

(Use Strategy 2: Translate from words to algebra.) When the given diagram has been labeled as above, then we know

$$3x = 39 \qquad \boxed{1}$$
$$xy = 65 \qquad \boxed{2}$$

From $\boxed{1}$ we have

$$x = 13 \qquad \boxed{3}$$

Substituting $\boxed{3}$ into $\boxed{2}$, we have

$$13y = 65$$
$$\text{or} \quad y = 5 \qquad \boxed{4}$$

The perimeter of the rectangle

$$= 2x + 2y$$
$$= 2(13) + 2(5)$$
$$= 36$$

(Math Refresher #200, #304, #308, and #431)

	First Place (6 points)	Second Place (4 points)	Third Place (2 points)
Game 1			
Game 2		Bob	
Game 3			Bob

24. Choice C is correct.

(Use Strategy 17: Use the given information effectively.) Carl can attain the *minimum* possible score by placing third in Game 1 and Game 2 and second in Game 3.

From the chart he would have 2, 2, and 4 points for each of these finishes.
Thus, minimum score = 2 + 2 + 4
    minimum score = 8 points

25. Choice D is correct. Two-fifths, or 40%, of the applicants fail on the examination. Of the 60% remaining, three-fourths fail to get into the program. $\frac{3}{4} \times 60\%$ = 45%. Thus, the total number of failures is equal to 40% + 45%, or 85%.

Or, to solve it algebraically:

Let x be the number of applicants.
$\frac{3}{5}x$ = applicants who passed the exam

$\frac{\frac{3}{5}x}{4} = \frac{3}{20}x$ = applicants who passed the exam and were accepted

$\frac{\frac{3}{20}x}{x} = \frac{3}{20}$ = % of all applicants who gain admission

$1 - \frac{3}{20} = \frac{17}{20} = 85\%$ = % who *fail* to gain admission

(Math Refresher #106)

What You Must Do Now to Raise Your GRE Score

1. Follow the directions on page 693 to determine your scaled score for the GRE Test you've just taken. These results will give you a good idea about how hard you'll need to study in order to achieve a certain score on the actual GRE.

2. Eliminate your weaknesses in each of the GRE test areas by taking the following Giant Steps toward GRE success:

Sentence Completion and Reading Part

Giant Step 1

Take advantage of the Sentence Completion and Reading Strategies that begin on page 136. Read again the Explanatory Answer for each of the Sentence Completion and Reading questions that you got wrong. Refer to the Reading Strategy that applies to each of your incorrect answers. Learn each of these strategies thoroughly. These strategies are crucial if you want to raise your GRE Verbal score substantially.

Giant Step 2

You can improve your vocabulary by doing the following:

1) Study the GRE 3,400-Word List beginning on page 377.

2) Take the 100 Tests to Strengthen Your Vocabulary beginning on page 426.

3) Study the Gruber Prefix-Root-Suffix List beginning on page 366.

4) Learn the Hot Prefixes and Roots beginning on page 717.

5) Read through the List of Standardized Test Words Appearing More Than Once beginning on page 371.

6) Look through the Most Important/Frequently Used GRE Words and Their Opposites beginning on page 373.

7) Learn the 3 Vocabulary Strategies beginning on page 168.

8) Read as widely as possible—not only novels. Nonfiction is important too…and don't forget to read newspapers and magazines.

9) Listen to people who speak well. Tune in to worthwhile TV programs.

10) Use the dictionary frequently and extensively—at home, on the bus, at work, etc.

11) Play word games—for example, crossword puzzles, anagrams, and Scrabble. Another game is to compose your own Sentence Completion questions. Try them on your friends.

Math Part

Giant Step 3

Make good use of the 25 Math Strategies that begin on page 72. Read again the solutions for each Math question that you answered incorrectly. Refer to the Math Strategy that applies to each of your incorrect answers. Learn each of these Math Strategies thoroughly. We repeat that these strategies are crucial if you want to raise your GRE Math score substantially.

Giant Step 4

You may want to take the **101 Most Important Math Questions You Need to Know How to Solve** test beginning on page 40 and follow the directions after the test for a basic math skills diagnosis.

For each Math question that you got wrong in the test, note the reference to the Math Refresher section beginning on page 185. This reference will explain clearly the mathematical principle involved in the solution of the question you answered incorrectly. Learn that particular mathematical principle thoroughly.

For Both the Math and Reading Parts

Giant Step 5

You may want to take the **Strategy Diagnostic Test** beginning on page 1 to assess whether you're using the best strategies for the questions.

For the Writing Part

Giant Step 6

Take a look at Part 8, the Analytical Writing Section, which describes the various item types in the Writing Section and sample questions with answers and explanations. Also make use of the Brief Review of English Grammar, Part 9.

If you do the job *right* and follow the steps listed earlier, you are likely to raise your GRE score substantially on each of the Verbal, Math, and Writing parts of the test.

I am the master of my fate:
I am the captain of my soul.

—From the poem "Invictus"
by William Ernest Henley

Appendix A: Hot Prefixes and Roots

Here is a list of the most important prefixes and roots that impart a certain meaning or feeling. They can be instant clues to the meanings of more than 110,000 words.

PREFIXES THAT MEAN "TO," "WITH," "BETWEEN," OR "AMONG"

PREFIX	MEANING	EXAMPLES
ad, ac, af, an, ap, as, at	to, toward	adapt—to fit into adhere—to stick to attract—to draw near
com, con, co, col	with, together	combine—to bring together contact—to touch together collect—to bring together coworker—one who works together with another worker
in, il, ir, im	into	inject—to put into impose—to force into illustrate—to put into example irritate—to put into discomfort
inter	between, among	international—among nations interact—to act among the people
pro	forward, going ahead	proceed—to go forward promote—to move forward

PREFIXES THAT MEAN "BAD"

PREFIX	MEANING	EXAMPLES
mal	wrong, bad	malady—illness malevolent—evil malfunction—poorly functioning

mis	wrong, badly	mistreat—to treat badly
		mistake—to get wrong

PREFIXES THAT MEAN "AWAY FROM," "NOT," OR "AGAINST"

PREFIX	MEANING	EXAMPLES
ab	away from	absent—not present, away abscond—to run away
anti	against	antifreeze—a substance used to prevent freezing antisocial—someone who is not social
de, dis	away from, down, the opposite of, apart, not	depart—to go away from decline—to turn down dislike—not to like dishonest—not honest distant—apart
ex, e, ef	out, from	exit—to go out eject—to throw out efface—to rub out, erase
in, il, ir, im	not	inactive—not active impossible—not possible illiterate—not literate irreversible—not reversible
non	not	nonsense—no sense nonstop—having no stops
ob	against, in front of	obstacle—something that stands in the way of obstinate—inflexible
un	not	unhelpful—not helpful uninterested—not interested

PREFIXES THAT DENOTE DISTANCE

PREFIX	MEANING	EXAMPLES
circum	around	circumscribe—to write or inscribe in a circle circumspect—very careful
equ, equi	equal, the same	equalize—to make equal equitable—fair, equal
post	after	postpone—to do after postmortem—after death
pre	before	preview—a viewing that goes before another viewing prehistorical—before written history
trans	across	transcontinental—across the continent transit—act of going across
re	back, again	retell—to tell again recall—to call back, to remember
sub	under	subordinate—under something else subconscious—under the conscious
super	over, above	superimpose—to put something over something else superstar—a star greater than other stars
un, uni	one	unity—oneness unanimous—sharing one view unidirectional—having one direction

ROOTS

ROOT	MEANING	EXAMPLES
cap, capt, cept, ceive	to take, to hold	captive—one who is held capable—to be able to take hold of things concept—an idea or thought held in mind receive—to take
cred	to believe	credible—believable credit—belief, trust
curr, curs, cours	to run	current—now in progress, running cursor—a moveable indicator recourse—running for help
dic, dict	to say	indicate—to say by demonstrating diction—verbal saying
duc, duct	to lead	induce—to lead to action aqueduct—a pipe or waterway that leads water somewhere
fac, fic, fect, fy	to make, to do	facile—easy to do fiction—something that has been made up satisfy—to make happy or to fulfill affect—to make a change in
jec, ject	to throw	project—to put forward trajectory—a path of an object that has been thrown
mit, mis	to send	admit—to send in missile—something that gets sent through the air

ROOT	MEANING	EXAMPLES
pon, pos	to place	transpose—to place across compose—to put into place many parts deposit—to place in something
scrib, script	to write	describe—to write or tell about scripture—a written tablet
spec, spic	to look	specimen—an example to look at inspect—to look over
ten, tain	to hold	maintain—to hold up or keep retentive—holding
ven, vent	to come	advent—a coming convene—to come together

Appendix B: Words Commonly Mistaken for Each Other

Review the following lists of words quickly and use a pencil to mark the pairs that you have trouble remembering. This way, you'll be able to focus your attention on these on subsequent reviews.

AGGRAVATE —to make worse
IRRITATE —to annoy

ALLUSION —indirect reference
ILLUSION —error in vision

ARBITER —a supposedly unprejudiced judge
ARBITRARY —prejudiced

ASCENT —upward movement
ASSENT —agreement; to agree

ASCETIC —self-denying
AESTHETIC —pertaining to the beautiful

BAN —prohibit
BANE —woe

CANVAS —coarse cloth
CANVASS —examine; solicit

CAPITAL —excellent; chief town; money; punishable by death or life imprisonment
CAPITOL —state house

CENSURE —find fault
CENSOR —purge or remove offensive passages

COMPLACENT —self-satisfied; smug
COMPLAISANT —kindly; submissive

COMPLEMENT —that which completes
COMPLIMENT —praise

CONSUL —diplomatic representative
COUNCIL —group of advisors
COUNSEL —advice

CONTEMPTIBLE —despicable
CONTEMPTUOUS —scornful

COSMOPOLITAN —sophisticated
METROPOLITAN —pertaining to the city

CREDIBLE	—believable
CREDITABLE	—worthy of praise
DEMURE	—pretending modesty
DEMUR	—hesitate; raise objection
DEPRECATE	—disapprove regretfully
DEPRECIATE	—undervalue
DISCREET	—judicious; prudent
DISCRETE	—separate and distinct
DISINTERESTED	—unprejudiced
UNINTERESTED	—not interested
DIVERS	—several
DIVERSE	—varied
ELICIT	—extract
ILLICIT	—unlawful
EMEND	—correct a text or manuscript
AMEND	—improve by making slight changes
EMINENT	—high in rank
IMMINENT	—threatening; at hand
EQUABLE	—even-tempered
EQUITABLE	—just
EXULT	—rejoice
EXALT	—raise; praise highly
FORMALLY	—in a formal manner
FORMERLY	—at a previous time
GORILLA	—large ape
GUERRILLA	—mercenary
GOURMET	—lover of good food
GOURMAND	—glutton
HAIL	—frozen pellets; to call; originate (from)
HALE	—strong, healthy
HEALTHY	—possessing health
HEALTHFUL	—bringing about health
IMPLY	—indicate or suggest
INFER	—draw a conclusion from
INCREDIBLE	—unbelievable
INCREDULOUS	—unbelieving
INDIGENT	—poor
INDIGENOUS	—native
INGENIOUS	—skillful; clever; resourceful
INGENUOUS	—frank; naïve

INTERNMENT	—imprisonment
INTERMENT	—burial
MAIZE	—corn
MAZE	—confusing network
MARTIAL	—warlike
MARITAL	—pertaining to marriage
MENDACIOUS	—lying
MERITORIOUS	—possessing merit; praiseworthy
PERSONAL	—private
PERSONABLE	—pleasant in appearance and manner
PERSPICACIOUS	—shrewd; acute
PERSPICUOUS	—clear; lucid
PRACTICAL	—sensible; useful
PRACTICABLE	—timely; capable of being accomplished
PRODIGAL	—wastefully lavish
PRODIGIOUS	—extraordinarily large
PROPHECY	—prediction
PROPHESY	—to predict
PROVIDED	—on condition that
PROVIDING	—furnishing; giving
REGAL	—royal
REGALE	—entertain lavishly
RESPECTFULLY	—with respect
RESPECTIVELY	—in the order already suggested
SANCTION	—authorize
SANCTITY	—holiness
SOCIAL	—pertaining to human society
SOCIABLE	—companionable; friendly
STATUE	—piece of sculpture
STATURE	—height
STATUTE	—a law
URBAN	—pertaining to the city
URBANE	—polished; suave
VENAL	—corrupt, mercenary
VENIAL	—pardonable

Essentials from
Dr. Gary Gruber

"Gruber can ring the bell on any number
of standardized exams."
—*Chicago Tribune*

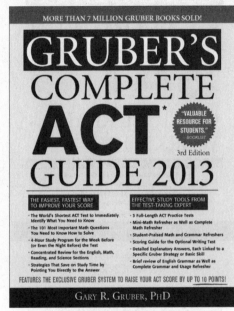

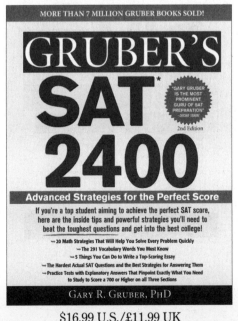
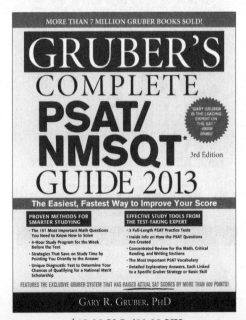

MyMaxScore Diagnostic

Online ACT/SAT Diagnostic from the #1 Test-Prep Expert—
Detailed Reporting Tailored to You!

My Ma₂ Score

New diagnostic program tests your ACT/SAT content knowledge with a full practice test and gives you a detailed report of how well you did on the full list of ACT/SAT topics.

Know exactly where to focus your study efforts!

Your online report shows you everything:

✔ **How well you did in each subject area**
✔ **How well you did on topics and subtopics within each subject area**
✔ **Which questions you got right and wrong**

In addition, MyMaxScore Diagnostic gives you access to Dr. Gruber's:

✔ **Test-taking strategies**
✔ **Topic/subtopic refresher lessons**
✔ **Explanations of correct answers**

You can even go back and review specific questions.

Don't have 3 hours to sit down and take the entire test?

No problem. You can interrupt the test and return to it later.

Don't need to study all of the subject areas?

No problem. You can choose which subject area test(s) to take.

Want to get help from your teacher or a private tutor?

No problem. You can print your report and show them just what you need to work on.

MyMaxScore Diagnostic gives you the
CONTROL and FLEXIBILITY
you need!

Check out MyMaxScore.com for more information.

Notes

_____

_____

_____

_____

_____

_____

_____

_____

_____

_____

_____

_____

_____

Notes

Notes

Notes

Notes